Dr. Tom Shinder's ISA Server 2006 Migration Guide

Debra Littlejohn Shinder
Dr. Thomas W. Shinder

With
Adrian F. Dimcev
James Eaton-Lee
Jason Jones
Steve Moffat

KEY	SERIAL NUMBER
001	HJIRTCV764
002	PO9873D5FG
003	829KM8NJH2
004	BAL923457U
005	CVPLQ6WQ23
006	VBP965T5T5
007	HJJJ863WD3E
008	2987GVTWMK
009	629MP5SDJT
010	IMWQ295T6T

PUBLISHED BY
Syngress Publishing, Inc.
Elsevier, Inc.
30 Corporate Drive
Burlington, MA 01803

Dr. Tom Shinder's ISA Server 2006 Migration Guide

Printed and bound in the United Kingdom
Transferred to Digital Printing, 2011

ISBN 13: 978-1-59749-199-0

Publisher: Amorette Pedersen   Page Layout and Art: SPi
Acquisitions Editor: Andrew Williams   Copy Editor: Edwina Lewis
Technical Editor: Dr. Thomas W. Shinder

For information on rights, translations, and bulk sales, contact Matt Pedersen, Commercial Sales Director and Rights, at Syngress Publishing; email m.pedersen@elsevier.com.

Lead Authors

Thomas W. Shinder, MD is an MCSE and has been awarded the Microsoft Most Valuable Professional (MVP) award for his work with ISA Server and is recognized in the firewall community as one of the foremost experts on ISA Server. Tom has consulted with major companies and organizations such as Microsoft Corp., Xerox, Lucent Technologies, FINA Oil, Hewlett-Packard, and the U.S. Department of Energy.

Tom practiced medicine in Oregon, Texas, and Arkansas before turning his growing fascination with computer technology into a new career shortly after marrying his wife, Debra Littlejohn Shinder, in the mid 90s. They co-own TACteam (Trainers, Authors, and Consultants), through which they teach technology topics and develop courseware, write books, articles, whitepapers and corporate product documentation and marketing materials, and assist small and large businesses in deploying technology solutions.

Tom co-authored, with Deb, the best selling *Configuring ISA Server 2000* (Syngress Publishing, ISBN: 1-928994-29-6), *Dr. Tom Shinder's ISA Server and Beyond* (Syngress, ISBN: 1-931836-66-3), and *Troubleshooting Windows 2000 TCP/IP* (Syngress, ISBN: 1-928994-11-3). He has contributed to several other books on subjects such as the Windows 2000 and Windows 2003 MCSE exams and has written hundreds of articles on Windows server products for a variety of electronic and print publications.

Tom is the "primary perpetrator" on ISAserver.org (www.isaserver.org), where he answers hundreds of questions per week on the discussion boards and is the leading content contributor.

Debra Littlejohn Shinder, MCSE, MVP is a technology consultant, trainer and writer who has authored a number of books on computer operating systems, networking, and security. These include *Scene of the Cybercrime: Computer Forensics Handbook,* published by Syngress, and *Computer Networking Essentials,* published by Cisco Press. She is co-author, with her husband, Dr. Thomas Shinder, of *Troubleshooting Windows 2000 TCP/IP,* the best-selling *Configuring ISA Server 2000, ISA Server and Beyond,* and *Configuring ISA Server 2004.* She also co-authored *Windows XP: Ask the Experts* with Jim Boyce.

Deb is a tech editor, developmental editor and contributor to over 20 additional books on subjects such as the Windows 2000 and Windows 2003 MCSE exams, CompTIA Security+ exam and TruSecure's ICSA certification. She formerly edited the Brainbuzz A+ Hardware News and currently edits Sunbelt Software's WinXP

News and VistaNews, with over a million subscribers, and writes a weekly column on Voice over IP technologies for TechRepublic/CNET. Her articles on various technology issues are regularly published on the CNET Web sites and Windowsecurity. com, and have appeared in print magazines such as Windows IT Pro (formerly Windows & .NET) Magazine and Law & Order Magazine.

She has authored training material, corporate whitepapers, marketing material, and product documentation for Microsoft Corporation, Hewlett-Packard, GFI Software, Sunbelt Software, Sony and other technology companies and written courseware for Powered, Inc and DigitalThink.

Deb currently specializes in security issues and Microsoft products; she has been awarded Microsoft's Most Valuable Professional (MVP) status in Windows Server Security for the last four years. A former police officer and police academy instructor, she lives and works with her husband, Tom, on a beautiful lake just outside Dallas, Texas and teaches computer networking and security and occasional criminal justice courses at Eastfield College (Mesquite, TX). You can read her tech blog at http://deb-tech. spaces.live.com.

Contributing Authors

Adrian F. Dimcev is a consultant specializing in the design and implementation of VPNs. Adrian also has extensive experience in penetration testing.

James Eaton-Lee lives in Scotland with his two fantastic children, lovely wife, and three cats. He works as a Security Consultant specializing in technology as diverse as IIS and IPCop, to VPNs and VoIP in applications ranging from enterprise wireless networks to internet banking platforms. He has worked with clients ranging from small consulting firms to manufacturing companies, offshore engineering firms, and some of the world's largest financial institutions. James is the co-author of IPCop: Closing Borders with Open Source, has written papers and given talks on topics relating to infrastructure security for groups including the British Computer Society and various Linux Users Groups, and is an MVP in the ISA Server category.

Jason Jones (BSc Hons., MCSE, MSCE: Security, MCP, CNE, MCNE) is the Principal Security Consultant for Silversands Limited. He currently provides senior-level strategic, architectural and technical consulting to all Silversands clients throughout the UK. Silversands are one of the UK's leading IT Solution and Service providers whose dedication, professionalism and attention to detail has won them four Microsoft Gold Certifications. Jason provides the driving force for the Microsoft Security competency at Silversands, to develop enterprise-wide technology solutions which turn customer's security goals into a reality. Jason's specialities focus around the Microsoft security arena with a high-level of expertise in using ISA Server to secure and protect Microsoft based products like Microsoft Exchange Server and Microsoft SharePoint Server. In addition, Jason also provides consultancy for all other aspects of Microsoft infrastructure security like Server Hardening, Microsoft Certificate Services and the adoption of Microsoft Security best practice across customer systems.

Jason has over 10 years of experience in the computer industry and has a wide range of technical knowledge, linked with a passion for IT security in order to provide customers with the very best level of security possible. Jason is also a moderator for ISAserver.org where he is able to share this passion with others, and help them realize the real-world potential of ISA Server.

Jason holds a bachelor's degree in Applied Mathematics from the University of Southampton, and resides in the south of England with his inspiring wife Tanya and his beautiful daughter Caitlin.

Steve Moffat is an MCSA and has worked in IT support services for the last 25 years. Steve has been employed in the UK by Digital, Experian, Computacenter (to name but a few). He has also consulted with major companies and organizations such as Zurich Insurance, Seagram's, Texaco, Peugeot, PriceWaterhouseCoopers, and the Bermuda Government. He now lives and works in paradise. Since moving to Bermuda in 2001 to work for Gateway Ltd as a senior engineer/consultant, he has gained a wife, Hannah, has formed his own company and is currently CEO & Director of Operations for The TLA Group Ltd. He specializes in ISA Server deployments & server virtualization. He is also the owner & host of the well known ISA Server web site, www.isaserver.bm

Contents

Introduction xxiii

Chapter 1 Network Security Basics 1
Introduction 2
Security Overview 2
Defining Basic Security Concepts 2
Knowledge is Power 3
Think Like a Thief 3
The Intrusion Triangle 4
Removing Intrusion Opportunities 5
Security Terminology 5
Addressing Security Objectives 7
Controlling Physical Access 8
Physical Access Factors 8
Protecting the Servers 9
Keeping Workstations Secure 9
Protecting Network Devices 10
Securing the Cable 11
Safely Going Wireless 12
Have Laptop, Will Travel 13
The Paper Chase 14
Removable Storage Risks 14
Physical Security Summary 15
Preventing Accidental Compromise of Data 15
Know Your Users 16
Educate Your Users 16
Control Your Users 16
Preventing Intentional Internal Security Breaches 16
Hiring and Human Resource Policies 17
Detecting Internal Breaches 17
Preventing Intentional Internal Breaches 18
Preventing Unauthorized External Intrusions 18
External Intruders with Internal Access 19
Tactical Planning 19

Recognizing Network Security Threats. 19

   Understanding Intruder Motivations 20

      Recreational Hackers. 20

      Profit-motivated Hackers 20

      Vengeful Hackers. 21

      Hybrid Hackers. 22

   Classifying Specific Types of Attacks. 22

      Social engineering attacks. 22

         What is social engineering? 22

         Protecting your network against social engineers. 23

      Denial of Service (DOS) Attacks. 24

         Distributed Denial of Service attacks 24

         DNS DOS attack 25

         SYN attack/LAND attack 25

         Ping of Death 27

         Teardrop. 27

         Ping Flood (ICMP flood) 27

         SMURF attack 28

         UDP bomb or UDP flood. 29

         UDP Snork attack. 29

         WinNuke (Windows out-of-band attack) 29

         Mail bomb attack 29

      Scanning and Spoofing. 30

         Port scan. 30

         IP half scan attack 32

         IP Spoofing. 32

      Source Routing attack 32

      Other protocol exploits 33

      System and software exploits 33

      Trojans, viruses and worms. 34

         Trojans 34

         Viruses 34

         Worms 35

Designing a Comprehensive Security Plan. 35

   Evaluating Security Needs 36

      Assessing the type of business 36

      Assessing the type of data. 37

      Assessing the network connections 37

      Assessing management philosophy 38

         Understanding management models. 38

Understanding Security Ratings 38
Legal Considerations. 39
Designating Responsibility for Network Security. 39
    Responsibility for Developing the Security Plan
    and Policies. 39
    Responsibility for Implementing and Enforcing
    the Security Plan and Policies 40
Designing the Corporate Security Policy. 40
    Developing an Effective Password Policy. 41
        Password Length and Complexity. 41
        Who creates the password?. 42
        Password Change Policy. 42
        Summary of Best Password Practices. 43
    Educating Network Users on Security Issues 43
Summary. 45

**Chapter 2 ISA Server 2006 Client Types and Automating
Client Provisioning** **47**
Introduction 48
Understanding ISA Server 2006 Client Types 48
    Understanding the ISA Server 2006 SecureNAT Client 50
        SecureNAT Client Limitations 52
        SecureNAT Client Advantages 56
        Name Resolution for SecureNAT Clients. 58
        Name Resolution and "Looping Back"
        Through the ISA Server 2006 Firewall. 58
    Understanding the ISA Server 2006 Firewall Client 62
        Allows Strong User/Group-Based Authentication for All
        Winsock Applications Using TCP and UDP Protocols 63
        Allows User and Application Information to be Recorded
        in the ISA Server 2006 Firewall's Log Files. 64
        Provides Enhanced Support for Network Applications,
        Including Complex Protocols That Require
        Secondary Connections. 64
        Provides "Proxy" DNS Support for Firewall Client Machines. 64
        The Network Routing Infrastructure Is Transparent
        to the Firewall Client 65
        How the Firewall Client Works 67
        Installing the Firewall Client Share 69

Installing the Firewall Client. 70
Firewall Client Configuration. 71
Centralized Configuration Options at the
ISA Server 2006 Firewall Computer 72
Enabling Support for Legacy Firewall
Client/Winsock Proxy Clients. 75
Client Side Firewall Client Settings. 76
Firewall Client Configuration Files 78
.ini Files 79
Advanced Firewall Client Settings 80
Firewall Client Configuration at the ISA Server 2006 Firewall 82
ISA Server 2006 Web Proxy Client 84
Improved Performance for the Firewall Client and
SecureNAT Client Configuration for Web Access 85
Ability to Use the Autoconfiguration Script to
Bypass Sites Using Direct Access 85
Allows You to Provide Web Access (HTTP/HTTPS/FTP
Download) without Enabling Users Access to Other Protocols 85
Allows You to Enforce User/Group-based
Access Controls Over Web Access 86
Allows you to Limit the Number of Outbound
Web Proxy Client Connections 92
Supports Web Proxy Chaining, Which Can Further
Speed Up Internet Access 93
ISA Server 2006 Multiple Client Type Configuration. 93
Deciding on an ISA Server 2006 Client Type. 95
Automating ISA Server 2006 Client Provisioning 96
Configuring DHCP Servers to Support Web Proxy
and Firewall Client Autodiscovery 97
Install the DHCP Server 98
Create the DHCP scope 98
Create the DHCP 252 Scope Option and Add It to the Scope 101
Configure the Client as a DHCP Client. 104
Configure the Client Browser to Use DCHP for Autodiscovery 105
Configure the ISA Server 2006 Firewall
to Publish Autodiscovery Information 105
Making the Connection. 106
Configuring DNS Servers to Support Web Proxy and
Firewall Client Autodiscovery 108
Creating the wpad Entry in DNS. 108

Configure the Client to Use the Fully-Qualified wpad Alias 111
Configure the client browser to use autodiscovery. 114
Configure the ISA Server 2006 Firewall to
    Publish Autodiscovery Information 114
Making the Connection Using DNS for Autodiscovery. 115
Automating Installation of the Firewall Client 116
Configuring Firewall Client and Web Proxy Client
    Configuration in the ISA Management Console. 117
Group Policy Software Installation. 121
Silent Installation Script 124
Systems Management Server (SMS). 125
One More Time 125

**Chapter 3 Installing and Configuring the
ISA Firewall Software. 127**
Pre-installation Tasks and Considerations. 128
System Requirements. 128
Configuring the Routing Table 130
DNS Server Placement 132
Configuring the ISA Firewall's Network Interfaces 134
Installation via a Terminal Services Administration Mode Session 138
Performing a Clean Installation on a Multihomed Machine 138
Default Post-installation ISA Firewall Configuration 145
The Post-installation System Policy. 146
Performing a Single NIC Installation (Unihomed ISA Firewall) 157
Quick Start Configuration for ISA Firewalls 159
Configuring the ISA Firewall's Network Interfaces. 161
IP Address and DNS Server Assignment 161
Configuring the Internal Network Interface. 162
Configuring the External Network Interface 163
Network Interface Order 163
Installing and Configuring a DNS Server on the
    ISA Server Firewall 164
Installing the DNS Service. 164
Installing the DNS Server Service on Windows Server 2003 164
Configuring the DNS Service on the ISA Firewall 165
Configuring the DNS Service in Windows Server 2003 165
Configuring the DNS Service on the
    Internal Network DNS Server. 168

Installing and Configuring a DHCP Server on the
    ISA Server Firewall 170
  Installing the DHCP Service 170
    Installing the DHCP Server Service on a Windows
    Server 2003 Computer 171
  Configuring the DHCP Service 171
Installing and Configuring the ISA Server 2006 Software 173
  Configuring the ISA Firewall 176
    DHCP Request to Server Rule 178
    DHCP Reply from Server Rule. 180
    Internal DNS Server to DNS Forwarder Rule 181
    Internal Network to DNS Server 182
    The All Open Rule 183
  Configuring the Internal Network Computers 184
  Configuring Internal Clients as DHCP Clients 184
Hardening the Base ISA Firewall Configuration
  and Operating System. 187
  ISA Firewall Service Dependencies 187
  Service Requirements for Common Tasks Performed
    on the ISA Firewall. 190
  Client Roles for the ISA Firewall 193
  ISA Firewall Administrative Roles and Permissions. 195
  Lockdown Mode 197
    Lockdown Mode Functionality 197
  Connection Limits 198
  DHCP Spoof Attack Prevention 200
One More Time 203

**Chapter 4 Creating and Using ISA 2006
Firewall Access Policy. 205**
ISA Firewall Access Rule Elements 208
  Protocols 208
  User Sets 209
  Content Types 210
  Schedules. 216
  Network Objects 217
Configuring Access Rules for Outbound Access
    through the ISA Firewall. 217
  The Rule Action Page 217
  The Protocols Page. 218

The Access Rule Sources Page 220
The Access Rule Destinations Page 221
The User Sets Page. 221
Access Rule Properties 222
    The General Tab 222
    The Action Tab 222
    The Protocols Tab 223
    The From Tab 225
    The To Tab 226
    The Users Tab 226
    The Schedule Tab 227
    The Content Types Tab 228
The Access Rule Context Menu Options 229
Configuring RPC Policy 230
Configuring FTP Policy 231
Configuring HTTP Policy 232
Ordering and Organizing Access Rules 232
How to Block Logging for Selected Protocols 233
Disabling Automatic Web Proxy Connections for
    SecureNAT Clients 234
Using Scripts to Populate Domain Name Sets 235
    Using the Import Scripts 237
Extending the SSL Tunnel Port Range for Web Access
    to Alternate SSL Ports 242
Avoiding Looping Back through the ISA Firewall
    for Internal Resources. 244
Anonymous Requests Appear in Log File Even When
    Authentication is Enforced For Web (HTTP Connections) 246
Blocking MSN Messenger using an Access Rule 246
Allowing Outbound Access to MSN Messenger via Web Proxy 249
Changes to ISA Firewall Policy Only Affects New Connections 250
Allowing Intradomain Communications through the ISA Firewall 251
One More Time 260

**Chapter 5 Publishing Network Services
with ISA 2006 Firewalls** **263**
Overview of Web Publishing and Server Publishing. 264
    Web Publishing Rules. 264
        Proxied Access to Web Sites Protectedby the ISA firewall. 265

Deep Application-Layer Inspection of Connections Made
to Published Web Sites. 265
Path Redirection 266
URL rewriting with ISA's Link Translation. 266
Ability to Publish Multiple Web Sites with a Single IP Address. 267
Pre-authentication of requests, and Authentication
Delegation to the published Site 267
Single Sign-On (SSO) for Published Web Sites 268
Support for SecurID Authentication 268
Support for RADIUS Authentication 268
Reverse Caching of Published Web Sites. 269
Support for Forwarding either the ISA Firewall's IP Address,
or the Original Web Client's IP Address to the Web Site 269
Ability to Schedule when Connections are
Allowed to Published Web Sites 270
Port and Protocol Redirection 270
Server Publishing Rules 271
Server Publishing Rules are a Form of Reverse NAT,
sometimes referred to as "Port Mapping" or
"Port forwarding" and do not Proxy the Connection 271
Almost All IP Level and TCP/UDP Protocols can be
Published using Server Publishing Rules 272
Server Publishing Rules do not Support Authentication
on the ISA Server 272
Application-Layer Filtering can be Applied to a Defined
Subset of Server Published Protocols 272
You can Configure Port Overrides to Customize the Listening
Ports and the Port Redirection. You can also Lock Down
the Source Ports the Requesting Clients use to Connect
to the Published Server 273
You can lock down who can Access Published Resources
using IP addresses 273
The External Client Source IP Address can be Preserved
or it can be Replaced with the ISA Firewall's IP address 273
Restrict connections to specific days and times 273
Support for Port Redirection or PAT (Port Address Translation). 274
Creating and Configuring Non-SSL Web Publishing Rules 274
The Select Rule Action Page 274
The Publishing Type Page. 275

The Server Connection Security Page. 276
The Internal Publishing Details Page (Part one). 277
The Internal Publishing Details Page(Part two) 279
The Public Name Details Page 281
The Select Web Listener Page and Creating an HTTP
    Web Listener 282
The Web Listener IP Addresses Page 284
The Authentication Settings Page 286
The Single Sign on Settings Page 290
The LDAP Settings Page. 291
The RADIUS Settings Page 293
SecurID Settings. 295
The Authentication Delegation Page 295
The User Sets Page. 298
Creating and Configuring SSL Web Publishing Rules 299
SSL Bridging 299
    SSL "Tunneling" versus SSL "Bridging" 300
    What about SSL-to-HTTP Bridging?. 300
    Enterprise and Standalone Certificate Authorities 301
    SSL-to-SSL Bridging and Web Site
        Certificate Configuration. 302
    Importing Web Site Certificates into the ISA Firewall's
        Machine Certificate Store 304
    Requesting a User Certificate for the ISA Firewall
        to Present to SSL Web Sites. 306
Creating an SSL Web Publishing Rule. 308
    The Internal Publishing Details Pages 309
    The Public Name Details Page. 311
    The Server Connection Security Page 311
    The Client Connection Security Page 312
    ISA 2004's Bridging Mode Page and ISA 2006 315
Configuring Advanced Web Listener Properties. 316
    The General Tab 316
    The Networks Tab. 316
    The Connections Tab. 316
    The Connections – Advanced Dialog 318
    The Certificates Tab. 318
    The Certificates – Advanced Dialog 319
    The Authentication Tab 319

Advanced Authentication Options Dialog Box 319
The Forms Tab 322
The Forms – Advanced Dialog 323
The SSO Tab 324
The Web Publishing Rule Properties Dialog Box 325
The General Tab 325
Action 326
From 327
To 328
Traffic 330
Listener 332
Public Name 332
Paths 333
Bridging 337
Users 338
Schedule 340
Link Translation 340
Authentication Delegation 341
Application Settings 343
Creating Server Publishing Rules 344
The Server Publishing Rule Properties Dialog Box 349
Server Publishing HTTP Sites 355
Creating Mail Server Publishing Rules 357
The Client Access: RPC, IMAP, POP3, SMTP Option 358
Publishing Exchange Web Client Access 360
One More Time 363

Chapter 6 Creating Remote Access and Site-to-Site
VPNs with ISA Firewalls **365**
Overview of ISA Firewall VPN Networking 366
Firewall Policy Applied to VPN Client Connections 368
Firewall Policy Applied to VPN Site-to-Site Connections 369
VPN Quarantine 370
User Mapping of VPN Clients 371
SecureNAT Client Support for VPN Connections 372
Site-to-Site VPN Using Tunnel Mode IPSec 373
Publishing PPTP VPN Servers 374
Pre-shared Key Support for IPSec VPN Connections 375
Advanced Name Server Assignment for VPN Clients 376
Monitoring of VPN Client Connections 377

An Improved Site-to-Site Wizard (New ISA 2006 feature) 377
The Create Answer File Wizard (New ISA 2006 Feature) 378
The Branch Office Connectivity Wizard (New ISA 2006 feature) 378
The Site-to-Site Summary (New ISA 2006 Feature) 379
Creating a Remote Access PPTP VPN Server 379
Enable the VPN Server 380
Create an Access Rule Allowing VPN Clients Access
to Allowed Resources 391
Enable Dial-in Access 392
Test the PPTP VPN Connection 395
Creating a Remote Access L2TP/IPSec Server 397
Issue Certificates to the ISA Firewall and VPN Clients 397
Test the L2TP/IPSec VPN Connection 403
Monitor VPN Clients 404
Using a Pre-shared Key for VPN Client
Remote Access Connections 406
Creating a PPTP Site-to-Site VPN 408
Create the Remote Site Network at the Main Office 411
The Network Rule at the Main Office 418
The Access Rules at the Main Office 418
Create the VPN Gateway Dial-in Account at the Main Office 419
Create the Remote Site Network at the Branch Office 421
The Network Rule at the Branch Office 423
The Access Rules at the Branch Office 424
Create the VPN Gateway Dial-in Account at the Branch Office 424
Activate the Site-to-Site Links 425
Creating an L2TP/IPSec Site-to-Site VPN 426
Enable the System Policy Rule on the Main Office Firewall
to Access the Enterprise CA 427
Request and Install a Certificate for the Main Office Firewall 428
Configure the Main Office ISA Firewall to use
L2TP/IPSec for the Site-to-Site Link 432
Enable the System Policy Rule on the Branch Office
Firewall to Access the Enterprise CA 434
Request and Install a Certificate for the Branch Office Firewall 435
Configure the Branch Office ISA Firewall to use
L2TP/IPSec for the Site-to-Site Link 437
Activate the L2TP/IPSec Site-to-Site VPN Connection 437
Configuring Pre-shared Keys for Site-to-Site
L2TP/IPSec VPN Links 439

IPSec Tunnel Mode Site-to-Site VPNs with Downlevel VPN Gateways 440
Using RADIUS for VPN Authentication and Remote Access Policy 440
   Configure the Internet Authentication Services (RADIUS) Server 441
   Create a VPN Clients Remote Access Policy 442
   Remote Access Permissions and Domain Functional Level 445
   Changing the User Account Dial-in Permissions 447
   Changing the Domain Functional Level 448
   Controlling Remote Access Permission via Remote Access Policy 449
   Enable the VPN Server on the ISA Firewall and
      Configure RADIUS Support 450
   Create an Access Rule Allowing VPN Clients Access
      to Approved Resources 453
   Make the Connection from a PPTP VPN Client 454
Using EAP User Certificate Authentication for Remote Access VPNs 456
   Configuring the ISA Firewall Software to
      Support EAP Authentication 457
   Enabling User Mapping for EAP Authenticated Users 459
   Issuing a User Certificate to the Remote Access
      VPN Client Machine 460
Supporting Outbound VPN Connections through the ISA Firewall 463
Installing and Configuring the DHCP Server and DHCP
   Relay Agent on the ISA Firewall 466
Summary 469

**Chapter 7 ISA 2006 Stateful Inspection
and Application Layer Filtering 471**
Introduction 472
Application Filters 472
   The SMTP Filter 473
   The DNS Filter 474
   The POP Intrusion Detection Filter 475
   The SOCKS V4 Filter 475
   The FTP Access Filter 477
   The H.323 Filter 477
   The MMS Filter 478
   The PNM Filter 478
   The PPTP Filter 478
   The RPC Filter 478
   The RTSP Filter 478

Web Filters 479
    The HTTP Security Filter (HTTP Filter) 479
        Overview of HTTP Security Filter Settings 480
            The General Tab 480
            The Methods Tab 482
            The Extensions Tab 484
            The Headers Tab 485
            The Signatures Tab 489
        HTTP Security Filter Logging 492
        Exporting and Importing HTTP Security Filter Settings 493
            Exporting an HTTP Policy from a Web Publishing Rule 493
            Importing an HTTP Policy into a Web Publishing Rule 494
        Investigating HTTP Headers for Potentially
            Dangerous Applications 495
        Example HTTP Security Filter Policies 499
        Commonly Blocked Headers and Application Signatures 503
    The ISA Server Link Translator 504
        Determining Custom Dictionary Entries 507
        Configuring Custom Link Translation Dictionary Entries 507
    The Web Proxy Filter 509
    The OWA Forms–Based Authentication Filter 510
    The RADIUS Authentication Filter 511
IP Filtering and Intrusion Detection/Intrusion Prevention 511
    Common Attacks Detection and Prevention 511
    DNS Attacks Detection and Prevention 512
    IP Options and IP Fragment Filtering 513
        Source Routing Attack 515
Summary 516

Chapter 8 Accelerating Web Performance with
ISA 2006 Caching Capabilities 517
Understanding Caching Concepts 518
    Web Caching Types 518
        Forward Caching 519
        Reverse Caching 519
            How Reverse Caching Reduces Bandwidth Usage 520
            How Reverse Caching Increases Availability of Web Content 520
    Web Caching Architectures 520
    Web Caching Protocols 523

Understanding ISA 2006's Web Caching Capabilities 523
    Using the Caching Feature 524
    Understanding Cache Rules 525
        Using Cache Rules to Specify Content Types
        That Can Be Cached. 526
        Using Cache Rules to Specify How Objects
        are Retrieved and Served from Cache 526
    Understanding the Content Download Feature 527
Configuring ISA 2006 as a Caching Firewall. 529
    Enabling and Configuring Caching. 529
        How to Enable Caching in Enterprise Edition 529
        How to Enable Caching in Standard Edition. 531
        How to Disable Caching in Enterprise Edition 531
        How to Disable Caching in Standard Edition 532
        How to Configure Properties. 532
        Configuring Which Content to Cache 532
        Configuring the Maximum Size of Objects in the Cache 533
        Configuring Whether Expired Objects
        Should be Returned from Cache. 534
        Allocating a Percentage of Memory to Caching 534
    Creating Cache Rules. 535
        How to Create a Cache Rule. 535
        How to Modify an Existing Cache Rule. 539
        How to Disable or Delete a Cache Rule. 541
        How to Change the Order of Cache Rules. 541
        How to Copy a Cache Rule 541
        How to Export and Import Cache Rules 542
    Configuring Content Downloads 544
        How to Ensure a Content Download Job Can Run 545
            Configuring the Local Host Network. 545
            Enabling the System Policy Rules. 547
            Running the Job Scheduler Service 548
        How to Create and Configure Scheduled
        Content Download Jobs 550
        How to Make Changes to an Existing Content Download Job 553
        How to Disable or Delete Content Download Jobs. 554
        How to Export and Import Content Download
        Job Configurations 554
        How to Run a Content Download Job Immediately. 555
Summary. 556

Chapter 9 Using ISA Firewall 2006's Monitoring, Logging, and Reporting Tools **557**

Introduction 558
Exploring the ISA 2006 Dashboard. 559
    Dashboard Sections. 561
        Dashboard Connectivity Section. 562
        Dashboard Services Section 563
        Dashboard Reports Section 564
        Dashboard Alerts Section 565
        Dashboard Sessions Section 566
        Dashboard System Performance Section 567
    Configuring and Customizing the Dashboard 569
Creating and Configuring ISA 2006 Alerts 570
    Alert–Triggering Events 570
    Viewing the Predefined Alerts. 573
    Creating a New Alert 573
    Modifying Alerts. 580
    Viewing Alerts that have been Triggered 581
Monitoring ISA 2006 Connectivity, Sessions, and Services 583
    Configuring and Monitoring Connectivity 583
        Creating Connectivity Verifiers. 584
        Monitoring Connectivity. 587
    Monitoring Sessions 591
        Viewing, Stopping and Pausing Monitoring of Sessions 591
        Monitoring Specific Sessions Using Filter Definitions 593
        Disconnecting Sessions. 596
        Exporting and Importing Filter Definitions. 596
    Monitoring Services 596
Working with ISA Firewall Logs and Reports 597
    Understanding ISA Firewall Logs 597
        Log Types 598
            Logging to an MSDE Database 598
            Logging to a SQL Server. 598
            Logging to a File. 599
        How to Configure Logging 600
            Configuring MSDE Database Logging 601
            Configuring Logging to a File 602
            Configuring Logging to a SQL Database 603
        How to Use the Log Viewer. 604
        How to Filter the Log Information. 605

Saving Log Viewer Data to a File 608
Exporting and Importing Filter Definitions 609
Generating, Viewing, and Publishing Reports with ISA 2006 609
How to Generate a One-Time Report 609
How to Configure an Automated Report Job 612
Other Report Tasks 615
How to View Reports 616
Publishing Reports 617
Using the ISA Firewall's Performance Monitor 618
Recommended Performance Counters 622
ISA Firewall 2004 Upgrade Considerations 622
Preserving Log Files Prior to Upgrade 623
File Logging 623
MSDE Logging 624
SQL Logging 625
Preserving SQL Logging Options Prior to Upgrade 626

Index 627

Introduction

What's New in ISA 2006 Firewalls

By Thomas W. Shinder MD, MVP

Many people who currently use ISA 2000 or 2004 will want to know why they should upgrade to ISA 2006 firewalls. While the upgrade from ISA Server 2000 to ISA 2004 was an easy one to sell because of the major improvements and changes made between ISA Server 2000 and ISA 2004, the changes included with ISA 2006 versus ISA 2004 are more incremental and provide a much smoother transition than the upgrade from 2000 to 2004.

If you take only a superficial look at the ISA 2006, the new features and capabilities seen in ISA 2006 compared to 2004 are difficult for you to see. The user interface is the same, the networking model is same, there have been no changes in terms of how the ISA firewall performs outbound access control, and there have been no changes to the core networking feature set.

The bulk of the improvements seen with the ISA 2006 firewall are focused on secure Web publishing. The other major difference between ISA 2006 and ISA 2004 is that ISA 2006 has a much more robust mechanism for handling worm flood attacks. Some ISA 2004 firewalls have suffered from worm and DNS flood attack situations. ISA 2006 includes built in mechanism to prevent exhaustion of non-paged pool memory so that even when under heavy denial of service type worm or DNS flood attacks, the ISA 2006 firewall will be able to stand up even when the ISA 2004 firewall might fall over and need to be rebooted.

When thinking about upgrading to the new ISA Firewall, consider the following:

- ISA 2006 worm and DNS flood protection will increase uptime and stability

- Significant enhancements have been made in increasing the security for remote access connections to Outlook Web Access (OWA), Outlook Mobile Access (OMA), Exchange ActiveSync (EAS) and RPC/HTTP (Outlook Anywhere). You will be able to do things such as customize the log on form, enable password changes from the log on form, and be able to automatically inform users of how many days there are until a password change is required in the log on form

- Those of you publishing SharePoint Portal servers may have frustrations and incomplete functionality when using ISA 2004. If you have SharePoint Portal Servers in place you will be able to get full functionality from your SPS deployments when publishing through an ISA 2006 firewall as it was purpose designed to provide secure remote access to SharePoint Portal Servers

- For all of you publishing Web sites, including Exchange and SharePoint Portal Server sites, you are now able to use forms-based authentication for any type of Web publishing scenario, and that editing the log on form is now completely supported by Microsoft

- For any of you publishing secure sites requiring pre-authentication at the ISA firewall, be aware that there are additional authentication mechanisms available, including LDAP authentication and RADIUS One-time password. Both these authentication methods allow the ISA firewall publishing the Web sites to be removed from the Active Directory domain but still authenticate users belonging to the domain. RADIUS OTP provides those of you who don't wish to use SecurID with another two-factor authentication option.

- Anyone interested in publishing a Web farm will benefit greatly by upgrading from ISA 2004 to ISA 2006. This is especially true for those of you who have front-end Exchange Servers and want to have two or more front-end Exchange Servers. The same is true for Client Access Servers. The ISA 2006 Web farm load balancing feature removes the requirement for you to make the FE/Client Access Server SecureNET clients when NLB was enabled on the FE Exchange Server array. In fact, ISA 2006 Web farm load balancing completely removes the requirement for NLB on the FE Exchange Server array or a third-party hardware load balancer.

While it might seem to you that there is a relatively small feature set on which to base upgrades from 2004 to 2006, the improvements included with ISA Server 2006 make it worth upgrading for any company that publishes Web sties. This might appear to you at first to represent a relatively small percentage of the entire ISA firewall feature set, but from my experience with thousands of ISA Firewall admins, it appears that ISA Server's largest deployment scenario is for secure reverse Web proxy, and this is exactly the feature set that the ISA Firewall development team has focused upon.

What's New and Improved in ISA Server 2006	
New Feature	**What it does**
Web Farm Load Balancing **NEW**	ISA 2006 Web Farm Load Balancing enables the ISA firewall administrator to publish a farm of Web servers that host the same content or perform similar roles. The ISA firewall provides both load balancing and fail over and fail back for the published Web farm and does not require NLB to enabled on the ISA firewall array or on the Web farm. You'll benefit from this feature because they do not need to enable NLB on the farm warm (which would require that the farm members be SecureNET clients) and you don't need to purchase an expensive external load balancer, such as F5.
Forms-based authentication support for all Web Publishing Rules **NEW**	In ISA 2004, Forms-based authentication was supported only for Outlook Web Access Web Publishing Rules. ISA Server 2006 expands its forms-based authentication support by enabling forms-based authentication for all Web sites published using Web Publishing Rules.
Kerberos Constrained Delegation **NEW**	In ISA 2004, User Certificate authentication could be performed by the ISA firewall, but the user's credentials could not be forwarded to the published Web server. This generated multiple authentication prompts. In ISA Server 2006, a user can pre-authenticate with the ISA firewall and then that users credentials can be delegated as Kerberos credentials to the published Web servers, thus avoiding multiple authentication prompts and improving the end-user experience.
Enhanced Delegation of Authentication support	ISA 2004 supported only delegation of basic authentication. ISA Server 2006 enhances support for authentication delegation by enabling credentials to be delegated as Kerberos, Integrated, Negotiate or basic. This increases the flexibility of deployment for ISA firewalls since many published Web servers do not support basic authentication. In addition, the increases security for Web Publishing scenarios where SSL to SSL bridging is not an option and prevents the clear text basic credentials from being intercepted on the wire.

Continued

New Feature	What it does
Separate name resolution from CONNECT name in Web Publishing Rules **NEW**	In ISA 2004, the same name was used for name resolution and the CONNECT name sent to the published Web server. This created a situation where the ISA firewall administrator had to create a split DNS, or enter a custom HOSTS file entry on the ISA firewall so that the CONNECT name resolved to the IP address of the published server on the internal network. ISA Server 2006 solves this problem by allowing you to specific a name or IP address that is separate from the CONNECT name used by the Web Publishing Rule.
Improved Exchange Server Web Publishing Rule Wizard	The ISA Server 2006 Exchange Server Web Publishing Wizard includes a number of improvements that makes publishing all versions of Exchange, from version 5.5 to 2007 easier than ever.
Integrated support for Password changes on log on form **NEW**	In ISA 2004, there was little or no support for allowing the users to change their passwords when using Forms-based authentication. ISA Server 2006 solves this problem by integrating the ability for a user to change his password right in the log on form. No special configuration tasks are required on the ISA firewall or published OWA Server
Integrated support for Password change notification on log on form **NEW**	In ISA 2004, there was no integrated support for providing users information about pending password expiration dates. ISA 2006 solves this problem by making the option available to the ISA firewall administrator to inform users of pending password expiration dates. You can customized the warning period by specifying the number of days in advance that you want users to be aware of password expiration.
Improved Mail Server Publishing Wizard	In ISA 2004, a single Mail Server Publishing Wizard was used to published both Exchange Web services and non-Web services. ISA Server 2006 breaks out Web from non-Web publishing tasks into two separate wizards, making it easier to publish non-Web protocols for your Exchange mail server.

New Feature	What it does
SharePoint Portal Server Publishing Wizard **NEW**	It was possible to publish SharePoint Portal Servers using ISA 2004, but the process was potentially complex and not all features were available from the Internet because of problem with link translation. ISA Server 2006 solves this problem with enhanced support for SharePoint Portal Server publishing and an updated link translation dictionary that takes all the complexity of successfully publishing a SharePoint Portal Server deployment.
Single Sign-on **NEW**	One of the most requested features that didn't make its way into ISA 2004 was single sign-on. In ISA 2004, users had to reauthenticate even if they were connecting to a Web server in the same domain as the original Web server. ISA Server 2006 solves this problem by enabling single sign-on on a per-listen/per-domain basis. If multiple Web sites belong to the same domain, and are published by the same Web listener, then users will not be required to reauthenticate and cached credentials are used.
Support for wildcard certificates on the published Web Server **NEW**	ISA 2004 supported wildcard certificates on its Web listener, but did not support wildcard certificates on the published Web server located behind the ISA firewall. ISA Server 2006 improves on wildcard certificate support by allowing the ISA firewall administrator to use a wildcard certificate on the published Web server.
Advanced Client Certificate Restrictions and Configurable Certificate Trust List **NEW**	A completely new feature included with ISA Server 2006 is Client Certificate Restrictions and configurable Certificate Trust List. The Client Certificate Restrictions feature allows you to set restrictions on the certificates users can provide when User Certificate authentication is enabled. Restrictions can be defined based on: ■ Issuer ■ Subject ■ Enhanced Key Usage ■ Extensions

Continued

New Feature	What it does
	In addition, you can set restrictions on the OID (object ID) presented by the User Certificate The Configurable Trust List option enables you to set specific trusted CAs on a per-Web Listener basis. This list of trusted CAs is separate and distinct from the ISA firewall machine's list of Trusted CAs. This enables the ISA firewall administrator to limit the User Certificates that can be used to authenticate with the ISA firewall to those issued only by a specific set of CAs, such as the company's private CAs. This allows you to implement User Certificate Authentication as a method to limit access only to corporate managed machines and devices, such as PDAs and PDA enabled phones.
Fall back to basic authentication for non-Web browser clients **NEW**	One of the major problems ISA firewall administrators had with ISA 2004 was that they needed to create two listeners, requiring two different certificates, to publish both RPC/HTTP and OWA sites when forms-based authentication was enabled on the OWA Web listener. ISA Server 2006 solves this problem by detecting the user-agent string in the client request and falling back to basic authentication when the client is not a Web browser. This allows you to publish OWA with forms-based authentication enabled and RPC/HTTP using the same Web listener. The end result is that if you have only a single external IP address, both OWA with FBA and RPC/HTTP can be published using that single IP address, something not possible with ISA 2004.
Enhanced Link Translation Dictionary	Link translation dictionaries are used to change the contents of pages returned to external users. This is helpful when Web applications imbed private computer names in responses sent to external clients, since external clients are not able to connect to servers using their Internal names. ISA Server 2006 includes an enhanced link translation dictionary that automatically populates itself based on settings in your Web Publishing Rules. This allows the ISA firewall administrator to provide a seamless experience for external users who need to access multiple sites published by the ISA firewall. For example, this feature allows OWA users to receive links to SharePoint Portal Server messages in their OWA e-mail and access those links automatically, without complex reconfiguration required on the OWA and SharePoint Portal Server or even on the ISA firewall itself.

New Feature	What it does
Cross array link translation **NEW**	Cross array link translation allows you to publish Web sites across multiple arrays and have the link translation dictionary available for all arrays in the same ISA Enterprise Edition enterprise group. This greatly simplifies large deployments by automatically populating the link translation list and avoiding the requirement for manual reconfiguration.
Improved CARP Support in ISA 2006 Enterprise Edition	Changes were made to the CARP algorithm with the release of ISA 2004 SP2. These changes have been carried over to ISA Server 2006 so that instead of requiring CARP exceptions to URLs you don't want to be load balanced, you now create CARP exceptions for URLs that you *do* want load balanced. This change was made within the context of another change included with ISA 2004 SP2, where instead of using the URL to predetermine which array member handled the request, the FQDN is now used instead. This prevents problems with session handling for connections that might be spread across multiple array members for specific URLs contained within the same page or session.
BITS Caching for Microsoft Update Sites	BITS caching for Microsoft Updates was introduced with ISA 2004 SP2. This feature has been carried over and included with ISA Server 2006. BITS caching for Microsoft updates greatly improves bandwidth utilization over site to site or WAN links, making more bandwidth available to branch offices that would otherwise be overwhelmed with update traffic from servers located at the main office or the Internet. Main office servers also benefit from bandwidth optimization provided by BITS update caching.
HTTP Compression support	Support for HTTP Compression was introduced in ISA 2004 SP2 and carried over to ISA Server 2006. HTTP compression allows the ISA firewall administrator to control from where clients can ask for HTTP compression and from what servers can return HTTP compression. HTTP compression is very useful in a branch office scenario where bandwidth to the main office is at a premium.
Diffserv QoS Support for HTTP communications	Diffserv QoS support was introduced with ISA 2004 SP2 and carried over to ISA Server 2006. Diffserv is a method that can be used on Diffserv enabled networks to give preference to certain packets over

Continued

New Feature	What it does
	others. The ISA firewall administrator can use Diffserv to prioritize packets destined to certain server over those of non-priority servers
Add multiple VIPs within the ISA Server management console NEW	ISA 2004 supported multiple VIP IP addresses. However, in order to add more than one VIP, the ISA firewall administrator had to drop out of the ISA management console and enter these IP addresses in the TCP/IP configuration of the NIC. ISA Server 2006 improves this situation by allowing the administrator to enter addition VIPs in the ISA management console.
Branch office Connectivity Wizard NEW	With ISA 2004, deploying branch office ISA firewalls was potentially complex, sometime requiring a site to site VPN connection to be configured and then trying to join the branch office ISA firewall to the domain after the site to site VPN tunnel was established. ISA Server 2006 takes the complexity out of branch office deployment by introducing a branch office deployment wizard, that enables the ISA firewall administrator to create a simple answer file that allows a non-technical user to plug a branch office ISA firewall device and run the answer file from a simple link.
Ability to assign multiple certificates to a single Web listener NEW	ISA 2004 allowed the ISA firewall administrator to bind only a single certificate to a Web listener. This was problematic when you wanted to use the same Web listener to publish multiple secure Web sties. ISA Server 2006 solves this problem by allowing you to bind multiple certificates to the same Web listener and assigning that Web listener to multiple Web Publishing Rules, enabling single sign-on and an improved end-user experience.
Support for customized forms for Forms-based authentication NEW	ISA 2004 supported forms-based authentication only for publishing OWA sites and customizing the form was not supported. With ISA Server 2006, you can now use forms-based authentication to publish any site and forms customization is supported.
LDAP authentication for Web Publishing Rules NEW	With ISA 2004, if the ISA firewall machine was not a member of the domain, the only viable method of pre-authenticating users at the ISA firewall was to use RADIUS authentication for Web Publishing Rules.

New Feature	What it does
	RADIUS is limited because it does not allow the administrator to leverage Active Directory Groups. With ISA Server 2006, you can use LDAP authentication for ISA firewalls that are not domain members and take advantage of Active Directory Groups. In addition, the ISA 2006 firewall can be configured to use multiple LDAP servers and rules can be configured to look at authentication strings and forward the authentication request to the appropriate LDAP server (Active Directory domain controller).
RADIUS One-Time Passwords (OTP) for Web Publishing Rules **NEW**	Another authentication option now available to non-domain member for Web Publishing Rules is RADIUS One-Time passwords (OTP). RADIUS OTP allows users to authenticate using a password that is valid on a single attempt and cannot be reused.
Improved cookie management	ISA 2004 did not provide an administrator accessible method for managing cookies on client machines connecting to published Web resources. With ISA Server 2006, the administrator is provided several options for controlling how cookies are validated and configurable credentials caching.
Enhanced Flood Mitigation Settings	ISA 2004 included a basic flood mitigation feature that helped protect the networks that the ISA firewall was connected, in addition to the ISA firewall machine itself. ISA Server 2006 builds on the ISA 2004 flood protection mechanism to help protect against more types of flood attacks
Customer Experience Program **NEW**	The customer experience program provides a mechanism where Microsoft can obtain information about how ISA Server is deployed and used in production environments. No personally identifiable information is sent to Microsoft, and this information is used to help Microsoft understand how to improve the product in service packs and future releases. The Customer Experience Program was first introduced with ISA 2004 SP2.
Support for Published Configuration Storage Servers **NEW**	ISA Server 2006 enables the administrator to connect to Configuration Storage Servers at the main office even when the site to site VPN connection between branch and main offices becomes unavailable. You can publish the main office Configuration Storage Server

Continued

New Feature	What it does
	and configure the branch office ISA firewall to connect to the published Configuration Storage Server over the Internet in the event that the site to site VPN connection becomes unavailable.
Enhanced support for SSL Accelerators in NLB Scenarios **NEW**	When an NLB array of ISA firewalls publishes secure SSL Web sites, the same Web site certificate must be installed on all the array members accepting incoming connections for the published Web site. This can be problematic when SSL accelerator cards are used and require that different certificates be bound to each SSL card in the NLB array. ISA Server 2006 supports binding different certificates to each card in the array to better support SSL accelerator cards.
Support for outbound SSL Bridging (add-on required) **NEW**	Although not a feature in the base product, ISA firewall administrators can significantly increase the network security by using an ISA Server add-on product named ClearTunnel (www.collectivesoftware.com) ClearTunnel enables the ISA firewall to perform application layer inspection on outbound SSL connections and prevents potential exploits from being downloaded from the Internet through an encrypted SSL tunnel. SSL connections outbound represent a major security threat to corporate networks today, so the ability to inspect outbound SSL communications is a great enhancement to the network security that ISA Server can provide.
Updated MOM Management Pack	ISA Server 2006 includes an updated MOM pack.
Improved Alerting	ISA Server 2006 builds on the configuration and security alerts includes with ISA 2004 and adds a number of new alerts that help information the ISA administrator of configuration issues, certificate issue, security issues, and threat triggers. The new alerts included with ISA Server 2006 will make it easier than ever to troubleshoot ISA firewall related problems.
Site to Site VPN Wizard and Unattended Answer File support	ISA Server 2000 included a comprehensive site to site VPN wizard that took the complexities out of configuring a site to site VPN connection. This feature

New Feature	What it does
NEW	was removed from ISA 2004. In ISA Server 2006, the site to site VPN wizard returns and makes creating site to site VPN connections easier than ever. In addition to simplifying the creation of a site to site VPN, the new ISA 2006 site to site VPN wizards allows the main office ISA firewall administrator to create a simple answer file that a non-technical users at a branch office can use to automatically connect the branch office ISA firewall to the main office corporate network.
Logging supports Referring Server **NEW**	A common complaint among ISA firewall administrators was the inability to log the referring server for connections made to servers published using Web Publishing Rules. ISA Server 2006 solves this problem by adding the ability to log the referring server in the ISA firewall's Web proxy log files.

In this book we'll go over many of these new features. However, some of the features are quite complex and do not lend themselves to coverage in a relatively short book. If there is a new feature that's not covered in the book and you want to know more about it, please visit www.isaserver.org and search the site. I am confident that you'll find the information that you need. If you don't find the feature of interest covered, please write to me at tshinder@isaserver.org and I will create an article that covers that feature or capability. Of course, as the owner of this book, you're always welcome to write to me about any questions you might have anything contained in this book.

Thanks!
Thomas W. Shinder MD, MVP – October 2007

Chapter 1

Network Security Basics

Solutions in this chapter:

- Security Overview
- Defining Basic Security Concepts
- Addressing Security Objectives
- Recognizing Network Security Threats
- Designing a Comprehensive Security Plan

☑ Summary

Introduction

Before you can understand firewalls and how ISA Server 2006 works, you need to look at the big picture: what we mean by network security in general – and Internet security in particular – why it's necessary, how we can create a comprehensive security policy to protect our networks from unauthorized access, and where ISA Server fits into that picture.

Network security is a big topic and is growing into a high profile (and often highly paid) Information Technology (IT) specialty area. Security-related websites are tremendously popular with savvy Internet users. The popularity of security-related certifications has expanded. Esoteric security measures like biometric identification and authentication – formerly the province of science fiction writers and perhaps a few ultra-secretive government agencies – have become commonplace in corporate America. Yet, with all this focus on security, many organizations still implement security measures in an almost haphazard way, with no well-thought-out plan for making all the parts fit together. Computer security involves many aspects, from protection of the physical equipment to protection of the electronic bits and bytes that make up the information that resides on the network.

In the next section, we will provide a brief overview of what we mean by "security" and how it applies to your computer network.

> **NOTE**
>
> This chapter focuses on generic computer and Internet security concepts and how to develop a comprehensive security plan for your organization. The rest of this book will discuss how ISA Server fits into that security plan.

Security Overview

The term *computer security* encompasses many related, yet separate, topics. These can be stated as *security objectives*, and include:

- Control of physical accessibility to the computer(s) and/or network
- Prevention of accidental erasure, modification or compromise of data
- Detection and prevention of intentional internal security breaches
- Detection and prevention of unauthorized external intrusions (hacking)

Network security solutions are loosely divided into three categories: *hardware, software* and *human*. In this chapter, we will provide an overview of basic security concepts. Then, we will examine the four security objectives and look at each of the three categories of security solutions.

Defining Basic Security Concepts

A generic definition of *security* is "freedom from risk or danger; safety" (The American Heritage Dictionary).

This definition is perhaps a little misleading when it comes to computer and networking security, as it implies a degree of protection that is inherently impossible in the modern connectivity-oriented computing environment.

This is why the same dictionary provides another definition specific to computer science: "The *level to which* a program or device is safe from unauthorized use [emphasis added]." Implicit in this definition is the caveat that the objectives of security and accessibility – the two top priorities on the minds of many network administrators – are, by their very natures, diametrically opposed. The more accessible your data is, the less secure it is. Likewise, the more tightly you secure it, the more you impede accessibility. Any security plan is an attempt to strike the proper balance between the two.

As in any other specialty field, security professionals speak a language all their own and understanding the concepts requires that you learn the jargon. At the end of this section, you will find a list of some common terms that you are likely to encounter in the IT security field.

Knowledge is Power

The above title is a famous hacker's motto (along with such other gems as "Information wants to be free," and the simplistic but optimistic, "Hack the world!"). However, it is a truism that applies not only to those attempting to gain access to data they aren't supposed to see, but also to those who are trying to protect themselves from the intruders. The first step in winning any battle – and network security *is* a battle over the ownership and control of your computer files – is the same as it's always been: "know thine enemy."

To protect your network resources from theft, damage, or unwanted exposure, you must understand who initiates these things, why, and how they do it. Knowledge will make *you* powerful, too – and better able to prevent unauthorized intrusions into your network. In the section entitled *Detecting and Preventing Unauthorized External Intrusions,* we will discuss the various motivations that drive different network intruders and the types of people who make a practice of "breaking and entering" networks.

The very best place to learn is from the hackers themselves. Many network administrators and even some security specialists eschew the books and websites that are written to a hacker audience or from the hacker's point of view. This may be because one fears "guilt by association" or believes that it would be somehow demeaning to hang out with the hackers. This attitude may be based on high moral ground, but strategically, it's a mistake.

Think Like a Thief

It is well known in law enforcement circles that the best criminal investigators are those who are best able to "get inside the mind" of the lawbreaker. Network intrusion detectives will find that the same is true – to prevent your network from falling prey to hackers, or to catch data thieves when they do get in, requires that you be able to adopt a mindset emulating theirs.

This means learning to anticipate the intruder's actions. First, you must determine *what* needs to be protected, and to what degree. A wealthy person not only establishes a general security perimeter by building fences around the house and locking doors and windows, but also places the most valuable items in a wall or floor safe. This provides multiple *layers* of protection. The practice of implementing multiple layers of protection is known as *defense in depth.*

ISA Server can be an important layer of protection in your organization's security plan.

The Intrusion Triangle

Borrowing again from the law enforcement community, crime prevention specialists use a model called the "Crime Triangle" to explain that certain criteria must exist before a crime can occur. We can adapt this same triangle to network security: the same three criteria must exist before a network security breach can take place. The three "legs" or points of the triangle are shown in Figure 1.1.

Figure 1.1 All three legs of the triangle must exist for a network intrusion to occur

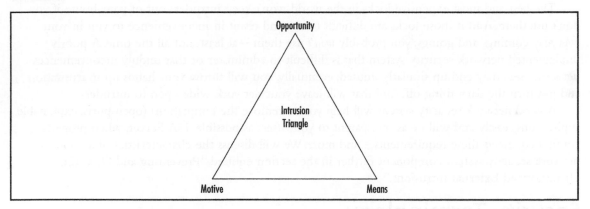

Let's look at each point individually:

■ **Motive:** An intruder must have a reason to want to breach the security of your network (even if the reason is "just for fun"); otherwise, he/she won't bother.

■ **Means:** An intruder must have the ability (either the programming knowledge, or, in the case of "script kiddies," the intrusion software written by others), or he/she won't be able to breach your security.

■ **Opportunity:** An intruder must have the chance to enter the network, either because of flaws in your security plan, holes in a software program that open an avenue of access, or physical proximity to network components; if there is no opportunity to intrude, the would-be hacker will go elsewhere.

If you think about the three-point intrusion criteria for a moment, you'll see that there is really only one leg of the triangle over which you, as the network administrator or security specialist, have any control. It is unlikely that you can do much to remove the intruder's *motive*. The motive is likely to be built into the type of data you have on the network or even the personality of the intruder him/herself. It is also not possible for you to prevent the intruder from having or obtaining the *means* to breach your security. Programming knowledge is freely available, and there are many experienced hackers out there who are more than happy to help out a less-sophisticated ones. The one thing that you *can* affect is the *opportunity* afforded the hacker.

Removing Intrusion Opportunities

Crime prevention officers tell members of the community that the "good guys" probably can't keep a potential burglar from wanting to steal, and they certainly can't keep the potential burglar from obtaining burglary tools or learning the "tricks of the trade." What citizens *can* do is take away, as much as possible, the opportunity for the burglar to target their own homes.

This means putting dead-bolt locks on the doors (and using them), getting a big, loud, unfriendly dog, installing an alarm system, and the like. In other words, as a homeowner, your goal is not to prevent the burglar from burglarizing, but to make your own home a less desirable target. As a network "owner," your objective is to "harden" your own network so that all those hackers out there who already have the motive and the means will look for an easier victim.

The best and most expensive locks in the world won't keep intruders out of your house if you don't use them. And if those locks are difficult to use and result in inconvenience to you in your everyday comings and goings, you probably *won't* use them – at least, not all the time. A poorly implemented network security system that is difficult to administer or that unduly inconveniences network users may end up similarly unused; eventually, you will throw your hands up in frustration and just turn the darn thing off. And that will leave your network wide open to intruders.

A good network security system will help you to remove the temptations (open ports, exploitable applications) easily and will be as transparent to your users as possible. ISA Server, when properly configured, meets these requirements – and more. We will discuss the characteristics of a good network security system component further in the section entitled "Preventing and Detecting Unauthorized External Intrusions."

Security Terminology

Every industry has its own "language," the jargon that describes concepts and procedures peculiar to the field. Computer networking is infamous for the "technotalk" and the proliferation of acronyms that often mystify outsiders. Specialty areas within an industry often have their own brands of jargon, as well, and the computer security sub-field is no exception.

It is not possible to provide a complete glossary of security-related terms within the scope of this chapter, but in this section, we will define some of the more common words and phrases that you may encounter as you begin to explore the fascinating world of computer security:

- **Attack** In the context of computer/network security, an attack is an attempt to access resources on a computer or a network without authorization, or to bypass security measures that are in place.

- **Audit** To track security-related events, such as logging onto the system or network, accessing objects, or exercising user/group rights or privileges.

- **Availability of data** Reliable and timely access to data.

- **Breach** Successfully defeating security measures to gain access to data or resources without authorization, or to make data or resources available to unauthorized persons, or to delete or alter computer files.

- **Brute force attack** Attempt to "crack" passwords by sequentially trying all possible combinations of characters until the right combination works to allow access.

- **Buffer**   A holding area for data.

- **Buffer overflow**   A way to crash a system by putting more data into a buffer than the buffer is able to hold.

- **CIA triad**   Confidentiality, Integrity, and Availability of data. Ensuring the confidentiality, integrity, and availability of data and services are primary security objectives that are often related to each other. See also *availability of data*, *confidentiality of data*, and *integrity of data*.

- **Confidentiality of data**   Ensuring that the contents of messages will be kept secret. See also *integrity of data*.

- **Countermeasures**   Steps taken to prevent or respond to an attack or malicious code.

- **Cracker**   A hacker who specializes in "cracking" or discovering system passwords to gain access to computer systems without authorization. See also *hacker*.

- **Crash**   Sudden failure of a computer system, rendering it unusable.

- **Defense-in-depth**   The practice of implementing multiple layers of security. Effective defense-in-depth strategies do not limit themselves to focusing on technology, but also focus on operations and people. For example, a firewall can protect against unauthorized intrusion, but training and the implementation of well-considered security policies help to ensure that the firewall is properly configured.

- **Denial of Service attack**   A deliberate action that keeps a computer or network from functioning as intended (for example, preventing users from being able to log onto the network).

- **Exposure**   A measure of the extent to which a network or individual computer is open to attack, based on its particular vulnerabilities, how well known it is to hackers, and the time duration during which intruders have the opportunity to attack. For example, a computer using a dialup analog connection has less exposure to attack coming over the Internet, because it is connected for a shorter period of time than those using "always-on" connections such as cable, DSL or T-carrier.

- **Hacker**   A person who spends time learning the details of computer programming and operating systems, how to test the limits of their capabilities, and where their vulnerabilities lie. See also *cracker*.

- **Integrity of data**   Ensuring that data has not been modified or altered, that the data received is identical to the data that was sent.

- **Least privilege**   The principle of least privilege requires that users and administrators have only the minimum level of access to perform their job-related duties. In military parlance, the principle of least privilege is referred to as *need to know*.

- **Malicious code**   A computer program or script that performs an action that intentionally damages a system or data, that performs another unauthorized purpose, or that provides unauthorized access to the system.

- **Penetration testing**   Evaluating a system by attempting to circumvent the computer's or network's security measures.

- **Reliability**   The probability of a computer system or network continuing to perform in a satisfactory manner for a specific time period under normal operating conditions.

- **Risk**   The probability that a specific security threat will be able to exploit a system vulnerability, resulting in damage, loss of data, or other undesired results. That is, a risk is the sum of the threat plus the vulnerability.

- **Risk management**   The process of identifying, controlling, and either minimizing or completely eliminating events that pose a threat to system reliability, data integrity, and data confidentiality.

- **Sniffer**   A program that captures data as it travels across a network. Also called a *packet sniffer*.

- **Social engineering**   Gaining unauthorized access to a system or network by subverting personnel (for example, posing as a member of the IT department to convince users to reveal their passwords).

- **TCSEC**   Trusted Computer System Evaluation Criteria. A means of evaluating the level of security of a system.

- **Technical vulnerability**   A flaw or bug in the hardware or software components of a system that leaves it vulnerable to security breach.

- **Threat**   A potential danger to data or systems. A threat agent can be a virus; a hacker; a natural phenomenon, such as a tornado; a disgruntled employee; a competitor, and other menaces.

- **Trojan horse**   A computer program that appears to perform a desirable function but contains hidden code that is intended to allow unauthorized collection, modification or destruction of data.

- **Virus**   A program that is introduced onto a system or network for the purpose of performing an unauthorized action (which can vary from popping up a harmless message to destroying all data on the hard disk).

- **Vulnerability**   A weakness in the hardware or software or security plan that leaves a system or network open to threat of unauthorized access or damage or destruction of data.

- **Worm**   A program that replicates itself, spreading from one machine to another across a network.

Once you are comfortable with the terminology, you can begin to address the individual objectives that will assist you in realizing your goal to create a secure network environment.

Addressing Security Objectives

If our security goal is to have complete control over what data comes into and goes out of our networks, we must define objectives that will help us reach that goal. We listed some general security objectives related to computer networks – especially those connected to an outside internetwork such as the Global Internet – as controlling physical access, preventing accidental compromise of data, detecting and preventing intentional internal security breaches, and detecting and preventing unauthorized external intrusions. In the following sections, we will examine each of these objectives in detail.

Controlling Physical Access

One of the most important, and at the same time most overlooked aspects of a comprehensive network security plan is physical access control. This matter is often left up to facilities managers or plant security departments, or it is outsourced to security guard companies. Network administrators frequently concern themselves with sophisticated software and hardware solutions that prevent intruders from accessing internal computers remotely, while doing nothing to protect the servers, routers, cable, and other physical components of the network from direct access.

Thinking Outside the Box About Security

In far too many supposedly security-conscious organizations, computers are locked away from employees and visitors all day, only to be left open at night to the janitorial staff, which has keys to all offices. It is not at all uncommon for computer espionage experts to pose as members of the cleaning crew to gain physical access to machines that hold sensitive data. This is a favorite ploy for several reasons:

- Cleaning services are often contracted out, and workers in the industry are often transient, so that company employees may not be easily aware of who is or isn't a legitimate employee of the cleaning company.
- Cleaning is usually done late at night, when all or most company employees are gone, making it easier to surreptitiously steal data.
- Cleaning crew members are often paid little or no attention by company employees, who take their presence for granted and think nothing of their being in areas where the presence of others might be questioned.

Physically breaking into the server room and stealing the hard disk on which sensitive data resides may be a crude method; nonetheless, it happens. In some organizations, it may be the easiest way to gain unauthorized access, especially for an intruder who has help "on the inside."

Physical Access Factors

It is important for you to make physical access control the "outer perimeter" of your security plan. This means:

- Controlling physical access to the servers
- Controlling physical access to networked workstations

- Controlling physical access to network devices

- Controlling physical access to the cable

- Being aware of security considerations with wireless media

- Being aware of security considerations related to portable computers

- Recognizing the security risk of allowing data to be printed out

- Recognizing the security risks involving floppy disks, CDs, tapes, and other removable media

Let's look at why each of these is important and how you can implement a physical security plan that addresses all these factors.

Protecting the Servers

File servers on which sensitive data is stored and infrastructure servers that provide mission critical services such as logon authentication and access control should be placed in a highly secure location. At the minimum, servers should be in a locked room where only those who need to work directly with the servers have access. Keys should be distributed sparingly, and records should be kept of issuance and return.

If security needs are high due to the nature of the business or the nature of the data, access to the server room may be controlled by magnetic card, electronic locks requiring entry of a numerical code, or even biometric access control devices such as fingerprint or retinal scanners. Both ingress and egress should be controlled – ideally with logs, video cameras, and/or other means of recording both who enters and who exits.

Other security measures include monitor detectors or other alarm systems, activated during non-business hours, and security cameras. A security guard or company should monitor these devices.

Keeping Workstations Secure

Many network security plans focus on the servers but ignore the risk posed by workstations with network access to those servers. It is not uncommon for employees to leave their computers unsecured when they leave for lunch or even when they leave for the evening. Often there will be a workstation in the receptionist area that is open to visitors who walk in off the street. If the receptionist must leave briefly, the computer – and the network to which it is connected – is vulnerable unless steps have been taken to ensure that it is secure.

A good security plan includes protection of all unmanned workstations. A secure client operating system such as Windows NT or Windows 2000 requires an interactive logon with a valid account name and password in order to access the operating system (unlike Windows 9x). This allows users to "lock" the workstation when they are going to be away from it so someone else can't just step up and start using the computer.

However, don't depend on access permissions and other software security methods alone to protect your network. If a potential intruder can gain physical access to a networked computer, he/she is that much closer to accessing your valuable data or introducing a virus onto your network.

Ensure all workstation users adhere to a good password policy, as discussed in the section entitled *Planning a Comprehensive Security Plan* later in this chapter.

Many modern PC cases come with some type of locking mechanism that will help prevent an unauthorized person from opening the case and stealing the hard disk. Locks are also available to prevent use of the floppy drive, copying data to diskette, and/or rebooting the computer with a floppy.

Protecting Network Devices

Hubs, routers, switches and other network devices should be physically secured from unauthorized access. It is easy to forget that just because a device doesn't have a monitor on which you can *see* data, this does not mean the data can't be captured or destroyed at that access point.

For example, a traditional Ethernet hub sends all data out every port on the hub. An intruder who has access to the hub can plug a packet-sniffing device (or a laptop computer with sniffer software) that operates in "promiscuous mode" into a spare port and capture data sent to any computer on the segment, as shown in Figure 1.2.

Figure 1.2 An intruder who has access to the hub can easily intercept data

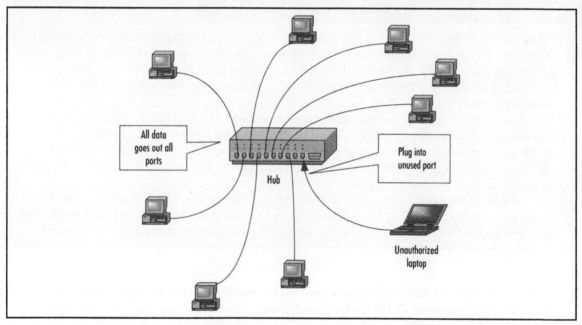

Although switches and routers are somewhat more secure, any device through which the data passes is a point of vulnerability. Replacing hubs with switches and routers makes it more difficult for an intruder to "sniff" on your network, but it is still possible to use techniques such as Address Resolution Protocol (ARP) spoofing. This is sometimes called *router redirection*, in which nearby machines are redirected to forward traffic through an intruder's machine by sending ARP packets that contain the router's Internet Protocol (IP) address mapped to the intruder's machine's MAC address. This results in other machines believing the intruder's machine is the router, and so they send their traffic to it. A similar method uses Internet Control Message Protocol (ICMP) router advertisement messages.

It is also possible, with certain switches, to overflow the address tables with multiple false Media Access Control (MAC) addresses or send a continuous flow of random garbage through the switch to trigger it to change from bridging mode to repeating mode. This means all frames will be broadcast on all ports, giving the intruder the same opportunity to access the data that he would have with a regular hub. This is called *switch jamming*.

Finally, if the switch has a special monitor port designed to be used with a sniffer for legitimate (network troubleshooting) purposes, an intruder who has physical access to the switch can simply plug into this port and capture network data.

Your network devices should be placed in a locked room or closet and protected in the same manner as your servers.

How Packet Sniffers Work

Packetsniffer/protocol analyzer devices and programs are not used solely for nefarious purposes, although intruders use them to capture unencrypted data and clear-text passwords that will allow them to break into systems. Despite the fact that they can be used to "steal" data as it travels across the network, they are also invaluable troubleshooting tools for network administrators.

The sniffer captures individual data packets and allows you to view and analyze the message contents and packet headers. This can be useful in diagnosing network communications problems and uncovering network bottlenecks that are impacting performance. Packet sniffers can also be turned against hackers and crackers and used to discover unauthorized intruders.

The most important part of the sniffer is the capture driver. This is the component that captures the network traffic, filters it (according to criteria set by the user), and stores the data in a buffer. The packets can then be analyzed and decoded to display the contents.

It is often possible to detect an unauthorized packet sniffer on the wire using a device called a Time Domain Reflectometer (TDR), which sends a pulse down the cable and creates a graph of the reflections that are returned. Those who know how to read the graph can tell whether unauthorized devices are attached to the cable and where.

Other ways of detecting unauthorized connections include monitoring hub or switch lights using Simple Network Monitoring Protocol (SNMP) managers that log connections and disconnections or using one of the many tools designed for the specific purpose of detecting sniffers on the network. There are also several techniques using Packet Internetwork Groper (ping), ARP, and DNS that may help you to catch unauthorized sniffers.

Securing the Cable

The next step in protecting your network data is to secure the cable across which it travels. Twisted pair and coaxial cable are both vulnerable to data capture; an intruder who has access to the cable can tap into it and eavesdrop on messages being sent across it. A number of companies make "tapping" devices.

Fiber optic cable is more difficult to tap into because it does not produce electrical pulses, but instead, uses pulses of light to represent the 0s and 1s of binary data. It is, however, possible for a sophisticated intruder to use an optical splitter and tap into the signal on fiber optic media.

Compromise of security at the physical level is a special threat when network cables are not contained in one facility but span a distance between buildings. There is even a name for this risk, "manhole manipulation," referring to the easy access intruders often have to cabling that runs through underground conduits.

Cable taps can sometimes be detected by using a TDR or optical TDR to measure the strength of the signal and determine where the tap is located.

Safely Going Wireless

Wireless media is becoming more and more popular as our society becomes more mobile, and many predict it will be next big thing in networking during the first years of the new millennium.

Large companies such as Cisco Systems, Lucent Technologies, Sun Microsystems, and Microsoft have invested large amounts of talent and money into the wireless initiative. Wireless Internet access based on the Wireless Access Protocol (WAP) is common in Europe and beginning to catch on in the U.S. Fixed wireless services are offered by communications giants such as AT&T and Sprint and companies such as Metricom (which offers the Ricochet wireless service).

Wireless networking offers several distinct advantages over traditional cabled networking. Laptop users can easily connect and disconnect as they come and go. Workers out in the field can maintain network communications in areas where there are no cables or phone lines. For professions such as policing, where employees work from a moving vehicle most of the time, wireless is the only way to stay connected to the department LAN. For telecommuters in rural areas where DSL and cable modem access are unavailable, wireless technologies such as satellite provide a broadband alternative to slow analog modems.

There are several different varieties of wireless networking, including:

- Radio (narrow band or spread spectrum)

- Satellite/microwave

- Laser/infrared

The most popular wireless technologies are radio-based and operate according to the IEEE 802.x standards. 802.11b (and increasingly, 802.11g, which is backwardly compatible with b) networks are becoming commonplace as commercial "hot spots" spring up in major cities and businesses and home computer users implement wireless networks because of their convenience. Wireless connectivity is available at hotels, airports, and even coffee shops and restaurants.

Despite the many benefits of these wireless technologies, they also present special problems, especially in the area of network security. Wireless is more vulnerable to inception of data than cabled media. Radio and microwave are known as broadcast media. Because the signals are transmitted across the airwaves, any receiver set to the correct frequency can easily eavesdrop on the communications.

The practice of "war driving" (going out with a wireless NIC-equipped laptop or handheld system and looking for open wireless networks to which they can connect) is a favorite pastime of hackers.

> **NOTE**
>
> Laser signals are not as easy to intercept; however, because laser is a line-of-sight technology, it is more limited in application – and lasers are much more sensitive to environmental factors, such as weather.

If security is a priority, any data sent via radio or microwave links should be encrypted.

Have Laptop, Will Travel

Portable computers – laptops, notebooks, and new fully functional handheld computers such as the Pocket PC and Palm machines – present their own security problems based on the very features that make them popular– their small size and mobility. Physical security for portable computers is especially important because it is so easy to steal the entire machine, data and all.

Luckily, there are a large number of companies that make theft protection devices and security software for laptops. Locks and alarms are widely available, along with software programs that will disable the laptop's functionality if it is stolen, or even help track it down by causing the computer to "phone home" the first time the portable computer is attached to a modem (see Figure 1.3).

Figure 1.3 Tracking programs help recover stolen portable computers

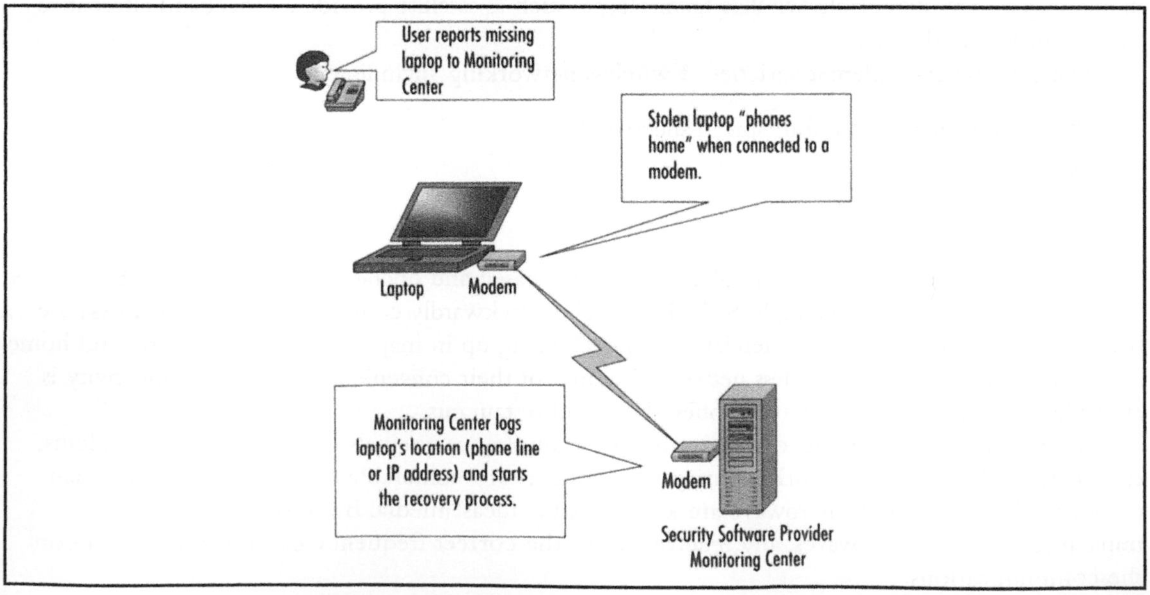

Some laptops come with removable hard disks. It is a good idea if you have highly sensitive data that must be accessed with your laptop to store it on a removable disk (PC Card disks and those that plug into the parallel port are widely available) and encrypt it. Separate the disk from the computer when it is not in use.

TIP

Theft recovery/tracking software for laptops includes Computrace www.computrace.com from Absolute Software Corporation, Alert PC www.sentryinc.com from Computer Sentry Software. TrackIT www.trackitcorp.com is a hardware anti-theft device for computer cases and other baggage.

The possibility of theft is not the only way in which laptops present a security risk. The threat to your network is that a data theft who is able to enter your premises may be able to plug a laptop into the network, crack passwords (or obtain a password via social engineering), and download data to the portable machine, which can then be easily carried away.

New handheld computers are coming with more security devices built in. For example, the Hewlett-Packard iPAQ 5555 includes biometric (fingerprint recognition) technology to prevent unauthorized users from accessing the data.

The Paper Chase

Network security specialists and administrators tend to concentrate on protecting data in electronic form, but you should recognize that intruders may also steal confidential digital information by printing it out or locating a hard copy that was printed by someone else. It does little good to implement strong password policies and network access controls if employees can print out sensitive material and then leave it lying on desks, stored in unlocked file cabinets, or thrown into an easily accessed trash basket. "Dumpster diving" (searching the trash for company secrets) is a common form of corporate espionage – and one that surprisingly often yields results.

If confidential data must be printed, the paper copy should be kept as physically secure as the digital version. Disposal should require shredding, and in cases of particularly high-security information, the shredded paper can be mixed with water to create a pulp that is impossible to put back together again.

Removable Storage Risks

Yet another potential point of failure in your network security plan involves saving data to removable media. Floppy diskettes, zip and jaz disks, tapes, PC cards, CDs and DVDs containing sensitive data must be kept physically secured at all times.

Don't make the mistake of thinking that deleting the files on a disk, or even formatting the disk, completely erases the data; it is still there until it has been overwritten and can be retrieved using special software.

NOTE

The residual physical representation of data that has been "erased," from which that data can be reconstructed, is called *data remanence*. Methods used to prevent this in high-security environments include degaussing, overwriting, and in extreme cases, physical destruction of the media. Degaussing involves use of a device that generates a magnetic field to reduce the magnetic state of the media to zero, which restores it to an unrecorded state. Software (sometimes referred to as "file shredder" software) is available to overwrite all sectors of a disk with random bits in order to prevent recovery of the data.

Although removable media can present a security threat to the network, it can also play a part in your overall security plan. Removable disks (including fully bootable large capacity hard disks installed in mobile "nesting" racks) can be removed from the computer and locked in a safe or removed from the premises to protect the data that is stored there.

Physical Security Summary

Ensuring a physically secure network environment is the first step in controlling access to your network's important data and system files, but it is only part of a good security plan. This is truer today than in the past, because networks have more "ways in" than they once did. A medium or large network may have multiple dial-in servers, VPN servers, and a dedicated full-time Internet connection. Even a small network is likely to be connected to the Internet part of the time.

Virtual intruders never set foot on your organization's property and never touch your computers. They can access your network from across the street or from halfway across the world. But they can do as much damage as the thief who breaks into your company headquarters to steal or destroy your data – and they are much harder to catch. In the following sections, we will examine specific network security risks, and how to prevent them.

Preventing Accidental Compromise of Data

The topic of network security may bring to mind a picture of evil corporate rivals determined to steal your company's most precious trade secrets or malevolent hackers bent on crashing your network and erasing all of your data just for the sheer joy of it. While these risks do exist, often the reality of network data loss is far less glamorous. A large proportion of erased, modified, or disclosed data is the result of the actions of employees or other authorized network personnel. And a large percentage of *that* is the result of *accidental* compromise of the data.

Unintended errors in entering data or accessing network resources or carelessness in use of the computers and network can cause loss of data or crashing of individual computers, the server, and even the network.

Your network security plan should address these unintended compromises, which can be just as disastrous as intentional breaches of security.

Know Your Users

To prevent accidental compromise of data, you should first know your users and their skill levels. Those with few technical skills should be given as little access as possible – allow them the access required to do their jobs, and no more (this philosophy is often referred to as the *principle of least privilege,* or, in government circles, as *need to know*.) Too many network users have, in all innocence, destroyed or changed important files while attempting to clear up space on their hard disks or troubleshoot a computer problem on their own.

Educate Your Users

Educating your users is one of the most important factors in eliminating or reducing such incidents, and an essential component of the multilayered "defense in depth" approach to security. This does not necessarily mean upgrading their technical skills (although it can). Turning all your users into power users may not be cost effective or otherwise desirable. What *is* essential is to train all of your network users in the proper procedures and rules of usage for the network.

Every person who accesses your company network should be aware of your user policies and should agree to adhere to them. This includes notifying technical support personnel immediately of any hardware or software problems, refraining from installing any unauthorized software on their machines or downloading files from the Internet without authorization, and never dialing up their personal ISPs or other networks or services from company machines without permission.

Control Your Users

In some cases, establishing clear-cut policies and making staffers and other users aware of them will be enough. In other cases, you will find that users are unable or unwilling to follow the rules, and you will have to take steps to enforce them – including locking down desktops with system/group policies and, with software such as ISA Server, implementing access rules and filtering to prevent unauthorized packets from being sent or received over the network.

Fortunately, most users will at least attempt to comply with the rules. A more serious problem is the "insider" who is looking to intentionally breach network security. This may be simply a maverick employee who doesn't like being told what to do, or it may be someone with a darker motive.

Preventing Intentional Internal Security Breaches

According to most computer security studies, as documented in RFC 2196, *Site Security Handbook,* actual loss (in terms of money, productivity, computer reputation, and other tangible and intangible harm) is greater for internal security breaches than for those from the outside. Internal attackers are more dangerous for several reasons:

- They generally know more about the company, the network, the layout of the building(s), normal operating procedure, and other information that will make it easier for them to gain access without detection.

- They usually have at least some degree of legitimate access and may find it easy to discover passwords and holes in the current security system.

- They know what information is on the network and what actions will cause the most damage.

We discuss common motivations behind intentional security breaches, both internal and external, in the section entitled *Recognizing Network Security Threats*. Preventing such problems begins with the same methods used to prevent unintentional compromises, but goes a step further.

To a large extent, unintended breaches can be prevented through education. The best way to prevent such breaches depends, in part, on the motivations of the employee(s) concerned.

Hiring and Human Resource Policies

A good "defense in depth" security strategy is multifaceted, involving technology, operations, and people. In many cases, the latter is the weakest link in the chain. Thus, prevention starts with good human resources practices. That means management should institute hiring policies aimed at recruiting persons of good character. Background investigations should be conducted, especially for key positions that will have more than normal user access.

The work environment should encourage high employee morale. In many cases, internal security breaches are committed as "revenge" by employees who feel underpaid, under-appreciated, and even mistreated. Employees who are enthusiastic about their jobs and feel valued by the organization will be much more likely to comply with company rules, including network security policies.

Another motivation for internal breaches is money. If the company engages in a highly competitive business, competitors may approach employees with lucrative offers for trade secrets or other confidential data. If you are in a field that is vulnerable to corporate espionage, your security policies should lean toward the "deny all access" model, in which access for a particular network user starts at nothing, and access is added on the basis of the user's need to know.

NOTE

The "deny all access" policy model is one of two basic starting points in creating a security policy. The other is "allow all access" in which all resources are open to a user unless there are specific reasons to deny access. Neither of these is "right" or "wrong," although the "deny all access" model is undisputedly more secure, and the "allow all access" model is easier to implement. From which of these starting points you work depends on the security *philosophy* of the organization.

Detecting Internal Breaches

Implementing auditing will help you detect internal breaches of security by recording specified security events. You will be able to track when objects (such as files or folders) are accessed, what user account was used to access them, when users exercise user rights, and when users log onto or off of the computer or network. Modern network operating systems such as Windows 2000 and XP/2003 include built-in auditing functionality.

WARNING

You should audit only those events that are necessary to track in keeping with your security policy. Auditing too many events (and access to too many objects) will have a negative impact on your computer's performance and will make relevant events more difficult to find in the security log.

If you choose to audit many events, or often-accessed objects, the security log can grow very large, very quickly. Windows allows you to set the maximum size in kilobytes for the security log by configuring its property sheet in the Event Viewer (right-click **Security Log** and select **Properties**). You can also choose whether to overwrite previous events when the maximum size is reached or to require manual clearing of the log.

Preventing Intentional Internal Breaches

Firewalls are helpful in keeping basically compliant employees from accidentally (or out of ignorance) visiting dangerous websites or sending specific types of packets outside the local network. However, they are of more limited use in preventing intentional internal security breaches. Simply limiting their access to the external network cannot thwart insiders who are determined to destroy, modify, or copy your data. Because they have physical access, they can copy data to removable media, to a portable computer (including tiny handheld machines), or perhaps even print it to paper and remove it from the premises that way. They may change the format of the data to disguise it and upload files to web-based data storage services.

In a high security environment, computers without floppy drives – or even completely diskless workstations – may be warranted. System or group policy can be applied that prevents users from installing software (such as that needed for a desktop computer to communicate with a Pocket PC or Palm Pilot). Cases can be locked, and physical access to serial ports, USB ports, and other connection points can be covered so removable media devices can't be attached. Other internal controls include physical measures such as key cards to limit entry to server rooms and other sensitive resources, as well as software controls such as user and group accounts, encryption, and so forth.

Intentional internal breaches of security constitute a serious problem, and company policies should treat it as such.

Preventing Unauthorized External Intrusions

External intrusions (or "hacking into the system") from outside the LAN has received a lot of attention in the media and thus is the major concern of many companies when it comes to network security issues. In recent years, there have been a number of high profile cases in which the web servers of prominent organizations (such as Yahoo and Microsoft) have been hacked. Attempts to penetrate sensitive government networks, such as the Pentagon's systems, occur on a regular basis. Distributed Denial of Service (Duos) attacks make front-page news when they crash servers and prevent Internet users from accessing popular sites.

There are psychological factors involved, as well. Internal breaches are usually seen by companies as personnel problems and handled administratively. External breaches may seem more like a "violation" and are more often prosecuted in criminal actions. Because the external intruder could come from anywhere, at any time, the sense of uncertainty and fear of the unknown may cause organizations to react in a much stronger way to this type of threat.

The good news about external intrusions is that the area(s) that must be controlled are much more focused. There are usually only a limited number of points of entry to the network from the outside. This is where a properly configured firewall can be invaluable, allowing authorized traffic into the network while keeping unauthorized traffic out. On the other hand, the popularity of firewalls ensures that dedicated hackers know how they work and spend a great deal of time and effort devising ways to defeat them.

Never depend on the firewall to provide 100 percent protection, even against outside intruders. Remember that in order to be effective, a security plan must be a multifaceted, multilayered one. We hope the firewall will keep intruders out of your network completely – but if they *do* get in, what is your contingency plan? How will you reduce the amount of damage they can do and protect your most sensitive or valuable data?

External Intruders with Internal Access

A special type of "external" intruder is the outsider who *physically* breaks into your facility to gain access to your network. Although not a true "insider," because he is not authorized to be there and does not have a valid account on the network, he has many of the advantages of those discussed in the section on internal security breaches.

Your security policy should take into account the threats posed by this "hybrid" type of intruder.

Tactical Planning

In dealing with network intruders, you should practice what police officers in defensive tactics training call "if/then thinking." This means considering every possible outcome of a given situation and then asking yourself, "*If* this happens, *then* what could be done to protect us from the consequences?" The answers to these questions will form the basis of your security policy.

This tactic requires that you be able to plan your responses in detail, which means you must think in specifics rather than generalities. Your security threat must be based in part on understanding the motivations of those initiating the attack and in part on the technical aspects of the type of attack that is initiated. In the next section, we will discuss common intruder motivations and specific types of network attacks.

Recognizing Network Security Threats

In order to effectively protect your network, you must consider the following question: from *whom* or *what* are you protecting it? In this section, we will approach the answer to that question from two perspectives:

- *Who*: types of network intruders and their motivations
- *What*: types of network attackers and how they work

These questions form the basis for performing a *threat analysis*. A comprehensive threat analysis is often the product of collaborative brainstorming among people who are knowledgeable about the business processes, industry, security, and so on. In fact, it is desirable that a threat analysis not be conducted solely by computer security experts, as this group might lack important "big picture" knowledge of the business and industry. The ability to think creatively is a key requirement for members of a threat analysis team.

First, we will look at intruder motivations and classify the different types of people who have the skill and desire to hack into others' computers and networks.

Understanding Intruder Motivations

There are probably as many different specific motives as there are hackers, but we can break the most common intruder motivations into a few broad categories:

- **Recreation** Those who hack into networks "just for fun" or to prove their technical prowess; often young people or "anti-establishment" types.

- **Remuneration** People who invade the network for personal gain, such as those who attempt to transfer funds to their own bank accounts or erase records of their debts; "hackers for hire" who are paid by others to break into the network; corporate espionage is included in this category.

- **Revenge** Dissatisfied customers, disgruntled former employees, angry competitors, or people who have a personal grudge against someone in the organization.

The scope of damage and extent of the intrusion is often – although by no means always–tied to the intruder's motivation.

Recreational Hackers

Recreational hackers are often teen hackers who do it primarily for the thrill of accomplishment. In many cases, they do little or no permanent damage, perhaps only leaving "I was here" type messages to "stake their claims" and prove to their peers that they were able to penetrate your network's security.

There are more malevolent versions of the fun-seeking hacker, however. These are the cyber-vandals, who get their kicks out of destroying as much of your data as possible, or causing your systems to crash.

Profit-motivated Hackers

Those who break into your network for remuneration of some kind – either directly or indirectly – are more dangerous. Because money is at stake, they are more motivated to accomplish their objective. And because many of them are "professionals" of a sort, their hacking techniques may be more sophisticated than the average teenage recreational hacker.

Monetary motivations include:

- Personal financial gain
- Third-party payment
- Corporate espionage

Those motivated by the last are usually the most sophisticated and the most dangerous. There is often *big* money involved in theft of trade secrets. Corporate espionage agents may be employees who have been approached by your competitors and offered money or merchandise, or even threatened with blackmail or physical harm.

In some instances, those working for competitors will go "undercover" and seek a job with your company in order to steal data that they can take back to their own organizations (to add insult to injury, these "stealth spies" are getting paid by your company at the same time they're working against you to the benefit of your competitor).

There are also "professional" freelance corporate spies. They may be contacted and contracted to obtain your company secrets, or they may do it on their own and auction it off to your competitors.

These corporate espionage agents are often highly skilled. They are technically savvy and intelligent enough to avoid being caught or detected. Fields that are especially vulnerable to the threat of corporate espionage include:

- Oil and energy
- Engineering
- Computer technology
- Research medicine
- Law

Any company that is on the verge of a breakthrough that could result in large monetary rewards or world-wide recognition, especially if the company's involvement is high profile, should be aware of the possibility of espionage and take steps to guard against it.

Vengeful Hackers

Persons motivated by the desire for revenge are dangerous, as well. Vengeance seeking is usually based on strong emotions, which means these hackers may go all out in their efforts to sabotage your network.

Examples of hackers or security saboteurs acting out of revenge include:

- Former employees who are bitter about being fired or laid off or who quit their jobs under unpleasant circumstances
- Current employees who feel mistreated by the company, especially those who may be planning to leave soon
- Current employees who aim to sabotage the work of other employees due to internal political battles, rivalry over promotions, and the like
- Outsiders who have grudges against the company, such as those at competing companies who want to harm or embarrass the company or dissatisfied customers
- Outsiders who have personal grudges against someone who works for the company, such as former girlfriend/boyfriends, spouses going through a divorce, and other relationship-related problems

Luckily, the intruders in this category are generally less technically talented than those in the other two groups, and their emotional involvement may cause them to be careless and take outrageous chances, which makes them easier to catch.

Hybrid Hackers

Of course, the three categories can overlap in some cases. A recreational hacker who perceives himself to have been mistreated by an employer or in a personal relationship may use his otherwise benign hacking skills to impose "justice" for the wrongs done to him, or a vengeful ex-employee or ex-spouse might pay someone else to do the hacking for him.

It is beneficial to understand the common motivations of network intruders because, although we may not be able to predict which type of hacker will decide to attack our networks, we can recognize how each operates and take steps to protect our networks from all of them.

Even more important in planning our security strategy than the type of *hacker,* however, is the type of *attack.* In the next section, we will examine specific types of network attacks and how you can protect against them.

Classifying Specific Types of Attacks

The *attack type* refers to *how* an intruder gains entry to your computer or network and *what he does* once he has gained entry. In this section, we will discuss some of the more common types of hack attacks, including:

- Social engineering attacks
- Denial of Service (DOS) attacks
- Scanning and Spoofing
- Source routing and other protocol exploits
- Software and system exploits
- Trojans, viruses and worms

When you have a basic understanding of how each type of attack works, you will be better armed to guard against them.

Social engineering attacks

Unlike the other attack types, *social engineering* does not refer to a technological manipulation of computer hardware or software vulnerabilities and does not require much in the way of technical skills. Instead, this type of attack exploits *human* weaknesses – such as carelessness or the desire to be cooperative – to gain access to legitimate network credentials. The talents that are most useful to the intruder who relies on this technique are the so-called "people skills," such as a charming or persuasive personality or a commanding, authoritative presence.

What is social engineering?

Social engineering is defined as *obtaining confidential information by means of human interaction* (Business Wire, August 4, 1998). You can think of social engineering attackers as specialized con artists. They gain the trust of users (or even better, administrators) and then take advantage of the relationship to find out the user's account name and password, or have the unsuspecting users log them onto the system. Because it is based on convincing a valid network user to "open the door," social engineering can successfully get an intruder into a network that is protected by high-security measures such as biometric scanners.

Social engineering is, in many cases, the easiest way to gain unauthorized access to a computer network. The Social Engineering Competition at a Defcon annual hackers' convention in Las Vegas attracted hundreds of attendants eager to practice their manipulative techniques. Even hackers who are famous for their technical abilities know that *people* make up the biggest security vulnerability on most networks. Kevin Mitnick, convicted computer crimes felon and celebrity hacker extraordinaire, tells in his lectures how he used social engineering to gain access to systems during his hacking career.

These "engineers" often pose as technical support personnel – either in-house, or pretending to work for outside entities such as the telephone company, the Internet Service provider, the network's hardware vendor, or even the government. They often contact their victims by phone, and they will usually spin a complex and plausible tale of why they need the users to divulge their passwords or other information (such as the IP address of the user's machine or the computer name of the network's authentication server).

Protecting your network against social engineers

It is especially challenging to protect against social engineering attacks. Adopting strongly worded policies that prohibit divulging passwords and other network information to anyone over the telephone and educating your users about the phenomenon are obvious steps you can take to reduce the likelihood of this type of security breach. Human nature being what it is, however, there will always be some users on every network who are vulnerable to the social engineer's con game. A talented social engineer is a master at making users doubt their own doubts about his legitimacy.

The "wannabe" intruder may regale the user with woeful stories of the extra cost the company will incur if he spends extra time verifying his identity. He may pose as a member of the company's top management and take a stern approach, threatening the employee with disciplinary action or even loss of job if he doesn't get the user's cooperation. Or he may try to make the employee feel guilty by pretending to be a low-level employee who is just trying to do his job and who will be fired if he doesn't get access to the network and get the problem taken care of right away. A really good social engineer is patient and thorough. He will do his homework, and will know enough about your company, or the organization he claims to represent, to be convincing.

Because social engineering is a human problem, not a technical problem, prevention must come primarily through education rather than technological solutions.

NOTE

For more information about social engineering and how to tell when someone is attempting to pull a social engineering scam, see the preview chapter entitled *Everything You Wanted to Know about Social Engineering – but were Afraid to Ask* at the "Happy Hacker" website, located at www.happyhacker.org/uberhacker/se.shtml.

Denial of Service (DOS) Attacks

Denial of Service (DOS) attacks are one of the most popular choices of Internet hackers who want to disrupt a network's operations. Although they do not destroy or steal data as some other types of attacks do, the objective of the DOS attacker is to bring down the network, denying service to its legitimate users. DOS attacks are easy to initiate; software is readily available from hacker websites and warez newsgroups that will allow anyone to launch a DOS attack with little or no technical expertise.

> **NOTE**
>
> *Warez* is a term used by hackers and crackers to describe bootlegged software that has been "cracked" to remove copy protections and made available by software pirates on the Internet, or in its broader definition, to describe any illegally distributed software.

In February of 2000, massive DOS attacks brought down several of the biggest websites, including Yahoo.com and Buy.com.

The purpose of a DOS attack is to render a network inaccessible by generating a type or amount of network traffic that will crash the servers, overwhelm the routers or otherwise prevent the network's devices from functioning properly. Denial of service can be accomplished by tying up the server's resources, for example, by overwhelming the CPU and memory resources. In other cases, a particular user/machine can be the target of denial of service attacks that hang up the client machine and require it to be rebooted.

> **NOTE**
>
> Denial of service attacks are sometimes referred to in the security community as "nuke attacks."

Distributed Denial of Service attacks

Distributed DOS (DDOS) attacks use intermediary computers called *agents* on which programs called *zombies* have previously been surreptitiously installed. The hacker activates these zombie programs remotely, causing the intermediary computers (which can number in the hundreds or even thousands) to simultaneously launch the actual attack. Because the attack comes from the computers running the zombie programs, which may be on networks anywhere in the world, the hacker is able to conceal the true origin of the attack.

Examples of DDOS tools used by hackers are TFN (Tribe FloodNet), TFN2K, Trinoo, and Stacheldraht (German for "barbed wire"). While early versions of DDOS tools targeted UNIX and Solaris systems, TFN2K can run on both UNIX and Windows systems.

It is important to note that DDOS attacks pose a two-layer threat. Not only could your network be the target of a DOS attack that crashes your servers and prevents incoming and outgoing traffic, but your computers could be used as the "innocent middle men" to launch a DOS attack against another network or site.

DNS DOS attack

The Domain Name System (DNS) DOS attack exploits the difference in size between a DNS query and a DNS response, in which all of the network's bandwidth is tied up by bogus DNS queries. The attacker uses the DNS servers as "amplifiers" to multiply the DNS traffic.

The attacker begins by sending small DNS queries to each DNS server, which contain the spoofed IP address (see *IP Spoofing* later in this chapter) of the intended victim. The responses returned to the small queries are much larger in size, so that if there are a large number of responses returned at the same time, the link will become congested and denial of service will take place.

One solution to this problem is for administrators to configure DNS servers to respond with a "refused" response, which is much smaller in size than a name resolution response, when they received DNS queries from suspicious or unexpected sources.

SYN attack/LAND attack

Synchronization request (SYN) attacks exploit the Transmission Control Protocol (TCP) "three-way handshake," the process by which a communications session is established between two computers. Because TCP, unlike User Datagram Protocol (UDP), is connection-oriented, a *session*, or direct one-to-one communication link, must be created before sending data. The client computer initiates communication with the server (the computer whose resources it wants to access).

The "handshake" includes the following steps:

1. The client machine sends a SYN segment.

2. The server sends an acknowledgement (ACK) message and a SYN, which acknowledges the client machine's request that was sent in step 1 and sends the client a synchronization request of its own. The client and server machines must synchronize each other's sequence numbers.

3. The client sends an ACK back to the server, acknowledging the server's request for synchronization. When both machines have acknowledged each other's requests, the handshake has been successfully completed and a connection is established between the two computers.

Figure 1.4 illustrates how the client/server connection works.

Figure 1.4 TCP uses a "three-way handshake" to establish a connection between client and server

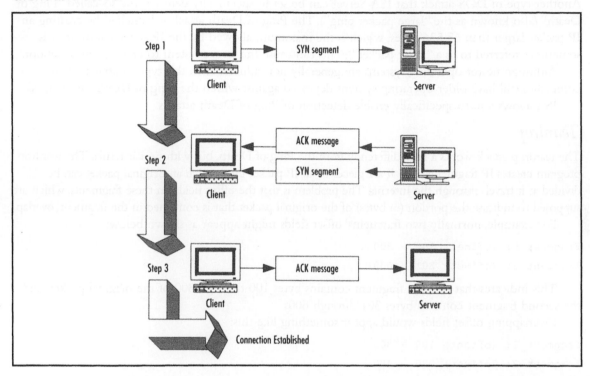

This is how the process normally works. A SYN attack uses this process to flood the system targeted with multiple SYN packets that have bad source IP addresses, which causes the system to respond with SYN/ACK messages. The problem comes when the system, waiting for the ACK message, puts the waiting SYN/ACK messages into a queue. The queue is limited in the number of messages it can handle, and when it is full, all subsequent incoming SYN packets will be ignored. In order for a SYN/ACK to be removed from the queue, an ACK must be returned from the client, or the interval timer must run out and terminate the three-way handshake process.

Because the source IP addresses for the SYN packets sent by the attacker are no good, the ACKs that the server is waiting for never come. The queue stays full, and there is no room for valid SYN requests to be processed. Thus service is denied to legitimate clients attempting to establish communications with the server.

The LAND attack is a variation on the SYN attack. In the LAND attack, instead of sending SYN packets with IP addresses that do not exist, the flood of SYN packets all have the same spoof IP address – that of the targeted computer.

The LAND attack can be prevented by filtering out incoming packets whose source IP addresses appear to be from computers on the internal network. ISA Server has preset intrusion detection functionality that allows you to detect attempted LAND attacks, and you can configure Alerts to notify you when such an attack is detected.

Ping of Death

Another type of DOS attack that ISA Server can be set to specifically detect is the so-called "Ping of Death" (also known as the "large packet ping"). The Ping of Death attack is launched by creating an IP packet larger than 65,536 bytes, which is the maximum allowed by the IP specification (this is sometimes referred to as a "killer packet"). This can cause the target system to crash, hang or reboot.

Although newer operating systems are generally not vulnerable to this type of attack, many companies still have older operating systems deployed against which the Ping of Death can be used.

ISA allows you to specifically enable detection of Ping of Death attacks.

Teardrop

The teardrop attack works a little differently from the Ping of Death, but with similar results. The teardrop program creates IP fragments, which are pieces of an IP packet into which an original packet can be divided as it travels through the Internet. The problem is that the offset fields on these fragments, which are supposed to indicate the portion (in bytes) of the original packet that is contained in the fragment, overlap.

For example, normally two fragments' offset fields might appear as shown below:

```
Fragment 1: (offset) 100 - 300
Fragment 2: (offset) 301 - 600
```

This indicates that the first fragment contains bytes 100 through 300 of the original packet, and the second fragment contains bytes 301 through 600.

Overlapping offset fields would appear something like this:

```
Fragment 1: (offset) 100 - 300
Fragment 2: (offset) 200 - 400
```

When the destination computer tries to reassemble these packets, it is unable to do so and may crash, hang or reboot.

Variations include:

- NewTear
- Teardrop2
- SynDrop
- Boink

All of these programs generate some sort of fragment overlap.

Ping Flood (ICMP flood)

The ping flood or ICMP flood is a means of tying up a specific client machine. It is caused by an attacker sending a large number of ping packets (ICMP echo request packets) to the Winsock or dialer software. This prevents it from responding to server ping activity requests, which causes the server to eventually timeout the connection. A symptom of a ping flood is a huge amount of modem activity, as indicated by the modem lights. This is also referred to as a *ping storm*.

The *fraggle attack* is related to the ping storm. Using a spoofed IP address (which is the address of the targeted victim), an attacker sends ping packets to a subnet, causing all computers on the subnet to respond to the spoofed address and flood it with echo reply messages.

NOTE

During the Kosovo crisis, the fraggle attack was frequently used by pro-Serbian hackers against U.S. and NATO sites to overload them and bring them down.

You can use programs such as NetXray or other IP tracing software to record and display a log of the flood packets. Firewalls can be configured to block ping packets to prevent these attacks.

SMURF attack

The Smurf attack is a form of "brute force" attack that uses the same method as the ping flood, but directs the flood of ICMP echo request packets at the network's router. The destination address of the ping packets is the broadcast address of the network, which causes the router to broadcast the packet to every computer on the network or segment. This can result in a very large amount of network traffic if there are many host computers, which can create congestion that causes a denial of service to legitimate users.

NOTE

The broadcast address is normally represented by all 1s in the host ID. This means, for example, that on class C network 192.168.1.0, the broadcast address would be 192.168.1.255 (255 in decimal represents 11111111 in binary), and in a class C network, the last or z octet represents the host ID. A message sent to the broadcast address is sent simultaneously to all hosts on the network.

In its most insidious form, the Smurf attacker spoofs the source IP address of a ping packet. Then both the network to which the packets are sent *and* the network of the spoofed source IP address will be overwhelmed with traffic. The network to which the spoofed source address belongs will be deluged with responses to the ping when all the hosts to which the ping was sent answer the echo request with an echo reply.

Smurf attacks can generally do more damage than other forms of DoS, such as SYN floods. The SYN flood affects only the ability of other computers to establish a TCP connection to the flooded server, but a Smurf attack can bring an entire ISP down for minutes or hours. This is because a single attacker can easily send 40–50 ping packets per second, even using a slow modem connection. Because each is broadcast to every computer on the destination network, that means the number of responses per second is 40–50 times the number of computers on the network – which could be hundreds or thousands. This is enough data to congest even a T-1 link.

One way to prevent a Smurf attack from using your network as the broadcast target is to turn off the capability to transmit broadcast traffic on the router. Most routers allow you to do this. To prevent your network from being the victim of the spoofed IP address, you will need to configure your firewall to filter out incoming ping packets.

UDP bomb or UDP flood

An attacker can use the UDP and one of several services that echo packets upon receipt to create service-denying network congestion by generating a flood of UDP packets between two target systems. For example, the UDP chargen service on the first computer, which is a testing tool that generates a series of characters for every packet that it receives, sends packets to another system's UDP echo service, which echoes every character it receives. By exploiting these testing tools, an endless flow of echos go back and forth between the two systems, congesting the network. This is sometimes called a *UDP packet storm*.

In addition to port 7, the echo port, an attacker can use port 17, the quote of the day service (quotd) or the daytime service on port 13. These services will also echo packets they receive. UDP chargen is on port 19.

Disabling unnecessary UDP services on each computer (especially those mentioned above) or using a firewall to filter those ports/services, will protect you from this type of attack.

UDP Snork attack

The snork attack is similar to the UDP bomb. It uses a UDP frame that has a source port of either 7 (echo) or 9 (chargen), with a destination port of 135 (Microsoft location service). The result is the same as the UDP bomb – a flood of unnecessary transmissions that can slow performance or crash the systems that are involved.

WinNuke (Windows out-of-band attack)

The out-of-band (OOB) attack is one that exploits a vulnerability in Microsoft networks, which is sometimes called the *Windows OOB bug*. The WinNuke program (and variations such as Sinnerz and Muerte) creates an out-of-band data transmission that crashes the machine to which it is sent. It works like this: a TCP/IP connection is established with the target IP address, using port 139 (the NetBIOS port). Then the program sends data using a flag called MSG_OOB (or Urgent) in the packet header. This flag instructs the computer's Winsock to send data called out-of-band data. Upon receipt, the targeted Windows server expects a pointer to the position in the packet where the Urgent data ends, with normal data following, but the OOB pointer in the packet created by WinNuke points to the end of the frame with no data following.

The Windows machine does not know how to handle this situation and will cease communicating on the network, and service will be denied to any users who subsequently attempt to communicate with it. A WinNuke attack usually requires a reboot of the affected system to reestablish network communications.

Windows 95 and NT 3.51 and 4.0 are vulnerable to the WinNuke exploit, unless the fixes provided by Microsoft have been installed. Windows 98/ME and Windows 2000 are not vulnerable to WinNuke, but ISA server allows you to enable detection of attempted OOB attacks.

Mail bomb attack

A mail bomb is a means of overwhelming a mail server, causing it to stop functioning and thus denying service to users. A mail is a relatively simple form of attack, accomplished by sending a massive quantity of email to a specific user or system. There are programs available on hacking sites on the Internet that allow a user to easily launch a mail bomb attack, automatically sending floods of email to a specified address while protecting the attacker's identity.

A variation on the mail bomb program automatically subscribes a targeted user to hundreds or thousands of high volume Internet mailing lists, which will fill the user's mailbox and/or the mail server. Bombers call this *list linking*. Examples of these mail bomb programs include Unabomber, extreme Mail, Avalanche, and Kaboom.

The solution to repeated mail bomb attacks is to block traffic from the originating network using packet filters. Unfortunately, this does not work with list linking because the originator's address is obscured; the deluge of traffic comes from the mailing lists to which the victim has been subscribed.

Scanning and Spoofing

The term *scanner*, in the context of network security, refers to a software program that is used by hackers to remotely determine what TCP/UDP ports are open on a given system, and thus vulnerable to attack. Administrators also use scanners to detect and correct vulnerabilities in their own systems before an intruder finds them. Network diagnostic tools such as the famous Security Administrator's Tool for Analyzing Networks (SATAN), a UNIX utility, include sophisticated port scanning capabilities.

A good scanning program can locate a target computer on the Internet (one that is vulnerable to attack), determine what TCP/IP services are running on the machine, and probe those services for security weaknesses.

NOTE

A common saying among hackers is: *a good port scanner is worth a thousand passwords.*

Many scanning programs are available as freeware on the Internet.

Port scan

Port scanning refers to a means of locating "listening" TCP or UDP ports on a computer or router and obtaining as much information as possible about the device from the listening ports. TCP and UDP services and applications use a number of *well-known ports*, which are widely published. The hacker uses his knowledge of these commonly used ports to extrapolate information.

For example, Telnet normally uses port 23. If the hacker finds that port open and listening, he knows that Telnet is probably enabled on the machine. He can then try to infiltrate the system, for example by guessing the appropriate password in a brute force attack.

Back to Basics: TCP/UDP Well Known Ports

The official well-known port assignments are documented in RFC 1700, available on the web at www.freesoft.org/CIE/RFC/1700/index.htm . The port assignments are made by the Internet Assigned Numbers Authority (IANA). In general, a service will use the same port number with UDP as with TCP, although there are some exceptions. The assigned ports were originally those from 0–255, but the number was later expanded to 0–1023.

Some of the most used well-known ports include:

- TCP/UDP port 20: FTP (data)
- TCP/UDP port 21: FTP (control)
- TCP/UDP port23: Telnet
- TCP/UDP port 25: SMTP
- TCP/UDP port 53: DNS
- TCP/UDP port 67: BOOTP server
- TCP/UDP port 68: BOOTP client
- TCP/UDP port 69: TFTP
- TCP/UDP port 80: HTTP
- TCP/UDP port 88: Kerberos
- TCP/UDP port 110: POP3
- TCP/UDP port 119: NNTP
- TCP/UDP port 137: NetBIOS name service
- TCP/UDP port 138: NetBIOS datagram service
- TCP/UDP port 139: NetBIOS session service
- TCP/UDP port 194: IRC
- TCP/UDP port 220: IMAPv3
- TCP/UDP port 389: LDAP

Ports 1024-65,535 are called *registered ports;* these numbers are not controlled by IANA and can be used by user processes or applications.

There are a total of 65,535 TCP ports (and the same number of UDP ports) used for various services and applications. If a port is open, it will respond when another computer attempts to contact it over the network. Port scanning programs such as *Nmap* are used to determine which ports are open on a particular machine. The program sends packets for a wide variety of protocols and, by examining which messages receive responses and which don't, creates a map of the computer's listening ports.

Port scanning in itself does no harm to your network or system, but it provides hackers with information they can use to penetrate the network.

IP half scan attack

"Half scans" (also called "half open scans" or FIN scans) attempt to avoid detection by sending only initial or final packets, rather than establishing a connection. A half scan starts the SYN/ACK process with a targeted computer, but does not complete it. Software that conducts half scans, such as Jakal, is called a *stealth scanner*.

Many port scanning detectors are unable to detect half scans; however, ISA Server provides IP half scan as part of its intrusion detection.

IP Spoofing

IP spoofing involves changing the packet headers of a message to indicate that it came from an IP address other than the true source. The spoofed address is normally a trusted port, which allows a hacker to get a message through a firewall or router that would otherwise be filtered out. Modern firewalls protect against IP spoofing.

Spoofing is used whenever it is beneficial for one machine to impersonate another. It is often used in combination with one of the other types of attacks. For example, a spoofed address is used in the SYN flood attack to create a "half open" connection, in which the client never responds to the SYN/ACK message because the spoofed address is that of a computer that is down or doesn't exist. Spoofing is also used to hide the true IP address of the attacker in Ping of Death, Teardrop and other attacks.

IP spoofing can be prevented by using Source Address Verification on your router, if it is supported.

Source Routing attack

TCP/IP supports *source routing,* a means that permits the sender of network data to route packets through a specific point on the network. There are two types of source routing:

- *Strict source routing:* the sender of the data can specify the exact route (rarely used).
- *Loose source record route (LSRR):* the sender can specify certain routers (hops) through which the packet must pass.

The source route is an option in the IP header that allows a sender to override routing decisions normally made by routers between the source and destination machines. Source routing is used by network administrators to map the network, or for troubleshooting routing and communications problems. It can also be used to force traffic through the route that will provide the best performance. Unfortunately, source routing can be exploited by hackers.

If the system allows source routing, an intruder can use it to reach private internal addresses on the LAN that normally would not be reachable from the Internet, by routing the traffic through another machine that is reachable from both the Internet and the internal machine.

Source routing can be disabled on most routers to prevent this type of attack.

Other protocol exploits

The attacks we have discussed so far involve exploiting some feature or weakness of the TCP/IP protocols. Hackers can also exploit vulnerabilities of other common protocols, such as Hypertext Transfer Protocol (HTTP), Domain Name System (DNS), Common Gateway Interface (CGI), and other commonly used protocols.

Active-X controls, Java script, and VBscript can be used to add animations or applets to web sites, but hackers can exploit these to write controls or scripts that allow them to remotely plant viruses, access data, or change or delete files on the hard disk of unaware users who visit the page and run the script. Many e-mail client programs have similar vulnerabilities.

System and software exploits

System and software exploits are those that take advantage of weaknesses of particular operating systems and applications (often called *bugs*). Like protocol exploits, they are used by intruders to gain unauthorized access to computers or networks or to crash or clog up the systems to deny service to others.

Common "bugs" can be categorized as follows:

- **Buffer overflows** Many common security holes are based on buffer overflow problems. Buffer overflows occur when the number of bytes or characters input exceeds the maximum number allowed by the programmer in writing the program.

- **Unexpected input** Programmers may not take steps to define what happens if invalid input (input that doesn't match program specifications) is entered. This could cause the program to crash or open up a way into the system.

- **System configuration bugs** These are not really "bugs," per se, but rather are ways of configuring the operating system or software that leaves it vulnerable to penetration.

Popular software such as Microsoft's Internet Information Server (IIS), Internet Explorer (MSIE) and Outlook Express (MSOE) are popular targets of hackers looking for software security holes that can be exploited.

Major operating system and software vendors regularly release security patches to fix exploitable bugs. It is very important for network administrators to stay up to date in applying these fixes and/or service packs to ensure that their systems are as secure as possible.

NOTE

Microsoft issues *security bulletins* and makes security patches available as part of TechNet. See the website at www.microsoft.com/technet/security/default.asp.

Trojans, viruses and worms

Intruders who access your systems without authorization or inside attackers with malicious motives may plant various types of programs to cause damage to your network. There are three broad categories of *malicious code*, as follows:

- Trojans
- Viruses
- Worms

We will take a brief look at each of these attack types.

Trojans

The name is short for "Trojan horse," and refers to a software program that appears to perform a useful function, but in fact, performs actions that the user of the program did not intend or was not aware of. Trojan horses are often written by hackers to circumvent the security of a system. Once installed, the hacker can exploit the security holes created by the Trojan to gain unauthorized access, or the Trojan program may perform some action such as:

- Deleting or modifying files
- Transmitting files across the network to the intruder
- Installing other programs or viruses

Basically, the Trojan can perform any action that the user has privileges and permissions to do on the system. This means a Trojan is especially dangerous if the unsuspecting user who installs it is an administrator and has access to the system files.

Trojans can be very cleverly disguised as innocuous programs, such as utilities or screensavers. A Trojan can also be installed by an executable script (Javascript, a Java applet, Active-X control, and others) on a web site. Accessing the site may initiate the installation of the program if the web browser is configured to allow scripts to run automatically.

Viruses

The most common use of the term "virus" is any program that is installed without the awareness of the user and performs undesired actions (often harmful, although sometimes merely annoying). Viruses may also replicate themselves, infecting other systems by writing themselves to any floppy disk that is used in the computer or sending themselves across the network. Viruses are often distributed as attachments to e-mail, or as macros in word processing documents. Some activate immediately upon installation, and others lie dormant until a specific date/time or a particular system event triggers them.

Viruses come in thousands of different varieties. They can do anything from popping up a message that says "Hi!" to erasing the computer's entire hard disk. The proliferation of computer viruses has also led to the phenomenon of the *virus hoax*, which is a warning – generally circulated via email or websites – about a virus that does not exist or that does not do what the warning claims it will do.

Viruses, however, present a real threat to your network. Companies such as Symantec and McAfee make anti-virus software that is aimed at detecting and removing virus programs. Because new viruses are being created daily, it is important to download new *virus definition files,* which contain information required to detect each virus type, on a regular basis to ensure that your virus protection stays up to date.

Worms

A worm is a program that can travel across the network from one computer to another. Sometimes different parts of a worm run on different computers. Technically, a worm – unlike a virus – can replicate itself without user interaction; however, much modern documentation makes little distinction between the two, or classifies the worm as a subtype of the virus. Worms make multiple copies of themselves and spread throughout a network. Originally the term *worm* was used to describe code that attacked multiuser systems (networks) while *virus* was used to describe programs that replicated on individual computers.

The primary purpose of the worm is to replicate. These programs were initially used for legitimate purposes in performing network management duties, but their ability to multiply quickly has been exploited by hackers who create malicious worms that replicate wildly, and may also exploit operating system weaknesses and perform other harmful actions.

Designing a Comprehensive Security Plan

Now that you have some understanding of basic security concepts and terminology, general security objectives, common motivation of network intruders, different types of specific attacks and how they are used, and an overview of available hardware and software solutions, you can begin to design a comprehensive security policy for your organization.

A widely accepted method for developing your network security plan is laid out in Request for Comments (RFC) 2196, *Site Security Handbook,* and attributed to Fites, et al (1989). It consists of the following steps:

- Identify what you are trying to protect.

- Determine what you are trying to protect it from.

- Determine how likely the anticipated threats are.

- Implement measures that will protect your assets in a cost-effective manner.

- Review the process continually and make improvements each time a weakness is discovered.

NOTE

The entire text of RFC 2196, which provides many excellent suggestions that focus primarily on the implementation phase, can be found on the web at www.faqs.org/rfcs/rfc2196.html.

It is important to understand that a security *plan* is not the same thing as a security *policy*, although the two words are sometimes used interchangeably. Your security policies (and there are likely to be many of them) grow out of the security plan. Think of policy as "law" or "rules," while the security plan is procedural; it lays out *how* the rules will be implemented.

Your security plan will generally address three different aspects of protecting your network:

1. *Prevention*: the measures that are implemented to keep your information from being modified, destroyed, or compromised.

2. *Detection*: the measures that are implemented to recognize when a security breach has occurred or has been attempted, and if possible, the origin of the breach.

3. *Reaction*: the measures that are implemented to recover from a security breach, to recover lost or altered data, to restore system or network operations, and to prevent future occurrences.

These can be divided into two types of actions: *proactive* and *reactive*. The first, prevention, is proactive because it takes place *before* any breach has occurred and involves actions that will, if successful, make further actions unnecessary. Unfortunately, our proactive measures don't always work. Reactive measures such as detection and reaction do, however, help us to develop additional proactive measures that will prevent future intrusions.

Regardless of how good your prevention and detection methods may be, it is essential that you have in place a reaction in case attackers do get through and damage your data or disrupt your network operations. As the old folk saying goes: "hope for the best, and plan for the worst."

Evaluating Security Needs

Before you can develop a security plan and policies for your organization, you must assess the security needs, which will generally be based on the following broad considerations:

- Type of business in which the organization engages
- Type of data that is stored on the network
- Type of connection(s) that the network has to other networks
- Philosophy of the organization's management

Each of these will play a part in determining the level of security that is desirable or necessary for your network.

Assessing the type of business

Certain fields have inherent high-security requirements. An obvious example is the military, or other government agencies that deal with defense or national security issues. Private companies with government defense contracts also fall into this category. Others may be less obvious:

- Law firms are bound by law and ethics to protect client confidentiality.
- Medical offices must protect patient records.
- Law enforcement agencies, courts, and other governmental bodies must secure information.

- Educational institutions store student records.

- Companies that gather information from individuals or organizations guarantee that the data will be kept confidential.

The competitive nature of the business is also a consideration. In a field such as biogenetic research, which is a "hot" market where new developments are being made on a daily basis, any of which could involve huge profits for the company that patents the idea, protecting trade secrets becomes vitally important.

Most businesses will have *some* data of a confidential nature on the network's computer systems, but the security requirements in some fields are much higher than others. This should be considered as you begin to develop your security plan.

Assessing the type of data

The second question to consider is what type of data is stored on your network, and where. You may find that a higher level of security is needed in one department or division than another. You may, in fact, want to divide the network physically, into separate subnets, to allow you to better control access to different parts of the company network independently.

Generally, payroll and human resource records (such as personnel files and insurance claim documents), company financial records (accounting documents, financial statements, tax documents), and a variety of other common business records will need to be protected. Even in cases where these documents are required to be made public, you will want to take steps to ensure that they can't be modified or destroyed. Remember that *data integrity,* as well as *data confidentiality and availability,* is protected by a good security plan.

Assessing the network connections

Your exposure to outside intruders is another consideration in planning how to implement security on your network. A LAN that is self-contained and has no Internet connectivity, nor any modems or other outside connections, will not require the degree of protection (other than physical security) that is necessary when there are many avenues "in" that an intruder can take.

Dialup modem connections merit special consideration. While a dialup connection is less open to intrusion than a fulltime dedicated connection – both because it is connected to the outside for a shorter time period, reducing the window of opportunity for intrusion, and because it will usually have a dynamic IP address, making it harder for an intruder to locate it on multiple occasions – allowing workstations on your network to have modems and phone lines can create a huge security risk.

If improperly configured, a computer with a dialup connection to the Internet that is also cabled to the internal network can act as a router, allowing outside intruders to access not just the workstation connected to the modem, but other computers on the LAN.

One reason for allowing modems at individual workstations is to allow users to dialup connections to other private networks. A more secure way to do this is to remove the modems and have the users establish a virtual private networking (VPN) connection with the other private network through the LAN's Internet connection.

The best security policy is to have as few connections from the internal network to the outside as possible, and control access at those entry points (called the *network perimeter*).

Assessing management philosophy

This last criteria is the most subjective, but can have a tremendous influence on the security level that is appropriate for your organization. Most companies are based on one (or a combination of more than one) management model.

Understanding management models

Some companies institute a highly structured, formal management style. Employees are expected to respect a strict chain of command, and information is generally disseminated on a "need to know" basis. Governmental agencies, especially those that are law-enforcementrelated, such as police departments and investigative agencies, often follow this philosophy. This is sometimes referred to as the paramilitary model.

Other companies, particularly those in the IT industry and other fields that are subject to little state regulation, are built on the opposite premise: that all employees should have as much information and input as possible, that managers should function as "team leaders" rather than authoritarian supervisors, and that restrictions on employee actions should be imposed only when necessary for the efficiency and productivity of the organization. This is sometimes called the "one big happy family" model. Creativity is valued more than "going by the book," and job satisfaction is considered an important aspect of enhancing employee performance and productivity.

In business management circles, these two diametrically-opposed models are called Theory X (traditional paramilitary style) and Theory Y (modern, team-oriented approach). Although there are numerous other management models that have been popularized in recent years, such as Management by Objective (MBO) and Total Quality Management (TQM), each company's management style will fall somewhere on the continuum between Theory X and Theory Y. The management model is based on the personal philosophies of the company's top decision-makers regarding the relationship between management and employees.

The management model can have a profound influence on what is or isn't acceptable in planning security for the network. A "deny all access" security policy that is viewed as appropriate in a Theory X organization may meet with so much resentment and employee dissatisfaction in a Theory Y company that it disrupts business operations. Always consider the company "atmosphere" as part of your security planning. If you have good reasons to implement strict security in a Theory Y atmosphere, realize that you will probably have to justify the restrictions to management and "sell" them to employees, whereas those same restrictions might be accepted without question in a more traditional organization.

Understanding Security Ratings

Security ratings may be of interest as you develop your company's security policy, although they are not likely to be important unless your organization works under government contract requiring a specified level of security.

The U.S. Government provides specifications for the rating of network security implementations in a publication often referred to as the *orange book,* formally called the *Department of Defense Trusted Computer System Evaluation Criteria,* or *TCSEC.* The *red book,* or *Trusted Network Interpretation of the TCSEC (TNI)* explains how the TCSEC evaluation criteria are applied to computer networks.

Other countries have security rating systems that work in a similar way. For example:

- CTPEC (Canada)
- AISEP (Australia)
- ITSEC (Western Europe)

To obtain a government contract in the U.S., companies are often required to obtain a C2 rating. A C2 rating has several requirements:

1. That the operating system in use be capable of tracking access to data, including both who accessed it and when it was accessed (as is done by the auditing function of Windows NT/2000)

2. That users' access to objects be subject to control (access permissions)

3. That users are uniquely identified on the system (user account name and password)

4. That security-related events can be tracked and permanently recorded for auditing (audit log)

If your organization needs a C2 rating for its systems, you should consult the National Computer Security Center (NCSC) publications to ensure that it meets all of the requirements.

Legal Considerations

Another important step in preparing to design your network security plan is to consider legal aspects that may affect your network. It is a good idea to have a member of your company's legal department who specializes in computer law to be involved in the development of your security plan and policies. If this is not possible, the written policies should be submitted for legal review before you put them into practice.

Designating Responsibility for Network Security

In any undertaking as complex as the development and implementation of a comprehensive corporate security plan and accompanying policies, it is vital that areas of responsibility be clearly designated.

Best practices dictate that no one person should have complete authority or control, and in an enterprise-level network, it would be difficult for any single person to handle all facets of developing and implementing the security plan anyway.

Responsibility for Developing the Security Plan and Policies

The initial creation of a good security plan will require a great deal of thought and effort. The policy will impact those at all levels of the organization, and soliciting input from as many representatives of different departments and job descriptions as is practical is desirable. An effective approach is to form a committee consisting of persons from several areas of the organization to be involved in creating and reviewing the security plan and policies.

The Security Planning Committee might include some or all of the following:

1. The network administrator and one or more assistant administrators

2. The site's security administrator

3. Department heads of various company departments or their representatives

4. Representatives of user groups that will be impacted by the security policies (for example, the secretarial staff or the data processing center)

5. A member of the legal department who specializes in computer and technology law

6. A member of the finance or budget department

Responsibility for Implementing and Enforcing the Security Plan and Policies

Security policies will generally be implemented and enforced by network administrators and members of the IT staff. Job descriptions and policies should designate exactly who is responsible for the implementation of which parts of the plan. There should be a clear-cut chain of command that specifies whose decision prevails in case of conflict.

In some cases – such as physical penetration of the network – the company security staff will become involved. There should be written, clearly formulated policies that stipulate which department has responsibility for which tasks in such situations.

The security plan should also address the procedures for reporting security breaches, both internally, and if the police or other outside agencies are to be brought in (as well as who is responsible for or has the authority to call in outside agents).

One of the most important factors in a good security policy is that it must be enforceable, and going a step further, it must be enforced. This is important for legal as well as practical reasons. If your company has policies in place that they routinely fail to enforce, this can be seen as an informal voiding of the policy, leaving the company legally liable for the actions of employees who violate the policy. If the policy can be enforced through technological means, this is preferred. If the policies must be enforced through reprimand or other actions against employees who violate them, there should be clearly worded, universally distributed written documentation of what constitutes a violation and what sanctions will result, as well as who is responsible for imposing such sanctions.

Designing the Corporate Security Policy

Designing a good corporate network security policy will differ, depending on the particular organization. However, there are common elements that should be addressed, including (but not limited to) the following:

■ Developing an effective password and authentication policy

■ Developing a privacy policy that sets forth reasonable expectations of privacy as to employees' e-mail, monitoring access to Web sites, access to users' directories and files, and so forth

■ Developing an accountability policy that defines responsibility concerning security issues, including policies regarding users' obligation to report security violations and the process for doing so

■ A network use statement that defines users' responsibilities in regard to accessing network resources, protection of password confidentiality, reporting of problems, and expectations as to availability of network resources

- A disaster protection and recovery policy that specifies policies for fault tolerance, scheduling of data backups and storage of backed-up data, failover plans for critical systems, and other related matters

It is beyond the scope of this chapter to provide detailed examples of all of the above. We will, however, address the first issue: how to go about developing an effective password policy and some of the factors that should be considered. The other policy areas should be addressed in similar depth and detail.

Developing an Effective Password Policy

In the networking world, passwords (in combination with user account names) are normally the "keys to the kingdom" that provide access to network resources and data. It may seem simplistic to say that your comprehensive security plan should include an effective password policy, but it is a basic component that is more difficult to implement than it might appear at first glance.

In order to be effective, your password policy must require users to select passwords that are difficult to "crack" – yet easy for them to remember so they don't commit the common security breach of writing the password on a sticky note that will end up stuck to the monitor or sitting prominently in the top desk drawer.

A good password policy is the first line of defense in protecting your network from intruders. Careless password practices (choosing common passwords such as "god" or "love" or the user's spouse's name; choosing short, all-alpha, one-case passwords, writing passwords down or sending them across the network in plain text) are like leaving your car doors unlocked with the keys in the ignition. Although some intruders may be targeting a specific system, many others are just "browsing" for a network that's easy to break into. Lack of a good password policy is an open invitation to them.

TIP

Expensive, sophisticated firewalls and other strict security measures (short of biometric scanning devices that recognize fingerprints or retinal images) will not protect you if an intruder has knowledge of a valid user name and password. It is particularly important to use strong passwords for administrative accounts.

Best practices for password creation require that you address the following:

- Password length and complexity
- Who creates the password?
- Forced changing of passwords

Let's discuss each of these considerations.

Password Length and Complexity

It's easy to define a "bad" password – it's one that can be easily guessed by someone other than the authorized user.

One way in which "crackers" (hackers who specialize in defeating passwords to break into systems) do their work is called the *brute force* attack. In this kind of attack, the cracker manually, or more often, using a script or specially written software program, simply tries every possible combination of characters until he finally hits upon the right one. It goes without saying that using this method, it will be easier to guess a short password than a longer one; there are more possible combinations. For this reason, most security experts recommend that passwords have a minimum required length (for example, eight characters). Modern network operating systems such as Windows 2000 allow domain administrators to impose such rules so that if a user attempts to set a password that doesn't meet the minimum length requirement, the password change will be rejected.

Who creates the password?

Network administrators may be tempted to institute a policy whereby they create all passwords and "issue" them to the users. This has the advantage of ensuring that all passwords will meet the administrator's criteria in regard to length and complexity. However, it has a few big disadvantages as well:

1. This places a heavy burden on administrators who must handle all password changes and be responsible for letting users know what their passwords are. Of course, you would not want to notify the user of his/her password via e-mail or other insecure channels. In fact, the best way to do so is to personally deliver the password information. In a large organization, this becomes particularly taxing if you have a policy requiring that passwords be changed on a regular basis (as you should; we will discuss this in the next section).

2. Users will have more difficulty remembering passwords that they didn't choose. This means they are more likely to write the passwords down, resulting in security compromises. Otherwise, they may have to contact the administrator frequently to be reminded of their passwords.

3. If the administrator creates all passwords, this means the administrator *knows* everyone's password. This may or may not be acceptable under your overall security policy. Some users (including management) may be uncomfortable with the idea that the administrator knows their passwords. Even though an administrator can generally access a user's account and/or files without knowing the password, it is less obvious to the users, and thus, less of a concern.

Allowing users to create their own passwords, within set parameters (length and complexity requirements) is usually the best option. The user is less likely to forget the password because he can create a complex password that is meaningless to anyone else, but which has meaning to him.

For example, it would be difficult for others to guess the password "Mft2doSmis." It has 10 characters, combines alpha and numeric characters, and combines upper and lower case in a seemingly random manner. To the user, it would be easy to remember because it means, "My favorite thing to do on Sunday morning is sleep."

Password Change Policy

Best practices dictate that users change their passwords at regular intervals, and after any suspected security breach. Windows 2000 allows the administrator to set a maximum password age, forcing users to change their passwords at the end of the specified period (in days). Password expiration periods can be set from 1 to 999 days. The default is 42 days.

NOTE

Individual user accounts that need to keep the same passwords can be configured so that their passwords never expire. This overrides the general password expiration setting.

Because it is the nature of most users to make their passwords as easy to remember as possible, you must institute policies to prevent the following practices, all of which can present security risks:

- Changing the password to a variation of the same password (for example, changing from Tag2mB to Tag3mB)

- Changing the password back and forth between two favored passwords each time a change is required (that is, changing from Tag2mB to VERoh9 and back again continuously)

- "Changing" the password to the same password (entering the same password for the new password as was already being used)

Administrators can use operating system features or third party software to prevent most of these practices. For example, in Windows 2000, you can configure the operating system to remember the user's password history, so that up to a maximum of the last 24 passwords will be recorded, and the user will not be able to change the password to one that has been used during that time.

Summary of Best Password Practices

- Passwords should have a minimum of eight characters.

- Passwords should not be "dictionary" words.

- Passwords should consist of a mixture of alpha, numeric and symbol characters.

- Passwords should be created by their users.

- Passwords should be easy for users to remember.

- Passwords should never be written down.

- Passwords should be changed on a regular basis.

- Passwords should be changed anytime compromise is suspected.

- Password change policies should prevent users from making only slight changes.

Educating Network Users on Security Issues

The best security policies in the world will be ineffective if the network users are unaware of them, or if the policies are so restrictive and place so many inconveniences on users that they go out of their ways to attempt to circumvent them.

The security plan itself should contain a program for educating network users – not just as to what the policies are, but *why* they are important, and how the users benefit from them. Users should also be instructed in the best ways to comply with the policies, and what to do if they are unable to comply or observe a deliberate violation of the policies on the part of other users.

If you involve users in the planning and policy-making stages, you will find it must easier to educate them and gain their support for the policies at the implementation and enforcement stages.

Summary

To get the most out of ISA's features, you must be able to recognize the security threats to which your network is subject and understand a little about the motivations of typical intruders. It is not necessary that you *be* a hacker in order to prevent your network from hacking attempts, but it *will* benefit you to know something about how unscrupulous hackers think and how they do their dirty work.

You must be aware of the different types of attacks with which you could be confronted, and understand how to protect your network from social engineering attacks, DoS attacks, scanning and spoofing, source routing and other protocol exploits, software and system exploits, and Trojans, viruses and worms.

There are a number of hardware-based security solutions available, and even more software-based firewalls on the market. You should have a basic understanding of the capabilities and limitations of each type, and how ISA Server compares – in features and cost – to some of the others. We think you will find that ISA Server offers an excellent value in comparison to competitive products, along with easy configurability and options to integrate third-party programs for even more functionality.

Your comprehensive security plan is integral to protecting your network from both internal and external threats. There is no "one size fits all" when it comes to corporate security plans and policies; yours should be based on the nature of the business in which your organization engages, the nature of the data stored on the network, the number and types of connections your network has to the "outside world," and the management philosophy regarding organizational structure.

A good security plan is one that meets the needs of IT administration, company management, and network users. The best way to ensure that your security plan meets these criteria is to involve persons from all levels of the organization in the planning process. Once you have a good, comprehensive security plan and corresponding policies worked out, you will be able to use ISA Server as an important element in your security plan, to implement and enforce those policies and provide monitoring, notification, and record-keeping to document the successful functioning of your security plan.

Chapter 2

ISA Server 2006 Client Types and Automating Client Provisioning

Solutions in this chapter:

- **Understanding ISA Server 2006 Client Types**

- **Automating ISA Server 2006 Client Provisioning**

- **Automating Installation of the Firewall Client**

Introduction

One of the most misunderstood, but most critical, issues relating to the installation and management of ISA Server 2006 firewalls is that of ISA Server 2006 client types. Some of these client types have a classic client/server relationship with the ISA Server. That is, the client makes a request for data from the server; the server subsequently performs the work of retrieving the data, and returning the data to the client. The client/server relationship is dependent on client software installed on the client computer that makes it possible to communicate with the particular services running on the server.

In the case of ISA Server, the client might request data in the form of a Web page on the Internet; the ISA Server would perform the work of retrieving the Web page and delivering it to the client. However, not all ISA Server 2006 clients have a classic client/server relationship with the firewall, and each client type accesses networks outside its own in a different fashion. Furthermore, some applications work with one ISA Server 2006 client type but not with another. It is critical to determine the ISA Server 2006 client type *before* you install and configure ISA Server 2006. Failure to implement the correct ISA Server 2006 client type can lead to the misconception that the firewall is not working correctly.

All machines connecting to resources by going through the ISA Server 2006 firewall are considered clients of the ISA Server 2006 firewall machine. This does not imply that all machines need to have client software installed or need their applications configured to connect directly with the ISA Server 2006 firewall computer. In the context of ISA Server 2006, the "client" does not always participate in the classic "client/server" relationship with the ISA Server 2006 firewall.

Understanding ISA Server 2006 Client Types

Computers that go through the ISA server to access resources outside their networks fall into one or more ISA Server 2006 client type categories. These are:

- The SecureNAT client
- The Firewall client
- The Web Proxy client

A single machine can be configured to act in multiple ISA Server 2006 client-type roles. For example, a Windows XP computer can be configured as a SecureNAT, Firewall and Web Proxy client. Another Windows XP computer can be configured as only a Firewall and Web Proxy client. A Linux machine can be configured as a SecureNAT client and Web Proxy client.

Table 2.1 provides an overview of the ISA Server 2006 client types, how each is installed or configured, which operating systems each supports, protocols supported by each, type of user-level authentication each supports, and special deployment considerations for each type.

Table 2.1 Overview of ISA Server 2006 Client Types

Feature	SecureNAT client	Firewall client	Web Proxy client
Installation of client software required?	No. SecureNAT clients require only a default gateway address that can route Internet-bound requests through the ISA Server 2006 firewall. The default gateway is set in the TCP/IP properties for the computer's network adapter.	Yes. The Firewall client software must be installed from an installation share on the network. The Firewall client installation share can be on the ISA Server 2006 firewall itself, or (preferably) on a File Server located somewhere on the network.	No. However, Web browsers on client computers must be configured to use the ISA Server 2006 firewall as their Web Proxy. The proxy is set in the Web browser's connection settings.
Operating system support	SecureNAT supports all operating systems. The SecureNAT client type can be used with Windows, MacOS, Unix, Linux, and any other operating system that supports TCP/IP networking.	The Firewall client supports all post-Windows 95 platforms, from Windows 98 to Windows Server 2003.	The Web Proxy client supports all platforms, but does so by way of a Web application. All Web browsers that can be configured to use a proxy server can function as Web Proxy clients.
Protocol support	All simple protocols are supported by SecureNAT. Complex protocols (those that require multiple connections) require that an application filter be installed on the ISA Server 2006 firewall machine.	The Firewall client supports all Winsock applications that use the TCP and UDP protocols; the Firewall client does not mediate non-TCP/UDP connections.	The Web Proxy client supports HTTP, HTTPS (SSL/TLS), and HTTP tunneled FTP (proxied FTP)
User-level authentication supported?	No. SecureNAT clients cannot authenticate with the ISA Server 2006 firewall unless the client applications support SOCKS 5 and a SOCKS 5 application filter is installed on the firewall.	Yes. The Firewall client enables strong user/group-based access control by transparently forwarding client credentials to the ISA Server 2006 firewall.	Yes. Web Proxy clients will authenticate with the ISA Server 2006 firewall if the firewall requests credentials. No credentials are sent if an anonymous access rule enabling the connection is available to the Web Proxy client.

Continued

Table 2.1 Continued

Feature	SecureNAT client	Firewall client	Web Proxy client
Deployment Considerations	All non-Windows operating systems can be configured as SecureNAT client if they require protocol access outside of HTTP/HTTPS and FTP. All post-Windows 95 Windows operating systems should be configured as Firewall clients if at all possible. All servers published via Server Publishing Rules should be configured as SecureNAT clients. Use SecureNAT on Windows clients only when outbound ICMP or PPTP is required.	All Windows operating systems that support Firewall client installation (post-Windows 95) should have the Firewall client installed unless there are technical or management barriers that prevent this. The Firewall client increases the overall level of security and accessibility for all machines with the Firewall client software installed.	All browsers should be configured as Web Proxy clients when authentication is required for Web (HTTP/HTTPS/FTP) access. If user authentication is not required, Web Proxy configuration is not required because the ISA Server 2006 firewall will provide transparent Web Proxy functionality for Firewall and SecureNAT clients.

Understanding the ISA Server 2006 SecureNAT Client

A SecureNAT client is any device configured with a default gateway address that can route Internet-bound connections through the ISA Server 2006 firewall. That is, the ISA Server role is closely related to the role of a router for outbound access. The SecureNAT client does not have a traditional client/server relationship with the ISA Server. There are three network scenarios in which the SecureNAT client is most commonly found:

- Simple
- Complex
- VPN client

A "simple network scenario" is one that has only a single subnet located behind the ISA Server 2006 firewall computer. For example, you have an ISA Server 2006 firewall sitting at the edge of the network with an interface directly connected to the Internet and a second interface connected to the Internal network. All the machines behind the ISA Server 2006 firewall are on a single subnet (for example, 10.0.0.0/8). There are no routers on the Internal network. Figure 2.1 depicts a typical simple network scenario.

Figure 2.1 SecureNAT Simple Network Scenario

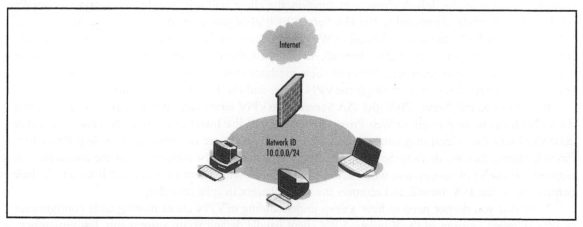

In the simple network scenario, the default gateway of the SecureNAT clients is configured as the IP address of the Internal interface of the ISA Server 2006 firewall. You can manually configure the default gateway address, or you can use DHCP to automatically assign addresses to the SecureNAT clients. The DHCP server can be on the ISA Server 2006 firewall itself, or it can be located on a separate machine on the Internal network.

In the "complex network scenario," the Internal network consists of multiple network IDs that are managed by a router or series of routers or layer 3 switch(s). In the case of the complex network, the default gateway address assigned to each SecureNAT client depends on the location of the SecureNAT client computer. The gateway address for the SecureNAT client will be a router that allows the SecureNAT client access to other networks within the organization, as well as the Internet. The routing infrastructure must be configured to support the SecureNAT client so that Internet-bound requests are forwarded to the Internal interface of the ISA Server 2006 firewall. Figure 2.2 depicts the SecureNAT complex network scenario.

Figure 2.2 SecureNAT Complex Network Scenario

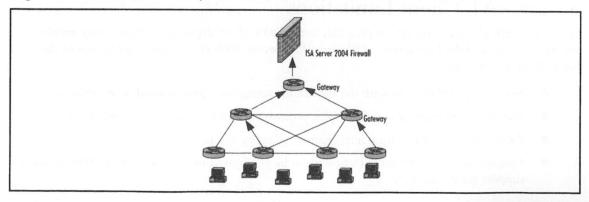

The "VPN client scenario" applies to machines that have created a VPN connection with the ISA Server 2006 firewall.

With ISA Server 2000, when a VPN client computer makes a connection with the VPN server, the client's routing table is changed so that the default gateway is an address on the VPN server. Unless changes are made to the default client configuration, the client will not be able to connect to resources on the Internet while connected to the ISA Server 2000 VPN server. It was possible to configure the ISA Server 2000 VPN client as a Firewall or Web Proxy client and allow the VPN client to access the Internet through the ISA Server 2000 firewall. Alternatively, the ISA Server 2000 VPN client could be configured to allow split tunneling. Either of these methods makes it possible for the client to be connected to internal resources through the VPN server and the Internet at the same time.

In contrast to ISA Server 2000, the ISA Server 2006 VPN server does not require you to configure the VPN clients to be Firewall or Web Proxy clients to access the Internet through the same ISA Server 2006 VPN server to which they connect. Because the VPN clients are not configured as Web Proxy or Firewall clients, they are de facto SecureNAT clients. This allows VPN users to access the corporate network via the VPN connection, while at the same time allowing them to access the Internet via their connection to the ISA firewall, and removes the risks inherent in split tunneling.

Note that you do not need to have a deep understanding of VPN client routing table configuration or how different versions of the Windows VPN client handle default route assignments. Just remember that when a VPN client creates a VPN connection with the ISA Server 2006 firewall/VPN server, that client will be able to connect to the Internet via the ISA Server 2006 firewall based on access rules that you configure.

WARNING

Split tunneling represents a significant security risk and should never be enabled on your VPN clients. ISA Server 2006 supports VPN client SecureNAT connections to the Internet through the same ISA Server 2006 firewall to which they connect, and thus, obviates the need for split tunneling. In addition, the ISA Server 2006 firewall enhances the SecureNAT client support for VPN clients and enables user/group-based access controls for VPN clients. We will discuss the issue of split tunneling and the risks it imposes, in addition to the enhanced SecureNAT client support for VPN clients, in detail in **Remote Access and Site-to-Site Virtual Private Networking.**

SecureNAT Client Limitations

While SecureNAT clients are the simplest ISA Server 2006 client types to configure, they are also the least capable and the least secure of the three ISA Server 2006 client types. Limitations of the SecureNAT client include:

- Inability to authenticate with the firewall for strong user/group–based access control

- Inability to take advantage of complex protocols without the aid of an application filter

- Dependency on the routing infrastructure to access the Internet

- Requirement for a Protocol Definition to be configured on the ISA Server 2006 firewall to support the connection

SecureNAT clients do not send credentials to the ISA Server 2006 firewall because, in order for credentials to be sent to the firewall, there must be a client software component to send them. The basic TCP/IP protocol stack does not provide for user authentication and requires an application component to send user credentials. Thus, Firewall and Web Proxy clients can send user credentials, but the SecureNAT client cannot. The Firewall client uses the Firewall client software to send user credentials, and Web browsers configured to use the ISA Server 2006 firewall as a Web Proxy have the built-in capability to send user credentials. This means you cannot use strong user/group-based outbound access controls for machines configured *only* as SecureNAT clients.

SecureNAT clients cannot connect to the Internet (or any other location through the ISA Server 2006 firewall) using complex protocols without the aid of an application filter installed on the ISA Server. A complex protocol is one that requires multiple primary or secondary connections. A classic case of a complex protocol would be FTP standard (Port) mode connections.

When the standard mode FTP client establishes a connection to the FTP server, the initial connection (the "control channel") is established on TCP port 20. The FTP client and server then negotiate a port number on which the FTP client can receive the data (the file to download), and the FTP server returns the data from its own TCP port 21 to the negotiated port. This inbound connection is a *new* primary connection request and not a response to a primary outbound connection made by the FTP client.

The firewall must be aware of the communications going on between the FTP standard mode client and the FTP server so that the correct ports are available for the new inbound connection request to the ISA Server 2006 firewall. This is accomplished on ISA Server 2006 via its intelligent FTP Access Application Filter. Figure 2.3 depicts the FTP standard mode client and server communications.

Figure 2.3 FTP Standard Mode Client/Server Communciations

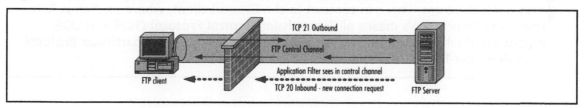

This limitation regarding complex protocols is especially problematic when it comes to Internet games and voice/video applications. These applications typically require multiple inbound and outbound primary connections. The SecureNAT client will not be able to use these applications unless there are specific application filters on the firewall to support them. In contrast, the Firewall client is easily able to handle applications that require multiple inbound and outbound primary connections without installing anything extra on the firewall.

Of course, there's an exception to every rule, and here's the exception to the statement above: Complex protocol support for SecureNAT clients is possible *if* the application installed on the SecureNAT client is designed to work with a SOCKS 4 proxy. In this case, the application is explicitly configured to communicate with the ISA Server 2006 firewall's SOCKS 4 service. The SOCKS 4 service can manage the connections on behalf of the SecureNAT client machine's application.

WARNING

Although SecureNAT clients running SOCKS 4 applications might be able to support complex protocols for the application that is configured to use the SOCKS proxy, the SOCKS proxy will *not* enable the client to benefit from user/group authentication. The SOCKS 4 proxy application filter on the ISA Server 2006 firewall does not accept user credentials that would enable user/group-based access control.

The SecureNAT client is dependent on the organization's routing infrastructure. Unlike the Firewall and Web Proxy clients, which send their Internet connection requests directly to the ISA Server 2006 firewall (and thus, only need to know the route to the Internal interface of the ISA Server 2006 firewall machine), the SecureNAT client depends on the routing infrastructure to forward Internet-bound requests to the Internal interface of the ISA Server 2006 firewall. If the connection encounters a router in the path that does not route Internet-bound connections through the ISA Server 2006 firewall, the connection attempt will fail.

TIP

There must be a protocol definition created on the ISA Server 2006 firewall for each protocol you want the SecureNAT client to access. This is true even when you configure an Access Rule that allows the SecureNAT client access to all protocols. For the SecureNAT client, "all protocols" means all protocols for which there are Protocol Definitions. This is in contrast to the Firewall client, where an Access Rule specifying all protocols means all Transmission Control Protocol (TCP) and UDP, regardless of whether or not there is a Protocol Definition for a particular protocol (including non-TCP/UDP, such as ICMP and IP-level protocols).

- Because of the limitations of SecureNAT, a computer should only be configured as a SecureNAT client when at least one of the following conditions exists: The machine does not support Firewall client software (non-Windows clients) and requires protocol support outside of what the Web Proxy client can provide (protocols other than HTTP/HTTPS and FTP upload).

- The machine requires outbound access to the ICMP and PPTP.

- For administrative or political reasons, you cannot install the Firewall client on machines that require protocol access outside of that provided by the Web Proxy client configuration.

Disadvantages of the SecureNAT configuration are summarized in Table 2.2.

Table 2.2 Disadvantages of the SecureNAT Client Configuration

Disadvantage	Implication
Inability to authenticate with the ISA Server 2006 firewall	The SecureNAT client is unable to send user credentials (user name and password) to the ISA Server 2006 firewall. This prevents the use of strong user/group-based outbound access control over Internet access. The only outbound access control available for SecureNAT clients is based on a client source IP address.
Inability to use complex protocols	Complex protocols require multiple primary and/or secondary connections. Internet games, voice/video applications, and instant messaging applications often require complex protocol support. The SecureNAT client cannot access Internet applications using complex protocols without the assistance of an application filter installed on the ISA Server 2006 firewall machine. The only exception to this is when the application installed on the SecureNAT client is configured to support SOCKS 4.
Dependency on the existing network routing infrastructure	The SecureNAT client does not forward connections directly to the ISA Server 2006 firewall. Instead, it depends on the organization's routing infrastructure. Each router along the path from the SecureNAT client to the ISA Server 2006 firewall must be aware that the path to the Internet is through the ISA Server 2006 firewall. This may require reconfiguring network routers with new gateways of last resort (default gateways).
User information is not included in the Firewall and Web Proxy logs	The user name is only included in Firewall and Web Proxy logs when a client sends that information to the ISA firewall. A client piece is *always* required to send user information to the firewall since there are no provisions in the layer 1 through 6 headers to provide this information. Only the Firewall client and Web Proxy client configurations can send user information to the ISA firewall and have this information included in the log files. SecureNAT client connections allow for logging of the source IP address, but user information is never recorded.

SecureNAT Client Advantages

Despite the limitations discussed in the foregoing section, you should not conclude that the SecureNAT client is all bad. In fact, some of the SecureNAT client's weaknesses also represent the SecureNAT client's strengths. Advantages of the SecureNAT client configuration include:

- Support for non-Windows client operating systems

- Support for non-TCP/UDP (PPTP and ICMP)

- No requirement for client software installation or configuration

The primary purpose of the SecureNAT client configuration is to enable non-Microsoft operating systems to access a broader range of protocols than is supported by the Web Proxy client configuration. The Firewall client works only with Windows operating systems. Thus, without the SecureNAT client configuration, the only protocols that would be available to non-Microsoft operating systems are those provided by the Web Proxy client configuration (HTTP/HTTPS and FTP upload).

The SecureNAT client has an important use for Microsoft operating systems, as well. The Firewall client software intercepts outbound TCP and UDP connections established by Winsock applications and forwards them to the ISA Server 2006 firewall. However, the Firewall client software does not evaluate non-TCP/UDP communications. Networking protocols such as ICMP and GRE (used for the PPTP VPN protocols) do not use UDP or TCP as a transport protocol, and thus, are not evaluated by the Firewall client. You must configure client computers as SecureNAT clients to support outbound access through the ISA Server 2006 firewall using these protocols.

One significant downside of this situation is that you cannot use user/group-based access controls over which hosts can create outbound connections using non-TCP/UDP protocols. For example, you might want to allow outbound PPTP VPN connections for a specific group of users. This is not possible because PPTP requires GRE; this bypasses the Firewall client software, and therefore, no user information is passed to the ISA Server 2006 firewall. If you create an outbound PPTP Access Rule that requires user authentication, the connection attempt will fail. The only method available to control an outbound PPTP connection is by source IP address. We will cover this subject in more detail in Chapter 5.

NOTE

ICMP is most commonly used by the ping utility, although other utilities such as tracert also use ICMP. GRE is required if you wish to allow clients outbound access to external VPN servers using the PPTP VPN protocols. In contrast, outbound VPN clients that use the L2TP/IPSec NAT Traversal (NAT-T) protocol do not have to be configured as SecureNAT clients. L2TP/IPSec NAT-T uses only UDP ports 500 and 4500 for outbound access to L2TP/IPSec NAT-T VPN servers. Because of this, you can use the Firewall client configuration to force strong user/group-based access controls over L2TP/IPSec VPN connections.

Probably the most common reason for implementing the SecureNAT client configuration is to avoid having to install or configure client software. Firewall and network administrators are loath to install software on client computers that imposes itself on the network stack. In addition, there is a perception that significant administrative overhead is involved with installing the ISA Server 2006 Firewall client and configuring the Web Proxy client, although in reality, there is not.

In fact, there is an extremely low likelihood that the Firewall client software will interfere with the networking components of any client software, and the administrative overhead is very small when you automate the Firewall client and Web Proxy client installation and configuration.

We will discuss how to automate client installation and configuration later in this chapter. Table 2.3 details the advantages of the SecureNAT client configuration.

Table 2.3 Advantages of the SecureNAT Client Configuration

Advantage	Implication
Provides additional protocol support for non-Windows operating systems	Non-Windows operating systems do not support the Firewall client software. If you wish to provide support for protocols other than those allowed via the Web Proxy client configuration (that is, HTTP/HTTPS/FTP upload), the SecureNAT configuration is your only option for non-Windows operating system clients such as Linux, UNIX, and Macintosh.
Support for non-TCP/UDP Protocols	The SecureNAT client is the only ISA Server 2006 client configuration that supports non-TCP/UDP protocols. Ping,tracert, and PPTP are some of the non-TCP/UDP protocols that require the SecureNAT client configuration. Note that you cannot exert strong user/group-based access controls for non-TCP/UDP protocols because the SecureNAT client configuration does not support user authentication.
Does not require client software installation or configuration	The SecureNAT client does not require that any software be installed or configured on the client computers. The only requirement is that the default gateway address on the client machine be configured so that Internet-bound requests are forwarded through the ISA Server 2006 firewall.
Best general configuration for published servers	When publishing a server to the Internet, the server often needs to not only accept connections from Internet-based hosts, but also needs to initiate new connections. The best example is an SMTP relay configured for both inbound and outbound relay. The SMTP relay does not need to be configured as a SecureNAT client to receive inbound connections from remote SMTP servers (because you have the option to replace the original source IP address of the Internet host with the IP address of the ISA Server 2006 firewall). However, the SMTP relay *does* need to be configured as a SecureNAT client to send outbound mail to Internet SMTP servers. We will cover this issue in more detail in Chapter 7.

Name Resolution for SecureNAT Clients

As we discussed earlier in the context of network services support, name resolution is a critical issue not only when installing the ISA Server 2006 firewall software on the server, but for all types of ISA Server 2006 clients. Each ISA Server 2006 client resolves names in its own way. The SecureNAT client resolves names for hosts on the Internal and External networks using the DNS server address configured on the SecureNAT client's own network interfaces.

The fact that the SecureNAT client must be able to resolve names based on its own TCP/IP configuration can pose challenges for Internet-connected organizations that require access to resources both while connected to the corporate network and when those same hosts must leave the Internal network and connect to corporate resources from remote locations. In addition, there are significant challenges when SecureNAT clients attempt to "loop back" through the ISA Server 2006 firewall to access resources on the Internal or other protected networks.

SecureNAT clients must be configured to use a DNS server that can resolve both Internal network names and Internet host names. Most organizations host their own DNS servers within the confines of the corporate network. In this case, the SecureNAT client should be configured to use the Internal DNS server that can resolve Internal network names, and then either perform recursion to resolve Internet host names, or use a DNS forwarder to resolve the Internet host names.

Name Resolution and "Looping Back" Through the ISA Server 2006 Firewall

Consider the example of an organization that uses the domain name *internal.net* for resources located on the Internal network behind the ISA Server 2006 firewall. The organization uses the same domain name to host resources for remote users and publishes those resources on the Internal network. For example, the company hosts its own Web server on the Internal network, and the IP address of that Web server on the Internal network is **192.168.1.10**.

The organization also hosts its own DNS resources and has entered the IP address **222.222.222.1** into the DNS database for the host name **www.internal.net.** External users use this name, **www.internal.net,** to access the company's Web server. The Web server is published using ISA Server 2006 Web Publishing Rules and external users have no problem accessing the published Web server.

The problem is that when SecureNAT clients on the Internal network try to reach the same Web server, the connection attempts always fail. The reason for this is that the SecureNAT clients are configured to use the same DNS server that is used by the external clients to resolve the name **www.internal.net.** This name resolves to the public address on the external interface of the ISA Server 2006 firewall that is used in the Web Publishing Rule. The SecureNAT client resolves the name **www.internal.net** to this address and forwards the connection to the external interface of the ISA Server 2006 firewall. The ISA Server 2006 firewall then forwards the request to the Web server on the Internal network.

The Web server then responds *directly to the SecureNAT client computer.* The reason for this is that the source IP address in the request forwarded by the ISA Server 2006 firewall to the Web Server on the Internal network is the IP address of the SecureNAT client. This causes the Web server on the Internal network to recognize the IP address as one on its local network and respond directly to the SecureNAT client. The SecureNAT client computer drops the response from the Web server because it sent the request to the public IP address of the ISA Server 2006 firewall, not to the IP address of the Web server on the Internal network.

The response is dropped because the SecureNAT client sees this as an unsolicited communication. Figure 2.4 depicts the SecureNAT client looping back through the ISA Server 2006 firewall.

Figure 2.4 SecureNAT "Loop Back"

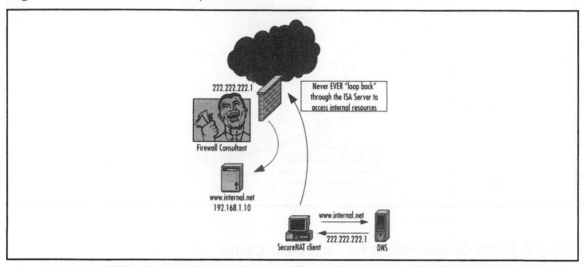

The solution to this problem is the split DNS infrastructure. In almost all cases in which the organization requires remote access to resources located on the Internal network, the split DNS infrastructure provides the solution to name resolution problems for SecureNAT and roaming clients (hosts that move between the Internal network and locations outside the corporate network).

In a split DNS infrastructure, the SecureNAT client is configured to use an Internal DNS server that resolves names for resources based on the resource's Internal network address. Remote hosts can resolve the same names, but the external hosts resolve the same names to the IP address on the external interface of the ISA Server 2006 firewall that publishes the resource. This prevents the SecureNAT client from looping back through the ISA Server 2006 firewall, and connection attempts to published servers succeed for the SecureNAT clients. Figure 2.5 demonstrates how the split DNS infrastructure solves the "looping back" issue for SecureNAT clients. Table 2.4 summarizes important DNS considerations for SecureNAT clients.

NOTE

For this reason, Web developers should never "hard code" IP addresses or names in links returned to Web users. For example, a Web developer might code a link that points to **http://192.168.1.1/info** into a Web page response to a user. Internal network clients can access this link because the IP address is that of the Web server on the Internal network, but remote access users will not be able to connect to this resource because the address is not accessible from the Internet. Many Java applications suffer from this type of poor coding, and even some Microsoft applications, such as SharePoint Portal Server (although some of these problems can be solved using the ISA Server 2006 firewall's Link Translator feature).

Figure 2.5 A Split DNS Solves the SecureNAT Paradox

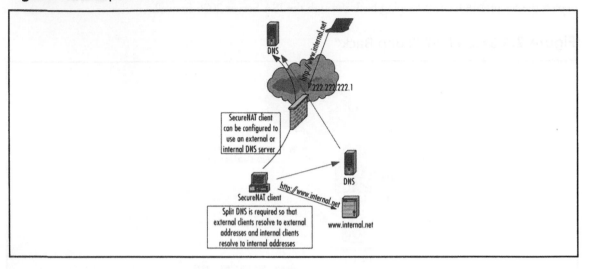

Table 2.4 DNS Considerations for SecureNAT Clients

SecureNAT DNS Consideration	Implications
Internal and external host name resolution	The SecureNAT client must be able to resolve all host names via its locally-configured DNS server address. The DNS server must be able to resolve Internal network names, as well as external Internet host names. If the DNS server that the SecureNAT client is configured to use is not able to resolve local names or Internet names, the name resolution request will fail and the connection attempt will be aborted.
Looping back through the ISA Server 2006 firewall	SecureNAT clients must not loop back through the ISA Server 2006 firewall to access Internal network resources. The most common situation where this occurs is when a server on the Internal network has been published to the Internet. The SecureNAT client is configured with a DNS server that resolves the name of the server to the IP address on the external interface of the ISA Server 2006 firewall. The SecureNAT client sends a connection request to that IP address and the connection request fails. The solution is to design and configure a split DNS infrastructure.

Table 2.4 Continued

SecureNAT DNS Consideration	Implications
Organizations with Internal DNS servers	Organizations with Internal DNS servers should configure those servers to resolve both internal and external host names. The Internal DNS servers are authoritative for the Internal network domain names. The DNS servers should be configured to either perform recursion against Internet DNS servers or use a forwarder to resolve Internet host names. Note that an organization may elect to use different servers for local and external name resolution, but the SecureNAT clients DNS point of contact must have a mechanism in place to resolve both internal and external names.
Organizations without Internal servers DNS	Smaller organizations may not have a DNS server on the Internal network. In this case, alternate methods are used for local name resolution, such as WINS, NetBIOS broadcast name resolution, or local HOSTS files. The SecureNAT clients should be configured to use a DNS located on the Internet (such as their ISP's DNS server) or configure a caching-only DNS server on the ISA Server 2006 firewall computer.
SecureNAT client cannot connect to the Internet	The most common reason for SecureNAT clients failing to connect to Internet resources is a name resolution failure. Check that the SecureNAT client is configured to use a DNS server that can resolve Internet host names. You can also use the **nslookup** utility to test name resolution on the SecureNAT client computer.
SecureNAT client cannot connect to servers on the Internal network	The most common reason for SecureNAT clients failing to connect to local resources using DNS host names is name resolution failure. Check that the DNS server configured on the SecureNAT client is able to resolve names on the Internal network. Note that if the SecureNAT client is configured to use an Internet-based DNS server (such as your ISP's DNS server), the SecureNAT client will not be able to resolve local DNS host names. This can be solved by configuring the SecureNAT client to use an Internal DNS server that can resolve local and Internet host names, or by using an alternate method of Internal network host name resolution.

Continued

Table 2.4 Continued

SecureNAT DNS Consideration	Implications
SecureNAT clients should be configured to use an Internal network DNS Server	Although small organizations may not have a DNS server responsible for name resolution on the Internal network, you should avoid using public DNS servers for your SecureNAT clients. Instead, configure the ISA Server 2006 firewall as a caching-only DNS server, and configure the SecureNAT clients to use the caching-only DNS server on the ISA Server 2006 firewall. Configure the caching-only DNS server on the ISA Server 2006 firewall to use a trusted DNS server, such as your ISP's DNS server, as a forwarder. This reduces the risks inherent from |allowing SecureNAT clients to communicate directly with Internet DNS servers. The caching-only DNS server on the ISA Server 2006 firewall can be configured to prevent common DNS exploits, such as cache poisoning.

Understanding the ISA Server 2006 Firewall Client

The Firewall client software is an optional piece of software that can be installed on any supported Windows operating system to provide enhanced security and accessibility. The Firewall client software provides the following enhancements to Windows clients:

- Allows strong user/group-based authentication for all Winsock applications using TCP and UDP protocols

- Allows user and application information to be recorded in the ISA Server 2006 firewall's log files

- Provides enhanced support for network applications, including complex protocols that require secondary connections

- Provides "proxy" DNS support for Firewall client machines

- Allows you to publish servers that require complex protocols without the aid of an application filter

- The network routing infrastructure is transparent to the Firewall client

Allows Strong User/Group-Based Authentication for All Winsock Applications Using TCP and UDP Protocols

The Firewall client software transparently sends user information to the ISA Server 2006 firewall. This allows you to create Access Rules that apply to users and groups and allow or deny access to any protocol, site, or content, based on a user account or group membership. This strong user/group-based outbound access control is extremely important. Not all users require the same level of access, and users should only be allowed access to protocols, sites, and content they require to do their jobs.

> **NOTE**
>
> The concept of allowing users access to only the protocols, sites, and content they require is based on the principle of *least privilege*. The principle of least privilege applies to both inbound and outbound access. For inbound access scenarios, Server and Web Publishing rules allow traffic from external hosts to Internal network resources in a highly controlled and monitored fashion. The same should be true for outbound access. In traditional network environments, inbound access is highly limited while users are allowed outbound access to virtually any resource they desire. This weak approach to outbound access control can put not only the corporate network at risk, but other networks as well, as Internet worms can easily traverse firewalls that do not restrict outbound access.

The Firewall client automatically sends user credentials (user name and password) to the ISA Server 2006 firewall. The user must be logged on with a user account that is either in the Windows Active Directory or NT domain, or the user account must be mirrored on the ISA Server 2006 firewall. For example, if you have an Active Directory domain, users should log on to the domain, and the ISA Server 2006 firewall must be a member of the domain. The ISA Server 2006 firewall is able to authenticate the user and allows or denies access based on the user's domain credentials.

If you do not have a Windows domain, you can still use the Firewall client software to control outbound access based on user/group. In this case, you must mirror the accounts that users log on to on their workstations to user accounts stored in the local Security Account Manager (SAM) on the ISA Server 2006 firewall computer.

For example, a small business does not use an Active Directory, but they do want strong outbound access control based on user/group membership. Users log on to their machine with local user accounts. You can enter the same user names and passwords on the ISA Server 2006 firewall, and the ISA Server 2006 firewall will be able to authenticate the users based on the same account information they use when they log on to their local machines.

Allows User and Application Information to be Recorded in the ISA Server 2006 Firewall's Log Files

A major benefit of using the Firewall client is that when the user name is sent to the ISA Server 2006 firewall, that user name is included in the ISA Server 2006 firewall's log files. This allows you to easily query the log files based on username and obtain precise information on that user's Internet activity.

In this context, the Firewall client provides not only a high level of security by allowing you to control outbound access based on user/group accounts, but also provides a high level of accountability. Users will be less enthusiastic about sharing their account information with other users when they know that their Internet activity is being tracked based on their account name, and they are held responsible for that activity.

Provides Enhanced Support for Network Applications, Including Complex Protocols That Require Secondary Connections

Unlike the SecureNAT client, which requires an application filter to support complex protocols requiring secondary connections, the Firewall client can support virtually any Winsock application using TCP or UDP protocols, regardless of the number of primary or secondary connections, without requiring an application filter.

The ISA Server 2006 firewall makes it easy for you to configure Protocol Definitions reflecting multiple primary or secondary connections and then create Access Rules based on these Protocol Definitions. This provides a significant advantage in terms of Total Cost of Ownership (TCO) because you do not need to purchase applications that are SOCKS proxy aware, and you do not need to incur the time and cost overhead involved with creating customer application filters to support "off-label" Internet applications.

Provides "Proxy" DNS Support for Firewall Client Machines

In contrast to the SecureNAT client, the Firewall client does not need to be configured with a DNS server that can resolve Internet host names. The ISA Server 2006 firewall can perform a "proxy" DNS function for Firewall clients.

For example, when a Firewall client sends a connection request for **ftp://ftp.microsoft.com,** the request is sent directly to the ISA Server 2006 firewall. The ISA Server 2006 firewall resolves the name for the Firewall client based on the DNS settings on the ISA Server 2006 firewall's network interface cards. The ISA Server 2006 firewall returns the IP address to the Firewall client machine, and the Firewall client machine sends the FTP request to the IP address for the **ftp.microsoft.com** FTP site. The ISA Server 2006 firewall also caches the results of the DNS queries it makes for Firewall clients. This speeds up name resolution for subsequent Firewall client connections to the same sites. Figure 2.6 shows the name resolution sequence for the Firewall client.

Figure 2.6 Firewall Name Resolution Sequence

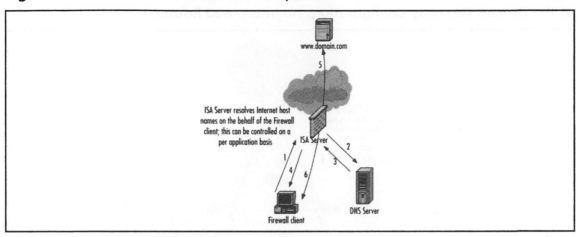

1. The Firewall client sends a request for ftp.microsoft.com.

2. The ISA Server 2006 firewall sends a DNS query to an Internal DNS server.

3. The DNS server resolves the name ftp.microsoft.com to its IP address and returns the result to the ISA Server 2006 firewall.

4. The ISA Server 2006 firewall returns the IP address of ftp.microsoft.com to the Firewall client that made the request.

5. The Firewall client sends a request to the IP address for ftp.microsoft.com and the connection is complete.

6. The Internet server returns requested information to the Firewall client via the Firewall client connection made to the ISA Server 2006 firewall.

The Network Routing Infrastructure Is Transparent to the Firewall Client

The final major benefit conferred by the Firewall client is that the routing infrastructure is virtually transparent to the Firewall client machine. In contrast to the SecureNAT client, which depends on its default gateway and the default gateway settings on routers throughout the corporate network, the Firewall client machine only needs to know the route to the IP address on the Internal interface of the ISA Server 2006 firewall. The Firewall client machine "remotes" or sends requests directly to the IP address of the ISA Server 2006 firewall. Since corporate routers are typically aware of all routes on the corporate network, there is no need to make changes to the routing infrastructure to support Firewall client connections to the Internet. Figure 2.7 depicts the "remoting" of these connections directly to the ISA Server 2006 firewall computer. Table 2.5 summarizes the advantages of the Firewall client application.

Figure 2.7 Firewall Client Connections to the ISA 2004 Firewall are Independent of the Default Gateway Configurations on Interposed Routers

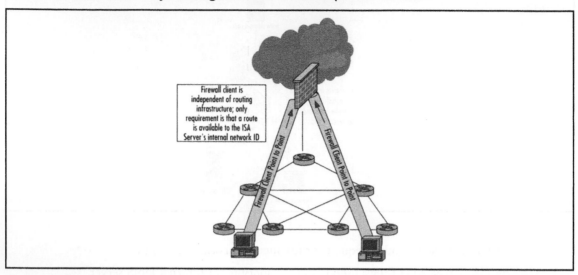

Table 2.5 Advantages of the Firewall Client Configuration

Firewall Client Advantage	Implication
Strong user/based authentication for Winsock TCP and UDP protocols	Strong user/based authentication for Winsock applications using TCP and UDP allows you fine-tuned granular control over outbound access and makes it possible for you to implement the principle of least privilege, which protocols not only your own network, but other corporations networks as well.
User name and application information is saved in the ISA Server 2006 firewall's logs	While strong user/group-based access controls increase the security the firewall provides for your network, user name and application name information saved in the ISA Server 2006 firewall's log increases the accountability and enables you to easily research what sites, protocols, and applications any user running the Firewall client software has accessed.
Enhanced support for network applications and protocols	The Firewall client can access virtually any TCP or UDP-based protocol, even those used by complex protocols that require multiple primary and/or secondary connections. In contrast, the SecureNAT client requires an application filter on the ISA Server 2006 firewall to be in place to support complex protocols. The overall effect is that the Firewall client reduces the TCO of the ISA Server 2006 firewall solution.

Table 2.5 Continued

Firewall Client Advantage	Implication
Proxy DNS support for Firewall clients	The ISA Server 2006 firewall can resolve names on behalf of Firewall clients. This offloads the Internet host name resolution responsibility from the Firewall client and allows the ISA Server 2006 firewall to keep a DNS cache of recent name resolution requests. This DNS proxy feature also enhances the security configuration for Firewall clients because it eliminates the requirement that the Firewall client be configured to use a public DNS server to resolve Internet host names.
Enables publishing servers that require a complex networking protocol	Web and Server Publishing Rules support simple protocols, with the exception of those that have an application installed on the ISA Server 2006 firewall, such as the FTP Access application filter. You can install Firewall client software on a published server to support complex protocols, such as those that might be required if you wished to run a game server on your network.
The network routing infrastructure is virtually transparent to the firewall client	Unlike the SecureNAT client, which relies on the routing infrastructure through the organization to use the ISA Server 2006 firewall as its Internet access firewall, the Firewall client only needs to know the route to the IP address on the Internal interface of the ISA Server 2006 firewall. This significantly reduces the administrative overhead of supporting the Firewall client versus the SecureNAT client.

How the Firewall Client Works

The details of how the Firewall client software actually works are not fully documented in the Microsoft literature. What we do know is that the ISA Server 2006 Firewall client, unlike previous versions, uses only TCP 1745 for the Firewall client *Control Channel*. Over this control channel, the Firewall client communicates directly with the ISA Server 2006 firewall service to perform name resolution and network application-specific commands (such as those used by FTP and Telnet). The firewall service uses the information gained through the control channel and sets up a connection between the Firewall client and the destination server on the Internet.

Note that the Firewall client only establishes a control channel connection when connecting to resources not located on the Internal network. In ISA Server 2000, the Internal network was defined by the Local Address Table (LAT). The ISA Server 2006 firewall does not use a LAT because of its enhanced multinetworking capabilities. Nevertheless, the Firewall client must have some mechanism in place to determine which communications should be sent to the firewall service on the ISA Server 2006 firewall and which should be sent directly to the destination host with which the Firewall client wants to communicate.

The Firewall client solves this problem using addresses defined by the **Internal Network**. The Internal network for any specific Firewall client consists of all the addresses reachable from the network interface that is connected to the Firewall client's own network. This situation gets interesting on a multihomed ISA Server 2006 firewall that has multiple Internal networks associated with different network adapters. In general, all hosts located behind the same network adapter (regardless of network ID) are considered part of the same **Internal** network and all communications between hosts on the same Internal network should bypass the Firewall client.

Addresses for the Internal network are defined during installation of the ISA Server 2006 firewall software, but you can create other "Internal" networks as required.

ISA Server 2006 Security Alert

You may have multiple interfaces on the same ISA Server 2006 firewall computer. However, only a single network may have the name **Internal**. The Internal network consists of a group of machines that have an implicit trust in each other (at least enough trust to not require a network firewall to control communications between them). You can have multiple Internal networks, but additional Internal networks cannot be included in the Internal address range of another Internal network.

The most significant improvement the ISA Server 2006 Firewall client has over previous versions of the Firewall client (Winsock Proxy Client 2.0 and ISA Server 2006 Firewall Client) is that you now have the option to use an encrypted channel between the Firewall client and the ISA Server 2006 firewall. Remember that the Firewall client sends user credentials transparently to the ISA Server 2006 firewall. The ISA Server 2006 Firewall client encrypts the channel so that user credentials will not be intercepted by someone who may be "sniffing" the network with a network analyzer (such as Microsoft Network Monitor or Ethereal). Note that you do have the option of configuring the ISA Server 2006 firewall to allow both secure encrypted and non-encrypted control channel communications.

For a very thorough empirical study on how the Firewall client application works with the firewall service in ISA Server 2000, check out Stefaan Pouseele's article **Understanding the Firewall Client Control Channel** at www.isaserver.org/articles/Understanding_the_Firewall_Client_Control_Channel.html.

Note

If Internet Protocol security (IPSec) transport mode is enabled for a network so that the Firewall client machine uses IPSec transport mode to connect to the ISA Server 2006 firewall, you may experience unusual and unpredictable connectivity issues. If Firewall clients in the network do not behave as expected, disable **IP routing** at the ISA Server 2006 firewall console. In the **Microsoft Internet Security** and **Acceleration Server 2004** management console, expand the server, and then expand the **Configuration** node; click the **General** node. In the details pane, click **Define IP Preferences**. On the **IP Routing** tab, verify that the **Enable IP Routing** check box is *not* selected. Note that disabling IP Routing can significantly degrade the performance of your SecureNAT clients.

Installing the Firewall Client Share

The Firewall client share contains the installation files for the Firewall client. Regardless of the method you use to distribute the Firewall client, you must install the Firewall client share on either the ISA Server 2006 firewall or a file server on the Internal network. We recommend that you do not install the Firewall client software on the ISA Server 2006 firewall.

When the Firewall client share is installed on the ISA Server 2006 firewall, a Firewall System Policy Rule (a type of Access Rule that is processed before using defined Access Rules) is created that allows a number of potentially dangerous protocols access to the firewall machine. These protocols include:

- Microsoft Common Internet File System (CIFS) (TCP)
- Microsoft CIFS (UDP)
- NetBIOS Datagram
- NetBIOS Name Service
- NetBIOS Session

In addition, File and Printer Sharing must be enabled on the Internal interface. These Microsoft File and Printer sharing services and protocols, as well as the Client for Microsoft Networks service, can pose a significant risk to the ISA Server 2006 firewall and should be disabled, if at all possible, on all ISA Server 2006 network interfaces. You can disable these services and still make the Firewall client share available to network users by installing the Firewall client share on another machine on the corporate network.

Do the following to install the Firewall client share on a file server on the Internal network:

1. Place the ISA Server 2006 CD into the CD tray on the file server.
2. Close the Autorun window when it appears.
3. Using windows explorer, browse the cd and copy the client folder to a network location of your choice and create the mspclnt share.
4. The default **Share Permissions** on the folder should be set to **Everyone Read**. The default NTFS permissions on the share should be:

- Administrators – Full Control
- Authenticated Users – Read & Execute, List Folder Contents and Read
- System – Full Control

Installing the Firewall Client

There are a number of methods you can use to install the Firewall client software. These include:

- Using an SMB/CIFS connection to a share on a file server
- Active Directory Group Policy Software Management
- Silent Installation Script
- Systems Management Server (SMS)

In this section, we will cover the manual installation of the Firewall client. Users who choose this method of installing the Firewall client software must be local administrators on the machine on which they install the software. For example, if the machine is a laptop computer that is also a member of the corporate domain, make sure the user has a local account on the laptop that is a member of the Administrators group. Have the user log off the domain and log on to the local computer. The user can then connect to the Firewall client share on the network file server. The user may need to enter network credentials when connecting to the File server if the laptop's local account the user is currently logged into is not mirrored on the file server or in the Active Directory (if the file server and the user are members of the same Active Directory domain).

All users of the computer have access to the Firewall client software after it is installed. That means the user can log off from the local account and log back in with domain credentials and still use the Firewall client software.

If you do not allow your users to be members of the Administrators group on their local machines, you must use one of the automated approaches that installs the Firewall client software *before* user log on. You can use Active Directory Group Policy Software Assignment or Systems Management Server (SMS) to accomplish this task.

Some things to take note of regarding installation of the Firewall client software:

- Do **not** install the Firewall client software on the ISA Server 2006 firewall machine.

- Do **not** install the Firewall client software on a domain controller or other network servers. The only exception to this rule is when you must publish a server that requires complex protocol support. For example, many game servers require multiple primary and secondary connections. In this case, the Firewall client must be installed on the published server

- The Firewall client software begins working immediately after installation is complete.

- You can install the Firewall client on any version of Windows (except Windows 95) as long as Internet Explorer 5.0 is installed.

Perform the following steps to install the Firewall client software from a file share on the Internal network:

The latest version can also be downloaded from Microsoft at https://www.microsoft.com/downloads/details.aspx?familyid=05C2C932-B15A-4990-B525-66380743DA89&displaylang=en

1. Click **Start** and then click **Run**.
2. In the **Run** dialog box, enter **\\FILESERVER\mspclnt\setup** (where FILESERVER is the name of the server having the mspclnt share) and click **OK**.
3. Click **Next** on the **Welcome to the Install Wizard for Microsoft Firewall Client** page.

4. Click **Next** on the **Destination Folder** page.

5. On the **ISA Server Computer Selection** page, select **Connect to this ISA Server computer**, and enter **remoteisa.msfirewall.org** in the text box below it. Click **Next**.

6. Click **Install** on the **Ready to Install the Program** page.

7. Click **Finish** on the **Install the Wizard Completed** page.

8. You will see the Firewall client icon in the system tray (see Figure 2.8). If there is an active TCP or UDP connection to a network that is not the Internal network, the icon will have a GREEN up-pointing arrow.

Figure 2.8 Firewall Client Icon

TIP

VPN clients can install the Firewall client software while connected to the network using a VPN client connection.

ISA SERVER 2006 SECURITY ALERT

Settings you specify during setup of the Firewall client apply to all user accounts on the client computer. Changes made in the Firewall Client dialog box on the Firewall client machine after installation are only applied to the logged-on user account. Changes are not applied to other users or to applications running under system accounts. In order to make a change in Firewall Client settings for all accounts after installation is complete, modify settings in the *Common.ini* and *Management.ini* files. These files are located in the **Documents and Settings\All Users\Application Data\Microsoft\Firewall Client 2004** folder. On Vista they are located at Users\Username\AppData\Local\Microsoft\Firewall Client 2004. You must restart the Firewall Client (FwcAgent) service on computers running Windows Server 2003, Windows XP, Windows 2000, and Windows NT after modifying Common.ini. You must restart the computer on computers running Windows 9x. Changes to Management.ini do not require a service or computer restart. We will discuss the Management.ini and Common.ini configuration files in more detail later in this section.

Firewall Client Configuration

There are two places where you can configure the Firewall client software: at the **Microsoft Internet Security and Acceleration Server 2006** management console and at the Firewall client computer itself. Configuration changes made in the **Microsoft Internet Security and Acceleration Server 2006** management console apply to all Firewall client computers, and those made at the client apply only to that individual client.

Centralized Configuration Options at the ISA Server 2006 Firewall Computer

Centralized Firewall client configuration options are carried out in the **Microsoft Internet Security and Acceleration Server 2004** management console. Firewall client configuration is done for each network configured to support Firewall client connections. Firewall client connections can be made from:

- Perimeter Networks
- Internal Networks

All other network types do not support Firewall client connections. When Firewall client connections are enabled for a network, incoming connections to TCP and UDP ports 1745 are enabled to the interface connected to that network.

You can reach the Firewall client configuration interface by opening the **Microsoft Internet Security and Acceleration Server 2004** management console, expanding the server name and then expanding the **Configuration** node. In the **Configuration** node, click the **Networks** node, and then click the **Networks** tab in the **Details** pane. Right click on the **Internal** network and click **Properties**.

On the **Firewall Client** tab, put a checkmark in the **Enable Firewall client support for this network** check box, as shown in Figure 2.9. In the **Firewall client configuration** frame, enter the name of the ISA Server 2006 firewall computer in the **ISA Server name or IP address** text box.

Figure 2.9 The Internal Network Properties Dialog Box

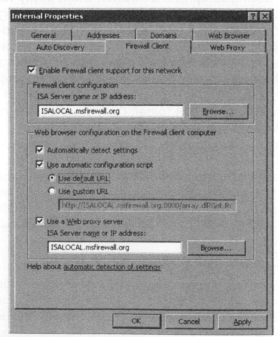

The default setting is to use the computer name (also known as the "NetBIOS" name). However, you should replace the NetBIOS name with the fully-qualified domain name (FQDN) of the ISA Server 2006 firewall. When you replace the computer name with the FQDN, the Firewall client machines can use the DNS to correctly resolve the name of the ISA Server 2006 firewall. This will avoid one of the most common troubleshooting issues with Firewall client connectivity. Make sure there is an entry for this name in your Internal network's DNS server. By default, all the interfaces on the ISA Server 2006 firewall will automatically register their names in the DNS, but if your DNS server does not support dynamic updates, you'll need to manually enter a Host (A) record for the ISA Server 2006 firewall.

NOTE

The most common problem ISA Server 2006 administrators encounter with the Firewall client is name resolution of the ISA Server 2006 firewall. If you do not have a DNS server on your network, use the IP address of the ISA Server 2006 firewall in the **ISA Server name or IP address** text box. Never use the default name that the software automatically enters into the text box This is a very common reason for Firewall client failures.

The Web Proxy client configuration settings are available in the **Web browser configuration on the Firewall client computer** frame. These settings will automatically configure the Web browser as a Web Proxy client *when the Firewall client is installed*. Note that you can change the settings later and the Web browsers will automatically update themselves with the new settings.

The **Automatically detect settings** option allows the Web browser to automatically detect the Web Proxy service and configure itself based on the settings you configure on the **Web Browser** tab of the **Internal Properties** dialog box. Note that autodetection relies on Web Proxy AutoDiscovery (WPAD) entries being placed in DNS and/or DHCP.

The **Use automatic configuration script** option allows you to assign a proxy autoconfiguration file (PAC) address to the Web browser. The Web browser will then connect to the location you specify or use the default location; the default location is on the ISA Server 2006 firewall machine itself. Note that when you use the default location, you obtain the same information you would receive if you had configured the Web browser to use the **Automatically detect settings** option.

The **Use default URL** option automatically configures the browser to connect to the ISA Server 2006 firewall for autoconfiguration information. You can use the **Use custom URL** option if you want to create your own PAC file that overrides the settings on the automatically-generated file at the ISA Server 2006 firewall. You can find more information on PAC files and proxy client autoconfiguration files in **Using Automatic Configuration and Automatic Proxy** at http://www.microsoft.com/technet/prodtechnol/ie/reskit/5/part5/ch21auto.mspx?mfr=true

The **Use a Web Proxy server** option allows you to configure the Web browser to use the ISA Server 2006 as its Web Proxy, but without the benefits of the autoconfiguration script. This setting provides higher Web browsing performance than the SecureNAT client configuration, but you do not benefit from the settings contained in the autoconfiguration script. The most important configuration settings in the autoconfiguration script include site names and addresses that should be used for *Direct Access*.

For this reason, you should avoid this option unless you do not wish to use Direct Access to bypass the Web Proxy to access selected Web sites.

NOTE

Web Proxy client Direct Access configuration allows you to bypass the Web Proxy for selected Web sites. Some Web sites do not conform to Internet standards (Java sites are the most common offenders), and therefore, do not work properly through Web Proxy servers. You can configure these sites for Direct Access and the client machine will bypass the Web Proxy and use an alternate method to connect to the destination Web site. In order for the client to use an alternate method to connect, the client machine must be configured as a Firewall and/or SecureNAT client.

Click the **Domains** tab, as shown in Figure 2.10.

Figure 2.10 The Domains Tab

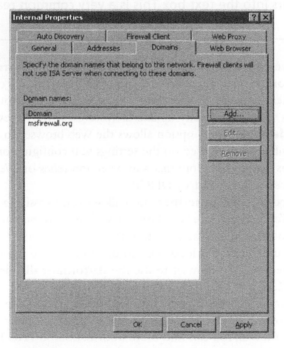

The **Domains** tab contains domains for which the Firewall client computer will not use the Firewall client software to establish a connection. The entries on the **Domains** tab have the same effect as adding machines in these domains to the Internal network (or whatever the network is named for which you are configuring Firewall client Properties). When a Firewall client makes a connection to a host that is located in one of the domains contained in the **Domains** tab, the Firewall client software is not used and the Firewall client machine attempts to connect directly to the destination host.

You can add domains by clicking the **Add** button, and choosing from the **Domain Properties** dialog box, as shown in Figure 2.11.

Figure 2.11 The Domain Properties Dialog Box

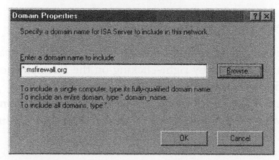

Note that you can use wildcards when specifying a domain. If you want to specify a single computer, just enter the fully-qualified domain name (FQDN) of that host. If you want to include all hosts in a single domain, then use an asterisk (*) just to the left of the leftmost period in the FQDN. If you want to avoid using the Firewall client for all domains, then just enter an asterisk. Click **OK** after making your entry.

You should always include all Internal network domains in the **Domains** tab, as you usually want to allow direct connections to hosts located in the same domain.

For example, if domain members are located on multiple subnets behind a single network interface representing a single network on the ISA Server 2006 firewall, you do *not* want hosts on the network to go through the ISA Server 2006 firewall to connect to hosts on the same network. This puts unneeded stress on the firewall, and the function of a network firewall is not to control these communications.

Enabling Support for Legacy Firewall Client/Winsock Proxy Clients

The ISA Server 2006 Firewall client uses a new and improved *Remote Winsock Proxy Protocol* that encrypts the communication channel between the Firewall client and the ISA Server 2006 firewall's Firewall service. This improves security because user credentials are transparently passed to the ISA Server 2006 firewall when the Firewall client makes an outbound connection request.

However, you have the option to allow non-encrypted Firewall client communications with the ISA Server 2006 firewall. This can provide you time to upgrade your existing Firewall client or Winsock Proxy 2.0 clients to the ISA Server 2006 Firewall client software.

Do the following to enable support for non-encrypted Firewall client connections from legacy Firewall/Winsock Proxy clients:

1. In the **Microsoft Internet Security and Acceleration Server 2006** management console, expand the server name, and then expand the **Configuration** node. Click on the **General** node.

2. On the **General** node, click the **Define Firewall Client Settings** link in the **Details** pane.

3. In the **Firewall Client Settings** dialog box, click the **Connection** node. Put a checkmark in the **Allow non-encrypted Firewall client connections** check box.

4.   Click **Apply,** and then click **OK**.

5.   Click **Apply** to save the changes and update the firewall policy.

6.   Click **OK** in the **Apply New Configuration** dialog box.

Client Side Firewall Client Settings

There are some configuration options available to users who have the Firewall client software installed. These options can be accessed by right-clicking on the Firewall client icon in the system tray and clicking the **Configure** command.

On the **General** tab (see Figure 2.12) of the **Microsoft Firewall Client for ISA Server 2006**, confirm that there is a checkmark in the **Enable Microsoft Firewall Client for ISA Server 2006** check box.

Figure 2.12 The Firewall Client Configuration Dialog box

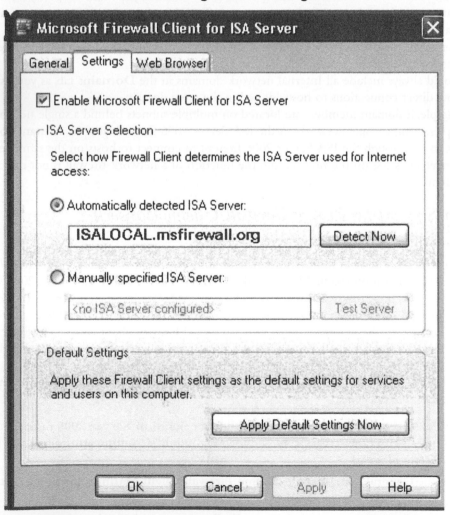

The **Automatically detect ISA Server** option takes advantage of a WPAD entry in a DHCP or DNS server to automatically detect the location of the ISA Server 2006 firewall, and then automatically obtain Firewall client configuration information.

Figure 2.13 illustrates the effect of clicking **Detect Now** button.

Figure 2.13 The Detecting ISA Server Dialog Box

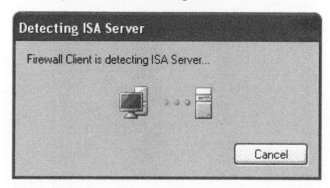

After the Firewall client finds the ISA Server 2006 firewall, you will see the dialog box shown in Figure 2.14.

Figure 2.14 The Detecting ISA Server Dialog Box

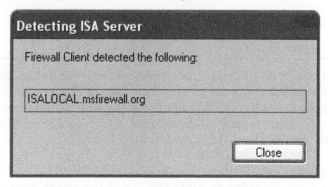

It's important to remember that autodetection will only work if you have configured a WPAD entry in a DHCP or DNS server. We will go through detailed procedures on how to configure the WPAD entries later in this chapter.

You also have the option to **Manually select ISA Server**. This option allows you to enter the IP address or DNS name of the ISA Server 2006 firewall and then click the **Test Server** button to find the firewall. When you enter an IP address, the client sends a request to TCP port 1745 and obtains the autoconfiguration information directly from the ISA Server 2006 firewall. Included in the autoconfiguration information is the name of the ISA Server 2006 firewall, which is listed in the **Detecting ISA Server** dialog box.

The Network Monitor trace shown in Figure 2.15 shows that a connection is made by the Firewall client and some of the information return to the Firewall client is shown in the Hex decode pane.

Figure 2.15 Firewall Client Packet Traces

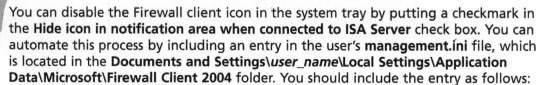

Click on the **Web Browser** tab. Here you have the option to **Enable Web browser automatic configuration**. This option pulls information from the Web browser configuration you set earlier in the **Microsoft Internet Security and Acceleration Server 2006** management console. Users can click the **Configure Now** button, which makes it easy for users who inadvertently change the browser settings to get back to the ideal configuration with a click of a button. For this reason, you should not disable the Firewall client icon in the system tray.

TIP

You can disable the Firewall client icon in the system tray by putting a checkmark in the **Hide icon in notification area when connected to ISA Server** check box. You can automate this process by including an entry in the user's **management.ini** file, which is located in the **Documents and Settings***user_name***\\Local Settings\\Application Data\\Microsoft\\Firewall Client 2004** folder. You should include the entry as follows:

[TrayIcon]
TrayIconVisualState=1

You can use a log-on script to place this file in the user's directory. More information on Firewall client configuration file settings are included in the next section.

Firewall Client Configuration Files

The Firewall Client software adopts the centralized settings you configured by the ISA Server 2006 computer. These settings determine things such as automatic Web Proxy client configuration, the ISA Server name, and ISA Server automatic detection. After the Firewall Client software is installed, ISA Server updates these client settings each time a client computer is restarted and every six hours after an initial refresh is made. The settings are also updated each time the user presses the **Test Server** button.

In addition to these settings, ISA Server automatically updates the Firewall client with information about IP addresses that the client should consider local (the "Internal" network for that particular Firewall client).

For almost all Winsock applications, the default Firewall client configuration works without any further configuration. However, there may be times when you want to modify the default settings. The Firewall client can be configured for each user and for each computer on the Firewall client computer. The configuration is done by making changes to .ini files, which are installed on the Firewall client computer.

You can change the default settings for all components after installation. The new configuration settings take effect only when the client configuration is refreshed.

.ini Files

The configuration information is stored in a set of files, which are installed on the Firewall client computer. When the Firewall client is installed, the following files (also seen in Figure 2.16) are created on the Firewall client computer:

- **common.ini**,   which specifies the common configuration for all applications

- **management.ini**,   which specifies Firewall client management configuration settings

Figure 2.16 Firewall Client Configuration Files

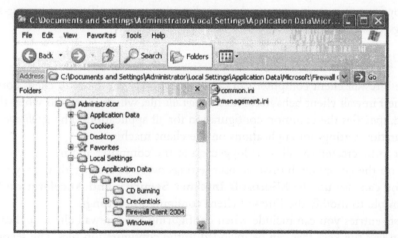

These files are created for all users logged on to the computer and may be created for each specific user on the computer. Per-user settings override the general configuration settings that apply to all users of the same Firewall client computer. These files are created in different locations, depending on the operating system. Unfortunately, we only have information on where these files are located on a Windows XP computer. You can use the **Search** function for your version of Windows to determine the location of the configuration files.

On Windows XP computers the files are located at:

- **\Documents and Settings\All Users\Application Data\Microsoft\Firewall Client 2004**

- **\Documents and Settings**_user_name_**\Local Settings\Application Data\Microsoft\ Firewall Client 2004** folder

In addition to these files, the user may create another file called **Application.ini**, which specifies configuration information for specific applications.

There is an order of precedence regarding how the configuration .ini files are evaluated by the Firewall client. The order of evaluation is:

1. .ini files in the user's folder are evaluated first. Any configuration settings here are used by the Firewall client to determine how the Firewall client and applications that depend on the Firewall client will behave.

2. The Firewall client looks next in the **Documents and Settings\All Users** folder. Any _additional_ configuration settings are applied. If a configuration setting specified contradicts the user-specific settings, it is ignored. The settings in the user's folder always take precedence.

3. The Firewall client detects the ISA Server computer to which it should connect and retrieves settings from the ISA Server 2006 firewall machine.

4. After retrieving the settings from the ISA Server 2006 firewall, the Firewall client examines the server-level settings. Any configuration settings specified on ISA Server are applied. If a configuration setting specified contradicts the user-specific or computer-specific settings, it is ignored.

Advanced Firewall Client Settings

The user on the Firewall client computer can create and modify the Firewall client configuration files and fine-tune the Firewall client behavior. The _common.ini_ file, which is created when the Firewall client is installed, specifies the common configuration for all applications. The _application.ini_ file controls configuration settings for applications on the client machine.

These files can be created for all users logged on to the computer and may be created for individual users on the computer. Individual user settings override settings that apply to all users of the computer. You can also use the **Microsoft Internet Security and Acceleration Server 2006** management console to modify the Firewall client configuration settings.

Table 2.6 lists entries you can include when configuring the Firewall client application settings. The first column lists the keys that can be included in the configuration files. The second column describes the values to which the keys can be set.

Be aware that some settings can be configured _only on the Firewall client_ computer and not via the **Microsoft Internet Security and Acceleration Server 2004** management console.

Table 2.6 Firewall Client Configuration File Settings

Entry	Description
ServerName	Specifies the name of the ISA Server computer to which the Firewall client should connect.
Disable	Possible values: 0 or 1. When the value is set to 1, the Firewall client application is disabled for the specific client application.
DisableEx	Possible values: 0 or 1. When the value is set to 1, the Firewall client application is disabled for the specific client application. Applies only to the Firewall client for ISA Server 2006. When set, overrides the Disable setting.
Autodetection	(Can be set only on the Firewall client computer.) Possible values: 0 or 1. When the value is set to 1, the Firewall client application automatically finds the ISA Server computer to which it should connect.
NameResolution	Possible values: L or R. By default, dotted decimal notation or Internet domain names are redirected to the ISA Server computer for name resolution and all other names are resolved on the local computer. When the value is set to R, all names are redirected to the ISA Server computer for resolution. When the value is set to L, all names are resolved on the local computer.
LocalBindTcpPorts	Specifies a Transmission Control Protocol (TCP) port, list, or range that is bound locally.
LocalBindUdpPorts	Specifies a User Datagram Protocol (UDP) port, list, or range that is bound locally.
RemoteBindTcpPorts	Specifies a TCP port, list, or range that is bound remotely.
RemoteBindUdpPorts	Specifies a UDP port, list, or range that is bound remotely.
ServerBindTcpPorts	Specifies a TCP port, list, or range for all ports that should accept more than one connection.
Persistent	Possible values: 0 or 1. When the value is set to 1, a specific server state can be maintained on the ISA Server computer if a service is stopped and restarted and if the server is not responding. The client sends a keep-alive message to the server periodically during an active session. If the server is not responding, the client tries to restore the state of the bound and listening sockets upon server restart.

Continued

Table 2.6 Continued

Entry	Description
ForceCredentials	(Can be set only on the Firewall client computer.) Used when running a Windows service or server application as a Firewall client application. When the value is set to 1, it forces the use of alternate user authentication credentials that are stored locally on the computer running the service. The user credentials are stored on the client computer using the Credtool.exe application that is provided with the Firewall client software. User credentials must reference a user account that can be authenticated by ISA Server, either local-to-ISA Server, or in a domain trusted by ISA Server. The user account is normally set not to expire. Otherwise, user credentials need to be renewed each time the account expires.
NameResolutionForLocalHost	Possible values are L (default), P, or E. Used to specify how the local (client) computer name is resolved, when the gethostbyname API is called. The LocalHost computer name is resolved by calling the Winsock API function gethostbyname() using the LocalHost string, an empty string, or a NULL string pointer. Winsock applications call gethostbyname(LocalHost) to find their local IP address and send it to an Internet server. When this option is set to L, gethostbyname() returns the IP addresses of the local host computer. When this option is set to P, gethostbyname() returns the IP addresses of the ISA Server computer. When this option is set to E, gethostbyname() returns only the external IP addresses of the ISA Server computer—those IP addresses that are not in the local address table.
ControlChannel	Possible values: Wsp.udp or Wsp.tcp (default). Specifies the type of control channel used.

Firewall Client Configuration at the ISA Server 2006 Firewall

While the configuration files stored at the local Firewall client machine remain a bit of a mystery at the time we write this book, the centralized configuration of the Firewall client done at the **Microsoft Internet Security and Acceleration Server 2006** management console remains as useful as it was in ISA Server 2000 & 2004. You can access the centralized Firewall client configuration interface by opening the **Microsoft Internet Security and Acceleration Server 2006** management console, then expanding the server name and the **Configuration** node. Click on the **General** node, and then click the **Define Firewall Client Settings** link.

Figure 2.17 The Define Firewall Client Settings link

Click the **Application Settings** tab. A list of the built-in Firewall client application settings is shown in Figure 2.18.

Figure 2.18 The Firewall Client Settings Dialog Box

These settings are applied to all Firewall clients who obtain their settings from the ISA Server 2006 firewall. For example, you can see a setting **outlook Disable 0.** This setting tells the Firewall client software to bypass the Firewall client settings for the Microsoft Outlook application. This is an important setting, which allows the Outlook client to receive the proper new mail notification messages.

One especially useful function of the Firewall client settings feature is to block applications. For example, you may want to block users from using the **kazaa.exe** application. You can use the **Disable** key to block the application. Do the following to block the **kazaa.exe** application:

1. In the **Firewall Client Settings** dialog box, on the **Application Settings** tab, click **New**.

2. In the **Application Entry Settings** dialog box, enter **Kazaa** (without the file extension) in the **Application** text box. Select **Disable** from the **Key** drop-down list. Select the value **1** from the **Value** list.

3. Click **OK**.

4. The new entry for **kazaa** appears in the **Settings** list. Click **Apply**, and then **OK**.

5. Click **Apply** (Figure 2.19) to save the changes and update the firewall policy.

Figure 2.19 Apply Changes to Firewall Configuration

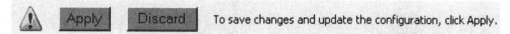

6. Click **OK** in the **Apply New Configuration** dialog box

At this point, any user that has the Firewall client software installed will not be able to use the **kazaa.exe** application.

WARNING

Users can get around this configuration by renaming the executable file. In order to completely block the **kazaa** application, you will need to configure the HTTP security filter and limit the users' access to only the HTTP protocol, or purchase a third-party application filter, such as the Akonix L7 for ISA Server product (www.akonix.com), that can detect peer-to-peer applications.

ISA Server 2006 Web Proxy Client

The Web Proxy client is any computer that has its browser configured to use the ISA Server 2006 firewall as its Web Proxy server. You do not need to add any new software to make a machine a Web Proxy client. The only requirement is that you configure the browser on the client machine to use the ISA Server 2006 firewall as its Web Proxy. The Web browser isn't the only application that can be configured as a Web Proxy client. Other applications, such as instant messengers and e-mail clients can also be configured as Web Proxy clients.

Advantages of the Web Proxy client configuration include:

- Improved performance for the Firewall client and SecureNAT client configuration for Web access

- Ability to use the autoconfiguration script to bypass sites using Direct Access

- Allows you to provide Web access (HTTP/HTTPS/FTP download) without enabling users access to other protocols

- Allows you to enforce user/group-based access controls over Web access

- Supports RADIUS authentication for outbound Web Proxy client requests

- Allows you to limit the number of outbound Web Proxy client connections

- Supports Web Proxy chaining, which can further speed up Internet access

Improved Performance for the Firewall Client and SecureNAT Client Configuration for Web Access

Web Proxy client machines communicate directly with the ISA Server 2006 firewall via the firewall's Web Proxy filter. The Web Proxy client connects directly to TCP port 8080 on the ISA Server 2006 firewall. TCP port 8080 is used by the ISA Server 2006 firewall's *Web Proxy listener*. The listener listens for outgoing Web requests and then exposes those communications to the firewall's Access Policies. This improves performance because connections from Firewall and SecureNAT clients must be passed to the Web Proxy filter instead of being received directly by the filter. You will find during your own testing that Web Proxy client computers access Web content noticeably faster.

Ability to Use the Autoconfiguration Script to Bypass Sites Using Direct Access

One of the most useful features of the Web Proxy client configuration is the ability to use Direct Access to bypass the Web Proxy filter for selected Web sites. This requires that the Web Proxy client computer be configured to use the autoconfiguration script. There are two ways you can configure the Web Proxy client to use the autoconfiguration script:

- Manually configure the client to use the autoconfiguration script
- Configure WPAD entries in DNS and /or DHCP and configure the Web Proxy client to use autodetection to access configuration information

You can manually configure the Web Proxy client browser to use the autoconfiguration script. Any application that pulls its own configuration from the Web browser settings can typically take advantage of the autoconfiguration script settings as well. Applications that do not pull their configuration from the Web browser are unlikely to be able to benefit from the autoconfiguration script settings.

A more efficient method of assigning the autoconfiguration script to the Web Proxy clients is to use WPAD entries in DNS and/or DHCP. The WPAD information will point the Web Proxy client to the IP address of the ISA Server 2006 firewall, from which the Web Proxy client will obtain autoconfiguration settings.

Support for the autoconfiguration script is critical for Web Proxy clients who want to access certain Java sites and also Hotmail e-mail. The autoconfiguration provides a centralized list of Web sites that should be accessed via Direct Access. When these sites are configured for Direct Access, the Web Proxy client computer will bypass the Web Proxy filter and allow other methods, such as the machine's SecureNAT and/or Firewall client configuration, to connect to the Web site.

Allows You to Provide Web Access (HTTP/HTTPS/FTP Download) without Enabling Users Access to Other Protocols

The Web Proxy client configuration allows you to provide Internet access to users who do not require the full range of Internet protocols to connect to the Internet. The Web Proxy client handles only the HTTP, HTTPS (SSL/TLS-over-HTTP) and HTTP-tunnel FTP download. If a user's computer is configured as *only* a Web Proxy client, that user will have access to those protocols and no others.

Web Proxy clients use a tunneled connection when they send their Internet requests to the ISA Server 2006 firewall. For example, when a user sends a request to **www.microsoft.com**, the Web Proxy client wraps this request in another HTTP header with the destination address being the ISA Server 2006 firewall computer's Internal interface and the destination port TCP 8080. When the ISA Server 2006 firewall receives the request, it removes the Web Proxy client's header and forwards the request to the Internet server at **www.microsoft.com**.

In the same way, when a Web Proxy client sends an FTP request to a site, such as **ftp://ftp.microsoft.com**, the Web Proxy client wraps the FTP request in the same HTTP header with the destination address of the Internal interface of the ISA Server 2006 firewall and the destination port TCP 8080. When the ISA Server 2006 firewall receives this request, it removes the HTTP header and forwards the request to the FTP server at **ftp.microsoft.com** as an actual FTP request, not an HTTP request. This is why we refer to the Web Proxy client's FTP support as HTTP-tunneled FTP.

NOTE

When using the Web Proxy client for FTP connections, the Web Proxy FTP client can perform only FTP *downloads*. In order to support FTP uploads the client machine will need to be configured as a SecureNAT or Firewall client.

Allows You to Enforce User/Group-based Access Controls Over Web Access

The Web Proxy client is able to send user credentials to the ISA Server 2006 firewall computer when required. In contrast to the Firewall client, which always sends user credentials to the ISA Server 2006 firewall, the Web Proxy client only sends credentials when asked to provide them. This improves performance, as authentication is only performed when required. If the Web Proxy client has access to an Access Rule that allows access to the site and content in the request, and if the Access Rule allows for anonymous access (allows "All Users" access to the rule), then the Web Proxy client does not send credentials and the connection is allowed (assuming that the Access Rule is an "allow" rule).

This feature explains many of the anonymous entries you have in your firewall log files. When the Web Proxy client sends a request to the ISA Server 2006 firewall, the first connection attempt does not include the Web Proxy client user credentials. This is logged as an anonymous request. If access to the site requires user credentials, then the ISA Server 2006 firewall will send an "access denied" message to the Web Proxy client machine and request the user to authenticate. Figure 2.20 illustrates that, at this point, the Web Proxy client has the option to authenticate using a number of different authentication protocols.

You can use the following authentication protocols for Web Proxy sessions:

- Windows-Integrated authentication
- Basic authentication
- Digest authentication

- Client Certificate authentication
- RADIUS authentication

> **WARNING**
>
> Web browsers can use Integrated, Basic, Digest, RADIUS, and Client Certificate authentication. It's important to note that Web browsers can only use Client Certificate authentication when connecting to published resources through a Web Publishing Rule. Web browser clients acting as Web Proxy clients cannot use Client Certificate authentication when accessing resources through the ISA Server 2006 firewall via an Access Rule.

Figure 2.20 The Authentication Dialog Box

Credentials are passed to the ISA Server 2006 firewall transparently when Integrated authentication is enabled. However, both the ISA Server 2006 firewall and the Web Proxy client must be members of the same domain, or the ISA Server 2006 firewall must use RADIUS authentication to connect to the Active Directory or Windows NT 4.0 user account database. You can also get transparent authentication if you mirror user accounts in the local Security Account Manager (SAM) on the ISA Server 2006 firewall computer. However, for any but the smallest of organizations, the administrative overhead and the security risks of mirroring user accounts can be unacceptably high.

SSL certificate authentication is currently not available for browser to Web Proxy server connections. You can use SSL certificate authentication when configuring Web Proxy chaining. In this setup, a downstream Web Proxy server forwards Web requests to an upstream Web Proxy server. The downstream ISA Server 2006 Web Proxy server can authenticate with the upstream server by presenting a client certificate to the upstream ISA Server 2006 Web Proxy server. This provides a very secure Web Proxy chaining configuration that is not easily attainable with other Web Proxy solutions.

Users are prompted for user name and password when only **Basic** authentication is used. If the Web Proxy client and the ISA Server 2006 firewall are not members of the same domain, or if RADIUS authentication is not used, then Basic authentication is the best solution.

A new feature included with ISA Server 2006 is the ability to use RADIUS for Web Proxy authentication. When RADIUS is enabled as an authentication protocol for Web Proxy clients, the ISA Server 2006 firewall does not need to be a member of the user domain. This provides a slightly higher level of security because an attacker who may take control of the ISA Server 2006 firewall will not be able to leverage domain credentials to attack users on the protected network behind the ISA Server 2006 firewall. When a domain user tries to authenticate for a Web connection, the ISA Server 2006 firewall that is not a member of the user domain forwards the authentication request to a RADIUS server on the Internal network. The RADIUS server forwards the request to an authentication server and then returns the response to the ISA Server 2006 firewall.

Note that when you configure the ISA Server 2006 firewall to support RADIUS authentication, the ISA Server 2006 firewall becomes a RADIUS client. You can use any RADIUS server, including Microsoft's RADIUS implementation, the Internet Authentication Server (IAS).

RADIUS authentication does require that you create a RADIUS server on the Internal network and configure the Web Proxy listener for the Web Proxy client's network to use the RADIUS server. In addition, there must be an Access Rule that allows the ISA Server 2006 firewall to communicate with the RADIUS server using the RADIUS protocol. There is a default firewall System Policy that allows RADIUS messages to the Internal network. If your RADIUS server is not located on the Internal network, you will need to configure the firewall System Policy to allow the RADIUS protocol to the RADIUS server at its alternate location.

We will go through the procedures required to create the RADIUS server and configure the RADIUS client later in this chapter. However, in order to support Web Proxy clients, you will need to perform the following:

- Configure the Outgoing Web Requests listener to use RADIUS authentication
- Configure the user account for Remote Access Permission or configure Remote Access Policy to enable access
- Configure the Remote Access Policy to support PAP authentication

Do the following to configure the Web Proxy listener on the Web Proxy client's Network to use RADIUS:

1. In the **Microsoft Internet Security and Acceleration Server 2006** management console, expand the server name and then expand the **Configuration** node. Click on the **Networks** node and right-click on the **Internal** network (assuming that the Web Proxy clients are located on the Internal network, you would choose the appropriate network in your own configuration). Click **Properties**.

2. In the **Internal Properties** dialog box, click the **Web Proxy** tab.

3. On the **Web Proxy** tab, click the **Authentication** button.

4. In the **Authentication** dialog box, remove the checkmarks from the all the other check boxes. You will see dialog boxes informing you that there are no authentication methods available. Confirm that you have only the **RADIUS** option selected (see Figure 2.21).

Figure 2.21 The Authentication Dialog Box

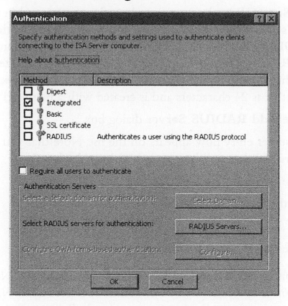

5. Click **RADIUS Servers**.

6. In the **Add RADIUS Server** dialog box, shown in Figure 2.22, enter a name or IP address for the RADIUS server in the **Server name** text box. If you enter a name, make sure that it's a fully-qualified domain name and that the ISA Server 2006 firewall can resolve that name to the correct IP address. Enter a description for the server in the **Server description** text box. Leave the **Port** and **Time-out (seconds)** values at their defaults unless you have a reason to change them. Confirm that there is a checkmark in the **Always use message authenticator** check box.

Figure 2.22 The Add RADIUS Server Dialog Box

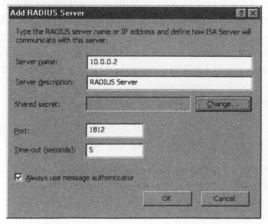

7. Click **Change**.

8. In the **Shared Secret** dialog box, enter and confirm a password in the **New secret** and **Confirm new secret** text boxes. This password is used to authenticate the RADIUS server and RADIUS client. Make sure that this is the same password you used when you configured the RADIUS client on the RADIUS server for the Internal network. Click **OK**. (NOTE: The RADIUS password should be long and complex; an ideal RADIUS password is one that is 24 characters and is created with a password generator application.)

9. Click **OK** in the **Add RADIUS Server** dialog box.

10. The RADIUS server entry now appears on the list. Note that you can create multiple RADIUS servers and they will be queried in the order listed.

11. Click **OK** in the **Authentication** dialog box.

12. Click **Apply** and **OK** in the **Internal Properties** dialog box.

13. Click **Apply** to save the changes and update the firewall policy.

14. Click **OK** in the **Apply New Configuration** dialog box.

The next step is to configure the user account to enable dial-in access. Note that this procedure is *not* required if the domain is in Windows 2000 or Windows Server 2003 Native Mode. The reason for this is that you can control access policy via Remote Access Policy, and the default setting for accounts controls access via Remote Access Policy when the domain is in Native Mode. For this reason, we highly recommend that you configure your Windows domains in Native Mode so that you do not need to enable each individual user account for dial-in access.

1. In the **Active Directory Users and Computers** console on a domain controller that contains the user accounts that you want to authenticate with Web Proxy RADIUS authentication, double-click on the account you want to allow to use RADIUS authentication.

2. In the user's **Properties** dialog box, click the **Dial-in** tab.

3. On the **Dial-in** tab, select the **Allow access** option.

4. Click **Apply**, and then click **OK**.

The user account is now able to use RADIUS for Web Proxy authentication.

The last step is to configure the Remote Access Policy so that PAP authentication is supported for Web Proxy client RADIUS authentication. It's important to note that PAP authentication is not secure, and you should use some method to protect the credentials as they as pass between the ISA Server 2006 firewall and the RADIUS server. The preferred method of protecting credentials is to use an IPSec transport mode connection.

Do the following to configure the Remote Access Policy:

1. At the IAS server on the Internal network, click **Start**, and point to **Administrative Tools**. Click **Internet Authentication Services**.

2. In the **Internet Authentication Services** console, click the **Remote Access Policies** node in the left pane of the console.

3. On the **Remote Access Policies** node, note that there are two Remote Access Policies in the right pane of the console. The first policy applies only to RAS connections from dial-up and VPN clients. The second policy, **Connections to other access servers** is the one used by the Web Proxy clients. Double-click **Connection to other access servers**.

4. In the **Connections to other access servers Properties** dialog box, click **Edit Profile**.

5. In the **Edit Dial-in Profile** dialog box, click the **Authentication** tab.

6. On the **Authentication** tab, put a checkmark in the **Unencrypted authentication (PAP, SPAP)** check box.

7. Click **Apply** and **OK**.

8. In the **Connections to other access servers Properties** dialog box (see Figure 2.23), confirm that the condition **Windows-Groups matches...** entry is included. This includes the groups of users who you want to have access to the Web Proxy service via RADIUS authentication. Use the **Add** button to add the group you want to have access. Also, confirm that the **Grant remote access permission** option is selected.

Figure 2.23 The Connections to other Access Servers Properties Dialog Box

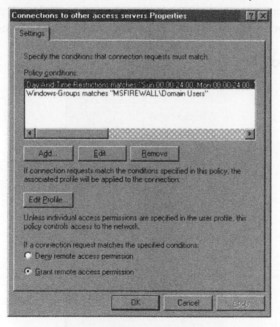

9. Click **Apply** and **OK** in the **Connections to other access server Properties** dialog box.

The policy will take effect immediately; you do not need to restart any equipment.

Allows you to Limit the Number of Outbound Web Proxy Client Connections

The number of Web Proxy client connections can be limited to a number that you specify. This can be helpful when you have limited bandwidth or you want to make sure that only a certain percentage of your users have access to the Internet at any single point in time.

You can access the configuration interface for the number of simultaneous Web Proxy client connections in the **Properties** dialog box of the network from which the Web Proxy clients access the Web. In the **Microsoft Internet Security and Acceleration Server 2004** management console, expand the server name, and then expand the **Configuration** node. Click the **Networks** node in the left pane of the console, and right-click the network in the **Details** pane. Click the **Properties** command.

In the network's **Properties** dialog box, click the **Web Proxy** tab. On the **Web Proxy** tab, click **Advanced**. In the **Advanced Settings** dialog box depicted in Figure 2.24, you can chose from the **Unlimited** and the **Maximum** options. When you select the **Maximum** option, you can enter a value for the maximum number of simultaneous connections. This also a **Connection timeout (seconds)** value that you can customize. The default value is **120** seconds. You can shorten or extend this value depending on your requirements. If you find that idle connections are using up the number of allowed simultaneous connections, you can shorten the timeout value. If you find that users complain about Web sessions being disconnected prematurely, you can extend the timeout value.

Figure 2.24 Advanced Settings

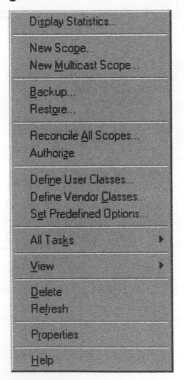

Supports Web Proxy Chaining, Which Can Further Speed Up Internet Access

Web Proxy chaining allows you to connect ISA Server 2006 and ISA Server 2000 firewall and Web Proxy servers to each other. The ISA Server firewall Web Proxy servers represent a chain, where the Web Proxy server farthest away from the centralized Internet access point represents the most "downstream" ISA Server Web Proxy and firewall server, and the ISA Server firewall and Web Proxy server closest to the centralized Internet connection is the most "upstream" ISA Server firewall Web Proxy server.

There are a number of scenarios where Web Proxy chaining can be configured. These scenarios include:

- Branch offices connecting to a main office ISA Server 2006 Web Proxy firewall server

- Campus networks with multiple workgroup/departmental LANs that connect to upstream ISA Server 2006 firewall Web Proxy servers upstream on a campus backbone or services network

- Back-to-back ISA Server 2006 firewall configurations where the downstream ISA Server 2006 firewall uses Web Proxy chaining to forward corporate network Web Proxy requests to the front-end ISA Server 2006 firewall. This configuration adds to the already-strong security of the back-to-back ISA Server 2006 firewall configuration.

We will go into these scenarios in detail in Chapter 8 "Accelerating Web Performance with ISA 2006 Caching Capabilities".

ISA Server 2006 Multiple Client Type Configuration

A common point of confusion among ISA Server 2006 firewall administrators is whether or not a machine can be configured as multiple ISA Server 2006 client types. Many ISA firewall administrators are under the impression that a single machine cannot be configured as a Web Proxy, Firewall, and SecureNAT client. This is a misconception. It is possible and sometimes preferred that a single computer be configured as all three types of ISA client.

The truth is that a single machine cannot be configured to *act* as both a Firewall client and a SecureNAT client. The reason for this is when a machine is configured as a Firewall client, all Winsock TCP and UDP communications are intercepted by the Firewall client software. Therefore, the SecureNAT client configuration does *not* have access to these communications. For non–Winsock TCP and UDP communications, and for all other non-TCP/UDP communications, the SecureNAT client handles the requests. For example, if the machine is configured as both a SecureNAT and Firewall client, the SecureNAT client configuration handles all ping, tracert and PPTP connections. Ping and tracert use ICMP, and PPTP uses GRE. Neither ICMP nor GRE uses TCP or UDP as a transport.

Table 2.7 describes the behavior of machines that are configured as multiple client types.

Table 2.7 Application Behavior on Multiple Client Configuration Machines

ISA Server 2006 Client Configuration	Application Behavior
SecureNAT and Firewall Client	Firewall client handles all TCP and UDP communications from Winsock applications. SecureNAT client handles all TCP/UDP communications from non-Winsock applications and all non-TCP/UDP communications
SecureNAT and Web Proxy Client	Web Proxy client handles all HTTP/HTTPS/FTP download communications from the Web Proxy client application. From non-Web Proxy client applications, the SecureNAT client handles the HTTP/HTTP/FTP connections (both download and upload). If the Web Proxy client-configured browser is not able to use the Web Proxy service to access FTP resources, the client will "fall back" on the SecureNAT client configuration. All other protocols are handled by the SecureNAT client configuration.
Firewall and Web Proxy Client	The Web Proxy client configuration handles all HTTP/HTTPS/FTP download from Web Proxy client-configured applications. The Firewall client handles all other Winsock TCP and UDP communications, including HTTP/HTTPS/FTP download and upload from applications not configured as Web Proxy clients. FTP download from Web Proxy clients can fall back on Firewall client configuration. No access to non-TCP/UDP protocols and no access to TCP and UDP protocols for non-Winsock applications.
SecureNAT, Firewall, and Web Proxy Client	Access to HTTP/HTTPS/FTP download via Web Proxy client configuration for applications configured as Web Proxy clients. Fall back to Firewall client configuration for FTP download if Web Proxy client configuration does not support connection. All TCP/UDP communications from Winsock applications handled by Firewall client. All other communications handled by SecureNAT client configuration.

Deciding on an ISA Server 2006 Client Type

The ISA Server 2006 client type you roll out depends on the level of functionality and level of security you require. Table 2.8 rates the various ISA Server 2006 clients, based on level of functionality, level of security, ease of deployment and management, and operating system compatibility.

Table 2.8 Grading Security, Functionality, Ease and Compatibility of ISA Server 2006 Client Types

Level of Functionality	Level of Security	Ease of Deployment and Management	Operating System Compatibility
Firewall client	Firewall client	SecureNAT client	SecureNAT client
SecureNAT client	Web Proxy client	Web Proxy client	Web Proxy client
Web Proxy	SecureNAT client	Firewall Client	Firewall client

Table 2.9 describes a number of parameters you should consider when selecting the ISA Server 2006 client type to use in your environment.

Table 2.9 Choosing the Appropriate ISA Server 2006 Client Type

You require:	Suggested ISA Server 2006 Client type:
No software deployment to network clients.	The SecureNAT and Web Proxy client. The SecureNAT client does not require software installation and only requires that you set the appropriate default gateway address. The Web Proxy client does not require client software installation; you only need to configure the Web Proxy applications to use the firewall as their Web Proxy server.
Only Web protocols: HTTP, HTTPS and FTP download through a Web browser and other Web Proxy-aware applications and Web caching.	Web Proxy client or SecureNAT client. Both of these clients will be able to benefit from the Web Proxy cache on the ISA Server 2006 firewall. The advantage to using the Web Proxy client over the SecureNAT client in this scenario is that the Web Proxy client will send user information to the ISA Server 2006 firewall and allow you to enforce strong user/group-based access control over what sites and content users access via the Web.
Authentication before allowing access. User name included in logs.	Firewall or Web Proxy client. The Web Proxy client enables you to enforce user/group-based strong access control over HTTP/HTTPS/FTP download connections via Web Proxy client applications. The Firewall client allows strong user/group-based access controls over all Winsock applications using TCP and UDP protocols. Whenever a user authenticates with the ISA Server 2006 firewall, that user's name is included in the logs.

Continued

www.syngress.com

Table 2.9 Continued

You require:	Suggested ISA Server 2006 Client type:
Servers published to the Internet using Web or Server Publishing Rules	SecureNAT or "non-ISA Server 2006 client". The published server must be configured as a SecureNAT client if the original Internet client IP address is retained in the communication reaching the published server. This is the default configuration for Server Publishing Rules. For Web Publishing Rules, the default is to replace the original client IP address with the IP address of the ISA Server 2006 firewall's Internal interface (the interface that lies on the same Network as the published server). When the original source IP address is replaced with the ISA Server 2006 firewall's IP address, the published server only needs to know the route to the Internal IP address of the ISA Server 2006 firewall that forwarded the request. Note that for both Web and Server Publishing Rules you have the option to preserve the original client IP address.
Support for non-Windows operating systems	SecureNAT and Web Proxy clients. All operating systems support the SecureNAT client configuration because the SecureNAT client only requires the appropriate default gateway address configuration. All operating systems running applications that support Web Proxy client configuration can connect to the ISA Server 2006 firewall via the Web Proxy client configuration.
Support for Internet games	Firewall client. Most Internet games require multiple primary and secondary connections. Only the Firewall client supports complex protocols that require secondary connections (unless there is an application filter installed on the ISA Server 2006 firewall to support that specific application).
Support for Voice/Video applications	Voice and video applications that do not require Session Initiation Protocol (SIP) generally require secondary connections (ISA Server 2006 does not support SIP signaling). Only the Firewall client supports secondary connections without the aid of an application filter.

Automating ISA Server 2006 Client Provisioning

There are several methods available for automating the Web Proxy and Firewall client configurations. These include:

- Configuring DHCP Servers to Support Web Proxy and Firewall Client Autodiscovery
- Configuring DNS Servers to Support Web Proxy and Firewall Client Autodiscovery

- Automating Web Proxy Client Configuration with Group Policy

- Automating Web Proxy Client Configuration with Internet Explorer Administration Kit (IEAK)

The following sections discuss how to automate the configuration of Web Proxy and Firewall clients using the Web Proxy AutoDiscovery (WPAD) protocol and Active Directory Group Policy. We will not go into the details of how to use the Internet Explorer Administration Kit to automate Web proxy client configuration.

Note that there are two primary methods for supporting Autodiscovery for Web Proxy and Firewall clients: DNS and DHCP. Table 2.10 provides information that will help you decide which method best fits your needs.

Table 2.10 DNS and DHCP Support for Web Proxy and Firewall Client Autodiscovery

DHCP	DNS
Client must be DHCP client	Client must be able to resolve DNS names on the Internal network
Internet Explorer 5.0 and above required	Internet Explorer 5.0 and above required
Must be able to send DHCPINFORM queries (Windows 2000, Windows XP, Windows Vista and Windows Server 2003 only)	Must be able to correctly qualify the unqualified name "WPAD" with a domain name to yield a FQDN that resolves to the ISA Server 2006 firewall's Internal IP address
User must be logged on as local administrator	Each domain must be configured with its own WPAD entry
ISA Server 2006 firewall can publish autodiscovery information on any available port	ISA Server 2006 firewall must publish autodiscovery information on TCP port 80
Each DHCP Server must be configured with a WPAD entry	Each DNS server must be configured with a WPAD entry. Branch offices may require a custom configuration to prevent Branch office clients from using the WPAD entry pointing to ISA Server 2006 firewalls at the Main office.

Configuring DHCP Servers to Support Web Proxy and Firewall Client Autodiscovery

DHCP clients can obtain autoconfiguration information from the ISA Server 2006 firewall computer by using DHCP Inform messages. The Firewall client and Web browser software can issue DHCP Inform messages to query a DHCP server for the address of a machine containing the autoconfiguration information. The DHCP server returns the address of the machine containing the autoconfiguration information, and the Firewall client or Web browser software requests autoconfiguration from the addresses returned by the DHCP server.

The DHCP server uses a special DHCP option to provide this information. In this section on configuring Web Proxy and Firewall clients to use DHCP to obtain autoconfiguration information via WPAD, we will discuss the following steps:

- Installing the DHCP server

- Creating the DHCP scope

- Creating the DHCP 252 scope option

- Configuring the client as a DHCP client

- Configuring the client browser to use autodiscovery

- Configuring the ISA Server 2006 firewall to publish autodiscovery information

- Making the connection

Install the DHCP Server

The first step is to install the DHCP server. Use the **Add/Remove Programs** applet in the **Control Panel** to install the DHCP Server service.

Create the DHCP scope

A DHCP scope is a collection of IP addresses that the DHCP server can use to assign to DHCP clients on the network. In addition, a DHCP scope can include additional TCP/IP settings to be assigned to clients, which are referred to as *DHCP options*. DHCP options can assign various TCP/IP settings such as a DNS server address, WINS server address, and primary domain name to DHCP clients.

Do the following on the DHCP server to enable the DHCP server and create the DHCP scope:

1. Click **Start**, and then select **Administrative Tools**. Click **DHCP**.

2. In the **DHCP** console, right click on your server name in the left pane of the console. Click on the **Authorize** command.

3. Click **Refresh** in the button bar of the console. You will notice that the icon to the left of the server name changes from a red, down-pointing arrow to a green, up-pointing arrow.

4. Right-click the server name in the left pane of the console again, and click the **New Scope** command.

5. Click **Next** on the **Welcome to the New Scope Wizard** page.

6. Enter a name for the scope on the **Scope Name** page. This name is descriptive only and does not affect the functionality of the scope. You can also enter a **Description** in the description box, if you wish. Click **Next**.

7. Enter a range of IP addresses that can be assigned to DHCP clients on the **IP Address Range** page. Enter the first address in the range into the **Start IP address** range text box

and the last IP address in the range in the **End IP address** text box. Enter the subnet mask for your IP address range in the **Subnet mask** text box.

8. In the example in Figure 2.25, the Internal network is on network ID 10.0.2/24. We do not want to assign all the IP addresses on the network ID to the DHCP scope, just a selection of them. So in this example, we enter **10.0.2.100** as the **Start IP address** and **10.0.2.150** as the end IP address and use a 24-bit subnet mask. Note that on production networks, it is often better to assign the entire network ID to the IP address range used in the scope. You can then create *exceptions* for hosts on the network that have statically-assigned IP addresses that are contained in the scope. This allows you to centrally manage IP address assignment and configuration using DHCP. Click **Next**.

Figure 2.25 Configuring the DHCP Scope IP Address Range

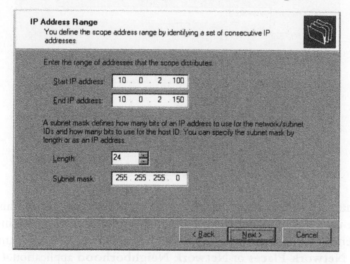

9. Do not enter any exclusions in the **Add Exclusions** dialog box. Click **Next**.

10. Accept the default settings on the **Lease Duration** page (8 days, 0 hours and 0 minutes), and click **Next**.

11. On the **Configure DHCP Options** page, select **Yes, I want to configure these options now,** and click **Next**.

12. Do not enter anything on the **Router (Default Gateway)** page. Note that if we were using SecureNAT clients on the network, we would enter the IP address of the Internal interface for the ISA Server 2006 firewall on this page. However, with the current scenario, we want to test *only* the Web Proxy and Firewall client configurations. Click **Next**.

13. On the **Domain Name and DNS Servers** page, enter the **primary domain name** you want to assign to DHCP clients, and the **DNS server address** you want the DHCP clients to use.

14. The **primary domain name** is a critical setting for your Firewall and Web Proxy clients. In order for autodiscovery to work correctly for Firewall and Web Proxy clients, these clients must be able to correctly fully qualify the unqualified name WPAD. We will discuss

this issue in more detail later. In this example, enter **msfirewall.org** in the **Parent domain** text box (see Figure 2.26). This will assign the DHCP clients the primary domain name msfirewall.org, which will be appended to unqualified names. Enter the IP address of the DNS server in the **IP address** text box. In this example, the IP address of the DNS server is **10.0.2.2**. Click **Add** after entering the IP address. Click **Next**.

Figure 2.26 Configuring the Default Domain Name for DHCP Clients

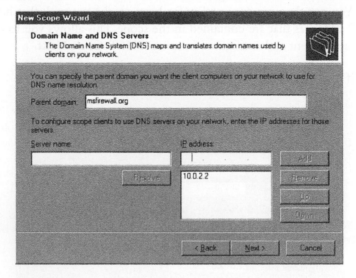

15. Do not enter a WINS server address on the **WINS Servers** page. In this example, we do not use a WINS server. However, WINS servers are very useful in VPN server environments if you wish your VPN clients to be able to browse the campus network using **My Network Places** or **Network Neighborhood** application. Click **Next**.

16. On the **Activate Scope** page, select **Yes, I want to activate this scope now**, and click **Next**.

17. Click **Finish** on the **Completing the New Scope Wizard** page.

18. In the right pane of the **DHCP** console, you see the two DHCP options you created in the Wizard, as seen in Figure 2.27.

Figure 2.27 Viewing the Scope Options

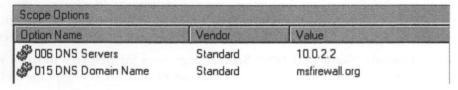

Option Name	Vendor	Value
006 DNS Servers	Standard	10.0.2.2
015 DNS Domain Name	Standard	msfirewall.org

The next step is to create a custom DHCP option that will allow DHCP clients to autodiscover Web Proxy and Firewall client settings.

Create the DHCP 252 Scope Option and Add It to the Scope

The DHCP scope option number 252 can be used to automatically configure Web Proxy and Firewall clients. The Web Proxy or Firewall client must be configured as a DHCP client, and the logged-on user must be a member of the local administrators group or Power users group (for Windows 2000). On Windows XP systems, the Network Configuration Operators group also has permission to issue DHCP queries (DHCPINFORM messages).

> **NOTE**
>
> For more information about the limitations of using DHCP for autodiscovery with Internet Explorer 6.0, please see KB article **Automatic Proxy Discovery in Internet Explorer with DHCP Requires Specific Permissions** at http://support.microsoft.com/default.aspx?scid=kb;en-us;312864

Do the following at the DHCP server to create the custom DHCP option:

1. Open the **DHCP** console from the **Administrative Tools** menu and right-click your server name in the left pane of the console. Click the **Set Predefined Options** command, shown in Figure 2.28.

Figure 2.28 Selecting the Set Predefined Options Command

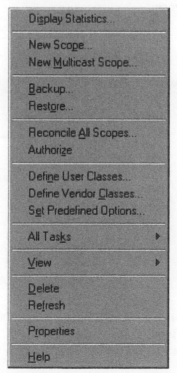

2. In the **Predefined Options and Values** dialog box (Figure 2.29), click **Add**.

Figure 2.29 The Predefined Options and Values Dialog Box

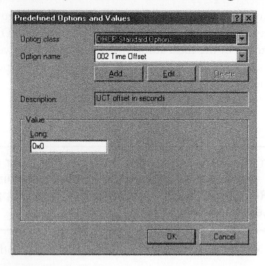

3. In the **Option Type** dialog box (Figure 2.30), enter the following information:
   Name: wpad
   Data type: String
   Code: 252
   Description: wpad entry
   Click **OK**.

Figure 2.30 The Option Type Dialog Box

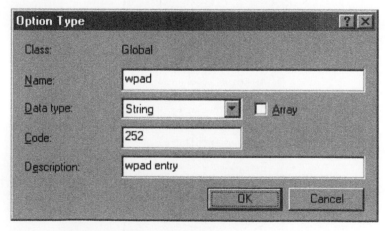

4. In the **Value** frame, enter the URL to the ISA Server 2006 firewall in the **String** text box. The format for this value is:

   http://ISAServername:Autodiscovery Port Number/wpad.dat

The default autodiscovery port number is TCP 80. You can customize this value in the **ISA Management** console. We will cover this subject in more detail later.

As shown in Figure 2.31, enter the following into the **String** text box: http://isa2.msfirewall.org:80/wpad.dat

Make sure to enter wpad.dat in all *lower case* letters. For more information on this problem, please refer to KB article **"Automatically Detect Settings" Does Not Work if You Configure DHCP Option 252** at http://support.microsoft.com/default. aspx?scid=kb;en-us;307502

Click **OK**.

Figure 2.31 Predefined Options and Values Dialog Box

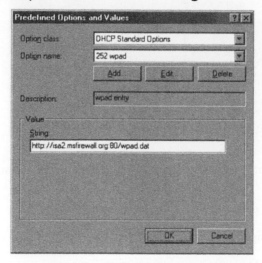

5. Right click the **Scope Options** node in the left pane of the console, and click the **Configure Options** command.

6. In the **Scope Options** dialog box (Figure 2.32), scroll through the list of **Available Options** and put a checkmark in the **252 wpad** check box. Click **Apply** and **OK**.

Figure 2.32 The Scope Options Dialog Box

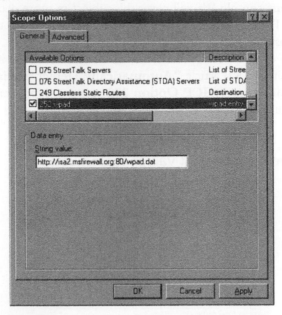

7. The **252 wpad** entry now appears in the right pane of the console under the list of **Scope Options**.

8. Close the **DHCP** console.

The next step is to configure the client computer as a DHCP client.

Configure the Client as a DHCP Client

In order to use DHCP to obtain autodiscovery information for Web Proxy and Firewall clients, the client computer must be configured as a DHCP client.

NOTE

In this example, we configure a Windows 2000 machine as a DHCP client. The procedure varies a bit with each client operating system. All Windows TCP/IP operating systems use DHCP as the default IP address configuration.

Do the following on the client machine to configure it as a DHCP client:

1. Right click **My Network Places** on the desktop, and click the **Properties** command.

2. Right click the **Local Area Connection** entry in the **Network and Dial-up Connections** window and click the **Properties** command.

3. In the **Local Area Connection Properties** dialog box, click the **Internet Protocol (TCP/IP)** entry and click **Properties**.

4. In the **Internet Protocol (TCP/IP) Properties** dialog box, select **Obtain an IP address automatically** and **Obtain DNS server address automatically**. Click **OK**.

5. Click **OK** in the **Local Area Connection Properties** dialog box.

6. Close the **Network and Dial-up Connections** window.

Now you're ready to configure the browser to use autodiscovery for automatically discovering its Web Proxy client settings.

Configure the Client Browser to Use DCHP for Autodiscovery

The browser must be configured to use autodiscovery before it can use the DHCP server option 252 to automatically configure itself. This is the default setting for Internet Explorer 6.0, but the default setting may have been changed at some time during the life of the browser on a particular machine. In the following example, we manually configure the browser to use autodiscovery to autoconfigure itself. We will discuss methods you can use to automatically set this option later.

Do the following on the Web Proxy client computer:

1. Right click on the **Internet Explorer** icon on the desktop and click **Properties**.

2. In the **Internet Properties** dialog box, click the **Connections** tab. Click the **LAN Settings** button.

3. In the **Local Area Network (LAN) Settings** dialog box, put a checkmark in the **Automatically detect settings** check box. Click **OK**.

4. Click **OK** in the **Internet Properties** dialog box.

ISA Server 2006 firewall must be configured to publish autodiscovery information before the Web Proxy client can obtain configuration information. That's the next step.

Configure the ISA Server 2006 Firewall to Publish Autodiscovery Information

All the settings required for the Web browser to configure itself are contained on the ISA Server 2006 firewall computer. By default, this option is disabled. You can enable publishing of autodiscovery information on the ISA Server 2006 firewall computer so that the Web Proxy client can obtain autoconfiguration settings.

Do the following on the ISA Server 2006 firewall computer to enable it to provide autoconfiguration information to Web Proxy and Firewall autodiscovery clients:

1. At this ISA Server 2006 firewall computer, open the **Microsoft Internet Security and Acceleration Server 2004** management console. Expand the server name in the left pane of the console, and then expand the **Configuration** node. Click the **Networks** node.

Figure 2.33 Accessing the Internal Network Properties Dialog Box

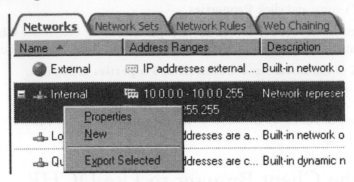

2. On the **Networks** node, click the **Networks** tab in the **Details** pane.

3. Right-click the **Internal** network on the **Networks** tab, and click **Properties** (see Figure 2.33).

4. In the **Internal Properties** dialog box, put a checkmark in the **Publish automatic discovery information** check box. In the **Use this port for automatic discovery request** text box, leave the default **port 80** as it is.

5. Click **Apply** and **OK**.

6. Click **Apply** to save the changes and update the firewall policy.

7. Click **OK** in the **Apply New Configuration** dialog box.

Making the Connection

All the components are now in place for the Web browser to automatically connect to the ISA Server 2006 firewall's Web Proxy service using autodiscovery.

Do the following on the Web Proxy client computer:

1. Open **Internet Explorer** and enter the URL for the Microsoft ISA Server site at **www.microsoft.com/isaserver**

2. A Network Monitor trace shows the DHCP Inform messages sent by the Web Proxy client. The Web Proxy client uses the DHCP Inform messages, such as the one shown in Figure 2.34 to obtain the autodiscovery address contained in the DHCP option 252 entry.

Figure 2.34 Viewing the DHCPINFORM Request

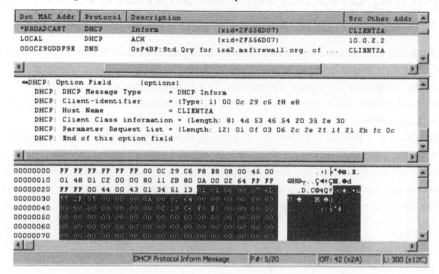

3. In Figure 2.35, you can see the ACK response to the Web Proxy client's DHCP inform message. In the bottom pane of the Network Monitor console, you can see that the DHCP server has returned the address you configured in the DHCP option 252 entry.

Figure 2.35 Viewing the contents of the DHCPINFORM request

```
000000F0  00 00 00 00 00 00 00 00 00 00 00 00 00 00 00 00   ................
00000100  00 00 00 00 00 00 00 00 00 00 00 00 00 00 00 00   ................
00000110  00 00 00 00 00 00 63 82 53 63 35 01 05 36 04 0A   ......cé5c5õ➊6➊⊞
00000120  00 02 02 01 04 FF FF FF 00 0F 0F 6D 73 66 69 72   .➌➌➌➍  .○○msfir
00000130  65 77 61 6C 6C 2E 6F 72 67 00 06 04 0A 00 02 02   ewall.org.�205.◐◐
00000140  FC 27 68 74 74 70 3A 2F 2F 69 73 61 32 2E 6D 73   ⌐'http://isa2.ms
00000150  66 69 72 65 77 61 6C 6C 2E 6F 72 67 3A 38 30 2F   firewall.org:80/
00000160  77 70 61 64 2E 64 61 74 00 FF                     wpad.dat.
```

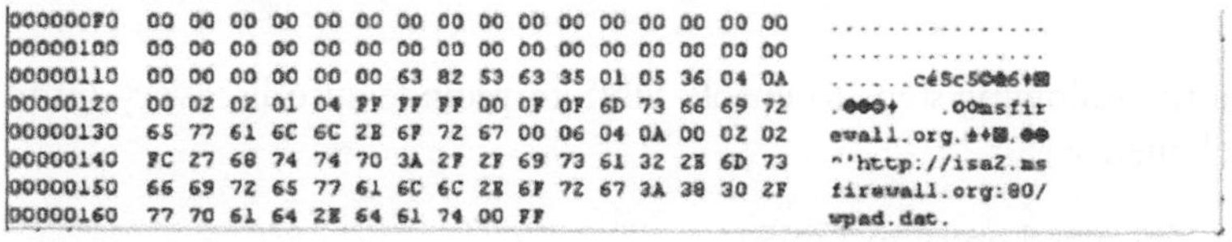

4. After the Web Proxy client receives the address of the ISA Server 2006 containing the autodiscovery settings, the next step is for it to resolve the name of the ISA Server 2006 firewall to its Internal IP address. Name resolution is critical for multiple aspects of ISA Server 2006 functioning, and this is another example of this fact. You can see in the Network Monitor (Figure 2.36) that the Web Proxy client has issued a query for isa2.msfirewall.org, which was the URL contained in the DHCP 252 option.

Figure 2.36 Viewing the WPAD DNS Query

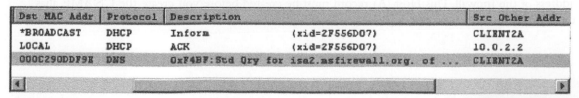

Configuring DNS Servers to Support Web Proxy and Firewall Client Autodiscovery

Another method that can be used to deliver autodiscovery information to Web Proxy and Firewall clients is DNS. You can create a wpad alias entry in DNS and allow browser clients to use this information to automatically configure themselves. This is in contrast to the situation we saw with the DHCP method, where the logged-on user needed to be a member of a specific group in the Windows operating system.

Name resolution is a pivotal component to making this method of Web Proxy and Firewall client autodiscovery work correctly. In this case, the client operating system must be able to correctly fully qualify the name *wpad*. The reason for this is that the Web Proxy and Firewall client only knows that it needs to resolve the name wpad; it does not know what specific domain name it should append to the query to resolve the name wpad. We will cover this issue in detail later –.

> **NOTE**
>
> In contrast to the DHCP method of assigning autodiscovery information to Web Proxy and Firewall clients, you do not have the option to use a custom port number to publish autodiscovery information when using the DNS method. You must publish autodiscovery information on TCP 80 when using the DNS method.

We will detail the following steps to enable DNS to provide autodiscovery information to Web Proxy and Firewall clients:

- Creating the wpad entry in DNS
- Configuring the client to use the fully-qualified wpad alias
- Configuring the client browser to use autodiscovery
- Making the connection

Creating the wpad Entry in DNS

The first step is to create a wpad alias entry in DNS. This alias points to a Host (A) record for the ISA Server 2006 firewall, which resolves the name of the ISA Server 2006 firewall to the Internal IP address of the firewall. This Host (A) record must be created before you create the CNAME alias entry. If you enable automatic registration in DNS, the ISA Server 2006 firewall's entry will already be entered into DNS. If you have not enabled automatic registration, you will need to create the Host (A) record for the ISA Server 2006 firewall manually. In the following example, the ISA Server 2006 firewall has automatically registered itself with DNS.

Do the following on the DNS server of the domain controller on the Internal network:

1. Click **Start** and select **Administrative Tools**. Click the **DNS** entry. In the **DNS** management console shown in Figure 2.37, right-click on the forward lookup zone for your domain, and click the **New Alias (CNAME)** command.

Figure 2.37 Selecting the New Alias (CNAME) Command

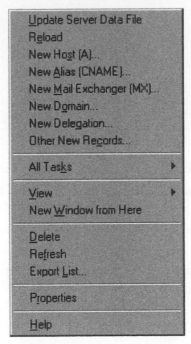

2. In the **New Resource Record** dialog box (Figure 2.38), enter **wpad** in the **Alias name** (uses parent domain if left blank) text box. Click the **Browse** button.

Figure 2.38 The New Resource Record Dialog Box

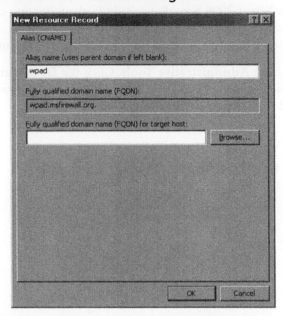

3. In the **Browse** dialog box, double-click on your server name in the **Records** list.

4. In the **Browse** dialog box, double-click on the **Forward Lookup Zone** entryin the **Records** frame.

5. In the **Browse** dialog box, double-click on the name of your forward lookup zone in the **Records** frame.

6. In the **Browse** dialog box, select the name of the ISA Server 2006 firewall in the **Records** frame. Click **OK**.

Figure 2.39 New Resource Dialog Box

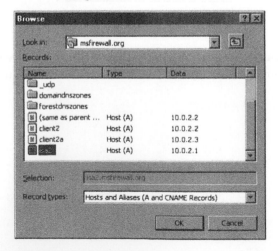

7. Click **OK** in the **New Resource Record** dialog box.

8. The **CNAME (alias)** entry appears in the right pane of the **DNS** management console.

Figure 2.40 Viewing the DNS WPAD Alias

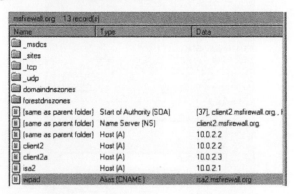

9. Close the **DNS Management** console.

Configure the Client to Use the Fully-Qualified wpad Alias

The Web Proxy and Firewall client needs to be able to correctly resolve the name *wpad*. The Web Proxy and Firewall client configurations are *not aware of the domain containing the wpad alias*. The Web Proxy and Firewall client operating system must be able to provide this information to the Web Proxy and Firewall client.

DNS queries must be *fully qualified* before the query is sent to the DNS server. A fully-qualified request contains a host name and a domain name. The Web Proxy and Firewall client only know the *host name* portion. The Web Proxy and Firewall client operating system must be able to provide the correct domain name, which it appends to the *wpad* host name, before it can send a DNS query to the DNS server.

There are a number of methods you can use to provide a domain name that is appended to the *wpad* name before the query is sent to the client operating system's DNS server. Two popular methods for doing this are:

- Using DHCP to assign a primary domain name
- Configuring a primary domain name in the client operating system's network identification dialog box.

We will detail these two methods in the following steps:

1. Right-click **My Computer** on the desktop, and click the **Properties** command.

2. In the **System Properties** dialog box, click the **Network Identification** tab. Click the **Properties** button.

3. In the **Identification Changes** dialog box (see Figure 2.41), click **More**.

Figure 2.41 The Identification Changes Dialog Box

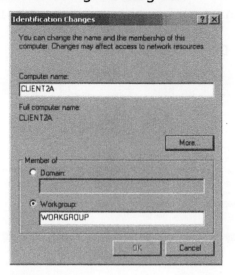

4. In the **DNS Suffix and NetBIOS Computer Name** dialog box shown in Figure 2.42, enter the domain name that contains your wpad entry in the **Primary DNS suffix of this computer** text box. This is the domain name that the operating system will append to the wpad name before sending the DNS query to the DNS server. By default, the primary domain name is the same as the domain name to which the machine belongs. If the machine is not a member of a domain, this text box will be empty. Note **Change primary DNS suffix when domain membership changes** is enabled by default. In the current example, the machine is not a member of a domain. Cancel out of each of the dialog boxes so that you do not configure a primary domain name at this time.

Figure 2.42 The DNS Suffix and NetBIOS Computer Name Dialog Box

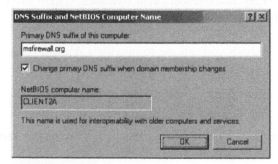

5. Another way to assign a machine a primary domain name is to use DHCP. A DHCP server can be configured to supply DHCP clients a primary domain name by configuring a DHCP scope option. We did this earlier when we created a scope on the DHCP server using the DHCP scope wizard. In the current example, the **DNS Domain Name** scope

option was set to deliver the domain name *msfirewall.org* to DHCP clients. This option (shown in Figure 2.43) has the same effect as manually setting the primary domain name. DHCP clients will append this name to unqualified DNS queries (such as those for wpad) before sending the DNS query to a DNS server.

Figure 2.43 Viewing Scope Options

Scope Options		
Option Name	Vendor	Value
006 DNS Servers	Standard	10.0.2.2
015 DNS Domain Name	Standard	msfirewall.org

6. Go to the DHCP client system and open a command prompt. At the command prompt, enter **ipconfig /all** and press **ENTER**. Notice that the machine has been assigned a **Connection-specific DNS Suffix** of **msfirewall.org**.

DHCP is the most efficient way to assign a primary DNS suffix to clients on your network, as seen in Figure 2.44. This feature allows you to automatically configure a DNS suffix on DHCP clients that connect to your network, which are not members of your Active Directory domain. These clients can still correctly resolve the wpad name based on your current DNS infrastructure without requiring them to join the domain or manually configuring them.

Figure 2.44 DHCP client configuration

```
C:\>ipconfig /all

Windows 2000 IP Configuration

        Host Name . . . . . . . . . . : CLIENT2A
        Primary DNS Suffix  . . . . . :
        Node Type . . . . . . . . . . : Hybrid
        IP Routing Enabled. . . . . . : No
        WINS Proxy Enabled. . . . . . : No
        DNS Suffix Search List. . . . : msfirewall.org

Ethernet adapter Local Area Connection:

        Connection-specific DNS Suffix  . : msfirewall.org
        Description . . . . . . . . . . . : AMD PCNET Family PCI Ethernet Ada
r #2
        Physical Address. . . . . . . . . : 00-0C-29-C6-F8-E8
        DHCP Enabled. . . . . . . . . . . : Yes
        Autoconfiguration Enabled . . . . : Yes
        IP Address. . . . . . . . . . . . : 10.0.2.100
        Subnet Mask . . . . . . . . . . . : 255.255.255.0
        Default Gateway . . . . . . . . . :
        DHCP Server . . . . . . . . . . . : 10.0.2.2
        DNS Servers . . . . . . . . . . . : 10.0.2.2
        Lease Obtained. . . . . . . . . . : Sunday, January 11, 2004 4:17:20 ]
        Lease Expires . . . . . . . . . . : Monday, January 19, 2004 4:17:20 ]

C:\>
```

Note that if you have multiple domains and clients on your Internal network that belong to multiple domains, you will need to create wpad CNAME alias entries for each of the domains. In addition, DNS support for WPAD entries can be a bit problematic when you have a single Internal network domain that spans WAN links. You can only enter a single WPAD entry per domain, and all hosts that fully qualify the WPAD entry with that domain name will receive the same server address. This can lead to Branch office hosts attempting to access the Internet via an ISA Server 2006 located at the Main office. The best solution to this problem is to create subdomains in the DNS that support Branch office clients.

Configure the client browser to use autodiscovery

The next step is to configure the browser to use autodiscovery. If you have not already done so, configure the Web browser to use autodiscovery to automatically configure itself to use the ISA Server 2006 firewall's Web Proxy service:

1. Right-click on the **Internet Explorer** icon on the desktop, and click **Properties**.

2. In the **Internet Properties** dialog box, click the **Connections** tab. Click the **LAN Settings** button.

3. In the **Local Area Network (LAN) Settings** dialog box, put a checkmark in the **Automatically detect settings** check box. Click **OK**.

4. Click **Apply**, and then click **OK** in the **Internet Properties** dialog box.

The next step is to configure the ISA Server 2006 firewall **Publish Autodiscovery Information** for autodiscovery Web Proxy and Firewall clients.

Configure the ISA Server 2006 Firewall to Publish Autodiscovery Information

Do the following on the ISA Server 2006 firewall computer to enable it to provide autoconfiguration information to Web Proxy and Firewall autodiscovery clients:

1. At the ISA Server 2006 firewall computer, open the **Microsoft Internet Security and Acceleration Server 2004** management console. Expand the server name in the left pane of the console, and then expand the **Configuration** node. Click the **Networks** node.

2. On the **Networks** node, click the **Networks** tab in the **Details** pane.

3. Right click the **Internal** network on the **Networks** tab, and click **Properties** (see Figure 2.45).

Figure 2.45 Accessing the Internal Network Properties Dialog Box

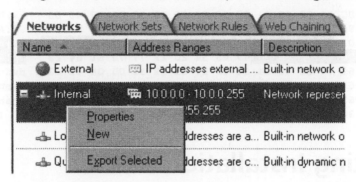

4. In the **Internal Properties** dialog box, put a checkmark in the **Publish automatic discovery information** check box. In the **Use this port for automatic discovery request** text box, leave the default port 80, as it is.

5. Click **Apply** and **OK**.

6. Click **Apply** to save the changes and update the firewall policy.

7. Click **OK** in the **Apply New Configuration** dialog box.

Making the Connection Using DNS for Autodiscovery

All the parts are now in place to allow the Web Proxy and Firewall client machine to use DNS to obtain autoconfiguration information. Perform the following steps on the Web Proxy client computer:

1. Open **Internet Explorer** and go to the **www.microsoft.com/isaserver/** home page.

2. A **Network Monitor** trace shows the Web Proxy client makes a DNS query for *wpad. msfirewall.org.* The DNS server responds to the query with the IP address (shown in Figure 2.46) of the ISA Server 2006 firewall computers.

Figure 2.46 Viewing DNS wpad Query Requests

Protocol	Description
DNS	0x406A:Std Qry for wpad.msfirewall.org. of type Host Addr on class INET addr.
DNS	0x406A:Std Qry Resp. for wpad.msfirewall.org. of type Host Addr on class INET
TCP	....S., len: 0, seq: 773548798-773548798, ack: 0, win:16384, src:

3. After it obtains the IP address of the ISA Server 2006 firewall computer and the port from which it can obtain autoconfiguration information, the Web Proxy client sends a request (see Figure 2.47) for wpad autoconfiguration information. You can see this request in the bottom pane of the Network Monitor Window, **GET /wpad.dat HTTP/1.1**.

Figure 2.47 Viewing the Details of a DNS wpad Query Request

```
00000000   00 0C 29 30 5B 64 00 0C 29 C6 F8 B8 08 00 45 00    . +)0[d. +)├°♣■.E.
00000010   00 96 00 61 40 00 80 06 B1 FD 0A 00 02 03 0A 00    .û.a@.Ç♣▲°⌐.♦♥⌐.
00000020   02 01 04 23 00 50 2E 1B 6A FF 16 22 EE 43 50 18    ☻☺♦#.P.←j ─"≥CP↑
00000030   44 70 6C 3E 00 00 47 45 54 20 2F 77 70 61 64 2E    Dpl>..GET /wpad.
00000040   64 61 74 20 48 54 54 50 2F 31 2E 31 0D 0A 41 63    dat HTTP/1.1.◙Ac
00000050   63 65 70 74 3A 20 2A 2F 2A 0D 0A 55 73 65 72 2D    cept: */*.◙User-
00000060   41 67 65 6E 74 3A 20 4D 6F 7A 69 6C 6C 61 2F 34    Agent: Mozilla/4
00000070   2E 30 20 28 63 6F 6D 70 61 74 69 62 6C 65 3B 20    .0 (compatible;
```

Automating Installation of the Firewall Client

The Firewall client software can be installed on virtually any 32-bit version of Windows except Windows 95. There are a number of compelling reasons for installing the Firewall client software on all machines that it supports:

- The Firewall client allows you to create user/group-based access controls for *all* TCP and UDP protocols. This is in contrast to the Web Proxy client configuration, which only supports HTTP, HTTPS and FTP.

- The Firewall client has access to all TCP and UDP-based protocols, including those requiring secondary connections. In contrast, the SecureNAT client does not support application protocols that require secondary connections *unless* there is an application filter to support it.

- The Firewall client provides much better performance than the SecureNAT client.

- The Firewall client sends application information to the ISA Server 2006 firewall service; this allows the Firewall service logs to collect application usage information and helps you determine which applications users are using to access Internet sites and services.

- The Firewall client sends user information to the Firewall service; this enables the ISA Server 2006 firewall to control access based on user account *and* record user information in the Firewall service's access logs. This information can be extracted and put into report form.

With these features, the Firewall client provides a level of functionality and access control that no other firewall in its class can match. For this reason, we always recommend that you install the Firewall client on any machine that supports the Firewall client software.

However, because the Firewall client configuration requires the Firewall client software to be installed, many firewall administrators are hesitant to avail themselves of the full feature set provided by the Firewall client. Many ISA Server 2006 firewall administrators don't have the time or the resources to "touch" (visit) each authorized computer on the corporate network in order to install the Firewall client software.

The solution to this problem is to automate the installation of the Firewall client. There are two methods that you can use. These methods require no additional software purchase and can greatly simplify the installation of the Firewall client software on large numbers of computers on the corporate network. These methods are:

- Group Policy-based software installation and management
- Silent installation script

In the following section, we will discuss these methods, as well as some key ISA Server client configuration settings that you should make in the **ISA Management** console.

Configuring Firewall Client and Web Proxy Client Configuration in the ISA Management Console

There are a few configuration options you should set for the Firewall client installation *before* you configure a Group Policy or a silent installation script to install the Firewall client software. These settings, made at the **Microsoft Internet Security and Acceleration Server 2006** management console, determine issues such as Firewall client autodiscovery behavior and whether (and how) the Web browser is configured during installation of the Firewall client.

Perform the following steps on the ISA Server 2006 firewall computer to configure these settings:

1. In the **Microsoft Internet Security and Acceleration Server 2006 management console**, expand the server name, and then expand the **Configuration** node.

2. Click the **Networks** node, and then click **Networks** on the **Details** tab. Right-click the Internal network, and click **Properties**.

3. In the **Internal Properties** dialog box, click the **Firewall Client** tab.

4. On the **Firewall Client** tab, put a checkmark in the **Enable Firewall client support for this network** check box. In the **Firewall client configuration** frame, enter the name of the ISA Server 2006 firewall computer in the **ISA Server name or IP address** text box. The default setting is the computer name. However, you should replace the computer (NetBIOS) name with the fully-qualified domain name of the ISA Server 2006 firewall. When you replace the computer name with the FQDN, the Firewall client machines can use DNS to correctly resolve the name of the ISA Server 2006 firewall. This will avoid one of the most common troubleshooting issues with Firewall client connectivity. Make sure there is an entry for this name in your Internal network's DNS server.

    The Web Proxy client configuration settings are available in the **Web browser configuration on the Firewall client computer** frame. These settings will automatically configure the Web browser as a Web Proxy client. Note that you can change the settings later, and the Web browsers will automatically update themselves with the new settings.

    The **Automatically detect settings** option allows the Web browser to detect the Web Proxy service and configure itself based on the settings you configure on the **Web Browser** tab of the **Internal Properties** dialog box, shown in Figure 2.48.

Figure 2.48 Internal Properties Dialog Box

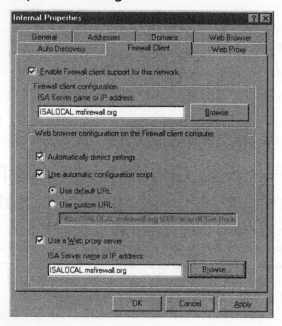

The **Use automatic configuration script** option allows you to assign a proxy autoconfiguration file (PAC) address to the Web browser. The Web browser will then query the location you specify or use the default location; the default location is on the ISA Server 2006 firewall machine. Note that when you use the default location, you obtain the same information you would receive if you had configured the Web browser to use the **Automatically detect settings** option. The **Use default URL** option automatically configures the browser to connect to the ISA Server 2006 firewall for autoconfiguration information. You can use the **Use custom URL** if you want to create your own PAC file that overrides the settings on the automatically-generated file at the ISA Server 2006 firewall. You can find more information on PAC files and proxy client autoconfiguration files in **Using Automatic Configuration and Automatic Proxy** at **http://www. microsoft.com/technet/prodtechnol/ie/reskit/5/part5/ch21auto.mspx?mfr=true**

The **Use a Web Proxy server** option allows you to configure the Web browser to use the ISA Server 2006 as its Web Proxy, but without the benefits of the autoconfiguration script information. This setting provides higher performance than the SecureNAT client configuration, but you do not benefit from the settings contained in the autoconfiguration script. The most important configuration settings in the autoconfiguration script include site names and addresses that should be used for *Direct Access*. For this reason, you should avoid this option unless you do not wish to use Direct Access to bypass the Web Proxy service to access selected Web sites.

> **NOTE**
>
> Web Proxy client Direct Access configuration allows you to bypass the Web Proxy service for selected Web sites. Some Web sites do not conform to Internet standards (Java sites are the most common offenders), and therefore, do not work properly through Web Proxy servers. You can configure these sites for Direct Access and the client machine will bypass the Web Proxy service and use an alternate means to connect to the destination Web site. In order for the client to use an alternate means to connect, the client machine must be configured as a Firewall and/or SecureNAT client.

5. Click the **Web Browser** tab, as shown in Figure 2.49. There are several settings in this dialog box that configure the Web Proxy clients via the autoconfiguration script. Note that in order for these options to take effect, you must configure the Web Proxy clients to use the autoconfiguration script either via autodiscovery and autoconfiguration or via a manual setting for the location of the autoconfiguration script.

    The **Bypass proxy for Web server in this network** option allows the Web browser to use Direct Access to directly connect to servers that are accessible via a *single label name*. For example, if the user accesses a Web server on the Internal network using the URL **http://SERVER1**, the Web Proxy client browser will *not* send the request to the ISA Server 2006 firewall. Instead, the Web browser will directly connect to the SERVER1 machine. This reduces the load on the ISA Server 2006 firewall and prevents users from *looping back* through the ISA Server 2006 firewall to access Internal network resources.

    The **Directly access computers specified in the Domains tab** option allows you to configure Direct Access to machines contained in the **Domains** tab. The **Domains** tab contains a collection of domain names that are used by the Firewall client to determine which hosts are part of the Internal network and bypass the ISA Server 2006 firewall when contacting hosts that are part of the same domain. The Web Proxy client can also use the domain on this list for Direct Access. We recommend that you always select this option as it will reduce the load on the ISA Server 2006 firewall by preventing Web Proxy clients from looping back through the firewall to access Internal network resources.

    The **Directly access these servers or domains** list is a list of computer addresses or domain names that you can configure for Direct Access. Click the **Add** button.

Figure 2.49 Web Browser Tab on the Internal Properties Dialog Box

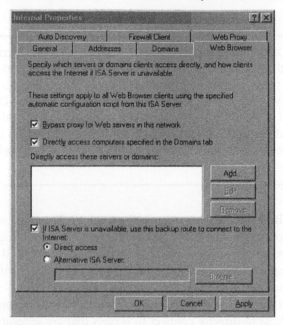

6. In the **Add Server** dialog box shown in Figure 2.50, you can select the **IP address within this range** option, and then enter an IP address or IP address range of machines that you want to Directly Access. You also have the option to select the **Domain or computer** option and enter the computer name or the FQDN of the machine that you want to access via Direct Access. A common domain name to enter for Direct Access is the **msn.com** domain, because this domain, along with the **passport.com** and the **hotmail.com** domains must be configured for Direct Access to simplify Web Proxy client connections to the Microsoft Hotmail site.

Figure 2.50 The Add Server Dialog Box

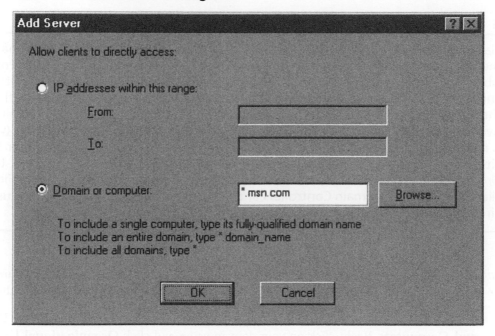

7. If the ISA Server is unavailable, **use this backup route to connect to the Internet** option allows machines configured as Web Proxy clients to use other means to connect to the Internet. Typically, this means that the Web Proxy client will leverage their SecureNAT or Firewall client configuration to connect to the Internet. If the machine is not configured as a SecureNAT and/or Firewall client, then no access will be allowed if the Web Proxy service becomes unavailable.

8. Click **Apply**, and then click **OK**, after making the changes to the configuration in the **Internal Properties** dialog box.

9. Click **Apply** to save the changes and update the firewall policy.

At this point the Firewall and Web Proxy client configuration is ready, and you can install the Firewall client on the client machines behind the ISA Server 2006 firewall and have these settings automatically configured on the clients.

Group Policy Software Installation

You might not wish to install the Firewall client on all machines. For example, domain controllers and published servers should not be configured as Firewall clients. You can gain granular control over Group Policy-based software installation by creating an organizational unit for Firewall clients and then configuring an Organization Unit (OU) group policy object to install the Firewall client only on computers belonging to that OU.

NOTE

Placing machines in a Firewall client's OU is only one possible solution. If you have the requisite Active Directory (AD) expertise, you may wish to link the Group Policy Object to a higher level (domain or site) if you don't want to move the computer to another OU and create a Group Policy for each OU. However, you may need to filter the Group Policy Object using Groups or WMI filters, which incurs its own administrative overhead. By default, all computers are placed in the computer container (which is not an OU), and that you must either link the Group Policy to the Domain or the Site, or create an OU and move the computer objects to the OU, and then link the Group Policy Object. Note that it's vital that not all machines be assigned the Firewall client software, as Domain Controllers and other server computers should not use the Firewall client unless it is absolutely required.

Perform the following steps on the domain controller to create the OU, and then configure software installation and management to install the Firewall client on machines belonging to the OU:

1. Click **Start**, and select the **Administrative Tools** menu. Click **Active Directory Users and Computers**. Right-click on your domain name, and click **Organizational Unit**.

2. In the **New Object – Organizational Unit** dialog box, enter a name for the OU in the **Name** text box. In this example, we will call the OU **FWCLIENTS**. Click **OK**.

3. Click on the **Computers** node in the left pane of the console. Right-click your client computer, and click the **Move** command.

4. In the **Move** dialog box, click the **FWCLIENTS** OU, and click **OK**.

5. Click on the **FWCLIENTS** OU. You should see the computer you moved into this OU.

6. Right-click the **FWCLIENTS** OU, and click the **Properties** command.

7. Click the **Group Policy** tab in the **FWCLIENTS** dialog box. Click the **New** button to create a **New Group Policy Object**. Select the **New Group Policy Object** and click **Edit**.

8. Expand the **Computer Configuration** node, and then expand the **Software Settings** node. Right-click on **Software** installation, point to **New** and click **Package**.

9. In the **Open** text box, type the path to the Firewall client's Microsoft installer package (.msi file) in the **File name** text box. In this example, the path is:

    \isa2\mspclnt\MS_FWC.MSI

    Where **isa2** is the NetBIOS name of the ISA Server 2006 firewall computer or the name of the file server hosting the Firewall client installation files; **mspclnt** is the name of the share on the ISA Server 2006 firewall computer that contains the Firewall client installation files, and **MS_FWC.MSI** is the name of the Firewall client Microsoft installer package. Click **Open** after entering the path.

Figure 2.51 Entering the Installer Path

10. In the **Deploy Software** dialog box, select the **Assigned** option (see Figure 2.52) and click **OK**. Notice that you do not have the **Published** option when installing software using the **Computer Configuration** node. The software is installed before the user logs on. This is critical because only local administrators can install the Firewall client software *if* there is a logged-on user. In contrast, you can assign software to machines without a logged-on user. Click **OK**.

Figure 2.52 Choosing the Assigned Option

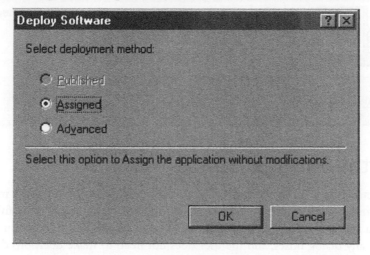

11. The new managed software package appears in the right pane of the console. All machines in the OU will have the Firewall client software installed when they are restarted. You can also manage the Firewall client software from here, as shown in Figure 2.53.

NOTE

For more details on how to take full advantage of Group Policy-based software installation and maintenance, please see the **Step-by-Step Guide to Software Installation and Maintenance** at **www.microsoft.com/windows2000/techinfo/ planning/management/swinstall.asp**

Figure 2.53 Managed Software

Name △	Version	Deployment state	Source
Microsoft Firewall Client	3.0	Assigned	\\isa2\mspclnt\MS_FWC.MSI

12. Close the **Group Policy Object Editor** and the **Active Directory Users and Computers** console.

13. When you restart the machines in the **FWCLIENTS** OU, you will see the log-on dialog box (Figure 2.54) provide information about how managed software is being installed on the Windows client operating system.

Figure 2.54 Logging On

Silent Installation Script

Another useful method you can use to install the Firewall client software on those machines that are not members of the domain is to use a silent installation script. This method is useful when the logged-on user is a member of the local administrator's group. The silent installation script does not expose the user to any dialog boxes, and the user does not need to make decisions during the installation process.

Open notepad; copy the following line into the new text document, and save the file as "fwcinstall.cmd":

msiexec /i \\ISA2\mspclnt\MS_FWC.msi /qn /l*v c:\mspclnt_i.log

The **\ISA2** entry is the computer name of the ISA Server 2006 firewall computer and will vary for each installation location. The rest of the line can be used exactly as listed above. Users can then go to a Web page, or click a link in an email message pointing them to this batch file. The process is very simple and only requires the user to click the link to run the script. The installation is completely transparent, and the only thing the user will see is a momentary command prompt window and the Firewall client icon in the system tray when the procedure is completed.

> **WARNING**
>
> The user must be a member of the *local* Administrator's group to install the Firewall client software. If the user is not a member of the local Administrator's group, the software installation will fail. You can get around this problem by assigning the Firewall client software to machines. The software is installed before user log-on, so there are no issues with who the logged-on user is at the time of installation.

Systems Management Server (SMS)

Organizations using Systems Management Server (SMS) 2003 can use the software distribution feature of SMS to deploy the Firewall client software. The Software distribution routine in SMS 2003 provides the ability to deploy Windows Installer (.msi) files to any computer that is assigned to the SMS environment in a manner similar to the Active Directory Group Policy software management feature. Do the following to deploy the Firewall client using SMS 2003:

1. Create a collection that includes all the machines on which you want the Firewall client installed. An SMS collection is a group of network objects, such as computers or users, which are treated as an SMS management group. You can configure requirements such as IP address, hardware configuration, or add clients directly by name to group all computers that require the Firewall client software.

2. Create a package by importing the Firewall client Windows file (**MS_FWC.msi**). The Windows Installer file automatically includes a variety of attended and unattended installation options that can be used on a per-system or per-user basis. Programs are also created to uninstall the client. The per-system programs are configured to install the client with administrative rights whether or not the user is logged on. The per-user programs install the client using the credentials of the logged-on user. This provides an advantage over the Group Policy method, which does not allow you to temporarily elevate privileges to install the Firewall client application.

3. Create an SMS advertisement, which specifies the target collection and program to install. In order to control deployment, you can schedule a time for the program to be advertised to collection members.

One More Time

A server is of little use without clients, but the ISA server is unusual in that there are a number of different ways that a computer can be configured to act as an ISA client. In fact, there are three distinct ISA client types: the SecureNAT client, the Firewall client and the Web Proxy client. Determining which is most appropriate in a given situation depends on a number of factors, including the client operating system, the protocols that need to be supported, and whether it is desirable or feasible to install client software on the client computers.

The SecureNAT client requires no software installation and no changes to the client computer's Web browser. By simply setting the client computer's TCP/IP settings so that the default gateway is that of the ISA server, any computer, running any popular operating system, can benefit from ISA Server 2006's firewall protections. This includes non-Microsoft operating systems such as Linux/UNIX and Macintosh, as well as older Microsoft operating systems, such as Windows 95, Windows 3.x and MS-DOS, which are not supported by the Firewall client software. All simple protocols are supported by SecureNAT, and even complex protocols can be supported by installing application filters on the ISA Server computer. SecureNAT is the logical choice when you have a variety of different client operating systems that need ISA's protection, and the client systems need to access protocols other than HTTP/HTTPS or FTP.

The Web Proxy client will also work with all operating system platforms, so long as a compatible Web browser (one that can be configured to use a proxy server) is installed. However, the Web Proxy client is much more limited in the protocols it supports; only HTTP/HTTPS and HTTP-tunneled FTP are supported. In many cases, this will be all that is needed, and indeed, this limitation acts as an extra security measure by preventing access to other applications. One advantage of the Web Proxy client over SecureNAT is its ability to authenticate with the ISA firewall (if the firewall requests credentials). SecureNAT clients are able to authenticate only with client applications that support SOCKS 5 and only if a SOCKS 5 application filter is installed on the ISA Server machine.

The Firewall client is the "client of choice" for modern Windows client machines – or at least, it should be. It can be installed on Windows 98 and all subsequent Windows operating systems, and it supports all Winsock applications that use TCP/UDP, including those that require complex protocols. No application filters are needed, reducing administrative overhead on the server side. Best of all, the Firewall client allows you to take advantage of strong user/group-based access controls, as credentials are sent to the ISA Server for authentication without any special configuration or action required on the part of the client. The Firewall client also gives administrators more control via logging of user and application information.

Client configuration problems are a common cause of access and security problems. However, configuring the Web Proxy client and installing the Firewall client don't have to be difficult or time-consuming. Both processes can be easily automated, and administrators have several automation methods from which to choose. DHCP servers can be configured to support Web Proxy and Firewall client autodiscovery, as can DNS servers. Installation can be automated via Group Policy or a silent installation script, or you can use the Internet Explorer Administration Kit (IEAK) to configure the Web Proxy client. If you have Systems Management Server (SMS) on your network, you can use it to deploy the Firewall client.

Selecting the correct client configuration and properly configuring the client computers is an essential ingredient in a successful deployment of ISA Server 2006, so it's important to understand the three client types and the step-by-step process for configuring each *before* you install your ISA Server.

Introduction

This chapter covers pre-installation and post-installation tasks and considerations for installing the ISA firewall software. These include:

- Resource Requirements
- Configuring the...

Chapter 3

Installing and Configuring the ISA Firewall Software

Solutions in this chapter:

- Pre-installation Tasks and Considerations

- Performing a Clean Installation on a Multihomed Machine

- Default Post-installation ISA Firewall Configuration

- Post-installation System Policy

- Quick Start Configuration for ISA Firewalls

- Hardening the Base ISA Firewall Configuration and Operating System

Pre-installation Tasks and Considerations

There are several key pre-installation and tasks and considerations you need to address before installing the ISA firewall software. These include:

- System Requirements
- Configuring the Routing Table
- DNS Server Placement
- Configuring the ISA Firewall's Network Interfaces
- Unattended Installation
- Installation via a Terminal Services Administration Mode Session

System Requirements

The following are requirements for installing the ISA firewall software:

- Intel or AMD system with a 773 megahertz (MHz) or higher processor
- Microsoft Windows Server 2003 32-bit operating system with Service Pack 1 (SP1) or Microsoft Windows Server 2003 R2 32-bit.
- A practical minimum of 512 MB of memory for non-Web caching systems, and 1000 MB for Web-caching ISA firewalls
- At least one network adapter; two or more network adapters are required to obtain stateful filtering and stateful application-layer inspection firewall functionality
- An additional network adapter for each network connected to the ISA Server computer
- One local hard-disk partition that is formatted with the NTFS file system, and at least 150 MB of available hard disk space (this is exclusive of hard-disk space you want to use for caching)
- Additional disk space, which ideally is on a separate spindle, if you plan on using the ISA firewall's Web-caching feature

Another important consideration is capacity planning. While the above reflects minimal system requirements for installing and running the ISA firewall software, the ideal configuration is obtained when you size the hardware to optimize the ISA firewall software performance for your site. Table 3.1 provides basic guidelines regarding processor, memory, disk space and network adapter requirements based on Internet link speed.

Table 3.1 Basic Processor, Memory, Disk Space and Network Adapter Requirements Based on Link Speed

Internet Link Bandwidth	Up to 5 T1	Up to 25 Mbps	Up to T3	90 Mbps	Notes
Processors	1	1	2	2/2	
Processor type	Pentium III750 megahertz (MHz) or higher	Pentium 4 3.0–4.0 gigahertz(GHz)	Xeon 3.0–4.0 GHz	Xeon Dual Core AMD Dual Core 2.0–3.0 GHz	You can use other processors with comparable power that emulate the IA-32 instruction set. In deployments requiring only stateful filtering ("stateful packet inspection" – that is, when there is no need for higher security stateful application-layer inspection), the Pentium 4 and Xeon processor recommen-dations reach LAN wire speeds.
Memory	512 MB	512 MB	1 GB	2 GB	With Web caching enabled, these requirements may be increased by approximately 256–512 MB.
Disk space	150 MB	2.5 GB	5 GB	10 GB	This is exclusive of hard-disk space you need to use for caching and logging.
Network adapter	10/100 Mbps	10/100 Mbps	100/1000 Mbps	100/1000 Mbps	These are the requirements for the network adapters not connected to the Internet.

Continued

Table 3.1 Continued

Internet Link Bandwidth	Up to 5 T1	Up to 25 Mbps	Up to T3	90 Mbps	Notes
Concurrent Remote-access VPN connections	150	700	850	2000	The Standard Edition of the ISA firewall supports a hard-coded maximum of 1000 concurrent VPN connections. The Enterprise Edition supports as many connections as are supported by the underlying operating system and has no ISA-based hard coded limitation.

For an exceptionally thorough and comprehensive discussion on ISA firewall performance optimization and sizing, please refer to the Microsoft document **ISA Server 2006 Performance Best Practices** at http://www.microsoft.com/technet/isa/2006/perf_bp.mspx

Configuring the Routing Table

The routing table on the ISA firewall machine should be configured before you install the ISA firewall software. The routing table should include routes to all networks that are not local to the ISA firewall's network interfaces. These routing table entries are required because the ISA firewall can have only a single default gateway. Normally, the default gateway is configured on the network interface that is used for the External Network. Therefore, if you have an internal or other Network that contains multiple subnets, you should configure routing table entries that ensure the ISA firewall can communicate with the computers and other IP devices on the appropriate subnets. The network interface with the default gateway is the one used to connect to the Internet, either direction or via upstream routers.

The routing table entries are critical to support the ISA firewall's "network-within-a-Network" scenarios. A network within a Network is a network ID located behind a NIC on the ISA firewall that is a non-local network.

For example, Figure 3.1 is an example of a simple network-within-a-Network scenario.

Figure 3.1 Network within a Network

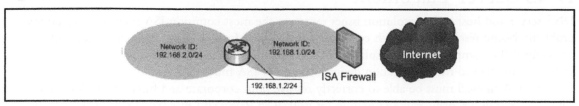

This small organization's IP addressing scheme uses two network IDs for the corporate network: 192.168.1.0/24 and 192.168.2.0/24. The network local to the ISA firewall's internal interface is 192.168.1.0/24. The network remote from the ISA firewall's internal interface is 192.168.2.0/24. A corporate network router separates the network and routes packets between these two network IDs.

The ISA firewall's networking model includes both of these networks as part of the same Network (Note: A capital "N" indicates an ISA firewall-defined network). You would naturally assume that the 192.168.1.0/24 would be an ISA-defined Network since it includes an entire network ID, but you might also assume that network ID 192.168.2.0/24 would be defined as a second ISA firewall-defined Network. That would be incorrect because the ISA firewall's Network model includes *all networks (all IP addresses)* reachable from a specific interface on the ISA firewall as being part of the same network.

The rationale behind this is that hosts on the same ISA-defined Network do not use the ISA firewall to mediate communications between themselves. It makes no sense for the ISA firewall to mediate communications between hosts on networks IDs 192.168.1.0/24 and 192.168.2.0/24, as this would require hosts to loop back through the firewall to reach hosts to which they should directly communicate.

In this example, there should be a routing table entry on the ISA firewall indicating that in order to reach network ID 192.168.2.0/24, the connection must be forwarded to IP address 192.168.2.1 on the corporate router. You can use either the RRAS console or the command line **ROUTE** and **netsh** commands to add the routing table entry.

The ISA firewall must know the route to *each* internal network ID. If you find that connections are not being correctly forwarded by the ISA firewall to hosts on the corporate network, confirm that there are routing table entries on the ISA firewall indicating the correct gateway for each of those network IDs.

ISA FIREWALL TIP

You can greatly simplify your ISA firewall Network definitions and routing table entries by creating a well-designed IP addressing infrastructure with proper subnet design that allows for route summarization.

DNS Server Placement

DNS server and host name resolution issues represent the most common ISA firewall connectivity problems. Name resolution for both corporate network and Internet hosts must be performed correctly. If the company's name resolution infrastructure isn't properly configured, one of the first victims of the flawed name resolution design will be the ISA firewall.

The ISA firewall must be able to correctly resolve both corporate and Internet DNS names. The ISA firewall performs name resolution for both Web Proxy and Firewall clients. If the firewall cannot perform name resolution correctly, Internet connectivity for both Web Proxy and Firewall clients will fail.

Correct name resolution for corporate network resources is also critical because the ISA firewall must be able to correctly resolve names for corporate network resources published via Web Publishing rules. For example, when you create a secure-SSL Web Publishing Rule, the ISA firewall must be able to correctly forward incoming connection requests to the FQDN used for the common name on the Web site certificate bound to the published Web server on the corporate network.

The ideal name resolution infrastructure is the split DNS. The split-DNS infrastructure allows external hosts to resolve names to publicly-accessible addresses and corporate network hosts to resolve names to privately-accessible addresses. Figure 3.2 depicts how a split-DNS infrastructure works to enhance name resolution for hosts inside your corporate network, as well as those that roam between the corporate network and remote locations on the Internet.

Figure 3.2 The Miracle of the Split-DNS Infrastructure

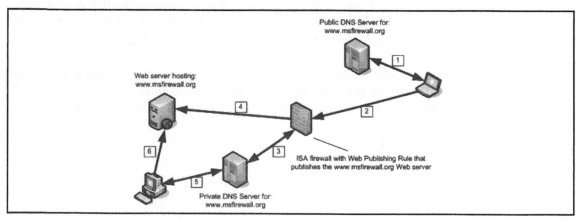

1.   A user at a remote location needs to access resources on the corporate Web server, www. msfirewall.org. The www.msfirewall.org Web server is hosted on an ISA firewall-Protected Network and published using an ISA firewall Web Publishing Rule. The remote user sends a request to www.msfirewall.org, and the name is resolved by the public DNS server authoritative for the msfirewall.org domain. The name is resolved to an IP address on the external interface of the ISA firewall used by the Web listener designated in the Web Publishing Rule.

2. The remote Web client sends the request to the IP address on the external interface used by the Web Publishing Rules Web listener.

3. The ISA firewall resolves the name www.msfirewall.org to the actual IP address bound to the www.msfirewall.org Web site on the corporate network by querying the Internal network DNS server authoritative for the msfirewall.org domain.

4. The ISA firewall forwards the connection to the actual IP address bound to the www.msfirewall.org Web site on the corporate network.

5. A host on the corporate network needs to access resources on the www.msfirewall.org Web site. The corporate user sends a request to the corporate DNS server that is authoritative for the msfirewall.org domain. The corporate DNS server resolves the name www.msfirewall.org to the actual IP address bound to the www.msfirewall.org Web site on the corporate network.

6. The Web client on the corporate network connects directly to the www.msfirewall.org Web server. The Web client doesn't loop back to reach the www.msfirewall.org Web site on the corporate network because Web Proxy clients are configured for direct access to resources on the msfirewall.org domain.

The split-DNS infrastructure provides transparent access to resources for users regardless of their location. Users can move between the corporate network and remote locations and use the same name to reach the same corporate resources. They don't need to reconfigure their mail clients, news clients, and other applications because *the same name* is used to access the resources regardless of location. Any organization needing to support users that roam between the corporate network and remote locations should implement a split DNS infrastructure.

Requirements for the split-DNS infrastructure include:

- A DNS server authoritative for the domain that resolves names for resources for that domain to the internal addresses used to access those resources.

- A DNS server authoritative for the domain that resolves names for resources in that domain to the publicly-accessible addresses used to access those resources.

- Remote users must be assigned DNS server addresses that forward requests for the domain to a public DNS server. This is easily accomplished using DHCP.

- Corporate users must be assigned DNS server addresses that forward requests for the domain to the private DNS server. This is easily accomplished using DHCP.

- The ISA firewall must be able to resolve names of published resources and all other resources hosted on a ISA firewall–Protected Network to the private address used to access that resource.

Most organizations that use the ISA firewall will have one or more internal DNS servers. At least one of those DNS servers should be configured to resolve both internal and Internet host names, and the ISA firewall should be configured to use that DNS server. If you have an internal network DNS server, you should never configure the ISA firewall's interfaces to use an external DNS server. This is a common mistake and can lead to slow or failed name resolution attempts.

ISA FIREWALL TIP

Check out Jim Harrison's article **Designing An ISA Server Solution on a Complex Network** at http://isaserver.org/tutorials/Designing_An_ISA_Server_Solution_on_a_Complex_Network.html for information on network designs supporting ISA firewalls.

Configuring the ISA Firewall's Network Interfaces

Perhaps one of the least understood ISA firewall configuration issues is how to correctly configure the IP addressing information on the ISA firewall's network interfaces. The reason for this is that name resolution issues have the potential for being complex, and fledging firewall administrators are often too busy to get lost in the details of DNS host name and NetBIOS name resolution.

There are two main networks interface configuration scenarios:

■ An established name-resolution infrastructure on the corporate network protected by the ISA firewall

■ *No* established name-resolution infrastructure on the corporate network protected by the ISA firewall

Tables 3.2 and 3.3 show the correct IP addressing information for both these scenarios in dual-homed ISA firewalls.

Table 3.2 Established Corporate Network Name-Resolution Infrastructure

Parameters	Internal Interface	External Interface
Client for Microsoft Networks	Enabled	Disabled
File and Print Sharing for Microsoft Networks	Enabled only if the ISA firewall hosts the Firewall client share	Disabled
Network Monitor Driver	Enabled when Network Monitor is installed on the ISA firewall (recommended)	Enabled when Network Monitor is installed on the ISA firewall (recommended)
Internet Protocol (TCP/IP)	Enabled	Enabled
IP address	Valid IP address on the network the internal interface is connected to	Valid IP address on the network the external interface is connected to. Public or private depending on your network infrastructure

Table 3.2 Continued

Parameters	Internal Interface	External Interface
Subnet mask	Valid subnet mask on the network the internal interface is connected to	Valid subnet mask on the network the external interface is connected to
Default gateway	NONE. Never configure a default gateway on any internal or DMZ interface on the ISA firewall.	IP address of upstream router (either corporate or ISP depending on next hop) allowing access to the Internet
Preferred DNS server	Internal DNS server that can resolve both internal and Internet host names	NONE. Do not enter a DNS server address on the external interface of the ISA firewall
Alternate DNS server	A second internal DNS server that can resolve both internal and Internet host names	NONE. Do not enter a DNS server address on the external interface of the ISA firewall.
Register this connection's addresses in DNS	Disabled. You should manually create entries on the Internal network DNS server to allow clients to resolve the name of the ISA firewall's internal interface.	Disabled
WINS	Enter an IP address for one more Internal network DNS server. Especially helpful for VPN clients who want to browse Internal network servers using NetBIOS name/browser service	NONE
WINS NetBIOS setting	Default	Disable NetBIOS over TCP/IP
Interface order	Top of interface list	Under internal interface

Table 3.3 *No* Established Corporate Network Name-Resolution Infrastructure

Parameters	Internal Interface	External Interface
Client for Microsoft Networks	Enabled	Disabled
File and Print Sharing for Microsoft Networks	Enabled only if the ISA firewall hosts the Firewall client share	Disabled

Continued

Table 3.3 Continued

Parameters	Internal Interface	External Interface
Network Monitor Driver	Enabled when Network Monitor is installed on the ISA firewall (recommended)	Enabled when Network Monitor is installed on the ISA firewall (recommended)
Internet Protocol (TCP/IP)	Enabled	Enabled
IP address	Valid IP address on the network the internal interface is connected to	Valid IP address on the network the external interface is connected to. Public or private depending on your network infrastructure. Alternatively, DHCP if required by ISP
Subnet mask	Valid subnet mask on the network the internal interface is connected to	Valid subnet mask on the network the external interface is connected to. May be assigned by ISP via DHCP
Default gateway	NONE. Never configure a default gateway on any internal or DMZ interface on the ISA firewalll	IP address of upstream router (either corporate or SP depending on next hop) allowing access to the Internet. May be assigned by ISP via DHCP
Preferred DNS server	External DNS server that can resolve Internet host names. Typically your ISP's DNS Server. **Note:** If the external interface uses DHCP to obtain IP addressing information, do not enter a DNSserver on the ISA firewall's internal interface.	None, unless assigned by ISP via DHCP.
Alternate DNS server	A second external DNS server that can resolve Internet host names **Note:** If the external interface uses DHCP to irewall unless assigned via obtain IP addressing information from your ISP, do not enter a DNS server on the ISA firewall's internal interface.	NONE. Do not enter a DNS server address on the external interface of the ISA DHCP by ISP.

Table 3.3 Continued

Parameters	Internal Interface	External Interface
Register this connection's addresses in DNS	Disabled	Disabled
WINS	NONE	NONE
WINS NetBIOS setting	Default	Disable NetBIOS over TCP/IP
Interface order	Top of interface list **Note:** If the external interface of the ISA firewall uses DHCP to obtain IP addressing information from your ISP, then do not move the internal interface to the top of the list.	Top of interface list if using ISP DHCP server to assign DNS server addresses

You should already be familiar with configuring IP addressing information for Windows Server interfaces. However, you may not be aware of how to change the interface order. The interface order is used to determine what name server addresses should be used preferentially.

ISA FIREWALL TIP

You can track which interface is connected to what Network by renaming your network interfaces in the Network and dial-up connections user interface. Right-click on the network interface, and click **rename**. Enter the new name for the interface. For example, on a simple trihomed ISA firewall, we often name the interfaces LAN, WAN, and DMZ.

Perform the following steps to change the interface order:

1. Right-click **My Network Places** on the desktop, and click **Properties**.

2. In the **Network and Dial-up Connections** window, click the **Advanced** menu, then click **Advanced Settings**.

3. In the **Advanced Settings** dialog box (Figure 3.3), click the internal interface in the list of **Connections** on the **Adapters and Bindings** tab. After selecting the internal interface, click the up-arrow to move the internal interface to the top of the list of interfaces.

Figure 3.3 The Advanced Settings Dialog Box

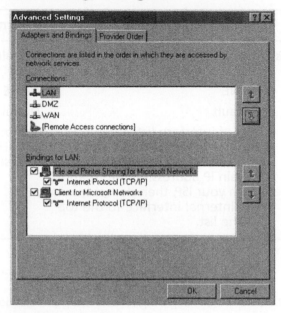

4.   Click **OK** in the **Advanced Settings** dialog box.

Installation via a Terminal Services Administration Mode Session

You can install the ISA firewall via an Admin mode Terminal services connection. After installing is complete, a System Policy rule is configured to allow RDP connections only from the IP address of the machine that was connected during the ISA firewall software installation. This is in contrast to the default System Policy setting when installing the ISA firewall software at the console, where any host on the Internal Network can initiate an RDP connection to the ISA firewalls Internal interface.

Performing a Clean Installation on a Multihomed Machine

The following steps demonstrate how to install the ISA Server 2006 software on a dual-homed (two Ethernet cards) Windows Server 2003 machine. This is a "clean machine" that has only the Windows Server 2003 software installed and the IP addressing information configured on each of the machine's interfaces. The routing table has also been properly configured on this machine.

Perform the following steps to install the ISA firewall software on the multihomed machine:

1.   Insert the ISA Server 2006 installation CD into the CD-ROM drive or connect to a network share point hosting the ISA Server 2006 installation files. If the installation routine does not

start automatically, double-click the **isaautorun.exe** file in the root of the installation files folder tree.

2. On the **Microsoft Internet Security and Acceleration Server 2006** page, click the link for **Review Release Notes** and read the release notes. The release notes contain very important and topical information regarding changes in basic firewall software functionality. This information may not be included in the Help file or elsewhere, so we highly recommend that you read this information. After reviewing the release notes, click the **Read Setup and Feature Guide** link. You may want to read the guide now, just review the major topics covered in the guide, or print it out. Click the **Install ISA Server 2006** link.

3. Click **Next** on the **Welcome to the Installation Wizard for Microsoft ISA Server 2006** page.

4. Select **I accept the terms in the license agreement option** on the **License Agreement** page. Click **Next**.

5. On the **Customer Information** page, enter your name and the name of your organization in the **User Name** and **Organization** text boxes. Enter your serial number in the **Product Serial Number** text box. If you installed an evaluation copy of the ISA firewall software and now are installing a licensed version, then backup your configuration using the ISA firewall's integrated backup tool and uninstall the evaluation version. Restart the installation of the licensed version of the software. Click **Next**.

6. On the **Setup Type** page (Figure 3.4), select **Custom**. If you do not want to install the ISA Server 2006 software on the C: drive, click **Change** to change the location of the program files on the hard disk. Click **Next**.

Figure 3.4 The Setup Type Page

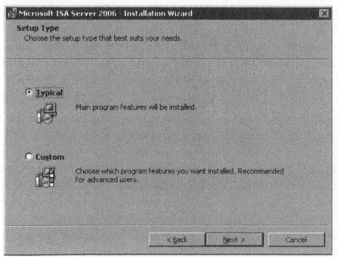

7. On the **Custom Setup** page (Figure 3.5), choose which components to install. By default, when you select **Custom**, the **Firewall Services**, **ISA Server Management**, and **Advanced Logging** features are installed. The **Advanced Logging** feature is MSDE logging, which provides superior log search and filtering features. Use the default settings, and click **Next**.

Figure 3.5 The Custom Setup Page

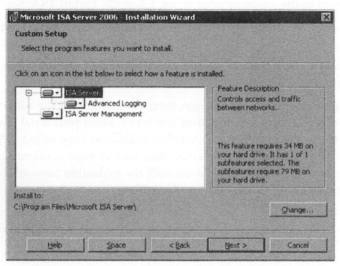

8. On the **Internal Network** page in Figure 3.6, click **Add**. The Internal Network is different from the internal network that was implied by the Local Address Table (LAT) was used by ISA Server 2000. In the case of ISA Server 2006, the Internal Network contains trusted network services with which the ISA firewall must communicate. Examples of such services include Active Directory domain controllers, DNS servers, DHCP servers, terminal servers, and management workstations. The firewall System Policy uses the Internal Network for a number of System Policy rules. We will look at the System Policy later in this chapter.

9. Define the addresses included on the default Internal Network on the Internal Network setup page. You can manually enter the addresses to be included in the Internal Network by entering the first and last addresses in the Internal Network range in the **From** and **To** text boxes and then clicking the **Add** button. A better way to configure the default Internal Network is to use **Select Network Adapter**. This allows the ISA firewall setup routine to use the routing table to determine addresses used for the default Internal Network. This is one reason why it is important to make sure that you have correctly configured your routing table entries before installing ISA. Click **Select Network Adapter**. (See Figure 3.6.)

Figure 3.6 The Internal Network Address Page

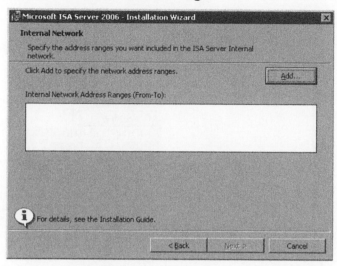

10.   In the **Addresses** dialog box, Select the internal network adapter. Add the address ranges based on your own internal range. In this example, we have renamed the network interfaces so that the interface name reflects its location. Click **OK**.

Figure 3.7 The Select Network Adapter Page

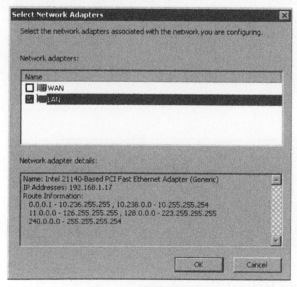

11.   If applicable, choose one of the predefines private subnets. (Figure 3.8, **Addresses**)

Figure 3.8 Automatic entry of various private subnets

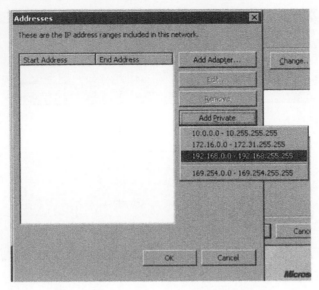

12.   Click **OK** on the **Addresses** dialog box, as shown in Figure 3.9.

Figure 3.9 Internal Network Address Ranges

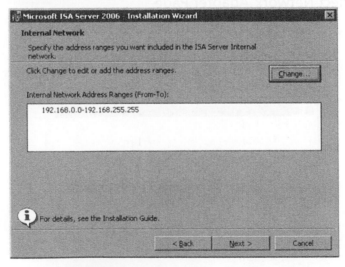

13.   Click **Next** on the **Internal Network** page.

14.   Put a checkmark by **Allow non-encrypted Firewall client connections** (Figure 3.10) if you want to support Firewall clients running previous versions of the Winsock Proxy

(Proxy Server 2.0) or the ISA Server 2000 Firewall client software. This will allow you to continue using the ISA Server 2000 Firewall client software as you migrate to ISA Server 2006. When you migrate your Firewall clients to the ISA 2006 version of the Firewall client, the channel between the Firewall clients and the ISA firewall will be encrypted. The ISA 2006 Firewall client software encrypts the user credentials that are transparently sent from the Firewall client machine to the ISA firewall. For best security practice, it is recommended that you deploy the latest version of the Firewall Client software. This can be downloaded from http://www.microsoft.com/downloads/details.aspx?displaylang=en& FamilyID=05c2c932-b15a-4990-b525-66380743da89

Click **Next**.

Figure 3.10 The Firewall Client Connection Settings Page

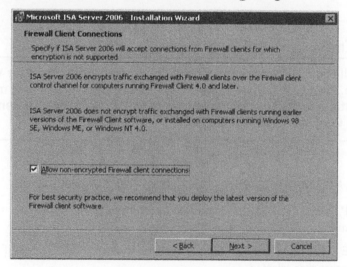

15. On the **Services** page, note that the **SNMP** and **IIS Admin Service** will be stopped during installation. If the **Internet Connection Firewall (ICF) / Internet Connection Sharing (ICF)**, and/or **IP Network Address Translation** (RRAS NAT service) services are installed on the ISA firewall machine, they will be disabled, as they conflict with the ISA firewall software.

16. Click **Install** on the **Ready to Install the Program** page.

17. On the **Installation Wizard Completed** page, click **Finish**.

18. Click **Yes** on the **Microsoft ISA Server** dialog box informing that you must restart the server (see Figure 3.11). Note that you will not need to restart the machine if you have installed the ISA firewall software on this machine before. The reason for the restart is that the TCP/IP stack is changed so that the dynamic port range of the TCP/IP driver is extended to 65535. If the installation routine recognizes that this range has already been extended, then the restart will not be required.

Figure 3.11 Warning Dialog Box regarding a Potential System Restart

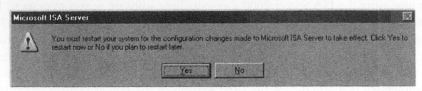

19.   Log on as an **Administrator** after the machine restarts.

20.   Click **Start**, and point to **All Programs**. Point to **Microsoft ISA Server**, and click **ISA Server Management**. The **Microsoft Internet Security and Acceleration Server 2006** management console opens and displays the **Welcome to Microsoft Internet Security and Acceleration Server 2006** page.

ISA FIREWALL TIP

You can install the ISA Management console on any Windows XP or Windows Server 2003 machine. System Policy will need to be configured so that the machine on which you install the Remote Management MMC is added to the **Remote Management Computers** Computer Set.

Three setup logs are created on the ISA firewall machine. These are:

- **ISAWRAP_*.log**   Provides information about installation success and failure and MSDE log files setup

- **ISAMSDE_*.log**   Provides detailed information about MSDE setup, if the Advanced Logging feature was selected

- **ISAFWSV_*.log**   Provides detailed information about the entire ISA firewall installation process

If you choose to not install certain components, such as Advanced Logging (MSDE logging), you can use the Control Panel's **Add/Remove Programs** applet to re-run the installation routine and install these additional components at a later time.

ISA FIREWALL ALERT

If the Microsoft Internet Authentication Service (IAS) was running on the machine during installation, you will need to restart the IAS service after installation completes.

Default Post-installation ISA Firewall Configuration

The ISA firewall installation routine incorporates the settings you entered during the setup Wizard process. The install routine also sets up some default settings for User Permissions, Network Settings, Firewall Policy, and others. Table 3.4 lists the settings that you did not explicitly define during the installation process.

We can quickly summarize the default post-installation configuration with the following:

- System Policies allow selected traffic to and from the ISA firewall itself.
- No traffic is allowed through the ISA firewall because there is only a single Deny-access rule.
- A route relationship is set between the VPN/VPN-Q Networks to the Internal Network.
- A NAT relationship is set between the Internal Network and the default External Network.
- Only Administrators can alter ISA firewall policy.

Table 3.4 Post-Installation ISA Firewall Settings

Feature	Post-installation Settings
User permissions	Members of the Administrators group on the local computer can configure firewall policy. If the ISA firewall is a member of the domain, domain admins are automatically added to the local administrators group.
Network settings	The following Network Rules are created by the installation wizard:
	Local Host Access
	Local Host Access defines a Route relationship between the Local Host network and all networks. Allow communications from the ISA firewall to all other hosts to be routed (does not use NAT; there would be no point to using NAT from Local Host to any Network).
	Internet Access
	Internet Access defines a Network Address Translation (NAT) relationship from the Internal network Quarantined VPN Clients network, and the VPN Clients network to the External network. NAT is used from these three Networks for any communications sourcing from them to the External Network. Access is allowed only if you configure the appropriate access policy.

Continued

Table 3.4 Continued

Feature	Post-installation Settings
	VPN Clients to Internal Network.
	VPN Clients to Internal Network defines a Route relationship between the VPN Clients Network and the Internal Network. Access is allowed only if you enable virtual private network (VPN) client access.
Firewall policy	A default Access Rule (named **Default Rule**) denies traffic between all networks.
System policy	The ISA firewall is secure by default. Some system policy rules are enabled to allow necessary services. You should review the system policy configuration and customize it so that only services critical to your specific deployment are enabled.
Web chaining	A default rule (named **Default Rule**) specifies that all Web Proxy client requests are retrieved directly from the Internet. That is to say, there is no Web chaining configured by default. Web chaining rules were called Web routing rules in ISA Server 2000.
Caching	The cache size is set to 0. All caching is therefore disabled. You will need to define a cache drive to enable Web caching.
Alerts	Most alerts are enabled. You should review and configure alerts in accordance with your specific networking needs.
Client configuration	Firewall and Web Proxy clients have automatic discovery enabled by default. Web browser applications on Firewall clients are configured when the Firewall client is installed.
Autodiscovery for Firewall and Web Proxy Clients	Publication of autodiscovery information is disabled by default. You will need to enable publication of autodiscovery information and confirm a port on which autodiscovery information is published.

The Post-installation System Policy

ISA Firewall Policy is a collection of Access Rules controlling access to and from the Local Host network. System Policy controls access to and from the *system*. You do **not** configure System Policy for network access between any other hosts. One of the most common errors made by new ISA firewall administrators is to use System Policy to control access from Protected Network hosts to non-Protected Network hosts.

Table 3.5 shows the list of System Policy rules and their status after installing the ISA firewall software. The **Order/Comments** column includes our advice regarding configuration of the specific System Policy Rule.

Table 3.5 Default Post-installation System Policy

Order/Comments	Name	Action	Protocols	From/Listener	To	Condition
1 Is the ISA firewall a member of the domain? If not, disable this rule.	Allow access to directory services for authentication purposes	Allow	LDAP LDAP (UDP) LDAP GC (global catalog) LDAPS LDAPS GC (Global Catalog)	Local Host	Internal	All Users
2 If no one is going to use the remote MMC to manage the ISA firewall, disable this rule.	Allow remote management from selected computers using MMC	Allow	Microsoft Firewall Control NetBIOS datagram NetBIOS Name Service NetBIOS Session RPC (all interfaces)	Remote Management Computers	Local Host	All Users
3 Confirm that the Remote Management Computers Computer Set has the addresses of the hosts that will manage the ISA firewall; if you don't want	Allow remote management from selected computers using Terminal Server	Allow	RDP (Terminal Services)	Remote Management Computers	Local Host	All Users
						Continued

Table 3.5 Continued

Order/Comments	Name	Action	Protocols	From/Listener	To	Condition
to allow RDP management of the ISA firewall, disable this rule.						
4 (Disabled by default) ■ Enable this rule if you want to log to SQL servers.	Allow remote logging to trusted servers using NetBIOS	Allow	NetBIOS Datagram NetBIOS Name Service NetBIOS Session	Local Host	Internal	All Users
5 Will you be using RADIUS authentication? If not, disable this rule.	Allow RADIUS authentication from ISA Server to trusted RADIUS servers	Allow	RADIUS RADIUS Accounting	Local Host	Internal	All Users
6 Will the ISA firewall be authenticating users? If not, disable this rule.	Allow Kerberos authentication from ISA Server to trusted servers	Allow	Kerberos-Sec (TCP) Kerberos-Sec (UDP)	Local Host	Internal	All Users
7 This rule must be enabled so that the ISA firewall can initiate DNS queries.	Allow DNS from ISA Server to selected servers	Allow	DNS	Local Host	All Networks (and Local Host)	All Users

#	Description	Name	Action	Protocols	From	To	Users
8	If the ISA firewall isn't going to act as a DHCP client, disable this rule.	Allow DHCP requests from ISA Server to all networks	Allow	DHCP (request)	Local Host	Anywhere	All Users
9	If the ISA firewall isn't going to act as a DHCP client, disable this rule.	Allow DHCP replies from DHCP servers to ISA Server	Allow	DHCP (reply)	Internal	Local Host	All Users
10	Confirm that you have configured the proper IP addresses for the Remote Management Computers Computer Set.	Allow ICMP (PING) requests from selected computers to ISA Server	Allow	Ping	Remote Management Computers	Local Host	All Users
11	This rule must be enabled so that the ISA firewall can carry out network management tasks via ICMP.	Allow ICMP requests from ISA Server to selected servers	Allow	ICMP Information Request ICMP Timestamp Ping	Local Host	All Networks (and Local Host Network)	All Users
12 (disabled by default)	This rule is automatically enabled when you enable the ISA firewall's VPN server component.	All VPN client traffic to ISA Server	Allow	PPTP	External	Local Host	All Users

Continued

Table 3.5 Continued

Order/Comments	Name	Action	Protocols	From/Listener	To	Condition
13 (disabled by default) This rule is automatically enabled when you enable a site-to-site VPN connection to this ISA firewall.	Allow VPN site-to-site traffic to ISA Server	Allow	NONE	External IPSec Remote Gateways	Local Host	All Users
14 (disabled by default) This rule is automatically enabled when you enable a site-to-site VPN connection to this ISA firewall.	Allow VPN site-to-site traffic from ISA Server	Allow	NONE	Local Host	External IPSec Remote Gateways	All Users
15 Will you be trying to access file shares from the ISA firewall? If not, disable this rule	Allow Microsoft CIFS from ISA Server to trusted servers	Allow	Microsoft CIFS (TCP) Microsoft CIFS (UDP)	Local Host	Internal	All Users
16 (disabled by default) ■ Enable this rule when you choose SQL logging.	Allow remote SQL logging from ISA Server to selected servers	Allow	Microsoft SQL (TCP) Microsoft SQL (UDP)	Local Host	Internal	All Users

	Name	Action	Protocols	From	To	Users
17 Unless you want to allow the ISA firewall to contact the Windows Update site itself, disable this rule. I prefer to download updates to a management machine, scan them, and then copy them out of band to the ISA firewall and install them from that.	Allow HTTP/HTTPS requests from ISA Server to specified sites	Allow	HTTP HTTPS	Local Host	System Policy Allowed Sites	All Users
18 (disabled by default) This rule is enabled when you create an HTTP/HTTPS connectivity verifier.	Allow HTTP/HTTPS requests from ISA Server to selected servers for connectivity verifiers	Allow	HTTP HTTPS	Local Host	All Networks (and Local Host Network)	All Users
19 (disabled by default) This rule is enabled if the Firewall client share is installed on the ISA firewall.	Allow access from trusted computers to the Firewall Client installation share on ISA Server	Allow	Microsoft CIFS (TCP) Microsoft CIFS (UDP) NetBIOS Datagram NetBIOS Name Service NetBIOS Session	Internal	Local Host	All Users

Continued

Table 3.5 Continued

Order/Comments	Name	Action	Protocols	From/Listener	To	Condition
20 (disabled by default) Enable this rule if you want to perform remote performance monitoring of ISA firewall.	Allow remote performance monitoring of ISA Server from trusted servers	Allow	NetBIOS Datagram NetBIOS Name Service NetBIOS Session	Remote Management Computers	Local Host	All Users
21 Unless you plan to access file shares from the ISA firewall, disable this rule.	Allow NetBIOS from ISA Server to trusted servers	Allow	NetBIOS datagram NetBIOS Name Service NetBIOS Sessions	Local Host	Internal	All Users
22 ■ Unless you plan to use RPC to connect to other servers, disable this rule.	Allow RPC from ISA Server to trusted servers	Allow	RPC (all interfaces)	Local Host	Internal	All Users
23 This rule allows the ISA firewall to send error reports to Microsoft.	Allow HTTP/HTTPS from ISA Server to specified Microsoft error reporting sites	Allow	HTTP HTTPS	Local Host	Microsoft Error Reporting sites	All Users
24 (disabled by default) This rule should	Allow SecurID authentication	Allow	SecurID	Local Host	Internal	All Users

	Action	Protocol	From	To	Users
be enabled if SecurID authentication is enabled. from ISA Server to trusted servers					
25 (disabled by default) ■ Enable this rule if you use MOM to monitor the ISA firewall. Allow remote monitoring from ISA Server to trusted servers, using Microsoft Operations Manager (MOM) Agent	Allow	Microsoft Operations Manager Agent	Local Host	Internal	All Users
26 (disabled by default) Enable this rule if you want the ISA firewall to access CRLs – required if the ISA terminates any SSL connections. Allow all HTTP traffic from ISA Server to all networks (for CRL downloads)	Allow	HTTP	Local Host	All Networks (and Local Host)	All Users
27 You should change this rule by allowing contact with a trusted NTP server in your organization. The Internal entry allows it to contact all servers anywhere in the world. Allow NTP from ISA Server to trusted NTP servers	Allow	NTP (UDP)	Local Host	Internal	All Users

Continued

Table 3.5 Continued

Order/Comments	Name	Action	Protocols	From/Listener	To	Condition
28 If you don't plan on using SMTP to send alerts, you should disable this rule. If you do plan on sending SMTP alerts, you should replace the Internal Destination with a specific computer that will accept SMTP messages from the ISA firewall.	Allow SMTP from ISA Server to trusted servers	Allow	SMTP	Local Host	Internal	All Users
29 (disabled by default) This rule is automatically enabled when Content Download Jobs are enabled.	Allow HTTP from ISA Server to selected computers for Content Download Jobs	Allow	HTTP	Local Host	All Networks (and Local Host)	System and Network Service
30 Unless you plan on using the remote MMC, disable this rule	Allow Microsoft Firewall Control communication to selected computers	Allow	All Outbound traffic	Local Host	Remote Manage-ment Computers	All Users

The ISA firewall's System Policy Rules are evaluated before any user-defined Access Rules in the order listed in the **Firewall Policy** first column. View the ISA firewall's System Policy by clicking **Firewall Policy** in the left pane of the console and then clicking the **Tasks** tab. In the **Tasks** tab, click **Show System Policy Rules**. Click **Hide System Policy Rules** when you're finished viewing the firewall's system policy.

ISA Firewall Warning

You can make changes to only some components of the ISA firewall's default System Policy. You will find that there are several instances where you cannot make changes to the ISA firewall's System Policy with the System Policy Editor.

You can edit the ISA firewall's System Policy by clicking **Edit System Policy** on the **Tasks** tab. This opens the **System Policy Editor,** as shown in Figure 3.12. For each System Policy Rule there is a **General** tab and a **From** or **To** tab. The **General** tab for each **Configuration Group** contains an explanation of the rule(s), and the **From** or **To** tab allows you to control protocol access to or from the ISA firewall machine itself.

Figure 3.12 The ISA Firewall's System Policy Editor

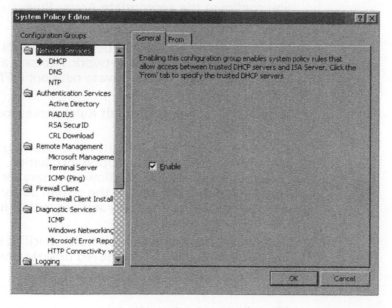

See Table 3.6 for post-installation ISA Firewall System Configuration default settings.

Table 3.6 Default Post-installation ISA Firewall System Configuration

Feature	Default Setting
User permissions	Members of the Administrators group on the local computer can configure firewall firewall is a member of the domain, then the Domain Admins global group is automatically included in the local machine's Administrators group.
Definition of Internal network	The Internal network contains IP addresses you specified during setup of the ISA firewall software.
Network Rules	**Local Host Access** Defines a route relationship between the Local Host network and all networks. All connections between the Local Host network (that is, the ISA firewall machine itself) are routed instead of NATed. **Internet Access** Defines a NAT (Network Address Translation) relationship between the Internal Network, Quarantined VPN Clients Network, and the VPN Clients Network – to the External network. From each of these three Networks to the Internet, the connection is NATed. Access is allowed only if you configure the appropriate Access Rules. **VPN Clients to Internal Network** Defines a route relationship between the VPN Clients Network and the Internal Network. Access is allowed only if you enable virtual private network (VPN) client access.
Firewall policy	A default rule (named **Default Rule**) denies traffic between all networks.
System policy	ISA Server is secure by default, while allowing certain critical services to function. Upon installation, some system policy rules are enabled to allow necessary services. We recommend that you review the system policy configuration and customize it so that only services critical to your specific deployment are enabled.
Web chaining	A default rule (named **Default Rule**) specifies that all Web Proxy client requests are retrieved directly from the Internet.
Caching	The cache size is set to 0. All caching is, therefore, disabled.
Alerts	Most alerts are active. We recommend that you review and configure the alerts in accordance with your specific networking needs.

Table 3.6 Continued

Feature	Default Setting
Client configuration	When installed or configured, Firewall and Web Proxy clients have automatic discovery enabled. Web browser applications on Firewall clients are configured when the Firewall client is installed.

Performing a Single NIC Installation (Unihomed ISA Firewall)

This ISA firewall software can be installed on a machine with a single network interface card. This is done to simulate the Proxy Server 2.0 configuration or the ISA Server 2000 caching-only mode. This 2006 ISA firewall does not have a caching-only mode, but you can strip away a significant level of firewall functionality from the ISA firewall when you install it in single-NIC mode.

When the ISA firewall is installed in single-NIC mode, you lose:

- Support for Firewall clients
- Support for full SecureNAT client security and functionality
- Server Publishing Rules
- All protocols except HTTP, HTTPS and HTTP-tunneled (Web proxied) FTP
- Remote Access VPN
- Site-to-Site VPN
- Multi-networking functionality (the entire IPv4 address space is the same network)
- Application-layer inspection except for HTTP

While this stripped version of the ISA firewall retains only a fraction of its ability to act as a network firewall protecting hosts on your corporate network, it does keep full firewall functionality when it comes to protecting itself. The ISA firewall will not be directly accessible to any host, external or internal, unless you enable system policy rules to allow access.

The NIC configuration on the unihomed ISA firewall should set the default gateway as the IP address of any current gateway on the network that allows the unihomed ISA firewall access to the Internet. All other non-local routes need to be configured in the unihomed ISA firewall's routing table.

If you only require a Web Proxy service to perform both forward and reverse proxy, then you can install the ISA firewall on a single NIC machine. The installation process differs a bit from what you find when the ISA firewall is installed on a multi-NIC machine.

Perform the following steps to install the ISA firewall software on a single-NIC machine:

1. Insert the ISA Server 2006 installation CD into the CD-ROM drive or connect to a network share point hosting the ISA Server 2006 installation files. If the installation routine does not

start automatically, double-click the **isaautorun.exe** file in the root of the installation files folder tree.

2. On the **Microsoft Internet Security and Acceleration Server 2004** page, click **Review Release Notes**, and read the release notes. The release notes contain very important and topical information regarding changes in basic firewall software functionality. This information may not be included in the Help file or elsewhere, so we highly recommend that you read it here. After reviewing the release notes, click **Read Setup and Feature Guide**. You may want to read the guide now, just review the major topics covered in the guide, or print it out. Click **Install ISA Server 2006**.

3. Click **Next** on the **Welcome to the Installation Wizard for Microsoft ISA Server 2006** page.

4. Select **I accept the terms in the license agreement option on the License Agreement** page. Click **Next**.

5. On the **Customer Information** page, enter your name and the name of your organization in the **User Name** and **Organization** text boxes. Enter your serial number in the **Product Serial Number** text box. If you installed an evaluation copy of the ISA firewall software and now are installing a licensed version, backup your configuration using the ISA firewall's integrated backup tool, and uninstall the evaluation version. Restart the installation of the licensed version of the ISA firewall software. Click **Next**.

6. On the **Setup Type** page, click the **Custom** option.

7. On the **Custom Setup** page you'll notice that the **Firewall Services**, **Advanced Logging**, and **ISA Server Management** options are selected by default. While you can install the **Firewall Client** share, keep in mind that the unihomed ISA firewall does not support Firewall or SecureNAT clients. The only client type supported is the Web Proxy client. However, if you have full service ISA firewalls on your network, you can install the Firewall client share on this machine and allow network clients to download the Firewall client software from the unihomed ISA firewall. There is no point to installing the SMTP message screener on the unihomed ISA firewall since this mode does not support Server Publishing Rules. Click **Next**.

8. On the **Internal Network** page click **Add**. On the **address ranges for internal network** page, click **Select Network Adapter**, as shown in Figure 3.13.

9. On the **Select Network Adapter** page, **Add the following private ranges** and **Add address ranges based on the Windows Routing Table** are selected. While you don't have to do anything is this checkbox, we recommend that you remove the checkmark from the **Add the following private ranges** option and put a checkmark in the box next to the single NIC installed on the unihomed ISA firewall. Click **OK**.

10. Click **OK** in the **Setup Message** dialog box informing you that the Internal Network was defined based on the routing table. This dialog box really doesn't apply to the unihomed ISA firewall, since all IP addresses in the IPv4 address range (except for the local host network ID)

are included in the definition of the Internal Network. The reason why the local host network ID is not included is that this address is included in the Local Host Network definition.

11. In the Internal network address range dialog box (Figure 3.13), you'll see that all IP addresses are included in the definition of the Internal network. Click **OK**.

Figure 3.13 The Internal Network Definition on the Unihomed ISA Firewall

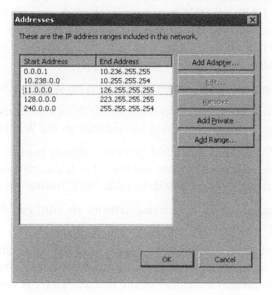

12. Click **Next** on the **Internal Network** page.
13. Click **Next** on the **Firewall Client Connection Settings** page. These settings don't mean anything because Firewall clients are not supported by the unihomed ISA firewall.
14. Click **Next** on the **Services** page.
15. Click **Install** on the **Ready to Install the Program** page.
16. Put a checkmark in the **Invoke ISA Server Management when the wizard closes** checkbox, and click **Finish**.

There are some significant limitations to the single NIC ISA firewall because there is no External network, there is lack of Firewall client support, and other factors. We discuss some of the implications of the unihomed ISA firewall and Access Policy related to this configuration in Chapter 7.

Quick Start Configuration for ISA Firewalls

Many of you will want to install and configure the ISA firewall as quickly as possible and then wait until later to get into the details of ISA firewall configuration. What you want to do is connect the ISA firewall to your network and your Internet connection, install the software, and create a rule that allows all hosts on your private network access to all protocols on the Internet as quickly as possible. Once you're up and running and connected to the Internet, you can then read the rest of this book at your leisure and get into the interesting and powerful configuration options available to you.

To help you, we have included a quick installation and configuration section. In order to make this a quick installation and configuration guide, we're making the following basic assumptions about your network:

- You don't have any other Windows servers on your network. While you can have other Windows services running Windows network services, this guide will include instructions on how to install DNS and DHCP services on the ISA firewall. If you already have a DNS server on your network, you do not need to install a DNS server on the ISA firewall. If you already have a DHCP server on your network, you do not need to install a DHCP server on the ISA firewall.

- We assume that you are installing ISA Server 2006 on Windows Server 2003.

- We assume you have installed Windows Server 2003 on a computer using the default installation settings and have not added any software to the Windows Server 2003 machine.

- We assume your Windows Server 2003 computer already has two Ethernet cards. One NIC is connected to the Internal Network and the other is directly connected to the Internet via a network router, or there is a DSL or cable NAT "router" in front of it.

- We assume that machines on the Internal network are configured as DHCP clients and will use the ISA Server 2006 firewall machine as their DHCP server.

- We assume the Windows Server 2003 machine that you're installing the ISA Server 2006 firewall software on is not a member of a Windows domain. While we recommend that you make the ISA firewall a member of the domain later, the computer running the ISA firewall software does not need to be a domain member. We make this assumption in this quick installation and setup guide because we assume that you have no other Windows servers on your network (you may have Linux, Netware, or other vendors servers, though).

Figure 3.14 shows the ISA firewall and its relationship to the internal and external networks. The internal interface is connected to a hub or switch on the internal network, and the external interface is connected to a hub or switch that also connects to the router.

We will perform the following procedures to get the ISA firewall quickly set up and configured:

- Configure ISA firewall's network interfaces.

- Install and configure a DNS server on the ISA Server 2006 firewall computer.

- Install and configure a DHCP server on the ISA Server 2006 firewall computer.

- Install and configure the ISA Server 2006 software.

- Configure the internal network computers as DHCP clients.

Figure 3.14 The Physical Relationships between the ISA Server 2006 Firewall and the Internal and External Networks

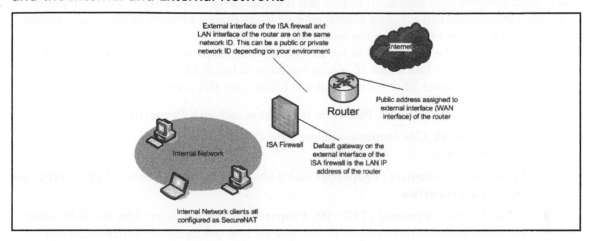

Configuring the ISA Firewall's Network Interfaces

The ISA firewall must have at least one *internal* network interface and one *external* network interface. To correctly configure the network interfaces on the ISA firewall:

- Assign IP addresses to the internal and external network interfaces.
- Assign a DNS server address to the internal interface of the ISA firewall.
- Place the internal interface on top of the network interface order.

IP Address and DNS Server Assignment

First, we will assign static IP addresses to the internal and external interfaces of the ISA firewall. The ISA firewall also requires a DNS server address bound to its internal interface. We will *not* need to use DHCP on any of the ISA firewall's network interfaces because the internal interface should always have a static IP address, and the external interface doesn't need to support a dynamic address because it's behind a router.

If your Internet account uses DHCP to assign your public address, your DSL or cable router can handle the task of obtaining and renewing the public address. In addition, if you use PPPoE or VPN to connect to your ISP, your router can also handle these tasks.

In this section, we discuss:

- Configuring the internal network interface, and
- Configuring the external network interface

Configuring the Internal Network Interface

The internal interface must have an IP address that is on the same network ID as other computers on the directly-attached network. This address must be in the private network address range, and the address must not already be in use on the network.

We will configure the ISA firewall to use its internal interface address as its DNS server address.

The ISA firewall must have a *static* IP address bound to its internal interface. Perform the following steps on the Windows Server 2003 machine that will become the ISA firewall:

1. Right-click **My Network Places** on the desktop, and click **Properties**.

2. In the **Network Connections** window, right-click the internal network interface, and click **Properties**.

3. In the network interface's **Properties** dialog box, click **Internet Protocol (TCP/IP)**, and then click **Properties**.

4. In the **Internet Protocol (TCP/IP) Properties** dialog box, select **Use the following IP address**. Enter the IP address for the internal interface in the **IP address** text box. Enter the subnet mask for the internal interface in the **Subnet mask** text box. Do *not* enter a default gateway for the internal interface.

5. Select **Use the following DNS server addresses**. Enter the IP address of the *internal* interface for the ISA firewall in the **Preferred DNS server** text box. This is the same number you entered in step 4 in the **IP address** text box. Click **OK** in the **Internet Protocol (TCP/IP) Properties** dialog box.

6. Click **OK** in the internal interface's **Properties** dialog box.

ISA FIREWALL WARNING

If you already have a DNS server on your internal network, you should configure the ISA firewall's internal interface to use the Internal Network DNS server's IP address. You then configure the DNS server on the Internal Network to resolve Internet host names. The Microsoft DNS server will automatically resolve Internet host names as long as the Root Hints file is primed with Internet DNS Root Servers. The default Access Rule we will create at the end of this quick install and configuration section will allow the DNS server outbound access to Internet DNS servers for host name resolution.

ISA FIREWALL ALERT

Never enter a default gateway address on the internal interface. An ISA firewall can have a single interface with a default gateway. Even if you have 17 NICs installed in the same ISA firewall, only one of those NICs can be configured with a default gateway. All other gateways must be configured in the Windows routing table.

Configuring the External Network Interface

Perform the following procedures to configure the IP addressing information on the external interface of the ISA firewall:

1. Right-click **My Network Places** on the desktop, and click **Properties**.

2. In the **Network Connections** window, right-click the external network interface, and click **Properties**.

3. In the network interface's **Properties** dialog box, click the **Internet Protocol (TCP/IP)** entry, and then click **Properties**.

4. In the **Internet Properties (TCP/IP) Properties** dialog box, select **Use the following IP address**. Enter the IP address for the external interface in the **IP address** text box. Enter the subnet mask for the external interface in the **Subnet mask** text box. Enter a **Default gateway** for the external interface in its text box. The default gateway is the LAN address of your router.

5. Click **OK** in the internal interface's **Properties** dialog box.

ISA FIREWALL TIP

You do not need to configure a DNS server address on the external interface. The DNS server address on the internal interface is the only DNS server address required.

Network Interface Order

The internal interface of the ISA Server 2006 computer is placed on top of the network interface list to ensure the best performance for name resolution. Perform the following steps to configure the network interface on the Windows Server 2003 machine:

Perform the following steps to change the network interface order:

1. Right-click **My Network Places** on the desktop, and click **Properties**.

2. In the **Network and Dial-up Connections** window, click the **Advanced** menu, then click **Advanced Settings**.

3. In the **Advanced Settings** dialog box (Figure 3.15), click the internal interface in the list of **Connections** on the **Adapters and Bindings** tab. After selecting the internal interface, click the up-arrow to move it to the top of the list of interfaces.

4. Click **OK** in the **Advanced Settings** dialog box.

Figure 3.15 The Advanced Settings Dialog Box

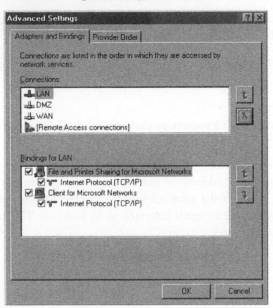

Installing and Configuring a DNS Server on the ISA Server Firewall

We will install a caching-only DNS server on the ISA firewall. This will allow machines on the Internal Network and the ISA firewall to resolve Internet host names. Note that you *do not* need to perform this step if you already have a DNS server on your internal network. Even if you already have a DNS server located on the internal network, you might consider configuring the ISA firewall computer as a caching-only DNS server and then configure computers on the internal network to use the ISA Server 2006 machine as their DNS server or configure the internal network computers to use your Internal Network DNS server and configure the Internal Network DNS server to use the ISA firewall as a DNS forwarder.

Installing the DNS Service

The DNS Server service is not installed by default on Windows server operating systems. The first step is to install the DNS Server service on the Windows Server 2003 machine that will be the ISA firewall.

Installing the DNS Server Service on Windows Server 2003

Perform the following steps to install the DNS Server service on a Windows Server 2003 computer:

1. Click **Start**, point to **Control Panel**, and click **Add or Remove Programs**.
2. In the **Add or Remove Programs** window, click **Add/Remove Windows Components**.

3. In the **Windows Components Wizard** dialog box, select **Networking Services** from the list of **Components**. *Do not put a checkmark in the checkbox!* After highlighting the **Networking Services** entry, click the **Details** button.

4. In the **Networking Services** dialog box, put a checkmark in the **Domain Name System (DNS)** checkbox, and click **OK**.

5. Click **Next** in the **Windows Components** dialog box.

6. Click **OK** in the **Insert Disk** dialog box. In the **Files Needed** dialog box, provide a path to the i386 folder from the Windows Server 2003 installation CD in the **Copy files from** text box, then click **OK**.

7. Click **Finish** on the **Completing the Windows Components Wizard** page.

8. **Close** the **Add or Remove Programs** window.

Configuring the DNS Service on the ISA Firewall

The DNS Server on the ISA firewall machine performs DNS queries for Internet host names on behalf of computers on the internal network. The DNS Server on the ISA firewall is configured as a *caching-only* DNS server. A caching-only DNS Server does not contain information about your public or private DNS names and domains. The caching-only DNS Server resolves Internet host names and caches the results; it does not answer DNS queries for names on your private internal network DNS zone or your public DNS zone.

ISA Firewall Note

DNS is an inherently complex topic. Do not be concerned if you do not completely understand the details of DNS operations. The DNS service will be correctly configured to resolve Internet host names when you complete the steps in this section.

If you have an internal network DNS server supporting an Active Directory domain, you can configure the caching-only DNS server located on the ISA firewall to refer client requests to your internal network domain to the DNS server on your internal network. The end result is that the caching-only DNS server on the ISA Server 2006 firewall computer will not interfere with your current DNS server setup.

Configuring the DNS Service in Windows Server 2003

Perform the following steps to configure the DNS service on the Windows Server 2003 computer:

1. Click **Start** and point to **Administrative Tools**. Click the **DNS** entry.

2. Right-click the server name in the left pane of the console, point to **View**, and click **Advanced**.

3. Expand all nodes in the left pane of the DNS console.

4. Right-click the server name in the left pane of the DNS console, and click the **Properties** option.

5. In the server's **Properties** dialog box, click **Interfaces**. Select **Only the following IP addresses**. Click any IP address that *is not* an IP address bound to the internal interface of the computer. After highlighting the non-internal IP address, click **Remove**. Click **Apply**.

6. Click the **Forwarders** tab, as shown in Figure 3.16. Enter the IP address of your ISP's DNS server in the **Selected domain's forwarder IP address list** text box, and then click **Add**. Put a checkmark in the **Do not use recursion for this domain** checkbox. This **Do not use recursion** option prevents the DNS server on the ISA firewall from trying to perform name resolution itself. The end result is if the forwarder is unable to resolve the name, the name resolution request stops. Click **Apply**.

ISA FIREWALL TIP

If you find that name resolution performance isn't as good as you expect, disable the **Forwarders** entry. While a well-managed ISP DNS server can significantly improve name resolution performance, a poorly-managed ISP DNS server can slow down your ISA firewall's ability to resolve Internet host names. In most instances, you'll get better performance using your ISP's DNS server because it will have a larger cache of resolved host names than your ISA firewall's caching-only DNS server.

Figure 3.16 The Forwarders Tab

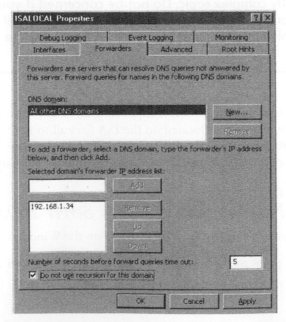

7. Click **OK** in the server's **Properties** dialog box.

8. Right-click the server name; point to **All Tasks**, and click **Restart**.

Perform the following steps *only if* you have an internal network DNS server that you are using to support an Active Directory domain. If you do not have an internal network DNS server and you do not need to resolve internal network DNS names, then bypass the following section on configuring a stub zone.

ISA FIREWALL WARNING

DO NOT perform the following steps if you do not already have a DNS server on your internal network. These steps are only for those networks already using Windows Server 2003 Active Directory domains.

1. The first step is to create the reverse lookup zone for the Internal Network where the Internal DNS server ID is located. Right-click the **Reverse Lookup Zones** node in the left pane of the console, and click **New Zone**.

2. Click **Next** on the **Welcome to the New Zone Wizard** page.

3. On the **Zone Type** page, select **Stub zone**, and click **Next**.

4. Select **Network ID**. On the **Reverse Lookup Zone Name** page, enter into the **Network ID** text box the ID for the network where the internal network DNS server is located, as shown in Figure 3.17. Click **Next**.

Figure 3.17 The Reverse Lookup Zone Name Page

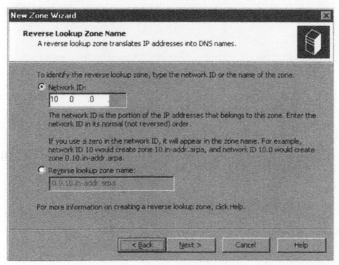

5. Accept the default file name on the **Zone File** page, and click **Next**.

6. On the **Master DNS Servers** page, enter the IP address of your internal network DNS server, and click **Add**. Click **Next**.

7.   Click **Finish** on the **Completing the New Zone Wizard** page.

8.   The next step is to create the forward lookup zone for the stub zone. Right-click the **Forward Lookup Zones** node in the left pane of the console, and click the **New Zone** command.

9.   Click **Next** on the **Welcome to the New Zone Wizard** page.

10. On the **Zone Type** page, select **Stub zone**, and click **Next**.

11. On the **Zone name** page, type the name of your internal network domain in the **Zone name** text box. Click **Next**.

12. On the **Zone File** page (Figure 3.18), accept the default name for the zone file, and click **Next**.

Figure 3.18 The Zone File Page

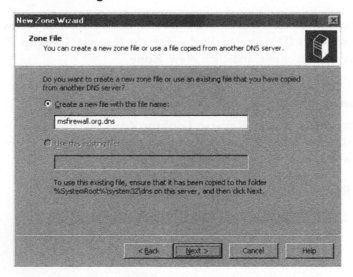

13. On the **Master DNS Servers** page, enter the IP address of your internal network's DNS server, and click **Add**. Click **Next**.

14. Click **Finish** on the **Completing the New Zone Wizard** page.

15. Right-click the server name in the left pane of the console; point to **All Tasks**, and click **Restart**.

Configuring the DNS Service on the Internal Network DNS Server

If your organization has an existing DNS infrastructure, you should configure your Internal network's DNS server to use the DNS server on the ISA Server 2006 firewall as its DNS forwarder. This provides a more secure DNS configuration because your Internal network DNS server never communicates directly with an untrusted DNS server on the Internet.

The Internal network DNS server forwards DNS queries to the DNS server on the ISA Server 2006 firewall, and the DNS server on the ISA Server 2006 resolves the name, places the result in its own DNS cache, and then returns the IP address to the DNS server on the Internal network.

ISA FIREWALL WARNING

Perform the following steps only if you have an internal DNS server and you have configured the ISA firewall's internal interface to use the internal DNS server. If you do not have an internal network DNS server, do *not* perform the following steps.

Perform the following steps on the *Internal network DNS server* to configure it to use the DNS server on the ISA firewall as its forwarder:

1. Click **Start** and point to **Administrative** tools, then click **DNS**.

2. In the **DNS Management** console, right-click the server name in the left pane of the console, and click **Properties**.

3. In the server's **Properties** dialog box, click the **Forwarders** tab, as shown in Figure 3.19.

4. On the **Forwarders** tab, enter the IP address on the Internal interface of the ISA Server 2006 firewall in the **Selected domain's forwarder IP address list** text box. Click **Add**.

5. The IP address for the internal interface of the ISA Server 2006 firewall appears in the list of forwarder addresses (Figure 3.19).

Figure 3.19 The Forwarders Tab

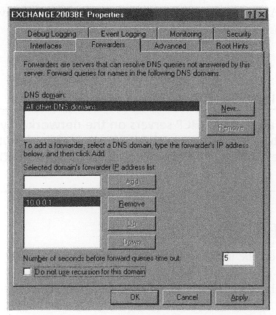

6. Put a checkmark in the **Do not use recursion for this domain** checkbox (Figure 3.20). This option prevents the Internal network DNS server from trying to resolve the name itself in the event that the forwarder on the ISA firewall is unable to resolve the name.

Figure 3.20 Disabling Recursion

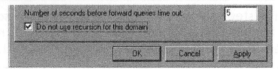

7. Click **Apply**, and then click **OK**.

Note that the DNS server on the Internal Network will not be able to resolve Internet host names yet. We still need to create an Access Rule allowing the DNS server access to the DNS server on the ISA firewall. We will create this Access Rule later in this section.

Installing and Configuring a DHCP Server on the ISA Server Firewall

Each of your computers needs an IP address and other information that allows them to communicate with each other and with computers on the Internet. The DHCP Server service can be installed on the ISA firewall and provide IP addressing information to Internal Network computers. We will assume that you need to use the ISA firewall as your DHCP server. If you already have a DHCP server on your network, you can bypass the following steps.

ISA FIREWALL WARNING

You must not have any other DHCP servers on the network. If you have another machine on the network acting as a DHCP server, disable the DHCP service on that machine so that the ISA Server 2006 firewall acts as your only DHCP server on the network.

Installing the DHCP Service

The DHCP Server service can be installed on Windows 2000 Server and Windows Server 2003 computers. The procedure varies slightly between the two operating systems. In this section, we discuss procedures for installing the DHCP Server service on Windows 2000 Server and Windows Server 2003 computers.

Installing the DHCP Server Service on a Windows Server 2003 Computer

Perform the following steps to install the DNS Server service on a Windows Server 2003 computer:

1. Click **Start**; point to **Control Panel**, and click **Add or Remove Programs**.

2. In the **Add or Remove Programs** window, click **Add/Remove Windows Components**.

3. In the **Windows Components Wizard** dialog box, select **Networking Services** from the list of **Components**. *Do not put a checkmark in the checkbox!* After highlighting the **Networking Services** entry, click the **Details** button.

4. In the **Networking Services** dialog box (Figure 3.21), put a checkmark in the **Dynamic Host Configuration Protocol (DHCP)** checkbox, and click **OK**.

Figure 3.21 The Networking Services Dialog Box

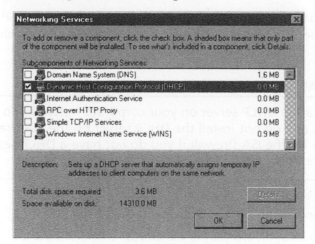

5. Click **Next** in the **Windows Components** dialog box.

6. Click **Finish** on the **Completing the Windows Components Wizard** page.

7. **Close** the **Add or Remove Programs** window.

Configuring the DHCP Service

The DHCP Server must be configured with a collection of IP addresses it can assign to machines on your private network. The DHCP Server also provides information in addition to an IP address, such as a DNS server address, default gateway, and primary domain name.

The DNS server and default gateway addresses assigned to your computers will be the IP address on the internal interface of the ISA firewall. The DHCP server uses a *DHCP scope* to provide this information to the internal network clients. You must create a DHCP scope that provides the correct IP addressing information to your internal network clients.

> **NOTE**
>
> The DHCP server must not assign addresses that are already in use on your network. You must create *exclusions* for these IP addresses. Examples of excluded IP addresses might be static or reserved addresses assigned to print servers, file servers, mail servers, or Web servers; these are just a few examples of devices or servers that always have the same IP address assigned to them. These addresses are permanently assigned to these servers and network devices. If you don't create exclusions for these addresses, the DHCP server will perform a gratuitous ARP, and when it finds this address in use, will move it into a *bad address* group. In addition, a well designed network will group computers into contiguous blocks of IP addresses. For example, all computers that need static addresses would be placed into one contiguous block.

Perform the following steps to configure the Windows Server 2003 DHCP Server with a scope that will assign the proper IP addressing information to the internal network clients:

> **ISA FIREWALL WARNING**
>
> If you already have a DHCP server on your corporate network, do not perform the following steps, and do not install the DHCP server on the ISA firewall. Only install the DHCP server on the ISA firewall if you do *not* have a DHCP server on your internal network.

1. Click **Start** and point to **Administrative Tools**. Click **DHCP**.

2. Expand all nodes in the left pane of the **DHCP** console. Right-click the server name in the left pane of the console, and click **New Scope**.

3. Click **Next** on the **Welcome to the New Scope Wizard** page.

4. Type **SecureNAT Client Scope** in the **Name** text box on the **Scope Name** page. Click **Next**.

5. On the **IP Address Range** page, enter the first IP address and the last IP address for the range in the **Start IP address** and **End IP address** text boxes. For example, if you are using the network ID 192.168.1.0 with a subnet mask of 255.255.255.0, then enter the start IP address as **192.168.1.1** and the end IP address as **192.168.1.254**. Click **Next**.

6. On the **Add Exclusions** page, enter the IP address of the internal interface for the ISA firewall in the **Start IP address** text box, and click **Add**. If you have servers or workstations on the network that have statically-assigned IP addresses that you do not want to change, add those addresses to the exclusions list. Click **Next** after adding all addresses you want to exclude from the DHCP scope.

7. Accept the default value on the **Lease Duration** page, and click **Next**.

8. On the **Configuring DHCP Options** page, select **Yes, I want to configure these options now,** and click **Next**.

9. On the **Router** page, enter the IP address of the internal interface for the ISA firewall, and click **Add**. Click **Next**.

10. On the **Domain Name and DNS Servers** page, enter the IP address of the internal interface for the ISA firewall in the **IP address** text box, and click **Add**. *If you have an Active Directory domain on the Internal network*, enter the name of your Internal network domain in the **Parent domain** text box. Do *not* enter a domain name in the **Parent domain** text box *unless* you have an existing Active Directory domain on the internal network. Click **Next**.

11. Do not enter any information on the **WINS Servers** page unless you already have a WINS server on the internal network. If you already have a WINS server, enter that IP address in the **IP address** text box. Click **Next**.

12. Select **Yes, I want to activate this scope now** on the **Activate Scope** page, and click **Yes**.

13. Click **Finish** on the **Completing the New Scope Wizard** page.

Installing and Configuring the ISA Server 2006 Software

We're now ready to install the ISA firewall software.

The following steps demonstrate how to install the ISA firewall software on a dual-homed Windows Server 2003 machine:

1. Insert the ISA Server 2006 installation media into the CD-ROM drive or connect to a network share hosting the ISA Server 2006 installation files. If the installation routine does not start automatically, double-click the **isaautorun.exe** file in the root of the installation files tree.

2. On the **Microsoft Internet Security and Acceleration Server 2004** page, click **Review Release Notes** and read the notes. The release notes contain useful information about important issues and configuration options. After reading the release notes, click **Read Setup and Feature Guide**. You don't need to read the entire guide right now, but you may want to print it to read later. Click **Install ISA Server 2004**.

3. Click **Next** on the **Welcome to the Installation Wizard for Microsoft ISA Server 2006** page.

4. Select **I accept the terms in the license agreement** on the **License Agreement** page. Click **Next**.

5. On the **Customer Information** page, enter your name and the name of your organization in the **User Name** and **Organization** text boxes. Enter your serial number in the **Product Serial Number** text box. Click **Next**.

6. On the **Setup Type** page, select the **Custom** option. If you do not want to install the ISA firewall software on the C: drive, click the **Change** button to change the location of the program files on the hard disk. Click **Next**.

7. On the **Custom Setup** page, choose the components to install. By default, the **Firewall Services**, **ISA Server Management**, and Advanced Logging are installed. To install the **Firewall Client Installation Share** so that we have the option later to install the Firewall client on Internal Network client machines, we will have to copy the client share directory from the ISAServer 2006 cd to a location of your choice and share it manually. The Firewall client adds a significant level of security to your network, and you should install the Firewall client on Internal network clients whenever possible. We discuss this issue in more detail in Chapter 5 on ISA Server client types. Click **Next**.

Figure 3.22 The Custom Setup Page

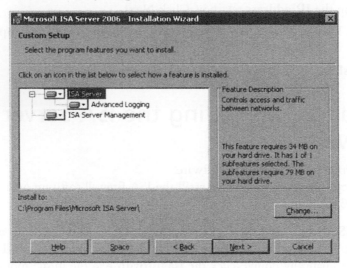

8. On the **Internal Network** page, click **Change**. The Internal network is different from the Local Address Table (LAT) used by ISA Server 2000. The Internal network contains trusted network services with which the ISA firewall must communicate. Examples of such services include Active Directory domain controllers, DNS, DHCP, terminal services client management workstations, and others. The firewall System Policy uses the Internal network definition in many of its System Policy Rules.

9. On the **Addresses** setup page, click the **Add Adapter** button.

10. Put a checkmark next to the adapter connected to the Internal network. In this example we have renamed the network interfaces so that the interface name reflects its location. Click **OK**.

Figure 3.23 The Select Network Adapter Page

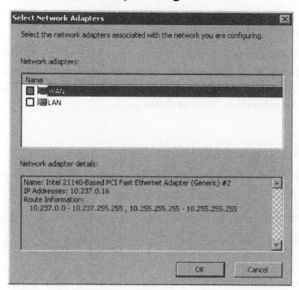

11. Click **OK** in the **Internal network address ranges** dialog box.

12. Click **Next** on the **Internal Network** page.

13. Put a checkmark by **Allow non-encrypted Firewall client connections** (Figure 3.10) if you want to support Firewall clients running previous versions of the Winsock Proxy (Proxy Server 2.0) or the ISA Server 2000 Firewall client software. This will allow you to continue using the ISA Server 2000 Firewall client software as you migrate to ISA Server 2006. When you migrate your Firewall clients to the ISA 2006 version of the Firewall client, the channel between the Firewall clients and the ISA firewall will be encrypted. The ISA 2006 Firewall client software encrypts the user credentials that are transparently sent from the Firewall client machine to the ISA firewall. For best security practice, it is recommended that you deploy the latest version of the Firewall Client software. This can be downloaded from http://www.microsoft.com/downloads/details.aspx?displaylang=en& FamilyID=05c2c932-b15a-4990-b525-66380743da89

14. On the **Services** page, note that the **SNMP** and **IIS Admin Service** will be stopped during installation. If the **Internet Connection Firewall (ICF) / Internet Connection Sharing (ICF)** and/or **IP Network Address Translation** services are installed on the ISA Server 2006 machine, they will be disabled, as they conflict with the ISA Server 2006 firewall software.

15. Click **Install** on the **Ready to Install the Program** page.

16. On the **Installation Wizard Completed** page, click **Finish**.

17. Click **Yes** on the **Microsoft ISA Server** dialog box informing that you must restart the server.

18. Log on as an **Administrator** after the machine restarts.

19. Click **Start** and point to **All Programs**. Point to **Microsoft ISA Server**, and click **ISA Server Management**. The **Microsoft Internet Security and Acceleration Server 2006** management console opens and displays the **Welcome to Microsoft Internet Security and Acceleration Server 2006** page.

Configuring the ISA Firewall

Now we're ready to configure Access Policy on the ISA firewall. We need to create the following five Access Rules:

- A rule that allows Internal Network clients access to the DHCP server on the ISA firewall.

- A rule that allows the ISA firewall to send DHCP messages to the hosts on the Internal network.

- A rule that allows the Internal Network DNS server to use the ISA firewall as its DNS server. Create this rule only if you have an Internal Network DNS server.

- A rule that allows Internal Network clients access to the caching-only DNS server on the ISA firewall. Use this rule if you do not have a DNS server on the Internal Network, or if you have a DNS server on the Internal Network and you want to use the ISA firewall as a caching-only DNS server with a stub zone pointing to your Internal Network domain.

- An "All Open" rule allowing Internal Network clients access to all protocols and sites on the Internet.

Tables 3.7 through 3.11 show the details of each of these rules.

Table 3.7 DHCP Request to Server

Name	DHCP Request to Server
Action	Allow
Protocols	DHCP (request)
From	Anywhere
To	Local Host
Users	All Users
Schedule	Always
Content Types	All content types
Purpose	This rule allows DHCP clients to send DHCP requests to the DHCP server installed on the ISA firewall.

Table 3.8 DHCP Reply from Server

Name	DHCP Reply from Server
Action	Allow
Protocols	DHCP (reply)
From	Local Host
To	Internal
Users	All Users
Schedule	Always
Content Types	All content types
Purpose	This rule allows the DHCP server on the ISA firewall to reply to DHCP requests made by Internal network DHCP clients.

Table 3.9 Internal DNS Server to Forwarder

Name	Internal DNS Server to DNS forwarder
Action	Allow
Protocols	DNS
From	DNS Server*
To	Local Host
Users	All Users
Schedule	Always
Content Types	All content types
Purpose	This rule allows the Internal network DNS server to forward queries to the DNS forwarder on the ISA Server 2006 firewall machine. **Create this rule only if you have an Internal Network DNS server.**

* User defined

Table 3.10 Internal Network to DNS Server

Name	Internal Network to DNS Server
Action	Allow
Protocols	DNS
From	Internal
To	Local Host
Users	All Users
Schedule	Always
Content Types	All content types

Continued

Table 3.10 Continued

Purpose	This rule allows Internal network clients access to the caching-only DNS server on the ISA firewall. Create this rule if you do not have an Internal Network DNS server, or if you have decided that you want to use the caching-only DNS server as your caching-only forwarder for all Internal Network clients, even when you have an Internal Network DNS server.

Table 3.11 All Open

Name	All Open
Action	Allow
Protocols	All Outbound Traffic
From	Internal
To	External
Users	All Users
Schedule	Always
Content Types	All content types
Purpose	This rule allows Internal network clients access to all protocols and sites on the Internet.

ISA FIREWALL WARNING

This last rule, **All Open**, is used only to get you up and running. This All Open rule allows you to test the ISA firewall's basic Internet connection ability, but does not provide any outbound access control in a manner similar to most hardware packet-filter firewalls. The ISA firewall provides advanced inbound and outbound protection, so you want to be sure to disable the All Open rule and create per user/group, per protocol and per site rules after your basic Internet connections through the ISA firewall are successful.

In addition to these Access Rules, you should configure the firewall System Policy to allow DHCP replies from External network DHCP servers.

DHCP Request to Server Rule

Perform the following steps to create the **DHCP Request to Server** rule:

1. In the **Microsoft Internet Security and Acceleration Server 2004** management console, expand the server name, and click **Firewall Policy**.

2. In the **Firewall Policy** node, click the **Tasks** tab in the Task pane. On the Task pane, click **Create a New Access Rule**.

3. On the **Welcome to the New Access Rule Wizard** page, enter **DHCP Request to Server** in the **Access Rule name** text box. Click **Next**.

4. On the **Rule Action** page, select **Allow**, and click **Next**.

5. On the **Protocols** page, select the **Selected protocols** option from the **This rule applies to** list, and click **Add**.

6. In the **Add Protocols** dialog box (Figure 3.24), click the **Infrastructure** folder. Double-click the **DHCP (request)** entry, and click **Close**.

Figure 3.24 The Add Protocols Dialog Box

7. Click **Next** on the **Protocols** page.

8. On the **Access Rule Sources** page, click **Add**.

9. In the **Add Network Entities** dialog box, click the **Computer Sets** folder. Double-click the **Anywhere** entry, and click **Close**.

10. Click **Next** on the **Access Rule Sources** page.

11. On the **Access Rule Destinations** page, click **Add**.

12. In the **Add Network Entities** dialog box, click the **Networks** folder, and double-click **Local Host**. Click **Close**.

13. Click **Next** on the **Access Rule Destinations** page.

14. On the **User Sets** page, accept the default entry, **All Users**, and click **Next**.

15. On the **Completing the New Access Rule Wizard** page, review the settings, and click **Finish**.

DHCP Reply from Server Rule

Perform the following steps to create the **DHCP Reply from Server** rule:

1. In the **Microsoft Internet Security and Acceleration Server 2004** management console, expand the server name, and click **Firewall Policy**.

2. In the **Firewall Policy** node, click the **Tasks** tab in the Task pane. On the Task pane, click **Create a New Access Rule**.

3. On the **Welcome to the New Access Rule Wizard** page, enter **DHCP Reply from Server** in the **Access Rule name** text box. Click **Next**.

4. On the **Rule Action** page, select **Allow**, and click **Next**.

5. On the **Protocols** page, select the **Selected protocols** option from the **This rule applies to** list, and click **Add**.

6. In the **Add Protocols** dialog box, click the **Infrastructure** folder. Double-click **DHCP (reply)**, and click **Close**.

7. Click **Next** on the **Protocols** page.

8. On the **Access Rule Sources** page, click **Add**.

Figure 3.25 The Protocols Page

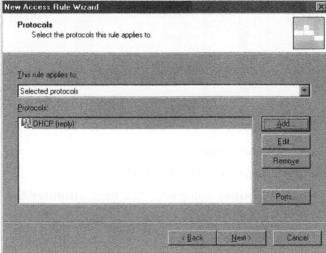

9. In the **Add Network Entities** dialog box, click the **Networks** folder. Double-click the **Local Host** entry, and click **Close**.

10. Click **Next** on the **Access Rule Sources** page.

11. On the **Access Rule Destinations** page, click **Add**.

12. In the **Add Network Entities** dialog box, click the **Networks** folder, and then double-click the **Internal** entry. Click **Close**.

13. Click **Next** on the **Access Rule Destinations** page.

14. On the **User Sets** page, accept the default entry, **All Users**, and click **Next**.

15. On the **Completing the New Access Rule Wizard** page, review the settings, and click **Finish**.

Internal DNS Server to DNS Forwarder Rule

Perform the following steps to create the **Internal DNS Server to DNS Forwarder** rule:

1. In the **Microsoft Internet Security and Acceleration Server 2004** management console, expand the server name, and click **Firewall Policy**.

2. In the **Firewall Policy** node, click the **Tasks** tab in the Task pane. On the Task pane, click **Create a New Access Rule**.

3. On the **Welcome to the New Access Rule Wizard** page, enter **Internal DNS Server to DNS Forwarder** in the **Access Rule name** text box. Click **Next**.

4. On the **Rule Action** page, select **Allow**, and click **Next**.

5. On the **Protocols** page, select the **Selected protocols** option from the **This rule applies to** list, and click **Add**.

6. In the **Add Protocols** dialog box, click the **Infrastructure** folder. Double-click the **DNS** entry, and click **Close**.

7. Click **Next** on the **Protocols** page.

8. On the **Access Rule Sources** page, click **Add**.

9. In the **Add Network Entities** dialog box (Figure 3.26), click the **New** menu, then click **Computer**.

Figure 3.26 Selecting the Computer Command

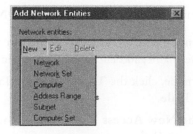

10. In the **New Computer Rule Element** dialog box, enter **Internal DNS Server** in the **Name** text box. Enter **10.0.0.2** in the **Computer IP Address** text box. Click **OK**.

11. In the **Add Network Entities** dialog box (Figure 3.27), click the **Computers** folder, and double-click **Internal DNS Server**. Click **Close**.

Figure 3.27 Selecting the New Computer Object

12. Click **Next** on the **Access Rule Sources** page.

13. On the **Access Rule Destinations** page, click **Add**.

14. In the **Add Network Entities** dialog box, click the **Networks** folder, and double-click **Local Host**. Click **Close**.

15. Click **Next** on the **Access Rule Destinations** page.

16. On the **User Sets** page, accept the default entry, **All Users**, and click **Next**.

17. On the **Completing the New Access Rule Wizard** page, review the settings, and click **Finish**.

Internal Network to DNS Server

Perform the following steps to create the **Internal Network to DNS Server** rule:

1. In the **Microsoft Internet Security and Acceleration Server 2006** management console, expand the server name, and click **Firewall Policy**.

2. In the **Firewall Policy** node, click the **Tasks** tab in the Task pane. On the Task pane, click **Create a New Access Rule**.

3. On the **Welcome to the New Access Rule Wizard** page, enter **Internal Network to DNS Server** in the **Access Rule name** text box. Click **Next**.

4. On the **Rule Action** page, select **Allow**, and click **Next**.

5. On the **Protocols** page, select the **Selected protocols** option from the **This rule applies to** list, and click **Add**.

6. In the **Add Protocols** dialog box, click the **Common Protocols** folder. Double-click the **DNS** entry, and click **Close**.

7. Click **Next** on the **Protocols** page.

8. On the **Access Rule Sources** page, click **Add**.

9. In the **Add Network Entities** dialog box, click the **Networks** folder. Double-click **Internal**, and click **Close**.

10. Click **Next** on the **Access Rule Sources** page.

11. On the **Access Rule Destinations** page, click **Add**.

12. In the **Add Network Entities** dialog box, click the **Networks** folder, and double-click **Local Host**. Click **Close**.

13. Click **Next** on the **Access Rule Destinations** page.

14. On the **User Sets** page, accept the default entry, **All Users**, and click **Next**.

15. On the **Completing the New Access Rule Wizard** page, review the settings, and click **Finish**.

The All Open Rule

Perform the following steps to create the **All Open** rule:

1. In the **Microsoft Internet Security and Acceleration Server 2006** management console, expand the server name, and click **Firewall Policy**.

2. In the **Firewall Policy** node, click the **Tasks** tab in the Task pane. On the Task pane, click **Create a New Access Rule**.

3. On the **Welcome to the New Access Rule Wizard** page, enter **All Open** in the **Access Rule name** text box. Click **Next**.

4. On the **Rule Action** page, select **Allow**, and click **Next**.

5. On the **Protocols** page, select **All outbound traffic** from the **This rule applies to** list, and click **Next**.

6. On the **Access Rule Sources** page, click **Add**.

7. In the **Add Network Entities** dialog box, click the **Networks** folder. Double-click **Internal**, and click **Close**.

8. Click **Next** on the **Access Rule Sources** page.

9. On the **Access Rule Destinations** page, click **Add**.

10. In the **Add Network Entities** dialog box, click the **Networks** folder, and double-click **External**. Click **Close**.

11. Click **Next** on the **Access Rule Destinations** page.

12. On the **User Sets** page, accept the default entry, **All Users**, and click **Next**.

13. On the **Completing the New Access Rule Wizard** page, review the settings, and click **Finish**.

Your Access Rule should look like those in Figure 3.28. Note that in this example, you do not need to reorder the rules. When you start creating advanced Access Rules to control inbound and outbound access, you may need to reorder rules to obtain the desired results.

Figure 3.28 The Resulting Firewall Policy

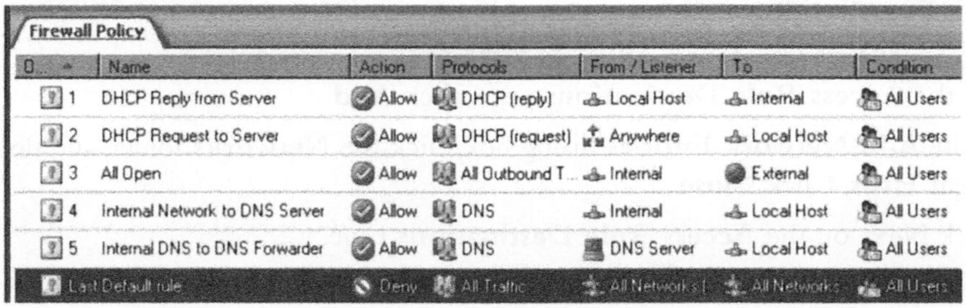

Configuring the Internal Network Computers

Internal Network computers are set up as ISA Server *SecureNAT* clients. A SecureNAT client is a machine with a default gateway address set to an IP address of a network device that routes Internet-bound requests to the internal IP address of the 2006 ISA Server 2006 firewall.

When Internal network computers are on the same network ID as the internal interface of the ISA firewall, the default gateway of the internal network computers is set as the internal IP address on the ISA firewall machine. This is how the DHCP scope on the DHCP server located on the ISA firewall is configured.

We will configure internal network computers that are on the same network ID as the internal interface of the 2006 ISA Server 2006 firewall and clients that may be located on network IDs that are not on the same network ID. This latter configuration is more common on larger networks that have more than one network ID on the internal network.

ISA FIREWALL NOTE

The "network ID" is part of the IP address. Network IDs are part of advanced TCP/IP networking concepts. Typically, SOHO networks have only one Network ID and you do not need to be concerned about knowing your network ID. If you have a router anywhere *behind* the ISA firewall, you need to understand network IDs.

Configuring Internal Clients as DHCP Clients

DHCP clients request IP addressing information from a DHCP server. In this section, you will find out how to configure the Windows (Server or Professional) client as a DHCP client. The procedure is similar for all Windows-based clients. Perform the following steps to configure the internal network client and a DHCP client:

1. Right-click **My Network Places** on the desktop, and click **Properties**.

2. In the **Network Connections** window, right-click the external network interface, and click **Properties**.

3. In the network interface's **Properties** dialog box, click the **Internet Protocol (TCP/IP)** entry, and click **Properties**.

4. In the **Internet Protocol (TCP/IP) Properties** dialog box (Figure 3.29), select **Obtain an IP address automatically**.

Figure 3.29 The Internet Protocol (TCP/IP) Properties Dialog Box

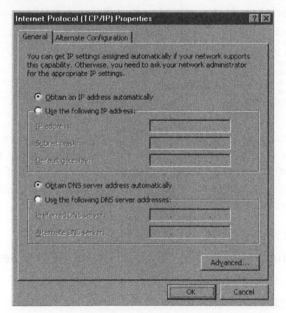

5. Select **Use the following DNS server addresses**. Enter the IP address of the internal interface in the **Preferred DNS server** text box. Click **OK** in the **Internet Protocol (TCP/IP) Properties** dialog box.

6. Click **OK** in the internal interface's **Properties** dialog box.

In Figure 3.30, you can see a Network Monitor trace of a Windows XP client sending a request to the caching-only DNS server on the ISA firewall for an Internal Network domain for which we created a stub zone. The following eight frames are in the trace:

1. The client sends a reverse lookup query to the DNS server for the IP address of the DNS server itself. This allows the client to ascertain the name of the DNS server.

2. The caching-only DNS server on the ISA firewall responds to the Windows XP client with the answer to the query made in frame #1.

3. The Windows XP client sends a query to the caching-only DNS server on the ISA firewall for www.msfireall.org. The msfireall.org domain is the name of the Internal Network domain.

4. An ARP broadcast is made by the ISA firewall to discover the IP address of the DNS server authoritative for the Internal Network domain.

5. The DNS server returns its IP address to the ISA firewall in an ARP broadcast.

6. The ISA firewall sends a query to the Internal DNS server to resolve the name of the Internal domain host.

7. The Internal DNS server returns the answer to the query to the ISA firewall.

8. The ISA firewall returns the response to the Windows XP client that made the original request.

Figure 3.30 DNS Queries in Network Monitor Trace

```
DNS       0x1:Std Qry for 1.0.0.10.in-addr.arpa. of type Dom. na...   10.0.0.5    10.0.0.1
DNS       0x1:Std Qry Resp. for 1.0.0.10.in-addr.arpa. of type D...   10.0.0.1    10.0.0.5
DNS       0x2:Std Qry for www.msfirewall.org. of type Host Addr ...   10.0.0.5    10.0.0.1
ARP_RARP  ARP: Request, Target IP: 10.0.0.2
ARP_RARP  ARP: Reply, Target IP: 10.0.0.1 Target Hdwr Addr: 000C...
DNS       0x30F8:Std Qry for www.msfirewall.org. of type Host Ad...   10.0.0.1    10.0.0.2
DNS       0x30F8:Std Qry Resp. Auth. NS is msfirewall.org. of ty...   10.0.0.2    10.0.0.1
DNS       0x2:Std Qry Resp. Auth. NS is msfirewall.org. of type ...   10.0.0.1    10.0.0.5
```

Figure 3.31 shows the domains cached on the caching-only DNS server located on the ISA firewall. You can enable the Advanced View in the DNS console and see the **Cached Lookups** node. After expanding the **.(root)** folder, you can see the domains for which the DNS server has cached DNS query information. If you double-click on any of the domains, you will see the actual resource records that the DNS server has cached.

Figure 3.31 DNS Domains Cached by the Caching-only DNS Server on the ISA Firewall

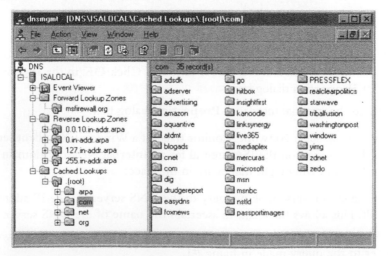

Hardening the Base ISA Firewall Configuration and Operating System

While the ISA firewall software does an exceptional job of protecting the firewall from attack, there are things you can do to further harden the ISA firewall configuration and the underlying operating system.

In this section, we'll discuss the following hardening and local security issues:

- **ISA firewall service dependencies** You need to know what services the ISA firewall depends on before disabling services on the firewall. In this section, we'll present the list of ISA firewall software dependencies.

- **Service requirements for common tasks performed on the ISA firewall** There are several maintenance tasks that you can run on the ISA firewall that depend on features provided by the underlying operating system. In this section, we'll examine some of these features and the services they depend upon.

- **Client roles for the ISA firewall client rules** This ISA firewall may need to act as a network client to a variety of network services. In this section, we'll review some of the network client roles and operating system services required for the ISA firewall to fulfill those roles.

- **ISA firewall administrative roles and permissions** Not all ISA firewall administrators are created equal. In this section, we'll discuss the ISA firewall administrative roles and how to provide users more granular control over the ISA firewall configuration and management.

- **ISA firewall lockdown mode** The ISA firewall needs to protect itself and the networks dependent on it in the event that an attack shuts down the ISA firewalls Firewall Service. In this section, we'll discuss the ISA firewall's Lockdown Mode.

ISA Firewall Service Dependencies

One of the more frustrating aspects of the ISA Server 2000 firewall was that there was never any definitive guidance regarding what services were required for full firewall functionality. Many ISA fans attempted to divine the service dependencies, but no hard and fast guidance was ever developed. To make life even more difficult for the ISA Server 2000 firewall administrator, the ISA Server 2000 System Hardening Templates invariably broke key features of the firewall and the underlying operating system.

These problems are corrected with the new ISA firewall. Now we know the exact services required by the ISA firewall software. Table 3.12 lists the core services that must be enabled for ISA Server and the ISA Server computer to function properly.

ISA FIREWALL WARNING

Do not use any of the default security templates included with the version of Windows on which you've installed the ISA firewall software. You should create your own custom security policy on the ISA firewall and then create a template based on that policy.

Table 3.12 Services on which the ISA Firewall Software Depends

Service name	Rationale	Startup mode
COM+ Event System	Core operating system	Manual
Cryptographic Services	Core operating system (security)	Automatic
Event Log	Core operating system	Automatic
IPSec Services	Core operating system (security)	Automatic
Logical Disk Manager	Core operating system (disk management)	Automatic
Logical Disk Manager Administrative Service	Core operating system (disk management)	Manual
Microsoft Firewall	Required for normal functioning of ISA Server	Automatic
Microsoft ISA Server Control	Required for normal functioning of ISA Server	Automatic
Microsoft ISA Server Job Scheduler	Required for normal functioning of ISA Server	Automatic
Microsoft ISA Server Storage	Required for normal functioning of ISA Server	Automatic
MSSQL$MSFW	Required when MSDE logging is used for ISA Server	Automatic
Network Connections	Core operating system (network infrastructure)	Manual
NTLM Security Support Provider	Core operating system (security)	Manual
Plug and Play	Core operating system	Automatic
Protected Storage	Core operating system (security)	Automatic

Table 3.12 Continued

Service name	Rationale	Startup mode
Remote Access Connection Manager	Required for normal functioning of ISA Server	Manual
Remote Procedure Call (RPC)	Core operating system	Automatic
Secondary Logon	Core operating system (security)	Automatic
Security Accounts Manager	Core operating system	Automatic
Server*	Required for ISA Server Firewall Client Share (and others depending on your requirements)*	Automatic*
Smart Card	Core operating system (security)	Manual
SQLAgent$MSFW	Required when MSDE logging is used for ISA Server (not installed when Advanced Logging is not selected during installation)	Manual
System Event Notification	Core operating system	Automatic
Telephony	Required for normal functioning of ISA Server	Manual
Virtual Disk Service (VDS)	Core operating system (disk management)	Manual
Windows Management Instrumentation (WMI)	Core operating system (WMI)	Automatic
WMI Performance Adapter	Core operating system (WMI)	Manual

* The startup mode for the Server service should be set as Automatic in the following circumstances:

- You install Firewall client installation share on the ISA firewall
- You use Routing and Remote Access Management, rather than ISA Server Management, to configure a virtual private network (VPN). Required if you want to use EAP user certificate authentication for demand-dial VPN connections and troubleshooting of demand-dial VPN connections
- IF other tasks or roles table require the Server service
- The startup mode for the Routing and Remote Access service is Manual. ISA Server starts the service only if a VPN is enabled. Note that the Server service is required only if you need access to Routing and Remote Access console (rather than Microsoft Internet Security and Acceleration Server 2006 management console) to configure a remote-access VPN or site-to-site.

Service Requirements for Common Tasks Performed on the ISA Firewall

Specific services must be enabled in order for the ISA firewall to perform necessary tasks. All services that are not used should be disabled. Table 3.13 lists a number of tasks the ISA firewall's underlying operating system may need to perform. Enable those services required to perform the tasks you want to perform on the ISA firewall and disable services responsible for tasks you will not be using.

Table 3.13 Services Required for Common Tasks Performed on the ISA Firewall

Task	Usage scenario	Services required	Startup mode
Application Installation locally using Windows Installer	Required to install, uninstall, or repair applications using the Microsoft Installer Service. Often required to install ISA firewall add-ins to enhance firewall functionality and protection	Windows Installer	Manual
Backup	Required if using NTBackup or other backup programs on the ISA firewall	Microsoft Software Shadow Copy Provider	Manual
Backup	Required if using NTBackup or other backup programs on the ISA firewall	Volume Shadow Copy	Manual
Backup	Required if using NTBackup or other backup program on the ISA firewall	Removable Storage Service	Manual
Error Reporting	Required for error reporting, which helps improve Windows reliability by reporting critical faults to Microsoft for analysis	Error Reporting Service	Automatic
Help and Support	Allows collection of historical computer data for Microsoft Product Support Services incident escalation	Help and Support	Automatic

Table 3.13 Continued

Task	Usage scenario	Services required	Startup mode
Host the Firewall client installation share	Required to allow computers SMB/CIFS connections to the ISA firewall to install the Firewall client software	Server	Automatic
MSDE logging	Required to allow logging using MSDE databases. If you do not enable the applicable service, you can log to SQL databases or to files. However, you will not be able to use the Log Viewer in off-line mode. Required only when ISA Advanced logging is installed	SQLAgent$MSFW	Manual
MSDE logging	Required to allow logging using MSDE databases. If you do not enable the applicable service, you can log to SQL databases or to files. However, you will not be able to use the Log Viewer in off-line mode. Required only when Advanced logging is installed	MSSQL$MSFW	Automatic
Performance Monitor – Background Collect	Allows background collecting of performance data on the ISA firewall	Performance Logs and Alerts	Automatic
Print to a remote computer	Allows printing from the ISA Server computer (not recommended)	Print Spooler	Automatic
Print to a remote computer	Allows printing from the ISA Server computer (not recommended that you send print jobs from the ISA firewall)	TCP/IP NetBIOS Helper	Automatic

Continued

www.syngress.com

Table 3.13 Continued

Task	Usage scenario	Services required	Startup mode
Print to a remote computer	Allows printing from the ISA Server computer (not recommended that you send print jobs from the ISA firewall)	Workstation	Automatic
Remote Windows administration	Allows remote management of the Windows server (not required for remote management of the ISA firewall software)	Server	Automatic
Remote Windows administration	Allows remote management of the Windows server (not required for remote management of the ISA firewall software)	Remote Registry	Automatic
Time Synchronization	Allows the ISA firewall to contact an NTP server to synchronize its clock. An accurate clock is important for event auditing and other security protocols.	Windows Time	Automatic
Remote Assistant	Allows the Remote Assistance feature to be used on this computer (not recommended that you run remote assistance sessions from the ISA firewall)	Help and Support	Automatic
Remote Assistant	Allows the Remote Assistance feature to be used on this computer (not recommended that you run remote assistance sessions from the ISA firewall)	Remote Desktop Help Session Manager	Manual
Remote Assistant	Allows the Remote Assistance feature to be used on this computer	Terminal Services	Manual

Client Roles for the ISA Firewall

The ISA firewall may need to act in the role of client to network services located on protected and non-protected Networks. Network client services are required for the ISA firewall to act in its role of network client. Table 3.14 lists possible network client roles the ISA firewall may act as, describes when they may be required, and lists the services that should be enabled when you enable the role.

ISA FIREWALL NOTE

You will also need to enable the automatic update services if you are using a WUS or SUS server on your network.

Table 3.14 Service Requirements Based on the ISA Firewall's Client Roles

Client role	Usage scenario	Services required	Startup mode
Automatic Update client	Select this role to allow automatic detection and update from Microsoft Windows Update.	Automatic Updates	Automatic
Automatic Update client	Select this role to allow automatic detection and update from Microsoft Windows Update.	Background Intelligent Transfer Service	Manual
DHCP client	Select this role if the ISA Server computer receives its IP address automatically from a DHCP server.	DHCP Client	Automatic
DNS client	Select this role if the ISA Server computer needs to receive name resolution information from other servers.	DNS Client	Automatic
Domain member	Select this role if the ISA Server computer belongs to a domain.	Network location awareness (NLA)	Manual

Continued

www.syngress.com

Table 3.14 Continued

Client role	Usage scenario	Services required	Startup mode
Domain member	Select this role if the ISA Server computer belongs to a domain.	Net logon	Automatic
Domain member	Select this role if the ISA Server computer belongs to a domain.	Windows Time	Automatic
Dynamic DNS registration	Select this role to allow the ISA Server computer to automatically register its name and address information with a DNS Server.	DHCP Client	Automatic
Microsoft Networking client	Select this role if the ISA Server computer has to connect to other Windows clients. If you do not select this role, the ISA Server computer will not be able to access shares on remote computers; for example, to publish reports.	TCP/IP NetBIOS Helper	Automatic
Microsoft Networking client	Select this role if the ISA Server computer has to connect to other Windows clients. If you do not select this role, the ISA Server computer will not be able to access shares on remote computers; for example, to publish reports.	Workstation	Automatic
WINS client	Select this role if the ISA. Server computer uses WINS-based name resolution	TCP/IP NetBIOS Helper	Automatic

After determining the appropriate service configuration for your ISA firewall, you can save the configuration in a Windows security template (.inf) file. Check www.isaserver.org for sample ISA security templates covering several common scenarios.

ISA Firewall Administrative Roles and Permissions

Not all firewall administrators should have the same level of control over the ISA firewall's configuration and management. The ISA firewall allows you to provide three levels of control over the firewall software based on the role assigned to the user.

The ISA firewall's Administrative Roles are:

- ISA Server Basic Monitoring
- ISA Server Extended Monitoring
- ISA Server Full Administrator

Table 3.15 describes the functions of each of these roles.

Table 3.15 ISA Firewall Administrative Roles

Role	Description
ISA Server Basic Monitoring	Users and groups assigned this role can monitor the ISA Server computer and network activity, but cannot configure specific monitoring functionality.
ISA Server Extended Monitoring	Users and groups assigned this role can perform all monitoring tasks, including log configuration, alert definition configuration, and all monitoring functions available to the ISA Server Basic Monitoring role.
ISA Server Full Administrator	Users and groups assigned this role can perform any ISA Server task, including rule configuration, applying of network templates, and monitoring.

Users assigned to these roles can be created in the ISA firewall's local SAM, or they can be domain users if the ISA firewall is a member of the Internal network Active Directory domain. Any users can be assigned to one of the ISA firewall's Administrative roles, and no special privileges or Windows permissions are required. The only exception to this is when a user needs to monitor the ISA Server performance counters using Perfmon or the ISA Server Dashboard; the user must be a member of the Windows Server 2003 Performance Monitors User group.

Each ISA Server role has a specific list of firewall administrator and configuration tasks associated with it. Table 3.16 lists some firewall tasks and the Administrative roles that are allowed to perform each task.

Table 3.16 ISA Firewall Tasks Assigned to ISA Firewall Administrative Roles

Activity	Basic Monitoring permissions	Extended Monitoring permissions	Full Administrator permissions
View Dashboard, alerts, connectivity, sessions, services	X	X	X
Acknowledge alerts	X	X	X
View log information		X	X
Create alert definitions		X	X
Create reports		X	X
Stop and start sessions and services		X	X
View firewall policy		X	X
Configure firewall policy			X
Configure cache			X
Configure VPN			X

ISA FIREWALL ALERT

Users with ISA Server Extended Monitoring permissions can export and import all configuration information, including secret configuration information. This means that they can potentially decrypt secret information.

To assign administrative roles, perform the following steps:

1. Click **Start**, point to **All Programs**, point to **Microsoft ISA Server**, and click **ISA Server Management**.

2. Click the server name in the left pane of the **Microsoft Internet Security and Acceleration Server 2006** management console. Click **Define Administrative Roles** on the **Tasks** tab.

3. On the **Welcome to the ISA Server Administration Delegation Wizard** page, click **Next**.

4. On the **Delegate Control** page, click **Add**.

5. In **Group (recommended) or User** dialog box, enter the name of the group or user to which the specific administrative permissions will be assigned. Click the down arrow in the **Role** drop-down list and select the applicable administrative role. Click **OK**.

6. Click **Next** on the **Delegate Control** page.

7. Click **Finish** on the **Completing the Administration Delegation Wizard** page.

8. Click **Apply** to save the changes and update the firewall policy.

9. Click **OK** in the **Apply New Configuration** dialog box.

Lockdown Mode

The ISA firewall sports a new feature that combines the need to isolate the firewall and all Protected Networks from harm in the event that the ISA firewall is attacked, to the extent that the Firewall services are shut down. The ISA firewall accomplishes a combination of protection and protective accessibility by entering *lockdown mode*.

Lockdown mode occurs when:

1. An attack or some other network or local host event causes the Firewall service to shut down. This can happen from a fault, or you can do it explicitly by configuring Alerts and then configuring an Alert Action that shuts down the Firewall service in response to the issue that triggered the Alert.

2. Lockdown mode occurs when the Firewall service is manually shut down. You can shut down the Firewall service if you become aware of an ongoing attack while configuring the ISA firewall and the network to effectively respond to the attack.

Lockdown Mode Functionality

When in lockdown mode, the following functionality applies:

1. The ISA Firewall's Packet Filter Engine (fweng) applies the lockdown firewall policy.

2. Firewall policy rules permits outgoing traffic from the Local Host network to all networks, if allowed. If an outgoing connection is established, that connection can be used to respond to incoming traffic. For example, a DNS query can receive a DNS response on the same connection. This does not imply that lockdown mode allows an extension of existing firewall policy for outbound access from the local host network. Only existing rules allowing outbound access from the local host network are allowed.

3. No new primary connections to the ISA firewall itself are allowed, unless a System Policy Rule that specifically allows the traffic is enabled. An exception is DHCP traffic, which is always allowed. DHCP requests (on UDP port 67) are allowed from the Local Host Network to all Networks, and DHCP replies (on UDP port 68) are allowed back in.

4. Remote-access VPN clients will not be able to connect to the ISA firewall. Site-to-site VPN connections will also be denied.

5. Any changes to the network configuration while in lockdown mode are applied only after the Firewall service restarts and the ISA firewall exits lockdown mode.

6. The ISA Server will not trigger any Alerts.

Connection Limits

The ISA firewall puts a limit on the number of connections made to or through it at any point in time. Connection limits allow the ISA firewall to block connections through the firewall for clients that may be infected with worms that attempt to establish large numbers of connections through the ISA firewall. Examples of such worms are mass mailing worms and the Blaster worm.

For Web Publishing Rules, you can customize a total number of connections limit by specifying a maximum number of concurrent connections in the Properties of the Web listener. Any new client requests will be denied when the maximum number of connections configured to the Web listener is reached.

You can limit the total number of UDP, ICMP, and other Raw IP sessions allowed by a Server Publishing Rule or Access Rule on a per-second basis. These limitations do not apply to TCP connections. When the specified number of connections is surpassed, new connections will not be created. Existing connections will not be disconnected.

You should begin by configuring low connection-limit thresholds. This enables the ISA firewall to limit malicious hosts from consuming resources on the ISA Server computer.

By default, connection limits for *non-TCP connections* are configured to 1000 connections *per second per rule* and to 160 connections *per client*.

Connection limits for TCP connections begin at 160 connections per client. You should not change these limits unless you notice that legitimate hosts are being blocked because the limiting is too low. You can determine if a host is being blocked because it has exceeded its connection limit by an associated Alert. The Alert will provide the IP address of the host exceeding its allowed number of connections.

Perform the following steps to configure connection limits:

1. Click **Start**, point to **All Programs**, point to **Microsoft ISA Server**, and click **ISA Server Management**.

2. Expand the server name in the left pane of the **Microsoft Internet Security and Acceleration Server 2006** management console, and expand the **Configuration** node. Click the **General** node.

3. Click **Configure Flood Mitigation Settings** in the details pane.

4. On the **Flood Mitigation** tab (Figure 3.32), click on each Edit button. You can then configure the number of **Connections created per second, per rule (non-TCP)** and **Connection limit per client (TCP and non-TCP)**. Some machines may need access in excess of these numbers, such as busy published servers. In that case, you can click **Add** and select a **Computer Set** to apply the **Customer connection limit** value.

New connections will not be created after the specified number of connections is exceeded. However, existing connections will not be disconnected. Up to 1000 new connections are allowed per rule, per second by default. When this default limit is exceeded, an alert is triggered.

Figure 3.32 The Connection Limits Dialog Box

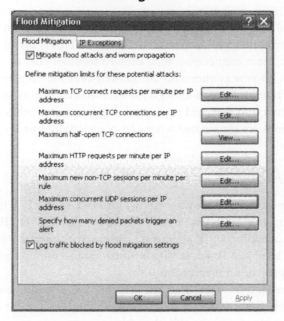

A log entry is recorded when the limit is exceeded:

- Action is Connection Denied

- Result code is FWX_E_RULE_QUOTA_EXCEEDED_DROPPED

You should limit the number of connections hosts can make to prevent flood attacks. Many requests are sent from spoofed source addresses when a UDP or IP flood attack occurs, and this can result in a denial of service.

Try the following when the limit is exceeded:

- If the malicious traffic appears to originate from an ISA firewall Protected Network, this may indicate a host on the Protected Network has a virus or worm infection. Immediately disconnect the computer from the network.

- Create a rule denying access to a computer set that includes the source IP addresses if the malicious traffic appears to originate from a small range of IP addresses on an external network.

- Evaluate the overall status of your network if the traffic appears to originate from a large range of IP addresses. Consider setting a smaller connection limit so that ISA Server can better protect your network.

If the limit has been exceeded due to a heavy load, consider setting a higher per-rule connection limit based on your analysis of your network's requirements.

In firewall chaining, and in some back-to-back ISA firewall scenarios, make sure to configure customized connection limits for the IP addresses of the chained server or back-end ISA firewall.

Also, if your system publishes more than one UDP-based or raw IP-based service to the External network, you should configure smaller limits to help keep your network secure from flood attacks.

You can limit the total number of UDP, ICMP, and other Raw IP connections allowed per client. You can specify custom limits to apply to specific IP addresses. This is useful when you want to allow specific servers to establish more connections than allowed to other clients.

For TCP connections, no new connections are allowed after the connection limit is exceeded. Make sure you set connection limits high enough for TCP-based services, such as SMTP, so that SMTP servers can send outbound mail and receive inbound mail. For other connections (Raw IP and UDP), older connections are terminated when the connection limit is exceeded so that new connections can be created.

DHCP Spoof Attack Prevention

Some of you may want to use DHCP on the external interface of the ISA firewall so that it can obtain IP addressing information from your cable or DSL company's DHCP server. You might encounter problems with obtaining an IP address on the external interface when that interface is configured to use DHCP to obtain IP addressing information. A common reason for this problem is the DHCP Spoof Attack prevention mechanism.

It's important to understand the DHCP attack prevention mechanism to solve this problem. For each adapter on which DHCP is enabled, the ISA firewall maintains the list of allowed addresses. There is an entry in the registry for each DHCP enabled adapter:

The registry key name is

```
HKLM\SYSTEM\CurrentControlSet\Services\Fweng\Parameters\DhcpAdapters\<Adapter's MAC>/
<Adapter's hardware type>
```

The values under the key are:

1. The adapter's name

2. The ISA network name of the adapter

3. The adapter's MAC address

4. ISA network addresses

5. The adapter's hardware type

Figure 3.33 shows an example of the registry key.

Figure 3.33 Registry Key for DHCP Attack Prevention

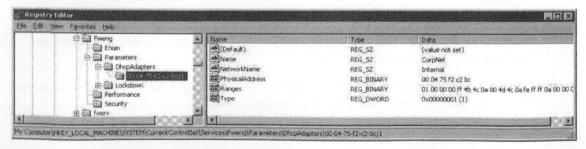

When the ISA firewall's driver sees a DHCP Offer message, it validates the offer using the following logic:

1. Using the DHCP "Client Ethernet Address" field and the "Hardware Type" field, the driver finds the corresponding registry key of the adapter.

2. If there is no registry key, the packet is allowed (this will be the case during initial setup of the ISA firewall software).

3. The driver verifies that "Your IP Address" field in the DHCP Offer contains an IP address within the addresses of the adapter's network element (as written in the registry).

4. If the verification fails, the packet is dropped, and an ISA alert is raised.

Figure 3.34 shows an example of a DHCP offer packet (the relevant fields are marked).

Figure 3.34 Network Monitor Capture of a DHCP Offer Packet

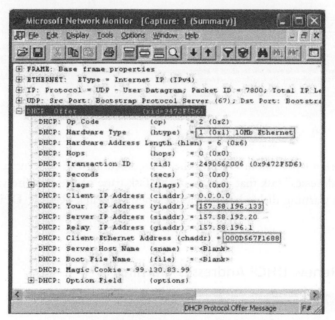

The invalid alert contains the following information (Figure 3.35).

Figure 3.35 An Invalid DHCP Offer Alert

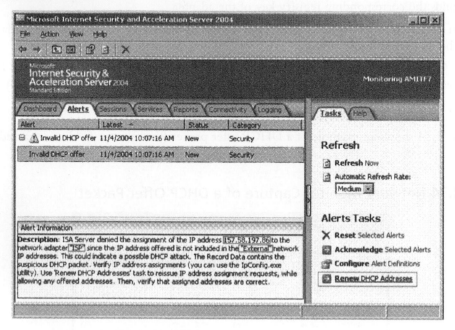

In case the network adapter should receive the offered address, the administrator should use the "Renew DHCP addresses" task that appears in the Task pane of the ISA firewall console. Figure 3.36 shows the warning dialog box you'll see when you click **Renew DHCP Addresses** in the Task pane.

Figure 3.36 The Renew DHCP Addresses Warning

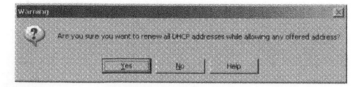

After clicking **Yes**, all registry keys related to DHCP attack prevention are deleted, and an "ipconfig /renew" is performed. This means that during this period, no offered address will be dropped by the driver (because there are no registry keys). Once the adapters receive their addresses, new registry keys are written with the new values, and the mechanism will be activated once again.

Dropped DHCP offers due to DHCP Attack Prevention may happen in the following scenarios:

1. If you have two DHCP adapters and you switched them. For example, the one that was connected to the internal network is now connected to the external network, and vice versa.

2. A DHCP adapter was moved to a different network. For example, ISA's external NIC was connected to a home network where another router made the connectivity to the ISP (and the Internet), and now you try replacing this router to use ISA's external NIC for connecting the ISP.

In such cases you need to use the **Renew DHCP Addresses** task, in order to allow the DHCP assignment. Note that once it's allowed, you will not need to allow it anymore. This procedure is needed only after changing the DHCP adapter in such a way that it becomes a member of a different ISA network element

One More Time

In this chapter, we discussed many issues related to planning and installing an ISA firewall. We also discussed default System Policy and Firewall configuration after installation is complete. A quick start configuration was discussed and described which will allow you to get up and running quickly.

Chapter 4

Creating and Using ISA 2006 Firewall Access Policy

Solutions in this chapter:

- ISA Firewall Access Rule Elements

- Configuring Access Rules for Outbound Access through the ISA Firewall

- Using Scripts to Populate Domain Name Sets

- Allowing Intradomain Communications through the ISA Firewall

The ISA firewall's Access Policy (also known as firewall policy) includes Web Publishing Rules, Server Publishing Rules and Access Rules. Web Publishing Rules and Server Publishing Rules are used to allow inbound access and Access Rules are used to control outbound access.

The concepts of inbound and outbound access are somewhat more confusing with the new ISA firewall, when compared to their interpretations in ISA Server 2000. The reason for this is that ISA Server 2000 was Local Address Table (LAT) based. The definitions of inbound and outbound access were relative to the LAT. Inbound access was defined as incoming connections from non-LAT hosts to LAT hosts (external to internal). In contrast, the new ISA firewall does not have a LAT and there is not a comparable concept of an "internal" network in the same way that there was an internal network defined by the LAT in ISA Server 2000.

In general, you should use Web Publishing Rules and Server Publishing Rules when you want to allow connections from hosts that are not located on an ISA firewall Protected Network to a host on an ISA firewall Protected Network. Access Rules are used to control access between any two networks. The only limitation is that you cannot create Access Rules to control access between networks that have a Network Address Translation (NAT) relationship when the initiating host is on the non-NAT'd site of the relationship.

For example, suppose you have a NAT relationship between the default Internal Network and the Internet. You can create Access Rules that control connections between the Internal Network and the Internet because the initiating hosts are on the NAT'd side of the network relationship. However, you cannot create an Access Rule between a host on the Internet and the Internal Network because the Internet hosts are on the non-NAT'd side of the network relationship.

In contrast, you can create Access Rules in *both* directions when there is a route relationship between the source and destination Networks. For example, suppose you have a route relationship between a DMZ segment and the Internet. In this case, you can create Access Rules controlling traffic between the DMZ and the Internet and you can also create Access Rules that control traffic between the Internet and the DMZ segment.

The main job of the ISA firewall is to control traffic between source and destination networks. The ISA firewall's Access Policy permits clients on the source network to access hosts on a destination network and Access Rules also can be configured to block hosts on a source network from connecting to hosts on a destination network. Access Policy determines how hosts access hosts on other networks.

This is a key concept. The source and destination hosts must be on different networks. The ISA firewall should never mediate communications between hosts on the same ISA network. We refer to this type of configuration as "looping back through the ISA firewall". You should never loop back through the ISA firewall to access resources on the same network.

When the ISA firewall intercepts an outbound connection request, it checks both network rules and firewall policy rules to determine if access is allowed. Network Rules are checked first. If there is no Network Rule defining a NAT or Route relationship between the source and destination networks, then the connection attempt will fail. This is a common reason for failed connections and it is something you should check for when Access Policy does not behave the way you expect it to.

Access Rules can be configured to apply to specific source and/or destination hosts. Clients can be specified either by IP address (for example, by using Computer or Computer Set Network Objects) or by user name. The ISA firewall processes the requests differently depending on which type of client is requesting the object and how the Access Rules are configured.

When a connection request is received by the ISA firewall, the first thing the ISA firewall does is check to see if there is a Network Rule defining the route relationship between the source and destination networks. If there is no Network Rule, the ISA firewall assumes that the source and destination networks are *not connected*. If there is a Network Rule defining a route relationship between the source and destination network, then the ISA firewall processes the Access Policy rules.

After the ISA firewall has confirmed that the source and destination networks are connected, Access Policy is processed. The ISA firewall processes the Access Rules in the Access Policy from the top down (System Policy is processed before user-defined Access Policy).

If an Allow rule is associated with the outbound connection request, the ISA firewall will allow the request. In order for the Allow rule to be applied, the characteristics of the connection request must match the characteristics defined by the Access Rule. The Access Rule will match the connection request if the connection request matches the following Access Rule parameters:

- Protocol
- From (source location, which can include a source port number)
- Schedule
- To (destination location, which can include addresses, names, URLs and other Network Objects)
- Users
- Content groups

If the settings for each of these parameters match those in the connection request, then the Access Rule will be applied to the connection. If the connection request doesn't match the parameters in the Access Rule, then the ISA firewall moves to the next rule in the firewall's Access Policy.

ISA Firewall Alert

If there are no System Policy or user-defined Access Rules that apply to the connection request, then the **Last Default rule** is applied. This rule blocks all communications through the ISA firewall.

If the Access Rule matches the parameters in the connection request, then the next step is for the ISA firewall to check the Network Rules once again to determine if there is a NAT or Route relationship between the source and destination Networks. The ISA firewall also checks for any Web chaining rules (if a Web Proxy client requested the object) or for a possible firewall chaining configuration (if a SecureNAT or firewall client requested the object) to determine how the request will be serviced.

ISA FIREWALL SECRET

Web Chaining Rules and Firewall Chaining both represent methods of ISA firewall routing. Web Chaining Rules can be configured to forward requests from Web Proxy clients to specific locations, such as upstream Web Proxy servers. Firewall chaining allows requests from SecureNAT and Firewall clients to be forwarded to upstream ISA firewalls. Both Web Chaining and Firewall Chaining Rules allow the ISA firewall to bypass its default gateway configuration for specific connection requests from Web Proxy and Firewall clients.

For example, suppose you have an ISA firewall with two NICs: one NIC is connected to the Internet and the other connected to the Internal Network. You have created a single "All Open" rule which allows all users access to all protocol to connect to all sites on the Internet.

This "All Open" policy would include the following rules on the ISA firewall:

- A Network Rule defining the route relationship between the source network (the Internal Network) and the destination Network (the Internet).

- An Access Rule allowing all internal clients access to all sites at all times, using any protocol.

The default configuration is to NAT between the default Internal Network and the Internet. However, you can Route between the Internal network (and any other network) and the Internet if you like (as long as you have public addresses on the network).

ISA Firewall Access Rule Elements

You construct Access Rules using Policy Elements. One of the major improvements in the new ISA firewall over ISA Server 2000 is the ability to create all Policy Elements "on the fly". That is, you can create all Policy Elements from within the New Access Rule Wizard. This greatly improves on ISA Server 2000, where you have to plan out your Policy Elements in advance and then create Protocol Rules and Publishing Rules *after* you configure your Policy Elements.

The ISA firewall includes the following Policy Elements:

- Protocols
- User Sets
- Content Types
- Schedules
- Network Objects

Protocols

The ISA firewall includes a number of built-in protocols that you can use right out of the box to create Access Rules, Web Publishing Rules and Server Publishing Rules.

In addition to the built-in protocols, you can create your own protocols by using the ISA firewall's New Protocol Wizard. The pre-built protocols cannot be modified or deleted. However, you can edit or delete protocols you create yourself. There are some protocols that are installed with application filters that cannot be modified, but they can be deleted. You do have the option to unbind application filters from protocols. For example, if you don't want Web requests for SecureNAT and Firewall clients to be forwarded to the Web Proxy filter, you can unbind the Web Proxy filter from the HTTP protocol. We'll examine this issue in more detail later in this chapter.

When you create a new Protocol Definition, you'll need to specify the following information:

- **Protocol Type.**   TCP, UDP, ICMP, or IP-level protocol. If you specify an ICMP protocol, then you'll need to include the ICMP type and code. Note that you cannot publish IP-level or ICMP protocols.

- **Direction.**   For UDP, this includes Send, Receive, Send Receive, or Receive Send. For TCP, this includes Inbound and Outbound. For ICMP and IP-level, this includes Send and Receive.

- **Port range.**   (for TCP and UDP protocols) This is a range of ports between 1 and 65535 that is used for the initial connection. IP-level and ICMP protocols do not use ports, as ports are part of the transport layer header.

- **Protocol number.**   (for IP-level protocols). This is the protocol number. For example, GRE uses IP protocol number 47.

- **ICMP properties.**   (for ICMP protocol). This is the ICMP code and type.

- (Optional) **Secondary connections.**   This is the range of ports, protocol types, and direction used for additional connections or packets that follow the initial connection. You can configure one or more secondary connections. Secondary connections can be inbound, outbound or both inbound and outbound.

NOTE

You cannot define secondary connections for IP-level primary protocols.

User Sets

In order to enable outbound access control, you can create Access Rules and apply them to specific Internet Protocol (IP) addresses or to specific users or groups of users. When Access Rules are applied to a user or group, the users will have to authenticate using the appropriate authentication protocol. The Firewall client always uses integrated authentication and always sends the user credentials transparently. The Web Proxy client can use a number of different authentication methods.

The ISA firewall allows you to group users and user groups together in User Sets or what we like to call "firewall groups". User sets include one or more users or groups from any authentication scheme supported by the ISA firewall. For example, a user set might include a Windows user, a user from a RADIUS namespace, and another user from the SecurID namespace. The Windows, RADIUS and SecurID namespaces all use different authentication schemes, but users from each of these can be included in a single User Set.

The ISA firewall comes preconfigured with the following user sets:

- **All Authenticated Users.**   This predefined user set represents all authenticated users, regardless of the method used to authenticate. An Access Rule using this set applies to authenticated users. When a rule applies to authenticated users, connections from SecureNAT clients will fail. An exception to this is when the SecureNAT client is also a VPN client. When a user creates a VPN connection to the ISA firewall, the VPN client automatically becomes a SecureNAT client. Although normally a SecureNAT client cannot send user credentials to the ISA firewall, when the SecureNAT client is also a VPN client, the VPN log on credentials can be used to authenticate the user.

- **All Users.**   This predefined User Set represents all users. A rule defined using this set will apply to all users, both authenticated and unauthenticated, and no credentials are required to access a rule configured to use this User Set. However, the Firewall client will always send credentials to the ISA firewall, even when authentication is not required. You'll see this in effect in the **Microsoft Internet Security and Acceleration Server 2006** management console, in the **Sessions** tab when a user name has a question mark next to it.

- **System and Network Service.**   This pre-built User Set represents the Local System service and the Network service on the ISA firewall machine itself. This User Set is used in some System Policy Rules.

Content Types

Content types specify Multipurpose Internet Mail Extensions (MIME) types and file extensions. When you create an access rule that applies to the HTTP protocol, you can limit what Content Types the Access Rule applies to. Content Type control allows you to be very granular when configuring Access Policy because you can control access not only on a protocol and destination basis, but also by specific content.

Content Type control only works with HTTP and tunneled FTP traffic. Content Type control will not work with FTP traffic that isn't handled by the ISA firewall's Web Proxy filter.

When an FTP request is made by a host on an ISA firewall Protected Network, the ISA firewall will check the file extension in the request. The ISA firewall then determines if the rule applies to a Content Type that includes the requested file extension and processes the rule accordingly. If the Content Type doesn't match, then the rule is ignored and the next rule in the Access Policy is checked.

When a host on an ISA firewall Protected Network makes an outbound HTTP request, the ISA firewall sends the request to the Web server via the Web Proxy filter (by default). When the Web server returns the requested Web object, the ISA firewall checks the object's MIME type (which is found in the HTTP header information) or its file extension (depending on the header information returned by the Web server.) The ISA firewall determines if the rule applies to the specified Content Type including the requested file extension, and processes the rule accordingly.

The ISA firewall comes with a pre-built list of Content Types that you can use right out of the box. You can also create your own Content Types. When you create your own Content Types, you should specify both MIME type and file extension.

For example, to include all Director files in a content type, select the following file name extensions and MIME types:

- .dir

- .dxr

- .dcr

- application/x-director

You can use an asterisk (★) as a wildcard character when configuring a MIME type. For example, to include all application types, enter **application/★**.

TIP

The wildcard character can be used only with MIME types. You *cannot* use wildcards for file extensions. You can use the wildcard only once and that is at the end of the MIME type after the slash (/).

The ISA firewall comes with the following pre-built Content Types:

- Application

- Application data files

- Audio

- Compressed files

- Documents

- HTML documents

- Images

- Macro documents

- Text

- Video

- VRML.

Controlling access via MIME type can be challenging because different MIME types are associated with different file name extensions. The reason for this is that the Web server controls the MIME type associated with the Web object returned to the user. While there is general agreement on how MIME types are defined, a Web site administrator has complete control over the MIME type associated with any content hosted by his Web server. Because of this, you will sometimes see that content that you had thought you had blocked using Content Types is not blocked. You can determine the MIME type used by the Web server returning the response by doing a Network Monitor trace. The HTTP header will show the MIME type returned by the Web server for the Web content requested by the requesting client.

The following table lists the Internet Information Services (IIS) default associations. You can use these for general reference.

Table 4.1 Default IIS MIME Types for common file extensions

File name extension	MIME type
.hta	application/hta
.isp	application/x-internet-signup
.crd	application/x-mscardfile
.pmc	application/x-perfmon
.spc	application/x-pkcs7-certificates
.sv4crc	application/x-sv4crc
.bin	application/octet-stream
.clp	application/x-msclip
.mny	application/x-msmoney
.p7r	application/x-pkcs7-certreqresp
.evy	application/envoy
.p7s	application/pkcs7-signature
.eps	application/postscript
.setreg	application/set-registration-initiation
.xlm	application/vnd.ms-excel
.cpio	application/x-cpio
.dvi	application/x-dvi
.p7b	application/x-pkcs7-certificates
.doc	application/msword
.dot	application/msword
.p7c	application/pkcs7-mime
.ps	application/postscript
.wps	application/vnd.ms-works
.csh	application/x-csh
.iii	application/x-iphone
.pmw	application/x-perfmon
.man	application/x-troff-man
.hdf	application/x-hdf
.mvb	application/x-msmediaview
.texi	application/x-texinfo
.setpay	application/set-payment-initiation
.stl	application/vndms-pkistl
.mdb	application/x-msaccess
.oda	application/oda

Table 4.1 Continued

File name extension	MIME type
.hlp	application/winhlp
.nc	application/x-netcdf
.sh	application/x-sh
.shar	application/x-shar
.tcl	application/x-tcl
.ms	application/x-troff-ms
.ods	application/oleobject
.axs	application/olescript
.xla	application/vnd.ms-excel
.mpp	application/vnd.ms-project
.dir	application/x-director
.sit	application/x-stuffit
.*	application/octet-stream
.crl	application/pkix-crl
.ai	application/postscript
.xls	application/vnd.ms-excel
.wks	application/vnd.ms-works
.ins	application/x-internet-signup
.pub	application/x-mspublisher
.wri	application/x-mswrite
.spl	application/futuresplash
.hqx	application/mac-binhex40
.p10	application/pkcs10
.xlc	application/vnd.ms-excel
.xlt	application/vnd.ms-excel
.dxr	application/x-director
.js	application/x-javascript
.m13	application/x-msmediaview
.trm	application/x-msterminal
.pml	application/x-perfmon
.me	application/x-troff-me
.wcm	application/vnd.ms-works
.latex	application/x-latex

Continued

Table 4.1 Continued

File name extension	MIME type
.m14	application/x-msmediaview
.wmf	application/x-msmetafile
.cer	application/x-x509-ca-cert
.zip	application/x-zip-compressed
.p12	application/x-pkcs12
.pfx	application/x-pkcs12
.der	application/x-x509-ca-cert
.pdf	application/pdf
.xlw	application/vnd.ms-excel
.texinfo	application/x-texinfo
.p7m	application/pkcs7-mime
.pps	application/vnd.ms-powerpoint
.dcr	application/x-director
.gtar	application/x-gtar
.sct	text/scriptlet
.fif	application/fractals
.exe	application/octet-stream
.ppt	application/vnd.ms-powerpoint
.sst	application/vndms-pkicertstore
.pko	application/vndms-pkipko
.scd	application/x-msschedule
.tar	application/x-tar
.roff	application/x-troff
.t	application/x-troff
.prf	application/pics-rules
.rtf	application/rtf
.pot	application/vnd.ms-powerpoint
.wdb	application/vnd.ms-works
.bcpio	application/x-bcpio
.dll	application/x-msdownload
.pma	application/x-perfmon
.pmr	application/x-perfmon
.tr	application/x-troff
.src	application/x-wais-source

Table 4.1 Continued

File name extension	MIME type
.acx	application/internet-property-stream
.cat	application/vndms-pkiseccat
.cdf	application/x-cdf
.tgz	application/x-compressed
.sv4cpio	application/x-sv4cpio
.tex	application/x-tex
.ustar	application/x-ustar
.crt	application/x-x509-ca-cert
.ra	audio/x-pn-realaudio
.mid	audio/mid
.au	audio/basic
.snd	audio/basic
.wav	audio/wav
.aifc	audio/aiff
.m3u	audio/x-mpegurl
.ram	audio/x-pn-realaudio
.aiff	audio/aiff
.rmi	audio/mid
.aif	audio/x-aiff
.mp3	audio/mpeg
.gz	application/x-gzip
.z	application/x-compress
.tsv	text/tab-separated-values
.xml	text/xml
.323	text/h323
.htt	text/webviewhtml
.stm	text/html
.html	text/html
.xsl	text/xml
.htm	text/html
.cod	image/cis-cod
.ief	image/ief
.pbm	image/x-portable-bitmap

Continued

Table 4.1 Continued

File name extension	MIME type
.tiff	image/tiff
.ppm	image/x-portable-pixmap
.rgb	image/x-rgb
.dib	image/bmp
.jpeg	image/jpeg
.cmx	image/x-cmx
.pnm	image/x-portable-anymap
.jpe	image/jpeg
.jfif	image/pjpeg
.tif	image/tiff
.jpg	image/jpeg
.xbm	image/x-xbitmap
.ras	image/x-cmu-raster
.gif	image/gif

Schedules

You can apply a Schedule to an Access Rule to control when the rule should be applied. There are three built-in schedules:

- **Work Hours**   Permits access between 09:00 (9:00 A.M.) and 17:00 (5:00 P.M.) on Monday through Friday (to this rule)
- **Weekends**   Permits access at all times on Saturday and Sunday (to this rule)
- **Always**   Permits access at all times (to this rule)

Note that rules can be allow or deny rules. The Schedules apply to all Access Rules, not just allow rules.

ISA FIREWALL WARNING

Schedules control only new connections that apply to an Access Rule. Connections that are already established are not affected by Schedules. For example, if you schedule access to a partner site during Work Hours, users will not be disconnected after 5PM. You will have to manually disconnect the users or script a restart of the firewall service.

Network Objects

Network Objects are used to control the source and destination of connections moving through the ISA firewall. We discussed the Network Objects Policy Elements in Chapter 1.

Configuring Access Rules for Outbound Access through the ISA Firewall

Access Rules always apply to outbound connections. Only protocols with a primary connection in either the outbound or send direction can be used in Access Rules. In contrast, Web Publishing Rules and Server Publishing Rules always use protocols with a primary connection with the inbound or receive direction. Access Rules control access from source to destination using outbound protocols.

In this section we'll go over in detail how to create an Access Rule and each of the options available to you when using the **New Access Rule Wizard,** along with additional options available to you in the **Properties** of the Access Rule.

To begin, open the **Microsoft Internet Security and Acceleration Server 2006** management console and expand the server name and click **Firewall Policy** node. Click the **Tasks** tab in the Task Pane and click the **Create New Access Rule** link. This brings up the **Welcome to the New Access Rule Wizard** page. Enter a name for the rule in the **Access Rule name** text box. In this example we'll create an "All Open" Access Rule that allows all traffic from all hosts outbound from the default Internal Network to the default External Network. Click **Next**.

ISA FIREWALL ALERT

The "All Open" rule we create in this example is for demonstration purposes only and for initial firewall testing. After you confirm that your ISA firewall successfully connects you to the Internet, you should disable the "All Open" rule and create Access Rules that match your network use policy. Outbound access control is just as important to your overall security posture as inbound access control. In fact, the ISA firewall's strong user/group based outbound access control is one feature that sets the ISA firewall apart from virtually any other firewall on the market today.

The Rule Action Page

On the **Rule Action** page you have two options: **Allow** or **Deny**. In contrast to ISA Server 2000, the new ISA firewall has the **Deny** option set as the default. In this example, we'll select the **Allow** option and click **Next, as shown in Figure 4.1**.

Figure 4.1 The Rule Action page

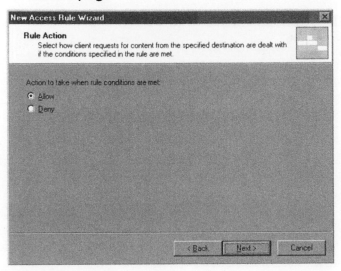

The Protocols Page

On the **Protocols** page, you decide what protocols should be allowed outbound from the source to destination location. You have three options in the **This rule applies to** list:

- **All outbound traffic** This option allows all protocols outbound. The effect of this option differs depending on the client type used to access this rule. For Firewall clients, this option allows all protocols outbound, including secondary protocols that are defined on the ISA firewall and some that are not defined. However, if a SecureNAT client attempts to connect via a rule that employs this option, outbound access will only be allowed for protocols that are included in the ISA firewall's **Protocols** list. If the SecureNAT client cannot connect to a resource when you use this protocol, try creating a new Protocol Definition on the ISA firewall to support the SecureNAT client's connection. However, if secondary connections are required, such as is the case with FTP, you must employ the Firewall client or create an application filter to support that protocol for SecureNAT clients.

- **Selected protocols** This option allows you to select the specific protocols to which you want this rule to apply. You can select from the default list of protocols included with the ISA firewall right out of the box, or you can create a new Protocol Definition "on the fly". You can select one protocol or multiple protocols for a single rule.

- **All outbound traffic except selected** This option allows you to enable all protocols outbound (dependent only the client type) *except* for specific protocols outbound. For example, you might want to allow Firewall clients outbound access to all protocols except those you explicitly want to deny because of corporate security policy, such as AOL Instant Messenger, MSN Messenger and IRC. See Figure 4.2.

Figure 4.2 The Protocols page

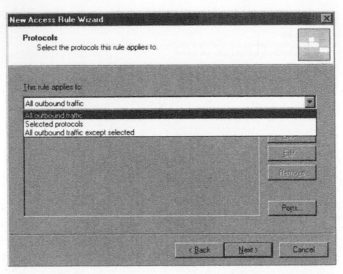

Highlight the **Selected Protocols** option and click the **Add** button. This brings up the **Add Protocols** dialog box. In the **Add Protocols** dialog box, you see a list of folders that group protocols based on their general use. For example, the **Common Protocols** folder contains protocols most commonly used when connecting to the Internet and the **Mail Protocols** folder is used to group protocols most commonly used when accessing mail services through the ISA firewall. The **User-Defined** folder contains all your custom protocols that you manually create on the ISA firewall. The **All Protocols** folder contains all protocols, both built-in and User-defined, configured on the ISA firewall.

Click the **All Protocols** folder and you'll see a list of all protocols configured on the ISA firewall. The ISA firewall comes with over 100 built-in Protocol Definitions you can use in your Access Rules, as shown in Figure 4.3.

Figure 4.3 The Add Protocols dialog box

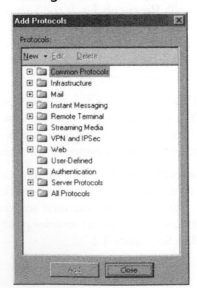

If you need to use a protocol for which there isn't already a Protocol Definition, you can create a new one now but clicking the **New** menu. Clicking the **New** menu will allow you the option to create a new **Protocol** or new **RPC Protocol**. See the section earlier in this chapter on how to create new Protocol Definitions.

Once you identify the protocol you want to include in the rule, double click on it. Double click on any other protocol you want to include in the rule and then click **Close** in the **Add Protocols** dialog box. In this example, we want to allow access to all protocols, so click close in the **Add Protocols** dialog box.

On the **Protocols** page, select the **All outbound traffic** option from the **This rule applies to** list and click **Next**.

The Access Rule Sources Page

On the **Access Rule Sources** page, select the source location to which this Access Rule should apply. Click the **Add** button to add the source of the communication for which this rule will apply.

In the **Add Network Entities** dialog box you can choose the source location of the communication to which this Access Rule applies. If none of the source locations listed in the **Add Network Entities** dialog box works for you, you can create a new Network Object by clicking the **New** menu. Double click the location to which you want the rule to apply. Note that you can choose more than one source location by double clicking on multiple Network Objects.

In this example, click on the **Networks** folder to expand the folder and then double click on the **Internal** Network entry. Click **Close** to close the **Add Network Entities** dialog box as shown in Figure 4.4.

Figure 4.4 The Add Network Entities dialog box

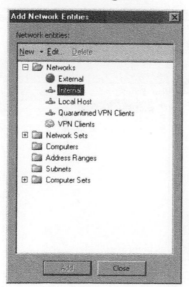

Click **Next** on the **Access Rule Sources** page.

The Access Rule Destinations Page

On the **Access Rule Destinations** page, select the destination for which you want this rule to apply. Click the **Add** button to add a destination location. The **Add Network Entities** dialog box appears and you can select a Network Object for the destination for which this Access Rule applies. As in the previous page of the Access Rule Wizard, you can create a new destination location by clicking the **New** menu and creating the new location.

   In this example, we'll click on the **Networks** folder and then double click on the **External** entry. Click **Close** to close the **Add Network Entities** dialog box. Click **Next** on the **Access Rule Destinations** page.

The User Sets Page

On the **User Sets** page, you can set the users to which this Access Rule applies. The default setting is **All Users**. If you want to remove this User Set or any other one from the list of users to which this rule applies, select the User Set and click the **Remove** button. You can also edit a user set in the list by clicking the **Edit** button.

   You can add a User Set to the list by clicking the **Add** button. In the **Add Users** dialog box, you can double click on a Firewall Group to which you want the rule to apply. You can also create new firewall groups by clicking the **New** menu and you can edit existing firewall groups by clicking the **Edit** menu.

   In this example, we'll use the default setting, **All Users**. Click **Close** in the **Add Users** dialog box and click **Next** on the **User Sets** page as shown in Figure 4.5.

Figure 4.5 The User Sets page

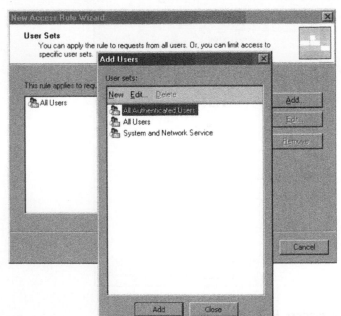

The **Completing the New Access Rule Wizard** page appears next. Review your settings and click **Finish**.

ISA FIREWALL NOTE

When you create a rule that allows outbound access for **All Users**, unauthenticated connections are allowed through the ISA firewall. A rule that applies to **All Users** can be used by SecureNAT clients. If an Access Rule requires authentication, SecureNAT client connections will fail because the SecureNAT client cannot authenticate.

Access Rule Properties

There are several options you can configure in an Access Rule that aren't exposed in the New Access Rule Wizard. You can select these options by going into the **Properties** dialog box of the Access Rule.

The **Properties** dialog box of an Access Rule contains the following tabs:

- The General tab
- The Action tab
- The Protocols tab
- The From tab
- The Users tab
- The Schedule tab
- The Content Types tab

Right click the Access Rule and click the **Properties** command.

The General Tab

The first tab you see is the **General** tab. You can change the name of the Access Rule by entering the new name in the **Name** text box. The rule can be enabled or disabled by placing or removing the checkmark in the **Enable** checkbox.

The Action Tab

The Action tab provides several options that were not exposed in the New Access Rule Wizard. The options available on the Action tab include:

- **Allow** Choose this option if you want connections matching the characteristics of this rule to be allowed through the ISA firewall
- **Deny** Choose this option if you want to connections matching the characteristics of this rule to be denied access through the ISA firewall

- **Redirect HTTP requests to this Web page**   Choose this option if you want HTTP requests matching the characteristics of this rule to be redirected to another Web page. This option is only available if the rule is a Deny rule. When the user attempts to access a denied site, the request is automatically redirected to a Web page you configure in the text box below this option. Make sure that you enter the complete URL to which you want the user to be redirected, such as http://corp.domain.com/accesspolicy.htm.

- **Log requests matching this rule**   Connection attempts matching the Access Rule are automatically logged after you create the rule. There may be times when you don't want to log all connections matching a particular rule. One example of when you would not want to log connections matching a rule is when you create a rule matching protocols you have little interest in investigating, such as NetBIOS broadcasts. Later in this chapter, we will describe a procedure you can use to reduce the size of your log files by creating an Access Rule that does not log connections matching NetBIOS broadcast protocols.

Figure 4.6 shows the contents of the Action tab.

Figure 4.6 The Action tab

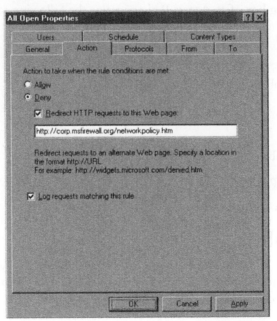

The Protocols Tab

The **Protocols** tab provides you many of the same options available in the New Access Rule Wizard. You have the same options in the **This rule applies to** list, which are: **Allow all outbound traffic**, **Selected protocols** and **All outbound traffic except selected**. You can use the **Add** button to add more protocols to the list. Use the **Remove** button to remove protocols that you select in the **Protocols** list and click the **Edit** button to edit protocols you select in the **Protocols** list.

NOTE

You can edit only user-defined protocols.

There are application filters that you can configure for any of the protocols you've included in the **Protocols** list on the **Protocols** tab. The filters available depend on the protocols you've included in the list. Click the **Filters** button to view the configurable filters for the list of protocols included in the Access Rule as shown in Figure 4.7.

Figure 4.7 The Protocols tab

You also have control over the source ports allowed to access resources through the ISA firewall via each Access Rule. Click the **Ports** button and you'll see the **Source Ports** dialog box. The default setting is **Allow traffic from any allowed source port**. However, if you have applications for which you can control the source port, or those that use default source ports (such as SMTP), then you can limit the source ports allowed to access the rule by selecting the **Limit access to traffic from this range of source ports** option and enter the **From** and **To** source ports that represent the first and last ports in a range of source ports you want to allow. See Figure 4.8.

Figure 4.8 The Source Ports dialog box

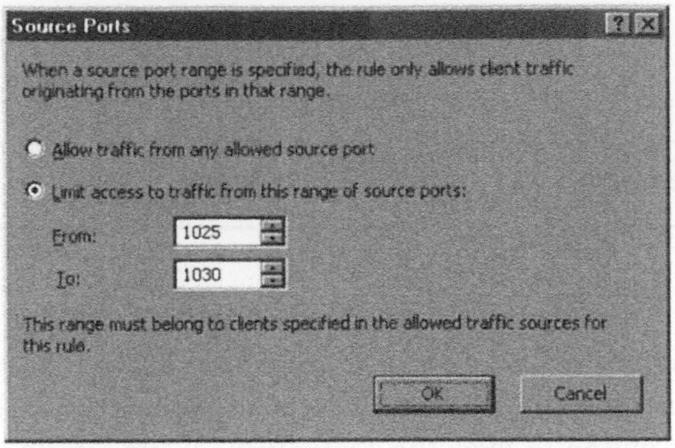

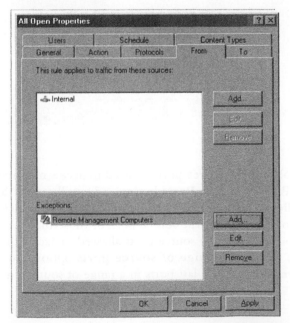

The From Tab

On the **From** tab you have options similar to those seen in the New Access Rule Wizard. However, an option not available in the Wizard is the ability to create an exception. If you want to add additional source locations for which this Access Rule should apply, click the **Add** button next to the **This rule applies to traffic from these sources** list. If you want to remove a source location, click the location and then click the **Remove** button. If you want to edit the characteristics of a location, click the **Edit** button.

You can apply this rule to all source locations in the **This rule applied to traffic from these sources** list *except* for certain source locations you specify in the **Exceptions** list. For example, suppose the Access Rule is configured to deny outbound access to the PPTP VPN protocol for all machines on the Internal Network. However, you want to allow machines that belong to the **Remote Management Computers** Computer Set access to this protocol. You can add the **Remote Management Computers** Computer Set to the list of **Exceptions** by clicking the **Add** button. Use the **Remove** and **Edit** button in the **Exceptions** list to remove and edit the locations in that list, as shown in Figure 4.9.

Figure 4.9 The From tab

The To Tab

The **To** tab provides similar functionality as that on the **Access Rule Destination** page of the New Access Rule Wizard. However, you have the additional option to set an Exception to the destinations included in the **This rule applies to traffic sent to these destinations** list.

For example, suppose you create an Access Rule that allows outbound access to the HTTP protocol for all External sites. However, you do not want to allow users access to the Hotmail Web mail site. You can create a Domain Name Set for the domains required for Hotmail access and then use the **Add** button in the **Exceptions** section to add the Hotmail Domain Name Set. The rule will then will allow HTTP access to all sites *except* the Hotmail site. See Figure 4.10.

Figure 4.10 The To Tab

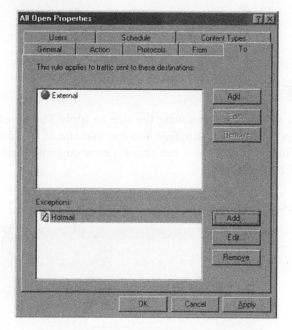

The Users Tab

The Users tab allows you to add firewall groups to which you want the Access Rule to apply, as shown in Figure 4.11. In addition, you have the option to add exceptions to the group to which the rule applies. For example, you could configure the rule to apply to **All Authenticated Users** but exclude other firewall groups, such as the built-in **System and Network Service** group.

Figure 4.11 The Users tab

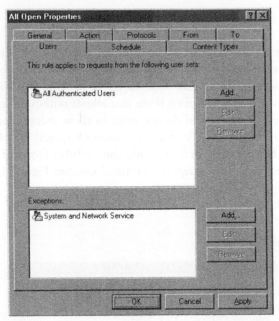

The Schedule Tab

On the **Schedule** tab, you set the times you want the rule to apply. The scheduling option isn't exposed in the New Access Rule Wizard interface. You can use one of the three default schedules: **Always**, **Weekends** or **Work hours,** or you can create a new custom schedule by clicking the **New** button, as illustrated by Figure 4.12.

Figure 4.12 The Schedule tab

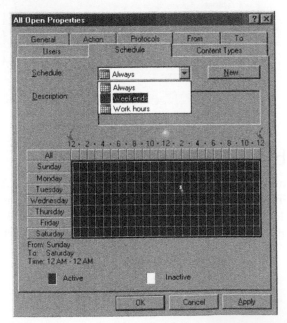

ISA FIREWALL WARNING

When you set a schedule for an Access Rule, the rule is applied only to new connections that match the characteristics of the rule. Active connections to which this rule applies will *not* be disconnected. This setting is analogous to the **Logon Hours** setting in the Active Directory. You will need to either wait until the users disconnect or their sessions time out, or you can manually disconnect the sessions in the **Microsoft Internet Security and Acceleration Server 2006** management console or via a script.

The Content Types Tab

Another option not exposed in the New Access Rule Wizard is the ability to apply content type control over the connection. On the **Content Types** tab, you can specify what content types will apply to the rule. Content Type constraints are only applied to HTTP connections; all other protocols ignore the settings on the Content Types tab.

The default setting is to have the rule apply to **All content types.** You can limit the content types the rule applies to by selecting the **Selected content types (with this option selected, the rule is applicable only HTTP traffic)** option and putting a checkmark in the checkboxes next to the content types to which you want the rule to apply. See Figure 4.13.

TIP

If you unbind the Web Proxy filter from the HTTP protocol and then allow Firewall or SecureNAT client connections access to this rule, the connection attempt may fail because content inspection is dependent on the Web Proxy filter.

Figure 4.13 The Content Types tab

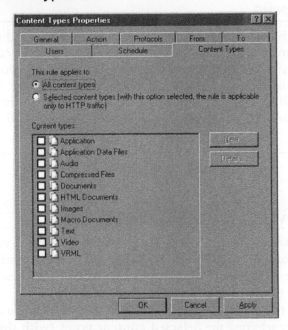

The Access Rule Context Menu Options

There are several options to choose from when you right click an Access Rule. These options include the following:

- **Properties**   This option brings up the Access Rule's **Properties** dialog box.
- **Delete**   This option deletes the Access Rule.
- **Copy**   This option allows you to copy an Access Rule and then paste a copy of the rule to the Firewall policy.
- **Paste**   This option allows you to paste an Access Rule that you've copied.
- **Export Selected**   This option allows you to export the Access Rule to an .xml file. You can then import this file to another ISA firewall to replicate the rule to another machine.
- **Import to Selected**   This option allow you to import an Access Rule from an .xml file to the position selected in the Access Policy.
- **Move Up**   This option allows you to move the rule up on the list of Access Rules.
- **Move Down**   This option allows you to move the rule down on the list of Access Rules.
- **Disable**   This option allows you disable the Access Rule while keeping it on the list of Access Rules and allows you to re-enable it later if you require it again.
- **Enable**   This option allows you to enable an Access Rule that you've disabled.

- **Configure HTTP**   This option appears when the Access Rule includes the HTTP protocol. The Configure HTTP option allows you to configure the HTTP Security Filter to exert access control over HTTP connections using the ISA firewall's advanced application layer inspection mechanisms.

- **Configure FTP**   This option appears when the Access Rule includes the FTP protocol. When it is selected, you are presented with a dialog box that allows you to enable or disable FTP uploads.

- **Configure RPC Protocol**   This option appears when the Access Rule includes an RPC protocol. When it is selected, you are presented with a dialog box that allows you to enable or disable strict RPC compliance (which has the effect of enabling or disabling DCOM connections).

TIP

The **Copy** option is very useful if you want to avoid using the New Access Rule Wizard to create new rules. Right click an existing rule and then click **Copy**. Right click the same rule and then click **Paste**. The pasted copy of the rule will have the same name as the original rule except that there will be a **(1)** appended to the name. You can then right click the rule and click **Properties** or you can double click the rule and then change the name and other characteristics of the rule. We find this useful when we're making small changes to Access Rules and do not want to lose the settings on the original rule. If the new rule doesn't work as expected, we can delete the new rule and return to the original rule. Try copying and paste rules a few times and see how this process works for you.

Configuring RPC Policy

When you create an Access Rule that allows outbound RPC, you have the option to configure RPC protocol policy. Access Rules that allow **All IP Traffic** also include RPC protocols. Right click the Access Rule and click **Configure RPC protocol** to configure RPC policy.

In the **Configure RPC protocol policy** dialog box, shown in Figure 4.14, you have a single option: **Enforce strict RPC compliance**. The default setting is enabled. When this setting is not enabled, the RPC filter will allow additional RPC type protocols, such as DCOM. If you find that some RPC-based protocols do not work correctly through the ISA firewall, consider disabling this option.

RPC policy is configured on a per-protocol basis. For example, you can enforce strict RPC compliance for one Access Rule and disable strict RPC compliance for another Access Rule in the ISA firewall's firewall policy.

Figure 4.14 The Configure RPC protocol policy dialog box

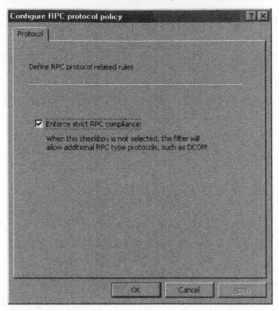

Configuring FTP Policy

When you created an Access Rule that allows the FTP protocol, you have the option to configure FTP policy. Right click the Access Rule and click the **Configure FTP** command. This brings up the **Configure FTP protocol policy** dialog box, shown in Figure 4.15. By default, the **Read Only** checkbox is enabled. When this checkbox is enabled, FTP uploads will be blocked. If you want to allow users to upload files using FTP, remove the checkmark from the checkbox.

FTP policy is configured on a per-rule basis.

Figure 4.15 The Configures FTP protocol policy dialog box

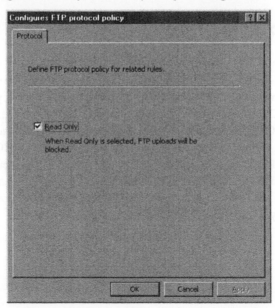

Configuring HTTP Policy

Whenever you create an Access Rule that allows HTTP connections, you have the option to configure HTTP policy. HTTP policy settings control the HTTP Security Filter. We discuss the configuration options available in the HTTP Security Filter in full detail in Chapter 7.

Ordering and Organizing Access Rules

The ordering of Access Rules is important to ensure that your Access Policy works the way you expect it to work. We recommend the follow ordering of Access Rules:

- Put Web Publishing Rules and Server Publishing Rules on the top of the list

- Place anonymous Deny Access Rules under the Web Publishing Rules and Server Publishing Rules. These rules do not require user authentication and do not require the client to be from a specific location (such as part of a Computer Set)

- Place anonymous Allow Access Rules under the Anonymous Deny Access Rules. These rules do not require user authentication and do not require the client to be from a specific location (such as part of a Computer Set)

- Place Deny Access Rules requiring authentication below the anonymous Allow Access Rules

- Place Allow Access Rules requiring authentication below the Deny Access Rules requiring authentication.

It is important that anonymous rules that apply to the same protocol as an authenticated access rule be applied first if it is your intent to allow anonymous access for that protocol. If you do not put the anonymous access rule before the authenticated Access Rule, then the connection request will be denied to the anonymous user (typically a SecureNAT client) for that protocol.

For example, suppose you have two Access Rules: one rule allows all users access to the HTTP protocol and the second rule allows members of the EXECS firewall group access to the HTTP, HTTPS, FTP, IRC and MSN Messenger protocols. If you place the rule allowing the EXECS group access before the anonymous access rule, then all HTTP connections outbound will require authentication and the anonymous access rule located under the authentication required rule will be ignored. However, if you had an anonymous access rule for the NNTP protocol under the rule allowing the EXECS outbound access to the HTTP, HTTPS, FTP, IRC and MSN Messenger protocols, then the anonymous NNTP connection would be allowed because the NNTP protocol doesn't match the characteristics of the rule allowing the EXECS users outbound access.

We found this model a bit confusing at first. When we first starting working with the ISA firewall, we assumed that when a rule applies to a particular firewall group, a connection request from a user that does not supply credentials to the ISA firewall would be ignored and the firewall would then continue down the list of rules until an anonymous Access Rule matching the connection parameters was found. However, this is *not* the case. Anonymous users might be considered members of the "Anonymous Users" group and that group does not match any group for which you might require authentication. Since the "Anonymous Users" group never matches an actual group, any rule for which authentication is required matching the connection request will be denied.

How to Block Logging for Selected Protocols

You may want to prevent the ISA firewall from logging information about certain protocols that reach the firewall. Common examples are the NetBIOS broadcast protocols: NetBIOS Name Service and NetBIOS Datagram. Both of these protocols regularly broadcast to the local subnet broadcast address and can fill the ISA firewall's Firewall Service log with information that isn't very useful to the ISA firewall administrator.

You can create an Access Rule that includes these protocols and then configure the Access Rule to not log information about connections associated with the rule. For example, you can perform the following procedure to block logging of these NetBIOS protocols:

1. In the **Microsoft Internet Security and Acceleration Server 2006** management console, expand the server name and click the **Firewall Policy** node.

2. In the Task Pane, click the **Tasks** tab and click the **Create New Access Rule** link.

3. On the **Welcome to the New Access Rule Wizard** page, enter a name for the rule in the **Access Rule name** text box. In this example, we'll name the rule **Block NetBIOS logging**. Click **Next**.

4. Select the **Deny** option on the **Rule Action** page and click **Next**.

5. On the **Protocols** page, select the **Selected protocols** option from the **This rule applies to** list. Click the **Add** button.

6. In the **Add Protocols** dialog box, click the **Infrastructure** folder. Double click the **NetBIOS Datagram** and **NetBIOS Name Service** entries. Click **Close**.

7. Click **Next** on the **Protocols** page.

8. On the **Access Rule Sources** page, click the **Add** button.

9. In the **Add Network Entities** dialog box, click the **Computer Sets** folder and then double click the **Anywhere** entry. Click **Close**.

10. Click **Next** on the **Access Rule Sources** page.

11. On the **Access Rule Destinations** page, click the **Add** button.

12. In the **Add Network Entities** dialog box, click the **Computer Sets** folder. Double click the **Anywhere** entry and click **Close**.

13. Click **Next** on the **Access Rule Destinations** page.

14. Click **Next** on the **User Sets** page.

15. Click **Finish** on the **Completing the New Access Rule Wizard** page.

16. Right click the **Block NetBIOS Logging** rule and click **Properties**.

17. In the **Block NetBIOS Logging Properties** dialog box, remove the checkmark from the **Log requests matching this rule** checkbox.

18. Click **Apply** and then click **OK**.

19. Click **Apply** to save the changes and update the firewall policy.

20. Click **OK** in the **Apply New Configuration** dialog box.

The rule you created in this example not only prevents logging of NetBIOS broadcasts, but prevents these protocols to and from the ISA firewall. Thus, you get two benefits from one rule!

Disabling Automatic Web Proxy Connections for SecureNAT Clients

There may be times when you want Firewall and SecureNAT client to bypass the Web Proxy service. By default, HTTP connections from SecureNAT and Firewall clients are automatically forwarded to the Web Proxy filter. The advantage of this configuration is that both SecureNAT and Firewall clients are able to benefit from the ISA firewall's Web Proxy cache (when caching is enabled on the ISA firewall).

The problem is that some Web sites are poorly written and are not compliant with CERN compliant Web proxies. You can solve this problem by configuring these sites for Direct Access and then unbinding the Web Proxy filter from the HTTP protocol.

Perform the following steps to disable automatic Web Proxy connections for Firewall and SecureNAT clients:

1. In the **Microsoft Internet Security and Acceleration Server 2006** management console, expand the server name and click the **Firewall Policy** node in the left pane of the console.

2. In the Task Pane, click the **Toolbox** tab. On the **Toolbox** tab, click the **Command Protocols** folder and double click the **HTTP** protocol.

3. In the **HTTP Properties** dialog box, click the **Parameters** tab.

4. On the **Parameters** tab, remove the checkmark from the **Web Proxy Filter** checkbox. Click **Apply** and then click **OK**.

5. Click **Apply** to save the changes and update the firewall policy.

6. Click **OK** in the **Apply New Configuration** dialog box.

One side effect of bypassing the Web Proxy filter is that HTTP Policy is not applied to the SecureNAT and Firewall clients. However, HTTP Policy is applied to machines that are explicitly configured as Web Proxy clients, even when the Firewall, SecureNAT and Web Proxy clients access the site using the same Access Rule.

For example, suppose you create a rule named **HTTP Access**. The **HTTP Access** Access Rule allows all users on the Internal network access to all sites on the External Network using the HTTP protocol. Let's say you configure HTTP Policy for this rule to block connections to the www.spyware. com domain. When Web Proxy clients attempt to connect to www.spyware.com, the connection will be blocked by the **HTTP Access** Access Rule. However, when the SecureNAT and Firewall clients attempt to access www.spyware.com via the **HTTP Access** rule (when the Web Proxy Filter is unbound from the HTTP protocol), that Access Rule will allow the SecureNAT and Firewall clients through.

Another side effect of unbinding the Web Proxy Filter from the HTTP Protocol Definition is that the configuration interface (**Configure HTTP policy for rule** dialog box) for the HTTP filter is removed from the **Microsoft Internet Security and Acceleration Server 2006** management console. For all rules that have an HTTP policy already configured, that policy is still enforced on Web Proxy clients. However, to change HTTP Policy on existing rule, or to configure HTTP policy on new Access Rules, you will need to re-bind the HTTP Filter to the HTTP Protocol Definition. You can then unbind the Web Proxy Filter again after configuring the HTTP policy.

Of course, you could just configure all clients as Web Proxy clients (which is our recommendation) and avoid the administrative overhead.

 ISA FIREWALL WARNING

The HTTP Policy configuration interface is also removed from Web Proxy rules when the Web Proxy Filter is unbound from the HTTP Protocol Definition.

Using Scripts to Populate Domain Name Sets

One of the ISA firewall's strong suits is its exceptional stateful application layer inspection. In addition to performing the basic task of stateful filtering (which even a simple 'hardware' firewall can do), the ISA firewall's strong application layer inspection feature set allows the ISA firewall to actually understand the protocols passing though the firewall. In contrast to traditional second generation hardware firewalls, the ISA firewall represents a third-generation firewall that is not only network aware, but application protocol aware.

The ISA firewall's stateful application inspection mechanism allows you to control access not just to "ports", but to the actual protocols moving through those ports. While the conventional "hardware" firewall is adept at passing packets using simple stateful filtering mechanisms that have been available since the mid 1990's, the ISA firewall's stateful application layer inspection mechanisms bring the ISA firewall into the 21st century and actually control application layer protocol access. This allows strong inbound and outbound access control based on the firewall's application layer awareness, rather than through simple "opening and closing" of ports.

One powerful example is the ability to control what sites users can access through the ISA firewall. You can combine this ability to control the sites users can access by adding strong user/group based access control as well as protocol control.

For example, you might have a group of users called "Web Users," and you might want to block access to a list of 1500 URLs or domains for those users. You can create an Access Rule that blocks only those 1500 sites and allows access to all other sites when members of that group authenticate with the ISA firewall.

Another example might be this: you want to create a block list of 5000 domains that you want to prevent all users except for domain admins from reaching via any protocol. You can create a Domain Name Set and then apply this Domain Name Set to an Access Rule blocking these sites.

The trick is to find a way to get those thousands of domains or URLs into Domain Name Sets and URL Sets. You can, of course, enter these URLs and domains manually using the built-in tools included in the ISA Management console. The problem with this approach is that you'll need to get your clicking thumb ready for a long weekend as you click your way through the user interface to add all of these domains and URLs.

A better way is to import the sites you want to include in your URL Sets and Domain Name Sets from a text file. There are a number of places on the Internet where you can find such files

(I won't mention any here because I don't want to create an implicit endorsement of any of them). Once you have a text file, you'll want use a script to import the entries in the text file into a URL Set or a Domain Name Set.

First, let's start with the scripts. The first script below is used to import the entries in a text file into a URL Set. Copy the information into a text file and then save it as **ImportURLs.vbs**.

```
< -----------------Start with the line below this one------->
Set Isa = CreateObject("FPC.Root")
Set CurArray = Isa.GetContainingArray
Set RuleElements = CurArray.RuleElements
Set URLSets = RuleElements.URLSets
Set URLSet = URLSets.Item("Urls")
Set FileSys = CreateObject("Scripting.FileSystemObject")
Set UrlsFile = FileSys.OpenTextFile("urls.txt", 1)
For i = 1 to URLSet.Count
  URLSet.Remove 1
Next
Do While UrlsFile.AtEndOfStream <> True
  URLSet.Add UrlsFile.ReadLine
Loop
WScript.Echo "Saving..."
CurArray.Save
WScript.Echo "Done"
< -----------------End with the line above this one--------->
```

The two entries in this file you need to change for your own setup are highlighted in yellow. In the line:

```
Set URLSet = URLSets.Item("Urls")
```

Change the **Urls** entry to the name of the URL Set you want to create on the ISA firewall. In the line:

```
Set UrlsFile = FileSys.OpenTextFile("urls.txt", 1)
```

Change the **urls.txt** entry to the name of the text file that contains the URLs you want to import into the ISA firewall's configuration.

The next script is used to import a collections of domains contained in a text file. Save the following information in a text file and name it **ImportDomains.vbs**.

```
< -----------------Start with the line below this one------->
Set Isa = CreateObject("FPC.Root")
Set CurArray = Isa.GetContainingArray
Set RuleElements = CurArray.RuleElements
Set DomainNameSets = RuleElements.DomainNameSets
Set DomainNameSet = DomainNameSets.Item("Domains")
```

```
Set FileSys = CreateObject("Scripting.FileSystemObject")
Set DomainsFile = FileSys.OpenTextFile("domains.txt", 1)
For i = 1 to DomainNameSet.Count
  DomainNameSet.Remove 1
Next
Do While DomainsFile.AtEndOfStream <> True
  DomainNameSet.Add DomainsFile.ReadLine
Loop
WScript.Echo "Saving…"
CurArray.Save
WScript.Echo "Done"
< ------------------End with the line above this one--------->
```

The two entries in this file you need to change for your own setup are shown below.
In the line:

```
Set DomainNameSet = DomainNameSets.Item("Domains")
```

Change the **Domains** entry to the name of the Domain Name Set you want to create on the ISA firewall.
In the line:

```
Set DomainsFile = FileSys.OpenTextFile("domains.txt", 1)
```

Change the **domains.txt** entry to the name of the text file that contains the domains you want to import into the ISA firewall's configuration.

Using the Import Scripts

Now let's see how the scripts work. The first thing you need to do is create the URL Set and the Domain Name Set in the **Microsoft Internet Security and Acceleration Server 2006** management console. This is easy and involves only a few steps.

First, we'll create a URL Set named **URLs**, since that's the default name in our script. Remember, you can change the URL Set name in the script if you like; just make sure you first create a URL Set in the **Microsoft Internet Security and Acceleration Server 2006** management console with the same name.

Perform the following steps to create a URL Set with the name **URLs**:

- In the **Microsoft Internet Security and Acceleration Server 2006** management console, expand the server name and then click on the **Firewall Policy** node.

- In the **Firewall Policy** node, click the **Toolbox** tab in the Task Pane. In the **Toolbox**, click the **Network Objects** tab.

- In the **Network Objects** tab, click the **New** menu and click **URL Set**.

- In the **New URL Set Rule Element** dialog box, shown in Figure 4.16, enter **URLs** in the **Name** text box. Click **OK**.

Figure 4.16 The New URL Set Rule Element dialog box

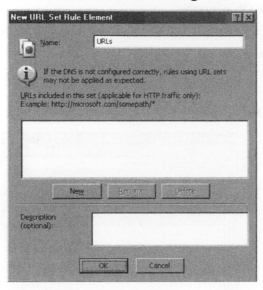

The URL Set now appears in the list of URL Sets, shown in Figure 4.17.

Figure 4.17 The URL Sets list

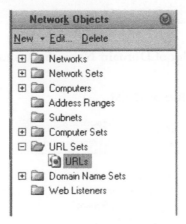

The next step is to create a Domain Name Set with the name **Domains**, which is the default name of the Set used in the ImportDomains script. Remember, you can use a different name for the Domain Name Set; just make sure the name is the same as the one you set in the script.

Perform the following steps to create the Domain Name Set with the name Domains:

1. In the **Microsoft Internet Security and Acceleration Server 2006** management console, expand the server name and then click on the **Firewall Policy** node.

2. In the **Firewall Policy** node, click the **Toolbox** tab in the Task Pane. In the **Toolbox**, click the **Network Objects** tab.

3. In the **Network Objects** tab, click the **New** menu and click **Domain Name Set**.

4. In the **New Domain Name Set Policy Element** dialog box, shown in Figure 4.18, enter **Domains** in the **Name** text box. Click **OK**.

Figure 4.18 The New Domain Set Policy Element dialog box

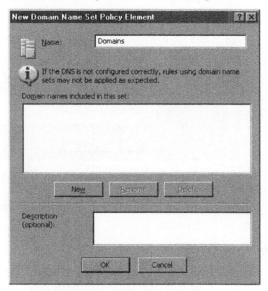

The new entry appears in the list of **Domain Name Sets,** shown in Figure 4.19.

Figure 4.19 The Domain Name Sets list

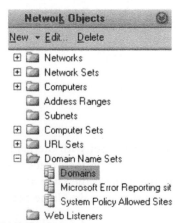

5. Click **Apply** to save the changes and update the firewall policy.

6. Click **OK** in the **Apply New Configuration** dialog box.

Now we need to create two text files: **urls.txt** and **domains.txt**. Those are the default names used in the scripts. You can change the names of the files, but make sure they match the names you configure in the scripts.

The **domains.txt** file will contain the following entries:

■ stuff.com

■ blah.com

■ scumware.com

The **urls.txt** file will contain the following entries:

```
http://www.cisco.com
http://www.checkpoint.com
http://www.sonicwall.com
```

Next, copy the script files and the text files into the same directory. In this example, we'll copy the script files and text files into the root of the C: drive. Double click on the **ImportURLs.vbs** file. You'll first see a dialog box that says **Saving,** as shown in Figure 4.20. Click **OK**.

Figure 4.20 Saving the information

Depending on how many URLs you're importing, it will be a few moments or a few minutes until you see the next dialog box, shown in Figure 4.21, which informs you that the import was completed. Click **OK**.

Figure 4.21 Finishing the procedure

Now we'll import the Domains. Double click the **ImportDomains.vbs** file. You'll see the **Saving** dialog box again. Click **OK**. A few moments to a few minutes later, you'll see the **Done** dialog box. Click **OK**.

Close the **Microsoft Internet Security and Acceleration Server 2006** management console if it is open. Now open the **Microsoft Internet Security and Acceleration Server 2006** management console and go to the **Firewall Policy** node in the left pane of the console.

ISA FIREWALL NOTE

You can avoid opening and closing the **Microsoft Internet Security and Acceleration Server 2006** management console by clicking the **Refresh** button in the **Microsoft Internet Security and Acceleration Server 2006** management console's button bar.

Click the **Toolbox** tab in the Task Pane and click the **Network Objects** bar. Click the **URL Sets** folder. Double click the **URLs** URL Set. You'll see that the URL Set was populated with the entries in your text file as shown in Figure 4.22. Cool!

Figure 4.22 URL Set entries

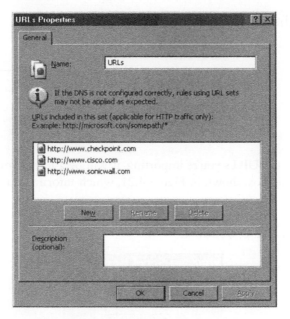

Click on the **Domain Name Sets** folder. Double click on the **Domains** entry. You'll see that the Domain Name Set is populated with domains you want to block, or allow, depending on your need. In this example we included a set of domains we'd like to block, shown in Figure 4.23.

Figure 4.23 Domain Name Set Properties

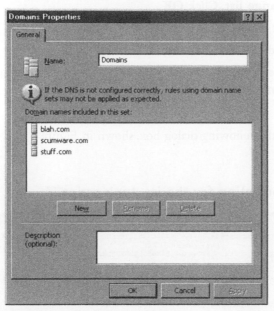

As you obtain more URLs, you can add them to the same text files and run the script again. The new entries will be added without creating duplicates of the domains or URLs that are already included in the Domain Name Set or URL Set.

Extending the SSL Tunnel Port Range for Web Access to Alternate SSL Ports

There will be times when your Web Proxy clients need to connect to SSL Web sites using an alternate port for the SSL link. For example, your users might try to access a banking Web site that requires an SSL connection on TCP port 4433 instead of the default port 443. This can also be problematic for SecureNAT and Firewall clients, since the default setting on the ISA firewall is to forward SecureNAT and Firewall client HTTP connections to the Web Proxy filter. Clients will see either a blank page or an error page indicating that the page cannot be displayed.

The problem here is that the Web Proxy filter only forwards SSL connections to TCP port 443. If clients try to connect to an SSL site over a port other than TCP 443, the connection attempt will fail. You can solve this problem by extending the SSL tunnel port range. However, to do so, you will need to download Jim Harrison's script at http://www.isatools.org, and enter the tunnel port range(s) you want the ISA firewall's Web Proxy component to use.

Perform the following steps to extend the ISA firewall's SSL tunnel port range:

1. Go to www.isatools.org and download the **isa_tpr.js** file and copy that file to your ISA firewall. *Do not use* the browser on the firewall. Download the file to a management workstation, scan the file, and then copy the file to removable media and then take it to the ISA firewall. Remember, you should *never* use client applications, such as browsers, e-mail clients, etc. on the firewall itself.

2. Double click the **isa_tpr.js** file. The first dialog box you see states **This is your current Tunnel Port Range list**. Click **OK**.

3. The NNTP port is displayed. Click **OK**.

4. The SSL port is displayed. Click **OK**.

5. Now copy the **isa_tpr.js** file to the root of the C: drive. Open a command prompt and enter the following:

```
isa_tpr.js /?
```

You will see the following dialog box, shown in Figure 4.24.

Figure 4.24 Help information for the isa_tpr.js script

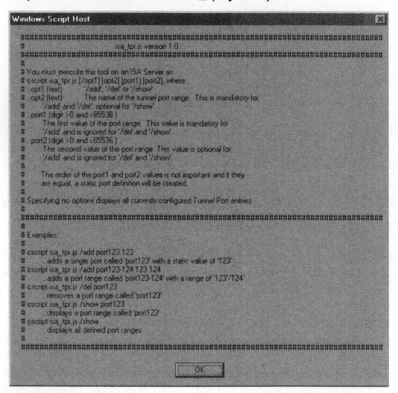

6. To add a new tunnel port, such as **8848,** enter the following command and press ENTER:

```
Cscript isa_tpr.js /add Ext8848 8848
```

You will see something like what appears in Figure 4.25 after the command runs successfully.

Figure 4.25 Running the isa_tpr.js script to add a port to the SSL tunnel port range

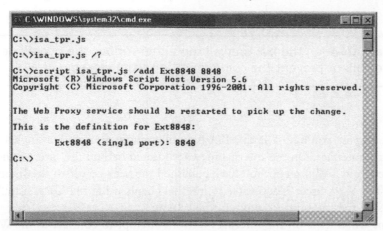

Alternatively, you can download the .NET application, **ISATpre.zip** file (written by Steven Soekrasno) from the www.isatools.org site and install the application on the ISA firewall. This application provides an easy to use graphical interface that allows you to extend the SSL tunnel port range. Figure 4.26 shows what the GUI for this application looks like.

Figure 4.26 Using Steven Soekrasno's .NET Tunnel Port Range extension application

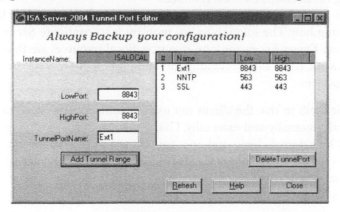

Avoiding Looping Back through the ISA Firewall for Internal Resources

A common error made by ISA firewall administrators involves allowing hosts on an ISA firewall Protected Network to loop back through the firewall to access resources on the same network where the client is located.

> **NOTE**
>
> Looping back through the ISA firewall can either reduce the overall performance of the ISA firewall, or prevent the communication from working at all.

For example, suppose you have a simple ISA firewall configuration with a single external interface and a single internal interface. On the Internal network located behind the internal interface, you have a SecureNAT client and a Web server. You have published the Web server to the Internet using a Web Publishing Rule. The Web server is accessible to internal clients using the URL http://web1 and to external clients using the URL http://www.msfirewall.org.

What happens when users on the Internal Network attempt to connect to the Web server using the URL www.msfirewall.org? If you don't have a split DNS in place, the clients on the Internal Network will resolve the name www.msfirewall.org to the IP address on the external interface of the ISA firewall that is listening for incoming connections to www.msfirewall.org. The host then will try to connect to the Internal resource by looping back through the ISA firewall via the Web Publishing Rule. If the client is a SecureNAT client, the connection attempt may fail (depending on how the ISA firewall is configured) or the overall performance of the ISA firewall is severely degraded because the firewall is handling connections for local resources.

You should always avoid looping back through the ISA firewall for resources located on the same network as the requesting host. The solution to this problem is to configure SecureNAT, Firewall and Web Proxy clients to use Direct Access for local resources (local resources are those contained on the same ISA firewall Network as the host requesting those resources). A Direct Access solution depends on the following components:

- Create a split DNS so that the clients can use the same domain name to reach the same resources both internally and externally. This requires two zones on two DNS servers. One zone is used by external clients and one zone is used by internal clients. The external client zone resolves names to the externally accessible address and the internal zone resolves names to internally accessible addresses. The key is that the zones are authoritative for the same domain name.

- Configure the properties of the network on which the Protected Network Web Proxy client is located to use Direct Access to reach both the IP addresses on the Internal network and the internal network domain names. This is done on the Web Proxy tab.

- Configure the properties of the network on which the Protected Network Firewall client is located to use Direct Access for internal domains.

Details of this configuration are included in Chapter 2 on ISA client installation and provisioning and in Chapter 1 on the ISA firewall's networking design.

Anonymous Requests Appear in Log File Even When Authentication is Enforced For Web (HTTP Connections)

A common question we encounter from ISA firewall admins relates to the appearance of anonymous connections from Web Proxy clients in the ISA firewall's Web proxy logs. These connections appear in spite of the fact that all rules are configured to require authentication. The short answer to this question is that this is normal and expected.

The long answer to this question involves how Web proxy clients normally communicate with authenticating Web proxy servers. For performance reasons, the initial request from the Web Proxy client is send *without* user credentials. If there is a rule that allows the connection anonymously, then the connection is allowed. If the client must authenticate first, then the Web proxy server sends back to the Web proxy client an access denied message (error 407) with a request for credentials. The Web proxy client then sends credentials to the ISA firewall and the user name appears in the log files.

Figure 4.27 shows the HTTP 407 response returned to the Web proxy client. On the right side of the figure, you'll see the ASCII decode of a frame taken from a Network Monitor trace. On the fifth line from the top, you'll see **HTTP/1.1 407 Proxy Authentication Required...** This is the 407 response the Web Proxy clients receive when an Access Rule requires authentication in order to connect to a Web site through the ISA firewall.

Figure 4.27 A 407 response is returned to the Web proxy client

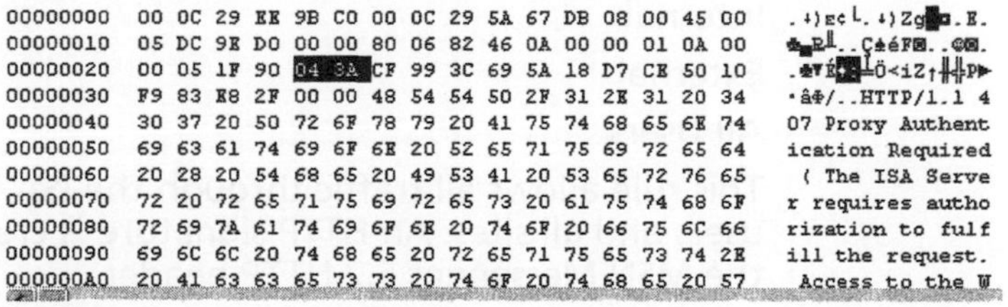

Blocking MSN Messenger using an Access Rule

Blocking dangerous applications is a common task for the ISA firewall. There are a number of methods you can use to block dangerous applications:

- Use the HTTP Security Filter to block the application if the application uses a Web (HTTP) connection to reach the site

- Use Domain Name Sets or URL Sets to block the sites the dangerous application needs to access to establish a connection

- Block the protocol, or do not allow access to the protocol, required by the dangerous application if the application uses a custom protocol

- If the application can use both a custom protocol and Web connection to access the Internet, then block the custom protocol and then use Domain Name Sets or URL Sets to block its ability to access the Internet using a Web connection

- Simplify your life by using the Principle of Least Privilege. When you use Least Privilege, you create rules to allow access. Anything not explicitly allowed is blocked. In this way, you'll almost never need to create a Deny rule of any kind

To demonstrate one method you can use to block dangerous applications, we'll create an Access Policy that blocks the MSN Messenger 6.2 application. The elements of the solution include the following:

- Create a Deny Rule that blocks the MSN Messenger Protocol
- Create an Access Rule that blocks the MSN Messenger HTTP header.

In this example, we will create an "all open" rule that allows all protocols outbound, but include a signature in the HTTP Security Filter that blocks the MSN Messenger. The second rule blocks the MSN Messenger protocol. Tables 4.2 and 4.3 show the properties of each Access Rule.

Table 4.2 All Open Rule with MSN Messenger 6.2 HTTP Security Filter signature

Setting	Value
Name	All Open -1
Action	Allow
Protocols	HTTP and HTTPS
From/Listener	Internal
To	External
Condition	All Users
Purpose	This rule allows all traffic through the ISA firewall to all users and all sites. An HTTP signature is created to block the MSN Messenger 6.2 HTTP header

Table 4.3 Access Rule that denies the MSN Messenger protocol

Setting	Value
Name	Deny Messenger Protocol
Action	Deny
Protocols	MSN Messenger
From/Listener	Internal
To	External
Condition	All Users
Purpose	Blocks the MSN Messenger Protocol TCP 1863

You can use the information given earlier in this chapter on how to create the Access Rules listed in Tables 4.2 and 4.3. The **Deny Messenger Protocol** Access Rule must be placed above the **All Open** rule. Deny rules should always be placed above allow rules. Your firewall policy should look something like that in Figure 4.28.

Figure 4.28 Firewall Policy to block MSN Messenger

O	▲	Name	Action	Protocols	From / Listener	To	Condition
	1	Deny Messenger Protocol	⊘ Deny	MSN Messenger	Internal	External	All Users
	2	All Open -1	✓ Allow	All Outbound Traffic	Internal	External	All Users
	3	Block NetBIOS Logging	⊘ Deny	NetBios Datagram / NetBios Name Service	Anywhere	Anywhere	All Users
	4	Web Publishing Rule	✓ Allow	HTTP	HTTP	10.0.0.2	All Users

After creating the Access Rules, right click on the **All Open -1** Access Rule and click the **Configure HTTP** command. In the **Configure HTTP policy for rule** dialog box, click the **Add** button. In the **Signature** dialog box, shown in Figure 4.29, enter the following information:

- **Name:**   Enter a name for the MSN Messenger blocking signature
- **Description (optional):**   Enter a description for the rule
- **Search in:**   Select the **Request headers** option from the drop down list
- **HTTP Header:**   Enter **User-Agent:** in the text box
- **Signature:**   enter **MSN Messenger** in the text box

Click **OK** to save the signature and click **OK** in the **Properties** dialog box. Click **Apply** to save the changes and update the firewall policy and Click **OK** in the **Apply New Configuration** dialog box.

Figure 4.29 The Signature dialog box

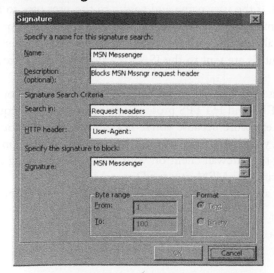

Figure 4.30 shows log file entries for the blocked connection from MSN Messenger. This first entry shows the connection using the MSN Messenger protocol being blocked and the third entry shows that the MSN Messenger connection was blocked by the HTTP Security Filter signature in the All Open rule.

Figure 4.30 Log file entries showing the HTTP Security Filter blocking the MSN Messenger connection

Destination Port	Protocol	HTTP Method	Action	URL	Rule	Filter Information
1863	MSN Messenger	·	Denied Connection	·	Deny Messenger Protocol	·
8080	http	GET	Allowed Connection	http://ISALOCAL/array.dll?Get.Routing.Script		
8080	http	POST	Denied Connection	http://gateway.messenger.hotmail.com/gatewa...	All Open -1	Blocked by the HTTP Security filter...

ISA FIREWALL TIP

A good way to filter for these types of events related to the HTTP Security Filter is to add the **HTTP Status** column in the ISA firewall's real-time log monitor.

Allowing Outbound Access to MSN Messenger via Web Proxy

The MSN Messenger can access the Internet using its own protocol, or it can tunnel its communications in an HTTP header. However, you will run into problems if you want Web Proxy clients to access the MSN Messenger site because of an authentication issue that hounds both the MSN Messenger and Hotmail applications.

When the MSN Messenger sends credentials to the MSN Messenger site, those credentials are also sent to the ISA firewall. If the user name and password the user uses to access the MSN Messenger site aren't the same as the credentials the user uses on the corporate network, then the connection will fail. If you allow anonymous access to the MSN Messenger site, then you won't have problems because no credentials are sent to the ISA firewall because the firewall won't challenge the user for credentials.

You can get around this issue by enabling an anonymous access rule for Web Proxy clients so that they can use the HTTP and HTTPS protocols to reach the sites required by the MSN messenger. This limits your exposure because you're not allowing anonymous access to all sites, just MSN Messenger. However, you do lose out on user/group based access control. You can easily solve this problem by using the Firewall client on your hosts and enforcing authentication via the Firewall client and configuring the MSN sites for Direct Access.

You will need to allow anonymous access to the HTTP protocol to the following sites:

```
Config.messenger.msn.com
Gateway.messenger.hotmail.com
Loginnet.passport.net
```

```
Loginnet.passport.com
207.46.110.0/24 (this is a Subnet Network Object)
```

We obtained this information by viewing the log file entries in the ISA firewall console's real time log viewer. The subnet and domains may change over time, so if you find that the rule no longer works, you'll need to check your log files and see what sites are required by the Messenger.

Table 4.4 shows the settings in the Access Rule allowing Web Proxy clients access to the MSN Messenger site.

Table 4.4 Settings for a MSN Messenger Web Proxy Access rule

Setting	Value
Name	MSN Messenger Web Proxy Access
Action	Allow
Protocols	HTTP and HTTPS
From/Listener	Internal
To	Messenger Subnet Messenger Sites
Condition	All Users
Purpose	This rule allows Web Proxy clients access to the MSN Messenger Sites without requiring authentication. This rule must be above all other rules that require authentication for the HTTP and HTTPS protocols.

Changes to ISA Firewall Policy Only Affects New Connections

After a client initiates a request, the ISA firewall maintains an active state in the firewall state table for the session which permits the response to return to the client. The active state permits the client to send new requests. The ISA firewall removes the active state from the state table after the session is idle for an unspecified period of time (usually a minute or two).

For example, try the following:

■ Open a command prompt on a host on a Protected Network and ping a host through the ISA firewall using the "ping –n IP address" command. The –n allows the ping to continue unabated during your test. When you're finished with your test, you can use the CTRL+C command to stop the ping. Make sure there is a rule that allows the host to ping the host through the ISA firewall.

■ On the ISA firewall, apply a Deny rule for the Ping protocol and place it above any rule that currently allows the ping through the ISA firewall.

■ The ping continues unabated even after the rule is applied. This is because there is an active state table entry for the ping from that client and the destination address being pinged.

- Open a second command prompt on the client that is pinging the remote host. Start a ping to a second host through the ISA firewall. The ping requests are denied because there is no state table entry for the ping protocol from that host to that destination host.

If you try to ping from a different client, the ping is denied.

Access Rules are applied immediately for *new* connections when you click **Apply** to save the changes and update firewall policy. To make changes apply to all existing connections, you can do either of the following:

- Disconnect existing sessions in the **Sessions** tab of the **Monitoring** node. To disconnect a session, open the **Microsoft Internet Security and Acceleration Server 2006** management console, click the **Monitoring** node, click the **Sessions** tab in the middle pane, click the session that you want to disconnect, and then click **Disconnect Session** on the **Tasks** tab.

- Another option is to restart the Microsoft Firewall service. In the **Microsoft Internet Security and Acceleration Server 2006** management console, click the **Monitoring** node, click the **Services** tab, click **Microsoft Firewall**, click **Stop Selected Service** on the **Tasks** tab, and then click **Start Selected Service** on the **Tasks** tab.

Allowing Intradomain Communications through the ISA Firewall

The new ISA firewall's enhanced support for directly attached DMZs has led to a lot of questions on how to allow intradomain communications through the ISA firewall from one network to another. You can now create multiple directly attached perimeter networks and allow controlled access to and from those perimeter networks. You can also safely put domain member machines on these DMZ segments to support a variety of new scenarios, such as dedicated network services segments that enforce domain segmentation.

For example, you might want to put an Internet facing Exchange Server or an inbound authenticating SMTP relay on a network services segment. In order to take advantage of the user database in the Active Directory, you need to join these machines to the Active Directory domain on the Internal network. Since the Internal network domain controllers are located on a network controlled by the ISA firewall, you need to configure the ISA firewall to allow the protocols required for intradomain communications.

TIP

Note that we don't "open ports" on the ISA firewall. The term "open ports" has its roots in simple packet filter based hardware firewalls. Since the ISA firewall is protocol aware, it can perform stateful filtering and stateful application layer inspection on all communications moving through the firewall. We highly recommend that you do *not* put your trust in only a simple packet filter hardware firewall to protect your critical corporate resources.

The basic network configuration used in this example is seen in Figure 4.31.

Figure 4.31 Basic network configuration for trihomed DMZ

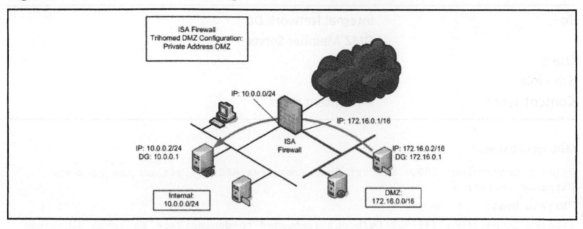

Table 4.5 shows the protocols required for intradomain communications, as well as other details included in an Access Rule we will create to support these communications.

Table 4.5 Protocols Required for Intradomain Communications

Name	Intradomain Communications
Action	Allow
Protocols	ADLogon/DirRep*
	Direct Host (TCP 445)**
	DNS
	Kerberos-Adm(UDP)
	Kerberos-Sec(TCP)
	Kerberos-Sec(UDP)
	LDAP (TCP)
	LDAP (UDP)
	LDAP GC (Global Catalog)
	RPC Endpoint Mapper (TCP 135)***
	NTP
	Ping
From	DMZ Member Server
	Internal Network DC

Table 4.5 Continued

Name	Intradomain Communications
To	Internal Network DC DMZ Member Server
Users	All
Schedule	Always
Content Types	All content types

*ADLogon/DirRep:

```
Primary Connection: 50000 TCP Outbound (requires RPC key set on the back-end
Exchange Server)
```

**Direct Host:

```
Primary Connection: 445 TCP Outbound (required to demonstrate an issue discussed
in this section
```

***RPC Endpoint Mapper

```
Primary Connection:  135 TCP Outbound (required to demonstrate an issue
discussed in this section)
```

RPC services configure themselves in the Registry with a universally unique identifier (UUID), which is similar in function to a globally unique identifier (GUID). RPC UUIDs are well-known identifiers (at least to RPC services), and are unique for each service.

When an RPC service starts, it obtains an unused high or ephemeral port, and registers that port with the RPC service's UUID. Some services choose a random high port while others try to always use the same high port if that port is not already in use. The high port assignment is static for the lifetime of the service and changes only after the machine or service is restarted.

When a client communicates with an RPC service, it doesn't know in advance which high port the service is using. Instead, the RPC client application establishes a connection to the server's RPC portmapper (endpoint mapper) service (on TCP 135) and requests the service it wants by using the service's specific UUID. The RPC endpoint mapper returns the corresponding high port number to the client and closes the connection endpoint mapper connection.

Finally, the client makes a new connection to the server, using the high port number it received from the endpoint mapper.

Because it's impossible to know in advance which port an RPC service will use, the firewall needs to permit all high ports through.

We want to limit the ports required for RPC to a single port. This allows us to know in advance what port to use and configure on the firewall. Otherwise, we would need to allow all high ports from the DMZ to the Internal network. We can limit the ports to a single port by making a Registry change on each domain controller. The Registry Key is:

```
HKEY_LOCAL_MACHINE\SYSTEM\CurrentControlSet\Services\NTDS\Parameters\
```

ISA FIREWALL NOTE

We actually do not need to do this, as the ISA firewall's RPC filter can dynamically control port access. The RPC filter listens to the RPC negotiations and then dynamically opens the required high port. However, we prefer to set the port manually as it makes it easier to analyze the logs and track the RPC communications moving between the DMZ segment and the Internal network. If the administrative overhead of setting a specific high port for RPC communications is too high, you can take advantage of the RPC filter and not worry about it. This is what we mean when we say the ISA firewall doesn't "open ports" – the ISA firewall actually understands the *protocols* required.

You need to add a DWORD value named **TCP/IP Port** and set the value to the port you want to use. You'll need to carry out this procedure on each of the domain controllers in your domain.

Perform the following steps on each of the domain controllers in your domain to limit the RPC replication port to **50000**:

1. Click **Start** and click **Run**. In the **Open** text box enter **Regedit** and click **OK**.
2. Go to the following Registry key:
3. HKEY_LOCAL_MACHINE\SYSTEM\CurrentControlSet\Services\NTDS\Parameters\
4. Click the **Edit** menu and point to **New**. Click **DWORD Value**.
5. Rename the entry from **New Value #1** to **TCP/IP Port**, then double click the entry.
6. In the **Edit DWORD Value** dialog box, select the **Decimal** option. Enter **50000** in the **Value data** text box. Click **OK**.
7. Restart the domain controller.

The ISA firewall allows you to control the route relationship between any two Networks. In this example, we will use a ROUTE relationship between the DMZ and the Internal network. Note that when you apply a Network Template to create a DMZ segment, the default route relationship is set as NAT. While there are some minimal advantages to using a NAT relationship, those advantages are outweighed by the limitations they impose in this scenario. If you used a Network Template, make sure to change the Network Rule that controls communications between the DMZ and Internal network to ROUTE as shown in Figure 4.32.

Figure 4.32 Configuring the Network Relationship

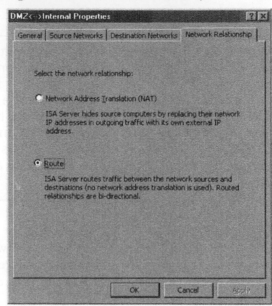

In the following example, we create a rule allowing intradomain communications between a single member server in the DMZ and a single domain controller on the Internal Network. We are using this scenario for simplicity's sake, but you are by no means limited to allowing communications between single servers.

For example, you might have several member server machines on the DMZ and multiple domain controllers on the Internal network. In this case, instead of creating computer objects representing single machines, you would create a Computer Set for the DMZ member servers and another Computer Set for the Internal Network domain controllers. You can then use the Computer Sets to control the Source and Destination locations for the intradomain communications rule.

ISA FIREWALL NOTE

In the following exercise, you will create two Protocol Definitions that are *not required* since there are built in Protocol Definitions to support our requirements. However, we will create these Protocol Definitions to illustrate some important points that we discuss at the end of the section.

Perform the following steps to create the intradomain communications rule that will allow machines in the DMZ segment to communicate with domain controllers on the Internal network:

1. In the **Microsoft Internet Security and Acceleration Server 2006** management console, expand the server name and then click the **Firewall Policy** node.

2. In the **Firewall Policy** node, click the **Tasks** tab on the Task Pane. Click the **Create a New Access Rule** link.

3. On the **Welcome to the New Access Rule Wizard** page, enter a name for the rule in the **Access Rule name** text box. In this example, we will call the rule **Member Server→Internal DC**. Click **Next**.

4. On the **Rule Action** page, select the **Allow** option and click **Next**.

5. In the **This rule applies to** list, select the **Selected protocols** option. Click the **Add** button.

6. In the **Add Protocols** dialog box, click the **All Protocols** folder. Double click the following protocols:

    ```
    DNS
    Kerberos-Adm (UDP)
    Kerberos-Sec (TCP)
    Kerberos-Sec (UDP)
    LDAP
    LDAP (UDP)
    LDAP GC (Global Catalog)
    NTP (UDP)
    Ping
    ```

7. Click the **New** menu and click **Protocol**.

8. On the **Welcome to the New Protocol Definition Wizard** page, enter **ADLogon/ DirRep** in the **Protocol Definition name** text box. Click **Next**.

9. On the **Primary Connection Information** page, click **New**.

10.   On the **New/Edit Protocol Connection** page, select **TCP** in the **Protocol type** list. Select **Outbound** in the **Direction** list. In the **Port Range** frame, enter **50000** in the **From** and **To** text boxes as shown in Figure 4.33. Click **OK**.

Figure 4.33 Creating a new Protocol Definitions

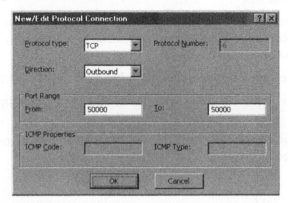

11.   Click **Next** on the **Primary Connection Information** page.

12.   Select the **No** option on the **Secondary Connections** page.

13.   Click **Finish** on the **Completing the New Protocol Definition Wizard** page.

14.   Click the **New** menu and click **Protocol**.

15.   On the **Welcome to the New Protocol Definition Wizard** page, enter **Direct Host** in the **Protocol Definition** name text box. Click **Next**.

16.   On the **Primary Connection Information** page, click **New**.

17.   On the **New/Edit Protocol Connection page**, select **TCP** in the **Protocol type** list. Select **Outbound** in the **Direction** list. In the **Port Range** frame, enter **445** in the **From** and **To** text boxes. Click **OK**.

18.   Click **Next** on the **Primary Connection Information** page as shown in Figure 4.34.

Figure 4.34 Configure the Primary Connection for the Protocol Definition

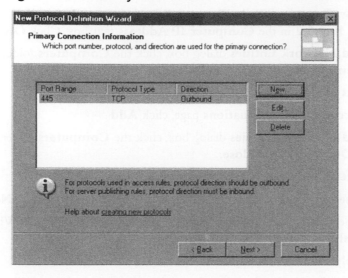

19.   Select the **No** option on the **Secondary Connections** page.

20.   Click **Finish** on the **Completing the New Protocol Definition Wizard** page.

21.   Click the **New** menu and click **Protocol**.

22.   On the **Welcome to the New Protocol Definition Wizard** page, enter **RPC Endpoint Mapper (TCP 135)** in the **Protocol Definition name** text box. Click **Next**.

23.   On the **Primary Connection Information** page, click **New**.

24.   On the **New/Edit Protocol Connection** page, select **TCP** in the **Protocol type** list. Select **Outbound** in the **Direction** list. In the **Port Range** frame, enter **135** in the **From** and **To** text boxes. Click **OK**.

25.   Click **Next** on the **Primary Connection Information** page.

26.   Select the **No** option on the **Secondary Connections** page.

27.   Click **Finish** on the **Completing the New Protocol Definition Wizard** page.

28.   In the **Add Protocols** dialog box, click the **User-Defined** folder. Double click the **ADLogon/DirRep, Direct Access** and **RPC Endpoint Mapper (TCP 135)** protocols. Click **Close**.

29.   Click **Next** on the **Protocols** page.

30.   On the **Access Rule Sources** page, click **Add**.

31.   In the **Add Network Entities** dialog box, click the **New** menu. Click **Computer**.

32.   In the **New Computer Rule Element** dialog box, enter **DMZ Member Server** in the **Name** text box. Enter **172.16.0.2** in the **Computer IP Address** text box. Click **OK**.

33. In the **Add Network Entities** dialog box, click the **New** menu. Click **Computer**.

34. In the **New Computer Rule Element** dialog box, enter **Internal DC** in the **Name** text box. Enter **10.0.0.2** in the **Computer IP Address** text box. Click **OK**.

35. In the **Add Network Entities** dialog box, click the **Computers** folder. Double click the **DMZ Member Server** entry. Click **Close**.

36. Click **Next** on the **Access Rule Sources** page.

37. On the **Access Rule Destinations** page, click **Add**.

38. In the **Add Network Entities** dialog box, click the **Computers** folder. Double click the **Internal DC** entry. Click **Close**.

39. Click **Next** on the **Access Rule Destinations** page.

40. On the **User Sets** page, accept the default entry, **All Users**, and click **Next**.

41. Review the settings on the **Completing the New Access Rule Wizard** page and click **Finish**.

42. Click **Apply** to save the changes and update the firewall policy.

43. Click **OK** in the **Apply New Configuration** dialog box, then you'll see what's shown in Figure 4.35 in the Firewall Policy tab.

Figure 4.35 Firewall Policy

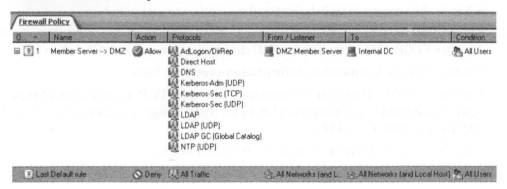

You can test the rule by joining a machine in the DMZ to the Active Directory domain on the Internal network and then logging into the domain after joining the domain. Note that this rule doesn't allow all protocols through from the member servers to the domain controllers. You will need to create other Access Rules for other protocols, and additional Access Rules for communications to other machines on other networks.

Figure 4.36 below shows some log file entries for communications between the member server and the domain controller on the Internal network. There are some entries in the log file that highlight some undocumented issues with the ISA firewall and its configuration.

Figure 4.36 Log file entries showing communications between member server and domain controller

Client IP	Destinat...	Destination Port	Protocol	Action	Rule	Source Network	Destination Net
172.16.0.2	10.0.0.2	445	Microsoft CIFS (TCP)	Closed...	Member Server <--> DMZ	DMZ	Internal
172.16.0.2	10.0.0.2	389	LDAP	Closed...	Member Server <--> DMZ	DMZ	Internal
172.16.0.2	10.0.0.2	88	Kerberos-Sec (UDP)	Initiated...	Member Server <--> DMZ	DMZ	Internal
172.16.0.2	10.0.0.2	50000	AdLogon/DirRep	Initiated...	Member Server <--> DMZ	DMZ	Internal
172.16.0.2	10.0.0.2	135	RPC (all interfaces)	Initiated...	Member Server <--> DMZ	DMZ	Internal
172.16.0.2	10.0.0.2	88	Kerberos-Sec (UDP)	Initiated...	Member Server <--> DMZ	DMZ	Internal
172.16.0.2	10.0.0.2	88	Kerberos-Sec (UDP)	Initiated...	Member Server <--> DMZ	DMZ	Internal
172.16.0.2	10.0.0.2	389	LDAP	Initiated...	Member Server <--> DMZ	DMZ	Internal
172.16.0.2	10.0.0.2	88	Kerberos-Sec (UDP)	Initiated...	Member Server <--> DMZ	DMZ	Internal
172.16.0.2	10.0.0.2	88	Kerberos-Sec (UDP)	Initiated...	Member Server <--> DMZ	DMZ	Internal
172.16.0.2	10.0.0.2	88	Kerberos-Sec (UDP)	Initiated...	Member Server <--> DMZ	DMZ	Internal
172.16.0.2	10.0.0.2	445	Microsoft CIFS (TCP)	Initiated...	Member Server <--> DMZ	DMZ	Internal
172.16.0.2	10.0.0.2	389	LDAP (UDP)	Initiated...	Member Server <--> DMZ	DMZ	Internal
172.16.0.2	10.0.0.2	389	LDAP (UDP)	Initiated...	Member Server <--> DMZ	DMZ	Internal
172.16.0.2	10.0.0.2	389	LDAP (UDP)	Initiated...	Member Server <--> DMZ	DMZ	Internal
172.16.0.2	10.0.0.2	445	Microsoft CIFS (TCP)	Closed...	Member Server <--> DMZ	DMZ	Internal

Notice on the first line the connection to TCP port 445. In the protocol column, the name of the protocol is **Microsoft CIFS (TCP)** and not **Direct Host**, which is the name of the Protocol Definition we created for that protocol. The reason for this is that the built-in protocols will be used preferentially in the event that you create a Protocol Definition that has the same settings as a built-in Protocol Definition.

In the fifth line from the top, you'll see a connection made to TCP port 135. The **Protocol** column lists this as the **RCP (all interfaces)** protocol, instead of the **RCP Endpoint Mapper** protocol that we created. Again, the reason for this is that there is a built-in **RPC (all interfaces)** protocol and it is used preferentially over the one we created. In addition, this built-in Protocol Definition automatically binds the ISA firewall's RPC filter, which adds a significant amount of protection for the RPC communications.

We do see one of our custom Protocol Definitions being used in the fourth line from the top. The **ADLogon/DirRep** Protocol Definition is used to communicate on the custom RPC port we configured in the Registry of the domain controller.

One More Time

In this chapter we discussed how the ISA firewall processes Access Policy and how to configure Access Rules to control outbound access through the ISA firewall. We also discussed a number of special topics in ISA firewall Access Policy that you can use to further lockdown your network.

You learned about the elements that make up the ISA firewall access rules, including protocols, user sets, content types, schedules and network objects. We discussed how you can create your own protocols or use those built into the ISA Server firewall. We also discussed the user sets (firewall groups) that come preconfigured in ISA Server: all authenticated users, all users, and system and network service. We talked about how content type control works with HTTP and tunneled FTP traffic, and you learned about the pre-built content types, as well as how to create your own content types. We also discussed how to apply schedules to access rules.

Next, we provided step by step details on how to create access rules and all the options that are available when creating or configuring a rule. You also learned how to bypass the Wizard and create new rules by copying and pasting, then making changes to an existing rule. We showed you how to configure RPC, FTP and HTTP policies, and how to order and organize your access rules.

We discussed using scripts to populate domain name sets, and provided a sample script that will allow you to import entries into a Domain Name set or URL set from a text file.

You learned about some specific examples of tasks you might want to perform, such as how to block MSN Messenger using an access rule and how to allow outbound access to MSN Messenger via Web Proxy.

In the next section, we discussed the details of creating and configuring a public address trihomed DMZ (perimeter) network. We discussed reasons for using access rules instead of publishing rules to allow access to DMZ hosts, and described how to publish a public address DMZ host using access rules and how to test the rules.

Finally, we covered how to allow intradomain communications through an ISA Server Firewall. We discussed protocols required for intradomain communications and showed you how to edit the registry on your domain controllers to limit ports required for RPC to a single port, in order to make it easier to analyze the logs.

Chapter 5

Publishing Network Services with ISA 2006 Firewalls

Solutions in this chapter:

- Overview of Web Publishing and Server Publishing
- Creating and Configuring Non-SSL Web Publishing Rules
- Creating and Configuring SSL Web Publishing Rules
- Creating Server Publishing Rules
- Creating Mail Server Publishing Rules

Overview of Web Publishing and Server Publishing

Web Publishing and Server Publishing Rules allow you to make servers and services on ISA firewall Protected Networks available to users on both protected and non-protected networks. Web and Server Publishing Rules allow you to make popular services, such as SMTP, HTTP, POP3, IMAP4, Exchange/OWA, NNTP, Terminal Services, and many more securely available to users on remote networks or on other Internal or Perimeter Networks.

Web Publishing Rules and Server Publishing Rules provide very different feature sets and are used for very different purposes. In general, Web Publishing Rules should be used to publish Web servers and services, and Server Publishing Rules should be used to publish non-Web servers and services. There are exceptions to these rules, and we will discuss these exceptions in this chapter.

We will begin the chapter with a discussion of the features and capabilities of Web and Server Publishing Rules. After this general overview of Web and Server Publishing Rules, we will go into the details of how to create and configure Web and Server Publishing Rules. We will then complete this chapter with several scenarios that demonstrate how Web and Server Publishing Rules are used on production networks.

Web Publishing Rules

Web Publishing Rules are used to publish Web sites and services. Web Publishing is sometimes referred to as "reverse proxying." When you publish a Web site, the ISA firewall's Web Proxy filter always intercepts the request and then proxies the request to the Web site published by the Web Publishing Rule.

Web Publishing Rules sport the following features:

- Proxied access to Web sites protected by the ISA firewall

- Deep application-layer inspection of connections made to published Web sites

- Path redirection

- URL Rewriting with ISA's Link Translation

- Ability to publish multiple Web sites with a single IP address

- Pre-authentication of requests, and Authentication Delegation to the published Site

- Single Sign-On (SSO) for Published Web Sites

- Support for SecurID authentication

- Support for RADIUS authentication

- Support for (Secure) LDAP authentication

- Reverse Caching of published Web sites

- Support for forwarding either the ISA firewall's IP address or the original client's IP address to the Web site

- Ability to schedule when connections are allowed to Published Web sites

- Port and Protocol Redirection
- Load-balancing of published websites performed by ISA itself

Let's look at each of these features in more detail.

Proxied Access to Web Sites Protected by the ISA firewall

Web Publishing Rules provide proxied access to Web sites located on an ISA firewall Protected Network. Any Network that is not part of the default External Network is considered an ISA firewall Protected Network. A proxied connection is more secure than a routed and NATed connection because the entire communication is deconstructed and reconstructed by the ISA firewall. This allows the ISA firewall to perform very deep application-layer inspection of Web requests made to published Web sites that have been published using Web Publishing Rules.

The ISA firewall's Web Proxy filter handles all incoming Web connections made through Web Publishing Rules. Even when you unbind the Web Proxy filter from the HTTP protocol definition, the Web Proxy filter is always enabled for Web Publishing Rules. This is a security decision made by the ISA firewall team. They determined that non-proxied incoming connections to Protected Network Web servers should always be proxied to allow for the highest degree of protection for published Web servers.

Deep Application-Layer Inspection of Connections Made to Published Web Sites

One of the major advantages of using Web Publishing Rules to publish Web sites on protected networks is the ISA firewall's ability to perform very deep application-layer inspection on all connections made to published Web sites. This deep application-layer inspection provides a high degree of protection against attacks exploiting flaws in the inspected protocol, including malicious code and attacks targeting the published webserver. This allows the ISA firewall to stop attacks at the perimeter and prevents the attacker from ever reaching the published Web server itself.

Deep application-layer inspection for Web requests is the responsibility of the ISA firewall's **HTTP Filter**. The ISA firewall's HTTP filter allows you to control virtually any aspect of an HTTP communication and block or allow connections based on almost any component of an HTTP communication.

Examples of how you can control connections to published Web sites include:

- Setting the maximum payload length, which guards against attacks involving large amounts of data submitted to databases or web servers in an HTTP POST request.
- Blocking high-bit characters, which are often indicative of a Buffer overflow attack. Enabling this option will only allow standard ASCII characters, but will prevent URLs using some international character sets from working.
- Verifying normalization, helping to protect against URL-encoding attacks by performing the decoding process on encoded characters such as %20 (whitespace) twice to detect, and block, attacks relying on double encoding. See http://www.owasp.org/index.php/Double_Encoding for more information on this attack class.

- Blocking responses containing Windows executable content

- Setting the exact HTTP methods that you want to allow to the published Web site and block all others

- Allowing only a specific list of file extensions

- Allowing only a specific list of Request or Response headers

- Creating fine-tuned signatures that can block connections based on Request URLs, Request headers, Request body, Response headers, or Response body

We will go into some of the details of the HTTP Security Filter (HTTP Filter) later in this chapter, and we will also go into the deep details of the HTTP Security Filter in Chapter 4 on the ISA firewall's application-layer filtering feature set.

Path Redirection

Web Publishing Rules allow you to redirect connections based on the path indicated by the external user. Path redirection allows you to redirect connections based on the user's indicated path to an alternate directory on the same Web server, or to another Web server entirely.

For example, a user sends a request to http://www.example.com/kits. You want the request to be forwarded to a server named **WEBSERVER1** and to a directory on the server named **/deployment_kits** in order to allow a partner without access to the intranet server **WEBSERVER1** to access information via the internet.

You can configure the Web Publishing Rule to direct the path in the request (which is **/kits**) to the path on the internal Web server, **/deployment_kits**.

You can also use path redirection to forward the request to another Web server entirely. For example, suppose users submit requests for the following sites:

- www.example.com/scripts

- www.example.com/deployment_kits

You can create two Web Publishing Rules, one for incoming requests to www.example.com/scripts and one for www.example.com/deployment_kits. The request for www.example.com/script can be redirected to a Web server named **WEBSERVER1**, and the second can be redirected to **WEBSERVER2**. We can even redirect the request to alternate paths on each Web server.

We will go over some examples of path redirection in the scenarios section of this chapter.

URL rewriting with ISA's Link Translation

The ISA firewall's link translator can rewrite the responses that published Web servers send to users making requests. The link translator is useful when publishing Web sites that include hard-coded URLs or references to images and intranet servers in their responses, where those URLs are not accessible from remote locations, or are published using a path redirection rule.

For example, if – as in the preceding example – http://webserver1/kits were published via an ISA server as http://www.example.com/deployment_kits, but included hard-coded links (with *absolute* rather than *relative* paths) to http://webserver1/kits/documents/somefile.txt, any request from a visitor to http://www.example.com/deployment_kits for somefile.txt would fail.

The link translator solves this problem by rewriting the responses returned to the user accessing the Web site. The link http://webserver1/kits/documents/somefile.txt is rewritten http://www.example.com/deployment_kits/documents/somefile.txt, which is accessible from the Internet.

This is commonly a feature enabled where intranet servers are published to the internet, or anywhere where the URLs being returned reference host or DNS names which are not resolvable (or which cannot be connected to) from the network the ISA Server is publishing to.

Link translation is also useful in some SSL scenarios. For example, when you are not using SSL from the ISA firewall to the Web server, but you are using SSL between the Web client on the Internet and the ISA firewall, the link translator can change the HTTP response returned by the Web server to an SSL response in the links presented to the user. This prevents the users from encountering broken links on the published Web page.

We will discuss the usages and configuration options of the link translator in this chapter and in detail in Chapter 4 on application-layer filtering.

Ability to Publish Multiple Web Sites with a Single IP Address

Link translation allows multiple applications such as Sharepoint instances or Live Communications Server's Communicator Web Access to be exposed as paths stemming from the same site, with a similar FQDN and SSL Certificate. In addition to this, web Publishing Rules allow you to publish multiple Web sites using a single IP address on the external interface of the ISA firewall using HTTP Host Headers.

The ISA firewall can do this because of its ability to perform stateful application-layer inspection. Part of the ISA firewall's stateful application-layer inspection feature set is its ability to examine the host header on the incoming request and make decisions on how to handle the incoming request based on that host header information.

For example, suppose you have a single IP address on the external interface of the ISA firewall. You want to publish two Web servers on an ISA firewall Protected Network. Users will access the Web sites using the URLs extranet.example.com and crm.example.com. All you need to do is create two Web Publishing Rules. One of the Web Publishing Rules will listen for incoming connections for extranet.example.com and forward those requests to the extranet.example.com server on the ISA firewall Protected Network, and the other Web Publishing Rule will listen for requests to crm.example.com and forward those requests to the Web site on the ISA firewall Protected Network responsible for the crm.example.com Web site.

The key to making this work, as we'll discuss later in this chapter, is to make sure that the public DNS resolves the fully-qualified domain names to the IP address on the external interface of the ISA firewall. Once the DNS issue is addressed, publishing two or two hundred Web sites with a single IP address is very simple using the ISA firewall's Web Publishing Rules.

Pre-authentication of requests, and Authentication Delegation to the published Site

Web Publishing Rules can be configured to authenticate users at the ISA firewall. ISA challenges clients to authenticate using a combination of three HTTP authentication methods (Basic, Digest, or Integrated), X.509 Client Certificate Authentication, or Forms-Based Authentication (FBA) (also referred to as HTML Form Authentication), also implementing Pre-Authentication.

This pre-authentication prevents unauthenticated connections from ever reaching the Web server. Pre-authentication blocks attackers and other malicious users from leveraging unauthenticated connections to exploit known and unknown weaknesses in Web servers and applications, significantly reducing the attack surface of the webserver.

One popular use of pre-authentication is for OWA Web sites. Instead of allowing unauthenticated connections from reaching the OWA Web site, the ISA firewall's Web Publishing Rule for the OWA Web site can be configured to authenticate the user. If the user successfully authenticates with the ISA firewall, then the connection request is passed to the OWA site. If the user cannot authenticate successfully with the ISA firewall, then the connection attempt is dropped at the firewall and never reaches the published Web site.

ISA 2006 enables the use of FBA (Forms-Based Authentication) for any site published with ISA, so Sharepoint sites, intranet pages, and any other web content can be exposed by ISA using FBA.

Pre-authentication also allows you to control who can access Web sites. You can configure Web Publishing Rules to allow only certain user groups to access the published Web site. So even if users are able to authenticate successfully, they will only be able to access the published Web site if they have permission to do so. In this way, the ISA firewall's Web Publishing Rules allow authentication and authorization for access to published Web sites.

The ISA firewall's delegation of basic authentication option allows the ISA firewall to authenticate the user and then forward the user credentials to the published Web site when the Web site request credentials. This prevents the user from being subjected to double authentication prompts. Instead of the user answering the Web site's request for authentication, the ISA firewall answers the request after successfully authenticating the user.

Single Sign-On (SSO) for Published Web Sites

Increasingly, organizations are deploying multiple web-based applications such as Outlook Web Access and Sharepoint as applications for users. Whilst deploying intranet pages and processes via the web greatly increases the convenience of working remotely, exposing multiple web applications through one ISA Server can require users to authenticate to each web application in turn.

Single Sign-On with ISA Server allows the user to authenticate once to the ISA Server, allowing the ISA Server itself to handle authentication from this point on. Single Sign-on is only supported.

Support for SecurID Authentication

RSA's SecurID is a two-factor authentication mechanism. Two-factor authentication increases security over simple password protection by requiring that the user use both something they know (their password) in addition to something they physically posses (the SecurID token) to authenticate.

The SecurID token itself is a small electronic device which generates a six-digit number based on a shared secret stored within the token itself, and on a backend server against which a firewall such as ISA authenticates the user. The ISA firewall comes with built-in support for SecurID authentication for Web servers and services published via Web Publishing Rules.

Support for RADIUS Authentication

Some organizations will choose to put the ISA firewall in a location where making the firewall a member of the user domain is not the best option. For example, if you have a back-to-back firewall configuration where the front-end firewall is an ISA firewall, you should not make the front-end ISA firewall a member of the user domain. You can still take advantage of the domain user database for authentication and authorization by using RADIUS for Web Publishing Rule authentication.

The ISA firewall can be configured as a RADIUS client to a RADIUS server on the corporate network. The RADIUS server can then be configured to authenticate users against the Active Directory or any other RADIUS-compliant directory on the corporate network. RADIUS authentication can be used for both inbound and outbound connections through the ISA firewall's Web Proxy filter. Setting up Web Publishing Rules using RADIUS is very easy and allows the ISA firewall support back-to-back firewall scenarios where the ISA firewall is the front-end firewall.

Radius can also be used to allow the ISA Firewall to authenticate against a directory services infrastructure or authentication provider not supported natively, or simply a third party radius solution.

Reverse Caching of Published Web Sites

The ISA firewall can cache responses from Web sites published via Web Publishing Rules. Once a user makes a request for content on the published Web site, that content can be cached (stored) on the ISA firewall. When subsequent users make requests for the same content on the published Web server, the content is served from the ISA firewall's Web cache instead of being fetched from the Web server itself.

Caching responses from published Web sites reduces the load on the published Web server and on any network segments between the ISA firewall and the published Web server. Since the content is served from the ISA firewall's Web cache, the published Web server isn't exposed to the processing overhead required to service those Web requests. As content is served from the ISA firewall's Web cache instead of the published Web site, network traffic between the ISA firewall and the published Web site is reduced, which increases overall network performance on the corporate network.

In the former case, an ageing webserver may have load reduced by caching. In the latter, an intranet page with largely static content may be accessed by clients in a branch office ostensibly over the local network, with ISA making efficient use of a slow WAN link.

You can also control the reverse caching on content. You may want users to always receive the freshest versions of content in some locations on your published Web server, while allowing the ISA firewall to cache other content on the published Web servers for a pre-defined time period. You can create cache rules on the ISA firewall in order to have fine-tuned control over what content is cached and how long that content is cached. Scheduled cache content download jobs also allow static content to be retrieved into the cache on a fixed schedule.

Support for Forwarding either the ISA Firewall's IP Address, or the Original Web Client's IP Address to the Web Site

One of the limitations with Web Publishing Rules in ISA Server 2000 was that logs on the published Web server always showed the IP address for the internal network adapter of the ISA Server. When you published Web servers using Web Publishing Rules, the source IP address of the client connecting to the published Web server was replaced with the internal IP address of the ISA Server. This was a major barrier to adoption for many potential ISA Server administrators because they already had sunk significant costs into log analysis software installed on the published Web servers. In addition, publishing load-balanced clusters via ISA is complicated when published web servers see all traffic coming from the ISA firewalls, rather than original IP addresses. With ISA 2000, the only option was to use Server Publishing Rules, which isn't a good option because Server Publishing Rules do not confer the same high level of security as Web Publishing Rules.

ISA 2004 and beyond give you the choice between forwarding the ISA firewall's IP address to the published Web server or forwarding the actual remote Web client's IP address to the published Web server. If you don't need the actual client's IP address in the Web server's log files, then use the default option, which is to replace the client IP address with the ISA firewall's network interface address. If you need to preserve the remote Web client's IP address, then you can choose the option to preserve the IP address.

We'll discuss the advantages and disadvantages of each approach when we cover the details of creating and configuring Web Publishing Rules later in this chapter.

Ability to Schedule when Connections are Allowed to Published Web Sites

ISA Firewall Web Publishing Rules allow you to control when users can access the published Web site. You may have some Web sites that you only want accessed during work hours, and other Web sites that have high bandwidth requirements that you only want accessed during off-hours. You can control when users access published Web sites by applying either built-in or custom schedules to your Web Publishing Rules.

Port and Protocol Redirection

Web Publishing Rules allow you to perform both protocol and port redirection. Port redirection allows the ISA firewall to accept a connection request on one port and then forward that request to an alternate port on the published Web server. For example, the ISA firewall can listen to incoming requests on its Web listener on TCP port 80 and then redirect that connection to TCP 8888 on the published Web server on the ISA firewall Protected Network.

You can also perform protocol redirection using Web Publishing Rules. In contrast to port redirection, where the only change is the destination port, the ISA firewall's support for protocol redirection allows you to publish FTP sites using Web Publishing Rules. The incoming HTTP GET request made to the Web Publishing Rule's Web listener is transformed to an FTP GET and forwarded to the published FTP site on a ISA firewall Protected Network. Web Publishing Rules support protocol redirection from HTTP to FTP.

Load-balancing of published websites performed by the ISA firewall itself

ISA 2006 introduces new functionality designed to publish web servers which serve the same content, commonly referred to as load-balanced, or clustered web servers. There are many third party software packages and hardware platforms which manage this, including Microsoft's own Network Load Balancing (NLB) (formerly Windows Load Balancing Services, or WLBS), which is designed to run on Windows servers themselves, which collectively form a load-balanced cluster, and hardware solutions from third party vendors.

Like the appliances, load-balancing with ISA is undertaken by the ISA firewall (or cluster of ISA firewalls) publishing the web sites, and requires no special backend logic (unlike NLB). ISA Web Farm Load Balancing can be configured to determine 'affinity' (i.e. Which web server a given client should communicate with) either by IP address or cookie – in the latter case, the ISA firewall itself inserts a cookie in the client's browser which is sent with each subsequent request. As with similar load balancing schemes, the ISA firewall includes configurable heart beating for determining the health of published web servers, and can be used to transparently remove and add servers from service without any visible disruption to clients.

Server Publishing Rules

Like Web Publishing Rules, you can use Server Publishing Rules to provide access to servers and services on ISA firewall Protected Networks. The following features and capabilities characterize Server Publishing Rules:

- Server Publishing Rules are a form of reverse NAT, sometimes referred to as "Port Mapping" or "Port forwarding" and do not proxy the connection.
- Almost all IP level and TCP/UDP protocols can be published using Server Publishing Rules.
- Server Publishing Rules do not support authentication on the ISA Server.
- Application-layer filtering can be applied to a defined subset of Server Published protocols.
- You can configure port overrides to customize the listening ports and the port redirection. You can also lock down the source ports the requesting clients use to connect to the published server.
- You can lock down who can access published resources using IP addresses.
- The external client source IP address can be preserved or can be replaced with the ISA firewall's IP address.
- Restrict connections to specific days and times.
- Support for "port redirection" (or PAT – Port address translation) where connections can be received on one port and redirected to another port, providing the same functionality as that seen in many "hardware" firewall solutions.

Let's look at each of these in a bit more detail.

Server Publishing Rules are a Form of Reverse NAT, sometimes referred to as "Port Mapping" or "Port forwarding" and do not Proxy the Connection

Server Publishing Rules are a form of either reverse NAT or port mapping, depending on whether you have a NAT or route relationship between the published server and the host that is connecting to the published server via the Server Publishing Rule. The Server Publishing Rule configures the ISA firewall to listen on a specific port and then forwards those connections to the published server on an ISA firewall Protected Network.

In contrast, Web Publishing Rules proxy the requests to the published Web server. Server Publishing Rules just change the source port and IP address before forwarding the connection to the published server. Proxied connections are completely deconstructed and reconstructed by the ISA firewall, and thus, confer a much higher level of application-layer inspection than Server Publishing Rules.

Almost All IP Level and TCP/UDP Protocols can be Published using Server Publishing Rules

Web Publishing Rules only accept HTTP and HTTPS connections and forward them as HTTP, HTTPS, or FTP connections. In contrast, Server Publishing Rules can be used to publish almost any IP Level, TCP, or UDP protocol. This provides a great deal of flexibility in what services can be made available to hosts via Server Publishing Rules.

Server Publishing Rules do not Support Authentication on the ISA Server

One of the major drawbacks of Web Publishing Rules compared to Server Publishing Rules is that Server Publishing Rules do not support pre-authentication at the ISA firewall. Authentication must be done by the server published by the Server Publishing Rule, and therefore unauthenticated clients have the ability to communicate with (and potentially compromise or attack) published servers.

Application-Layer Filtering can be Applied to a Defined Subset of Server Published Protocols

Deep stateful application-layer inspection for connections made through Web Publishing Rules is performed by the ISA firewall's HTTP filter. Server Publishing Rules also support application-layer inspection through the use of Application Filters. The ISA firewall comes out of the box with the following application filters:

- DNS (security filter)
- FTP Access Filter
- H.323 Filter
- MMS Filter
- PNM Filter
- POP Intrusion Detection Filter (security filter)
- PPTP Filter
- RPC Filter (security filter)
- RTSP Filter
- SMTP Filter (security filter)
- SOCKS v4 Filter
- Web Proxy Filter (security filter)

A number of these filters are used to mediate complex protocols in the same way that NAT editors allow the use of complex protocols through a NAT device. Examples of types of access filters are the H.323 Filter, the MMS Filter, and the RTSP filter. In contrast, there are several application filters whose main job is to secure connections made through the ISA firewall by performing compliance testing against the connection. Example of these security filters are the DNS filter, POP Intrusion Detection Filter, and the RPC Filter.

Some of the application-layer filters perform both duties. They mediate complex protocol management for SecureNAT clients, and they also secure the connections they mediate. Filters fitting into this category include the FTP Access Filter and the RPC Filter.

We will cover application-layer filters in detail in Chapter 4.

You can Configure Port Overrides to Customize the Listening Ports and the Port Redirection. You can also Lock Down the Source Ports the Requesting Clients use to Connect to the Published Server

Within each Server Publishing Rule is the ability to control the listening port, the destination port, and the port that the requesting client can use as a source port to access the Server-Published server. This provides you very granular control over port redirection (port mapping) for any server you publish using Server Publishing Rules.

You can lock down who can Access Published Resources using IP addresses

Although Server Publishing Rules do not allow you to pre-authenticate users at the ISA firewall, you can configure Server Publishing Rules to limit IP addresses that can connect to the published server via the Server Publishing Rule. This type of IP address-based access control is used for publishing servers that should have limited access. An example of such a server is a Terminal Server on the corporate network that only administrators located at pre-defined addresses can access.

The External Client Source IP Address can be Preserved or it can be Replaced with the ISA Firewall's IP address

In ISA Server 2000, Server Publishing Rules always preserved the original client IP address when it forwarded the connections to the published server on the internal network. ISA 2004 and 2006 allow you to choose to either preserve the original client IP address or replace the original client IP address with the IP address of the ISA firewall itself.

Restrict connections to specific days and times

Like Web Publishing Rules, Server Publishing Rules can be put on a schedule so that connections can only be established to the published server during the times allowed by the schedule. You can use one of the built-in schedules ("Always", "Weekends", and "Work Hours") or create your own custom schedules.

Support for Port Redirection or PAT (Port Address Translation)

Like Web Publishing Rules, Server Publishing Rules allow you to customize how connections are forwarded to the published server and what ports are used to accept and forward the connection requests. For example, you might want to accept incoming connections for your private SMTP server on TCP port 26 and forward them to TCP port 27 on a published SMTP server. You can do this using the ISA firewall's port redirection (PAT) feature.

Creating and Configuring Non-SSL Web Publishing Rules

You can create Web Publishing Rules by using the ISA firewall Web Publishing Rule Wizard. The Web Publishing Rule Wizard walks you through the steps of creating a Web Publishing rule that allows you to publish Web servers and services on any ISA firewall Protected Network. In this section, we will go through the Web Publishing Rule Wizard and discuss the options you're presented with and the implications of those options.

In this section, we'll focus on Web Publishing Rules that do not require SSL-secured connections. SSL security requires additional steps, and we'll cover those steps in the next section where we focus on secure SSL Web Publishing Rules.

To start the Web Server Publishing Rule Wizard with ISA 2006 *Standard Edition,* open the **Microsoft Internet Security and Acceleration Server 2006** management console, and expand the server name. Click the **Firewall policy** node.

To start the Web Server Publishing Rule Wizard with ISA 2006 *Enterprise Edition*, open the **Microsoft Internet Security and Acceleration Server 2006** management console, and expand the 'arrays' node. Expand the array you wish to edit the firewall policy for, and click on the **Firewall Policy** node.

Within the **Firewall Policy** node, click the **Tasks** tab within the **Tasks Pane**. On the **Tasks** tab, click the **Publish Web Sites** link.

You'll first encounter the **Welcome to the New Web Publishing Rule Wizard** page. On this page, you'll enter a name for the rule in the **Web publishing rule name** text box. Click **Next**.

The Select Rule Action Page

On the **Select Rule Action** page, you have the option to **Allow** or **Deny** connections to the published Web server. Note that the default option on the **Select Rule Action** page is **Allow**. This is in contrast to the default action on the Access Rule Wizard, where the default action is **Deny**. Most Web Publishing Rules will allow access to Web sites and specific paths within those Web sites. However, you can create Web Publishing Rules that deny access to fine-tune Web Publishing Rules that allow access. Choose the **Allow** option and click **Next**. Figure 5.1 below shows the default option on the Select Rule Action page.

Figure 5.1 The Select Rule Action Page

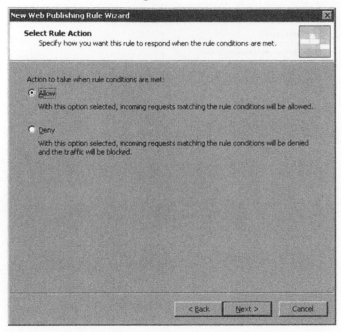

The Publishing Type Page

On the **Publishing Type** page, you configure which websites ISA exposes, and how it exposes them. As you can see in figure 5.2, there are three available options in this dialog:

- Publish a single Web site or load balancer
- Publish a server farm of load balanced Web Servers
- Publish multiple web sites

Figure 5.2 The Publishing Type Page

The first option was the only option available under ISA 2004. The second option is new to ISA 2006, and allows you to publish multiple web servers serving external content, balancing load between the websites, and (for websites which establish sessions with specific clients) can ensure clients continue using the same website ("affinity"). The third option allows the configuration of host's header-based publishing in ISA 2006 during the web publishing wizard itself.

We will first continue through the web publishing wizard assuming we are publishing one website (i.e. with the first option selected), before discussing the other two forms of web publishing.

The Server Connection Security Page

The **Server Connection Security** page is also new to ISA 2006, and provides an interface to existing functionality (the ability to publish an SSL or non_SSL website), but in a more prominent place. ISA 2006 provides us with entirely new options for specifying an SSL certificate while we create the rule itself.

The two options in this screen should be fairly self-explanatory, and are depicted in **Figure 5.3**.

Figure 5.3 The Server Connection Security Page

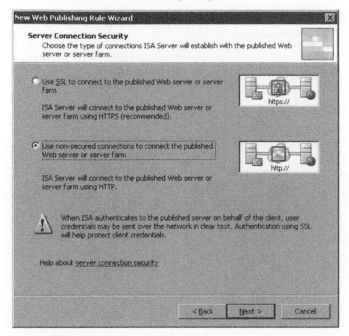

As we are publishing an HTTP site to begin with, we pick **Use non-secured connections to connect the published Web server or server farm** here. The ISA firewall will automatically pick the correct ports to use, but you may also go into properties for the publishing rule and edit which port it connects to under the **Bridging** tab after creating the rule. We will cover this later.

The Internal Publishing Details Page (Part one)

The two **Internal Publishing Details** pages replace the **Define Website to Publish** dialog in ISA 2004. On these pages you provide information about the Web site on the ISA firewall Protected Network. As you'll see in Figure 5.4, you have the following options on the first page:

- Internal Site Name
- Computer name or IP address

NOTE

Many issues with ISA Web Publishing Rules are caused by poorly thought-out DNS and Certificate Configuration. Make sure you're aware ahead of time which certificates you're using where, and the *Common Name* of the certificates you're using match the FQDNs used to access published sites, and the web servers being published by the ISA firewall. Keep this in mind when we get to publishing secure Web sites later in this chapter.

Figure 5.4 The Internal Publishing Details (Internal Site Name) Page

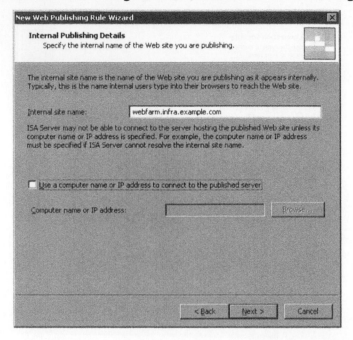

The **Internal Site Name** is the FQDN that clients on the ISA Protected Network use to connect to the website directly. In the example, we're using the URL *https://webfarm.infra.example.com*, an internal intranet site used clients on a corporate LAN. We will be publishing this externally via the ISA firewall as *https://extranet.example.com*. In the example, we will be publishing an internal site to the internet using a different URL on the Internet to one the Protected Network, referred to as *split DNS* – we'll discuss the virtues of this later.

In some instances, you may be publishing a site externally using the same URL on the internet as on the ISA firewall Protected Network. To work around this, you may enter the IP address or a host name for the web server you're publishing in the **Computer name or IP address** text box. If you use a FQDN, make sure that the ISA firewall is able to resolve that name to the Web server's IP address on the corporate network and *not* the IP address on the external interface of the ISA firewall. This is a very common error among ISA firewall administrators. You can ensure that the name is properly resolved to the private address of the Web server by creating a split DNS infrastructure or by using a HOSTS file entry on the ISA firewall.

One of the primary advantages of using a FQDN in the **Computer name or IP address** field is that the Web site name shows up in the URL field in the ISA firewall's Web Proxy log. If you use an IP address, only the IP address of the published server will appear in this field and make log analysis more difficult to perform efficiently.

The Internal Publishing Details Page (Part two)

The second **Internal Publishing Details** page presents you with the following options, displayed in Figure 5.5:

- Path Name
- Forward the original host header instead of the actual one

Figure 5.5 The Internal Publishing Details (Path Name) Page

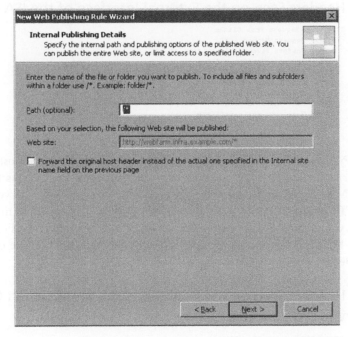

In the **Path** text box, you enter the paths you want accessible on the published Web server. If you simply want to make an entire web server available, then (as in the example) you can use the **/*** wildcard.

If, however, you want to make available only a specific subset of your internal web server available (for instance, /public/*, but not any other content at the root of the web server (/*), or the /private/* subdirectory), you can simply enter this path in the **Path** box. This option can work as a substitute for, or in addition to access controls on the Web Server itself.

Although this wizard page only allows you to enter a single path, we'll see later that we can enter the **Properties** dialog box of the Web Publishing Rule and create additional paths and even path redirections.

The **Web Site** box isn't a text box, so you can't enter anything in it. Instead, it shows you the URL that will be accessible on the published Web site (the **Internal Site Name** textbox from the previous screen with the **Path** suffixed).

In this example, we entered **webfarm.infra.example.com** for the **Internal Site Name** textbox and chose to forward the host header as per the **Internal Site Name** field.

The **Forward the original host header instead of the actual one specified in the Internal site name field on the previous page** option is an interesting option which may be unclear without a detailed understanding of HTTP.

What means in practice is that instead of the host header value in the **Computer name or IP address** text box being sent to the published server, the actual host header in the request sent by the external user is forwarded to the published Web server. This is an important issue if you are hosting multiple Web sites on a single Web server and differentiate the Web sites by using different host headers for each one.

You can see the effects of forwarding, or not forwarding, the original host headers in Figures 5.6, 5.7, and 5.8. In Figure 5.6 below, you see the host headers as seen on the external interface of the ISA firewall from a client connection request for **www.msfirewall.org**. The **HTTP: Host = www.msfirewall.org** host header appears in the network monitor trace.

Figure 5.6 HTTP Headers Seen on the External Interface of the ISA Firewall

```
⊟ HTTP: GET Request from Client
   ─ HTTP: Request Method =GET
   ─ HTTP: Uniform Resource Identifier =/
   ─ HTTP: Protocol Version =HTTP/1.1
   ─ HTTP: Accept = image/gif, image/x-xbitmap, image/jpeg, image/pjpeg, */*
   ─ HTTP: Accept-Language =en-us
   ─ HTTP: Accept-Encoding =gzip, deflate
   ─ HTTP: User-Agent =Mozilla/4.0 (compatible; MSIE 6.0; Windows NT 5.1)
   ─ HTTP: Host =www.msfirewall.org
   └ HTTP: Connection =Keep-Alive
```

When the Web Publishing Rule is configured to not forward the original Host header, and an IP address (or an alternate name) is used in the **Computer name or IP address** text box, you will see on the Network Monitor trace, in Figure 5.7, taken on the published Web server that the Host header entry is **HTTP: Host =10.0.0.2**, which isn't the Host header contained in the original client address. It's the entry we put in the **Computer name or IP address** text box. Figure 5.7 below shows an example of HTTP headers seen on the Published Web Server when the original Host header is not forwarded.

Figure 5.7 HTTP Headers Seen on the Published Web Server when Original Host Header is not Forwarded

```
⊟ HTTP: GET Request from Client
   ─ HTTP: Request Method =GET
   ─ HTTP: Uniform Resource Identifier =/
   ─ HTTP: Protocol Version =HTTP/1.1
   ─ HTTP: Reverse-Via = ISALOCAL
   ─ HTTP: Host =10.0.0.2
   ─ HTTP: If-None-Match ="0325lecdac21:af2"
   ─ HTTP: User-Agent =Mozilla/4.0 (compatible; MSIE 6.0; Windows NT 5.1)
   ─ HTTP: If-Modified-Since =Sat, 22 Feb 2003 00:48:30 GMT
   ─ HTTP: Accept = image/gif, image/x-xbitmap, image/jpeg, image/pjpeg, */*
   ─ HTTP: Accept-Language =en-us
   └ HTTP: Connection =Keep-Alive
```

However, when we enable **Forward the original host header instead of the actual one (specified above)**, Figure 5.8 shows what appears on the published Web server. In this case, the Network Monitor trace shows that the host header seen on the Web server is **HTTP: Host = www.msfirewall.org**. See Figure 5.8 below for headers seen on the published Web server when the original Host header is forwarded.

Figure 5.8 HTTP Headers Seen on the Published Web Server when Forwarding the Original Host Header

```
⊟ HTTP: GET Request from Client
   ⋯ HTTP: Request Method =GET
   ⋯ HTTP: Uniform Resource Identifier =/
   ⋯ HTTP: Protocol Version =HTTP/1.1
   ⋯ HTTP: Reverse-Via = ISALOCAL
   ⋯ HTTP: Host =www.msfirewall.org
   ⋯ HTTP: If-None-Match ="0325lecdac21:af2"
   ⋯ HTTP: User-Agent =Mozilla/4.0 (compatible; MSIE 6.0; Windows NT 5.1)
   ⋯ HTTP: If-Modified-Since =Sat, 22 Feb 2003 00:48:30 GMT
   ⋯ HTTP: Accept = image/gif, image/x-xbitmap, image/jpeg, image/pjpeg, */*
   ⋯ HTTP: Accept-Language =en-us
   ⋯ HTTP: Connection =Keep-Alive
```

The Public Name Details Page

On the **Public Name Details** page, you enter information about what FQDNs or IP addresses users will use to connect to the published Web site via this Web Publishing Rule. You have the following options on this page:

- Accept requests for
- Public Name
- Path (optional)

The **Accept requests for** drop-down list provides you with two choices: **Any domain name** and **This domain name (type below)**. If you choose **Any domain name**, any requests for a domain name or IP address are accepted by the Web listener for this rule. This is *strongly discouraged* for security reasons, as not requiring an HTTP hosts header corresponding to the name of the site will allow requests to be made to the web listener by IP address alone, by users (or scripts) who do not have a legitimate request. This increases your exposure to automated worms or scans.

For example, some prevalent worms will send requests to the TCP port 80 or to bogus domain names (such as www.worm.com) to the IP address used by the Web listener for this rule. If you select **Any domain name**, then the Web listener will accept these as valid requests and continue processing them. This is in spite of the fact that you are not hosting any resources for the bogus domain name the worm or the malicious user uses to access the IP address the Web listener is using on the external interface of the ISA firewall.

A better option, and the one we recommend that you always use for your Web Publishing Rules, is **This domain name (type below)**. When you choose this option, you enter the exact domain name that must be included in the users request to the Web listener. If you want to accept requests only for the www.msfirewall.org domain, then incoming requests for http://1.1.1.1 or http://www.worm.com will be dropped because they do not match the domain name you want this rule to apply to. The one minor disadvantage this configuration option carries is that in the event that you wish to connect to the site directly by IP address (if DNS is down, or has not yet been configured, for instance), you cannot do this straight from the browser, and will have to edit the hosts file on your workstation instead.

When you select **This domain name (type below)**, you must enter the domain name you want this rule to accept in the **Public name** text box. In this example, we entered the FQDN

extranet.example.com. The **Public Name Details** Wizard page allows you to enter only a single domain name, but you can add more domain names after the wizard is completed. However, we highly recommend that you use a single domain name per Web publishing rule.

The **Path (optional)** text box allows you to restrict the path(s) that users can access via this Web Publishing Rules. You might want to allow users access to only specific directories on your Web site and not to the entire site. Although you can only enter a single path on the **Public Name Details** page (Figure 5.9 below), you can enter additional paths after the wizard is completed, in the **Properties** dialog box for this rule.

Figure 5.9 The Public Name Details page

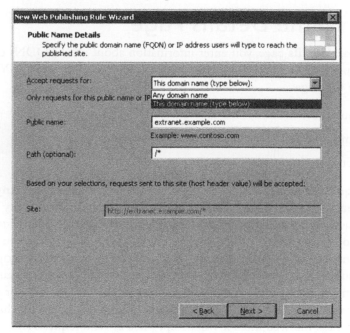

The Select Web Listener Page and Creating an HTTP Web Listener

You assign a Web listener to the Web Publishing Rule on the **Select Web Listener** page. A Web listener is a Network Object you use in Web Publishing Rules. The Web listener "listens" on an interface or IP address that you choose for incoming connections to the port you define. For example, for our Web publishing rule that allows HTTP public access to the extranet.example.com site, we will create a Web listener that listens on the external interface of the ISA firewall using the IP address that external users resolve *extranet.example.com* to.

NOTE

We assume in the above example that the external interface of the ISA firewall has a public address bound to it. The situation is slightly different if you have a firewall in front of the ISA firewall and have a NAT relationship between the front-end firewall and the ISA firewall. In that case, external clients would resolve the name *extranet. example.com* to the public address on the front-end firewall that is mapped to the IP address used on the Web listener on the back-end ISA firewall.

You have two options on the **Select Web Listener** page if there are listeners already configured on the ISA firewall:

- Edit
- New

Edit allows you to configure existing Web listeners, and **New** allows you to create a new Web listener. Figure 5.10 illustrates this dialog with a pre-existing listener in place. In the following section we will step through the process required to create the web listener pictured, and will start by clicking **New**.

Figure 5.10 The Select Web Listener Page

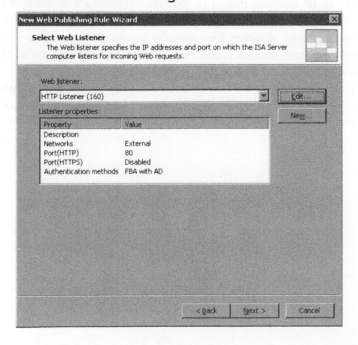

On the **Welcome to the New Web Listener Wizard** page, enter a name for the Web listener in the **Web listener name** text box. In this example, we'll name the Web listener **HTTP Listener (.160)** (since we have multiple IP addresses bound to ISA's external interface, this identifies the last octet in the IP address to help disambiguate between Web Listeners). Click **Next**.

On the **Client Connection Security** page, as with the connection from ISA to the Published Web Site, we have the option to choose whether our connection uses HTTP or HTTPS. In this instance, however, the choice affects how traffic from internet-based clients to the ISA Server are made. We pick **Do not Require SSL secured connections with clients** and hit **Next**.

The Web listener accepts incoming connections automatically on the default ports - TCP port **80** in the case of HTTP, and **443** in the case of HTTPS. You can change this port to any port you like, as long as it does not collide with a socket already in use on the ISA firewall. The wizard provides no means to do this, and you must change this after creating the Web Listener. We will cover this further on in the chapter.

The Web Listener IP Addresses Page

On the **Web Listener IP Addresses** page, select the Networks and IP addresses on those Networks that you want the listener to listen on. In ISA 2006, we can also choose to enable compression for web listeners.

Recall that each interface on the ISA firewall represents a Network, and all IP addresses reachable from that interface are considered part of that Network. The Web listener can listen on any Network defined on the ISA firewall.

In this example, we want to accept incoming connections from Internet users, so we'll select the **External** network by putting a checkmark in its checkbox. At this point, the Web listener will accept connection requests to all IP addresses bound to the external interface of the ISA firewall. We recommend that if you have multiple IP addresses bound to an interface that you configure the Web listener to use only one of those addresses. This provides you greater flexibility because you can customize the properties of each listener. If you allow the listener to listen on all IP addresses on the interface, then a single set of listener properties will be assigned to it.

In ISA 2006, we also gain the ability here to enable or disable http gzip compression for this web listener. Previously in versions of ISA 2004 pre-SP2, this could not be done without losing some of ISA's application-layer inspection capabilities.

Figure 5.11 The IP Addresses page

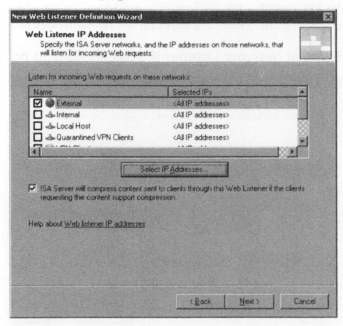

Click **Select IP Addresses** on the **Web Listener IP Addresses** page, as shown in Figure 5.11, to progress to the **Network Listener IP Selection** page. On this page (Figure 5.12) you have three options:

- All IP addresses on the ISA Server computer that are in the selected network
- The default IP address on the ISA Server computer in the selected network
- Specified IP addresses on the ISA Server computer in the selected network

All IP addresses on the ISA Server computer that are in the selected network is the default and is the same as checking the checkbox on the previous page without making any customizations. This option allows the listener to listen on all addresses bound to the interface representing the Network(s) you select. When you select more than one Network, the Web listener will listen on IP addresses bound to each of the Networks you select.

Default IP Addresses for network adapters in this network allows the listener to accept connections to the *primary* IP address bound to the Network interface. The primary address is the first address on the list of addresses bound to the Network interface. This is also the interface that is used for connections *leaving* that interface.

Specified IP addresses on the ISA Server computer in the selected network allows you to select the specific IP addresses you want the listener to use. The available IP addresses for the Network appear in the **Available IP addresses** section. You select the IP address you want the Web listener to use, and click **Add**; it then appears in the **Selected IP Addresses** section.

The example in Figure 5.12 demonstrates the Network centric nature of the ISA firewall – the **Available IP Addresses** list will display all IP addresses that correspond to the selected network, irrespective of which network adapters they are bound to. The default External Network includes *all IP addresses that are not defined as part of a Network*, which may include DMZ addresses if they are not configured within ISA as a separate network.

We can see in Figure 5.12 that there are a number of contiguous IP addresses bound to the external interface of the ISA firewall – but we have only picked one of the addresses for this particular publishing rule. Click **OK**. Then click **Next** on the **IP Addresses** page.

Figure 5.12 The External Network Listener IP Selection dialog box

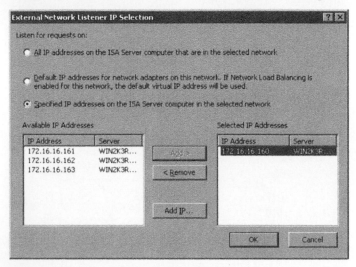

The Authentication Settings Page

The next screen within the Web Listener wizard ISA presents us with is the **Authentication Settings** page in Figure 5.13 is another new wizard page.

Figure 5.13 The Authentication Settings page

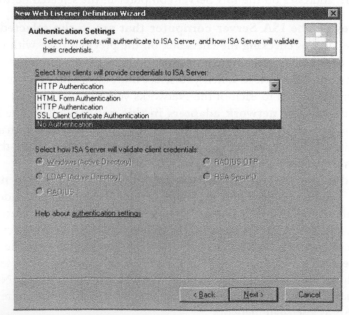

We will be enabling *HTML Form Authentication*, validated against *Windows (Active Directory)*. *HTML Form*, or *Forms-Based Authentication* in ISA 2006 provides a large number of possible back-ends and authentication types, and from the client to the ISA firewall is implemented using HTML forms and cookies, which – unlike with HTTP authentication - allow the administrator to configure timeouts after which the user must authenticate.

ISA FIREWALL ALERT

Here, we are configuring ISA to allow authentication over HTTP. By default, the ISA firewall does not allow this to happen, even though it appears to be a valid configuration in the User Interface – it must also be separately enabled in the **Authentication – Advanced** dialog discussed at the end of this section. If you do not have end-to-end encryption of client credentials, particularly over the internet, you should very carefully consider whether or not you should be allowing authentication to take place over HTTP.

Table 5.1 describes each of the authentication methods available for Web listeners and a short description of the important characteristics of each method.

Table 5.1 Web Listener Authentication Methods

Authentication Method	Details
Basic	■ Supported by all Web clients and servers
	■ User names and passwords are encoded (Base64), but not encrypted. Easy to obtain with any network analyzer
	■ Can be encrypted using SSL
	■ Supports backend authentication against a variety of authentication providers, including Active Directory (possibly the most common choice), but also LDAP, RADIUS, RADIUS with One-Time Passwords, and RSA SecurID
Digest	■ Credentials sent as one-way hash
	■ Web browser must support HTTP 1.1
	■ Requires domain controller to store password using reversible encryption
	■ WDigest encryption also supported (Windows Server 2003 only)
	■ User name and domain name case sensitive
	■ When both ISA firewall and DC are Windows Server 2003, Digest is used by default

Continued

Table 5.1 Continued

Authentication Method	Details
	■ Windows NT 4.0 user accounts do not support Digest authentication
	■ Can only be used with Active Directory as a backend authentication provider
Integrated	■ Uses NTLM, Kerberos and Negotiate authentication mechanisms
	■ User name and password hashed before sending
	■ Logged-on user credentials automatically sent to ISA firewall
	■ If logged-on user not authenticated, log-on dialog box appears
	■ Log-on dialog box continues to appear until valid credentials are entered or **CANCEL** is selected
	■ Can only be used with Active Directory as a backend authentication provider
RADIUS	■ RADIUS both authenticates and authorizes
	■ RADIUS users must enter credentials in DOMAIN\User format
	■ ISA firewall uses MD5 hash of the shared secret to authenticate with RADIUS server to encrypt user name, password, and characteristics of the connection
	■ Recommended to use IPSec to secure channel between ISA firewall and RADIUS server
	■ RADIUS servers configured on the ISA firewall are used for all rules and objects that use RADIUS authentication. You cannot configure separate lists of RADIUS servers for VPN and Web listener authentication. However, you can select separate RADIUS servers from the list for Web Publishing Rules and VPN authentication
	■ When using RADIUS for Web Publishing Rules, make sure you enable forwarding of basic authentication credentials in the Web Publishing Rule.
RADIUS OTP	■ New to ISA 2006
	■ As with RADIUS, uses a radius server, but
SecurID	■ Two-factor authentication
	■ Physical token and PIN (personal ID number) required

Table 5.1 Continued

Authentication Method	Details
	■ RSA ACE/Agent runs on ISA firewall
	■ RSA ACE/Agent passes credentials to RSA/ ACE server
	■ Cookie placed on user's browser after successful authentication; cookie is held in memory and not written to disk. Cookie removed from memory when browser closed
	■ Use SSL to secure connection between Web browser and ISA firewall when using SecurID authentication
	■ Refer to ISA Server 2004 Help for details of configuration
	■ Cannot be used in combination with other authentication methods.
OWA Forms-based	■ Used to publish Outlook Web Access (OWA)
	■ ISA firewall generates HTML-based logon form
	■ Cookie sent to browser when authentication successful
	■ Credential information not cached on client browser
	■ Users must reauthenticate if browser is closed, leave the OWA Web site
	■ Can set session time-out limits
	■ SSL connection between browser and ISA firewall recommended
	■ Can change password during session, but must reauthenticate after password change
	■ Can only be used with RADIUS authentica tion after a hotfix is applied. Check out http://support.microsoft.com/default.aspx?scid=kb;enus;884560 for details on this configuration.
Forms-Based Authentication	■ New to ISA 2006
	■ Enables the use of Forms-Based Authentication against non-OWA published sites, such as sharepoint portals and intranet pages.
	■ Supports the use of AD, LDAP, RADIUS, and RADIUS OTP backends.
	■ Allows for custom session timeouts
SSL Certificate	■ Users authenticate by presenting user certificates
	■ Most secure form of authentication

The authentication option you select applies only if you limit access to the Web Publishing Rule to a user or group. If you allow All Users access to the Web Publishing Rule, then the authentication option is ignored. These authentication options apply only to authentication performed by the ISA firewall itself, *not* to authentication that may be required by the published Web site. We will discuss authentication against the target webserver and Authentication Delegation later.

Some authentication methods (*HTTP Digest* and *Integrated* Authentication, and *SSL Client Certificate Authentication*) require that the ISA firewall be a member of a domain. This is not a significant issue unless you have a back-to-back firewall configuration where the front-end firewall is an ISA firewall (the back-end firewall can be any kind of firewall you like, including ISA firewalls). If the ISA firewall is on the front-end and you want to authenticate users at the front-end server, LDAP Authentication (or Radius Authentication) should be used. LDAP Authentication is a new feature in ISA 2006, and allows you to authenticate from the ISA firewall to one (or more than one) domain without being a member of that domain. Note that if you are using a back to back ISA Firewall configuration, no authentication should take place on the front-end ISA Firewall and the back-end ISA Firewall, which is a domain member, should do the authentication.

When the ISA firewall is on the back-end, we always recommend that you make the firewall a member of the Active Directory domain so that you can leverage the many security advantages inherent in domain membership. However, if there are political reasons why the back-end ISA firewall cannot be made a member of the domain, you can still leverage LDAP and RADIUS authentication in the scenario, too, although realize that by doing so, you reduce the overall security posture of the ISA Firewall.

In ISA 2006, the screens prompting for Radius/Radius OTP Server Settings and LDAP Server Settings (if you pick any of these options as the backend authentication provider) are prompted for after the Single Sign-On Settings, and these screens will be covered later.

The Single Sign on Settings Page

If we hit **Next** on the **Authentication Settings** dialog, we come to the **Single Sign on Settings** dialog, pictured in Figure 5.18. Also new to ISA 2006, the **Single Sign On** feature allows ISA to sign on to multiple websites after the user has authenticated to one. This allows simple, one-login access to sites such as Outlook Web Access (OWA), Office Communications Server Communicator Web Access (CWA), Sharepoint Portal Server, or any number of other web applications. This greatly simplifies the user experience and increases efficiency & security.

The **Single Sign on Settings** dialog presents you with only one choice – the **SSO Domain Name**. This is an important option, as the Domain Name is used in the domain attribute of the cookie provided to the client when it logs into the published site via Forms-Based Authentication. In our case, we set this to *.example.com*

ISA FIREWALL ALERT

The cookie created by ISA SSO can be read by any site within the domain specified in the **SSO Domain Name** field, and therefore providing a domain such as *.com* which is a superset of your domain name, whilst convenient, would allow any site with a domain name ending in .com to read the SSO cookie. It is highly important, then, to make the SSO Domain Name setting as specific as you can (and ideally, do not allow it to encompass any domain you do not have total control over).

Figure 5.14 The Single Sign On Settings Page

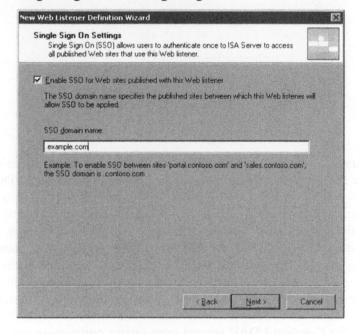

The LDAP Settings Page

As mentioned earlier, after the **Single Sign On Settings** page, if we have selected the **LDAP**, **Radius**, or **Radius (OTP)** backend authentication providers for our web listener authentication, we will now be prompted for further details of these settings if we have not previously configured LDAP authentication on other web listeners.

In the following section, we will explore the additional pages within the wizard having selected either of these options will present us with.

Figure 5.15 The LDAP Settings Page

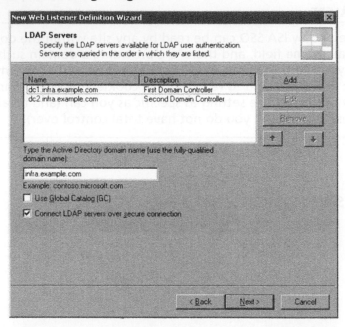

The **LDAP Servers** Page prompts you to enter details for your Infrastructure's LDAP Servers as well as which Active Directory domain name should be used for authentication. The LDAP Servers configured when you setup your first LDAP-enabled web listener are referred to as the *Default Set* – if you require different LDAP servers for different web listeners, you can define many sets of LDAP servers, and change the name of the default set, in properties for your web listener.

By default, this dialog does not check the **Connect LDAP servers over secure connection** option – without this selected, the queries sent by the ISA firewall to your domain controllers will be unencrypted LDAP queries sent to TCP Port 389 on the target LDAP Server. This option must be enabled in order to enable the *'Change Password'* function when publishing Outlook Web Access. When enabled, connections are encrypted LDAPS connections, made over TCP Port 636.

If you do enable the **Connect LDAP servers over secure connection**, you will need to ensure that you have a certificate installed in the *Personal, Local Machine* Certificate store for each domain controller. The simplest way to do this is using certificate auto enrolment with an *Enterprise CA*, but you could also do this with a Standalone (or third party) Certificate Authority (or even commercial certificates).

Without appropriately configured certificates installed, and the root certificate which issued those certificates stored in the ISA Server Local Computer Account's Trusted Root Certificate Store, connections to the target LDAP Server will fail.

If the option **Connect LDAP servers over secure connection** is not checked, you should ensure that your LDAP traffic is encrypted by IPSec or otherwise protected.

The **Use global catalog** option is optional, and if your LDAP servers are Global Catalog servers nullifies the requirement to provide an Active Directory Domain Name. This option, however, *will prevent Password Management from functioning properly.* Without **Connect LDAP servers over secure**

connection enabled, queries to LDAP Servers with the **Use global catalog** option enabled will be made to TCP Port 3268. With this option enabled, connections are made on TCP Port 3269.

In order to enable Password Management for OWA FBA, you will also need to specify a username and password that the ISA Firewall can use to bind to the LDAP server and access information inaccessible to an anonymous user. This setting does not appear in the wizard, and must be enabled in the main GUI. This topic will be covered later on in the chapter.

Finally, LDAP support is only for Microsoft Active Directory domain controller. The ISA Firewall does not support other types of LDAP servers.

The RADIUS Settings Page

If we enable RADIUS or RADIUS (OTP) authentication from ISA, we will be prompted when creating our web listener to specify the servers to which we want to authenticate. ISA will authenticate to any standard RADIUS Server, including Microsoft's (confusingly abbreviated) IAS Radius Server.

As mentioned earlier, RADIUS enables you to pre-authenticate users at the ISA firewall before authenticating to the target web server, without requiring ISA to be a member of the same domain as the target web server (or indeed any domain).

Figure 5.16 The RADIUS Servers Page

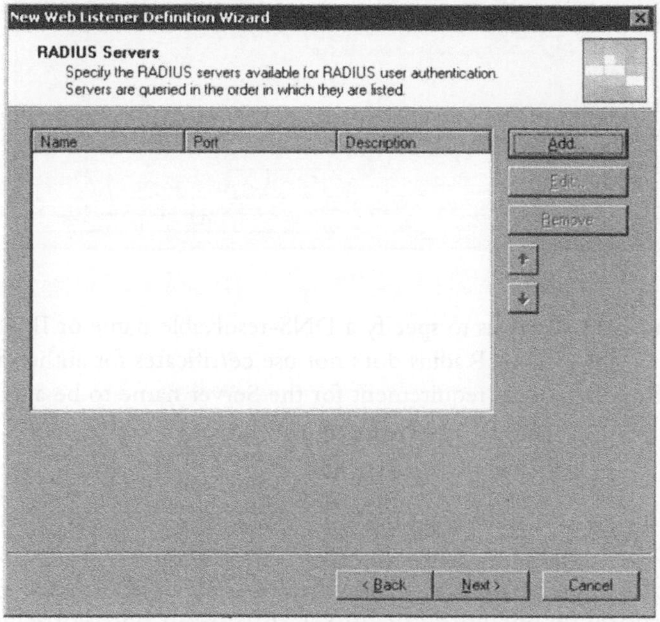

Hitting the **Add** button in this dialog presents us with Figure 5.17, the **Add Radius Server** dialog. This allows us to add the configuration settings for one Radius Server, and gives us the following options:

- Server Name
- Server Description

- Shared Secret
- Authentication Port
- Time-out (seconds)
- Always use message authenticator

Figure 5.17 The Add Radius Server Page

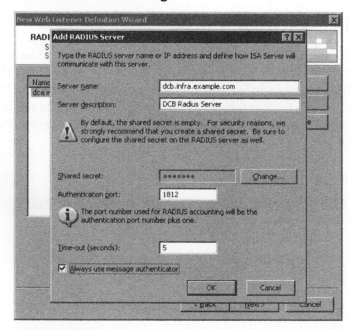

The **Server name** field allows us to specify a DNS-resolvable name or IP address for the radius server we need to use. Unlike LDAP, Radius does not use certificates for authentication or encryption, and therefore there is no requirement for the Server name to be a FQDN matching the Computer Account Certificate, and IP addresses can be used.

ISA FIREWALL ALERT

Although simpler than LDAP Authentication, RADIUS also has the disadvantage that it cannot inherently be encrypted using SSL. Although passwords are hashed when sent over RADIUS, you should still as a best practice protect your RADIUS traffic with IPSec if your Radius servers support this. At an absolute minimum, you should firewall connections to your RADIUS servers such that only authorized RADIUS clients such as ISA firewalls may connect, use strong shared secrets, enable the **Message Authenticator** option, and strictly control access to your DMZ/Protected network segments.

The **Description** field allows you to provide an annotation for your entry. The **Shared Secret** setting is used to hash passwords sent via RADIUS, and should be of adequate length and complexity to make brute force attacks impractical.

By default, RADIUS uses UDP port 1812 for authentication traffic, and the **Authentication Port** field allows you to specify the port that should be used. Microsoft IAS Server, in line with many other third party radius packages, uses the standard port. The **Time-out** setting allows you to control how long ISA will wait before moving to the next radius server in the set.

The **Always use Message Authenticator** option adds an extra layer of security to the RADIUS protocol, allowing the target RADIUS server to verify the source of the RADIUS traffic by including data encrypted using the shared secret specified earlier. This option should be enabled if your RADIUS Server supports it. Microsoft IAS Server on Windows 2003 supports this option, and then corresponding server-side option to be enabled in IAS is the **Client must always send the signature attribute in the request** option.

At this point, we hit the end of the Web Listener Wizard, and can click **Next** and **Finish** to proceed. At this point, we can see our new web listener listed in the **Select Web Listener** page illustrated in Figure 5.10. If we wish to edit advanced properties of the web listener before finishing the web publishing wizard, we can do this here by hitting the *Edit* button with the Web Listener selected. This will be covered later.

SecurID Settings

If you use SecurID to authenticate your website, you are not prompted for further settings during the completion of the Web Publishing Rule Wizard, and there are few options in the ISA GUI for RSA ACE server settings, or other details that are obviously required in order to configure the ISA Server to authenticate against the ACE Server.

In order to complete the setup of the ISA firewall, you will need to appropriately configure the RSA ACE Server, and install the *sdconf.rec* file provided by the ACE Server onto the ISA firewall, and place it in the *%systemroot%\system32* directory.

Full configuration of SecurID and ACE are outside our scope, as SecurID is a complex technology, but there is a useful *RSA Test Authentication Utility* which you can use to check your RSA Configuration and ensure that ISA is able to authenticate to your ACE Servers downloadable from http://www. microsoft.com/downloads/details.aspx?FamilyID=7b0ca409-55d0-4d33-bb3f-1ba4376d5737& DisplayLang=en.

The Authentication Delegation Page

The next page we are presented with is the **Authentication Delegation** page. This screen is also new to ISA, and controls how our ISA server authenticates to the server published to clients. The **Authentication Delegation** page is illustrated in Figure 5.18.

Figure 5.18 The Authentication Delegation Page

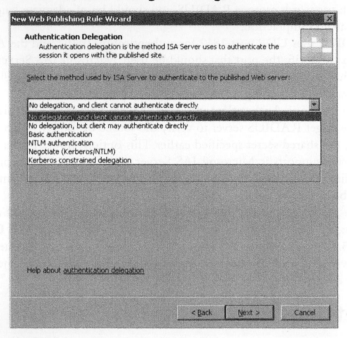

The **Select the method...** dropdown in this dialog allows you to dictate how authentication to the target web server takes place, and ISA 2006 introduces a variety of options for Authentication Delegation to the published web server, including *Kerberos Constrained Delegation*, both as part of the *Negotiate* and *Kerberos constrained delegation* options.

The following methods can be used for this second stage of the login process, from the ISA Server to the published Web Server:

Table 5.2 Authentication Delegation Methods

Authentication Method	Details
No delegation, and client cannot authenticate directly	■ ISA will not attempt to authenticate to the target webserver ■ Any content which is not enabled for 'anonymous access' will be inaccessible to the ISA Server (and therefore the client)
No delegation, but client may authenticate directly	■ Any challenge for authentication from the target webserver will be passed directly back to the client by the ISA Server.
Basic Authentication using ISA 2004.	■ This method was the only method allowed ■ Credentials supplied to ISA are forwarded to the published webserver using the 'basic' HTTP authentication method.

Table 5.2 Continued

Authentication Method	Details
NTLM Authentication	■ Credentials supplied to ISA are used to authenticate to the published webserver using the NTLM challenge/response protocol (see http://msdn2.microsoft.com/en-us/library/Aa378749.aspx for more information)
Negotiate (Kerberos/NTLM)	■ Also referred to as 'Integrated Authentication' for IIS
	■ ISA picks which method to use from a list of available methods provided by the webserver.
	■ In the case of IIS, this allows the ISA Server to pick Kerberos authentication, but if this is unavailable, fallback to NTLM authentication.
	■ In order to use this option, the appropriate SPN must be configured within Active Directory.
	■ This choice offers a balance of security and flexibility (the Kerberos protocol can be used, but if there are any problems, other negotiated protocols exist as a fallback)
Kerberos Constrained Delegation	■ Although Kerberos is a poor choice for authentication used over the internet, it can be used to authenticate from ISA Server to published websites.
	■ This is the securest choice, and can be used to provide end to end authentication without the use of stored and forwarded passwords (the user can authenticate to the ISA Server via certificates, for instance).
	■ In order to use this option, the appropriate SPN must be configured within Active Directory.
	■ ISA, the target webserver, and the client user account must all be within the same Active Directory Domain (KCD does not support cross-domain/forest trusts)
	■ Domain must be at Windows 2003 native level

We select *Negotiate (Kerberos/NTLM)*, and then hit **Next** to proceed to the last page in the Web Publishing Wizard.

The User Sets Page

On the **User Sets** page (Figure 5.19), configure whether authentication is required to access the Web server published by this Web Publishing Rule. The default setting for http:// rules is **All Users**, which means that authentication is not required to access the Web server published by this Web Publishing Rule. Click **Add** if you want to require authentication. You will be presented with the **Add Users** dialog box where you can select the User Set representing the users you want the rule to apply to.

Note that the **All Users** option only means that authentication is not required when the Web listener is not configured to require authentication. To configure the Web Publishing Rule to allow the user of anonymous credentials, use the **All Users** user set. Figure 5.19 below shows the options for the User Sets page.

Figure 5.19 The User Sets page

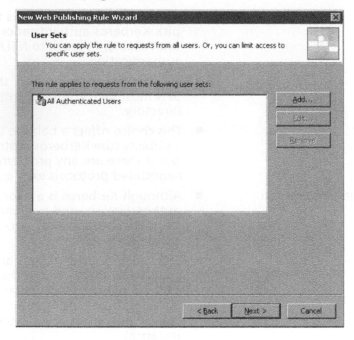

We will discuss User Sets, how to create them, and how to use them in Chapter 4. Click **Next** on the **User Sets** page, and then click **Finish** on the **Completing the New Web Publishing Rule Wizard** page.

Creating and Configuring SSL Web Publishing Rules

You can publish secure Web servers using SSL Web Publishing Rules. Publishing Secure Web servers requires a bit more work up front because you need to obtain a Web site certificate for the published Web site, bind that certificate to the Web site on the published Web server and then bind a Web site certificate to the ISA firewall so that it can impersonate the Web server. This allows the ISA firewall to provide very high security for SSL Web sites published via Web Publishing Rules. Fortunately, ISA 2006 includes several improvements to the way SSL Web Publishing Rules are configured which simplifies their configuration and troubleshooting.

In this section we'll discuss the following:

- SSL Bridging
- Importing Web site certificates into the ISA Firewall's machine certificate store
- Requesting a Web site certificate for the ISA Firewall to present to SSL Web sites
- Creating SSL Web Publishing Rules

SSL Bridging

SSL Bridging is an ISA firewall feature that allows the ISA firewall to perform stateful application-layer inspection on SSL connections made to Web-published Web servers on an ISA firewall Protected Network. This unique feature allows the ISA firewall to provide a level of stateful application-layer inspection uncommon amongst other firewalls in its class.

SSL bridging prevents intruders from hiding exploits within an encrypted SSL tunnel. Conventional stateful-filtering firewalls (such as most "hardware" firewalls on the market today) cannot perform stateful application-layer inspection on SSL connections moving through them. These hardware stateful-filtering firewalls see an incoming SSL connection, check the firewall's Access Control List, and if there is an ACL instructing the stateful packet filter-based firewall to forward the connection to a server on the corporate network, the connection is forwarded to the published server without any inspection for potential application-layer exploits.

The ISA firewall supports two methods of SSL bridging:

- SSL–to–SSL bridging
- SSL–to–HTTP bridging

SSL–to–SSL bridging provides a secure SSL connection from end to end. SSL–to–HTTP bridging ensures a secure connection between the Web client and the ISA firewall, and then allows a clear text connection between the ISA firewall and the published Web server.

In order to appreciate how the ISA firewall works with SSL in protecting your Web server, let's look at the life cycle of a communication between the Web client on the Internet and the Web site on the ISA firewall Protected network:

1. The OWA client on the Internet sends a request to the ISA firewall's external interface.
2. An SSL session is negotiated between the Web client on the Internet and the ISA firewall's external interface.

3. *After* the SSL session is established, the Web client sends the username and password to the ISA firewall. The SSL tunnel that has already been established between the Web client and ISA firewall protects these credentials.

4. The request is decrypted *before* the request is forwarded by the ISA firewall to the published Web server. The decrypted packets received from the Web client are examined by the ISA firewall and subjected to stateful application-layer inspection via the ISA firewall's HTTP security filter and any other application-layer inspection filters you've installed on the ISA firewall. If the ISA firewall finds a problem with the request, it is dropped.

5. If the request is acceptable, the ISA Server firewall re-encrypts the communication and sends it over a *second* SSL connection established between the ISA firewall and the published Web site on the ISA firewall Protected Network.

6. The published Web server decrypts the packet and replies to the ISA firewall. The Web server encrypts its response and sends it to the ISA firewall.

7. The ISA firewall decrypts the response received from the published Web server. It evaluates the response in the same way it did in step 4. If something is wrong with the response, the ISA firewall drops it. If the response passes stateful application-layer inspection, the ISA firewall re-encrypts the communication and forwards the response to the Web client on the Internet via the SSL session the Internet Web client has already established with the ISA firewall.

SSL "Tunneling" versus SSL "Bridging"

The ISA firewall actually participates in *two* different SSL sessions when SSL-to-SSL bridging is used:

-   An SSL session between the Web client and the external interface of the ISA firewall

-   A second SSL session between an internal interface of the ISA firewall and the published Web server

The typical stateful packet-filter firewall only forwards connections for published SSL sites. This is sometimes referred to as "SSL tunneling." The conventional stateful filtering firewall accepts SSL communications on its external interface and forwards them to the published SSL server. Application-layer information in the communication is completely hidden inside the SSL tunnel because the packet filter-based firewall has no mechanism to decrypt, inspect, and re-encrypt the data stream. Because traditional stateful filtering firewalls are unable to make allow and deny decisions based on knowledge of the contents of the encrypted tunnel, it passes viruses, worms, buffer overflows and other exploits from the Web client to the published Web site.

What about SSL-to-HTTP Bridging?

The ISA firewall can also perform SSL-to-HTTP bridging. In the SSL-to-HTTP bridging scenario, the connection between the Web client and the external interface of the ISA firewall is protected in the SSL tunnel. The connection between the ISA firewall's internal interface and the published Web server on the corporate network is sent "in the clear" and not encrypted. This helps performance because avoids the processor overhead incurred for the second SSL link.

However, you have to consider the implications of SSL-to-HTTP bridging. Steve Riley (http://www.microsoft.com/technet/treeview/default.asp?url=/technet/columns/security/askus/auaswho.asp), a Program Manager on the ISA Server team at Microsoft, has mentioned that the external user connecting to the published Web site using SSL has an implicit agreement and expectation that the entire transaction is protected. We agree with this assessment. The external Web client enters into what can arguably be considered a "social contract" with the published Web server, and part of that contract is that communications are protected from "end to end."

SSL-to-SSL bridging protects the data with SSL and the ISA Server firewall services from end to end. SSL-to-HTTP bridging protects the data from the OWA client and while it's on the ISA Server firewall, but it is not safe once it's forwarded from the ISA Server firewall and the OWA site on the internal network.

Enterprise and Standalone Certificate Authorities

The topic of Certificate Authorities (CAs) and PKI (Public Key Infrastructure) is usually enough to drive many administrators away from even considering SSL. There are a number of reasons for this:

- The available documentation on certificate authorities and PKI, in general, is difficult to understand.

- The subject has the potential to be extremely complex.

- You need to learn an entirely new vocabulary to understand the CAs and PKI. Often the documentation on these subjects doesn't define the new words, or they use equally arcane terms to define the arcane term for which you're trying to get the definition.

- There doesn't seem to be any support for the network and firewall administrator who just wants to get a CA setup and running so that he can use certificates for SSL and L2TP/IPSec authentication and encryption.

We not going to do an entire course on PKI and the Microsoft CA, but we do want to help you understand some of the decisions you need to make when deciding what type of Certificate Authority to install and use.

PKI, or Public Key Infrastructure, refers to the system through which keys, which may be used for a range of purposes from securing an SSL website to logging onto a website, are issued to clients, verified, and protected. Central to any PKI, whether the public infrastructures run by authorities such as Verisign and Cacert or a private corporate infrastructure, is the role of the CA.

A CA, or Certificate Authority, is a piece of server infrastructure which contains a *Root Certificate* trusted by all users of the PKI, and which can be used to issue certificates to clients automatically, or on request. Most CAs will have some form of web enrolment interface to simplify this process.

There are many third-party PKI packages, such as those from Entrust and RSA. These packages are typically highly capable, although expensive. Microsoft's implementation of PKI is referred to as *Certificate Services*, and ships with Server editions of Windows. Unless you have very complex requirements, chances are Certificate Services will probably do what you want, and it has several benefits if you have pre-existing Microsoft infrastructure (such as Active Directory) which you wish to integrate it with.

Certificate Services can be installed in one of four roles:

- Enterprise Root CA

- Enterprise Subordinate CA

- Standalone Root CA

- Standalone Subordinate CA

Enterprise Root and Enterprise Subordinate CAs can only be installed on Active Directory member servers. If you want to install a CA on a non-domain member (or wish to disassociate your PKI from Active Directory), then install a Standalone Root or Standalone Subordinate CA. If you install a single Certificate Server, you'll install it as an Enterprise Root or Standalone Root. Subordinate CAs are used in organizations managing multiple CAs.

- You can use the **Certificates MMC standalone snap-in** to obtain machine or user certificates – the snap-in is only available to domain member computers.

- You can configure Group Policy to automatically issue machine and user certificates via *autoenrollment* – this feature is only available to domain member computers.

- You can use the Web enrollment site to obtain certificates via a Web interface. (This can also be installed on a non-CA if you wish to split this role from that of the CA)

The **Certificates MMC snap-in** or autoenrollment can't be used to obtain certificates from Standalone CAs. The only way to obtain a certificate from a Standalone CA is to request one from the Standalone CA's Web enrollment site. You must fill out a form and then submit the request. The certificate is not immediately issued, because the only thing the CA knows about the requestor is what's put in the form. Someone needs to "eyeball" the request and then manually approve the request. The requestor then needs to use the browser to return to the Web enrollment site and download the certificate.

The Enterprise CA is less hassle because it has information about the requestor. Since the request is for a computer or user in the domain, someone has already qualified the domain user or computer and deemed that member worthy of a certificate. The Enterprise CA assumes you have administrative control over all domain member users and computers and can evaluate the validity of the certificate requests against the information available to it in the Active Directory. With an Enterprise CA, *Autoenrollment* can be configured via *Group Policy* to configure groups of computers, or users, to automatically apply for (and install) certificates for purposes such as SSL and IPSec without any manual administrative work on individual machines.

For these reasons, we recommend you use enterprise CAs. We will assume that you're using an enterprise CA for the remainder of this discussion.

For more information on Certificate Authorities and PKI, check out Microsoft's PKI page at www.microsoft.com/windowsserver2003/technologies/pki/default.mspx

SSL-to-SSL Bridging and Web Site Certificate Configuration

One of the most common reasons that ISA firewall admins give up on SSL, and SSL-to-SSL bridging is the problems they may experience in getting the SSL connections to work correctly. The most common reason for this is a configuration error that involves the relationship between the certificate configuration and the Web Publishing Rule used to publish the Web site.

Figure 5.20 provides details of the SSL-to-SSL bridged connection to a public Outlook Web Access Web site.

Figure 5.20 SSL-to-SSL bridging

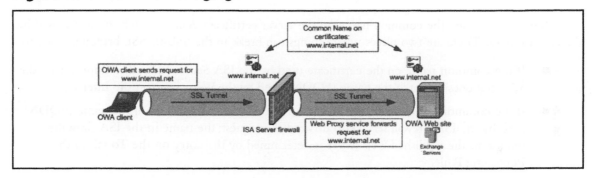

1. The Web client sends the request https://www.internal.net/exchange/ to the external interface of the ISA Server firewall publishing the OWA 2003 Web site

2. The ISA firewall checks its Web Publishing Rules to see if there is a Web Publishing Rule containing a Destination Set with the FQDN www.internal.net and the path **/exchange**. If there is a Web Publishing Rule matching this FQDN and path, the connection will be handled based on the forwarding instructions included in the Web Publishing Rule. However, *before* the ISA firewall can evaluate the URL, the SSL session must be established. The **common name** *on the certificate* the ISA firewall uses to impersonate the OWA Web site must be the *same* as the FQDN used by the Web client to connect to the site. In this example, the common name on the certificate the ISA firewall uses to impersonate the OWA Web site must be www.internal.net so that it matches the FQDN the external OWA client uses in its request.

3. The ISA firewall decrypts the packets, examines them, and then attempts to create a new SSL connection between itself and the internal OWA Web site. Just like when the external OWA client connects to the external interface of the ISA Server firewall, the ISA Server firewall's Web Proxy service acts as a client to the OWA 2003 Web site on the internal network. The request the Web Proxy service sends to the OWA 2003 site on the internal network must match the **common name** on the certificate on the OWA Web site. That is why we must configure the request to be forwarded to www.internal.net when we configure the Web Publishing Rule. We'll go over this important fact again when we discuss the configuration of the Web Publishing Rule.

4. The packets are forwarded to the Web site after the SSL session is established between the ISA firewall and the Web server on the internal network.

ISA FIREWALL NOTE

All machines participating in the SSL sessions (the Web client, the ISA firewall, and the Web site) must have the CA certificate of the root Certificate Authority in its **Trusted Root Certification Authorities** certificate store.

Things break when the common name on the server certificate doesn't match the name used by the client request. There are two places where things can break in the SSL-to-SSL bridging scenario:

- If the common name on the certificate used by the ISA Server firewall to impersonate the Web site doesn't match the name (FQDN) used by the Web client on the Internet

- If the common name on the certificate on the Web site doesn't match the name (FQDN) used by the ISA firewall service to forward the request; the name in the ISA firewall's request to the published Web server is determined by the entry on the **To** tab in the Web Publishing Rule.

Keep these facts in mind as we work through our SSL-to-SSL bridging Web Publishing Rule later.

ISA FIREWALL ALERT

You will encounter the dreaded **Internal Server Error 500** if there is a mismatch between the name in the request and the name on the certificate.

Importing Web Site Certificates into the ISA Firewall's Machine Certificate Store

The ISA firewall must be able to impersonate the published Web server so that it identifies itself to the remote Web client as the published Web server. The mechanism behind this impersonation is a common name on the Web site certificate. We must install the Web site certificate on the ISA firewall to accomplish this task.

The first step is to export the Web site certificate from the secure Web server's Web site. The IIS console has an easy-to-use Certificate Wizard where you can export the Web site certificate. When you export the Web site certificate, make sure that you include the private key. One of the most common reasons for failure in secure Web Publishing Rules is that the Web site certificate was not exported with its private key.

The Web site certificate is then imported into the ISA firewall's machine certificate store. Once the Web site certificate is imported into the ISA firewall's machine certificate store, it will be available to bind to a Web listener. You'll know that the certificate wasn't properly imported if you're unable to bind the certificate to a Web listener.

Perform the following steps to import the Web site certificate into the ISA firewall's machine certificate store:

1. Copy the Web site certificate to the ISA firewall machine.

2. Click **Start**, and then click the **Run** command. In the **Run** dialog box, enter **mmc** in the **Open** text box, and click **OK**.

3. In the console, click **File**, and then click **Add/Remove Snap-in**.

4. In the **Add/Remove Snap-in** dialog box, click **Add**.

5. In the **Add Standalone Snap-in** dialog box, click **Certificates** in the list of **Available Standalone Snap-ins**, and click **Add**.

6. On the **Certificates Snap-in** page, select the **Computer account** option and click **Next**.

7. On the **Select Computer** page, select **Local computer (the computer this console is running on)** and click **Finish**.

8. Click **Close** in the **Add Standalone Snap-in** dialog box.

9. Click **OK** in the **Add/Remove Snap-in** dialog box.

10. Expand the **Certificates (Local Computer)** node in the left pane of the console.

11. Expand the **Personal** node in the left pane of the console.

12. Right-click the **Certificates** node, point to **All Tasks** and click **Import**.

13. Click **Next** on the **Welcome to the Certificate Import Wizard** page.

14. On the **File to Import** page, use the **Browse** button to find the certificate you copied to the ISA firewall. Click **Next** after the certificate appears in the **File name** text box.

15. Enter the password you assigned to the Web site certificate in the **Password** text box on the **Password** page. Do *not* mark the certificate as exportable. Click **Next**.

16. Accept the default setting, **Place all certificates in the following store** on the **Certificate Store** page. Click **Next**.

17. Click **Finish** on the **Completing the Certificate Import Wizard** page.

18. Click **OK** on the **Certificate Import Wizard** dialog box.

19. The Web site certificate and the CA certificate appear in the right pane of the console. The CA certificate has the same name as the entry in the **Issued by** column.

20. Right-click the CA certificate and click **Cut**.

21. Expand the **Trusted Root Certification Authorities** node in the left pane of the console.

22. Right-click the **Certificates** node and click **Paste**. If the **Paste** command does not appear, repeat step 20, and then try again.

23. Return to the **Personal\Certificates** node in the left pane of the console and double-click the Web site certificate.

24. In the **Certificate** dialog box, click the **Certification Path** tab. The CA certificate should not have a red "x" on it. If there is a red "x" on the CA certificate that indicates that the CA certificate was not successfully imported into the **Trusted Root Certification Authorities** node.

25. Close the **Certificate** dialog box.

26. Close the **mmc** console. Do not save the console.

Now that the Web site certificate is imported into the machine's certificate store, it'll be available to bind to the Web listener used in the SSL Web Publishing Rule.

Requesting a User Certificate for the ISA Firewall to Present to SSL Web Sites

The ISA firewall can be configured to present a user certificate to Web sites that require user certificates before connecting to the site. These user certificates are also referred to as *client certificates*. The published Web site can be configured to require that the client certificate be presented before a connection is allowed. Client certificates can be mapped to user accounts. This allows for user certificate authentication. However, you can require user certificates and then provide log on credentials via alternate authentication methods.

You can request a user certificate for the ISA firewall's Firewall Service and then configure the Web Publishing Rule to present this certificate when Web sites request a client certificate. The first step is to request a certificate for the ISA firewall's Firewall Service account.

In the following example we will use the certificates MMC to import a certificate for the ISA firewall's Firewall service account. We cannot use the Certificates MMC to request a certificate for the account, but we can import a user certificate using the Web enrollment site.

In order to request a certificate for the ISA firewall from the Web enrollment site, we must first create a user account for the ISA firewall. Create a user account name **isafirewall** in the Active Directory prior to performing the following procedures.

Perform the following steps to request a certificate for the Firewall service account:

1. At the ISA firewall machine, open the **Microsoft Internet Security and Acceleration Server 2006** management console, expand the server name, and click the **Firewall Policy** node.

2. Click the **Tasks** tab in the Task pane. On the **Tasks** tab, click the **Show System Policy Rules** link.

3. In the list of **System Policy Rules**, right-click Rule 2 **Allow all HTTP traffic from ISA Server to all networks (for CRL downloads)**, and click **Edit System Policy**.

4. On the **General** tab of the **System Policy Rule for CRL Download**, check the **Enable** checkbox. Click **OK**.

5. Click **Apply** to save the changes and update the firewall policy.

6. Click **OK** in the **Apply New Configuration** dialog box.

7. Open Internet Explorer on the ISA firewall and enter the URL http://<certificateserver>/ certsrv, where **certificateserver** is the name or IP address of the enterprise CA on the corporate network.

8. In the **Connect to** dialog box, enter the credentials of the **isafirewall** account and click **OK**.

9. Click **Add** in the Internet Explorer dialog box, creating the blocking of the site.

10. Click **Add** in the **Trusted site** dialog box. Click **Close**.

11. On the **Welcome** page, click the **Request a certificate** link.

12. On the **Request a Certificate** page, click the **User Certificate** link.

13. On the **User Certificate – Identifying Information** page, click **Submit**.

14. Click **Yes** in the **Potential Scripting Violation** dialog box.

15. Click **Yes** in the dialog box informing you that you're sending information to the Web server.

16. On the **Install this certificate** page, click the **Install this certificate** link.

17. Click **Yes** in the **Potential Scripting Violation** dialog box.

18. Click the **Tools** menu in the browser, and click **Internet Options**.

19. In the **Internet Options** dialog box, click the **Content** tab.

20. On the **Content** tab, click **Certificates**.

21. In the **Certificates** dialog box, click **isafirewall** and click **Export**.

22. Click **Next** on the **Welcome to the Certificate Export Wizard** page.

23. On the **Export Private Key** page, select **Yes, export the private key**, and click **Next**.

24. On the **Export File Format** page, *remove* the checkmark from the **Enable strong protection** checkbox. Place a checkmark in the **Include all certificates in the certification path if possible** checkbox. Click **Next**.

25. On the **Password** page, enter a password and confirm the password for the certificate file. Click **Next**.

26. On the **File to Export** page, enter a path in the **File name** text box. In this example, we'll enter the file name **c:\isafirewallcert**. Click **Next**.

27. Click **Finish** on the **Completing the Certificate Export Wizard** page.

28. Click **OK** in the **Certificate Export Wizard** dialog box.

29. Click **Close** in the **Certificates** dialog box.

30. Click **OK** in the **Internet Options** dialog box.

Now we'll import the certificate into the Firewall service account:

1. Click **Start** and then click **Run**. In the **Run** dialog box, enter **mmc** in the **Open** text box, and click **OK**.

2. In the console, click **File**, and then click **Add/Remove Snap-in**.

3. In the **Add/Remove Snap-in** dialog box, click **Add**.

4. In the **Add Standalone Snap-in** dialog box, click **Certificates** in the list of **Available Standalone Snap-ins**, and click **Add**.

5. On the **Certificates snap-in** page, select the **Services account** option, and click **Next**.

6. On the **Select Computer** page, select **Local Computer (the computer this console is running on)**, and click **Next**.

7. On the **Select a service account to manage on the local computer** page, select **Microsoft Firewall** from the **Service account** list, and click **Finish**.

8. Click **Close** in the **Add Standalone Snap-in** dialog box.

9. Click **OK** in the **Add/Remove Snap-in** dialog box.

10. In the console, expand the **Certificates – Service** node and right-click **fwsrv\Personal**. Point to **All Tasks** and click on **Import**.

11. On the **Welcome to the Certificate Import Wizard** page, click **Next**.

12. On the **File to Import** page, click **Browse** to find the location of the user certificate file you exported from the browser. Click **Next**.

13. Enter the password you assigned the certificate in the **Password** text box. Do not put a checkmark in the **Mark this key as exportable** checkbox. You might also want to delete the certificate from the Web browser on the ISA firewall so that this certificate cannot be stolen by individuals who obtain physical access to the ISA firewall. Click **Next**.

14. On the **Certificate Store** page, use the default setting **Place all certificates in the following store**, and click **Next**.

15. Click **Finish** on the **Completing the Certificate Import Wizard** page.

16. Click **OK** in the **Certificate Import Wizard** dialog box.

The certificate is now associated with the Firewall service account. You might want to disable the System Policy Rule we created earlier so that you don't inadvertently use the browser on the ISA firewall. Remember, you should avoid using the browser, and all other client applications, on the firewall.

Creating an SSL Web Publishing Rule

Now that our certificates are in place, we can create the SSL secure Web Publishing Rule. There are two main differences between this process in ISA 2006, namely:

- There is no choice regarding tunneled and bridged rules

- The SSL and non-SSL publishing wizards have been merged

We will cover these differences, as well as re-exploring the **Internal Publishing Details** pages and **Public name details** pages, which have added implications for us when publishing SSL websites.

In ISA 2004, we had the choice as to whether to *tunnel* or *bridge* SSL Web Publishing Rules. ISA 2006 **does not give you this choice**, preferring instead to default to bridging SSL published websites.

This provides us with a wizard which has been tweaked to provide us only with the securer option - **SSL Bridging** provides a secure end-to-end encrypted SSL connection while at the same time allowing the ISA firewall to perform both stateful packet inspection (like any conventional "hardware" firewall) and stateful application-layer inspection.

SSL Tunneling with ISA 2004 bypassed the ISA firewall's stateful application-layer inspection functionality and reduced the overall level of security for the publishing rule that is provided by a conventional stateful packet inspection "hardware" firewall. The omission of this form of publishing rule from the wizard should not prove a problem for many people, as there were very few reasons to use this option save for unusual situations such as those in which you publish applications that are not compliant with HTTP 1.1 Web Proxies. If you must publish an SSL website in tunneled mode, you must now do this via the Server Publishing Wizard.

One exception to this best practice is when you have a back to back ISA Firewall configuration. In this case, the front-end ISA Firewall should use SSL tunneling to the back-end ISA Firewall. The SSL connection is then terminated on the back-end ISA Firewall and SSL to SSL bridging can be done there.

Unlike ISA 2004, ISA 2006 does not give us separate SSL and non-SSL publishing wizards; instead, the same wizard presents us with choices as to whether to use SSL or not. We have choices regarding this in two main places:

- The **New Web Publishing Rule Wizard - Server Connection Security** Page, in which we can choose how to connect to the published Web Server

- The **New Web Listener – Client Connection Security** Page, in which we can choose how the Web Listener will service client connections

ISA 2004 presented these choices to us in a subtly different way, allowing us to pick one of three options on the **Bridging Mode** page of the SSL Publishing Wizard:

- Secure connection to clients

- Secure connection to Web server

- Secure connection to clients and Web server

These three options are still possible in ISA 2006, but are the resultant effect of the combination of the **Server Connection Security** and **Client Connection Security** pages.

We'll cover these two distinctions in the Web Publishing Rule Wizard for the differing types of rule, and then go over how to accomplish with ISA 2006 what could be accomplished on the **Bridging Mode** page.

In our original Web Publishing Rule, we published a site on the ISA Protected Network, *http://webfarm.infra.example.com* as *http://extranet.example.com* to clients on the internet. In this example, we'll go over the changes to the process were we to decide, instead, to publish *https://webfarm.infra. example.com* as *https://extranet.example.com*, either instead of, or in addition to, the http:// rules. Recall our recommendation that *additional* Web Listeners be configured to publish the same sites as *http://* and *https://*, rather than a single Web Listener configured to handle both.

The Internal Publishing Details Pages

On the **Internal Publishing Details** pages, you have the following options on the first and second pages respectively:

First:

- Internal Site Name
- Computer Name or IP Address

Second:

- Path
- Site
- Forward the original host header instead of the actual one specified in the Internal Site name field on the previous page

The **Computer name or IP address** text box includes the IP address or name for the published Web server. This is a critical entry for SSL publishing because the name in this text box *must match the common name on the Web site certificate on the Web server*. If the name you enter in the **Computer name or IP address** text box doesn't match the common name on the Web site certificate, the connection attempt will fail, and the user will see a **500 Internal Server** error.

In our example, as the common name on the Web site certificate bound to the published Web site is **webfarm.infra.example.com**, then you *must* enter **webfarm.infra.example.com** in the **Computer name or IP address** text box. If you enter the IP address or NetBIOS name of the server, the connection will fail because the name doesn't match the common name on the Web site certificate.

Forward the original host header instead of the actual one (specified above) works the same way as it does when you publish non-SSL sites. However, you must be careful with this option because if the remote user uses a FQDN that is different than the common name on the Web site certificate, the connection attempt will fail.

For example, if you *have enabled* this option, if the remote user enters **https://extranet. example.com** to access the published Web site through the ISA firewall, then the ISA firewall will use **extranet.example.com** instead of **webfarm.infra.example.com** when it proxies the connection to the published Web site, and the connection will fail with a 500 error. For this reason, we recommend that you use the same name from end to end for your Web Publishing Rules. However, this isn't required because if you *do not enable* the **Forward the original host header instead of the actual one specified in the Internal Site name field on the previous page** option, and you use the same name from end to end, then the name the external user uses to access the Web site is the same as the common name on the Web site certificate.

The key to success is that the name in the **Computer name or IP address** text box matches the common name on the Web site certificate on the published Web site, and the ISA firewall resolves the name in the **Computer name or IP address** text box to the *internal* address, *not* the public address used by the Web listener, for that site. In this example, the name **webfarm.infra.example. com** must resolve to the *internal* or non-public address. That is to say, the *actual* address bound to the Web site on the corporate networks.

The **Path** text box is used in the same way it's used for non-SSL connections. See the section in this chapter on publishing non-secure Web sites for details of this option. The **Web Site** box lists the URL of the site that will be published on the Internal network.

The Public Name Details Page

On the **Public Name Details** (Figure 5.9) page, you define what names users can use to access the published Web site via this Web Publishing Rule. The **Public Name Details** page includes the following options:

- Accept requests for
- Public name
- Path (optional)
- Site

The **Accept requests for** drop-down list allows you to choose either **This domain name (type below)** or **Any domain name**. As we mentioned in our earlier discussion on non-SSL publishing, the **Any domain name** option is a low security option and should be avoided, if at all possible. This option allows the Web Publishing Rule to accept incoming requests using any IP address or FQDN that can reach the IP address that the Web listener for the Web Publishing Rule uses. The preferred option is **This domain name (type below)**. This option limits the name remote users can use when accessing the Web site published by this Web Publishing Rule.

You enter the name the remote user uses to access the published Web site in the **Public name** text box. This is a critical option. You must enter the name that the remote user uses to access the Web site, and the name *must match the common name on the Web site certificate bound to the Web listener* used by this rule.

We recommend that you export the Web site certificate bound to the published Web site and import that certificate into the ISA firewall's machine certificate store. When you do this, you can bind the original Web site certificate to the Web listener used by this Web Publishing Rule. You would then use the same name from end to end.

For example, if the Web site certificate used on the published Web site has the common name **crm.example.com**, and you export that Web site certificate and bind it to the Web listener used by this Web Publishing Rule, you should use the same name, **crm.example.com**, in the **Public name** text box. Remote users must be able to resolve this name to the address on the ISA firewall that the Web listener used by this rule accepts incoming secure connections.

The **Path** text box allows you to set what paths are accessible on the published Web site. For more details on how to use the **Path** option, review our discussion of this subject in the non-SSL Web publishing section of this chapter.

The Server Connection Security Page

On the **Server Connection Security** page (Figure 5.3), we can choose how to connect to the target web server. As mentioned earlier in the chapter, there is an implicit understanding when a user connects to an SSL-secured site that traffic from their computer to the site is protected against interlopers. If you publish a site via SSL which is sent over plaintext on your internal network, consider the security implications very carefully.

We choose **Use SSL to connect to the published Web server or server farm** to secure the connection between ISA and the target webserver. There is no additional configuration in the wizard that we are provided with as a result of this option.

The Client Connection Security Page

The **Client Connection Security** page in the **New Web Listener** wizard allows us to choose which ports, and using which protocol the web listener listens on – HTTP on port 80, or HTTPS on port 443.

After selecting **Require SSL Secured Connections with clients** on this page, we proceed as with a non-SSL rule to the **Web Listener IP Addresses** page, to select which networks and IP addresses the web listener should accept requests from. The next page we are presented with, however, is an SSL rule-specific page, the **Listener SSL Certificates** wizard page, illustrated in Figure 5.21.

Figure 5.21 The Listener SSL Certificates dialog box

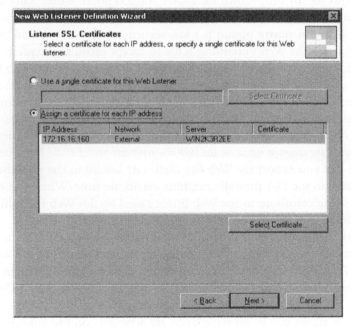

The **Listener SSL Certificates** dialog is new to ISA 2006, and provides simplified certificate management during the wizard itself. This wizard dialog allows you to specify either a single certificate for the web listener, or an individual certificate for each IP address selected in the publishing rule.

ISA FIREWALL ALERT

You cannot configure SSL on the listener unless you have a machine certificate stored in the ISA firewall's machine certificate store.

If we click the **Select Certificate** button, we open the **Select Certificate** dialog box, displayed in figure 5.22 which shows us which certificates are available for the listener, and in the lower **Certificate Installation Details** whether or not the selected certificate is valid for our purposes and correctly installed. The dialog defaults to displaying only valid certificates as shown in Figure 5.22.

Figure 5.22 The Select Certificate Dialog

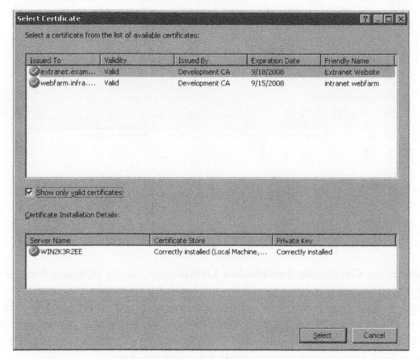

If we deselect the **Show only valid certificates** option and select an invalid certificate (in this instance, a root certificate with corresponding private key, since as this is not a production ISA Server, it is also functioning as a Standalone Certificate Authority)

Figure 5.23 The Select Certificate dialog

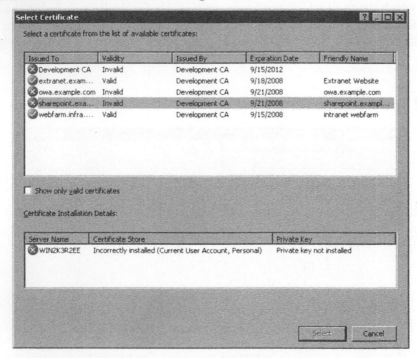

As you can see, the **Certificate Installation Details** pane clearly indicates that the selected certificate is *Incorrectly installed*, and does not have an installed Private key.

This dialog greatly simplifies the certificate assignment process by giving you a clear indication as to whether or not your certificate is installed in the correct location and is of the correct type – Figure 5.24 shows the **Certificate Installation Details** for a certificate which is correctly installed (and has a private key), but which is inappropriate for a web listener:

Figure 5.24 The Select Certificate dialog with invalid certificates selected

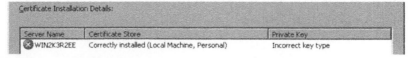

Hitting **Select** in the **Select Certificate** dialog once we have the correct certificate selected in the **Certificate Installation Details** pane, we can hit **Next** on the **Listener SSL Certificates** page, and proceed to the **Authentication Settings** Web Listener Wizard page which we have already covered.

ISA 2004's Bridging Mode Page and ISA 2006

The three options on the **Bridging Mode** page of the SSL Publishing Wizard can be configured as follows in ISA 2006:

- Secure connection to clients
- Secure connection to Web server
- Secure connection to clients and Web server

The **Secure connection to clients** option in ISA 2004 can be configured in ISA 2006 by choosing **Require SSL secured Connections with Clients** in the **Client Connection Security** dialog, and the **Use non-secured connections to connect the published Web server or farm** option in the **Server Connection Security** dialog displayed in figure 5.3.

This combination of settings sets the connection up as SSL-to-HTTP bridging. This option secures the connection between the Web client and the ISA firewall, but allows the connection to travel in unsecured free text between the ISA firewall and the published Web server. We highly recommend against this practice, unless you use an alternate method of securing the connection between the ISA firewall and the published Web server (such as IPSec or a dedicated link between the ISA firewall and the Web server where the cable itself would need to be compromised in the fashion of a "vampire tap" such as cutting the cable and wiring each side of the twisted pairs to a listening device acting as a "man in the middle," or by picking up the signal using a Time Domain Reflectometer).

We do realize that there is always a trade-off between security and performance and the implicit contract you have with users who assume their connection is secure from end to end. If you believe that you have a strong, defensible reason for not using an end-to-end connection, then SSL-to-HTTP bridging is possible with the ISA firewall. Depending on the Web application you publish, you may need to use the ISA firewall's Link Translator feature to get things working properly. We'll talk more about the Link Translator in Chapter 4.

The **Secure connection to Web server** option in ISA 2004 can be configured in ISA 2006 by choosing **Do not require SSL secured Connections with** Clients in the **Client Connection Security** dialog, and the **Use SSL to connect to the published Web Server or server farm** option in the **Server Connection Security** dialog.

This combination of settings allows you to perform HTTP-to-SSL bridging. The connection between the Web client is sent over HTTP, and the connection between the ISA firewall and the Web server is sent via SSL. This is a somewhat unusual scenario, where the client is on a more trusted network than the networks in the path between the ISA firewall and the published server. An example of this type of scenario is where a branch office has an ISA firewall connecting it to the main office using a dedicated WAN link. You can publish the main office Web server at the branch office ISA firewall and secure the connection over the WAN link to the main office and finally to the destination Web server.

The **Secure connection to clients and Web server** option in ISA 2004 can be configured in ISA 2006 by choosing **Require SSL secured Connections with Clients** in the **Client Connection Security** dialog, and the **Use SSL to connect to the published Web Server or server farm** option in the **Server Connection Security** dialog.

This option is the most secure and preferred option. This enables SSL-to-SSL bridging where the connection between the Web client and the ISA firewall is secured by SSL, and the connection between the ISA firewall and the published Web server is also secured by SSL. The ISA firewall is able to perform stateful application-layer inspection on the contents of the SSL connection when you use SSL bridging, while at the same time providing an end-to-end encrypted connection.

Configuring Advanced Web Listener Properties

There are many configuration items which may be applied to Web Listeners which do not appear in the wizard used to create them. In this section we will explore these additional options

The following tabs and dialogs are present in the properties dialog for a web listener, and tabs/dialogs which allow us to change settings not in the wizard are *italicized*.

- General
- Networks
- Connections
- *Connections – Advanced Dialog*
- Certificates
- *Certificates – Advanced Dialog*
- Authentication
- *Authentication – Advanced Dialog*
- *Forms*
- *Forms – Advanced Dialog*
- SSO

The General Tab

The *General Tab* allows us to change the **Name** and **Description** of the Web Listener. It is not pictured.

The Networks Tab

The *Networks Tab* allows us to change which networks the Web Listener is configured for, and which IP addresses within that network the Web Listener should use which are bound to the corresponding Interfaces in ISA Server.

By hitting the **Address** button, we can open the **External Network Listener IP Selection** dialog, pictured in Figure 5.12, allowing us to change the IP addresses to which the Web Listener binds.

The Connections Tab

The Connections tab of the Web Listener Properties dialog allows you to change which port the HTTP Listener is configured to accept connections on, as well as configure the same web listener to service HTTP and HTTPS requests. We recommend that you configure your HTTP and SSL listeners separately.

ISA FIREWALL ALERT

A socket is a combination of a transport protocol (TCP or UDP), an IP address, and a port number. Only one process can bind itself to a socket. If another process on the ISA firewall is using the same socket that you want to use for your Web listener, then you will need to disable the other process using the socket, or choose another port number for the Web listener to use. This is a common problem for ISA firewall administrators who attempt to publish Web resources located on the ISA firewall itself. As mentioned many other times in this book, you should *never* run services on the ISA firewall other than the ISA firewall services, services that the ISA firewall depends upon, and add-on services that enhance the ISA firewall's stateful application-layer inspection abilities.

Figure 5.25 The Connections Tab

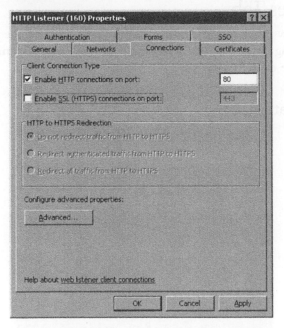

The **HTTP to HTTPS** Redirection allows you to force clients who browse to the URL of the web listener using http:// to be redirected to the https:// URL. This option requires that you enable both port 80 and 443 in the web listener under **Client Connection Type**.

When this option is enabled, the ISA Firewall will send an *HTTP/1.x 302 Object Moved* response back to clients who hit the http:// URL, causing the client browser to redirect to URL specified in the *Location* HTTP Header.

```
HTTP/1.x 302 Object Moved
Date: Fri, 21 Sep 2007 16:58:17 GMT
Connection: Keep-Alive
Content-Length: 0
Location: https://extranet.example.com/
```

The Connections – Advanced Dialog

If we click on the **Advanced** button, we reach the **Connections – Advanced** dialog, which allows us to configure the maximum number of clients which can be connected to the web listener at one time, and the connection timeout.

NOTE

Connection Limits are useful for throttling traffic. They can also be configured at the ISA Firewall level, and any TCP connection settings configured here will take precedence over the Web Listener connection settings.

The Certificates Tab

The Certificates Tab allows us to reconfigure the certificate options specified during the creation of the Web Listener, choosing either a **Single certificate for this web listener** or by choosing to **Assign a certificate for each IP address**.

Figure 5.26 Certificates Tab

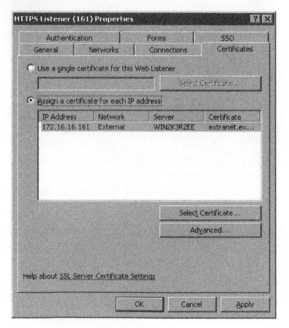

The Certificates – Advanced Dialog

By clicking the **Advanced** button on the **Certificates Tab** displayed in Figure 5.26, you can gain access to the one **Advanced Certificate option, Certificate per server on all IP addresses**.

If you use a hardware load balancer and require a separate certificate per server, even on addresses allocated to an NLB Interface, this option can be enabled to manage certificates on a server-by-server basis, rather than at the Array Level.

The Authentication Tab

The Authentication Tab allows you to configure the form of **Client Authentication Method** used by the Web Listener, configure which **Authentication Validation Method** to use, and **Configure Validation Servers** if using an authentication method that utilizes hardcoded validation servers, such as LDAP or RADIUS authentication.

Advanced Authentication Options Dialog Box

The **Authentication – Advanced** function can be reached by hitting the **Advanced** button on the **Authentication** tab.

With only HTTP enabled on the web listener, the **Advanced Authentication Options** dialog appears as in Figure 5.27, and has only one tab, the **Authentication Preferences** tab. With HTTPS also enabled, two additional tabs appear, the **Client Certificate Trust list** and **Client Certificate Restrictions** tabs, pictured in Figure 5.28 and 5.29.

Figure 5.27 Advanced Authentication Options – Authentication Preferences

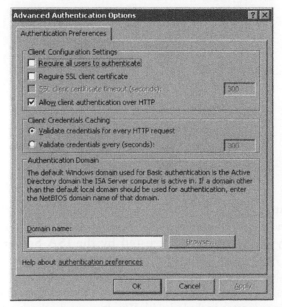

If you do not need to accept anonymous requests for this HTTP Listener, you can check the **Require all users to authenticate** option. As mentioned earlier in the chapter, ISA does not by default allow HTTP traffic to be used for authentication, and as such, the **Allow client authentication over HTTP** option comes **disabled** by default. In order to allow authentication over HTTP as we have earlier, this option should be enabled as displayed in Figure 5.26.

ISA FIREWALL ALERT

Only enable this option if traffic is protected by other means, such as a load balancer or SSL terminator in front of the ISA Firewall.

Client Credentials Caching and Authentication Domain can be configured to meet your requirements, whilst other options on this screen will be explored in the SSL Web Publishing section.

Figure 5.28 Advanced Authentication Options – Client Certificate Trust List

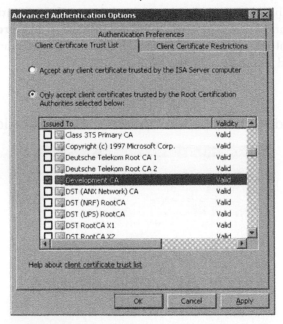

The **Client Certificate Trust List** tab affects how ISA handles User (client) certificates presented if we have SSL enabled, and accept client certificate authentication. By default, ISA has this setting configured to **Accept any client certificate trusted by the ISA Server computer**.

The list of Certificate Authorities ISA comes pre-populated with come from the Local Machine Trusted Root Certificates Store, and are shipped with Windows (and updated periodically with optional Windows Updates). The list includes Certificate Authorities such as Verisign and Equifax who have applied to have their certificates included with Windows, and who have passed a third-party audit.

So long as they adhere to the processes and procedures of the CA, anyone can buy a User certificate from many of these Trusted CAs, so if we enable User Certificate authentication with ISA, we automatically open the floodgates to allow any users of any of these Trusted Root CAs to authenticate to our ISA firewall. This may or may not be what we want to happen – if it isn't, and we run our own CA from which we would like users to have certificates issued, we can select the **Only accept client certificates trusted by the Root Certification Authorities selected below** option, and select our CA, as pictured in Figure 5.28.

Figure 5.29 Advanced Authentication Options – Client Certificate Restrictions

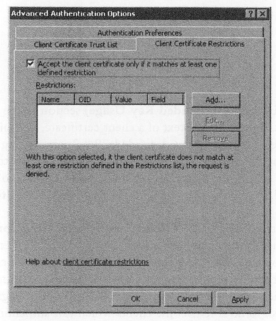

The **Client Certificate Restrictions** tab allows you to supply a filter to be applied to certificates used to authenticate to the ISA Server Web Listener. This provides more granular control over certificates than the **Client Certificate Trust List** can provide.

The restrictions that can be specified apply to one of the following four fields within the certificate itself:

■ Issuer – *ie. The CA which issued the certificate*

■ Subject – *ie. To whom the certificate is issued, including the CN.*

■ Enhanced Key Usage

■ Extensions

The **Issuer** field in the certificate indicates the CA which issued the certificate, for instance the Issuer field for the certificate used for https://www.microsoft.com is:

```
CN = Microsoft Secure Server Authority
DC = Redmond
```

```
DC = corp
DC = Microsoft
DC = com
```

The **Subject** field in the certificate indicates to whom the certificate is issued. As with the **Issuer** field, this takes the form of a comma-separated Distinguished Name, and contains the **CN**, or **Canonical Name** of the certificate, which is identical to the FQDN of the site the certificate is used for, if the certificate is used for Web Publishing.

```
CN = www.microsoft.com
OU = mscom
O = Microsoft
L = Redmond
ST = washington
C = US
```

The **Enhanced Key Usage** (or **Extended Key Usage**) section of the certificate defines what purposes the certificate has. Within the context of a client certificate, this might, for instance, include the Smart Card Logon object identifier *1.3.6.1.4.1.311.20.2.2* – restricting the client certificates usable to authenticate to the ISA Server to those which are stored on smartcards.

The X.509 Certificate specification includes provision for extensions to the specification made using the **Extensions** field. In popular these include the **Keyusage** and **AlternativeNames** extensions.

As we have demonstrated, although the **Client Certificate Restrictions** dialog is well tucked-away and appears simple, due to the complex nature of certificates, the potential for restricting User Certificates is extremely powerful. We have not covered the full breadth of configuration options this dialog presents us with, but the documentation for your PKI implementation should supply more information on how certificates can be used, and how you may wish to begin to use this feature.

Although if all you wish to do is restrict the clients which can authenticate to domain or corporate clients, the **Client Certificate Trust List** may be perfectly adequate, if you wish to use Smartcard-enabled clients or specify more granular restrictions, **Client Certificate Restrictions** provides you with many options.

The Forms Tab

The **Forms** tab, which is pictured in Figure 5.30, allows configuration of **Forms-Based Authentication**, if this is in use on the Web Listener.

Figure 5.30 The Forms Tab

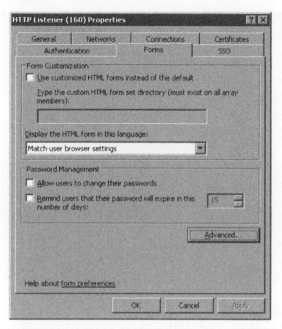

Form Customization allows users of Microsoft ISA Server to provide custom branding for the Forms-Based Authentication Interface, and configure language settings. The specifics of customizing the FBA Web Interface will not be covered here. **Password Management** can be enabled where authentication is performed against LDAP or integrated Active Directory back-ends, and when enabled, allows the user to pick an *I want to change my password after logging on* option whilst logging on via FBA.

The Forms – Advanced Dialog

The **Advanced** button on this tab allows us to open the **Advanced Form Options** dialog box, pictured in Figure 5.31. This dialog allows us to configure options pertaining to the cookies and timeouts used by Forms-Based Authentication.

Figure 5.31 The Forms – Advanced Dialog

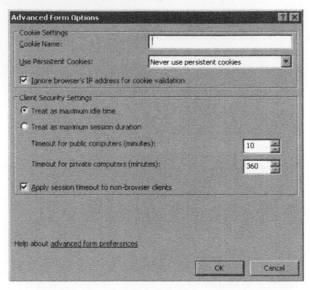

The **Cookie Name** settings allows you to configure your ISA firewall to provide specifically named cookies, as well as configuring whether or not **Persistent cookies** are used. **Persistent cookies** are cookies which remain in the user's browser after the browser is closed; using the default settings, *Never use persistent cookies,* cookies for Forms-Based Authentication are cleared when the browser is closed.

The **Ignore browser's IP address for cookie validation** option dictates whether or not the ISA firewall will allow users to authenticate using the same cookie using more than one IP address. If you have users who may use connections with IP addresses which change, such as mobile users or users behind proxy server arrays, it is recommended that you leave this option enabled, or users will be forced to re-authenticate.

The **Client Security Settings** pane allows you to configure timeout settings for FBA clients who select either *public* or *private* as their location, as well as how the Timeout is applied – as an *idle time* (ie. Time elapsing between actions performed by the user within the user interface) or *session time* (ie. Time elapsing after logon).

You may wish to pick *maximum session duration* to force users to re-authenticate after a fixed time period for increased security. This option should be considered carefully, as it may inconvenience users.

The **non-browser clients** option applies these timeout settings to non-browser clients, such as *RPC-over-HTTP/Outlook Anywhere* or *Activesync* clients.

The SSO Tab

The Single Sign-On tab allows you to change settings for SSO specified during the Listener Setup Process. Principally, this means the **SSO Domains** which dictate which domains the SSO cookie inserted by the Web Listener into the user's browser post –authentication is valid for.

As mentioned earlier, this should be as specific as possible – ie. *.example.com* in our example, *not* *.com*. Note also that SSO works only within the context of a single web listener – not cross-web-listener.

The Web Publishing Rule Properties Dialog Box

The new Web Publishing Rule appears in the **Firewall Policy** list. Right-click the **Web Publishing Rule**, and click **Properties**. The Web Publishing Rules **Properties** dialog box has fourteen tabs, two of which are new to ISA 2006, and which are *italicized*:

- General
- Action
- From
- To
- Traffic
- Listener
- Public Name
- Paths
- Bridging
- Users
- Schedule
- Link Translation
- *Authentication Delegation*
- *Application Settings*

Let's look at the options in each of these tabs. You'll find that as with the **Properties** dialog box for the Web Listener, there are many options on these tabs that were not exposed in the Web Publishing Rule Wizard.

The General Tab

On this tab, you can change the name of the Web Publishing Rule by entering a name in the **Name** text box. You can also enter a description for the rule in the **Description (optional)** text box. You can enable or disable the Web Publishing Rule in the **Enable** checkbox, as shown in Figure 5.32.

Figure 5.32 The General tab

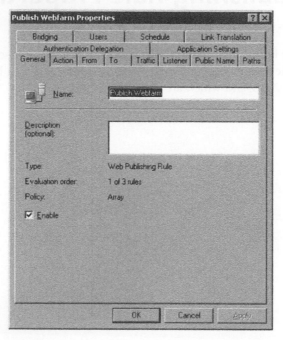

Action

On the **Action** tab (Figure 5.33) you either **Allow** or **Deny** access to the site configured in the Web Publishing Rule.

If you choose to **Deny** requests, you can redirect denied requests to a URL of your choice. This can be used for, for instance, exempting particular parts of a published site from being accessible via untrusted networks, or as a quick workaround for a particular security hole at a higher level than the ISA firewall is able to protect against, such as a vulnerability in a web application.

This can be accomplished simply by creating an identical publishing rule above the pre-existing publishing rule, but with paths matching only the portions of the site which should be denied, with an **Action** of **Deny**, and with the **Redirect HTTP Requests to this Web Page** field populated with a target to redirect to. This might be the root of your site, or a 'denied' page. Include the full URL as displayed in the '*Address*' bar of the browser.

ISA FIREWALL ALERT

If you use an **Action:Deny** rule to exempt access to certain portions of a site, ensure that your **Deny** rule is *above* the existing rule to ensure that an *allow* rule does not match first – the ISA firewall will use the first matching rule to service a request, and not evaluate all rules. If you use rules for this purpose, you should ensure you name your rules in a logical manner and document your firewall ruleset to avoid confusion. Wherever possible, define publishing rules which *allow specific paths*, rather than defining /* rules and positioning deny rules above them.

You also have the option to **Log requests matching this rule**. If you find that your log files are getting too large and the site being accessed by the rule isn't of any particular interest to you, then you might consider not logging requests handled by this rule. However, we do not recommend that you disable logging for any publishing rules because most of these rules represent connections from untrusted Networks.

Click **Apply** on the Action tab, shown in Figure 5.33, to save the changes you make on this tab.

Figure 5.33 The Action Tab

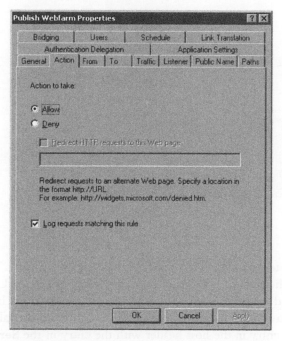

From

On the **From** tab, configure locations where you want the Web Publishing Rule to accept connections for the Published Site. The default location is **Anywhere**, which means that any host that can reach the IP address or addresses used for the Web listener can access this Web Publishing Rule.

You can limit access to this Web Publishing Rule by clicking **Anywhere** and then clicking **Remove**. After removing the **Anywhere** entry, click **Add**. In the **Add Network Entities** dialog box, click the folder that contains the Network Object you want to allow access to the Web Publishing Rule.

There is also the option to fine-tune access to the rule by setting exceptions in the **Exceptions** frame. For example, you might want to allow access to the Web Publishing Rule to all Networks *except* for hosts on the Network where the published server is located. This is generally a good idea because you do not want corporate network hosts looping back through the ISA firewall to connect to resources located on the corporate network.

Click **Apply** on the **From** page, Figure 5.34 below, after making your changes.

Figure 5.34 The From tab

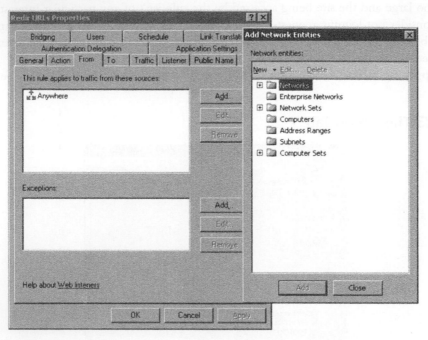

To

The **To** tab is one of the most important tabs in the **Properties** dialog box. The reason for this is that the entry you put in the **Server** text box defines the host name in the URL that Web Publishing Rule sends to the published Web site. The entry you put in the **Server** text box replaces the host header that was included in the original client request sent to the ISA firewall. If you don't want the ISA firewall to replace the entry in the host header with the entry in the **Server** text box, then put a checkmark in the **Forward the original host header instead of the actual one (specified above)** checkbox.

Another important option on the **To** tab is the ability to specify how the ISA firewall proxies the requests to the server listed in the **Server** text box. You have two options:

■ Requests appear to come from the ISA Server computer

■ Requests appear to come from the original client

Requests appear to come from the ISA Server computer is useful when you don't want to make the published Web server a SecureNAT client. One of the primary disadvantages of the SecureNAT client configuration is that the entire routing infrastructure must be aware that the ISA firewall should be the gateway to IP addresses clients of the web publishing rule come from. If this is an internet-facing publishing rule, this essentially requires making the ISA Firewall the default gateway, or configuring a very messy routing table on the published Web Servers.

Many organizations have an established routing infrastructure, and they don't want to make the ISA firewall the route of last resort for all hosts on the network. You can get around this problem by allowing the ISA firewall to replace the remote host's IP address with its own. When the published server returns its response, it only needs to know the route to the local interface on the ISA firewall. It doesn't need a route to the Internet and doesn't need to make the ISA firewall its default gateway.

Requests appear to come from the original client allows the ISA firewall to preserve the IP address of the remote host sending the request for published Web site resources. There are several advantages to this approach – in small environments, log-reporting software on the Web server itself frequently prompts this configuration, as you will be able to report on the actual IP addresses of the hosts connecting to the Web site. If you don't select this option, it will appear in the Web site's log files that all connections are coming from the ISA firewall's IP address.

In larger environments, load balancing software such as Microsoft Network Load Balancing frequently handles '*affinity*' (ie. Which webserver services which request) based on IP address – if all requests to webservers come from just one of the ISA firewall's IP addresses (or a small number of addresses), all requests made through a particular publishing ISA firewall will bind to a particular web server. While it is possible to work around this problem (using ISA 2006's own new-found understanding of load balancing of target web servers and *cookie-based affinity*, for instance), this is a problem which it is easier for many organizations to solve using the **Requests appear to come from the original client** option, with ISA in the routing chain.

One issue with this approach is that if you enable reverse proxy for the published Web site, you will notice a number of requests sourcing from the ISA firewall itself, and you might misinterpret this as the ISA firewall failing to preserve the IP address of the requesting host. This is not true, and there is no bug or problem with this ISA firewall software in this regard. The issue is that when performing reverse proxy, the ISA firewall serves the responses from its cache. However, the ISA firewall, in its role as reverse Proxy server, needs to check on the status of the objects on the Web site, and this status check generates requests from the ISA firewall's address to the published Web site, which subsequently appears in the Web site's logs.

For this reason and more, we prefer to perform Web site activity analysis on the ISA firewall's Web Proxy service logs instead of the Web site logs themselves. There are exceptions to this rule, but for sites that are public sites only and not accessed by internal users, the Web Proxy logs on the ISA firewall provide the most rich and most accurate information.

Options for the **To** tab are shown in Figure 5.17 below.

ISA FIREWALL TIP

We recommend that you use a FQDN in the **Server** text box on the **To** tab. This will allow the Web Proxy log to include this name in the log file entries and make it easier for you to audit access to the published servers. In addition, the FQDN will appear in any reports you create.

Figure 5.35 The To Tab

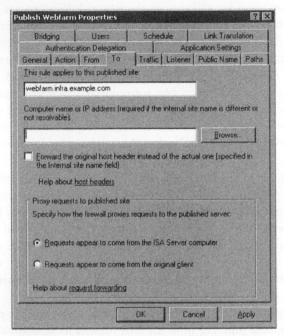

Traffic

On the **Traffic** tab, you'll see a list of protocols allowed by this Web Publishing Rule. The protocols are not configurable on this tab. Instead, the allowed protocols are determined by the protocol support set on the Web listener configured for this publishing rule.

Notify HTTP users to use HTTPS instead will be disabled if you do not have HTTP and HTTPS enabled on the web listener. A similar, but separate, setting can be enabled on the Web Listener itself – using the **HTTP to HTTPS Redirection** option on the **Connections** tab, covered earlier in the chapter. If you enable this option on the Web Listener, the **Notify HTTP users to use HTTPS instead** option will also be disabled.

When the **Notify HTTP users to use HTTPS instead** option is available, it allows the ISA firewall to return an error page to the user accessing the Web site through the Web Publishing Rule showing that HTTPS, instead of HTTP, should be used – the error message seen by clients is depicted in Figure 5.36.

It's a common error for users to enter HTTP, instead of HTTPS, when accessing secure Web sites. Fortunately, it takes less than three seconds to resubmit the request by adding an "s" to the protocol in the request. Forcing users to enter the correct protocol also encourages users to use correct Internet hygiene.

Whether you choose to redirect users from HTTP to HTTPS, or display an error and force them to alter the URL manually is up to you.

Figure 5.36 The Notify HTTP users to use HTTPS instead client experience

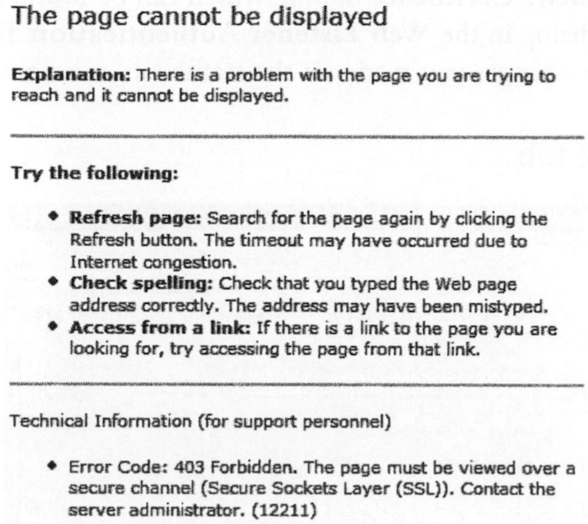

The page cannot be displayed

Explanation: There is a problem with the page you are trying to reach and it cannot be displayed.

Try the following:

♦ **Refresh page:** Search for the page again by clicking the Refresh button. The timeout may have occurred due to Internet congestion.
♦ **Check spelling:** Check that you typed the Web page address correctly. The address may have been mistyped.
♦ **Access from a link:** If there is a link to the page you are looking for, try accessing the page from that link.

Technical Information (for support personnel)

♦ Error Code: 403 Forbidden. The page must be viewed over a secure channel (Secure Sockets Layer (SSL)). Contact the server administrator. (12211)

Require 128-bit encryption for HTTPS traffic allows you to control the level of encryption security for SSL connections to the published Web site. All modern Windows clients support 128-bit encryption right out of the box, but there are outdated Windows clients and non–Windows clients that do not support 128-bit encryption, and you might want to block connections from these relatively unsecure clients.

ISA FIREWALL TIP

Enabling the **Require 128-bit encryption for HTTPS traffic** option will not actually prevent connections from being made using sub-standard ciphers, but rather negotiates SSL using the cipher supported by the older client, and then delivers an error message to the client over the https channel before ending the connection.

If you wish to disable the ciphers altogether (causing older clients to fail to negotiate the SSL channel, the error being dictated by the error handling in the client itself, http://support.microsoft.com/kb/245030 will explain how to do this – but on a machine level; this cannot be done on a rule-by-rule basis.

See http://blogs.isaserver.org/pouseele/2007/03/25/require-128-bit-encryption-for-https-traffic-with-isa-server-2006-part2/ for further exploration of this issue.

The **Require SSL Client Certificate** option is only enabled if the Web Listener for the publishing rule is *not* set to either **No authentication** or **SSL Client Certificate Authentication**. You can use this option to configure SSL User Certificate authentication *in addition to* other authentication methods – but the rule is only processed after the client authenticates via HTTP Basic or Forms-Based Authentication.

If you want to ensure that users have SSL User Certificates in order to connect at all, you should enable the **Require SSL Client Certificate** option, which can be found in the **Advanced Authentication Options** dialog in the **Web Listener Authentication Tab**.

Click **Apply** to save the changes you made on the traffic tab, as before.

Figure 5.37 The Traffic tab

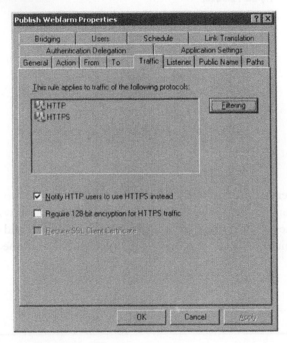

Listener

On the **Listener** tab, you can view the characteristics of the listener currently in use by the Web Publishing Rule, and you can change the properties of the listener here, as well, by clicking **Properties**. You can also create a new Web listener by clicking **New** and then applying the new listener to this Web Publishing Rule.

If you have already created multiple Web listeners on this ISA firewall, you can change the listener used by the Web Publishing Rule by clicking the down arrow on the **This rule applies to requests received on the following listener** drop-down box.

Click **Apply** after you make changes on the **Listener** tab.

Public Name

The **Public Name** tab allows you to view and configure the names that can be used to access the Web server published via this Web Publishing Rule. In the Web Publishing Rule we created in this example, we chose the name **extranet.example.com** for the public name that can be used to access the Web server. If a request comes in on the Web listener used by this Web Publishing Rule for a FQDN that is different from this one, this rule will ignore the connection request. Note that if this Web listener is used by other Web Publishing Rules, the incoming request will be compared to the **Public Name** entries in those other Web Publishing Rules. If no Web Publishing Rule includes a **Public Name** that matches that in the Host header of the incoming Web request, the connection will be dropped.

Also, note that a single Web Publishing Rule can be used for multiple host names. The key to success is to make sure that each of these host names resolves to the IP address or addresses that the Web listener bound to this rule is listening on. However, this also means that the same Paths, Bridging, Users, Schedule, and other settings would be applied to the connections coming in to the Web site. This might not always be the case, and this is why we recommend that you create separate Web Publishing Rules for each site that you publish.

You can **Add** a new Public name to the list by clicking **Add**, and you can **Remove** or **Edit** a selected public name by clicking **Edit** and **Remove**.

Click **Apply** when you have made your desired changes to the **Public Name** tab, as shown in Figure 5.38.

Figure 5.38 The Public Name Tab

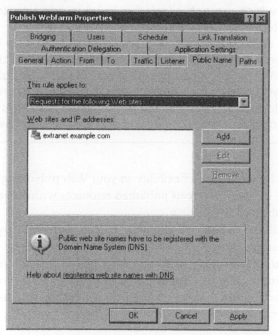

Paths

The **Paths** tab allows you to control how requests to different paths included in the requests are handled by the Web Publishing Rule. You'll notice in the path list that there are two columns: the **External Path** and the **Internal Path** column.

The **External Path** is the path in the request made by the user accessing the Web site through this Web Publishing Rule. For example, if a user enters the URL http://extranet.example.com/docs into the browser, then the external path is **/docs**. If a user enters the URL http://extranet.example. com/graphics into the browser, then the external path is **/graphics**.

The **Internal** path is the path that the ISA firewall will forward the request to based on the entry for the **External** path. For example, suppose we set the **External Path** as **/docs** and the **Internal Path** as **/publicdocuments**. When the user enters the URL http://extranet.example. com/docs into the browser, and the ISA firewall's Web listener for this rule accepts the connection for the request, then the ISA firewall will forward the request to the site listed in the **To** tab to the path **/publicdocuments**. If the entry in the **To** tab is **10.0.0.2**, then the ISA firewall forwards the request to the published Web server as **http://10.0.0.2/publicdocuments**.

ISA FIREWALL TIP

Carefully consider Web Publishing rules, particularly complex rules involving paths, to ensure that you leave yourself with the most simple, supportable combination of rules. When publishing rules contain path redirection rules, as is the case here, you need to ensure that you do not break links, hrefs, stylesheets, or other elements within web pages which use paths (*relative links*) in addition to those which are hard-coded (so-called *absolute links*).

Much dynamic web-content, such as Sharepoint sites, have expectations regarding how they're accessed, and can be setup specifically for alternative / extranet access on a different paths. Where this is not possible, consider the use of ISA Link Translation. As always, ensure you document and carefully name your ISA rules (and make use of the description field, particularly to include initials of the rule's creator, dates, or references to other sources, such as documentation and internal wiki pages.)

Path redirection provides you a lot of flexibility in your Web publishing rules and allows you to simplify the paths external users use to access published resources without requiring you to change directory names on the published Web server.

If you want access to all the folders and files under a particular directory, enter the path using the **/path/*** format. If you want to allow access to a single file in a path, enter the path in the **/path** format. For example, if you want to allow access to all the files in the **documents** directory on the Web server, enter for the **Internal** path **/documents/***. If you want to allow access to only the **names.htm** file in the **documents** directory, then enter the path as **/documents/names.htm**. An example of the **Paths** tab is shown below in Figure 5.39.

Figure 5.39 The Paths Tab

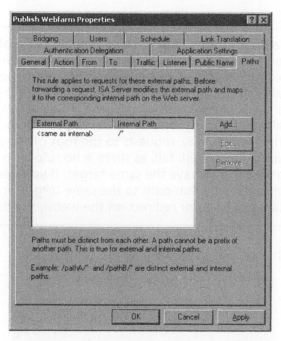

Click **Add** to add a new path. In the **Path mapping** dialog box, enter an *internal path* for **Specify the folder on the Web site that you want to publish. To publish the entire Web site, leave this field blank** text box. Next, select either the **Same as published folder** or **The following folder** option, as shown in Figure 5.40 below. If external users enter the same path, select the **Same as published folder**. If the users will enter a different path, select **The following folder** and enter the alternate path in the text box.

Figure 5.40 The Path Mapping Dialog Box

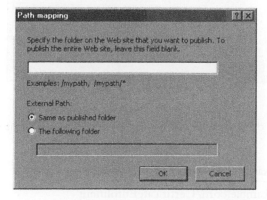

ISA FIREWALL TIP

Many ISA firewall administrators wish to redirect to the root of the Web site based on the path entered by the user. For example, if the user enters the URL http://extranet.example.com/firewalldocs, then the request should be forwarded to the root of the internal Web server. You can do this by entering the external path as **/firewalldocs/*** and the internal path as **/** as seen in Figure 5.41 below. All connections made to the **firewalldocs** directory are now redirected to the root of the server.

Note that configured this way, requests to the root of the published site (http://extranet.example.com/) will fail, as there is no rule with an 'external path' of /* - paths cannot overlap or have the same target. If you need to publish the root of a website (/*) and redirect a sub-path to the same target, you'll need to use a '*Deny*' rule as explained earlier, or redirect on the webserver itself.

Figure 5.41 Redirecting to the Web Root Using a Path

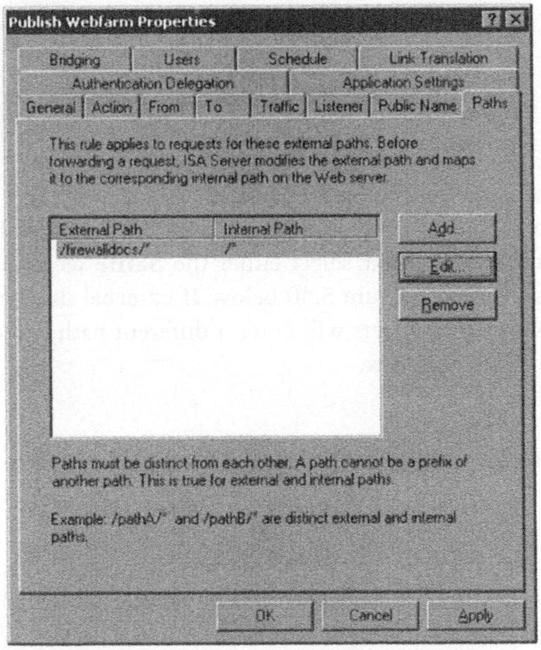

Another thing you can do with path statements is redirect to different servers. For example, take the following URLs:

- http://extranet.example.com/ContentManagement
- http://extranet.example.com/CertificateEnrolment
- http://extranet.example.com/Purchasing

All three URLs point to the same FQDN and only differ in the path. You can create three Web Publishing Rules, each one using the same **Public Name** and each one including a different path configuration and a different server on the **To** tab. When a user makes a request using one of these three URLs, the request will be forwarded to the appropriate server based on the settings on the **Public Name**, **Paths**, and **To** tabs.

ISA FIREWALL TIP

It's very common for organizations to use different FQDNs, IP addresses and certificates to publish different applications such as OWA, Sharepoint, and other intranet applications such as Content Management and Human Resources web applications. Path rules provide a highly attractive alternative to publishing each application on a separate IP address. Costs for certificates, IP address ranges, and general management and administration costs will be greatly reduced.

ISA 2006 presents another significant benefit to this approach – the use of one web listener means that Single Sign On will work across all of your applications, so users will only have to login once.

Bridging

The **Bridging** tab, as shown in Figure 5.42, allows you to configure port or protocol redirection for the Web Publishing Rule. You have the following options:

- Web Server
- Redirect requests to HTTP port
- Redirect requests to SSL port
- Use a certificate to authenticate to the SSL Web server
- FTP server
- Use this port when redirecting FTP requests

The **Web Server** option configures the Web Publishing Rule to forward HTTP or HTTPS requests. There is no protocol redirection with this option.

The **Redirect requests to HTTP port** option when checked allows you to redirect incoming HTTP requests for this Web Publishing Rule and Web listener to the published Web server using the port in the text box to the right of this option. The default port is TCP port **80**. You can choose any other port you like for the redirect. This allows you to use alternate port numbers on the published Web sites while still accepting requests on the default HTTP port used by the Web listener (although you do not need to use the default HTTP port on the Web listener if you have configured the Web listener to listen on an alternate port).

Redirect requests to SSL port allows you to redirect requests to the specified SSL port. Note that you can select both the HTTP and SSL checkboxes. When this is the case, incoming traffic is routed through its corresponding protocol and port. For example, if the incoming request is HTTP, then the request is forwarded to the HTTP port. If the incoming request is SSL, the request is forwarded to the SSL port. You can change the SSL port the request is forwarded to, which is helpful if you have SSL sites published on alternate ports. Note that you will have to have certificates on the published Web Server configured appropriately for this scenario.

One of the most misunderstood options in the ISA firewall's user interface is **Use a certificate to authenticate to the SSL Web server**. This option is *not* used by the ISA firewall to accept incoming SSL connections from users connecting to the published Web server. This option allows you to configure the ISA firewall to present a *user certificate* to the published Web site when the Web site requires user certificate authentication. The user certificate is bound to the Firewall service on the ISA firewall and enables the ISA firewall to present a user certificate for authentication to the Web site.

The **FTP server** option allows the Web Publishing Rule to perform protocol redirection. The incoming request can be either HTTP or HTTPS, and the connection is redirected as an FTP GET request to the published FTP site. Using SSL-to-FTP bridging is useful when providing remote access to FTP sites requiring authentication. Since FTP sites support only Basic authentication, you can protect user credentials by using an SSL link to the external interface of the ISA firewall. The **Bridging** tab is shown in Figure 5.43 below.

Figure 5.42 The Bridging Tab

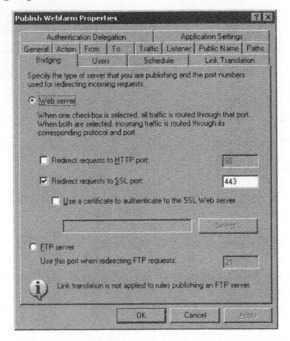

Users

The **Users** tab allows you to configure which users can access the published Web site via the Web Publishing Rule. Anyone can access the Web site through the ISA firewall when **All Users** are allowed access. However, this means that all users can get through the ISA firewall and have the unauthenticated requests forwarded to the published Web site. The Web site itself may require authentication. The user will still need to successfully authenticate with the Web site if the Web site requires authentication.

You can require authentication at the ISA firewall by removing the **All Users** group and adding any other user group via the **Add** button. The default groups included with the ISA firewall are **All Users**, **All Authenticated Users**, and **System and Network Service**. You can add your own firewall groups and fine-tune your authentication scheme. We'll talk more about firewall groups and how to use them in Chapter 4 on Creating and Configuring Firewall Policy for Outbound Access. See how to configure the **Users** tab in Figure 5.43.

Figure 5.43 The Users Tab

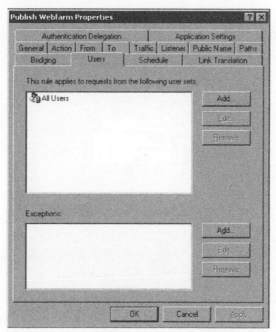

The ability to authenticate users at the ISA firewall provides a significant security advantage. Authenticating at the ISA firewall prevents unauthenticated connections from ever reaching the published Web server. Attackers and other malicious users and code can potentially leverage the unauthenticated connection to attack the published server. Authenticating at the firewall first removes the potential security risk.

Note that you can also require authentication at the Web site, so that users are required to authenticate at both the ISA firewall and at the Web site. In some circumstances, users will be presented with two log-on dialog boxes: the first authentication request is made by the ISA firewall, and the second authentication request is made by the published Web site.

You can avoid a dual authentication prompt by taking advantage of ISA's **Authentication Delegation**. Since ISA 2006 greatly increases the firewall's capabilities for delegation of authentication details, the '*Delegation of Basic authentication*' setting provided on this tab in ISA 2004 has been replaced by the **Authentication Delegation** tab.

Schedule

On the **Schedule** tab (Figure 5.44) you can configure schedules that control when users can connect to the published Web site. There are three default schedules:

- **Always** The Web site is always available through the Web Publishing Rule.
- **Weekends** All day Saturday and Sunday
- **Work hours** Monday through Friday 9:00 A.M. to 5:00 P.M.

You can also create your own custom schedules. We cover this issue in Chapter 4 on outbound access policies.

Figure 5.44 The Schedule tab

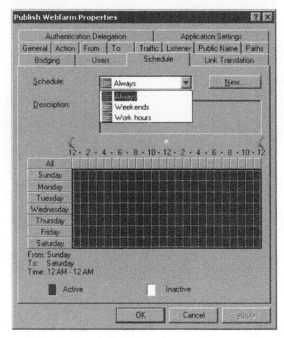

Link Translation

The ISA firewall's Link Translation feature allows you to rewrite the URLs returned by the published Web servers. URL rewriting is useful when you publish Web sites that hard code links in Web pages they return to users, and those links are not reachable from external locations.

For example, suppose we visit a Web site using the URL http://extranet.example.com. The http://extranet.example.com home page contains hard-coded links in the form of http://server1/users and http://server1/computers. When the Internet user clicks on one of these links, the connection fails because the Internet user isn't able to correctly resolve the name **server1** to the IP address on the external interface of the ISA firewall.

The ISA firewall's Link Translation feature allows you to rewrite the links containing **server1** to **extranet.example.com**. When the Web server returns the home page of the extranet.example.com site, the external user no longer sees the URLs with **server1** in them because the ISA firewall rewrote those URLs to include **extranet.example.com** instead of **server1**. The external user is now able to click on the links and access the content on the Web server. See Figure 5.45.

Figure 5.45 The Link Translation Tab

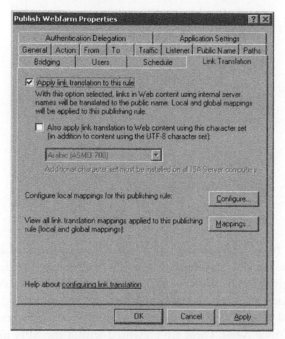

ISA 2006 introduces **global** and **local** mappings, allowing mappings to be applied at a higher level than the Web Publishing rule. Enterprise editions of ISA 2006 also include **Cross array link translation.** The newly introduced **Mappings** button allows us to view mappings defined at local and global level in the web browser.

We go into more detail in about the ISA firewall's Link Translator in Chapter 4.

Authentication Delegation

Authentication Delegation is entirely new to ISA 2006. As we discussed earlier, there are a range of options for authenticating to published Web Servers, whilst in ISA 2004, we only had *delegation of basic authentication*. To this end, ISA introduces a new tab for Authentication Delegation settings, pictured in Figure 5.46.

Figure 5.46 The Authentication Delegation Tab

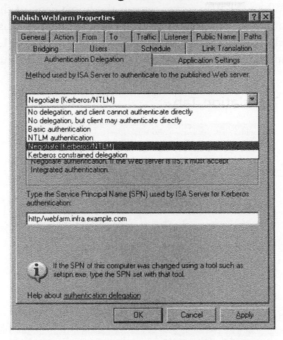

As we can see, if the *Negotiate (Kerberos/NTLM)* or *Kerberos constrained delegation* options are picked, we are asked for a **Service Principal Name**. As we discussed earlier, authenticating via Kerberos requires the registration of the SPN against which the ISA Server's computer account should be able to authenticate as users within Active Directory.

A **Service Principal Name**, or **SPN**, is made up of four components – *Service Type, Instance Name, Port Number, and Service Name*. These are presented within the SPN like so:

ServiceType / InstanceName : PortNumber / ServiceName

By default, computers have SPNs registered for their hostname and FQDN within Active Directory. These can be modified and viewed using the **Delegation** tab in the properties for the computer account, or using the **setspn** command line tool:

```
> setspn -l Machine1
Registered ServicePrincipalNames for
CN=Machine1, CN=Computers, DC=infra, DC=example, DC=com:
HOST/Machine1
HOST/Machine1.infra.example.com
```

Machines with kerberized services, such as LDAP, ADAM, or Exchange, will have additional SPNs. In order to allow our ISA Server, with a hostname of ISA01, authenticate via Kerberos Constrained Delegation to https://webfarm.infra.example.com, we would need to issue an setspn command as follows:

```
setspn -a http/webfarm.infra.example.com.com ISA01
Registering ServicePrincipalNames for
CN=ISA01, CN=Computers, DC=infra, DC=infra, DC=com
```

```
http/webfarm.infra.example.com ISA01
Updated object
```

Full coverage of the use of SPNs and AD for Kerberos Constrained Delegation is outside the scope of this book; for further documentation on the use of SPNs and Constrained Delegation, and the full implications of registering SPNs against machine accounts, see Tom Shinder's article on how to publish sites using Kerberos Constrained Delegation at http://www.isaserver.org/tutorials/Configuring-ISA-Firewalls-ISA-2006-RC-Support-User-Certificate-Authentication-using-Constrained-Delegation-Part2.html

Application Settings

The **Application Settings** tab allows you to configure several options pertaining to Forms-Based Authentication, as follows:

- Use customized HTML forms instead of the default
- Published server logoff URL
- Logon type provided to the Exchange server

The **Use customized HTML forms instead of the default** option allows you to customize the FBA login prompt. FBA Forms can be customized in order to apply your own branding to the login page, and display pre-authentication messages or disclaimers. ISA ships with two sets of customized forms, the **ISA** set (which are the default for web publishing rules), and the **Exchange** set (which are the default for exchange publishing rules).

Customizations to HTML forms can range in complexity from simple textual changes to full branding and tailoring to suit your requirements, and the full scope of form modification is outwith our scope. If you need to learn more about this, the ISA Server 2006 Technet site is a good starting point: http://www.microsoft.com/technet/isa/2006/html_forms.mspx.

The **Published server logoff URL** is an interesting option. Although if you publish Sharepoint or Outlook Web Access you will see a **Logoff** button, many applications which you may wish to publish via Forms-Based Authentication will not allow you to logoff in the same way as either of these two applications. The ISA firewall inserts a cookie into the user's browser during the FBA logon process which is used to determine whether or not the user is logged in, the login functions of published applications will not remove this cookie, even if it does remove an application-specific logon cookie.

When the user browses back to the site then, the ISA firewall's cookie continues to persist in the user's browser. The cookie can be used to re-authenticate to the published site until it is cleared by the browser or by the ISA firewall. In order to work around this issue, the ISA firewall allows you to specify a URL which causes the ISA firewall itself to effect the logoff process, and invalidate the cookie so that it cannot be used to re-authenticate to the site. If your application uses a custom logoff URL, such as */page.aspx?=logoff*, you can populate the **Published server logoff URL** with this value, and cause ISA to logoff at the same time as the logoff function within your application is triggered.

The **Logon type provided to the Exchange server** option allows you to enable, or disable, the **private** login type, which effects different settings for maximum login time.

Creating Server Publishing Rules

Creating Server Publishing Rules is simple compared to Web Publishing Rules. The only things you need to know when creating a Server Publishing Rule are:

- The protocol or protocols you want to publish

- The IP address where the ISA firewall accepts the incoming connections

- The IP address of the Protected Network server you want to publish

A Server Publishing Rule uses protocols with the primary connection set as **Inbound**, **Receive** or **Receive/Send**. For example, if you want to publish an SMTP server, the Protocol Definition for that protocol must be for SMTP, TCP port 25 Inbound. Outbound Protocol Definitions are used for Access Rules.

The ISA firewall comes with a number of built-in Server Publishing Protocol Definitions. Table 5.3 lists these built-in Protocol Definitions.

Table 5.3 Server Publishing Protocol Definitions

Protocol Definition	Usage
DNS Server	TCP 53 Inbound UDP 53 Receive/Send DNS Security Filter Enabled Domain Name System Protocol - Server. An inbound protocol used for server publishing. This Protocol Definition also allows for DNS zone transfer
Exchange RPC Server	TCP 135 Inbound RPC Security Filter enabled Only Exchange RPC interfaces are exposed (Exchange RPC UUIDs) Used for publishing Exchange server for RPC access from External network.
FTP Server	TCP 21 Inbound FTP Access Filter enabled File Transfer Protocol - Server. An inbound protocol used for server publishing. Both PASV and PORT modes are supported.
HTTPS Server	TCP 443 Inbound Secure HyperText Transfer Protocol - Server. An inbound protocol used for server publishing. Used for publishing SSL sites when Web Publishing Rules and enhanced security is not required.

Table 5.3 Continued

Protocol Definition	Usage
IKE Server	UDP 500 Receive/Send Internet Key Exchange Protocol - Server. An inbound protocol used for server publishing. Used for IPSec passthrough.
IMAP4 Server	TCP 143 Inbound Protocol (IMAP) - Server. An inbound protocol used for server publishing.
IMAPS Server	TCP 993 Inbound Secure Interactive Mail Access Protocol (IMAP) - Server. An inbound protocol used for server publishing.
IPSec ESP Server	IP Protocol 50 Receive/Send IPSec ESP Protocol - Server. An inbound protocol used for server publishing. Used for IPSec passthrough.
IPSec NAT-T Server	UDP 4500 Receive/Send IPSec NAT-T Protocol - Server. An inbound protocol used for server publishing. Used for NAT Traversal for L2TP/IPSec and other RFC-compliant NAT traversal connections for IPSec.
L2TP Server	UDP 1701 Receive/Send Layer 2 Tunneling Protocol - Server. An inbound protocol used for server publishing. Used to publish the L2TP/IPSec control channel.
Microsoft SQL Server	TCP 1433 Inbound Microsoft SQL Server Protocol
MMS Server	TCP 1755 Inbound UDP 1755 Receive MMS Filter enabled Microsoft Media Server Protocol - Server. An inbound protocol used for server publishing.
MS Firewall Secure Storage Server	TCP 2172 Inbound Protocol used to publish the Configuration Storage servers over SSL.
MS Firewall Storage Server	TCP 2171 Inbound TCP 2172 Inbound Protocol used to publish the Configuration Storage servers

Continued

Table 5.3 Continued

Protocol Definition	Usage
NNTP Server	TCP 119 Inbound Network News Transfer Protocol - Server. An inbound protocol used for server publishing.
NNTPS Server	TCP 563 Inbound Secure Network News Transfer Protocol - Server. An inbound protocol used for server publishing.
PNM Server	TCP 7070 Inbound PNM Filter enabled Progressive Networks Streaming Media Protocol - Server. An inbound protocol used for server publishing.
POP3 Server	TCP 110 Inbound Post Office Protocol v.3 - Server. An inbound protocol used for server publishing.
POP3S Server	TCP 995 Inbound Secure Post Office Protocol v.3 - Server. An inbound protocol used for server publishing.
PPTP Server	TCP 1723 Inbound PPTP Filter enabled Point-to-Point Tunneling Protocol - Server. An inbound protocol used for server publishing.
RDP (Terminal Services) Server	TCP 3389 Inbound Remote Desktop Protocol (Terminal Services) - Server
RPC Server (all interfaces)	TCP 135 Inbound RPC Filter enabled Remote Procedure Call Protocol - Server. An inbound protocol used for server publishing (All RPC interfaces). Used primarily to intradomain communications through the ISA firewall.
RTSP Server	TCP 554 Inbound Real Time Streaming Protocol - Server. An inbound protocol used for server publishing. Used by Windows Media Server services Windows Server 2003
SMTP Server	TCP 25 Inbound SMTP Security Filter enabled

Table 5.3 Continued

Protocol Definition	Usage
	Simple Mail Transfer Protocol - Server. An inbound protocol used for server publishing.
SMTPS Server	TCP 465 Inbound Secure Simple Mail Transfer Protocol - Server. An inbound protocol used for server publishing.
Telnet Server	TCP 23 Inbound Telnet Protocol - Server. An inbound protocol used for server publishing.

Any of the protocols in Table 5.3 can be used right out of the box for a Server Publishing Rule.

In the following example, we'll create a Server Publishing Rule for an RDP server on the default Internal Network. This could be a Windows XP client with Remote Desktop enabled, or it could be a Windows 2000 or 2003 Server with Terminal Services enabled.

Note that in production use, you should avoid publishing anything but a Windows 2003 SP1 or above Terminal Server since all other versions of RDP servers do not support server authentication. Only Windows 2003 SP1 and above support RDP over TLS and certificate based server authentication.

1. In the **Microsoft Internet Security and Acceleration Server 2006** management console, expand the server name, and then click the **Firewall Policy** node. Click the **Tasks** tab in the **Task** pane, and click **Publish Non-Web Server Protocols**.

2. On the **Welcome to the New Server Publishing Rule Wizard** page, enter a name for the rule in the **Server Publishing Rule name** text box. In the example, we'll name the rule **SPR – Terminal Server**. Click **Next**.

3. On the **Select Server** page, enter the IP address of the published server on the ISA firewall Protected Network in the **Server IP address** text box. In this example, we'll enter 10.0.0.2. You can also click **Browse** to find the server, but the ISA firewall will need to be able to resolve the name of that server correctly. Click **Next**.

4. On the **Select Protocol** page (Figure 5.47 below), click the down-arrow for the **Selected protocol** list, and click the **RDP (Terminal Services) Server** protocol. You can see the details of the selected protocol in the **Properties** dialog box. You can also change the ports used to accept the incoming connections and the ports used to forward the connection to the published Web server. Click **Ports**.

Figure 5.47 The Select Protocol Page

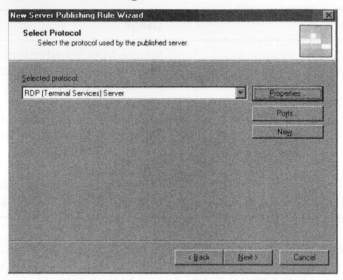

5.   The following options are available to you in the **Ports** dialog box.

- **Publish using the default port defined in the Protocol Definition**   This option allows the ISA firewall to listen on the default port defined in the Protocol Definition for the selected protocol. In the current example, the RDP Protocol Definition listens on TCP port 3389. Using this option the ISA firewall listens on TCP port 3389 on the IP address you set for the listener for this Server Publishing Rule. This is the default setting.

- **Publish on this port instead of the default port**   You can change the port number used to listen for incoming requests. This allows you to override the port number in the Protocol Definition. For example, we might want the ISA firewall to listen for incoming RDP connections on TCP port 8989. We could select **Publish on this port instead of the default port**, and then enter the alternate port, **8989**, in the text box next to this option.

- **Send requests to the default port on the published server**   This option configures the ISA firewall to forward the connection using the same port the ISA firewall received the request on. In this example, the RDP Server Publishing Rule accepts incoming RDP connections on TCP port 3389. The connection is then forwarded to port 3389 on the published server. This is the default setting.

- **Send requests to this port on the published server**   This option allows you to perform port redirection. For example, if the ISA firewall accepts incoming requests for RDP connections on TCP port 3389, you can redirect the connection to an alternate port on the published RDP server, such as TCP port 89.

- **Allow traffic from any allowed source port**   This allows the ISA firewall to accept incoming connections from clients that use any source port in their requests to the published server. This is the default setting, and most applications are designed to accept connections from any client source port.

- **Limit access to traffic from this range of source ports**   You can limit the source port that the application connecting to the published server uses by selecting this option. If your application allows you to configure the source port, you can improve the security of your Server Publishing Rule by limiting connections from hosts using a specific source port and entering that port in the text box associated with this option. You can also list a range of allowed source ports if you want to allow multiple hosts to connect to the server.

Click **OK** after making any changes. In this example, we will not change the listener or forwarded port number.

6. On the **Network Listener IP Addresses** page, you can select the Network(s) where you want the ISA firewall to listen for incoming connections to the published Web site. The **IP Addresses** page for Server Publishing Rules works the same way as that used by Web Publishing Rules. For more information on how to use the options on this page, review the discussion about the **IP Address** page earlier in this chapter. In this example, we'll select **External** by putting a checkmark in the **External** checkbox. Click **Next**.

7. Click **Finish** on the **Completing the New Server Publishing Rule Wizard** page.

8. Click **Apply** to save the changes and update the firewall policy.

9. Click **OK** in the **Apply New Configuration** dialog box.

The Server Publishing Rule Properties Dialog Box

You can fine-tune the Server Publishing Rule by opening the Server Publishing Rules **Properties** dialog box. Double-click the Server Publishing Rule to open the **Properties** dialog box. The first tab you'll encounter is the **General** tab. Here you can change the name of the Server Publishing Rule and provide a description for the rule. You can also enable or disable the rule by changing the status of the **Enable** checkbox. The General tab is shown in Figure 5.48 below.

Figure 5.48 The General Tab

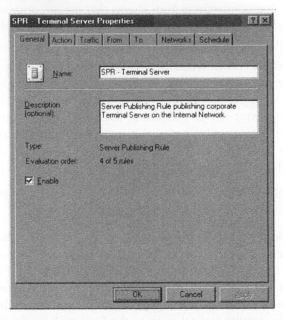

On the **Action** tab, set the rule for whether or not to log connections that apply to this rule. We recommend that you always log connections made via a Server Publishing Rule. However, if you have a reason why you do not want to log these connections (for example, privacy laws in your country do not allow logging this information), you can disable logging by removing the checkmark from the **Log requests matching this rule** checkbox shown in Figure 5.49 below.

Figure 5.49 The Action Tab

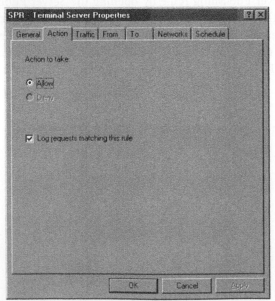

On the **Traffic** tab you can change the protocol used for the Server Publishing Rule by clicking the down arrow in the **Allow network traffic using the following protocol** drop-down list. You can create a new Protocol Definition for a Server Publishing Rule by clicking **New**, and you can view the details of the Protocol Definition used in the Server Publishing Rule by clicking **Properties**. You can also customize the source and destination ports allowed by the Server Publishing Rule using the **Ports** button. See options for the Traffic tab in Figure 5.50 below.

ISA FIREWALL TIP

As there is no "tunneled" option when creating Web Publishing Rules with ISA Server 2006, if you wish to publish SSL web servers in tunneled mode, you may do this using a Server Publishing Rule with the HTTPS protocol selected. We do not recommend that you do this unless absolutely necessary, as by doing so you lose a significant portion of the ISA firewall's protective capabilities.

Figure 5.50 The Traffic Tab

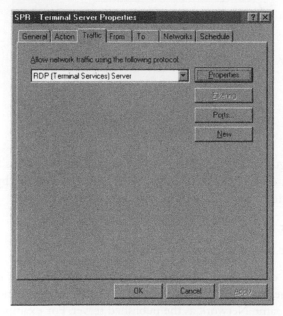

You can control what hosts can connect to the published server using settings on the **From** tab. The default location allows hosts from **Anywhere** to connect to the published server via this rule. However, connections will only be allowed from hosts that can connect via Networks configured on the **Networks** tab. So, while hosts from **Anywhere** can connect to the published server, connections are still limited to those hosts who can connect via the interface(s) responsible for the Networks listed on the **Networks** tab.

You can get more granular access control over who can connect to the published server by removing the **Anywhere** option and allowing a more limited group of machines access to the published server. Click **Anywhere**, and then click **Remove**. Then click **Add**, and select a Network Object defining the group of machines you want to allow access to the published server.

You can further fine-tune access control by setting exceptions to the list of allowed hosts and adding them to the **Exceptions** list. Click **Add** in the **Exceptions** section. See Figure 5.51 for options on the From tab.

Figure 5.51 The From Tab

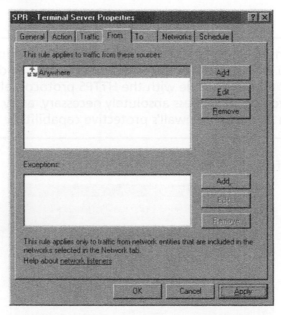

On the **To** tab, configure the IP address of the server published via this Server Publishing Rule. You can also control what client IP address is seen by the published server by your selection in the **Request for the published server** frame. You have two options:

- Requests appear to come from the ISA Server computer
- Requests appear to come from the original client

Requests appear to come from the ISA Server computer allows the published server to see the source IP address of the incoming connection to the IP address on the network interface on the ISA firewall that is on the same Network as the published server. For example, if the published server is on the Internal network, and the ISA firewall's interface on the Internal Network is **10.0.0.1**, then the published server will see the source IP address of the incoming connection as **10.0.0.1**.

This option is useful when you do not want to make the published server a SecureNAT client. The SecureNAT client is one where the machine is configured with a default gateway address that routes all Internet-bound connections through the ISA firewall. If you do not want to change the default gateway address on the published server, then use **Requests appear to come from the ISA Server computer**. The only requirement is, if the published server is on a different subnet from the ISA firewall, the published server needs to be able route to the IP address that the ISA firewall uses when it forwards the connection to the published server.

If you want the published server to see the actual client IP address, select **Requests appear to come from the original client**. This option requires that the published server be configured as a SecureNAT client. The reason why the machine must be configured as a SecureNAT client is that since the client IP address is from a non-local network, the published server must be configured such that traffic destined to the client's IP address be routed via the ISA firewall. In most networks, this will mean that the server is required to have a default gateway that routes Internet-bound communications through the ISA firewall. Figure 5.52 illustrates the options on the **To** tab.

Figure 5.52 The To Tab

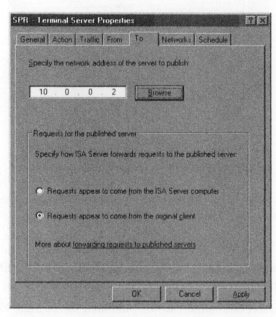

On the **Networks** tab, you can configure which Networks the ISA firewall can listen on to accept incoming connections to the published server. In this example, we set the Server Publishing Rule to accept incoming connections from hosts on the **External** Network (the default External Network includes all addresses that aren't defined in any other Network on the ISA firewall).

You can configure the ISA firewall to listen on any Network. For example, you can configure the Server Publishing Rule to listen for connections on the VPN Clients Network. VPN clients can then connect to the published server via this Server Publishing Rule. The Networks tab is shown in Figure 5.53 below.

Figure 5.53 The Networks Tab

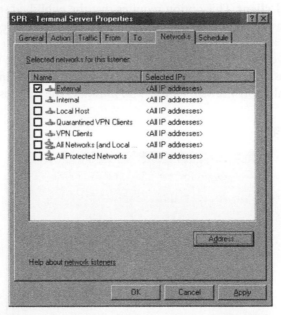

On the **Schedule** tab, you can set when connections can be made to the published server. There are three default schedules:

- **Always**   Users can always connect to the published server.

- **Weekends**   Users can connect to the published server from 12:00 A.M. to 12:00 A.M. Saturday and Sunday.

- **Work hours**   Users can connect to the published server from 9:00 A.M. to 5:00 P.M. Monday through Friday.

You can also create your own schedule using the **New** button. We'll talk more about creating schedules in Chapter 4. Note that schedules control when users can connect to the published server, but they do not drop existing connections. The reason for this is that users who connected to the published server connected when connections are allowed, and they may have ongoing work that would be disturbed if the connection where arbitrarily halted by the schedule.

ISA FIREWALL ALERT

You can script a disconnect using **Scheduled** Tasks by stopping the Microsoft Firewall service and restarting it if you must stop all connections going through the ISA firewall at a specific time. Beware, however – this will stop *all* connections going through the ISA firewall.

The Schedule tab is shown in Figure 5.54 below.

Figure 5.54 The Schedule Tab

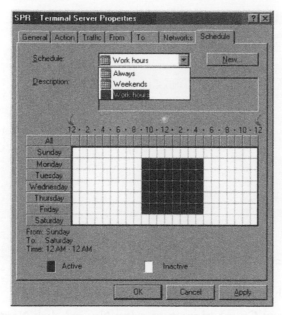

Server Publishing HTTP Sites

You might have noticed when going over the list of Protocol Definitions used for Server Publishing Rules that there wasn't a Protocol Definition for HTTP Server. There is a Protocol Definition for HTTPS servers, but not for HTTP. If you want to create a Server Publishing Rule for HTTP server publishing, you will need to create your own HTTP Server Protocol Definition.

We recommend that you always use Web Publishing Rules to publish Web sites, but there may be times when you want to publish a Web site that isn't compliant with Web Proxy servers. In this case, you will need to use a Server Publishing Rule instead of a Web Publishing Rule.

Perform the following steps to create the Protocol Definition for HTTP Server publishing:
<<TODO – Check in 2006 VM>>

1. In the **Microsoft Internet Security and Acceleration Server 2006** management console, expand the server name and click the **Firewall Policy** node. Click the **Toolbox** tab in the **Task** pane, and click the **Protocols** header.

2. Click the **New** menu and click **Protocol**.

3. On the **Welcome to the New Protocol Definition Wizard** page, enter **HTTP Server** in the **Protocol Definition name** text box, and click **Next**.

4. On the **Primary Connection Information** page, click **New**.

5. On the **New/Edit Protocol Connection** page (Figure 5.55), set the **Protocol type** to **TCP** and the **Direction** to **Inbound**. In the **Port range** frame, set the **From** and **To** values to **80**. Click **OK**.

Figure 5.55 The New/Edit Protocol Connection Dialog Box

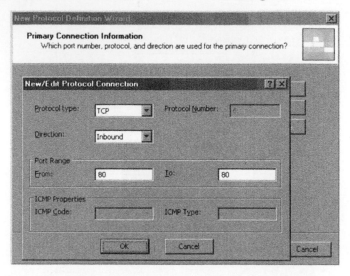

6. Click **Next** on the **Primary Connection Information** page.

7. On the **Secondary Connections** page, select **No**, and click **Next**.

8. Click **Finish** on the **Completing the New Protocol Definition Wizard** page.

9. Click **Apply** to save the changes and update the firewall policy.

10. Click **OK** in the **Apply New Configuration** dialog box.

11. The new **HTTP Server** Protocol Definition (Figure 5.56) appears in the list of **User-Defined** Protocol Definitions.

Figure 5.56 The New HTTP Server Protocol Definition

<<TODO – Entire Mail Publishing Section>>

Creating Mail Server Publishing Rules

The ISA firewall includes two wizards for publishing Mail Servers right out of the box. You can use the Mail Server Publishing Wizard to publish the following mail-related services:

- Secure Exchange RPC

- IMAP4 and Secure IMAP4

- POP3 and Secure POP3

- SMTP and Secure SMTP

The Mail Server Publishing Wizard creates the appropriate Web or Server Publishing Rules required to allow access to the published mail server through the ISA firewall. You can access the Mail Server Publishing Wizard by clicking on the **Firewall Policy** node in the left pane of the **Microsoft Internet Security and Acceleration Server 2006** management console and clicking the **Tasks** tab in the **Task** pane. Click the **Publish a Mail Server** link.

On the **Welcome to the New Mail Server Publishing Rule Wizard** page, enter a name for the rule in the **Mail Server Publishing Rule name** text box. Give the rule a meaningful name so that you'll be able to identify the purpose of the rule. You may create several Web or Server Publishing Rules based on your selections, so keep this in mind when naming the rule. You can always rename the rules after the Wizard is completed. Click **Next**.

On the **Select Access Type** page (Figure 5.57 below), you have the following options:

- Client access: RPC, IMAP, POP3, SMTP

- Server-to-server communication: SMTP, NNTP

Figure 5.57 The Select Access Type page

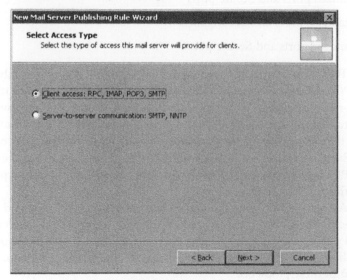

The **Client access: RPC, IMAP, POP3, SMTP** option publishes these protocols using Server Publishing Rules. You can publish one or more of these protocols when you select this option.

The **Server-to-server communication: SMTP, NNTP** option publishes these two protocols. You can select one or both.

Because the options available differ based on the selection you make on this page, we will cover each one separately in the following sections.

ISA FIREWALL ALERT

Unless you enable SSL for these three protocols, SMTP, POP, and IMAP are not secure protocols for your users to access their mail with, and even with SSL enabled, you will provide a subset of exchange functionality to users. Combined with a well-designed DNS infrastructure, *RPC-over-HTTP*, now known as *Outlook Anywhere*, is the best way to allow Outlook clients to access an Exchange Server over the internet.

Not only does it offer a full range of exchange functionality, but as it's HTTP based, you benefit from the full suite of ISA's protection mechanisms for Web Traffic when published via the web, and gives your users a seamless experience in and out of the office.

The Client Access: RPC, IMAP, POP3, SMTP Option

Select this option and click **Next**. On the **Select Services** page you have the following options:

- Outlook (RPC)
- POP3: Standard ports and Secure ports
- IMAP4: Standard ports and Secure ports
- SMTP: Standard ports and Secure ports

The **Outlook (RPC)** option creates a Server Publishing Rule that allows inbound access for secure Exchange RPC connections. Secure Exchange RPC publishing allows Outlook 2000, 2002, and 2003 to "just work," regardless of where the user is located. When combined with a well-designed split DNS infrastructure, users can roam between the corporate network and remote locations, open Outlook, and access their e-mail transparently without requiring reconfiguration of their e-mail application. Secure Exchange RPC is a very secure publishing protocol, and you can configure the Secure Exchange RPC Server Publishing Rule to force Outlook clients to encrypt their communications to the Exchange Server.

The **POP3, IMAP4,** and **SMTP** options allow you to publish both secure and non–secure versions of these protocols. Secure versions of these protocols use SSL to encrypt both user credentials and data. The ISA firewall will publish these protocols using Server Publishing Rules, but you must configure the Exchange Server with the appropriate Web site certificates to complete the configuration if you want to use the secure version of these protocols.

ISA FIREWALL TIP

The latest version of Exchange, Exchange 2007, includes a new role, the *Edge Server* role, specifically designed to act as a DMZ-based SMTP relay for exchange, capable of providing "message hygiene" services such as anti-virus and anti-spam, with the ability to reject mail not for legitimate recipients – but without being a member of your Domain Infrastructure. If considering a new deployment of exchange, or enhancing your existing messaging security infrastructure, this functionality is worth considering. The SMTP Message Screener is no longer included with the ISA Firewall. Microsoft expects you to use an Edge Exchange Server in its place.

On the **Select Server** page, enter the IP address of the published server on the corporate network in the **Select Server** text box. Click **Next**.

On the **IP Addresses** page, select the Network representing the Interface that should accept connection requests for the published server. You can limit the IP address used to accept the incoming connection if you have multiple addresses bound to any of these interfaces by clicking the **Address** button. For more information on how to configure the settings on the **IP Addresses** page, see the discussion on this subject in the Server Publishing Rules section of this chapter. Click **Next**.

Click **Finish** on the **Completing the New Mail Server Publishing Rule Wizard** page. Click **Apply** to save the changes and update the firewall policy. Click **OK** in the **Apply New Configuration** dialog box.

You can enhance the security for your secure Exchange RPC publishing rule by forcing the Outlook clients to use a secure connection. Right-click the **Exchange RPC Server** rule, and click **Configure Exchange RPC**. Put a checkmark in the **Enforce Encryption** checkbox, click **Apply** and then click **OK**. See Figure 5.58 below.

Figure 5.58 The Configure Exchange RPC Policy Dialog Box

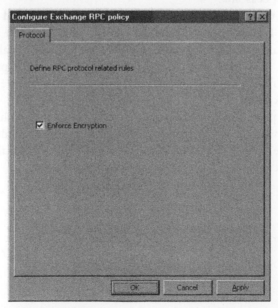

Publishing Exchange Web Client Access

Whereas ISA 2004 handled publishing Exchange's HTTP-based services via the **Publish Mail Servers** wizard, ISA 2006 has a separate wizard for this. The wizard not only lets you publish the four following services:

- Outlook Web Access
- Outlook Mobile Access
- Outlook Anywhere (RPC-over-HTTP),
- ActiveSync

ISA 2006 is also aware of four different versions of exchange, each of which gives you different permutations of these four options – Exchange 5.5, 2000, 2003, and 2007. The options you have for each version of exchange are as follows:

Exchange 5.5 – Only Outlook Web Access

Exchange 2000 – Only Outlook Web Access

Exchange 2003 – OWA, OMA, RPC-over-HTTP, Activesync.

Exchange 2007 – OWA, RPC-over-HTTP, Activesync.

While ISA 2006 will configure a Web Client Access for Exchange 2003 supporting all four services, Exchange 2007 requires that each be setup using a different rule (although these can use the same web listener).

Here, we will run through this process for OWA Publishing of Exchange 2007. You can access the Web Client Access Publishing Wizard by clicking on the **Firewall Policy** node in the left pane of the **ISA firewall console** and clicking the **Tasks** tab in the **Task** pane. Click the **Publish Exchange Web Client Access** link.

On the **Welcome to the New Exchange Publishing Rule Wizard** page, enter a name for the rule in the **Exchange Publishing Rule name** text box. Give the rule a meaningful name so that you'll be able to identify the purpose of the rule. You may create several Web or Server Publishing Rules based on your selections, particularly if you publish multiple Exchange 2007 services, so keep this in mind when naming the rule. You can always rename the rules after the Wizard is completed. Click **Next**.

The **Select Services** page, pictured in Figure 5.59, lets you pick which version of Exchange you wish to publish, as well as which services you wish to publish. As we have already discussed, we can only pick one service if we choose to publish Exchange 2007. We pick **Outlook Web Access**, and **Exchange 2007**, and click **next**.

Figure 5.59 The Select Services page

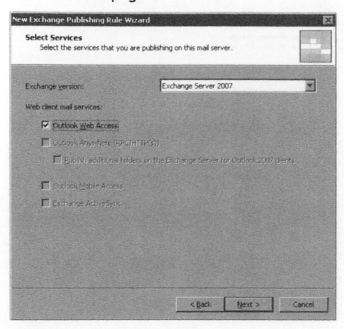

In the **Publishing Type** dialog, we pick which type of server we wish to publish, as with our earlier publishing rules – our choices here are **Publish a single Web site or load balancer**, or **Publish a server farm of load balanced web servers**. As we have only one Exchange Client Access Role Server here, we choose **Publish a single Web Server or load balancer**, and click **Next**.

In the **Server Connection Security** dialog, we have a choice of connection methods to the target Client Access Role Exchange 2007 server. We discussed this option earlier when dealing with SSL and non-SSL Web Publishing Rules. As we have SSL configured for our Exchange Server, we pick **Use SSL to connect to the published Web server or server farm**, and hit **Next**.

In the **Internal Publishing Details** dialog, we can specify the **Internal Site Name** and **Computer name or IP address**. We discussed these settings within the context of SSL web publishing rules earlier, and as we are publishing an SSL-enabled web service on the exchange server, we enter the full FQDN of the exchange server, matching the certificate installed on it. We enter **exchangeCA01.infra.example.com** into the **Internal site name** box pictured in Figure 5.60, and hit **Next** to continue.

Figure 5.60 The Internal Publishing Details page

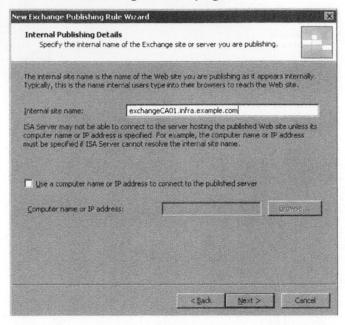

In the **Public Name Details** page, we have the option to **Accept requests for** *Any domain name*, or for *This domain name*. As we have discussed earlier, *This domain name* is the more secure choice, as our ISA Server will only accept requests specifically for the domain name we wish to publish on the internet. We enter **owa.example.com**, and hit next.

In the **Select Web Listener** dialog, we have to configure a new SSL web listener; see the section on secure Web Publishing Rules in this chapter for more information on this subject. Once we have configured or chosen the Web Listener we wish to use, we hit **Next.**

In the **Authentication Delegation** dialog, we select **Negotiate (Kerberos/NTLM)**, and hit next. If you use Kerberos Constrained Delegation, you will need to configure an appropriate SPN within Active Directory, as discussed in the SSL Web Publishing section earlier. We hit **Next**.

In the **User sets** dialog, we choose the default option of **All Authenticated users**, and hit next. Within Exchange itself, you must enable OWA (and other services, such as Outlook Anywhere) on a mailbox-by-mailbox basis, but if you wish to only allow specific security groups to access OWA through the ISA Server as an additional restriction, or in order to grant certain users access to OWA within the corporate network but not from the internet, you may pick an alternative group here. We hit **Next**.

Click **Finish** on the **Completing the New Mail Server Publishing Rule Wizard** page. Click **Apply** to save the changes and update the firewall policy. Click **OK** in the **Apply New Configuration** dialog box.

Our rule now appears within the ISA 2006 Firewall Policy, pictured in Figure 5.61. By repeating the process, we can publish all of the services supported by Exchange 2006 on the same Web Listener.

Figure 5.61 The Exchange Publishing Rule

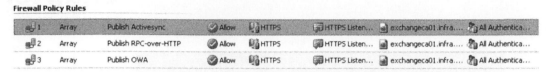

One More Time

In this chapter we discussed methods you can use to provide secure access to servers and services protected by the ISA firewall. The two primary methods of providing secure remote access to corporate services are Web Publishing Rules and Server Publishing Rules. Web Publishing Rules can be used to publish HTTP, HTTPS, and FTP servers. Server Publishing Rules can publish almost any other protocol. We discussed the details of Web and Server Publishing and how to configure and create Web and Server Publishing Rules.

Chapter 6

Creating Remote Access and Site-to-Site VPNs with ISA Firewalls

Solutions in this chapter:

- Overview of ISA Firewall VPN Networking
- Creating a Remote Access PPTP VPN Server
- Creating a Remote Access L2TP/IPSec Server
- Creating a PPTP Site-to-Site VPN
- Creating a L2TP/IPSec Site-to-Site VPN
- IPSec Tunnel Mode Site-to-Site VPNs with Downlevel VPN Gateways
- Using RADIUS for VPN Authentication and Remote Access Policy
- Using EAP User Certificate Authentication for Remote Access VPNs
- Supporting Outbound VPN connections through the ISA Firewall
- Installing and Configuring the DHCP Server and DHCP Relay Agent on the ISA Firewall

- ☑ Summary

Overview of ISA Firewall VPN Networking

Virtual private networking (VPN) has grown in popularity until it has become a standard for companies that have telecommuters, executives, and salespeople who need network access when on the road, and/or partners and customers who need access to resources on the corporate network. The purpose of VPN networking is to allow remote access to resources on the corporate network that would otherwise only be available if the user were directly connected to the corporate LAN. With a VPN connection, the user has a "virtual" point-to-point link between the remote VPN user and the corporate network. The user can work as if he/she were on site; applications and services running on the users' computers treat the VPN link as if it were a typical Ethernet connection. The Internet over which the client is connected to the corporate network is completely transparent to the users and applications.

One of the major advantages of using a VPN connection instead of a client/server Web application is that VPN users at remote locations can potentially access all of the protocols and servers on the corporate network. This means your users can access the full range of services on Microsoft Exchange Servers, Microsoft SharePoint Servers, Microsoft SQL Servers, and Microsoft Office Communication Servers just as they do when they are directly connected to the network at the corporate location. VPN client software is built into all modern Windows operating systems. A VPN user does not need any special software to connect to each of these services, and it's not necessary to create special proxy applications to allow your users to connect to these resources.

ISA Server 2000 was the first Microsoft firewall to provide tightly integrated VPN configuration and management. ISA 2000 firewall included easy-to-use wizards that made it simple to create remote access and site-to-site (gateway-to-gateway) VPN connections to the ISA 2000 firewall/VPN server. However, there were still some improvements that could be made. The ISA 2000 VPN server still required the firewall administrator to spend a significant amount of time fine-tuning the VPN server configuration via the Routing and Remote Access console.

ISA 2004 significantly enhanced the VPN components that were included with the Windows 2000 and Windows Server 2003 Routing and Remote Access Services (RRAS). An administrator could enable, configure, and manage the VPN server and gateway components directly from the ISA 2004 firewall management console, rather than having to go back and forth between the ISA MMC and the RRAS MMC. You rarely needed to use the Routing and Remote Access console to configure VPN components.

Other improvements to VPN functionality in ISA 2004 included:

- Firewall Policy Applied to VPN Client Connections
- Firewall Policy Applied to VPN Site-to-Site Connections
- VPN Quarantine
- User Mapping of VPN Clients
- SecureNAT Client Support for VPN Connections
- Site-to-Site VPN using Tunnel Mode IPSec

- Publishing PPTP VPN Servers

- Pre-shared Key Support for IPSec VPN Connections

- Advanced Name Server Assignment for VPN Clients

- Monitoring of VPN Client Connections

ISA 2000 had a comprehensive VPN site-to-site wizard. However this disappeared with ISA 2004. With ISA 2004, after running the site-to-site wizard, additional steps, like creating access rules and network rules were required. With ISA 2006 things have changed. While retaining the good things brought by ISA 2004, ISA 2006 includes new features like:

- An improved site-to-site wizard which simplify the creation of a site-to-site connection. We will discuss it later in this chapter.

- The Create Answer File Wizard

- The Branch Office Connectivity Wizard

- The site-to-site summary

One of the core deployment scenarios for ISA 2006 Firewall is the branch office security gateway. ISA 2006 includes along with the improved VPN site-to-site wizard and the especially designed wizards for the branch office, other technologies like BITS caching (available on ISA 2004 SP2 too), HTTP compression (available on ISA 2004 SP2 too), DiffServ (a method for packet prioritization, available on ISA 2004 SP2 too) and others. You can check all these at Microsoft site (http://www.microsoft.com/forefront/edgesecurity/bos.mspx).

SSL VPNs have gained increased popularity. The weaknesses of PPTP forced companies to migrate to other high security VPN remote access solutions. L2TP/IPSec represents such a solution. Properly designed SSL VPNs are an alternative to IPSec in terms of security and tend to offer better connectivity when you are behind restrictive firewalls (IPSec might be blocked) or behind poor NAT devices (which tend to break the NAT-T process). Unfortunately ISA 2006 does not include an SSL VPN component. However, IAG 2007, a new Microsoft product, offers a true SSL VPN solution. IAG 2007 integrated with ISA 2006, represents a single, powerful appliance for network perimeter defense, network separation, remote access and application-layer protection (for both SSL and IPSec connections), full control of inbound and outbound traffic. The two combined include technologies like advanced stateful packet inspection, circuit filtering, application-layer inspection and Web proxy. IAG 2007 also offers advanced VPN Quarantine options.

Another missed feature on ISA 2004 was support for AES (Advanced Encryption Standard). Things have not changed with ISA 2006 and AES is still not here.

With ISA 2006 Microsoft is pushing harder on L2TP/IPSec for both site-to-site connections and remote access. This protocol, for site-to-site connections, provides a "Highly Secure" connection method as compared to "IPSec tunnel mode" which offers "High Security and Interoperabilty with third party VPN vendors". We will discuss later in this chapter the two protocols.

Firewall Policy Applied to VPN Client Connections

When a VPN remote-access client establishes a connection with the VPN server, the VPN client acts like a machine that is directly connected to the corporate network. This virtual link to the corporate network enables the remote VPN user to access almost every resource on the corporate network, limited only by the access controls configured on the servers and workstations. However, this power to access virtually any resource on the corporate network can be a security risk. Generally, you should not allow users to have a full range of access to corporate resources when they connect over a remote access VPN connection. That's because these users might be connecting from computers that aren't within your control and don't conform to corporate software and security policies, or they may be connecting from computers that are on untrusted networks, such as hotel broadband networks. You have no way of knowing whether these machines pose a threat to your network.

Your VPN policy should stipulate that only highly-trusted users who are connecting from known trusted machines on known trusted networks are allowed unfettered access to the corporate network over a remote-access VPN link. Examples of users who might be granted such access include your network, security, and firewall administrators, and perhaps some highly-placed executives. All other users should be restricted to accessing only the subset of network resources that they need to do their jobs when connected via the VPN link.

For example, many firewall administrators allow users to connect over VPN so that they can use the full Outlook 2000/2002/2003/2007 MAPI client to access a Microsoft Exchange Server. Microsoft Exchange provides several different methods for remotely accessing Exchange Server resources. These include the SMTP, POP3, IMAP4, Outlook Web Access (OWA), Exchange ActiveSync and OMA services. However, users like to keep the broad range of options available to them when using the full Outlook MAPI client.

There are basically three ways to satisfy users' needs in this situation:

- Publish the Exchange Server using the ISA Server secure RPC Server Publishing Rule
- Have your users use the Outlook 2003/Exchange 2003 RPC over HTTP protocol
- Grant your users VPN access to the corporate network

The ISA firewall's secure RPC Server Publishing mechanism enables remote Outlook MAPI clients to connect to the full range of Microsoft Exchange Server services from any remote location. The only problem is that, for security reasons, many firewalls and ISPs have blocked access to the RPC port mapper port (TCP 135). This port is required to make the initial secure connection to the Exchange Server using a secure Exchange RPC publishing rule, but the Blaster worm, which exploited this port, caused most administrators to shut it down. Consequently, RPC publishing has lost much of its former utility.

RPC over HTTP(S) can solve this problem by encapsulating the RPC connection inside an HTTP header. This allows the Outlook MAPI client to send requests to the Exchange Server using HTTP. HTTPS is generally allowed by all corporate firewalls and ISPs, since it is used for Web communications. The problem with this solution is that not all organizations have upgraded to Outlook 2003/2007 and Exchange Server 2003 or 2007.

Granting users VPN access will circumvent the limitations of the other solutions, but providing such access can pose a security risk when all VPN clients can access the entire network. The ideal solution is to enforce Access Policy on VPN clients, based on user/group accounts. This way, users can access only the servers and protocols they require.

ISA 2004/2006 is the only VPN server solution that gives administrators this level of access control. When VPN clients connect to the VPN server, those clients are placed on a built-in network entity called the *VPN Clients Network*. The ISA 2004/2006 firewall treats this network like any other network, which means strong user- and group-based access controls can be placed on data that travels between the VPN Clients Network and the corporate network.

All you need to do is create the user accounts and create an access policy on the ISA 2004/2006 firewall/VPN server that limits what machines and protocols the users/groups can access and use, and all those network devices are protected from the VPN remote-access users.

This feature seems to eliminate the need for SSL VPNs (except in those circumstances where remote users are behind extremely restrictive firewalls that block all but HTTP and SSL connections outbound) and other proprietary remote-access solutions aimed at providing per protocol, per server, per user/group access to corporate network resources. Most commercial broadband networks at hotels and conference centers allow outbound PPTP and L2TP/IPSec via NAT Traversal. This way, you can provide remote access for your VPN users without the security threat that typically accompanies VPN client connections.

Firewall Policy Applied to VPN Site-to-Site Connections

A site-to-site VPN connection connects two or more networks (instead of an individual client and a network) over the Internet. Using a VPN site-to-site link can create substantial cost savings in comparison to dedicated WAN links that use dedicated circuits (for example, linking two sites via T-1).

To use a VPN site-to-site link, each site requires a VPN gateway and a relatively inexpensive Internet connection. When the VPN gateways establish connections with one another, the site-to-site VPN link is established. Then the users on each end can communicate with other networks over the VPN site-to-site link just as they would with a routed connection on their own network. The VPN gateways act as routers and route the packets to the appropriate network.

VPN site-to-site connections use the same technologies as do client-to-server (remote access) VPN connections – and traditionally suffered from the same security problem. That is, all users had access to the entire network to which their own network was connected. The only thing that kept users out of network resources for which they had no permission to access was local access controls on the servers.

Site-to-site VPN connections are typically set up between branch office and main office networks. Providing branch office users with access to the entire main office network can pose a major security threat.

The ISA 2004/2006 firewall/VPN server can solve this problem by controlling outbound data that travels through the site-to-site link. Users at the branch office can be limited to only the resources on the main office network required to do their jobs, and thus, prevented from accessing other computer resources on the main network. As with remote-access VPN clients, the users at the branch office should only be allowed to use the specific protocols they need on the servers they are allowed to access.

VPN site-to-site connections that take advantage of strong user and group-based access controls can save money without sacrificing security.

VPN Quarantine

VPN Quarantine (VPN-Q) was a new feature in ISA 2004 that allowed administrators to screen VPN client machines before allowing them access to the corporate network. The VPN Quarantine feature included with ISA 2004 was similar to the Network Quarantine feature found in Windows Server 2003 RRAS. On paper this feature looked great, but failed in real deployment scenario. It was only a basic framework. Frustration erupted through network administrators who were trying to deploy it on their networks. In the end VPN-Q turn into a big disappointment.

In order to use VPN-Q, you must create a CMAK (Connection Manager Administration Kit) package that includes a VPN-Q client and a VPN-Q client-side script. The client runs the script and reports the results to the VPN-Q server component on the ISA 2004/2006 firewall/VPN server. The VPN client is moved from the "VPN Quarantine" network to the "VPN Clients" network if the script reports that the client meets the software requirements for connecting to the network. You can set different access policies for hosts on the VPN Quarantine network versus the VPN Clients network.

The need of the script was a big issue. Microsoft provided some basic scripts (and an assistance quarantine tool), but to turn these scripts into a real checking system, hard and intense work was needed. Creating CMAC profiles requires additional work in order to make sure you have set everything properly. Also the user could release himself from the quarantine by running a command with some parameters and a shared secret (found in clear within the script) and he would have full access to the network without running any checks.

The ISA 2004 firewall extended the functionality of the Windows Server 2003 RRAS Quarantine controls because the Windows Server 2003 RRAS Quarantine feature did not let you set policy-based access controls. The RRAS Quarantine used simple "port-based" access controls, but it this didn't really provide any level of serious security. The ISA 2004 firewall aimed to apply strong firewall policy-based access controls over hosts on the VPN Quarantine network and exposes these connections to the ISA 2004 firewall's sophisticated application-layer filters.

Experienced programmers could turn the dream of the VPN-Q into reality. However not everybody is a programmer or has the resources to hire one. Another option, which is available for ISA 2006 too, is to use a commercial third party add-on solution that does not require any coding, scripting or similar activities.

VPN Quarantine is still available on ISA 2006. No improved wizard.

To enable Quarantine Control:

1. Open the **Microsoft Internet Security and Acceleration Server 2006** management console and expand the server name and Configuration. Click on the **Network** node.

2. Select the **Networks** tab, and then select the **Quarantined VPN Clients** network.

3. On the **Tasks** tab, click **Edit Selected Network**. On the **Quarantine** tab, **select Enable Quarantine Control**.

The same two options:

- **Enable quarantine according to RADIUS server policies.** The Routing and Remote Access policy determines whether the connection request is passed to ISA 2006. After the policy has been verified, the client can join the VPN Clients network. Windows 2003 VNP-Q is used.

- **Enable quarantine according to ISA Server policies.** In this scenario, ISA 2006 determines whet her to quarantine the VPN user. The Quarantined VPN Clients network is used, for which you can set firewall policy. You can exempt the user you want from quarantine. Although ISA 2006 brings the VPN-Q, the minimum system requirements according to ISA's 2006 section from Microsoft site are set to Windows 2003 SP1 or Windows 2003 R2, so the old discussion of ISA 2004 installed Windows 2000 which can benefit from VPN-Q is of no use.

As said before, IAG 2007 comes by default with a great list of checking options that a VPN client must pass before it can join the network. The developers have done the work for you, delivering a final version and not a half done job, like the case of VPN-Q. ISA 2006 VPN-Q remains a promise that Microsoft never fulfilled.

User Mapping of VPN Clients

User mapping is a feature that allows you to map virtual private network (VPN) clients connecting to ISA Server using an authentication method that is not based on "Windows authentication" to the Windows Active Directory namespace (There are two general types of users in ISA. The first one is the Active Directory user or group, the second type is the non-Windows user. Non-Windows users are users who are authenticated using an authentication scheme other than that of Active Directory. Each non-Windows user is defined by a user name and a namespace that identifies the applicable authentication scheme (http://msdn2.microsoft.com/en-us/library/ms812609.aspx).

For example when EAP-TLS is used, and the ISA firewall is a domain member, no RADIUS server, the VPN client and ISA firewall authenticate themselves by presenting a user certificate (issued by an Enterprise CA) and respectively a server certificate. The client certificate contains a user name attribute. The ISA firewall can map this user name with the corresponding Windows User from Active Directory. Therefore with user mapping enabled and configured, Firewall policy access rules specifying user sets for Windows users and groups are also applied to authenticated users who use EAP-TLS authentication. We will discuss EAP-TLS later in this chapter. Default firewall policy access rules will not be applied to users from namespaces that are not based on Windows, unless you define user mapping for users.

The user mapping feature extends the strong user/group-based access controls you can apply to VPN clients that use an authentication method other than Windows (we understand by Windows authentication related to VPN clients, for example, protocols like ms-chapv2, which use explicit Windows User credentials(user name and password), and ISA, domain member, can validate these credentials against Active Directory).

This is important because Windows authentication of domain users is only available when the ISA 2006 firewall belongs to the domain that contains the users' accounts, or to a domain that is trusted by the user accounts' domain. If the ISA 2006 firewall does not belong to a domain, then Windows authentication is used only for user accounts stored on the ISA 2006 firewall machine itself.

With user mapping, you can use RADIUS authentication of domain users, and you can apply user/group-based access control over VPN clients who authenticate via RADIUS. Without user mapping, you would not have access to strong user/group-based access control, and Access Policies from the VPN Clients Network to the Internal network would be limited to controlling protocol and server access to all users connecting to the VPN.

SecureNAT Client Support for VPN Connections

When a VPN client connects to the VPN server, the routing table on the VPN client changes so that the default gateway is the IP address of the VPN server. This causes a potential problem for VPN clients in that, while they are connected to the VPN, they cannot access resources on the Internet at the same time.

A problem with the ISA 2000 firewall/VPN server was that, for VPN clients to access resources on the Internet, you had to choose from one of the three following options:

- Enabling split tunneling on the VPN client

- Installing the Firewall Client software on the VPN client machines

- Configuring the Dial-up and Virtual Private Network settings of the VPN connection with Proxy Server settings (this enables browsing with Internet Explorer only when the client is connected to the VPN).

Split tunneling refers to a configuration where the VPN client machine is *not* configured to use the default gateway on the remote network. The default setting for Microsoft VPN clients is to use the default gateway for the remote network. A VPN requires two connections: first, a connection is made to the Internet (with broadband or other always-on technology, this connection does not have to be manually established each time); second, the VPN connection is made *over* the Internet connection. When VPN clients are configured not to use the default gateway, they can access resources on the corporate network through the VPN connection, and they can also access resources on the Internet via the Internet connection that was established by the VPN client machine *before* the VPN connection took place.

There are some serious security threats that occur when the VPN client machine can access the Internet directly while at the same time being able to access the corporate network via the VPN link. This allows the VPN client computer to completely bypass all Internet access policies that were configured on the ISA 2000 firewall for the duration of the VPN connection. Split tunneling is like allowing users on the corporate network to have local modem connections along with their connections to the LAN. The modem connections would completely bypass the ISA 2000 firewall policy and allow the workstation access to the Internet that would not otherwise be allowed by the ISA 2000 firewall policies. This creates a potential for downloading worms, viruses, and other dangerous content. A malicious user on the Internet would even be able to route exploits from an outside computer through the machine that is performing split tunneling and into the corporate network.

Because of this risk, it was important to provide an alternate method of allowing VPN clients Internet access while connected to the ISA 2004/2006 firewall/VPN server. The preferred alternative with ISA 2000 is to install the firewall client software on the VPN client machine. The Firewall Client will forward requests directly to the ISA Server firewall's internal IP address and does not require split tunneling to allow the client computer to connect to the Internet. In addition, the Firewall Client exposes the VPN client machine to the ISA 2000 firewall access policies.

ISA 2004/2006 firewall/VPN servers solve the problem of split tunneling without requiring installation of the Firewall client by enabling Internet access for VPN SecureNAT clients. The VPN clients are SecureNAT clients of the ISA 2004/2006 firewall by default, because they use the firewall as their default gateway. The ISA 2004/2006 firewall/VPN server can use the log-on credentials of the VPN client to apply strong user- and group-based access controls in order to limit the sites, content, and protocols that the VPN client machines will be allowed to access on the Internet.

TIP

Even though the Firewall client software is not required on VPN client computers to allow them to access the Internet through the ISA 2004/2006 firewall machine, you might still want to install the Firewall client on VPN client machines if you want to support complex protocols that require one or more secondary connections. SecureNAT clients can't use complex protocols that require secondary connections unless there is an application filter to support the secondary connections. Firewall client machines can access any TCP or UDP protocol, even those that require secondary connections, without the requirement of the Application Filter.

An alternative to using the Firewall client on the VPN client is to configure the Dial-up and Network settings of the VPN client connection object in Internet Explorer with Proxy Server settings. If you are using ISA 2000, you can configure the VPN connection object with the same Web Proxy settings that are used by internal clients. However, this approach allows VPN clients to use HTTP, HTTP(S) and FTP (download only) protocols for Internet access. This same feature is available when connecting to ISA 2004/2006 Firewall/VPN servers.

Site-to-Site VPN Using Tunnel Mode IPSec

With ISA 2000, VPN remote-access clients could use PPTP or L2TP/IPSec to connect to the ISA 2000 VPN server, and other VPN gateways could connect to the ISA 2000 VPN gateway and establish site-to-site VPN links between two geographically separate networks. However, most third-party VPN gateways (such as Cisco or other popular VPN gateway solutions) did not support PPTP or L2TP/ IPSec for VPN site-to-site connections. Instead, they required IPSec tunnel mode VPN connections.

If you had an ISA 2000 firewall/VPN server on both sites, it was simple to create a highly secure L2TP/IPSec VPN connection between the two sites or a less secure PPTP VPN connection. However, if you had a third-party VPN gateway at the main office, and you wanted to install an ISA 2000

VPN gateway at a branch office, you couldn't establish a site-to-site VPN connection to the main office VPN gateway because the main office VPN gateway didn't support PPTP or L2TP/IPSec connections, and ISA 2000 didn't support IPSec tunnel mode connections for site-to-site links.

ISA 2004/2006 firewalls solve this problem because you can now use IPSec tunnel mode for site-to-site links between an ISA 2004/2006 VPN gateway and a third-party VPN gateway. You can still use PPTP or high security L2TP/IPSec to create site-to-site links between two ISA Server firewall/VPN gateways, but ISA 2004/2006 enables you to use a lower security IPSec tunnel mode connection to connect to third party VPN gateways.

NOTE

IPSec tunnel mode is supported only for site-to-site VPN connections. Client-to-server remote-access VPN connections still use only PPTP or L2TP/IPSec. When using IPSec tunnel mode, you should be aware that it is vulnerable to several well-known exploits, whereas L2TP/IPSec requires stronger authentication (two levels of authentication, machine and user) and is not as vulnerable to these attacks. Also L2TP/IPSec can use FQDN for the VPN endpoints and DDNS if one endpoint does not have a fixed IP address. L2TP/IPSec provides data compression. Thus, when you have a choice, L2TP/IPSec is the preferred VPN protocol set for site-to-site VPN connections. IPSec tunnel mode provides data confidentiality, per packet connectionless integrity (proof of the fact that data has not been altered in transit), per packet data origin authentication (proof that the data was sent by the right peer) and replay-attack protection. Connectionless integrity and data origin authentication are commonly known as "integrity". IPSec tunnel mode provides one level of authentication, machine (through IKE). The strongest symmetric encryption algorithm for IPSec tunnel mode present on ISA 2006 is 3DES. Note that ISA 2006 supports the Diffie-Hellman Group 2048. Not every third-party VPN gateway does so.

Publishing PPTP VPN Servers

In ISA 2000, Server Publishing Rules limited you to publishing servers that required only TCP or UDP protocols. In other words, you could not publish servers that required non-TCP or UDP protocols, such as ICMP or GRE. This meant you could not publish a PPTP server because it uses the GRE protocol, which is a non-TCP or UDP protocol. The only alternative with ISA 2000 was to put these servers on a perimeter network segment and use packet filters to allow the required protocols to and from the Internet.

ISA 2004/2006 has solved this problem. You can create Server Publishing Rules for any IP protocol using ISA 2004/2006. This includes Server Publishing Rules for GRE. The ISA 2004/2006 Firewall's enhanced PPTP filter allows inbound and outbound access. The inbound access support meant you could publish a PPTP VPN server located behind an ISA 2004/2006 Firewall.

Pre-shared Key Support for IPSec VPN Connections

A Public Key Infrastructure (PKI) is necessary in high-security environments so that computer and user certificates can be issued to the computers that participate in an IPSec-based VPN connection. Digital certificates are used for machine (computer) authentication for L2TP/IPSec remote access and gateway-to-gateway connections, and for IPSec tunnel mode connections. Certificates can also be used for user authentication for both PPTP and L2TP/IPSec connections.

Setting up a PKI is not a simple task, and many network administrators do not have the time or the expertise to implement one quickly. In that case, there is another way to benefit from the level of security provided by IPSec-protected VPN connections.

With ISA 2004/2006, you can use pre-shared keys instead of certificates when you create remote access and site-to-site VPN connections. All VPN client machines running the updated L2TP/IPSec VPN client software can use a pre-shared key to create an L2TP/IPSec remote-access VPN client connection with the ISA 2004/2006 firewall/VPN server. Windows 2000 and Windows Server 2003 VPN gateways can also be configured to use a pre-shared key to establish site-to-site links.

WARNING

Pre-shared keys for IPSec-based VPN connections should be used with caution (recommended only for testing). Certificates are still the preferred method.

Using pre-shared keys for L2TP/IPSec remote access with ISA 2004/2006 means that all the VPN clients will use the same pre-shared key. Therefore it cannot function as an effective secret. In this situation, neither the client nor the server identifies itself during IKE authentication (machine authentication); it is only known that both parties are a member of the group with knowledge of the pre-shared key. This permits anyone with access to the group pre-shared key to act as a man-in-the-middle. MS-CHAPv2, since it provides mutual authentication can prevent the MITM attack. However, since MS-CHAPv2 is relatively weak and can expose user credentials (the attacker can run a dictionary attack, if the password is weak it will be cracked). This weakness is advertised in RFC3193 (L2TP/IPSec).

So be aware that a single remote-access server can use only one pre-shared key for all L2TP/IPSec connections that require a pre-shared key for authentication. You must issue the same pre-shared key to all L2TP/IPSec VPN clients connecting to the remote-access server using a pre-shared key. Unless you distribute the pre-shared key within a Connection Manager profile (CMAK), each user will have to manually enter the pre-shared key into the VPN client software settings. This reduces the security of the L2TP/IPSec VPN deployment and increases the probability of user error and increased number of support calls related to L2TP/IPSec connection failures.

> **WARNING**
>
> If the pre-shared key on the ISA 2004/2006 firewall/VPN server is changed, a client with a manually configured pre-shared key will not be able to connect using the L2TP/IPSec pre-shared key until the key on the client machine is also changed.

Despite its security drawbacks, the ability to easily use pre-shared keys to create secure L2TP/IPSec connections to the ISA 2004/2006 firewall/VPN server is still popular among firewall administrators. Pre-shared keys are an ideal "stop gap" measure that you can put into place immediately and use while in the process of putting together a certificate-based Public Key Infrastructure. When the PKI is complete, you can then migrate the clients from pre-shared keys to high-security computer and user certificate authentication.

Advanced Name Server Assignment for VPN Clients

The ISA 2000 VPN server/gateway was based on the VPN components included with the Windows 2000 and Windows Server 2003 Routing and Remote Access Services. The RRAS VPN services allow you to assign name server addresses to VPN remote access clients. Proper name server assignment is very important to VPN clients because incorrect name server assignments can render the VPN client unable to connect to either Internal network resources or resources located on the Internet.

Alternatively, it is possible to configure the VPN client connectoid with the IP addresses of WINS and DNS server. You can automate this process by using the Connection Manager Administration Kit to distribute these settings. Client-side name server assignment requires that each connectoid object be manually configured or that you use CMAK to distribute these settings.

It is possible to distribute name resolution settings from the VPN server. However, if you wanted to distribute name server settings to a VPN client from the ISA 2000 VPN server, you had to use one of the following:

- Name server addresses that were bound to one of the network interfaces on the ISA Server 2000 firewall machine

- Name server addresses provided to the VPN client via DHCP options (this was available only if the DHCP Relay Agent was installed on the ISA 2000 firewall/VPN server)

You might sometimes want to assign VPN clients name server addresses that are not based on the network interface configuration on the firewall/VPN server, and you might not want to install the DHCP Relay Agent on the firewall. Unfortunately, if this was the case, you were out of luck with ISA 2000 because it did not support this scenario.

Good news: ISA 2004/2006 firewall/VPN servers do not have this problem because they allow you to override the name server settings on the ISA 2004/2006 firewall/VPN server and issue custom name server addresses to the VPN clients. This can be done within the ISA 2004/2006 management console; you don't have to enter the RRAS console to create the custom configuration.

Monitoring of VPN Client Connections

The ISA 2000 VPN server was limited by the logging and monitoring capabilities of the Windows 2000 and Windows Server 2003 RRAS VPN. Determining who connected to the network via a VPN connection required that you sift through text files or database entries. And that's not all; because the firewall did not manage the VPN remote-access client connections, there was no central mechanism in place at the firewall to allow you to determine which resources were being accessed by VPN remote-access clients.

ISA 2004/2006 solves this problem by applying firewall policy to *all* connections to the firewall, including VPN connections. You can use the real-time log viewer to look at ongoing VPN remote-access client connections and filter it to view only VPN client connections. If you log to an MSDE database, you can query the database to view an historical record of VPN connections. With ISA 2004/2006 firewall/VPN servers, you not only get complete information about who connected to the ISA 2004/2006 firewall/VPN, but you also get information about what resources those users connected to and what protocols they used to connect to those resources.

For example, you can filter VPN criteria in the log viewer if you are using live logging and are logging to a file. What you can't do with file-based logging is use the ISA firewall's log viewer to query the archived data. However, you can still filter and monitor real-time VPN connections in the log viewer. In addition, you can filter VPN connections in both the Sessions view and the Log view.

In the **Tasks** tab in the Task pane of the **Virtual Private Networks (VPN)** node in the **Microsoft Internet Security and Acceleration Server 2006** management console, you can click on a link that allows you to monitor the VPN client and gateway connections. If you choose this option, make sure you back up the default filter settings so that you can return to your baseline filtering configuration.

This ISA 2004/2006 logging and monitoring feature is a big improvement over the logging and monitoring features included with ISA 2000 and is also much better than the standalone Windows 2000 and Windows Server 2003 Routing and Remote Access Service VPN.

ISA 2004 SP3 brought to ISA 2004 the following capabilities: Improved Log Viewer, Enhanced Log Filtering, Improved Management of Log Filters and a new Diagnostic Logging. These features are currently unavailable on the ISA 2006 Firewall but are expected to be available with the soon to be released ISA 2006 SP1.

An Improved Site-to-Site Wizard (New ISA 2006 feature)

The improved site-to-site wizard simplifies the creation of a site-to-site connection. Now the creation of the site-to-site connection is almost completely automated. Within the wizard you can define the required network rule (or you can opt to define it later), the access rules (or you can opt to define it later) and for example if you use certificate authentication (machine, L2TP/IPSec or IPSec tunnel mode) ISA can enable for you the System Policy named "Allow HTTP from ISA Server to selected networks for downloading updated Certificate Revocation Lists (CRL)".

In the case of PPTP and L2TP/IPSec, new with ISA 2006, if this is the first VPN connection (no VPN client access configured or other site-to-site connections defined), the wizard allows you to specify the IP Address assignment (either static or dynamic) and the incoming authentication method for L2TP/IPSec (in case you select as the outgoing authentication method pre-shared keys, you can allow or not for incoming authentication pre-shared keys).

When ISA 2006 is the Answering Gateway for PPTP and L2TP/IPSec site-to-site connections, still the same policies (address assignment, the incoming authentication method for IKE, the user authentication method) that apply to VPN clients are applied to VPN gateways like in the case of ISA 2004.

In the case of IPSec tunnel mode, the remote VPN gateway IP address is automatically included in the remote site IP address range (the same thing must be done at the remote VPN server). The omission of this IP address from the definition of the remote site caused issues with IPSec tunnel mode site-to-site connections in the ISA 2004 days. If you tried to ping or access resources from the local ISA firewall located on the remote site you could not until you manually perform this step on both gateways. For example, in case of testing connectivity with ping, you only received a Negotiating IP Security reply.

We will discuss later in this chapter the improved site-to-site wizard from ISA 2006.

The Create Answer File Wizard (New ISA 2006 Feature)

The Create Answer File Wizard creates an answer file at the main office ISA 2006 Enterprise Edition Firewall which will be used to setup the site-to-site VPN at the branch office. The wizard also gives you the option to make the branch office ISA Firewall a domain member. A simple and non-technical user can run the answer file to automatically connect the branch office ISA firewall to the main office network. The Create Answer File Wizard can only be used with IPSec tunnel mode and L2TP/IPSec site-to-site VPN connections.

The Branch Office Connectivity Wizard (New ISA 2006 feature)

Automated branch office ISA firewall deployment tool: The Branch Office Connectivity Wizard (the **appcfgwzd.exe** application) which is run at the branch office using the answer file created at the main office in order to setup the branch office ISA firewall. With ISA 2004, the branch office scenario represented a problem. It required an experienced ISA Firewall administrator to be available at the branch office to create the site-to-site connection, to bring up the tunnel and eventually to try and join the branch ISA Firewall to the domain, an ISA firewall best practice. When an answer file is available at the branch office the process is automated.

However the Branch Office Connectivity Wizard can be run without the answer file at the branch office by manually enter the configuration details.

The Branch Office Connectivity Wizard can only be used with IPSec tunnel mode and L2TP/IPSec site-to-site connections.

The Branch Office Connectivity Wizard represents a big improvement of ISA 2006 Enterprise Edition over ISA 2004.

The Site-to-Site Summary (New ISA 2006 Feature)

While on ISA 2004 you had an IPSec policy summary for IPSec tunnel mode site-to-site, now with ISA 2006 all three types of VPN site-to-site connections benefit from a site-to-site summary which allows you to quickly view what you have configured. It is very useful since it describes the local settings and also it suggests you the required settings at the other end of the tunnel.

Creating a Remote Access PPTP VPN Server

A remote access VPN server accepts VPN calls from VPN client machines. A remote access VPN server allows *individual client machines and users* access to corporate network resources after the VPN connection is established. In contrast, a VPN gateway connects entire networks to each other and allows multiple hosts on each network to connect to other networks through a VPN site-to-site link.

You can use any VPN client software that supports PPTP or L2TP/IPSec to connect to a VPN server. The ideal VPN client software is the Microsoft VPN client, which is included with all versions of Windows. However, if you wish to use L2TP/IPSec with pre-shared keys and NAT traversal support, you should download and install the updated L2TP/IPSec client from the Microsoft download site for older Windows OSs. We'll go over the details on how to obtain this software later in the chapter.

In this section, we'll go over the procedures required to create a PPTP remote access VPN server on the ISA firewall. The specific steps we'll perform include:

- Enabling the ISA Firewall's VPN Server component
- Creating an Access Rule allowing VPN Clients access to the Internal network
- Enabling Dial-in Access for VPN User Accounts
- Testing a PPTP VPN Connection

ISA Firewall Warning

While PPTP and MPPE are secure VPN protocols that can be used by organizations that do not want to use PKI and L2TP/IPSec, the level of security provided by PPTP/MPPE is directly related to the complexity of the user credentials and the PPP user authentication protocol. You should use only complex user passwords with MS-CHAPv2 or EAP user certificate authentication. This is due to the fact that PPTP encrypts data being transmitted but does not encrypt information being exchanged during negotiation. PPTP only provides per-packet data confidentiality. PPTP is defined in RFC2637 (Point to Point Tunneling Protocol), RFC3078 (MMPE, Microsoft Point to Point Encryption), RFC3079 (Deriving Keys for use with MPPE). Keep in mind that every of these RFCs does "not specify an Internet standard of any kind". This means that PPTP is not an Internet Standard. The strongest encryption algorithm available for data encryption is RC4 using 128-bit session keys. PPTP should not be used anymore for strong security even with EAP-TLS because of the relative weakness of its encryption algorithm.

Enable the VPN Server

You need to turn on the VPN server component, as it is disabled by default. The first step is to enable the VPN server feature and configure the VPN server components. You do this in the **Microsoft Internet Security and Acceleration Server 2006** management console and *not* in the RRAS console.

Most of the problems we've seen with the ISA firewall VPN configuration *were* related to fledgling ISA firewall administrators using the RRAS console to configure the VPN components. While there will be times when we want to use the RRAS console, the vast majority of the configuration for the ISA firewall's VPN server and VPN gateway is done in the **Microsoft Internet Security and Acceleration Server 2006** management console.

! ISA FIREWALL WARNING

You want to do most of your VPN server and gateway configuration in the **Microsoft Internet Security and Acceleration Server 2006** management console because the ISA firewall settings will overwrite most of the settings you create in the RRAS console. For more information on this issue, check out **Interoperability of Routing and Remote Access and Internet Security and Acceleration Server 2004** at http://support.microsoft.com/default.aspx?scid=kb;en-us;838374

Perform the following steps to enable and configure the ISA 2006 VPN Server:

1. Open the **Microsoft Internet Security and Acceleration Server 2006** management console and expand the server name. Click on the **Virtual Private Networks (VPN)** node.

2. Click on the **Tasks** tab in the Task pane. Click the **Enable VPN Client Access** link (Figure 6.1). With ISA 2006 you cannot enable VPN Client access until you define the IP address assignment method. Scroll bellow into the **Configure Access Networks Options** and see how you can define Address Assignment (Figure 6.10). You will receive a warning when you click **Enable VPN Client Access** if **Address Assignment** was not configured (Figure 6.2).

Figure 6.1 The Enable VPN Client Access link

Figure 6.2 Warning About address assignment

3. Click **Apply** to save the changes and update the firewall policy.

4. Click **OK** in the **Saving Configuration Changes** dialog box.

5. Click the Configure VPN Client Access link on the Tasks tab.

6. On the **General** tab in the **VPN Clients Properties** dialog box, change the value for the **Maximum number of VPN clients allowed** from **5** to **10**. The Standard Edition of the ISA firewall supports up to 1000 concurrent VPN connections. This is a hard-coded limit and it is locked-in regardless of the number of VPN connections supported by the Windows operating system on which the ISA firewall is installed. In contrast, the Enterprise edition of the ISA firewall does not have a hard-coded limit and supports the number of VPN connections supported by the base operating system. The exact number is unclear, but we do know that when the ISA firewall is installed on the Enterprise version of Windows Server 2003, you can create over 16,000 PPTP connections and over 30,000 L2TP/IPSec VPN connections to the ISA firewall. The General tab is shown in Figure 6.3.

Figure 6.3 The General Tab

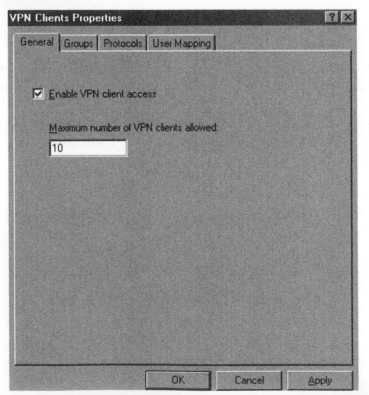

Make sure that you will have at least the number of IP addresses available to VPN clients as the number you list in the **Maximum number of VPN clients allowed** text box. Determine the number of VPN clients you want to connect to the ISA firewall, and then add one more for the ISA firewall itself. That's the number you want to enter into this text box.

1. Click on the **Groups** tab (Figure 6.4). On the **Groups** tab, click **Add**.

2. In the **Select Groups** dialog box, click the **Locations** button. In the **Locations** dialog box, click **msfirewall.org,** and click **OK**.

3. In the **Select Group** dialog box, enter **Domain Users** in the **Enter the object names to select** text box. Click **Check Names**. The group name will be underlined when it is found in the Active Directory. Click **OK**.

Figure 6.4 The Groups Tab

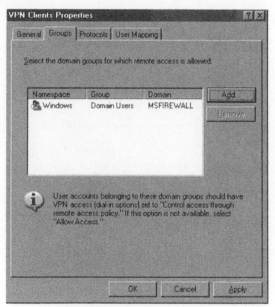

You can enter local groups that are configured on the ISA firewall machine itself, or you can use domain groups. The ISA firewall will use only domain Global Groups, it will not use Domain Local Groups. You configure domain Global Groups on the **Groups** tab *only* when the ISA firewall is a member of the domain. If the ISA firewall is not a member of the domain, then you can use RADIUS authentication to allow domain Global Groups access to the ISA firewall's VPN server. We will cover the details of configuring RADIUS authentication for VPN remote-access connections later in this chapter.

ISA FIREWALL ALERT

The domain functionality must be set to Windows 2000 Native or higher in order to be able to **Control access through remote access policy,** or the users/group must be created on the ISA firewall's own SAM.

Another thing to keep in mind is that when you control access to the VPN server via a domain (or local) group, the users must have remote access permission. We'll discuss that issue later in this chapter.

1. Click the **Protocols** tab. On the **Protocols** tab, put a checkmark in the **Enable PPTP** check box only, as shown in Figure 6.5.

Figure 6.5 The Protocols Tab

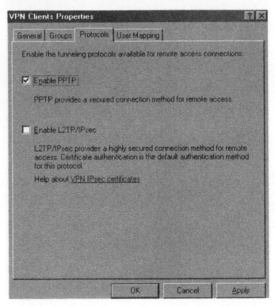

2. Click the **User Mapping** tab. Put a checkmark in the **Enable User Mapping** check box. Put a checkmark in the **When username does not contain a domain, use this domain** check box. Enter **msfirewall.org** in the **Domain Name** text box. Note that these settings will only apply when using RADIUS/EAP authentication. These settings are ignored when using Windows authentication (such as when the ISA 2006 firewall machine belongs to the domain and the user explicitly enters domain credentials). Click **Apply** and **OK.** You may see a **Microsoft Internet Security and Acceleration Server 2006** dialog box informing you that you need to restart the computer for the settings to take effect. If so, click **OK** in the dialog box. The User Mapping tab is shown in Figure 6.6.

Figure 6.6 The User Mapping tab

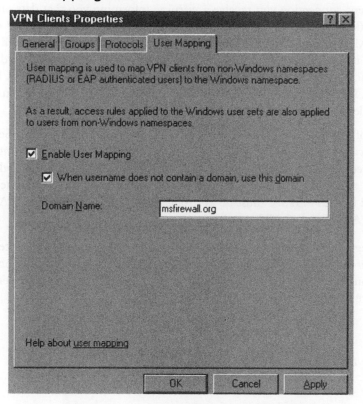

You can prevent all VPN connections to your ISA firewall if you enable user mapping and *do not* make the ISA firewall a member of the domain (Error 619). User mapping can be used when the ISA firewall is a member of your domain, and you use RADIUS authentication to support authentication for users that belong to multiple domains or if you use EAP-TLS authentication. You can enable user mapping to support creating user/group-based access control over users who log on via RADIUS and map those user accounts to accounts in the domain the ISA firewall belongs to, and then create Access Rules using those accounts by creating **User Sets** on the ISA firewall. In case of EAP-TLS (no RADIUS), when ISA is a domain member the user name from the certificate can be mapped to a Windows Active Directory account.

In case ISA does not belong to the domain (workgroup mode) you can use user mapping with RADIUS authentication (example IAS, Active Directory integrated) as long as you are using authentication protocols like PAP or SPAP (very weak protocols) enabled on ISA (if not you receive Error 919) and enabled on the RADIUS server and you specify a simple user name (just Administrator and not Administrator@msfirewall.org) when the client connects. Also you need to mirror the groups/accounts on ISA (if not you will not be able to connect) in order to apply group based firewall policy (i.e., use these local groups for the rules). You need user mapping only when you create group-based access rules. If you use user-based access rules then you can define **User Sets** with RADIUS namespace on ISA. Keep in mind that:

- In case of PPTP, PAP means that credentials will be sent in clear. When you configure the VPN client connection you receive a warning informing you that data encryption will not be used (keys used to encrypt data can only be obtain when MS-CHAP or MS-CHAPv2 is used, MMPE cannot be used with PAP and SPAP). So you need to tell the client to connect using no encryption. The RADIUS server must be configured to accept connections that use no encryption and to use PAP and/or SPAP. If not Error 742 will be received. PPTP is weak at its best, so using PAP and SPAP will make it useless (credentials sent in clear, no data encryption).

- In case of L2TP/IPSec keys used to encrypt data are obtained from IPSec, the PPP authentication is protected by IPSec ESP, so the RADIUS server does not need to be configured to use no encryption and you do not receive any warning when selecting PAP or SPAP at the client side. The second level of authentication, user authentication (PPP), provided by L2TP/IPSec must be as strong as possible and PAP and SPAP are as weak as possible. Again an unfeasible scenario.

In case of using EAP-TLS with a RADIUS server, ISA workgroup mode, once again you can use user mapping if you select "Use a different name for the connection" when configuring the client connection and you do not specify the domain name (the user/groups accounts need to be mirrored on ISA). See Figure 6.7 and Figure 6.8.

Figure 6.7 Use a different name for the connection

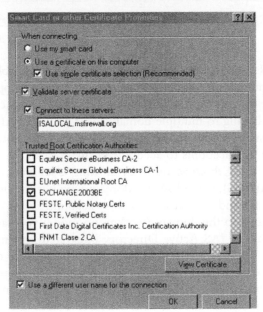

Figure 6.8 Enter a simple user name

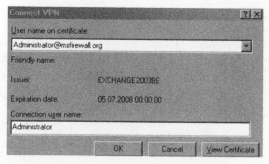

In ISA's help file there is a strong recommendation that PAP, SPAP and CHAP to remain disabled.

Therefore, we can conclude that if you want group-based firewall access policies you must make ISA a domain member and enable user mapping when EAP-TLS or RADIUS (IAS, Active Directory integrated) authentication is used. Since ISA is a domain member the RADIUS server is not needed. One remote access scenario when you would need a RADIUS server (and the ISA firewall is domain member) is when you might have a small group of users using PPTP and other group(s) using the stronger L2TP/IPSec and you want to explicitly specify who can use PPTP, due to security issues. You can create the required Remote Access Policies on the RADIUS server and create user/groups based firewall policies (access rules) on ISA with user mapping. Currently with ISA 2006 Firewall is not possible of doing that from the ISA's GUI.

We will discuss the user mapping subject in more detail later in this chapter and also discuss how to use apply user/group-based access control over VPN clients that log on via RADIUS.

We will go over the details of how User Mapping works with EAP user certificate authentication later in the chapter.

3. On the **Tasks** tab, click **Select Access Networks**.

4. In the **Virtual Private Networks (VPN) Properties** dialog box, click **Access Networks**. Note that the **External** checkbox is selected. This indicates that the external interface is listening for incoming VPN client connections. If you want internal users to connect to the ISA firewall, select **Internal**. You also have the options to allow VPN connections from All Networks (and Local Host) Network and All Protected Networks. The Virtual Private Networks Properties dialog box is shown in Figure 6.9, Select and Configure Access Networks Options.

Figure 6.9 Select and Configure Access Networks Options

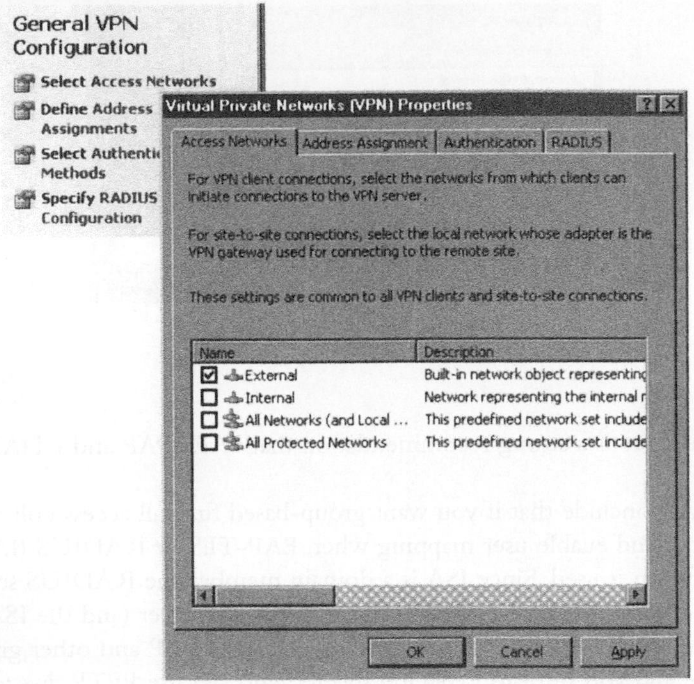

The ability to select VPN connections from multiple networks can be useful when you have unsecured networks located behind the ISA firewall. For example, suppose you have a trihomed ISA firewall that has an external interface, an Internal interface, and a WLAN interface. You use the WLAN for users who bring in laptops that are not managed by your organization. You also require users who have managed computers to use the WLAN segment as well when they bring laptops that are moved between the corporate network and untrusted networks.

You configure Access Rules on the ISA firewall to prevent connections from the WLAN segment. However, you configure Access Rules that allow VPN connections on the WLAN interface to connect to resources on the corporate Internal network. In this way, no users connected to the WLAN segment are able to access resources on the corporate Internal network segment except those corporate users who can VPN into the WLAN interface on the ISA firewall and present the proper credentials to complete a VPN link.

Another scenario where you might want to allow a VPN connection into the ISA firewall is when the ISA firewall is acting as a front-end firewall. In that case, you probably do not want to allow direct RDP or remote MMC connections to the ISA firewall. What you can do is allow RDP connections *only from VPN Clients* and then allow VPN clients RDP access to the Local Host Network. In this way, a user must establish a secure VPN connection to the front-end ISA firewall before an RDP connection can be established. Hosts connecting via any other means are denied access to the RDP protocols. Nice!

5. Click the **Address Assignment** tab (Figure 6.10). Select *Internal* from the **Use the following network to obtain DHCP, DNS and WINS services** drop down list box. This is a critical setting as it defines the network on which access to the DHCP is made.

Figure 6.10 The Address Assignment Tab

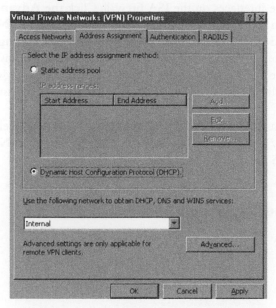

Note that this isn't your only option. You can select any of the adapters on the ISA firewall from **Use the following network to obtain DHCP, DNS and WINS services.** The key issue is that you select the adapter that has the correct name server information on it, and the most likely candidate is the Internal interface of the ISA firewall.

You also have the option to use a **Static address pool** to assign addresses to the VPN clients. The problem with using a static address pool is, if you assign *on subnet* addresses (addresses in the same network ID as one of the interfaces on the ISA firewall), you will need to remove those addresses from the definition of the Network to which the ISA firewall is connected.

For example, suppose the ISA firewall has two network interfaces: an external and an internal interface. The internal interface is connected to your default Internal Network and the Internal Network ID is 10.0.0.0/24. If you want to assign VPN clients addresses in the Internal Network address range using a static address pool, such as 10.0.0.200 to 10.0.0.211(total of 10 addresses), you will need to manually remove those addresses from the definition of the Internal Network before you can create a static address pool with these addresses. If you try to create a static address pool with these *on subnet* addresses, you'll see the following error (Figure 6.11).

Figure 6.11 A Network Warning Dialog Box

You can assign name server addresses to VPN clients that are independent of the name server configuration on any of the interfaces on the ISA firewall. Click the **Advanced** button, and you'll see the **Name Resolution** dialog box. The default settings are **Obtain DNS server addresses using DHCP configuration** and **Obtain WINS server addresses using DHCP configuration**. Of course, you cannot obtain DHCP options for VPN clients unless you install and configure a DHCP Relay Agent on the ISA firewall. The ISA firewall's RRAS service will only obtain blocks of IP addresses for the VPN clients, not DHCP options. We will discuss this issue in more detail later in this chapter.

If you want to avoid installing the DHCP Relay Agent, you can still deliver custom DNS and WINS server addresses to VPN clients by selecting **Use the following DNS server addresses** and **Use the following WINS server addresses**. See Figure 6.12.

Figure 6.12 The Name Resolution Dialog Box

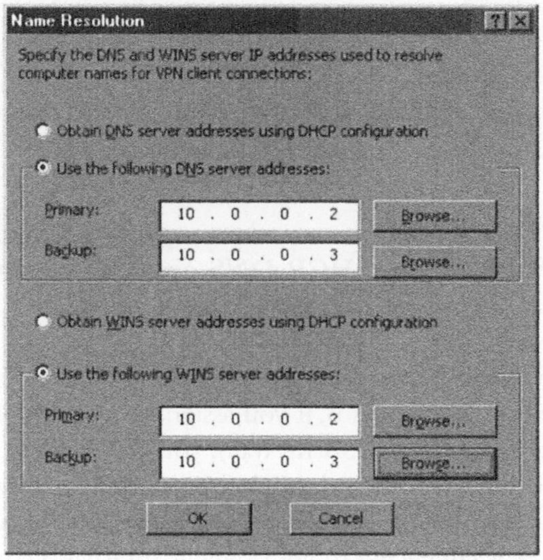

6. Click on the **Authentication** tab. Note that the default setting enables only **Microsoft encrypted authentication version 2 (MS–CHAPv2)**. Note the **Allow custom IPSec policy for L2TP connection** checkbox. If you do not want to create a public key infrastructure (PKI), or, you are in the process of creating one but have not yet finished, you can enable this checkbox and enter a **pre-shared** key. You should also enable a custom IPSec policy pre-shared key if you want to create a site-to-site VPN connection with pre-shared keys. We'll discuss this issue in detail later in this chapter. For the highest level of authentication security, enable the **Extensible authentication protocol (EAP) with smart card or other certificate** option. We will discuss later in this chapter how to configure the ISA firewall and VPN clients to use User Certificates to authenticate to the ISA firewall. Figure 6.13 shows the Authentication tab options.

Figure 6.13 The Authentication Tab

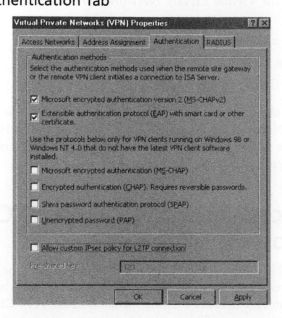

7. Click the **RADIUS** tab. Here you can configure the ISA 2006 firewall VPN server to use RADIUS to authenticate the VPN users. The advantage of RADIUS authentication is that you can leverage the Active Directory's (and other directories) user database to authenticate users without requiring the ISA firewall to be a member of a domain. See Figure 6.14. We'll go over the details of how to configure RADIUS support for VPN user authentication later in this chapter.

Figure 6.14 Virtual Private Networks Properties

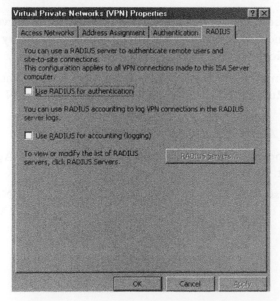

8. Click **Apply** in the **Virtual Private Networks (VPN) Properties** dialog box and then click **OK**.

9. Click **Apply** to save the changes and update the firewall policy.

10. Click **OK** in the **Saving Configuration Changes** dialog box.

11. Restart the ISA firewall machine.

The ISA firewall will obtain a block of IP addresses from the DHCP Server on the Internal network when it restarts. Note that on a production network where the DHCP server is located on a network segment remote from the ISA 2006 firewall, all interposed routers will need to have BOOTP or DHCP relay enabled so that DHCP requests from the firewall can reach the remote DHCP servers.

Create an Access Rule Allowing VPN Clients Access to Allowed Resources

The ISA firewall will be able to accept incoming VPN connections after the restart. However, VPN clients cannot access any resources because there are no Access Rules allowing the VPN clients to get to anything. You must create Access Rules allowing members of the VPN Clients network access to the resources you want them to access. This is a stark contrast to other combined firewall/VPN server solutions in that the ISA firewall VPN server applies stateful packet and application-layer inspection on all VPN client connections.

In the following example, you will create an Access Rule allowing all traffic to pass from the VPN Clients network to the Internal network. In a production environment, you would create more restrictive access rules so that users on the VPN Clients network have access only to resources they require. Later in this chapter, we will demonstrate how you can configure a more restrictive Access Policy using user/group-based access control on VPN clients.

Perform the following steps to create an unrestricted-access VPN client Access Rule:

1. In the **Microsoft Internet Security and Acceleration Server 2006** management console, expand the server name and click the **Firewall Policy** node. Right-click the **Firewall Policy** node, point to **New** and click **Access Rule**.

2. In the **Welcome to the New Access Rule Wizard** page, enter a name for the rule in the **Access Rule name** text box. In this example, enter **VPN Client to Internal**. Click **Next**.

3. On the **Rule Action** page, select **Allow** and click **Next**.

4. On the **Protocols** page, select **All outbound traffic** in the **Apply the rule to this protocols** list. Click **Next**.

5. On the **Access Rule Sources** page, click **Add**. In the **Add Network Entities** dialog box (Figure 6.15), click the **Networks** folder and double-click on **VPN Clients**. Click **Close**.

Figure 6.15 The Add Network Entities Dialog Box

6. Click **Next** on the **Access Rule Sources** page.

7. On the **Access Rule Destinations** page, click **Add**. In the **Add Network Entities** dialog box, click the **Networks** folder, and double-click **Internal**. Click **Close**.

8. On the **User Sets** page, accept the default setting, **All Users**, and click **Next**.

9. Click **Finish** on the **Completing the New Access Rule Wizard** page.

10. Click **Apply** to save the changes and update the firewall policy.

11. Click **OK** in the **Saving Configuration Changes** dialog box. The VPN client policy is now the top-listed Access Rule in the Access Policy list as shown in Figure 6.16.

Figure 6.16 VPN Client Policy

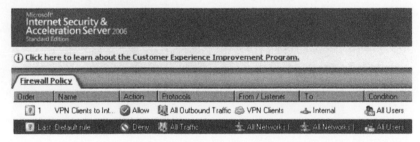

At this point VPN clients that successfully authenticate and have Dial-in permission will be able to access all resources, using any protocol, on the Internal network.

Enable Dial-in Access

In non-native mode Active Directory domains, all user accounts have dial-in access *disabled* by default. You must enable dial-in access on a *per account* basis for these non-native mode Active Directory domains. In contrast, native-mode Active Directory domains have dial-in access controlled by *Remote Access Policy* by default. Windows NT 4.0 domains always have dial-in access controlled on a per user account basis.

In the lab environment used in this book, Active Directory is in Windows Server 2003 mixed mode, so we will need to manually change the dial-in settings on each domain user account that requires access to the VPN server.

Perform the following steps on the domain controller to enable Dial-in access for the Administrator account:

1. Click Start and point to Administrative Tools. Click Active Directory Users and Computers.

2. In the Active Directory Users and Computers console, click on the Users node in the left pane. Double-click on the Administrator account in the right pane of the console.

3. Click on the Dial-in tab. In the Remote Access Permission (Dial-in or VPN) frame, select Allow access as shown in Figure 6.17. Click Apply and OK.

Figure 6.17 The account dial-in tab

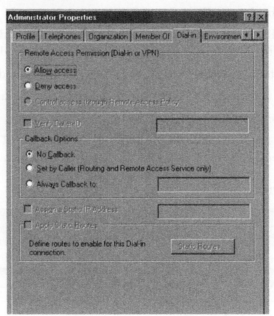

4. Close the Active Directory Users and Computers console.

Another option is to create groups on the ISA firewall itself. You can create local users on the ISA firewall and then place those users into groups. This method allows you to use the default setting on the user accounts created on the ISA firewall, where the default dial-in setting is **control access via Remote Access Policy**.

While this option doesn't scale very well, it's a viable option for those organizations that have a limited number of VPN users and who don't want to use RADIUS or don't have a RADIUS server to use.

Perform the following steps to create a user group that has access to the ISA firewall's VPN server:

1. On the ISA firewall, right-click **My Computer** on the desktop and click **Manage**.

2. In the **Computer Management** console, expand **System Tools**, and expand the **Local Users and Groups** node. Right-click the **Groups** node, and click **New Group**.

3. In the **New Group** dialog box, enter a name for the group in the **Group Name** text box. In this example, we'll name the group **VPN Users**. Click **Add**.

4. In the **Select Users** dialog box, click **Advanced**.

5. In the **Select Users** dialog box, select the users or groups you want to make part of the **VPN Users** group. In this example, we'll select **Authenticated Users**. Click **OK**.

6. Click **OK** in the **Select Users** dialog box.

7. Click **Create**, and then **Close**.

Now let's configure the ISA firewall's VPN server component to allow access to members of the **VPN Users** group:

1. In the **Microsoft Internet Security and Acceleration Server 2006** management console, expand the server name, and then click **Virtual Private Networking (VPN)**. Click **Configure VPN Client Access** on the **Tasks** tab in the Task pane.

2. In the **VPN Clients Properties Groups** tab, click **Add**.

3. In the **Select Groups** dialog box, enter **VPN Users** in the **Enter the object name to select** text box, and click **Check Names**. The group name will be underlined when it's found. Click **OK**.

We enter the local **VPN Users** group in the **Groups** tab in this example because VPN access can be controlled via the **Control access through Remote Access Policy** setting on the user accounts of users in the local SAM of the ISA firewall. You can also enter domain users and groups (when the ISA firewall is a member of the user domain) when the domain supports Dial-in access via Remote Access Policy. We will talk more about domain users and groups and Remote Access Policy later in this chapter. See Figure 6.18 for controlling permission via Remote Access Policy.

Figure 6.18 Controlling permission via Remote Access Policy

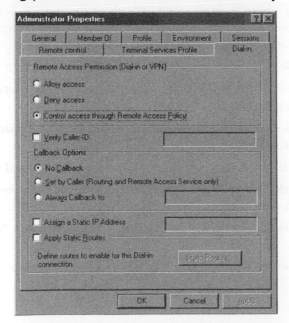

4. Click **Apply**, and then click **OK** in the **VPN Client Properties** dialog box (Figure 6.19).

Figure 6.19 The Groups Tab

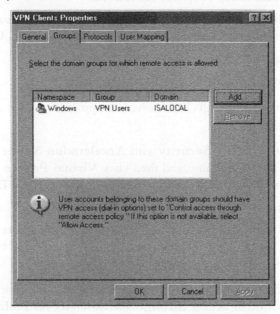

5. Click **Apply** to save the changes and update the firewall policy.

6. Click **OK** in the **Saving Configuration Changes** dialog box.

Test the PPTP VPN Connection

The ISA 2006 VPN server is now ready to accept VPN client connections. Set up the VPN connectoid on your VPN client, and then establish the VPN connection to the ISA firewall. In this book's test lab, we use a Windows XP client running Service Pack 2.

Perform the following steps to test the VPN Server:

1. On the Windows XP external client machine, right-click **My Network Places** on the desktop, and click **Properties**.

2. **Click Create a new connection wizard** in the **Network Connections** window, **Network Tasks panel**.

3. Click **Next** on the **Welcome to the New Connection Wizard** page.

4. On the **Network Connection Type** page, select **Connect to the network at my workplace**, and click **Next**.

5. On the **Network Connection** page, select the **Virtual Private Network connection**, and click **Next**.

6. On the **Connection Name** page, enter **VPN** in the **Company Name** text box, and click **Next**.

7. On the **VPN Server Selection** page, enter the IP address on the external interface of the ISA firewall (in this example, the external IP address is 192.168.1.70) in the **Host name or IP address** text box. Click **Next**.

8. On the **Connection Availability** select **Create this connection for My use only.** Click **Next**.

9. Click **Finish** on the **Completing the New Connection Wizard** page.

10. In the **Connect VPN** dialog box, enter the user name **Administrator** and the password for the administrator user account. (**NOTE:** If the ISA firewall is a member of a domain, enter the machine name or the domain name before the user name in the format NAMEusername, depending on whether the account is a local ISA firewall account or a domain account). Click **Connect**.

11. The VPN client establishes a connection with the ISA 2006 VPN server. Click **OK** in the **Connection Complete** dialog box informing that the connection is established.

12. Double-click the connection icon in the system tray, and click **Details**. You can see that **MPPE 128** encryption is used to protect the data and the IP address assigned to the VPN client (Figure 6.20). Click **Close**.

Figure 6.20 Details of PPTP connection

13. If you're using the lab setup for this book, click **Start** and **Run**. In the **Run** dialog box, enter **\\EXCHANGE2003BE** in the **Open** textbox, and click **OK**. The shares on the domain controller computer appear. Close the windows displaying the domain controller's contents. Note that we were able to use a single label name to connect to the domain controller because the ISA firewall assigned the VPN client a WINS server address. A single label name would also work via a DNS query if the VPN client machine were configured to fully qualify single label names with the correct domain name.

14. Right-click the connection icon in the system tray, and click **Disconnect**.

Creating a Remote Access L2TP/IPSec Server

In the last section, we discussed the procedures required to enable and configure the ISA firewall's VPN server component to allow remote access VPN client PPTP connections. In the following section, we'll build on the configuration we created in the last section and configure the ISA firewall to support a L2TP/IPSec remote access VPN client connection.

We'll perform the following procedures to allow L2TP/IPSec remote access VPN client connections to the ISA firewall:

- Issue certificates to the ISA 2006 firewall and VPN clients
- Test a L2TP/IPSec VPN connection
- Monitor VPN Client Connections

Issue Certificates to the ISA Firewall and VPN Clients

You can significantly improve the level of security on your VPN connections by using the L2TP/IPSec VPN protocol. The IPSec encryption protocol provides a number of security advantages over the Microsoft Point-to-Point Encryption (MPPE) protocol used to secure PPTP connections. While the ISA firewall supports using a pre-shared key to support the IPSec encryption process, this should be considered a low-security option and should be avoided if possible.

ISA FIREWALL WARNING

L2TP/IPSec provides data confidentiality, per packet connectionless integrity (proof of the fact that data has not been altered in transit), per packet data origin authentication (proof that the data was sent by the right peer) and replay-attack protection. Connectionless integrity and data origin authentication are commonly known as "integrity". L2TP/IPSec provides two levels of authentication: machine (through IKE) and user (PPP authentication). L2TP/IPSec is defined in RFC3193 which specifies "an Internet standards track protocol". The standardization state and status of this protocol is referred to as "Internet Official Protocol Standards". Due to the weaknesses of PPTP, L2TP/IPSec must be the protocol choice for VPN remote access. L2TP/IPSec uses a stronger encryption algorithm then PPTP, 3DES. If you want to comply with **NIST Guidelines for Public-Key Sizes** (http://csrc.nist.gov/publications/nistpubs/800-57/SP800-57-Part1.pdf, see Table2) you need to enable Diffie-Hellman Group 2048 (http://support.microsoft.com/kb/818043)

Also remember the security issues previously discussed regarding the use of L2TP/IPSec with pre-shared keys.

ISA FIREWALL NOTE

Windows 2000-based client computers, located behind a NAT device, that have update 818043 installed can connect to a "public" (not NAT-ed) L2TP/IPSec VPN server. Windows XP Service Pack 2-based computers, located behind a NAT device, by default can connect to a "public" (not NAT-ed) VPN server. Computers that run Microsoft Windows XP Service Pack 2 SP2 cannot connect by default to a L2TP/IPSec VPN server located behind a NAT device. If the ISA 2006 Firewall is located behind a NAT device and also the Windows XP SP2-based client computer is behind a NAT device, you must set the **AssumeUDPEncapsulationContextOnSendRule** registry value to **2**. Check this support link: http://support.microsoft.com/kb/818043. In case of Windows Vista, when the ISA 2006 firewall is located behind a NAT device you must also edit the registry on the Vista-based computer. Check this support link: http://support.microsoft.com/kb/926179.

   ISA 2006 on Windows 2003 R2 SP2, supports multiple L2TP/IPSec VPN clients located behind the same NAT device. If Windows 2003 SP2 is not installed, then no more then one or two clients can successfully connect. Also the NAT device must not break the NAT-T process (cheap NAT devices might do so).

However, if you just aren't in the position to roll out a PKI, then a pre-shared key for L2TP/IPSec is still a viable option. Just be aware that it lowers the level of security for your L2TP/IPSec connections compared to those created using machine certificates. The secure IPSec solution is to use computer certificates on the VPN server and VPN clients. We'll discuss using pre-shared keys after going through the procedures for using certificate authentication for the L2TP/IPSec connection.

The first step is to issue a computer certificate to the ISA firewall. There are a number of methods you can use to request a computer certificate. In the following example, we will use the **Certificates** stand-alone MMC snap-in. Note that you can only use the Certificate MMC snap-in when the ISA firewall is a member of the same domain where an enterprise CA is installed. If the ISA firewall is not a member of a domain where there is an enterprise CA, then you can use the Web enrollment site to obtain a machine certificate.

In order for the stand-alone MMC snap-in to communicate with the certificate authority, we will need to enable an "all open" rule that allows all traffic from the Local Host network to the Internet network. We will disable this rule after the certificate request is complete.

Perform the following steps on the ISA 2006 firewall to request a certificate from the enterprise CA on the Internal network:

1. In the **Microsoft Internet Security and Acceleration Server 2006** management console, expand the server name in the left pane, and then click the **Firewall Policy** node. Click the **Tasks** tab in the Task pane, and then click **Create Access Rule**.

2. On the **Welcome to the New Access Rule Wizard** page, enter a name for the rule in the **Access Rule name** text box. In this example, we will enter **All Open from Local Host to Internal**. Click **Next**.

3. On the **Rule Action** page, select **Allow**, and click **Next**.

4. On the **Protocols** page, accept the default selection, **All outbound traffic**, and click **Next**.

5. On the **Access Rule Sources** page, click **Add**. In the **Add Network Entities** dialog box, click the **Networks** folder. Double-click **Local Host**, and click **Close**.

6. On the **Access Rule Destinations** page, click **Add**. In the **Add Network Entities** dialog box, click the **Networks** folder. Double-click **Internal**, and click **Close**.

7. On the **User Sets** page, accept the default setting, **All Users**, and click **Next**.

8. Click **Finish** on the **Completing the Access Rule Wizard** page.

9. Right-click the **All Open from Local Host to Internal** Access Rule, and click the **Configure RPC Protocol** command.

10. In the **Configure RPC protocol policy** dialog box, remove the checkmark from the **Enforce strict RPC compliance** checkbox. Click **Apply**, and then click **OK**.

11. In the **Microsoft Internet Security and Acceleration Server 2006** management console, expand the **Configuration** node, and click on the **Add-ins** node. Right-click on the **RPC Filter** entry in the Details pane, and click **Disable**.

12. In the **ISA Server Warning** dialog box, select **Save the changes and restart the services**. Click **OK**.

13. Click **Apply** to save the changes and update the firewall policy.

14. Click **OK** in the **Saving Configuration Changes** dialog box.

15. Click **Start** and the **Run** command. Enter **mmc** in the **Open** text box, and click **OK**.

16. In **Console1**, click the **File** menu and the **Add/Remove Snap-in** command.

17. In the **Add/Remove Snap-in** dialog box, click **Add**.

18. In the **Add Standalone Snap-in** dialog box, select the **Certificates** entry from the **Available Standalone Snap-ins** list. Click **Add**.

19. On the **Certificates snap-in** page, select **Computer account**.

20. On the **Select Computer** page, select **Local computer**.

21. Click **Close** in the **Add Standalone Snap-in** dialog box.

22. Click **OK** in the **Add/Remove Snap-in** dialog box.

23. In the left pane of the console, expand **Certificates (Local Computer)** and click on **Personal**. Right-click on the **Personal** node. Point to **All Tasks**, and click **Request New Certificate**.

24. Click **Next** on the **Welcome to the Certificate Request Wizard** page.

25. On the **Certificate Types** page, select the **Computer** entry in the **Certificate types** lists, and click **Next**.

26. On the **Certificate Friendly Name and Description** page, enter a name in the **Friendly name** text box. In this example, enter **Firewall Computer Certificate**. Click **Next**.

27. Click **Finish** on the **Completing the Certificate Request Wizard** page.

28. Click **OK** in the dialog box informing you that the certificate request was successful.

29. Return to the **Microsoft Internet Security and Acceleration Server 2006** management console, and expand the computer name in the left pane. Click on the **Firewall Policy** node. Right-click on the **All Open from Local Host to Internal** Access Rule, and click **Disable**.

30. In the **Microsoft Internet Security and Acceleration Server 2006** management console, expand the **Configuration** node, and click on the **Add-ins** node. Right-click on the **RPC Filter** entry in the Details pane, and click **Enable**.

31. Click **Apply** to save the changes and update the firewall policy

32. In the **ISA Server Warning** dialog box, select **Save the changes and restart the services**. Click **OK**.

33. Click **OK** in the **Saving Configuration Changes** dialog box.

ISA FIREWALL SECRET

If you do not disable the RPC filter before attempting to request a certificate from the **Certificates** MMC, the certificate request will fail. If you then disable the RPC filter after requesting the certificate, the request will fail again. You will need to restart the ISA firewall in order to request the certificate. The moral of this story? Do *not* request the certificates from the **Certificates** MMC before you disable the RPC filter.

Note that you will not need to manually copy the enterprise CA certificate into the ISA firewall's **Trusted Root Certification Authorities** certificate store because CA certificate is automatically installed on domain members. If the firewall were not a member of the domain where an enterprise CA is installed, then you would need to manually place the CA certificate into the **Trusted Root Certification Authorities** certificate store.

ISA FIREWALL TIP

Check out the ISA 2000 VPN Deployment Kit documentation for detailed information on how to obtain certificates using the Web enrollment site and how to import the CA certificate into the ISA firewall's Trusted Root Certification Authorities machine certificate store. Find the Kit at the ISAserver.org Web site at http://www.isaserver.org/articles/isa2000vpndeploymentkit.html

The next step is to issue a computer certificate to the VPN client computer. In this example, the VPN client machine is not a member of the domain. You need to request a "computer" certificate using the enterprise CA's Web enrollment site and manually place the enterprise CA certificate into the client's **Trusted Root Certification Authorities** machine certificate store. The easiest way to accomplish this is to have the VPN client machine request the certificate when connected via a PPTP link.

ISA FIREWALL NOTE

In a production environment, untrusted client machines must not be issued computer certificates. Only managed computers should be allowed to install computer certificates. Domain members are managed clients and, therefore, under the organization's administrative control. We strongly encourage you to **not** allow users to install their own certificates on unmanaged machines. The computer certificate is a security principle and is not meant to provide free access to all users who wish to have one.

Perform the following steps to request and install the CA certificate:

1. Establish a PPTP VPN connection to the ISA firewall.

2. Open **Internet Explorer**. In the **Address** bar, enter **http://10.0.0.2/certsrv** (where 10.0.0.2 is the IP address of the CA on the Internal Network), and click **OK**.

3. In the **Enter Network Password** dialog box, enter **Administrator** in the **User Name** text box and enter the Administrator's password in the **Password** text box. Click **OK**.

VISTA NOTE

Certificate Services Web enrollment pages from Windows 2003 SP1 and SP2 won't work with Windows Vista. In case of SP1 you will receive the Downloading ActiveX control message in the Web browser window. In case of SP2 you will receive a message that states that the Web pages must be updated.
http://support.microsoft.com/kb/922706
    One quick solution to this is to request and install the certificate on a Windows XP-based machine and then export it along with the private key. Manually import it on the Vista-based computer.

4. Click **Request a Certificate** on the **Welcome** page.

5. On the **Request a Certificate** page, click **advanced certificate request**.

6. On the **Advanced Certificate Request** page, click **Create and submit a request to this CA**.

7. On the **Advanced Certificate Request** page, select the **Administrator** certificate from the **Certificate Template** list. Place a checkmark in the **Store certificate in the local computer certificate store** checkbox. Click **Submit**.

ISA FIREWALL NOTE

The "Administrator" template or a simple "User" template can be used for the "machine" certificate on the client side (even on ISA side) for IKE authentication as long as the certificate is placed in the Local computer certificate store. By default only administrators have access to this store.

8. Click **Yes** in the **Potential Scripting Violation** dialog box.

9. On the **Certificate Issued** page, click **Install this certificate**.

10. Click **Yes** on the **Potential Scripting Violation** page.

11. Close the browser after viewing the **Certificate Installed** page.

12. Click **Start,** and then click **Run**. Enter **mmc** in the **Open** text box, and click **OK**.

13. In **Console1**, click the **File** menu, and click the **Add/Remove Snap-in** command.

14. Click **Add** in the **Add/Remove Snap-in** dialog box.

15. In the **Add Standalone Snap-in** dialog box, select the **Certificates** entry from the **Available Standalone Snap-ins** list. Click **Add**.

16. Select **Computer account** on the **Certificates snap-in** page.

17. Select **Local computer** on the **Select Computer** page.

18. Click **Close** in the **Add Standalone Snap-in** dialog box.

19. Click **OK** in the **Add/Remove Snap-in** dialog box.

20. In the left pane of the console, expand **Certificates (Local Computer) Personal**. Click on **Personal****Certificates**. Double-click on **Administrator** certificate in the right pane of the console.

21. In the **Certificate** dialog box, click **Certification Path**. At the top of the certificate hierarchy seen in the **Certification path** frame is the root CA certificate. Click the **EXCHANGE2003BE** certificate at the top of the list. Click **View Certificate**.

22. In the CA certificate's **Certificate** dialog box, click the **Details** tab. Click **Copy to File**.

23. Click **Next** on the **Welcome to the Certificate Export Wizard** page.

24. On the **Export File Format** page, select **Cryptographic Message Syntax Standard – PKCS #7 Certificates (.P7B)**, and click **Next**.

25. On the **File to Export** page, enter **c:\cacert** in the **File name** text box. Click **Next**.

26. Click **Finish** on the **Completing the Certificate Export Wizard** page.

27. Click **OK** in the **Certificate Export Wizard** dialog box.

28. Click **OK** in the **Certificate** dialog box. Click **OK** again in the **Certificate** dialog box.

29. In the left pane of the console, expand the **Trusted Root Certification Authorities** node, and click **Certificates**. Right-click **\Trusted Root Certification Authorities\ Certificates**. Point to **All Tasks**, and click **Import**.

30. Click **Next** on the **Welcome to the Certificate Import Wizard** page.

31. On the **File to Import** page. Use the **Browse** button to locate the CA certificate you saved to the local hard disk, and click **Next**.

32. On the **Certificate Store** page, accept the default settings, and click **Next**.

33. On the **Completing the Certificate Import Wizard** page, click **Finish**.

34. In the **Certificate Import Wizard** dialog box informing you that the import was successful, click **OK**.

35. Disconnect from the VPN server. Right-click on the connection icon in the system tray, and click **Disconnect**.

Test the L2TP/IPSec VPN Connection

Now that both the ISA firewall and the VPN client machines have machine certificates, you can test a secure L2TP/IPSec remote-access client VPN connection to the firewall. The first step is to restart the Routing and Remote Access Service so that it registers the new certificate.

Perform the following steps to enable L2TP/IPSec support:

1. In the **Microsoft Internet Security and Acceleration Server 2006** management console, expand the server name, and click **Virtual Private Networking (VPN)**.

2. Click **Configure VPN Client Access** on the **Tasks** tab in the Task panel. Click the **Protocols** tab. On the **Protocols** tab, put a checkmark in the **Enable L2TP/IPSec** check box.

3. Click **Apply**, and then you will be prompted to enable the **System Policy** rule "**Allow all HTTP traffic from ISA server to all networks (for CRL downloads)**" (Figure 6.21). Click **Yes**. The click **OK**.

Figure 6.21 Enable the System Policy

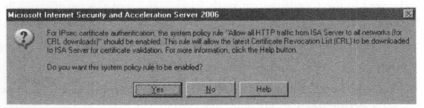

4. Click **Apply** to save the changes and update the firewall policy.

5. Click **OK** in the **Saving Configuration Changes** dialog box.

6. Restart the ISA firewall machine.

The next step is to start the VPN client connection:

1. From the VPN client computer, open the VPN client connectoid. Click **Properties**. In the **VPN Properties** dialog box, click **Networking**. On the **Networking** tab, change the **Type of VPN** to **L2TP/IPSec VPN**. Click **OK**.

2. Initiate the VPN connection to the ISA firewall.

3. Click **OK** in the **Connection Complete** dialog box informing you that the connection is established.

4. Double-click on the connection icon in the system tray.

5. In the **ISA VPN Status** dialog box (Figure 6.22), click the **Details** tab. You will see an entry for **IPSEC Encryption**, indicating that the L2TP/IPSec connection was successful.

6. Click **Close** in the **ISA VPN Status** dialog box.

Figure 6.22 L2TP/IPSec Connection Details

Monitor VPN Clients

The ISA firewall allows you to monitor the VPN client connections. Perform the following steps to see how you can view connections from VPN clients:

1. In the **Microsoft Internet Security and Acceleration Server 2006** management console, expand the server name, and click the **Virtual Private Networks (VPN)** node. Click the **Tasks** tab in the Task pane, and click **Monitor VPN Clients (Figure 6.23)**. Note that this option will change the nature of the Sessions filter. You might want to back up your current sessions filter so that you can get back to it after the VPN filter is created.

Figure 6.23 The Monitor VPN Clients Link

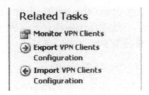

2. You are moved to the **Sessions** tab in the **Monitoring** node. Here you can see that the sessions have been filtered to show only the **VPN Client** connections.

3. Click on the **Dashboard** tab. Here you can see in the **Sessions** pane the **VPN Remote Client** connections (Figure 6.24).

Figure 6.24 The ISA Firewall Dashboard (New)

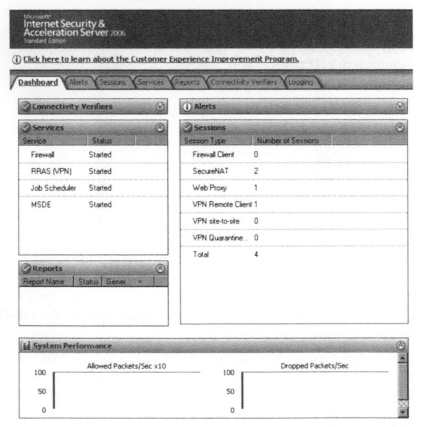

4. You can also use the real-time logging feature to see VPN client connections. Click on the **Logging** tab, and then click the **Tasks** tab in the Task pane. Click **Start Query**. You can use the filter capabilities to focus on specific VPN clients or only the VPN Clients network. Figure 6.25 shows the log file entries.

Figure 6.25 Log File Entries for the VPN Client Connection

9/7, 9/7/2007 11:06:31 AM	255.255.255.255	138	NetBios Datagram	Denied Connection	Default rule	10.0.0.108		VPN Clients	Local Host
9/7, 9/7/2007 11:06:31 AM	10.0.0.2	137	NetBios Name Ser...	Initiated Connection	VPN Client to Internal	10.0.0.108		VPN Clients	Internal
9/7, 9/7/2007 11:06:31 AM	10.0.0.2	53	DNS	Closed Connection	VPN Client to Internal	10.0.0.108	Administrator	VPN Clients	Internal
9/7, 9/7/2007 11:06:31 AM	10.0.0.2	0	Ping	Initiated Connection	VPN Client to Internal	10.0.0.108	Administrator	VPN Clients	Internal

As said before the new logging features brought by the ISA 2004 SP3 are not available on ISA 2006 Firewall.

Using a Pre-shared Key for VPN Client Remote Access Connections

As mentioned earlier in this chapter, you can use pre-shared keys for IPSec authentication if you don't have a PKI setup. The ISA firewall can be configured to support both pre-shared keys and certificates for VPN remote access client connections. The VPN client must support pre-shared keys for IPSec authentication. You can download the updated Windows L2TP/IPSec VPN client at http://download.microsoft.com/download/win98/Install/1.0/W9XNT4Me/EN-US/msl2tp.exe. This VPN client, a free download, allows Windows 9X, Windows Millennium and Windows 2000 client operating systems to use L2TP/IPSec with pre-shared keys.

The ISA firewall must be configured to support pre-shared keys. Perform the following steps to configure the ISA firewall to support pre-shared keys for IPSec authentication:

1. In the Microsoft Internet Security and Acceleration Server **2006** management console, expand the server name, and click the Virtual Private Networking (VPN) node.

2. Click the Select Authentication Methods link on the Tasks tab in the Task pane.

3. In the Virtual Private Networks (VPN) Properties dialog box, put a checkmark in the Allow **custom IPSec** policy for L2TP connection checkbox. Enter a pre-shared key in the Pre-shared key text box. Make sure that the key is complex and contains letters, numbers, and symbols (see Figure 6.26). Make the key at least 17 characters in length.

Figure 6.26 The Authentication Tab

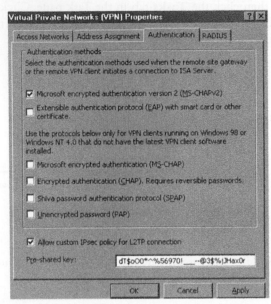

4. Click **Apply**, and then click **OK** in the **ISA** 2006 dialog box informing you that the Routing and Remote Access Service must be restarted. Click **OK** in the **Virtual Private Networking (VPN) Properties** dialog box.

5. Click **Apply** to save the changes and update the firewall policy.

6. Click **OK** in the **Saving Configuration Changes** dialog box.

You need to configure the VPN client to support a pre-shared key. The procedures will vary with the client you're using. The following describes how to configure the Windows XP VPN client to use a pre-shared key:

1. Open the VPN connectoid that you use to connect to the ISA firewall and click the **Properties** button.

2. In the connectoid's **Properties** dialog box, click the **Security** tab.

3. On the **Security** tab, click the **IPSec Settings** button.

4. In the **IPSec Settings** dialog box, put a checkmark in the **Use a pre-shared key for authentication** checkbox, and then enter the key in the **Key** text box as shown in Figure 6.27. Click **OK**.

Figure 6.27 Enter a pre-shared key on the L2TP/IPSec client

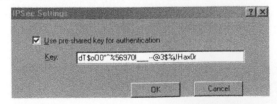

5. Click **OK** in the connectoid's **Properties** dialog box.

6. Connect to the ISA firewall. You can see that the pre-shared key is used for the IPSec connection by viewing the connection's characteristics in the **IPSec Security Monitor** MMC snap-in (Figure 6.28).

Figure 6.28 Viewing IPSec Information in the IPSec MMC

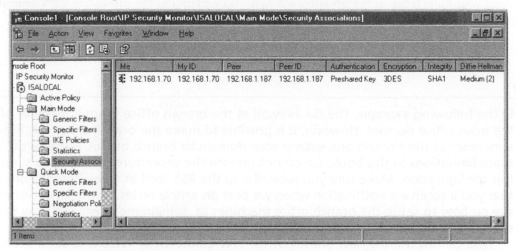

Creating a PPTP Site-to-Site VPN

Site-to-site VPNs allow you to connect entire networks to one another. This can lead to significant cost savings for organizations that are using dedicated frame relay links to connect branch offices to the main office, or branch offices to one another. The ISA firewall supports site-to-site VPN networking using the following VPN protocols:

- PPTP (Point-to-Point Tunneling Protocol)

- L2TP/IPSec (Layer Two Tunneling Protocol over IPSec)

- IPSec Tunnel Mode

The most secure VPN protocol for site-to-site VPNs is the L2TP/IPSec VPN protocol. L2TP/IPSec allows you to require both machine and user authentication. If you connect two ISA 2004/2006 Firewalls you should use LT2P/IPSec. IPSec tunnel mode should only be used when you need to connect to down-level VPN gateways. The major problem with IPSec tunnel mode *might be* that most down-level VPN gateway vendors require you to use a pre-shared key instead of certificate authentication, and there are a number of exploits that can take advantage of this situation (In the case of ISA 2004/2006 you must use a very long, complex and unguessable pre-shared key and you will stay out of trouble, ISA is using only IKE Main Mode and not IKE Aggressive Mode).

The use of PPTP should be avoided (it is the weakest VPN protocol available on ISA 2006).

Creating a site-to-site VPN used to be a complex process in ISA 2004 days, because of the number of steps involved. However, with the ISA 2006 new site-to-site wizard, you'll find that setting up a site-to-site VPN is a lot easier than you think. In this section we'll begin with creating a site-to-site

VPN using the PPTP VPN protocol. After we establish the PPTP link, we'll use the link to connect to the Web enrollment site on the enterprise CA at the main office network and install a machine certificate on the branch office ISA firewall.

In the following exercise, the main office ISA firewall is named **ISALOCAL**, and the branch office ISA firewall is named **REMOTEISA**. We will be used the lab network setup described in Chapter 4, so if you don't recall the details of the lab setup, you should take a look at it now. Refreshing your knowledge of the lab setup will help you understand the site-to-site VPN procedures we'll be carrying out.

> **NOTE**
>
> In the following example, the ISA firewall at the branch office is not a member of the main office domain. However, it is possible to make the branch office ISA firewall a member of the domain and extend your domain to branch offices. Because of space limitations in this book, we cannot go into the procedures required to support this configuration. Make sure you subscribe to the RSS feed at www.isaserver.org so that you'll receive a notification when we post an article series on the ISAserver.org site on how to setup the branch office machines as domain members and how to extend your domain into branch offices.
>
> You cannot use the new Branch Office VPN Connectivity Wizard to set a site-to-site VPN connection using the weak PPTP protocol.
>
> Another important consideration in the following walkthrough is that we are using DHCP to assign IP addresses to VPN clients and gateways. You can use either DHCP or a static address pool. However, if you choose to use a static address pool and you assign *on subnet* IP addresses to VPN clients and gateways, then you will need to remove those addresses from the definition of the Internal Network (or any other Network for which these might represent overlapping addresses).

You'll need to perform the following steps to get the PPTP site-to-site VPN working (note that with the new ISA 2006 ISA Firewall, most of them are automatically done using the improved site-to-site VPN wizard):

- **Create the Remote Network at the Main Office** A Remote Site Network is what the ISA firewall uses for site-to-site VPN connections. Whenever you connect the ISA firewall to another network using a site-to-site VPN, you must first create the Remote Site Network. The Remote Site Network is then used in Access Rules to control access to and from that Network. The Remote Site Network we create at the main office will represent the IP addresses used at the branch office network.

- **Create the Network Rule at the Main Office** A Network Rule controls the route relationship between Networks. We will configure the site-to-site Network so that there is a Route relationship between the main office and the branch office. We prefer to use Route relationships because not all protocols work with NAT.

- **Create the Access Rules at the Main Office** The Access Rules at the main office will allow all traffic from the main office to reach the branch office and all the traffic from the branch office to reach the main office. On your production network, you will likely want to lock down your rules a bit so that branch office users can only access the information they require at the main office. For example, if branch office users only need to access the OWA sites at the main office, then create Access Rules that only allow users access to the HTTPS protocol to the OWA server.

- **Create the VPN Gateway Dial-in Account at the Main Office** We must create a user account that the branch office ISA firewall can use to authenticate with the main office ISA firewall. This account is created on the main office ISA firewall. When the branch office ISA firewall calls the main office ISA firewall, the branch office will use this user name and password to authenticate with the main office. The branch office ISA firewall's demand-dial interface is configured to use this account.

- **Create the Remote Network at the Branch Office** Once the site-to-site VPN configuration is done at the main office, we move our attention to the branch office's ISA firewall. At the branch office ISA firewall, we begin by creating the Remote Site Network that represents the IP addresses in use at the main office. We'll use this Network Object to control traffic moving to and from the main office from the Branch office.

- **Create the Network Rule at the Branch Office** As we did at the main office, we need to create a Network Rule controlling the route relationship for communications between the branch office network and the main office network. We'll configure the Network Rule so that there is a Route relationship between the branch office and the main office.

- **Create the Access Rules at the Branch Office** We will create two Access Rules on the branch office ISA firewall. One allows all traffic to the branch office to reach the main office, and the second rule allows all traffic from the main office to reach the branch office. In a production environment you might wish to limit what traffic can leave the branch office to the main office. Note that you can set these access controls at either or both the branch office and the main office ISA firewall. We prefer to implement the access controls at both sites, but the access controls at the main office are more important because you often may not have change controls tightly regulated at the branch offices.

- **Create the VPN Gateway Dial-in Account at the Branch Office** We need to create a user account on the branch office ISA firewall that the main office ISA firewall can use to authenticate when it calls the branch office ISA firewall. The demand-dial interface on the main office ISA firewall uses this account to authenticate with the branch office ISA firewall.

- **Activate the Site-to-Site Links** We'll activate the site-to-site VPN connection by initiating a connection from a host on the branch office to a host on the main office network.

Create the Remote Site Network at the Main Office

We begin by configuring the ISA firewall at the main office. The first step is to configure the Remote Site Network in the **Microsoft Internet Security and Acceleration Server 2006** management console.

Perform the following steps to create the Remote Site Network at the main office ISA firewall:

1. Open the Microsoft Internet Security and Acceleration Server **2006** management console and expand the server name. Click Virtual Private Networks (VPN).

2. Click on the Remote Sites tab in the Details pane. Click on the Tasks tab in the Task pane. Click **Create VPN** Site-**to-Site Connection**.

3. On the Welcome to the **Create VPN Site-to-Site Connection** Wizard page, enter a name for the remote network in the *Site-to-Site network* name text box. In this example, we will name the remote network Branch. This name is very important because this will be the name of the demand-dial interface created on the ISA firewall at the main office, and it will be the name of the user account that the branch office ISA firewall will use to connect to the main office ISA firewall. Click Next.

On the VPN Protocol page, you have the choice of using IP Security protocol (IPSec tunnel mode, Layer Two Tunneling Protocol (L2TP) over IPSec and Point-to-Point Tunneling Protocol. If you have certificates installed on the main and branch office firewalls, or if you plan to install them in the future, choose the L2TP/IPSec option (you can use the pre-shared key until you get the certificates installed). Do *not* use the IPSec option unless you are connecting to a third-party VPN gateway (because of the low security conferred by IPSec tunnel mode site-to-site links which typically depend on pre-shared keys). In this example, we will configure a site-to-site VPN using PPTP, so select the **Point-to-Point Tunneling Protocol (PPTP)** (as shown in Figure 6.29). Click **Next**.

Figure 6.29 Selecting the VPN Protocol

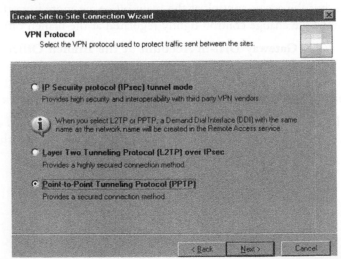

4. A user warning will appear informing you that you must specify a user account at the remote site. The user name must match the name of this site-to-site connection (Branch), the same name as the demand dial interface on this machine. See Figure 6.30. This user account will be created on the main office, with the Dial-in permissions. Click **OK**.

Figure 6.30 PPTP User Warning

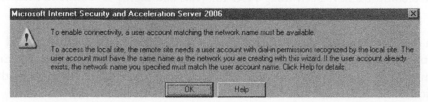

5. With the new ISA 2006 wizard if you did not set the IP Address Assignment method you will be prompted to do it now within the **Local Network VPN Settings** page. If you have a DHCP server select the **Dynamic Host Configuration protocol** (recommended). See Figure 6.31. This will automatically set the Internal Network as the network from where it will be obtain DHCP, DNS and WINS services.

ISA FIREWALL NOTE

The IP address assignment in case of PPTP and L2TP/IPSec will apply to VPN clients and also to VPN gateways. So any changes that you made **on General VPN Configuration** in the **Task** tab of the **Remote Sites** (authentication methods, address assignment, pre-shared key) will reflect into the **VPN General VPN Configuration** of **VPN Clients** in the **Task** tab and vice-versa.

Figure 6.31 Set Address Assignment

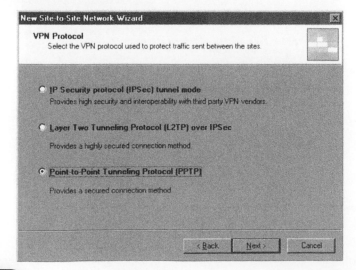

6.   On the **Remote Site Gateway** page, enter the IP address on the external interface of the remote ISA firewall. In this example, the IP address is **192.168.1.71**, so we will enter this value into the text box.

Note that you can also use a fully-qualified domain name in this text box. This is helpful if the branch office uses a dynamic address on its external interface and you use a DDNS service like TZO (www.tzo.com). We have been using TZO for years and highly recommend their service. Click **Next**.

7.   On the **Remote Authentication** page, put a checkmark in the **Allow Local site to initiate connections to remote site using this user account** checkbox. Enter the name of the account that you will create on the remote ISA firewall to allow the main office ISA firewall to authenticate to the branch office ISA firewall.

In this example, the user account will be named **Main** (the user account much match the name of the demand-dial interface created on the remote site; we haven't created that demand-dial interface yet, but we will when we configure the branch office ISA firewall). The **Domain** name is the computer name of the branch office ISA firewall, which in this example is **REMOTEISA** (if the remote ISA firewall were a domain controller, you would use the domain name instead of the computer name, since there are no local accounts stored on a domain controller). Enter a password for the account and confirm the password as shown in Figure 6.32. Make sure that you write down the password so you will remember it when you create the account later on the branch office ISA firewall. Click **Next**.

Figure 6.32 Setting Dial-in Credentials

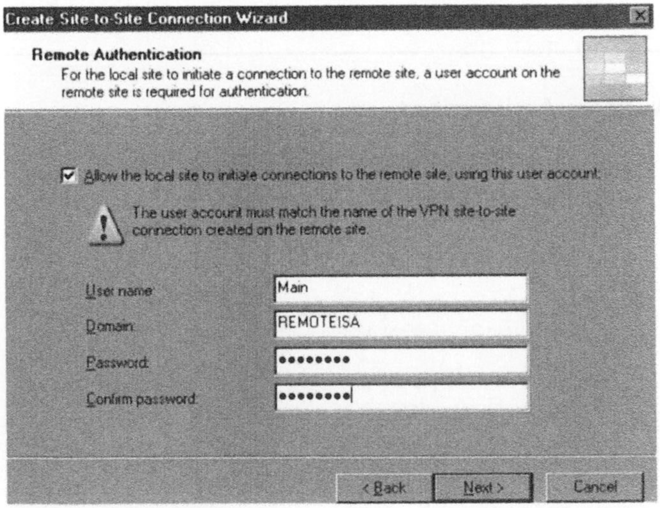

8. Read the information on the **Local Authentication** page, and click **Next**.

The information on this page reminds you that you must create a user account on this ISA firewall that the branch office ISA firewall can use to authenticate when it initiates a site-to-site VPN connection. If you forget to create the user account, the authenticate attempt will fail and the site-to-site VPN link will not establish.

9. Click **Add** on the **Network Addresses** page. In the **IP Address Range Properties** dialog box, enter **10.0.1.0** in the **Starting address** text box. Enter **10.0.1.255** in the **Ending address** text box. Click **OK**.

This is a critical step in your site-to-site VPN configuration. You should include all addresses on the Remote Site Network. While you might create Access Rules that allow access only to a subset of addresses on that network, you should still include all addresses in use on that network. Also, keep in mind any network IDs that are reachable from the branch office ISA firewall. For example, there may be multiple networks reachable from the LAN interface (any of the internal or DMZ interfaces of the branch office ISA firewall). Include all those addresses in this dialog box. See Figure 6.33.

Figure 6.33 Configuring the IP Address Range for the Remote Site Network

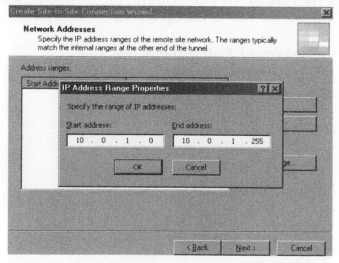

10. Click **Next** on the **Network Addresses** page.

11. With the new ISA 2006 wizard you can define the required network rule in the **Site-to-Site Network Rule** page. A route relationship will be defined between Branch and Internal. See Figure 6.34. Accept and click **Next**.

Figure 6.34 Site-to-site Wizard: Define the Network Rule

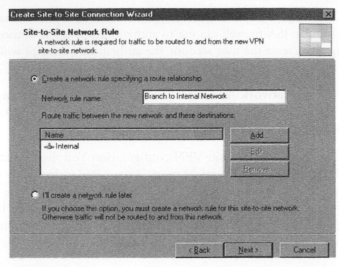

12. With the new ISA 2006 wizard you can define the required access rule for allowing communications between the Branch Network and the Internal Network in the **Site-to-Site Network Access Rule** page. See Figure 6.35. Select **All outbound traffic** in the **Apply the rule to these protocols** list. Click **Next**.

Figure 6.35 Site-to-site Wizard: Define the Access Rule

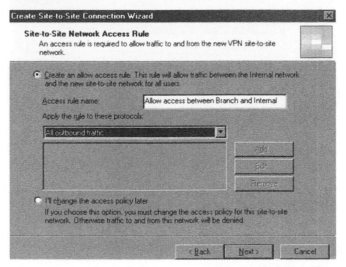

13. Click **Finish** on the **Completing the New VPN Site-to-Site Network Wizard** page.

14. A new window, **The Remaining VPN Site-to-Site Tasks** dialog box will appear. It tells us that we need to define a local account name Branch that will be used by the remote ISA Firewall to authenticate against the local ISA Firewall (in case the remote ISA is acting as the Calling Gateway and local ISA as the Answering Gateway). See Figure 6.36. Click **OK**.

Figure 6.36 The user account to be defined

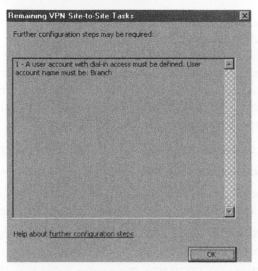

15. Click **Apply** to save the changes. As you have seen, with ISA 2006 you completed many tasks on the fly.

16. You can check the site-to-site summary by right-clicking on the new Branch remote site and click Summary. The site-to-site summary is shown in Figure 6.37.

Figure 6.37 The Site-to-Site Summary

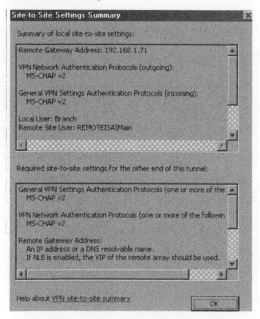

If you scroll **the Summary of local site-to-site settings** you will see a **Routable Local IP Addresses** field. This one comprises IP addresses from 10.0.0.0 to 10.0.0.255(the main office ISA Internal Network). It tells you that you have a network rule in place between the remote site and the

Internal Network. Also you can check the incoming and outgoing authentication protocols, the local and remote users. So the small summary can be very useful.

One thing you must do at the main office ISA is to disable automatic DNS registration on the demand-dial interfaces for the ISA 2006 Firewall using the RRAS console. The changing of the DDNS registration for the demand-dial interface is not overwritten by the ISA Firewall VPN configuration. When the demand-dial interface registers with the DDNS, it can causes problems.

Perform the following steps at the main office ISA Firewall:

1. Click **Start**, point to **Administrative Tools** and click **Routing and Remote Access**.

2. In the **Routing and Remote Access** console, expand the server name.

3. Click on the **Network Interfaces** node in the left pane of the console. Right click on the **Branch** entry in the right pane of the console and click **Properties**.

4. In the **Branch Properties** dialog box, click the **Networking** tab and then click the **Properties** button.

5. On the **Internet Protocol (TCP/IP) Properties** dialog box, click the **Advanced** button.

6. In the **Advanced TCP/IP Settings** dialog box, click the **DNS** tab. On the **DNS** tab, remove the checkmark from the **Register this connection's addresses in DNS** checkbox. Click **OK**. See Figure 6.38.

7. Click **OK** in the **Internet Protocol (TCP/IP) Properties** dialog box. Click **OK** in the **Branch Properties** dialog box.

8. Close the **Routing and Remote Access** console.

Figure 6.38 Register this connection's addresses in DNS checkbox

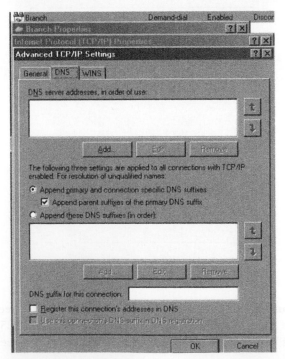

The Network Rule at the Main Office

The ISA firewall must know how to route packets to the branch office network. There are two options: **Route** and **NAT**. A Route relationship routes packets to the branch office and preserves the source IP address of the clients making a connection over the site-to-site link. A NAT relationship replaces the source IP address of the client making the connection. In general, the route relationship provides a higher level of protocol support, but the NAT relationship provides a higher level of security because it hides the original source IP address of the host on the NATed side.

One important reason for why you might want to use a Route relationship is if you plan to have domain members on the Remote Site Network. Kerberos authentication embeds the source IP address in the payload and has no NAT editor or application filter to make this work.

In Figure 6.39 you can see the network rule, with a route relationship, created by the site-to-site wizard.

Figure 6.39 The Network Relationship Page

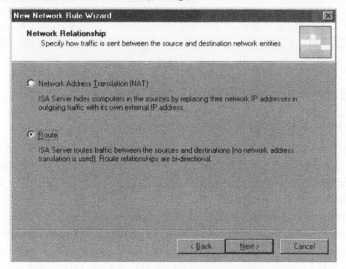

The Access Rules at the Main Office

We want hosts on both the main and branch office networks to have full access to all resources on each network. We must create Access Rules allowing traffic from the main office to the branch office and from the branch office to the main office.

NOTE

In a production environment, you would lock down access quite a bit and allow branch office users access only to the resources they require at the main office. In addition, you may not wish to allow main office users access to any resources at the branch office. Or perhaps you want to limit access from the main office to the branch office to only members of the Administrators group.

Figure 6.40 shows the resulting firewall policy after we have run the site-to-site wizard were we created the access rule allowing communications between the branch office and the main office.

Figure 6.40 The Resulting Firewall Policy

Create the VPN Gateway Dial-in Account at the Main Office

You must create a user account on the main office firewall that the branch office firewall can use to authenticate the site-to-site VPN link. This user account *must have the same name* as the demand-dial interface on the main office computer. You will later configure the branch office ISA 2006 to use this account when it dials the VPN site-to-site link.

User accounts and demand-dial interface naming conventions are a common source of confusion for ISA firewall administrators. The key here is that the calling VPN gateway must present credentials with a user name *that is the same as the name of the demand-dial interface answering the call*. In Figure 6.31, you can see how this works when the main office calls the branch office and when the branch office calls the main office.

The name of the demand dial interface at the main office is **Branch**. When the branch office calls the main office, the user account the branch office uses to authenticate with the main office ISA firewall is **Branch**. Because the name of the user account is the same as the name of the demand-dial interface, the main office ISA firewall knows that it's a remote VPN gateway making the call, and the ISA firewall does *not* treat this as a remote access VPN client connection.

When the main office calls the branch office, it presents the user credentials of a user named **Main**, which is the same name as the demand-dial interface on the branch office ISA firewall. Because the name of the user account presented during authentication is the same as the name of the demand-dial interface, the branch office ISA firewall knows that this is a VPN gateway connection (VPN router) and not a remote access client VPN connection. Figure 6.41 shows the demand dial interface configuration.

Figure 6.41 Demand Dial Interface Configuration on Local and Remote Sites

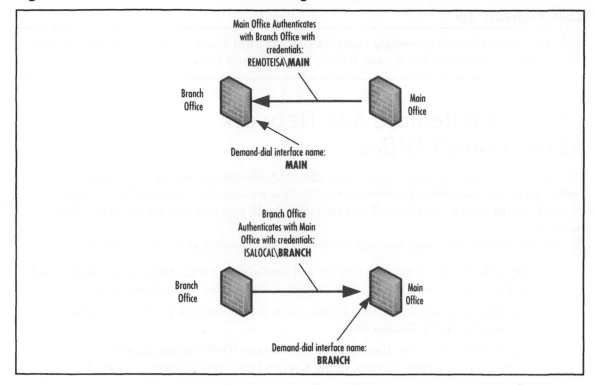

Perform the following steps to create the account the remote ISA 2006 firewall will use to connect to the main office VPN gateway:

1. Right-click **My Computer** on the desktop, and click **Manage**.

2. In the **Computer Management** console, expand the **Local Users and Groups** node. Right-click the **Users** node, and click **New User**.

3. In the **New User** dialog box, enter the name of the main office demand-dial interface. In our current example, the demand-dial interface is named **Branch**. Enter **Branch** into the text box. Enter a **Password** and confirm the **Password**. Write down this password because you'll need to use it when you configure the branch office ISA firewall. Remove the checkmark from the **User must change password at next logon** checkbox. Place checkmarks in the **User cannot change password** and **Password never expires** checkboxes. Click **Create**.

4. Click **Close** in the **New User** dialog box.

5. Double-click the **Branch** user in the right pane of the console.

6. In the **Branch Properties** dialog box, click the **Dial-in** tab. Select **Allow access**.

7. Click **Apply**, and then click **OK**.

8. Restart the ISA firewall computer.

ISA FIREWALL TIP

You should use an extremely complex password for these accounts, which includes a mix of upper and lower case letters, numbers, and symbols.

Create the Remote Site Network at the Branch Office

We can now turn our attention to the branch office ISA firewall. We will repeat the same steps we performed on the main office ISA firewall, but this time we begin by creating a Remote Site Network on the branch office firewall that represents the IP addresses used on the main office network.

Perform the following steps to create the Remote Site Network at the branch office:

1. Open the Microsoft Internet Security and Acceleration Server **2006** management console and expand the server name. Click the Virtual Private Networks (VPN) node.

2. Click Remote Sites in the Details pane. Click Tasks in the Task pane. Click **Create VPN Site-to-Site VPN Connection**.

3. On the Welcome to the **Create VPN Site-to-Site VPN Connection** Wizard page, enter a name for the remote network in the **Site-to-Site** Network name text box. In this example, we will name the remote network Main. Click Next.

4. On the VPN Protocol page, select Point-to-Point Tunneling Protocol (PPTP), and click Next. Click **OK** on the warning box.

5. Select the IP address assignment method on the Local Network VPN Settings page. If you have a DHCP server on the branch office you can specify "**Dynamic Host Configuration Protocol**". If not you must use static, say 10.0.1.252 to 10.0.1.255. Attention, you must exclude this IP addresses from the Internal Network range. Therefore define the Internal Network range as 10.0.1.0 to 10.10.0.251.

6. On the Remote Site Gateway page, enter the IP address on the external interface of the main office ISA firewall. In this example, the IP address is 192.168.1.70, so we will enter this value into the text box. Click Next.

7. On the Remote Authentication page, put a checkmark by **Allow** Local site **to** initiate connections to remote site using **this user account**. Enter the name of the account that you created on the main office ISA firewall to allow the branch office VPN gateway access.

In this example, the user account is named **Branch** (the user account much match the name of the demand-dial interface created at the main office). The Domain name is the name of the remote ISA 2006 firewall computer, which, in this example, is **ISALOCAL** (if the remote ISA firewall was a domain member and the user was a domain user, you would use the *domain name* instead of the computer name). Enter the password for the account and confirm the password as shown in Figure 6.42. Click **Next**.

Figure 6.42 Configure Dial-in Credentials

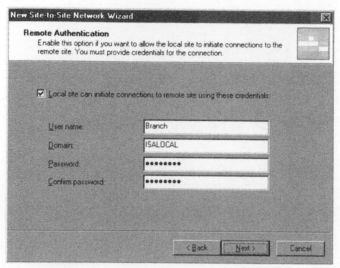

1. Click Add on the Network Addresses page. In the IP Address Range Properties dialog box, enter 10.0.0.0 in the Starting address text box. Enter 10.0.0.255 in the Ending address text box. Click OK.

2. Click Next on the Network Addresses page.

3. Create the Network Rule on the Site-to-Site Network Rule page between Internal and the remote site. Click Next.

4. Define the Access Rule on the Site-to-Site Network Access Rule between Main and Internal. Select All outbound traffic in the Apply the rule to this protocols list. Click Next.

5. Click Finish on the Completing the New VPN Site-to-Site Network Wizard page.

6. The new window, The Remaining VPN Site-to-Site Tasks dialog box will appear. It tells you that you need to define a local account name Main that will be used by the remote main office ISA Firewall to authenticate against the branch office ISA Firewall. Click OK.

7. Click Apply to save the changes.

8. Right-click on the new Main remote site and click **Summary** in order to quickly check the settings of the site-to-site connection. Figure 6.43 shows the **site-to-site summary**.

Figure 6.43 Site-to-Site Summary

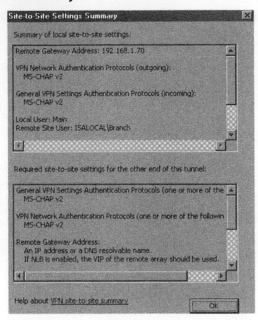

One thing you could do at the branch office ISA is to disable automatic DNS registration on the demand-dial interfaces for the ISA 2006 Firewall using the RRAS console. Just in case you later add the branch ISA 2006 Firewall to the domain.

The Network Rule at the Branch Office

The network rule was already created for you by the site-to-site wizard. Figure 6.44 shows the network rule.

Figure 6.44 The Network Rule

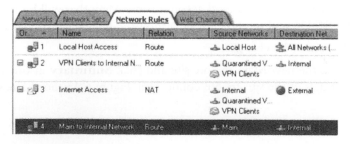

The Access Rules at the Branch Office

The access rule was already created for you by the site-to-site wizard. See Figure 6.45.

Figure 6.45 The Resulting Firewall Policy

Create the VPN Gateway Dial-in Account at the Branch Office

We must create a user account the main office VPN gateway can use to authenticate when it initiates the VPN site-to-site connection to the branch office. The user account must have the same name as the demand-dial interface created on the branch office machine, which, in this example, is **Main**.

Perform the following steps to create the account the main ISA 2006 firewall will use to connect to the branch office VPN gateway:

1. Right-click **My Computer** on the desktop, and click **Manage**.

2. In the **Computer Management** console, expand the **Local Users and Groups** node. Right-click the **Users** node, and click **New User**.

3. In the **New User** dialog box, enter the name of the main office demand-dial interface. In our current example, the demand-dial interface is named **Main**. Enter **Main** into the text box. Enter a **Password** and confirm the **Password**. This is the same password you used when you created the Remote Site Network at the Main office. Remove the checkmark from the **User must change password at next logon** checkbox. Place checkmarks in the **User cannot change password** and **Password never expires** checkboxes. Click **Create**.

4. Click **Close** in the **New User** dialog box.

5. Double-click the **Main** user in the right pane of the console.

6. In the **Main Properties** dialog box, click the **Dial-in** tab (Figure 6.46). Select **Allow access**. Click **Apply**, and then click **OK**.

Figure 6.46 The Dial-in Tab

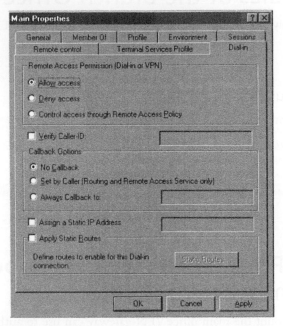

7. Restart the ISA firewall computer.

Activate the Site-to-Site Links

Now that both the main and branch office ISA firewalls are configured as VPN routers, you can test the site-to-site connection.

Perform the following steps to test the site-to-site link:

1. At the remote client computer behind the remote ISA 2006 firewall machine, click **Start**, and then click **Run**.

2. In the **Run** dialog box, enter **cmd** in the **Open** text box, and click **OK**.

3. In the command prompt window, enter **ping –t 10.0.0.2**, and press ENTER

4. You will see a few pings time out, and then the ping responses will be returned by the domain controller on the main office network.

5. Perform the same procedures at the domain controller at the main office network, but this time ping **10.0.1.2**.

TIP

If the site-to-site connection fails, check to make sure that you have defined valid IP address assignments to VPN clients and gateways. A common reason for failure of site-to-site VPN connections is that the ISA firewalls are not able to obtain an address from a DHCP server, and there are no addresses defined for a static address pool. When this happens, the ISA firewall assigns VPN clients and gateways IP addresses in the autonet range (169.254.0.0/16). When both gateways are assigned addresses in the autonet range, both machines' demand-dial interfaces are located on the same network ID and this causes the site-to-site link to fail.

Creating an L2TP/IPSec Site-to-Site VPN

We recommend that you use L2TP/IPSec as your VPN protocol for site-to-site VPN connections. L2TP/IPSec is more secure than PPTP and IPSec tunnel mode. However, to ensure that you have a secure site-to-site VPN connection using L2TP/IPSec, you must use machine certificates on all ISA firewall VPN gateways.

We can leverage the PPTP VPN site-to-site link we created in the previous section to allow the branch office ISA firewall access to the Web enrollment site of the enterprise CA located on the main office network.

We will perform the following procedures to enable the L2TP/IPSec site-to-site VPN link:

■ **Enable the System Policy Rule on the Main office firewall to access the enterprise CA** We will enable a system policy rule that allows the ISA firewall to connect from the Local Host Network to all Networks. While, ostensibly, this rule is to allow for CRL checking, we can use it to allow the ISA firewall at the main office access to the Web enrollment site on the Internal network.

■ **Request and install a Web site certificate for the Main office firewall** Once we connect to the Web enrollment site, we will request an Administrator certificate that we will install into the main office's local machine certificate store. We will also install the enterprise CA's certificate into the main office ISA firewall's Trusted Root Certification Authorities machine certificate store.

■ **Configure the main office ISA firewall to use L2TP/IPSec for the site-to-site link** The Remote Site Network configuration that defines the branch office Network is set to use PPTP for the site-to-site link. We need to change this so that L2TP/IPSec is used instead of PPTP.

■ **Enable the System Policy Rule on the Branch office firewall to access the enterprise CA** For the same reason we did so on the main office ISA firewall, we need to enable a System Policy rule that will allow the branch office's Local Host Network access to the Web enrollment site on the main office network.

- **Request and install a Web site certificate for the Branch office firewall** When the PPTP site-to-site link is established, the branch office ISA firewall will be able to connect to the Web enrollment site over that connection. We will install an Administrator certificate on the branch office firewall in its machine certificate store, and install the CA certificate for the main office enterprise CA in the branch office ISA firewall's Trusted Root Certification Authorities machine certificate store.

- **Configure the branch office ISA firewall to use L2TP/IPSec for the site-to-site link** The Remote Site Network representing the main office network must be configured to use L2TP/IPSec instead of PPTP for the site-to-site link.

- **Establish the IPSec Site-to-Site Connection** After we install the certificates and make the changes to the ISA firewall configurations, we'll trigger the site-to-site link and see the L2TP/IPSec connection in the ISA firewall's Monitoring node.

- **Configuring Pre-shared keys for Site-to-Site L2TP/IPSec VPN Links** This is an optional procedure. While we prefer that everyone use certificates for machine authentication, we realize that this is not always possible. We discuss the procedures you can use to support pre-shared key authentication for your L2TP/IPSec site-to-site VPN links.

Enable the System Policy Rule on the Main Office Firewall to Access the Enterprise CA

The ISA 2006 firewall is locked down by default and only a very limited set of protocols and sites are allowed outbound from the ISA firewall immediately after installation. As for any other communications moving through the ISA firewall, Access Rules are required to allow the firewall access to *any* network or network host. We will need to configure the ISA firewall at the main office with an Access Rule allowing it HTTP access to the Web enrollment site. We could create an Access Rule, or we could enable a System Policy rule. Creating an Access Rule allowing access from the Local Host Network to the enterprise CA using only the HTTP protocol would be more secure, but it's easier to enable the System Policy rule. In this example, we will enable a System Policy Rule that allows the firewall access to the Web enrollment site.

Perform the following steps to enable the System Policy rule on the Main Office firewall:

1. In the **Microsoft Internet Security and Acceleration Server 2006** management console, expand the server name, and click the **Firewall Policy** node.

2. Right-click **Firewall Policy**; point to **View**, and click **Show System Policy Rules**.

3. In the System Policy Rule list, double-click **Allow HTTP from ISA Server to all networks (for CRL downloads).** This is System Policy Rule #*18*.

4. In the **System Policy Editor** dialog box, check the **Enable** checkbox on the **General** tab as shown in Figure 6.47. Click **OK**.

Figure 6.47 Configuring System Policy

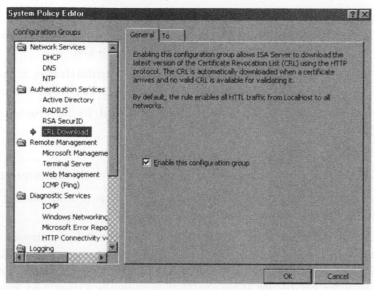

5. Click **Apply** to save the changes and update the firewall policy.

6. Click **OK** in the **Saving Configuration Changes** dialog box.

7. Click **Show/Hide System Policy Rules** (on the far right of the button bar in the MMC console) to hide System Policy.

Figure 6.48 and Figure 6.49 The Show/Hide System Policy Rules Button

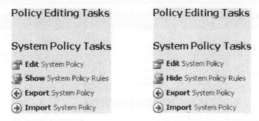

Request and Install a Certificate for the Main Office Firewall

The next step is to request a certificate from the enterprise CA's Web enrollment site. After obtaining the certificate, we will copy the CA certificate into the ISA firewall's **Trusted Root Certification Authorities** certificate store.

Perform the following steps on the main office ISA firewall to request and install the certificates:

1. Open **Internet Explorer**. In the **Address** bar, enter **http://10.0.0.2/certsrv** (where 10.0.0.2 is the IP address of the enterprise CA), and click **OK**.

2. In the **Enter Network Password** dialog box, enter **Administrator** in the **User Name** text box, and enter the **Administrator's** password in the **Password** text box. Click **OK**.

3. In the **Internet Explorer** security dialog box, click **Add**. In the **Trusted Sites** dialog box, click **Add** and **Close**.

4. Click **Request a Certificate** on the **Welcome** page.

5. On the **Request a Certificate** page, click **advanced certificate request**.

6. On the **Advanced Certificate Request** page, click **Create and submit a request to this CA**.

7. On the **Advanced Certificate Request** page, select the **Administrator** certificate from the **Certificate Template** list as shown in Figure 6.50. Remove the checkmark from the **Mark keys as exportable** checkbox. Place a checkmark in the **Store certificate in the local computer certificate store** checkbox as shown in Figure 6.51. It is recommended to use **Key Sizes** of 2048 bits. Click **Submit**.

Figure 6.50 The Advanced Certificate Request Page

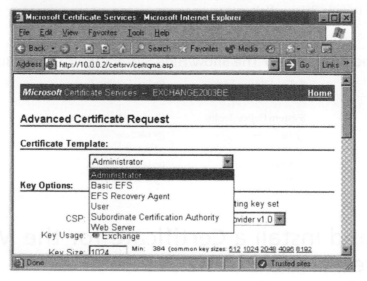

Figure 6.51 The Store Certificate in the Local Computer Certificate Store Option

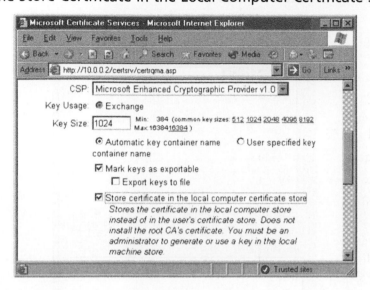

8. Click Yes in the Potential Scripting Violation dialog box.

9. On the Certificate Issued page, click Install this certificate.

10. Click Yes on the Potential Scripting Violation page.

11. Close the browser after viewing the Certificate Installed page.

12. Click Start, and then click Run. Enter mmc in the Open text box, and click OK.

13. In Console1, click the File menu, and then click Add/Remove Snap-in.

14. Click Add in the Add/Remove Snap-in dialog box.

15. Select the Certificates entry in the Available Standalone Snap-ins list in the Add Standalone Snap-in dialog box. Click Add.

16. Select Computer account on the Certificates snap-in page.

17. Select Local computer on the Select Computer page.

18. Click Close in the Add Standalone Snap-in dialog box.

19. Click OK in the Add/Remove Snap-in dialog box.

20. In the left pane of the console, expand Certificates (Local Computer), and then expand Personal. Click on PersonalCertificates. Double-click on the Administrator certificate in the right pane of the console.

21. In the Certificate dialog box, click the Certification Path tab. The root CA certificate is at the top of the certificate hierarchy seen in the Certification path frame. Click the EXCHANGE2003BE certificate (which is the CA that issued the Administrator certificate) at the top of the list. Click View Certificate (Figure 6.52).

Figure 6.52 The Certificate Path Tab

22. In the CA certificate's **Certificate** dialog box, click the **Details** tab. Click **Copy to File**.

23. Click **Next** in the **Welcome to the Certificate Export Wizard** page.

24. On the **Export File Format** page, select **Cryptographic Message Syntax Standard – PKCS #7 Certificates (.P7B)**, and click **Next**.

25. On the **File to Export** page, enter **c:cacert** in the **File name** text box. Click **Next**.

26. Click **Finish** on the **Completing the Certificate Export Wizard** page.

27. Click **OK** in the **Certificate Export Wizard** dialog box.

28. Click **OK** in the **Certificate** dialog box. Click **OK** again in the **Certificate** dialog box.

29. In the left pane of the console, expand **Trusted Root Certification Authorities** and click the **Certificates** node. Right-click **Trusted Root Certification Authorities\ Certificates**; point to **All Tasks**, and click **Import**.

30. Click **Next** on the **Welcome to the Certificate Import Wizard** page.

31. On the **File to Import** page, use **Browse** to locate the CA certificate you saved to the local hard disk, and click **Next**.

32. On the **Certificate Store** page, accept the default settings, and click **Next**.

33. Click **Finish** on the **Completing the Certificate Import Wizard** page.

34. Click **OK** in the **Certificate Import Wizard** dialog box informing you that the import was successful.

Configure the Main Office ISA Firewall to use L2TP/IPSec for the Site-to-Site Link

The Remote Site Network on the main office ISA firewall representing the branch office network is configured to use PPTP for the site-to-site connection. We need to change this to L2TP/IPSec. Perform the following steps to make the change:

1. In the **Microsoft Internet Security and Acceleration Server 2006** management console, expand the server name, and then click the **Virtual Private Networks (VPN)** node in the left pane of the console.

2. On the **Virtual Private Networks (VPN)** node, click the **Remote Sites** tab in the Details pane. Double-click the **Branch** Remote Site Network entry.

3. In the **Branch Properties** dialog box, **Protocol** tab, select the **L2TP/IPSec (provides a highly secure connection method)** option. Click **Apply** and then click **OK**.

4. Do *not* apply the new configuration to the Firewall Policy yet. This will break our PPTP site-to-site link, and we need this PPTP site-to-site link to stay up until we have installed a certificate on the branch office ISA firewall. After the branch office ISA firewall has been configured, and then you can apply the changes to the Firewall Policy at the main office.

5. Take a look at the **site-to-site summary** (Figure 6.53). It gives you information about the incoming and outgoing authentication methods (for both IKE and PPP), about the remote and local user, the remote IP address ranges and the routable local IP addresses (we have a network rule between Branch and Internal).

Figure 6.53 L2TP/IPSec site-to-site summary

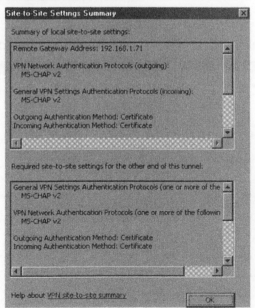

If this was the first site-to-site connection, because you do not want to use PPTP at all and you were using the new site-to-site wizard, then you would have the chance to specify the incoming L2TP/IPSec authentication method (in case you select as the outgoing authentication method the pre-shared key because you currently do not have certificates installed), either allowing or not the pre-shared key for incoming connections, within the site-to-site wizard (Figure 6.55). The same options, like in case of PPTP, specify address assignment, define the network rules and access rules are available for L2TP/IPSec VPN site-to-site connections. As you can see from Figure 6.54 the default outgoing method is certificate authentication.

Figure 6.54 The Outgoing L2TP/IPSec Authentication method

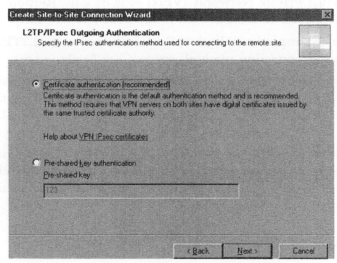

Figure 6.55 The Incoming L2TP/IPSec Authentication method

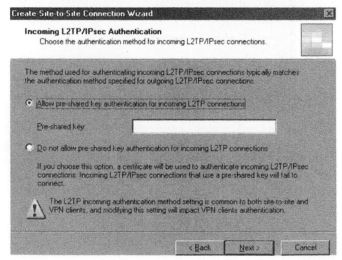

If you use certificates, ISA 2006 will also give you the option to enable System Policy #18 within the site-to-site wizard (Figure 6.56).

Figure 6.56 Enable the System Policy

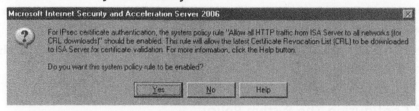

In case of certificate authentication ISA would inform you that you need to assign a proper certificate to ISA and to make available (publish) the CRL within the **Remaining VPN site-to-site Tasks** (Figure 6.57).

Figure 6.57 Remaining Tasks

Enable the System Policy Rule on the Branch Office Firewall to Access the Enterprise CA

Now we'll switch our attention to the branch office ISA firewall. We need to enable the System Policy Rule allowing the branch office firewall to connect to the enterprise CA on the main office network.

Perform the following steps to enable the System Policy rule on the branch office firewall:

1. In the **Microsoft Internet Security and Acceleration Server 2006** management console, expand the server name, and click the **Firewall Policy** node.

2. Right-click **Firewall Policy**; point to **View**, and click **Show System Policy Rules**.

3. In the System Policy Rule list, double-click **Allow HTTP from ISA Server to all networks (for CRL downloads).** This is System Policy Rule #*18*.

4. In the **System Policy Editor** dialog box (Figure 6.58), put a checkmark in the **Enable** checkbox on the **General** tab. Click **OK**.

Figure 6.58 Configuring The System Policy

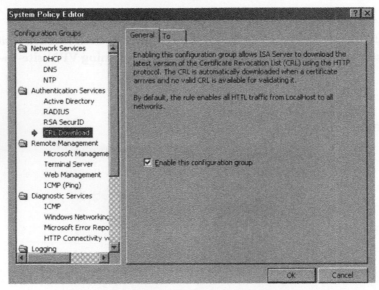

5. Click **Apply** to save the changes and update the firewall policy.

6. Click **OK** in the **Saving Configuration Changes** dialog box

Request and Install a Certificate for the Branch Office Firewall

Now we'll request a certificate for the branch office firewall. After we obtain the certificate, we will copy the CA certificate into the machine's **Trusted Root Certification Authorities** certificate store. Perform the following steps on the branch office ISA firewall to request and install the certificates:

1. Open **Internet Explorer**. In the Address bar, enter **http://10.0.0.2/certsrv**, and click **OK**.

2. In the **Enter Network Password** dialog box, enter **Administrator** in the **User Name** text box, and enter the **Administrator's** password in the **Password** text box. Click **OK**.

3. In the **Internet Explorer** security dialog box, click **Add**. In the **Trusted Sites** dialog box, click **Add and Close**.

4. Click **Request a Certificate** on the **Welcome** page.

5. On the **Request a Certificate** page, click **advanced certificate request**.

6. On the **Advanced Certificate Request** page, click **Create and submit a request to this CA**.

7. On the **Advanced Certificate Request** page, select the **Administrator** certificate from the **Certificate Template** list. Remove the checkmark from the **Mark keys as exportable** checkbox. Place a checkmark in the **Store certificate in the local computer certificate store** checkbox. Click **Submit**.

8. Click **Yes** in the **Potential Scripting Violation** dialog box.

9. On the **Certificate Issued** page, click **Install this certificate**.

10. Click **Yes** on the **Potential Scripting Violation** page.

11. Close the browser after viewing the **Certificate Installed** page.

12. Click **Start** and **Run**. Enter **mmc** in the **Open** text box, and click **OK**.

13. In **Console1**, click the **File** menu, and then click **Add/Remove Snap-in**.

14. Click **Add** in the **Add/Remove Snap-in** dialog box.

15. Select the **Certificates** entry from the **Available Standalone Snap-ins** list in the **Add Standalone Snap-in** dialog box. Click **Add**.

16. Select **Computer account** on the **Certificates snap-in** page.

17. Select **Local computer** on the **Select Computer** page.

18. Click **Close** in the **Add Standalone Snap-in** dialog box.

19. Click **OK** in the **Add/Remove Snap-in** dialog box.

20. In the left pane of the console, expand **Certificates (Local Computer)**, then expand **Personal**. Click on **\Personal\Certificates**. Double-click on the **Administrator** certificate in the right pane of the console.

21. In the **Certificate** dialog box, click the **Certification Path** tab. The root CA certificate is at the top of the certificate hierarchy seen in the Certification path frame. Click the **EXCHANGE2003BE** certificate at the top of the list. Click **View Certificate**.

22. In the CA certificate's **Certificate** dialog box, click **Details**. Click **Copy to File**.

23. Click **Next** in the **Welcome to the Certificate Export Wizard** page.

24. On the **Export File Format** page, select **Cryptographic Message Syntax Standard – PKCS #7 Certificates (.P7B)**, and click **Next**.

25. On the **File to Export** page, enter **c:\cacert** in the **File name** text box. Click **Next**.

26. Click **Finish** on the **Completing the Certificate Export Wizard** page.

27. Click **OK** in the **Certificate Export Wizard** dialog box.

28. Click **OK** in the **Certificate** dialog box. Click **OK** again in the **Certificate** dialog box.

29. In the left pane of the console, expand the **Trusted Root Certification Authorities** node, and click **Certificates**. Right-click the **\Trusted Root Certification Authorities\ Certificates** node; point to **All Tasks** and click **Import**.

30. Click **Next** on the **Welcome to the Certificate Import Wizard** page.

31. On the **File to Import** page, use **Browse** to locate the CA certificate you saved to the local hard disk, and click **Next**.

32. On the **Certificate Store** page, accept the default settings, and click **Next**.

33. Click **Finish** on the **Completing the Certificate Import Wizard** page.

34. Click **OK** on the **Certificate Import Wizard** dialog box informing you that the import was successful.

Configure the Branch Office ISA Firewall to use L2TP/IPSec for the Site-to-Site Link

The Remote Site Network at the branch office ISA firewall representing the main office network is configured to use PPTP for the site-to-site connection. We need to change this to L2TP/IPSec. Perform the following steps to make the change:

1. In the **Microsoft Internet Security and Acceleration Server 2006** management console, expand the server name, and then click the **Virtual Private Networks (VPN)** node in the left pane of the console.

2. On the **Virtual Private Networks (VPN)** node, click the **Remote Sites** tab in the Details pane. Double-click the **Main** Remote Site Network entry.

3. In the **Main Properties** dialog box, **Protocol** tab, select **L2TP/IPSec (provides a highly secure connection method)**. Click **Apply**, and then click **OK**.

4. Click **Apply** to save the changes and update the firewall policy.

5. Click **OK** in the **Saving Configuration Changes** dialog box.

6. Now you can save the changes to the Firewall Policy at the main office.

Activate the L2TP/IPSec Site-to-Site VPN Connection

Let's see if our L2TP/IPSec site-to-site VPN connection works:

1. First, you need to restart the **Routing and Remote Access Service** on both ISA firewalls so that the **Routing and Remote Access Service** recognizes the certificate.

2. In the **Microsoft Internet Security and Acceleration Server 2006** management console, expand the server name and click the **Monitoring** node.

3. On the **Monitoring** node, click the **Services** tab. Right-click the **Routing and Remote Access Service**, and click **Stop**.

4. When the service is stopped, right-click it again, and click **Start**.

5. From a host on the branch office network, ping the domain controller on the main office network.

6. When you receive ping responses, go to the branch office ISA firewall and open the **Microsoft Internet Security and Acceleration Server 2006** management console. Expand the server name, and then click the **Monitoring** node.

7. On the **Monitoring** node, click the **Sessions** tab. On the **Sessions** tab, right-click any of the column headers, and then click the **Application Name** entry (see Figure 6.59).

Figure 6.59 Adding the Application Name column

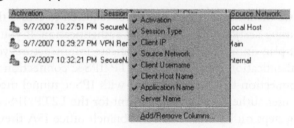

8. In the **Application Name** column you'll see that an L2TP/IPSec connection was established (see Figure 6.60).

Figure 6.60 Viewing the L2TP/IPSec

Activation	Session Type	Client IP	Source Network	Client Username	Client Host Name	Application Name
9/7/2007 10:27:51 PM	SecureNAT	192.168.1.71	Local Host		192.168.1.71	
9/7/2007 10:29:27 PM	VPN Remote Site	10.0.2.2	Main	Main	192.168.1.70	VPN (L2TP/IPSec)

> **NOTE**
>
> In the following example, the ISA firewall at the branch office is not a member of the main office domain. However, it is possible to make the branch office ISA firewall a member of the domain and extend your domain to branch offices.
>
> With ISA 2006 Enterprise Edition, the new Create Answer File Wizard enables you to create an answer file at the main office ISA 2006 Firewall EE, answer file that allows you to make the branch ISA 2006 Firewall EE a domain member. This answer file will be used at the branch office with the new Branch Office Connection Wizard. This automates the entire process of creating the VPN site-to-site connection at the branch office, since all the required settings are provided within the answer file. A simple user can run the wizard and the branch office ISA Firewall will be connected to the main office ISA Firewall.

Because of space limitations in this book, we cannot go into the procedures required to support this configuration. Make sure you read at www.isaserver.org the following seven parts of the article, *Creating a Site to Site VPN using the ISA 2006 Firewall Branch Office Connection Wizard*.
http://www.isaserver.org/tutorials/Creating-VPN-ISA-2006-Firewall-Branch-Office-Connection-Wizard-Part1.html

Configuring Pre-shared Keys for Site-to-Site L2TP/IPSec VPN Links

In the previous example, we demonstrated the procedures required to create the site-to-site L2TP/IPSec connection using certificates for computer authentication. If you don't have a PKI in place yet, or if you do not plan on implementing a certificate infrastructure, you can use pre-shared keys for the computer authentication component of L2TP/IPSec connection establishment. This provides a more secure connection than you would see with IPSec tunnel mode and pre-shared keys, because you still have the user authentication requirement for the L2TP/IPSec connection.

Perform the following steps on both the main and branch office ISA firewalls to enable pre-shared keys for the site-to-site VPN connection:

1. In the **Microsoft Internet Security and Acceleration Server 2006** management console, expand the server name, and then click the **Virtual Private Networking (VPN)** node in the left pane of the console.

2. On the **Virtual Private Networking (VPN)** node, click the **VPN Clients** tab in the Details pane. Or you can click **Remote Sites** too. As said before the changes will reflect from **VPN Clients** to **Remote Sites** and vice-versa.

3. Click the **Tasks** tab in the Task pane. Click the **Select Authentication Methods** link.

4. In the **Virtual Private Networks (VPN) Properties** dialog box, put a checkmark in the **Allow custom IPSec policy for L2TP connection** checkbox and enter the pre-shared key (for incoming authentication).

5. Click **Apply** and then click **OK**.

6. Double-click the remote site. In the **remote site Properties**, **Protocols** tab, put a check into the "**Use pre-shared key IPSec authentication instead of certificate authentication**" check box and enter the pre-shared key (for outgoing authentication). If, for example the pre-shared key (for outgoing authentication) is 12345 on the main ISA Firewall, then on the branch ISA Firewall the pre-shared key for incoming authentication must be 12345 (make sure you use a very long, complex and unguessable pre-shared key).

7. Click **Apply** and then click **OK**.

8. Click **Apply** to save the changes and update the firewall policy.

9. Click **OK** in the **Saving Configuration Changes** dialog box.

IPSec Tunnel Mode Site-to-Site VPNs with Downlevel VPN Gateways

One of the major improvements that the ISA 2004/2006 firewall has over ISA Server 2000 is that it can be configured to use IPSec tunnel mode for site-to-site VPN connections. Most third-party VPN gateways require that you use IPSec tunnel mode for site-to-site VPN connections. It was very difficult to find a third-party VPN gateway that would work with ISA Server 2000. But with the ISA 2004/2006 firewall, you can establish an IPSec tunnel mode site-to-site link with just about any third-party VPN gateway.

Because of the number of third-party VPN gateways available on the market today, it's not possible for us to go into detail on how to configure the ISA firewall to connect to each of these devices. The good news is that Microsoft has published a comprehensive set of documents on how to connect the ISA firewall to a number of popular VPN gateways. At the time of this writing, there are documents on how to connect the ISA firewall to the following VPN gateways:

- Cisco PIX
- Astaro Linux
- SmoothWall Express
- Generic third-party gateways

You can find these documents and more on the Microsoft ISA 2004 VPN documentation site at http://www.microsoft.com/isaserver/techinfo/guidance/2004/vpn.asp

As said before the wizard for IPSec tunnel mode is also updated, so you can specify the network rule and access rules, enable the System Policy for CRL download(in case of authentication with certificates) and the wizard automatically adds for you the remote VPN server IP address into the remote site IP address ranges.

Using RADIUS for VPN Authentication and Remote Access Policy

We prefer to not join front-end ISA firewalls to the user domain. The reason for this is that the network segments between the front-end ISA firewall and back-end firewalls are unauthenticated DMZ segments, and we want to avoid passing domain information through those segments as much as possible.

When the ISA firewall is not a member of the user domain, we must use a mechanism other than Windows to authenticate and authorize domain users. The ISA firewall can authenticate VPN users with RADIUS (Remote Access Dial-In User Service). The RADIUS Protocol allows the ISA 2006 firewall to forward user credentials of a RADIUS server on the Internal network. The RADIUS server sends the authentication request to an authentication server, such as an Active Directory domain controller. The Microsoft implementation of RADIUS is the Internet Authentication Service (IAS).

In addition to authenticating users, the IAS server can be used to centralize Remote Access Policy. For example, if you have six ISA firewall/VPN servers under your administrative control, you can apply the same Remote Access Policy to all these machines by creating policy on an IAS server on your network.

The ISA firewall is not limited to working with just IAS, and it supports all types of RADIUS servers. However, the Microsoft IAS server is included with all Windows 2000 and Windows Server 2003 server family products, which makes it very convenient to use for any Microsoft shop.

In this section we will discuss procedures required to enable RADIUS authentication and RADIUS Remote Access Policy for VPN clients. We will carry out the following procedures:

- Configure the IAS Server

- Create a VPN Clients Remote Access Policy

- Enable the VPN Server on the ISA 2006 firewall and configure RADIUS Support

- Create a VPN Client Access Rule

- Make the connection from a PPTP VPN client

Configure the Internet Authentication Services (RADIUS) Server

If you have not installed the IAS server, you can install it now using the **Add/Remove Programs** Control Panel applet on your Windows 2000 or Windows Server 2003 machines on the Internal Network. You need to configure the IAS server to communicate with the Active Directory and then instruct the IAS server to work with the ISA 2006 firewall/VPN server machine. In our current example, the IAS server is installed on the domain controller on the Internal Network (EXCHANGE2003BE).

Perform the following steps to configure the IAS server:

1. Click Start; point to Administrative Tools, and click on Internet Authentication Services.

2. In the Internet Authentication Services console, right-click on the Internet Authentication Service (Local) node in the left pane of the console. Click the Register Server in Active Directory command.

3. This setting allows the IAS Server to authenticate users in the Active Directory domain. Click OK in the Register Internet Authentication Server in Active Directory dialog box.

4. Click OK in the Server registered dialog box. This dialog box informs you that the IAS Server was registered in a specific domain and if you want this IAS Server to read users' dial-in properties from other domains, you'll need to enter this server into the RAS/IAS Server Group in that domain. This automatically places the machine in the RAS and IAS Server Group in the Active Directory. If you want to register the server in another domain, you must place it in the RAS and IAS Servers group in that domain or use the command netsh ras add registeredserver *Domain IASServer* command.

5. Right-click on the RADIUS Clients node in the left pane of the console, and click the New RADIUS Client command.

6. In the New RADIUS Client dialog box, type in a Friendly name for the ISA firewall. You can use any name you like. In this example we'll use the DNS host name of the ISA firewall, which is ISALOCAL. Enter either the FQDN or the IP address of the ISA 2006

firewall/VPN server in the Client address (IP or DNS) dialog box. Do not enter a FQDN if your ISA firewall has not registered its internal interface IP address with your internal DNS server. You can use the Verify button to test whether the IAS Server can resolve the FQDN. Click Next.

7. On the Additional Information page, leave the RADIUS Standard entry in the Client-Vendor drop-down list box. Your ISA firewall will use this setting. Enter a complex shared secret in the Shared secret text box, and confirm it in the Confirm shared secret text box. The shared secret should be a complex string consisting of upper and lower case letters, numbers, and symbols. Put a checkmark in the Request must contain the Message Authenticator attribute checkbox. This option enhances the security of the RADIUS messages passed between the ISA firewall and IAS servers. Click Finish. See Figure 6.61.

ISA FIREWALL SECURITY ALERT

The shared secret should be very long and complex. We recommend that it be at least 20 characters and contain a mix of upper and lower case letters, numbers, and symbols.

Figure 6.61 Configuring the Shared Secret

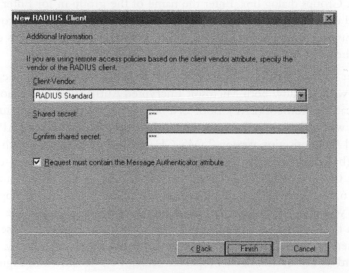

Create a VPN Clients Remote Access Policy

We're now ready to create a Remote Access Policy on the IAS Server. Remote Access Policies configured on the IAS Server are applied to VPN client connections made to the ISA firewall when the ISA firewall is configured to use RADIUS authentication and policy, and when the

ISA firewall is configured as a RADIUS client. Fortunately for us, the Windows Server 2003 IAS server has a Remote Access Policy Wizard that makes it easy to create a secure VPN client Remote Access Policy.

Perform the following steps to create a VPN client Remote Access Policy on the IAS Server:

1. In the Internet Authentication Service console, right-click on the Remote Access Policies node, and click the New Remote Access Policy command.

2. Click Next on the Welcome to the New Remote Access Policy Wizard page.

3. On the Policy Configuration Method page, select Use the wizard to set up a typical policy for a common scenario. In the Policy name text box, type a name for the policy. In this example, we'll call it VPN Access Policy. Click Next.

4. Select the VPN option on the Access Method page. This policy is used for all VPN connections. You have the option to create separate policies for PPTP and L2TP/IPSec VPN links. However, to create separate policies for PPTP and L2TP/IPSec connections, you'll need to go back to the previous page in the Wizard and create two custom policies. In this example, we apply the same policy to all remote access VPN connections. Click Next.

5. You can grant access to the VPN server based on user or group. The best access control method is on a per-group basis because it entails less administrative overhead. You can create a group such as VPN Users and allow them access, or allow all your users access. In this example, we will select the Group option and click the Add button. This brings up the Select Groups dialog box. Enter the name of the group in for Enter the object name to select, and click Check names to confirm that you entered the name correctly. In this example, use the Domain Users group. Click OK in the Select Groups dialog box and Next in the User or Group Access dialog box.

6. Select user authentication methods you want to allow on the Authentication Methods page. You may wish to allow both Microsoft Encrypted Authentication version 2 and Extensible Authentication Protocol (EAP). Both EAP and MS-CHAP version 2 authentication are secure, so we'll select both the Extensible Authentication Protocol (EAP) and Microsoft Encrypted Authentication version 2 (MS-CHAPv2) checkboxes. Click the down arrow from the Type (based on method of access and network configuration) drop-down list and select the Smart Card or other certificate option, then click the Configure button (as shown in Figure 6.62). In the Smart Card or other Certificate Properties dialog box, select the certificate you want the server to use to identify itself to VPN clients. The self-signed certificate appears in the Certificate issued to drop-down list. This certificate is used to identify the server when VPN clients are configured to confirm the server's validity. Click OK in the Smart Card or other Certificate Properties dialog box (as shown in Figure 6.63), and then click Next.

Figure 6.62 The Authentication Method Page

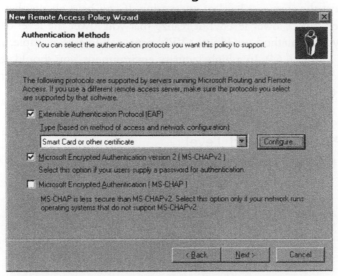

Figure 6.63 The Smart Card or other Certificate Properties Dialog Box

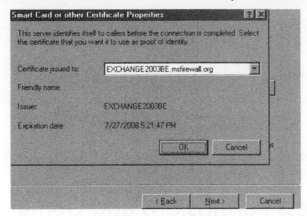

NOTE

If you do not see the certificate in the **Smart Card or other Certificate Properties** dialog box, then restart the RADIUS server and start over. The certificate will then appear in the dialog box after the restart. If you still do not see the certificate, this indicates that either the machine does not have a machine certificate installed on it, or that it has a machine certificate, but it does not trust the CA issuing the certificate. Double-check the machine certificate and the machine's Trusted Root Certification Authorities certificate stores to confirm that you have both these certificates installed.

7. Select the level(s) of encryption you want to enforce on VPN connections. All Microsoft clients support the strongest level of encryption. If you have clients that don't support 128 bit encryption, select lower levels, but realize that you lower the level of security provided by the encryption method used by the VPN protocol. In this example, we'll select all three options (see Figure 6.64). In a high-security environment, you should select on the strongest encryption option. Just make sure all your VPN clients support this level of encryption. Click **Next**.

Figure 6.64 The Policy Encrypted Level

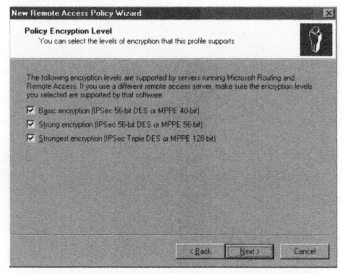

8. Review your settings on the Completing the New Remote Access Policy Wizard page and click Finish.

Remote Access Permissions and Domain Functional Level

The new Remote Access Policy requires the connection be a VPN connection. The VPN protocol can be either PPTP or L2TP/IPSec. The VPN client must use MS-CHAP v2 or EAP-TLS to authenticate, and the client must support the level of encryption set in the Remote Access Policy. The user must belong to the **Domain Users** group in the domain specified in the Remote Access Policy.

The next step is to configure Remote Access Permissions. Remote Access Permissions are different than Remote Access Policies.

When a VPN user calls the ISA firewall, the parameters of the connection are compared against Remote Access Policy (the remote access policy can be either on the ISA firewall itself or on a IAS server). Remote Access Policies are represented as a hierarchical list. The policy on top of the list is evaluated first, then the second-listed policy is evaluated, then the third, and so forth.

The VPN client's connection parameters are compared to the *conditions* in the policy. In the remote access policy we created above, there were two conditions:

- The connection type is a virtual connection, and
- The user is a member of the **Domain Users** group.

If the connection request matches both of those conditions, then Remote Access Permissions are determined. Remote access permissions are determined differently depending on the type of domain the user account belongs to.

Windows Server 2003 domains do not use the Mixed and Native Mode designations you might be familiar with in Windows 2000. Windows Server 2003 supports domains of varying *functional levels*. If all the domain controllers in your domain run Windows Server 2003, the default functional level is *Windows 2000 mixed*. All user accounts are denied VPN (Dial-up) access by default in Windows 2000 Mixed Mode functional level. In Windows 2000 Mixed Mode, *you must configure each user account* to have permission to log on to the VPN server. The reason is that user account permissions override Remote Access Policy permissions in Mixed Mode domains.

If you want to control Remote Access Permissions via Remote Access Policy, you must raise the domain functional level to Windows 2000 Native or Windows Server 2003. The default Remote Access Permission in Windows 2000 and Windows Server 2003 domains is **Control access through Remote Access Policy**. Once you are able to use Remote Access Policy to assign VPN access permission, you can take advantage of group membership to allow or deny VPN access to the VPN server.

When a VPN connection matches the *conditions* in the Remote Access Policy, and the user is granted access via either the user account Dial-in settings or Remote Access Policy, then the VPN connection parameters are compared to a number of settings defined by the *Remote Access Profile*. If the incoming connection does not comply with the settings in the Remote Access Profile, then the next Remote Access Policy is compared to the connection. If no policy matches the incoming connection's parameters, the VPN connection request to the ISA firewall is dropped.

The VPN Remote Access Policy you created earlier includes all the parameters required for a secure VPN connection. Your decision now centers on how you want to control Remote Access Permissions:

- **Enable Remote Access on a per group basis:** this requires that you run in Windows 2000 Native or Windows Server 2003 functional level
- **Enable Remote Access on a per user basis:** supported by Windows 2000 Native, Windows 2000 Mixed and Windows Server 2003 functional levels
- **Enable Remote Access on both a per user and per group basis:** this requires Windows 2000 Native or Windows Server 2003 functional level; granular user-based access control overriding group-based access control is done on a per user basis

Procedures required to allow *per user* and *per group* access include:

- Change the **Dial-in** permissions on the user account in the Active Directory to control Remote Access Permission on a per user basis.
- Change the domain functional level to support Dial-in permissions based on Remote Access Policy.
- Change the Permissions settings on the Remote Access Policy.

Changing the User Account Dial-in Permissions

You enable dial-in permissions on a per account basis, or create Remote Access Policies that can be configured to enable dial-in permissions to entire groups.

Perform the following steps if you want to control access on a per user basis, or if you have no other choice because of your domain's functional level:

1. Click Start; point to Administrative Tools, and click on Active Directory Users and Computers.

2. In the Active Directory Users and Computers console, expand your domain name and click on the User node.

3. Double-click on the Administrator account in the right pane of the console. In the user account Properties dialog box, click on the Dial-in tab. The default setting on the account is Deny access. You can allow VPN access for the account by selecting the Allow access option. Per user account settings override permissions set on the Remote Access Policy. Notice the Control access through Remote Access Policy option is disabled. This option is available only when the domain is at the Windows 2000 or Windows Server 2003 functional level. Make no changes to the account setting at this time. See Figure 6.65.

Figure 6.65 Changing the Dial-in Permissions

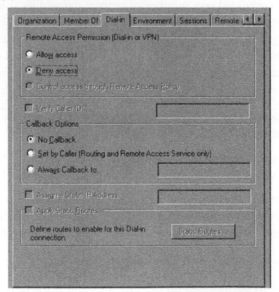

4. Click **Cancel** to escape this dialog box.

Changing the Domain Functional Level

If you want to control access on a per group basis, you will need to change the default domain functional level. Perform the following steps to change the domain functional level:

1. On a domain controller in your domain, open the Active Directory Domains and Trusts console. Click Start; point to Administrative Tools and click on Active Directory Domains and Trusts.

2. In the Active Directory Domains and Trusts console, right-click on your domain, and click on the Raise Domain Functional Level command.

3. In the Raise Domain Functional Level dialog box, click the down arrow in the Select an available domain functional level drop-down list and select either Windows 2000 native or Windows Server 2003, depending on the type of domain functional level your network can support. In this example, we will select the Windows Server 2003 option. Click the Raise button after making your selection (as shown in Figure 6.66).

Figure 6.66 The Raise Domain Functional Level

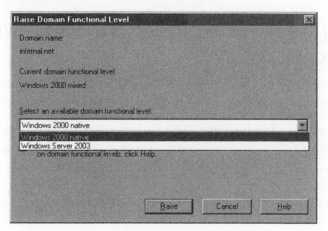

4. Click **OK** in the **Raise Domain Functional Level** dialog box. This dialog box explains that the change affects the entire domain and after the change is made, it cannot be reversed.

5. Click **OK** in the **Raise Domain Functional Level** dialog box informing you that the functional level was raised successfully. Note that you do not need to restart the computer for the changes to take effect. However, the default Remote Access Permission will not change for user accounts until Active Directory replication is completed. In this example, we will restart the computer. Restart the computer now and log in as Administrator.

6. Return to the **Active Directory Users and Computers** console and double-click on a user account. Click on the **Dial-in** tab in the user's **Properties** dialog box. Notice how the **Control access through Remote Access Policy** option is enabled and selected by default (Figure 6.67).

Figure 6.67 Controlling Access via Remote Access Policy

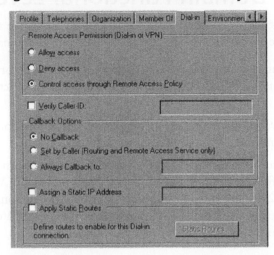

Controlling Remote Access Permission via Remote Access Policy

Now that we have the option to control access via Remote Access Policy (instead of a per user account basis), let's see how VPN access control via Remote Access Policy is performed:

1. Click Start; point to Administrative Tools, and click Internet Authentication Service.

2. Click Remote Access Policies in the left pane of the console. You will see the VPN Access Policy and two other built-in Remote Access Policies. You can delete the other policies if you require only VPN connections to your ISA firewall. Right-click on Connections to other access servers, and click Delete. Repeat with Connections to Microsoft Routing and Remote Access server.

3. Double-click on the VPN Access Policy in the right pane of the console. In the VPN Access Policy Properties dialog box there are two options that control access permissions based on Remote Access Policy:

    ■ Deny remote access permission

    ■ Grant remote access permission

Notice that this dialog box does inform you that the user account settings override the Remote Access Permission settings: **Unless individual access permissions are specified in the user profile, this policy controls access to the network**. Select the **Grant remote access permission** to allow members of the **Domain Users** group access to the VPN server (Figure 6.68).

Figure 6.68 Remote Access Policy Properties

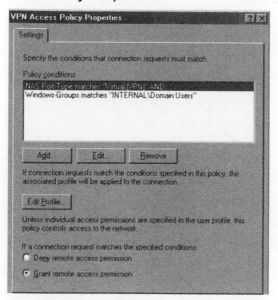

4. Click **Apply** and then click **OK** in the **VPN Access Policy Properties** dialog box to save the changes

Enable the VPN Server on the ISA Firewall and Configure RADIUS Support

After the RADIUS server is installed and configured and Remote Access Policies are in place, we can start configuring the ISA firewall. First, we will first enable the VPN server component and then configure the VPN server to support RADIUS authentication.

Perform the following steps to enable the VPN server and configure it for RADIUS support:

1. In the Microsoft Internet Security and Acceleration Server **2006** management console, expand the server name, and click on Virtual Private Networks (VPN).

2. Click the Tasks tab in the Task pane. Click Enable VPN Client Access.

3. Click Configure VPN Client Access.

4. In the VPN Clients Properties dialog box, put a checkmark in the Enable VPN client access checkbox. Configure the number of VPN clients you want to allow in the Maximum number of VPN allowed text box.

5. Click the Protocols tab. Put checkmarks in the Enable PPTP and Enable L2TP/**IPSec** checkboxes. Click Apply and then click OK. (Figure 6.69).

Figure 6.69 Enabling the VPN Protocols (New)

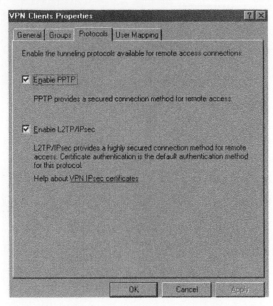

6. Click the Specify RADIUS Configuration link on the Tasks tab.

7. On the RADIUS tab in the Virtual Private Networks (VPN) Properties dialog box (Figure 6.70), put a checkmark in the Use RADIUS for authentication checkbox.

Figure 6.70 Configuring RADIUS Authentication

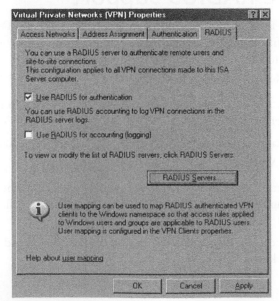

8. Click the **RADIUS Servers** button. In the **RADIUS** dialog box, click **Add**.

9. In the **Add RADIUS Server** dialog box, enter the name of the IAS server machine in the **Server name** text box. In this example, the name of the IAS server is **EXCHANGE2003BE.msfirewall.org**. Enter a description of the server in the **Server description** text box. In this example, enter the description **IAS Server**. Click the **Change** button (Figure 6.71).

Figure 6.71 The Add RADIUS Server Dialog Box

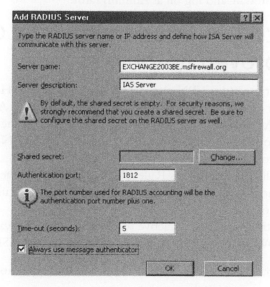

10. In the **Shared Secret** dialog box, enter a **New Secret** and then **Confirm new secret**. Make sure this is the *same secret* you entered in the RADIUS client configuration at the IAS server machine. Click **OK**.

11. Click **OK** in the **Add RADIUS Server** dialog box.

12. Click **OK** in the **RADIUS Servers** dialog box (Figure 6.72).

Figure 6.72 RADIUS Server Dialog Box

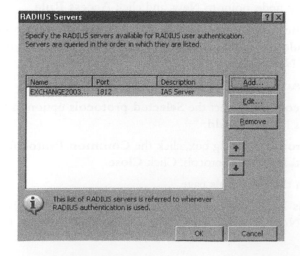

13. Click Apply in the Virtual Private Networks (VPN) Properties dialog box. Click OK in the ISA 2006 dialog box informing you that the Routing and Remote Access Service may restart. Click OK in the Virtual Private Networks (VPN) Properties dialog box.

14. Click Apply to save the changes and update the firewall policy.

15. Click OK in the **Saving** Configuration **Changes** dialog box.

16. Restart the ISA firewall, and log on as Administrator.

Create an Access Rule Allowing VPN Clients Access to Approved Resources

The ISA firewall can accept incoming VPN connections after the restart. However, the VPN clients cannot access any resources on the Internal network because there are no Access Rules enabling this access. You must create an Access Rule allowing machines belonging to the VPN clients network access to the Internal network. In contrast to other combined firewall VPN server solutions, the ISA firewall applies access controls for network access to VPN clients.

In this example, we will create an Access Rule allowing VPN clients access to the OWA server on the Internal network and no other servers. In addition, we'll limit the users to using only HTTP when making the connection.

This type of configuration would be attractive to organizations that want to allow secure remote access to their corporate OWA site, but that do not want to use SSL-to-SSL bridging because:

■ There may be potential vulnerabilities in the SSL/TLS encryption implementations, and

■ They want to allow non-encrypted communications through the corporate network to enable internal network IDS to evaluate the connections.

We will demonstrate other ways you can implement access control on VPN clients using user/group members later in this chapter.

Perform the following steps to create an unrestricted access VPN clients Access Rule:

1. In the **Microsoft Internet Security and Acceleration Server 2006** management console, expand the server name and click the **Firewall Policy** node. Right-click the **Firewall Policy** node, point to **New**, and click **Access Rule**.

2. In the **Welcome to the New Access Rule Wizard** page, enter a name for the rule in the **Access Rule name** text box. In this example, we will name the rule **OWA for VPN Clients**. Click **Next**.

3. On the **Rule Action** page, select **Allow**, and click **Next**.

4. On the **Protocols** page, select the **Selected protocols** option in the **Apply the rule to this protocols** list. Click **Add**.

5. In the **Add Protocols** dialog box, click the **Common Protocols** folder, and double-click the **HTTP** and **HTTPS** Protocols. Click **Close**.

6. Click **Next** on the **Protocols** page.

7. On the **Access Rule Sources** page, click **Add**. In the **Add Network Entities** dialog box, click the **Networks** folder, and double-click **VPN Clients**. Click **Close**.

8.   Click **Next** on the **Access Rule Sources** page.

9.   On the **Access Rule Destinations** page, click **Add**. In the **Add Network Entities** dialog box, click the **New** menu, and click **Computer**.

10. In the **New Computer Rule Element** dialog box, enter the name of the OWA server in the **Name** text box. In this example, we'll name it **OWA Server**. Enter the IP address of the OWA server in the **Computer IP Address** text box. Click **OK**.

11. Click the **Computers** folder and double-click the **OWA Server** entry. Click **Close**.

12. Click **Next** on the **Access Rule Destinations** page.

13. On the **User Sets** page, accept the default setting, **All Users**, and click **Next**.

14. Click Finish on the **Completing the New Access Rule Wizard** page.

15. Click **Apply** to save the changes and update the firewall policy.

16. Click **OK** in the **Saving Configuration Changes** dialog box. The **OWA for VPN Clients** policy is now the top-listed Access Rule in the Access Policy list (Figure 6.73).

Figure 6.73 The resulting firewall policy

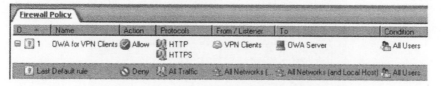

Make the Connection from a PPTP VPN Client

All the elements are in place to support RADIUS authentication for VPN clients. In the following exercise you will establish a PPTP VPN connection from an external network VPN client.

Perform the following steps to connect to the VPN server via RADIUS authentication:

1.   In the **Dial-up and Network Connections** window on the external network client, create a new VPN connectoid. Configure the connectoid to use the IP address **192.168.1.70** as the address of the VPN server. Log on with the user name **Administrator**.

2.   Click **OK** in the dialog box informing you that the VPN connection is established.

3.   At the domain controller machine, click **Start** and point to **Administrative Tools**. Click **Event Viewer**.

4.   In the **Event Viewer**, click on the **System** node in the left pane of the console. Double-click on the **Information** entry with the source as **IAS**. (See Figure 6.74)

Figure 6.74 Event Viewer Entry

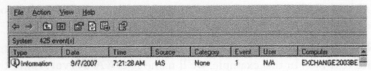

5.   In the **Event Properties** dialog box, you will see a **Description** of the log-on request. The information indicates that the RADIUS server authenticated the request and includes the RADIUS-specific information sent to the domain controller. Review this information and close the **Event Properties** dialog box (Figure 6.75).

Figure 6.75 Log-On Request Details

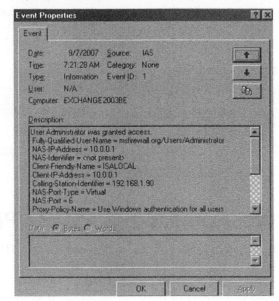

6.   At the ISA firewall, you can see log file entries specific to this VPN request. Note the PPTP and the RADIUS connections (Figure 6.76).

Figure 6.76 Log File Entries for VPN RADIUS Authentication

192.168.1.90	192.168.1.70	1723	PPTP	Initiated Connection	Allow VPN client traffic to ISA Server
192.168.1.90	192.168.1.70	0	PPTP	Initiated Connection	Allow VPN client traffic to ISA Server
10.0.0.1	10.0.0.2	1812	RADIUS	Initiated Connection	Allow RADIUS authentication from ISA Server to trusted RADIUS servers
10.0.0.108	10.0.0.109	0	WAN Miniport (PPTP)	Initiated VPN Connection		Administrator

7. At the ISA firewall server, you can see the VPN client session in the **Sessions** tab in the **Monitoring** node of the **Microsoft Internet Security and Acceleration Server 2006** management console (Figure 6.77).

Figure 6.77 VPN Session Appears in Sessions Section

Activation	Session Type	Client IP ▲	Source Network	Client Username	Client Host Name	Application Name
9/7/2007 7:41:34 AM	SecureNAT	10.0.0.1	Local Host		10.0.0.1	
9/7/2007 7:47:05 AM	SecureNAT	192.168.1.90	External		192.168.1.90	
9/7/2007 7:47:10 AM	VPN Client	10.0.0.106	VPN Clients	Administrator		VPN (PPTP)

8. At the VPN client computer, disconnect the VPN connection.

9. If you run a **Network Monitor** session on the RADIUS server, you can see that a single RADIUS **Access Request** is sent from the ISA firewall to the RADIUS server and a single **Access Accept** message is sent to the ISA firewall from the RADIUS server (Figure 6.78).

Figure 6.78 RADIUS Messages in Network Monitor Trace

Protocol	Description	Src Other Addr	Dst Other Addr
RADIUS	Message Type: Access Request(1)	ISALOCAL	EXCHANGE2003BE
RADIUS	Message Type: Access Accept(2)	EXCHANGE2003BE	ISALOCAL

If you want to create user-based firewall policies while ISA is not a domain member and you are authenticating against the RADIUS server you can create **User Sets** belonging to the RADIUS namespace on ISA. But you must use weak protocols like PAP and SPAP in order that users to be able to access resources.

Using EAP User Certificate Authentication for Remote Access VPNs

You can significantly enhance the security of your ISA firewall's VPN remote access client connections by using EAP user certificate authentication. User certificate authentication requires that the user possess a user certificate issued by a trusted certificate authority.

Both the ISA firewall and the remote access VPN client must have the appropriate certificates assignment to them. You must assign the ISA firewall a machine certificate that the firewall can use to identify itself. Users must be assigned user certificates from a certificate authority that the ISA firewall trusts. When both the remote access client machine presenting the user certificate and the ISA firewall contain a common CA certificate in their Trusted Root Certification Authorities certificate stores, the client and server trust the same certificate hierarchy.

The steps required to support user certificate authentication for remote access client VPN connections to the ISA firewall include:

- Issuing a machine certificate to the ISA firewall

- Configuring the ISA firewall software to support EAP authentication

- Enabling User Mapping for EAP authenticated users

- Configuring the Routing and Remote Access Service to support EAP authentication

- Issuing a user certificate to the remote access VPN client machine

We have discussed the procedures for issuing a machine certificate to the ISA firewall in other chapters in this book and in the ISA Deployment Kits at www.isaserver.org, so we will not reiterate that procedure here. Instead, we'll start with configuring the ISA firewall software to support EAP authentication, and then discuss how to configure the RRAS service and the clients.

ISA FIREWALL NOTE

The following exercises assume that you have already enabled and configured the ISA firewall's VPN server component before enabling EAP authentication support. Also note that this option is only available when the ISA firewall is a member of a domain. This provides another compelling reason for making the ISA firewall a domain member.

Configuring the ISA Firewall Software to Support EAP Authentication

Perform the following steps to configure the ISA firewall to support EAP authentication:

1. In the **Microsoft Internet Security and Acceleration Server 2006** management console, expand the server name, and click **Virtual Private Networks (VPN)** in the left pane of the console.

2. While in **Virtual Private Networks (VPN)**, click the **Tasks** tab in the Task pane. On the **Tasks** tab, click **Authentication Methods**.

3. In the **Virtual Private Networks (VPN) Properties** dialog box, put a checkmark in the **Extensible authentication protocol (EAP) with smart card or other certificate (ISA Server must belong to a domain)** checkbox (Figure 6.79).

Figure 6.79 Setting EAP Authentication

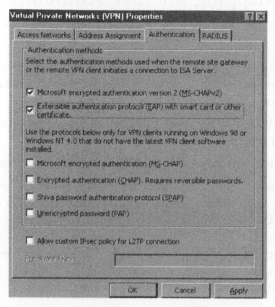

4. Read the information in the Microsoft Internet Security and Acceleration Server *2006* dialog box. The dialog box reports that EAP authenticated users belong to the RADIUS namespace and are not part of the Windows namespace. To apply user-based access rules to these users you can either define a RADIUS user set for them or you can use user mapping to map these users to the Windows namespace. If user mapping is enabled, access rules applied to the Windows users and group will be applicable to EAP authenticated users.

This is important information and describes the real utility of the User Mapping feature we discussed earlier in this chapter. Because EAP authentication doesn't use "Windows" authentication, you cannot by default apply user/group access policy on VPN clients authenticating with EAP user certificates. However, if we enable User Mapping for these users and map the user names of the EAP certificate authenticated users to domain users, then the same access rules that you apply to users who log on using Windows authentication will be applied to the EAP user certificate authenticated users. We'll go over the procedures of enabling and configuring User Mapping in the next procedures in this section.

5. Click **OK** (as shown in Figure 6.80) to acknowledge that you read and understand this information.

Figure 6.80 Warning about User Mapping and EAP

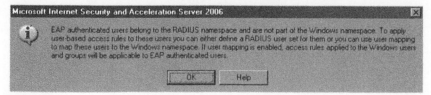

6. Click **Apply**, and then click **OK**.

Enabling User Mapping for EAP Authenticated Users

Perform the following steps to enable and configure User Mapping for EAP certificate authenticated users:

1. In the **Microsoft Internet Security and Acceleration Server 2006** management console, expand the server name, and click **Virtual Private Networks (VPN)** in the left pane of the console.

2. While in **Virtual Private Networks (VPN)**, click the **Tasks** tab in the Task pane. Click **Configure VPN Client Access** in the **Tasks** tab.

3. In the **VPN Clients Properties** dialog box, click the **User Mapping** tab.

4. On the **User Mapping** tab, put a checkmark in the **Enable User Mapping** checkbox. Put a checkmark in the **When username does not contain a domain, use this domain**. In the **Domain Name** text box, enter a domain name for the domain that the ISA firewall belongs to. This allows the ISA firewall to map the user name of the EAP certificate-authenticated user to accounts in that domain, and then rules applying to those users will apply to the EAP-authenticated users in the same way as they would if the users had authenticated using traditional "Windows" authentication.

5. Click **Apply** and then click **OK** (Figure 6.81).

Figure 6.81 Enabling User Mapping for EAP Authentication

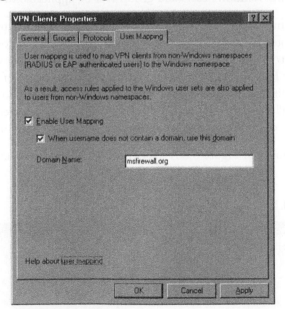

6. Click **Apply** to save the changes and update the firewall policy.

7. Click **OK** in the **Saving Configuration Changes** dialog box.

Issuing a User Certificate to the Remote Access VPN Client Machine

The VPN remote access client machines need to obtain user certificates and be configured to use the certificates to authenticate with the ISA firewall's remote access VPN server.

Perform the following steps to obtain a user certificate for the remote access VPN client:

1. Open **Internet Explorer**. In the **Address** bar, enter the URL for your certificate authority's Web enrollment site, and press **ENTER**.

2. Enter **Administrator** (or any name for which you want to obtain a user certificate) in the **User Name** text box. Enter the **Administrator's** password in the **Password** text box. Click **OK**.

3. On the **Welcome** page of the CA's Web enrollment site, click **Request a certificate**.

4. On the **Request a Certificate** page, click **User Certificate**.

5. Click **Submit** on the **User Certificate – Identifying Information** page.

6. Click **Yes** in the **Potential Scripting Violation** dialog box informing you that the Web site is requesting a new certificate on your behalf.

7. On the **Certificate Issued** page, click **Install this certificate**.

8. Click **Yes** in the **Potential Scripting Violation** dialog box informing you that the Web site is adding one or more certificates.

9. Close Internet Explorer.

We can configure the VPN connectoid to use user certificate authentication now that we have a user certificate installed on the remote access VPN client machine:

1. In the **Dial-up and Network Connections** window on the external network client, create a new VPN connectoid. Configure the connectoid to use the IP address **192.168.1.70** as the address of the VPN server.

2. When you complete the connection Wizard, you will see the **Connect** dialog box. Click **Properties**.

3. In the connectoid's **Properties** dialog box, click the **Security** tab. On the **Security** tab (Figure 6.82), select **Advanced (custom settings)**. Click **Settings**.

Figure 6.82 The Security Tab

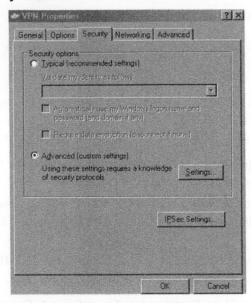

4.   In the Advanced Security Settings dialog box (Figure 6.83), select Use Extensible Authentication Protocol (EAP). Click Properties.

Figure 6.83 Enabling EAP Authentication

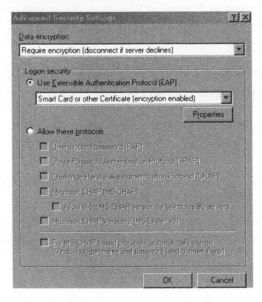

5.   In the Smart Card or other Certificate Properties dialog box, select Use a certificate on this computer. Place a checkmark by Validate server certificate. Place a checkmark by Connect **to these servers,** and enter the server name of the authentication server. In this example, the

server name is ISALOCAL.msfirewall.org (*the CN from the ISA certificate*), so enter that name in the text box. In the Trusted root certificate authority list, select the name of the CA that issued the certificates. In this example, the CA name is EXCHANGE2003BE, so select that option. Click OK in the Smart Card or other Certificate Properties dialog box (Figure 6.84).

Figure 6.84 The Smart Card or other Certificate Properties Dialog Box

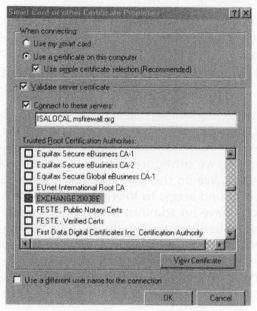

6. Click **OK** in the **Advanced Security Settings** dialog box.

7. Click **OK** in the connectoid's **Properties** dialog box.

8. A **Connect** dialog box appears which contains the name on the user certificate you obtained from the CA (Figure 6.85). Click **OK**.

Figure 6.85 Selecting the User Certificate for EAP User Authentication

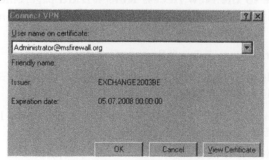

The VPN link will establish, and you'll be authenticated by the DC on the corporate network.

Supporting Outbound VPN Connections through the ISA Firewall

You can configure the ISA firewall to allow outbound access to VPN servers on the Internet. The ISA firewall supports all true VPN protocols, including PPTP, L2TP/IPSec, and IPSec NAT Traversal (NAT-T).

The ISA firewall can pass PPTP VPN connections from any Protected Network to the Internet with the help of its PPTP filter. The ISA firewall's PPTP filter intercepts the outbound PPTP connection from the Protected Network client and mediates the GRE (Generic Routing Encapsulation/IP Protocol 47) Protocol and the PPTP control channel (TCP 1723) communications. The only thing you need to do is create an Access Rule allowing outbound access to PPTP.

ISA FIREWALL SECURITY ALERT

In the following example, we configure outbound access to PPTP only from **Remote Management Computers**. We do this to emphasize that only highly-trusted hosts should be allowed outbound access to VPN servers. The VPN client connects to a network that you likely have no administrative control over. The VPN client acts as a potential security bridge between your network and the remote network. Therefore, you must be very strict on what machines are allowed outbound VPN access. This example also allows a connection to a specific VPN server. You should always pre-qualify VPN servers where your users connect to reduce the overall negative security impact outbound VPN connections can have on your corporate network.

Perform the following steps to allow outbound PPTP access through the ISA firewall:

1. In the **Microsoft Internet Security and Acceleration Server 2006** management console, expand the server name, and click **Firewall Policy**.

2. In the **Firewall Policy** node, click **Create Access Rule** on the **Tasks** tab in the Task pane.

3. On the **Welcome to the New Access Rule Wizard** page, enter a name for the rule in the **Access Rule name** text box. In this example, enter **Outbound PPTP for Administrators**. Click **Next**.

4. On the **Rule Action** page, select **Allow**, and click **Next**.

5. On the **Protocols** page, select the **Selected protocols** option from the **Apply the rule to this protocols** list. Click **Add**.

6. In the **Add Network Entities** dialog box, click the **VPN and IPSec** folder and double-click the **PPTP** entry. Click **Close**.

7. Click **Next** on the **Protocols** page.

8. In the **Add Network Entities** dialog box, click the **Computer Sets** folder and double-click the **Remote Management Computers** entry. Click **Close**.

9. Click **Next** on the **Access Rule Sources** page.

10. On the **Access Rule Destinations** page, click **Add**.

11. In the **Add Network Entities** dialog box, click the **New** menu, and then click **Computer**.

12. In the **New Computer Rule Element** dialog box, enter a name for the external VPN server in the **Name** text box. Enter the IP address of the authorized VPN server in the **Computer IP Address** text box. In this example, enter **Authorized VPN Server**. Click **OK**.

13. Click the **Computers** folder and double-click the **Authorized VPN Server** entry. Click **Close**.

14. Click **Next** on the **Access Rule Destinations** page.

15. Click **Next** on the **User Sets** page.

16. Click **Finish** on the **Completing the New Access Rule Wizard** page.

ISA FIREWALL SECRET

Because the PPTP VPN protocol requires GRE (an IP level protocol that does not use TCP or UDP as a transport), machines configured as only Firewall and/or Web Proxy clients will not be able to connect to Internet VPN servers using PPTP. The machine must also be configured as a SecureNAT client to successfully complete the PPTP connection. The result is that you can not use strong user/group-based access controls to limit which users can use PPTP connections to Internet VPN servers. An alternative is to use Computer Objects or Computer Address Set Objects and achieve outbound access control for PPTP using the client's IP address. The same is true for IPSec NAT-T protocols (although for different reasons), as you'll see in the following discussion.

All modern IPSec-based VPN clients support some type of NAT traversal. The Microsoft L2TP/IPSec client supports the IETF Internet draft (http://www.ietf.org/internet-drafts/draft-ietf-ipsec-nat-t-ike-08.txt) for supporting IPSec through NAT devices. While historically a number of non-Microsoft VPN vendors fragmented the IPSec NAT-T market by implementing proprietary NAT-T solutions for their VPN clients, most of them are following Microsoft's lead and are implementing the IETF draft recommendations for their VPN clients and servers.

Now NAT-T is standardized in RFC3947 (Negotiation of NAT-Traversal in the IKE) and RFC3948 (UDP Encapsulation of IPSec ESP Packets). ISA 2006, like ISA 2004 is based on the draft implementation and thus does not return the VID (Vendor ID) based on RFC3947 (the content of the payload is the MD5 hash of RFC 3947. The exact content in hex for the payload is 4a131c81070 358455c5728f20e95452f), just the VID for the draft. Windows Vista is the first Windows OS that is based on the new RFC. Vista will return both VIDs (for draft and RFC).

RFC-compliant NAT traversal requires that you allow outbound UDP 500 and UDP 4500 (the L2TP tunnel is protected(encapsulated) by IPSec ESP and thus it will never be seen by the intermediate device, UDP 1701 must be enabled at the VPN endpoint) through the ISA firewall. UDP port 500 is for the Internet Key Exchange (IKE) negotiation and UDP 4500 for UDP Encapsulation of IPSec ESP packets. For this reason, you might expect that using RFC-compliant IPSec NAT-T would allow you to control outbound VPN access on a user/group basis since most UDP and TCP protocols use Winsock.

Unfortunately, this is not the case for the Microsoft L2TP/IPSec NAT-T and most other IPSec NAT-T protocols because the NAT-T client is implemented as a *shim* in the Windows TCP/IP protocol stack and allows it to bypass the Winsock interface.

ISA FIREWALL SECURITY ALERT

Not all IPSec NAT-T implementations are RFC-compliant and use proprietary UDP or TCP NAT-T headers. In order to support outbound access for these proprietary, non-RFC IPSec NAT-T VPN clients, you'll need to understand the protocols required by these clients and make sure that both client and server are configured to support the same IPSec NAT-T protocols. For a detailed discussion of this problem and possible solutions, please review Stefaan Pouseele's excellent article **How to Pass IPSec Traffic Through ISA Server** at http://isaserver.org/articles/IPSec_Passthrough.html

Perform the following steps to allow RFC-compliant IPSec NAT-T VPN connections (such as the Windows L2TP/IPSec client) through the ISA firewall:

1. In the **Microsoft Internet Security and Acceleration Server 2006** management console, expand the server name and click **Firewall Policy**.

2. In the **Firewall Policy** node, click **Create Access Rule** on the **Tasks** tab in the Task pane.

3. On the **Welcome to the New Access Rule Wizard** page, enter a name for the rule in the **Access Rule name** text box. In this example, we'll name it **Outbound L2TP/IPSec NAT-T for Administrators**. Click **Next**.

4. On the **Rule Action** page, select **Allow** and click **Next**.

5. On the **Protocols** page, select the **Selected protocols** option from the **Apply the rule to this protocols** list. Click **Add**.

6. In the **Add Network Entities** dialog box, click the **VPN and IPSec** folder and double-click the **IKE Client(for UDP 500)** and **IPSec NAT-T Client(for UDP 4500)** entries. Click **Close**.

7. Click **Next** on the **Protocols** page.

8. On the **Access Rule Sources** page, click **Add**.

9. In the **Add Network Entities** dialog box, click the **Computer Sets** folder and double-click the **Remote Management Computers** entry. Click **Close**.

10. Click **Next** on the **Access Rule Sources** page.

11.   On the **Access Rule Destinations** page, click **Add**.

12.   In the **Add Network Entities** dialog box, click **New** and **Computer**.

13.   In the **New Computer Rule Element** dialog box, enter a name for the external VPN server in the **Name** text box. Enter the IP address of the authorized VPN server in the **Computer IP Address** text box. In this example, enter **Authorized VPN Server**. Click **OK**.

14.   Click the **Computers** folder, and double-click **Authorized VPN Server**. Click **Close**.

15.   Click **Next** on the **Access Rule Destinations** page.

16.   Click **Next** on the **User Sets** page.

17.   Click **Finish** on the **Completing the New Access Rule Wizard** page.

Installing and Configuring the DHCP Server and DHCP Relay Agent on the ISA Firewall

Many smaller organizations may wish to install a DHCP server on the ISA firewall itself (not recommended). This allows smaller companies the ability to automatically assign IP addressing information to hosts on the corporate network without requiring them to install the DHCP server on a separate server on the corporate network. Many of these companies may have only one other Windows Server on their network, and that server is often a Windows domain controller.

However there are potential negative security implications of putting a DHCP server on a Windows domain controller (http://support.microsoft.com/default.aspx?scid=kb;en-us;816592). You should not install any additional services on ISA 2006 Firewall (like DHCP server, DNS server) because this would increase the attack surface area.

The ISA firewall has a System Policy that enables the firewall itself to be a DHCP client. There are two System Policy Rules listed in Table 6.1.

Table 6.1 System Policy Rules Enabling the ISA Firewall to be a DHCP Client

Rule #	Rule Name	Action	Protocols	From/Listener	To	Condition
9	Allow DHCP requests from ISA Server to all networks	Allow	DHCP (request)	Local Host	Anywhere	All Users
10	Allow DHCP replies from DHCP servers to ISA Server	Allow	DHCP (reply)	Internal	Local Host	All Users

The DHCP System Policy Rules allow DHCP requests from the ISA firewall, and DHCP replies from the Internal Network to the ISA firewall. These rules won't help us when we want to run the DHCP server on the ISA firewall itself because we want to allow DHCP requests *from the Internal Network* to the ISA firewall. We also want to allow DHCP Replies *from the ISA firewall* to the Internal Network. We'll need to create Access Rules to allow the required DHCP communications to and from the ISA firewall.

Perform the following steps to create the Access Rules allowing DHCP Requests to the ISA firewall and DHCP Replies from the ISA firewall:

1. In the **Microsoft Internet Security and Acceleration Server 2006** management console, expand the server name, and click the **Firewall Policy** node.

2. In the **Firewall Policy** node, click **Create Access Rule** on the **Tasks** tab in the Task pane.

3. On the **Welcome to the New Access Rule Wizard** page, enter a name for the rule in the **Access Rule name** text box. In this example, enter **DHCP Request**. Click **Next**.

4. On the **Rule Action** page, select **Allow** and **Next**.

5. On the **Protocols** page, select the **Selected protocols** option from the **Apply the rule to this protocols** list. Click **Add**.

6. In the **Protocols** dialog box, click the **Infrastructure** folder and double-click the **DHCP (request)** entry. Click **Close**.

7. Click **Next** on the **Protocols** page.

8. On the **Access Rule Sources** page, click **Add**.

9. In the **Add Network Entities** dialog box, click the **Networks** folder and double-click the **Internal** entry. If you want clients from multiple Protected Networks to access the DHCP server on the ISA firewall, make sure to include those Networks, too. Click **Close**.

10. Click **Next** on the **Access Rule Sources** page.

11. On the **Access Rule Destinations** page, click **Add**.

12. In the **Add Network Entities** dialog box, click the **Networks** folder, and double-click the **Local Host** network.

13. Click **Next** on the **Access Rule Destinations** page.

14. Click **Next** on the **User Sets** page.

15. Click **Finish** on the **Completing the New Access Rule Wizard** page.

16. Next, we'll create the rule for the DHCP reply from the ISA firewall:

17. In the **Microsoft Internet Security and Acceleration Server 2006** management console, expand the server name, and click the **Firewall Policy** node.

18. In the **Firewall Policy** node, click **Create Access Rule** on the **Tasks** tab in the Task pane.

19. On the **Welcome to the New Access Rule Wizard** page, enter a name for the rule in the **Access Rule name** text box. In this example, we'll name it **DHCP Reply**. Click **Next**.

20. On the **Rule Action** page, select **Allow** and click **Next**.

21. On the **Protocols** page, select the **Selected protocols** option from the **Apply the rule to this protocols** list. Click **Add**.

22. In the **Protocols** dialog box, click the **Infrastructure** folder and double-click the **DHCP (reply)** entry. Click **Close**.

23. Click **Next** on the **Protocols** page.

24. On the **Access Rule Sources** page, click **Add**.

25. In the **Add Network Entities** dialog box, click the **Networks** folder and double-click the **Local Host** entry. Click **Close**.

26. Click **Next** on the **Access Rule Sources** page.

27. On the **Access Rule Destinations** page, click **Add**.

28. In the **Add Network Entities** dialog box, click the **Networks** folder and double-click the **Internal** network. If you want the ISA firewall to respond to clients from multiple Protected Networks to access the DHCP server on the ISA firewall, make sure to include those Networks, too. Click **Close**.

29. Click **Next** on the **Access Rule Destinations** page.

30. Click **Next** on the **User Sets** page.

31. Click **Finish** on the **Completing the New Access Rule Wizard** page.

NOTE

For more details about how to set up the DHCP Relay agent on ISA in order to provide to VPN clients DHCP options refer to the following www.isaserver.org article: *Enabling DHCP Relay for ISA Firewall VPN Clients*at http://www.isaserver.org/tutorials/2004dhcprelay.html

   You cannot assign a DNS suffix search list through DHCP options (Domain Search Option, Option Code 119, and RFC3397) to your VPN Clients. This is currently not supported by the Microsoft DHCP server and by the Windows Clients. Only connection-specific DNS suffix. The DNS suffix search list must be pushed through GPO.

Summary

In this chapter, we discussed the ISA 2006 firewall's VPN remote access server and VPN gateway features. The VPN remote access server supports both PPTP and L2TP/IPSec connections from remote access VPN clients. The ISA 2006 firewall's VPN gateway supports IPSec tunnel mode, PPTP and L2TP/IPSec connections from other VPN gateways. We also discussed other topics related to the ISA firewall's support for VPN clients and gateways, including EAP authentication and DHCP server configuration.

Chapter 7

ISA 2006 Stateful Inspection and Application Layer Filtering

Solutions in this chapter:

- Application Filters
- Web Filters

☑ Summary

Introduction

The ISA firewall is able to perform both stateful filtering and stateful application layer inspection. Its stateful filtering feature set makes it a network layer stateful firewall in the same class as any hardware firewall that performs stateful filtering at the network and transport layers. Stateful filtering is often referred to as *stateful packet inspection*, which is a bit of a misnomer because packets are Layer 3 entities, and to assess connection state, Layer 4 information must be assessed.

However, in contrast to traditional packet filter-based stateful hardware firewalls, the ISA firewall is able to perform stateful application layer inspection, which enables it to fully inspect the communication streams passed by it from one network to another. In contrast to stateful filtering where only the network and transport layer information is filtered, true stateful inspection requires that the firewall be able to analyze and make decisions on all layers of the communication, including the most important layer, the application layer.

The Web filters perform stateful application layer inspection on communications handled by the ISA firewall's Web Proxy components. The Web Proxy handles connections for HTTP, HTTPS (SSL), and HTTP tunneled FTP connections. The Web filters take apart the HTTP communications and expose them to the ISA firewall's application layer inspection mechanisms, examples of which include the HTTP Security filter and the OWA forms-based authentication filter.

The Application filters are responsible for performing stateful application layer inspection on non-HTTP protocols, such as SMTP, POP3, and DNS. These application layer filters also take apart the communication and expose them to deep stateful inspection at the ISA firewall.

Web and Application filters can perform two duties:

- Protocol access
- Protocol security

Protocol access allows access to protocols that require secondary connections. Complex protocols may require more than one connection, either inbound or outbound through the ISA firewall. SecureNAT clients require these filters to use complex protocols because the SecureNAT client does not have the power of the Firewall client. In contrast to the Firewall client that can work together with the ISA firewall to negotiate complex protocols, the SecureNAT client is a simple NAT client of the ISA firewall and requires the aid of application filters to connect using these complex protocols (such as FTP or MMS).

Protocol security protects the connections moving through the ISA firewall. Protocol security filters such as the SMTP and DNS filters inspect the communications that apply to those filters and block connections that are deemed outside of secure parameters. Some of these filters block connections that may represent buffer overflows (such as the DNS and SMTP filters), and some of them perform much deeper inspection and block connections or content based on policy (such as the SMTP Message Screener).

Application Filters

The ISA firewall includes a number of Application filters. In this section, we discuss:

- SMTP filter
- DNS filter

- POP Intrusion Detection filter
- SOCKS V4 filter
- FTP Access filter
- H.323 filter
- MMS filter
- PNM filter
- PPTP filter
- RPC filter
- RTSP filter

The SMTP Filter

The ISA firewall's SMTP filter configuration interface can be accessed by opening the **Microsoft Internet Security and Acceleration Server 2006** management console, expand the server name, and then expand the **Configuration** node. Click the **Add-ins** node. In the Details Pane, double-click the **SMTP Filter**. Click the **SMTP Commands** tab. (See Figure 7.1.)

The settings on the **SMTP Commands** tab are mediated by the SMTP filter component. The SMTP Message Screener does not evaluate SMTP commands and does not protect against buffer overflow conditions. The commands in the list are limited to a predefined length. If an incoming SMTP connection sends a command that exceeds the length allowed, the connection is dropped. In addition, if a command that is sent over the SMTP channel is not on this list, it is dropped. (See Figure 7.1.)

Figure 7.1 The SMTP Commands Tab

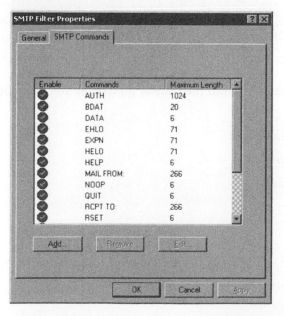

The DNS Filter

The ISA firewall's DNS filter protects the DNS server published by the ISA firewall using Server Publishing Rules. You can access the configuration interface for the DNS filter's attack prevention configuration page in the **Intrusion Detection** dialog box. Expand the server name and then expand the **Configuration** node. Click the **General** node.

In the Details Pane, click the **Enable Intrusion Detection and DNS Attack Detection** link. In the **Intrusion Detection** dialog box, click the **DNS Attacks** tab. On the **DNS Attacks** tab, put a checkmark in the **Enable detection and filtering of DNS attacks** checkbox. (See Figure 7.2.)

Figure 7.2 The DNS Attacks Tab

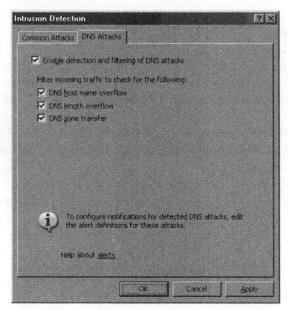

Once detection is enabled, you can then enable prevention. You can protect yourself from three attacks:

- DNS host name overflow
- DNS length overflow
- DNS zone transfer

The **DNS host name overflow** and **DNS length overflow** attacks are DNS denial-of-service (DoS) type attacks. The DNS DoS attack exploits the difference in size between a DNS query and a DNS response, in which all of the network's bandwidth is consumed by bogus DNS queries. The attacker uses the DNS servers as "amplifiers" to multiply the DNS traffic.

The attacker begins by sending small DNS queries to each DNS server that contains the spoofed IP address of the intended victim. The responses returned to the small queries are much larger, so if a large number of responses are returned at the same time, the link will become congested and denial of service will take place.

One solution to this problem is for administrators to configure DNS servers to respond with a "refused" response, which is much smaller than a name resolution response, when they receive DNS queries from suspicious or unexpected sources.

You can find detailed information for configuring DNS servers to prevent this problem in the U.S. Department of Energy's Computer Incident Advisory Capability information bulletin J-063, available at www.ciac.org/ciac/bulletins/j-063.shtml.

The POP Intrusion Detection Filter

The POP Intrusion Detection filter protects POP3 servers you publish via ISA firewall Server Publishing Rules from POP services buffer overflow attacks. There is no configuration interface for the POP Intrusion Detection filter.

The SOCKS V4 Filter

The SOCKS v4 filter is used to accept SOCKS version 4 connection requests from applications written to the SOCKS version 4 specification. Windows operating systems should never need to use the SOCKS filter because you can install the Firewall client on these machines to transparently authenticate to the ISA firewall and support complex protocol negotiation.

For hosts that cannot be configured as Firewall clients, such as Linux and Mac hosts, you can use the SOCKS v4 filter to support them. The SOCKS v4 filter is disabled by default. To enable the filter, open the **Microsoft Internet Security and Acceleration Server 2006** management console, expand the server name, and then expand the **Configuration** node. Click the **Add-ins** node. In the Details Pane, right-click the **SOCKS V4** filter and click **Enable**.

You will need to configure the SOCKS V4 filter to listen on the specific network(s) for which you want it to accept connections. Double-click the **SOCKS V4** filter. In the **SOCKS V4 Filter Properties** dialog box, click the **Networks** tab. On the **Networks** tab, you can configure the **Port** on which the SOCKS filter listens for SOCKS client connections. Next, put a checkmark in the checkbox next to the network for which you want the SOCKS filter to accept connections. Click **Apply** and then click **OK**. (See Figure 7.3.)

Figure 7.3 The SOCKS V4 Filter Properties Dialog Box

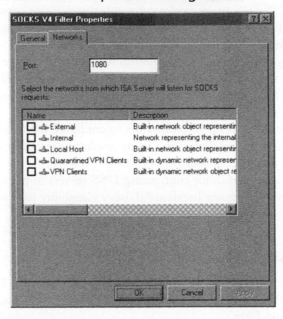

The SOCKS v4 filter supports SOCKS v4.3 client applications. The SOCKS filter is a generic sockets filter that supports all client applications that are designed to support the SOCKS v4.3 specification. The SOCKS filter performs duties similar to that performed by the Firewall client. However, there are some significant differences between how SOCKS and the Firewall client work:

- The Firewall client is a generic Winsock Proxy client application. All applications designed to the Windows Sockets specification will automatically use the Firewall client.

- The SOCKS filter supports applications written to the SOCKS v4.3 specification.

- When the Firewall client is installed on the client machine, all Winsock applications automatically use the Firewall client, and user credentials are automatically sent to the ISA firewall. In addition, the Firewall client will work with the ISA firewall service to manage complex protocols that require secondary connections (such as FTP, MMS, and many others).

- The SOCKS client must be configured on a per-application basis. Each application must be explicitly configured to use the ISA firewall as its SOCKS server. When the application is configured to use the ISA firewall as its SOCKS server, the SOCKS filter will manage complex protocols for the SOCKS client application.

- The SOCKS 4.3a filter included with the ISA firewall does not support authentication. SOCKS 5 introduced the capability to authenticate the client application that attempts to access content through the SOCKS proxy.

We always recommend that you use the Firewall client because of the impressive advantages it provides by allowing you the ability to authenticate all Winsock connections made through the ISA firewall. However, SOCKS is a good "second best" when you cannot install the Firewall client.

The FTP Access Filter

The FTP Access filter is used to mediate FTP connections between Protected Network clients and FTP servers on the Internet, and from external hosts and published FTP servers. The FTP Access filter supports both PASV and PORT (passive and standard) mode FTP connections.

The FTP Access filter is required for SecureNAT clients because FTP uses secondary connections for PORT-mode FTP connections. FTP is a complex protocol that requires outbound connections from the FTP PORT-mode client and new secondary inbound connections from the FTP server. While the Firewall client does not require application filter support for secondary connections, SecureNAT clients do require application layer filter support, which is why the ISA firewall dev team included the FTP Access application filter.

ISA FIREWALL SECRET

If you plan to support PORT-mode FTP client connections, make sure that IP Routing is enabled on the ISA firewall (the default setting). When IP Routing is enabled, the secondary connections are handled in kernel mode rather than user mode. This kernel-mode handling of the secondary connections (which are data transfers from the FTP server to the FTP client) will significantly increase performance.

Stefaan Pouseele, an ISA Server MVP, has written an excellent article on the FTP protocol and how FTP challenges firewall security. Check out his article, *How the FTP Protocol Challenges Firewall Security* at http://isaserver.org/articles/How_the_FTP_protocol_Challenges_Firewall_Security.html.

There is no configuration interface for the FTP Access filter. However, if there is an Access Rule that applies to FTP connection, the right click menu on the Access Rule will allow you to **Configure FTP**. The **Configure FTP** option allows you to control whether or not FTP uploads are allowed.

The H.323 Filter

The H.323 filter is used to support H.323 connections through the ISA firewall. To configure the H.323 filter, open the **Microsoft Internet Security and Acceleration Server 2006** management console and expand the server name. Next, expand the **Configuration** node and click the **Add-ins** node. Double-click the **H.323 Filter** entry in the Details Pane.

In the **H.323 Filter Properties** dialog box, click the **Call Control** tab. You have the following options:

- Use this Gatekeeper
- Use DNS gateway lookup and LRQs for alias resolution
- Allow audio
- Allow video
- Allow T120 and application sharing

Click the **Networks** tab. On the **Networks** tab, put a checkmark in the checkbox to the left of the networks on which you want the H.323 filter to accept connections requests.

The MMS Filter

The MMS filter supports Microsoft Media Services connections through the ISA firewall for Access Rules and Server Publishing Rules. The MMS filter is an access filter that allows SecureNAT client access to the complex protocols and secondary connections required to connect to Microsoft Media Services hosted content. Firewall clients do not require the help of the MMS filter to connect to MMS servers. There is no configuration interface for the MMS filter.

The PNM Filter

The PNM filter supports connections for the Progressive Networks Media Protocol from Real Networks. The PNM filter is an access filter allowing SecureNAT client access to the complex protocols and secondary connection required to connect to Progressive Networks Media servers. There is no configuration interface for the PNM filter.

The PPTP Filter

The PPTP filter supports PPTP connections through the ISA firewall for outbound connections made through Access Rules and inbound connections made through Server Publishing Rules. The ISA firewall's PPTP filter differs from the ISA Server 2000 PPTP filter in that it supports both inbound and outbound PPTP connections. The ISA Server 2000 PPTP filter only supports outbound PPTP connections.

The PPTP filter is required by both SecureNAT and Firewall clients. In fact, a machine located on an ISA firewall protected network must be configured as a SecureNAT client to use the PPTP filter to connect to PPTP VPN servers through the ISA firewall. The reason for this is that the Firewall client does not mediate non-TCP/UDP protocols. The PPTP VPN protocol requires the use of the Generic Routing Encapsulation (GRE) protocol (IP Protocol 47) and TCP protocol 1723. The TCP session is used by PPTP for tunnel management.

When the outbound access to the PPTP protocol is enabled, the PPTP filter automatically intercepts the GRE and TCP connections made by the PPTP VPN client. You do not need to create an Access Rule allowing outbound access to TCP 1723 for VPN clients.

The RPC Filter

The RPC filter is used to mediate RPC connections to servers requiring Remote Procedure Calls (RPCs) for both outbound connections using Access Rules and inbound connections using Server Publishing Rules. This includes secure Exchange RPC publishing.

There is no configuration interface for the RPC filter.

The RTSP Filter

The RTSP filter supports Microsoft Real Time Streaming Protocol connections through the ISA firewall for Access Rules and Server Publishing Rules. The RTSP filter is an access filter that allows SecureNAT client access to the complex protocols and secondary connections required to connect to Microsoft Real

Time Streaming Protocol hosted content (such as that on Windows Server 2003 Microsoft Media Servers). Firewall clients do not require the help of the MMS filter to connect to MMS servers.

There is no configuration interface for the RTSP filter.

Web Filters

ISA firewall Web filters are used to mediate HTTP, HTTPS, and FTP tunneled (Web proxied) connections through the ISA firewall. In this section, we discuss the following Web filters:

- HTTP Security filter
- ISA Server Link Translator
- Web Proxy filter
- SecurID filter
- OWA Forms-based Authentication filter

The HTTP Security Filter (HTTP Filter)

The ISA firewall's HTTP Security filter is one of the key application layer filtering and inspection mechanisms included with the ISA firewall. The HTTP Security filter allows the ISA firewall to perform application layer inspection on all HTTP communications moving through the ISA firewall and block connections that do not match your HTTP security requirements.

The HTTP Security filter is tightly tied to the Web Proxy filter. When the Web Proxy filter is bound to the HTTP protocol, all communications outbound through the ISA firewall with a destination port of TCP 80 are subjected to the HTTP Security filter's deep application layer inspection. We'll see later how to unbind the Web Proxy filter from the HTTP protocol if you do not want all communications to be scrubbed by the HTTP Security filter.

The HTTP Security filter is applied on a per-rule basis, and you can apply different HTTP filtering properties on each rule that allows outbound HTTP communications. This provides you very granular, fine-tuned control over what type of connections can move over the HTTP channel. In addition, you can bind the Web Proxy filter to other ports and enforce HTTP Security Filter policy over connections moving over alternate ports. This provides you another potent weapon against users and applications that try to subvert your network and Firewall Security policy by tunneling Web connections over alternate ports.

In this section, we discuss:

- Overview of HTTP Security Filter Settings
- HTTP Security Filter Logging
- Disabling the HTTP Security Filter for Web Requests
- Exporting and Importing HTTP Security Filter Settings
- Investigating HTTP Headers for Potentially Dangerous Applications
- Example HTTP Security Filter Policies
- Commonly Blocked Application Signatures
- The Dangers of SSL Tunneling

Overview of HTTP Security Filter Settings

The HTTP Security filter includes a number of tabs that allow you precise control over what HTTP communications are allowed through the ISA firewall on a per-rule basis. Configuration of the HTTP Security filter is done on the following tabs:

- General
- Methods
- Extensions
- Headers
- Signatures

The General Tab

On the **General** tab, you can configure the following options (see Figure 7.4):

- Maximum header length
- Payload length
- Maximum URL length
- Verify normalization
- Block high bit characters
- Block responses containing Windows executable content

Figure 7.4 The General Tab

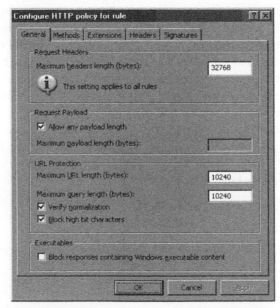

The **Maximum headers length (bytes)** option allows you to configure the maximum length of all headers included in a request HTTP communication. This setting applies to *all* rules that use the HTTP Security filter. This setting protects you from attacks that try to overflow Web site buffers by sending excessively long headers to the Web server. If you set the value too low, some applications on your site might not work correctly. If you set it too high, intruders may be able to construct a special HTTP request that could exploit known and unknown buffer overflow issues with your Web site or Web server. You might want to start with a value of 10,000 bytes and work upward from there. Your Web site administrator should be able to help you with the maximum header length required for sites your ISA firewall protects.

In the **Request Payload** frame, you have the option to **Allow any payload length** or to set a specific maximum payload length. The payload is the part of the HTTP communication that is not part of the HTTP header or command structure. For example, if you allow users to post content to your Web site (an ordering form or a discussion forum), you can set a limit on the length of their posts by unchecking the **Allow any payload length** checkbox and entering a custom value in the **Maximum payload length (bytes)** text box. Again, you may want to discuss your Web site's requirements with your Web site administrator or Web programmer to get specific details on maximum payload length requirements for your protected Web sites.

There are several options in the **URL Protection** frame. The **Maximum URL length (bytes)** option allows you to set the maximum URL that the user can send through the ISA firewall when making a request through the firewall for a Web site. Exploits can send excessively long URLs in an attempt to execute a buffer overflow or other attack against a Web server. The default value is **10240**, but you can increase or decrease this value based on your own site's custom requirements. The **Maximum query length (bytes)** value allows you to set the maximum length of the query portion of the URL. The query part of the URL appears after a question mark (?) in the request URL. The default value is **10240**, but you can make it longer or shorter, based on your requirements. Keep in mind that the **Maximum URL length** must be longer than the **Maximum query length** because the query is part of the URL.

The **Verify normalization** option is also included in the **URL Protection** frame. *Normalization* is the process of decoding so-called "escaped" characters. Web servers can receive requests that are encoded using escaped characters. One of the most common examples is when there is a space in the URL, as in the URL http://msfirewall.org/Dir%20One/default%20file.htm. The %20 is an "escape" character representing a "space." The problem is that bad guys can also encode the "%" character and perform what is called "double encoded" requests. Double encoding can be used to attack Web servers. When the **Verify Normalization** option is selected, the HTTP Security filter will normalize or decode the request twice. If the request of the first and second decodings is not the same, the HTTP Security filter will drop the request. This prevents "double encoding" attacks. You should enable this feature, but keep in mind that poorly designed Web sites and Web applications are not always security aware, and may actually accept and require double encoded requests. If that is the case for sites you want to access on the Internet or for sites you publish through the ISA firewall, you will need to disable this option.

The **Block high bit characters** option allows you to block HTTP requests that include URLs with high bit characters in them. High bit characters are used by many languages that use extended character sets, so if you find that you can't access Web sites that use these extended character sets in their URLs, you will need to disable this option.

The **Block responses containing Windows executable content** option allows you to prevent users from downloading files that are Windows executable files (such as .exe files, but any file extension can be used on a Windows executable). The HTTP Security filter is able to determine if the file is a Windows executable because the response will begin with an **MZ**. This can be very helpful when you need to prevent your users from downloading executables through the ISA firewall.

ISA FIREWALL TIP

Remember that your HTTP policy is configured on a per-rule basis. Because you can configure HTTP policy on a per-rule basis, you can enable these settings for some rules, and disable them for other rules. This per-rule HTTP policy configuration option provides you a great deal of flexibility in what content is available from specific sites to specific users at specific times.

The Methods Tab

You can control what HTTP methods are used through an Access Rule or Web Publishing Rule using the settings on the **Methods** tab (see Figure 7.5). You have three options:

- Allow all methods
- Allow only specified methods
- Block specified methods (allow all others)

Figure 7.5 The Methods Tab

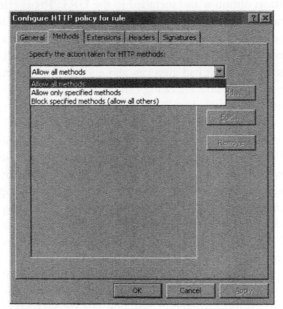

HTTP methods are HTTP commands that hosts can send to a Web server to perform specific actions; for example, GET, PUT, and POST. There are others that you, as a network and firewall administrator might not be familiar with, such as HEAD, SEARCH, and CHECKOUT. There are other methods that are proprietary and used by specific Web applications, such as Outlook Web Access. The **Allow all methods** option allows you to allow HTTP methods used in an HTTP communication through the ISA firewall.

ISA FIREWALL SECRET

Other HTTP methods you'll encounter when allowing access to Microsoft applications include RPC_IN_DATA and RPC_OUT_DATA, which are used for securely publishing RPC over HTTP for Outlook 2003 clients. However, remember that the filter only *blocks* communications set in the HTTP policy filter, so be careful not to block methods you might require, even when you're not completely sure what the exact methods you might require will be. We recommend that you thoroughly test your filter settings and discuss with the Web application admins and developers what methods are required.

The **Allow only specified methods** option allows you to specify the exact methods you want to allow through the ISA firewall. If you can identify what methods are required by your Web site and Web application, then you can allow those only and block any other method. Other methods could be used to compromise your Web site, so if they're not needed, block them.

The **Block specified methods (allow all others)** option allows you to allow all methods except those specific methods you want to allow. This option provides you a bit more latitude in that even if you don't know all the methods your site might require, you might know some that are definitely not required. One example might be the POST method. If you don't allow users to post content to your Web site, then there's no reason to allow the POST method, and you can explicitly block it.

When you select either the **Allow only specified methods** or the **Block specified methods (allow all others)** option, you need to click the **Add** button to add the method you want to allow or block. The **Method** dialog box appears after clicking the **Add** button.

In the **Add** dialog box, you enter the method in the **Method** text box (Figure 7.6). You might also want to add a description of this method in the **Description** text box. This helps you remember what the method does and helps the next person who might need to manage your ISA firewall and isn't aware of the insides of the HTTP protocol command set.

Figure 7.6 The Methods Dialog Box

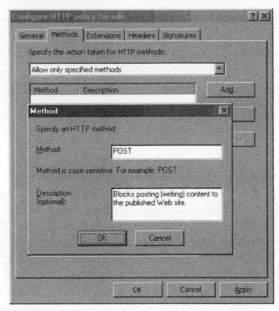

The Extensions Tab

On the **Extensions** tab, you have the following options (see Figure 7.7):

- Allow all extensions
- Allow only specified extensions
- Block specified extensions (allow all others)
- Block requests containing ambiguous extensions

Figure 7.7 The Extensions Tab

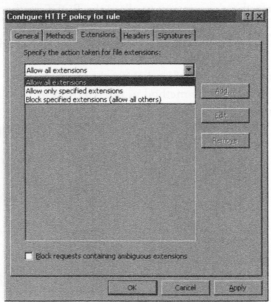

You can control what file extensions are allowed to be requested through the ISA firewall. This is extremely useful when you want to block users from requesting certain file types through the ISA firewall. For example, you can block users from accessing .exe, .com, .zip, and any other file extension through the ISA firewall.

The **Allow all extensions** option allows you to configure the Access Rule or Web Publishing Rule to allow users access to any type of file based on file extension through the ISA firewall. The **Allow only specified extensions** option allows you to specify the precise file extensions that users can access through the ISA firewall. The **Block specified extensions (allow all others)** option allows you to block specified file extensions that you deem dangerous.

If you select the **Allow only specified extensions** or **Block specified extensions (allow all others)** option, you need to click the **Add** button and add the extensions you want to allow or block.

The **Extension** dialog box appears after you click the **Add** button. Enter the name of the extension in the **Extension** text box. For example, if you want to block access to .exe files, enter **.exe**. Enter a description if you like in the **Description (optional)** text box. Click **OK** to save the new extension. (See Figure 7.8.)

Figure 7.8 The Extensions Dialog Box

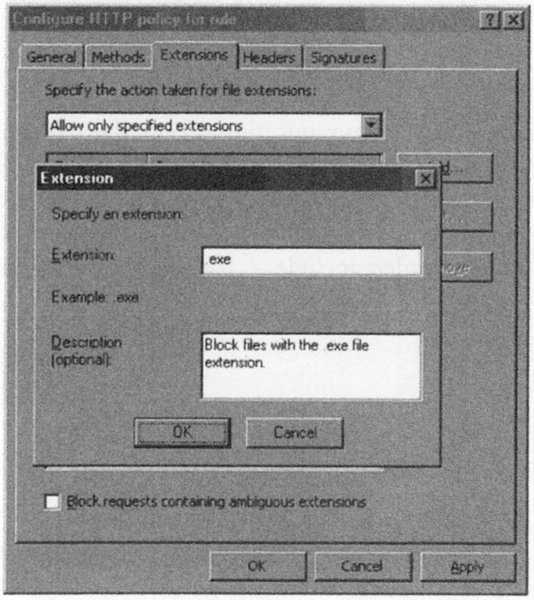

The Headers Tab

On the **Headers** tab, you have the following options (see Figure 7.9):

- Allow all headers except the following
- Server header
- Via header

Figure 7.9 The Headers Tab

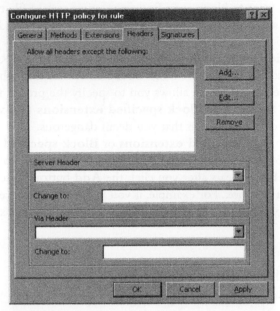

An HTTP header contains HTTP communication specific information that is included in HTTP requests made from a Web client (such as your Web browser) and HTTP responses sent back to the Web client from a Web server. These headers perform multiple functions that determine the status or state of the HTTP communications and other characteristics of the HTTP session.

Examples of common HTTP headers include:

- Content-length
- Pragma
- User-Agent
- Accept-Encoding

You can accept all HTTP headers or you can block certain specific HTTP headers. There are certain HTTP headers you might always want to block, such as the P2P-Agent header, which is used by many peer-to-peer applications. If you want to block a specific HTTP header, click the **Add** button.

In the **Header** dialog box, select either the **Request headers** or **Response headers** option from the **Search in** drop-down list. In the **HTTP header** text box, enter the HTTP header you want to block. Click **OK**. (See Figure 7.10.)

Figure 7.10 The Header Dialog Box

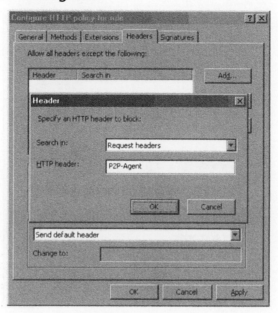

You can configure the Server Header returned in the HTTP responses by making a selection in the **Server Header** drop-down list. The Server Header is an HTTP header that the Web server sends back to the Web client informing the client of the type of Web server to which the client is connecting. Intruders can use this information to attack a Web server. You have the options to:

- Send original header
- Strip header from response
- Modify header in response

The **Send original header** option lets the header sent by the Web server go unchanged. The **Strip header from response** option allows the ISA firewall to remove the Server Header, and the **Modify header in response** allows you to change the header. You should change the header to confuse the attacker. Since this header isn't required by Web clients, you can change it to something like **Private** or **CompanyName** or anything else you like.

These options all help to prevent (or at least slow down) attackers. Attackers will have to expend more effort and use alternate methods to "fingerprint" your Web server. (See Figure 7.11.)

Figure 7.11 The Server Header Option

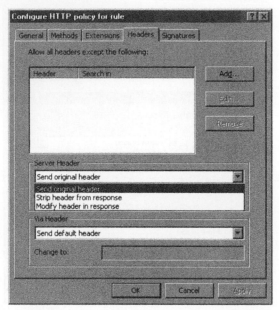

The **Via Header** option allows you to control the Via Header sent to the Web client. When Web Proxy servers are located between a client and Web server, the Web Proxy server will insert a Via Header in the HTTP communication informing the client that the request was handled by the Web Proxy server in transit. Each Web Proxy server in the request path can add its own Via Header, and each sender along the response path removes its own Via Header and forwards the response to the server specified in the next Via Header on the Via Header "stack." The **Via Header** settings allows you to change the name your ISA firewall includes in its own Via Header and enables you to hide the name of your ISA firewall. The default setting is for your ISA firewall to include its own Computer name in the Via Header.

You have two options:

- Send default header
- Modify header in request and response

The **Send default header** option leave the Via Header unchanged. The **Modify header in request and response** option allows you to change the name included in the Via Header inserted by your ISA firewall. We recommend that you change this to hide the actual name of your ISA firewall to prevent attackers from learning the actual name of your ISA firewall machine. (See Figure 7.12.)

Enter the alternate Via Header in the **Change To** text box.

Figure 7.12 The Via Header

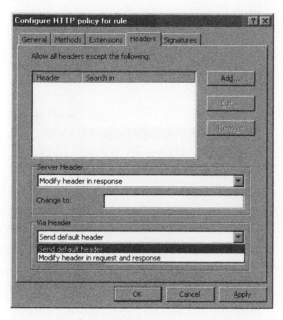

The Signatures Tab

The **Signatures** tab allows you to control access through the ISA firewall based on HTTP signatures you create. These signatures are based on strings contained in the following components of an HTTP communication:

- Request URL
- Request headers
- Request body
- Response headers
- Response body

You access the **Signature** dialog box by clicking the **Add** button. (See Figure 7.13.)

Figure 7.13 The Signatures Tab

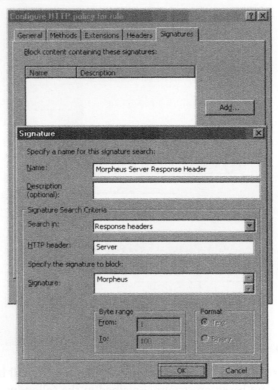

In the **Signature** dialog box, enter a name for the signature in the **Name** text box and a description of the signature in the **Description** text box. This is especially helpful so that you know the purpose and rationale for this signature.

In the **Search in** drop-down list, select where you want the ISA firewall to search for the specified string. You have the follow options:

■ **Request URL** When you select this option, you can enter a string that when found in the Web client's request URL, the connection is blocked. For example, if you wanted to prevent all requests to sites that have the string **Kazaa** in the URL included in the Web client's request, you enter **Kazaa** in the **Signature** text box.

■ **Request headers** When you select this option, you enter the specific HTTP header you want the ISA firewall to check in the **HTTP header** text box and then enter the string in the header you want the ISA firewall to block in the **Signature** text box. For example, if you want to block eDonkey P2P applications, you can select this option and then **User-Agent** in the **HTTP header** text box. In the **Signature** text box, you then enter **ed2k**. Note that this option gives you more granular control than you would have if you just blocked headers in the **Headers** tab. If you block a specific header in the **Headers** tab, you end up blocking all HTTP communications that use that specific header. By creating a signature that incorporates a specific header, you can allow that HTTP header for all communications that do not include the header value you enter for the signature.

- **Request body**   You can block HTTP communications based on the body of the Web request outside of that contained in the HTTP commands and headers. While this is a very powerful feature, it has the potential to consume a great deal of resources on the ISA firewall computer. For this reason, you need to configure the byte range you want the ISA firewall to inspect in the **Byte range From** and **To** text boxes. We don't have any explicit recommendations on specific entries you might want to include in this section, but will provide updates on www.isaserver.org when we do.

- **Response headers**   When you select this option, you enter the specific HTTP header you want to block based on the HTTP response returned by the Web server. You enter the specific HTTP header in the **HTTP header** text box and the HTTP header value in the **Signature** text box.

- **Response body**   The response body option works the same as the **Request body** option, except it applies to the content returned to the Web client from the Web server. For example, if you want to block Web pages that contain specific strings that are identified as dangerous or inappropriate, you can create a signature to block those strings. Keep this in mind when reading about the latest Web-based attack and create a signature that blocks connections that employ such an attack.

Figure 7.14 shows some example signatures blocking some commonly encountered applications that might be considered a major security risk for corporate networks.

Figure 7.14 Example Signatures

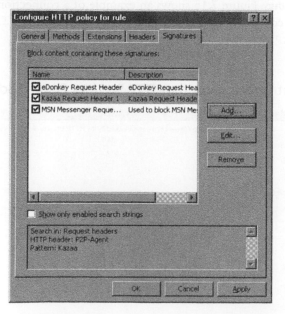

ISA FIREWALL TIP

Another signature you might want to create is one that blocks the **<iframe src="?"/>** string in the response body. This string can potentially peg the processor on the victim machine and hang the operating system.

HTTP Security Filter Logging

How do you know if your security filters are working? One way to determine the effectiveness of the entries you've made in the HTTP Security filter is to use the ISA firewall's built-in log viewer. Perform the following steps to configure the ISA firewall's built-in log viewer to view HTTP Security Filter actions:

1. In the **Microsoft Internet Security and Acceleration Server 2006** management console, expand the server name and click the **Monitoring** node in the left pane of the console.

2. In the **Monitoring** node, click the **Logging** tab. In the **Tasks** tab of the Task Pane, click the **Start Query** link.

3. Right-click one of the column headers and click the **Add/Remove Columns** command.

4. In the **Add/Remove Columns** dialog box, click the **Filter Information** entry in the **Available Columns** list and click **Add**. The **Filter Information** entry now appears in the list of **Displayed columns**. Click **OK**.

5. Issue a request from a client behind the ISA firewall that would be blocked by your HTTP Security Filter settings. Figure 7.15 shows an example of a connection that was blocked because the URL contained a string that was disallowed by the HTTP Security filter.

Figure 7.15 Log File Entries Showing the HTTP Security Filter Blocking a Connection

Client IP	Destinatio	Destination Port	Protocol	HTTP Method	URL	Filter Information
10.0.0.5	10.0.0.1	8080	http	GET	http://www.cisco.com/	Blocked by the HTTP Security filter: URL contains sequences which are disallowed
10.0.0.5	10.0.0.1	8080	Unidentifie...	·	·	·
10.0.0.1	10.0.0.2	53	DNS	·	·	·
192.168.1.70	192.168.1.34	53	DNS	·	·	·
10.0.0.5	10.0.0.1	8080	Unidentifie...	·	·	·
10.0.0.5	10.0.0.1	8080	http	GET	http://www.cisco.com/	Blocked by the HTTP Security filter: URL contains sequences which are disallowed

Exporting and Importing HTTP Security Filter Settings

An HTTP policy can be exported from or imported into an Access Rule that uses the HTTP protocol or a Web Publishing Rule. The **HttpFilterConfig.vbs** script in the SDK kit located at http://www.microsoft.com/downloads/details.aspx?familyid=16682C4F-7645-4279-97E4-9A0C73 C5162E&displaylang=en can be used to export an existing HTTP policy that has already been configured in an Access Rule or Web Publishing Rule or an HTTP policy that has already been exported to a file can be imported into an existing Access Rule or Web Publishing Rule.

The **HttpFilterConfig.vbs** script greatly simplifies configuration of complex HTTP policies that include multiple entries for parameters such as signature, file extensions, and headers. We recommend that you export your HTTP policies after you create them in the **Microsoft Internet Security and Acceleration Server 2006** management console.

In this section, we discuss how you can export and import an HTTP policy from and to a Web Publishing Rule.

ISA FIREWALL TIP

Jim Harrison, the Godfather of ISA firewall scripting, has several attack prevention tools and scripts on his site that automatically configure an HTTP policy as part of the attack prevention and mitigation configuration. Check out Jim's fantastic ISA firewall tools Web site at www.isatools.org.

Exporting an HTTP Policy from a Web Publishing Rule

HTTP policies can be exported from an Access Rule or Web Publishing Rule using the **HttpFilterConfig.vbs** file located on the ISA 2006 CD-ROM. Follow these steps to export the HTTP policy from an existing Web Publishing Rule:

1. Copy the **HttpFilterConfig.vbs** file to the root of the C: drive.

2. Open a command prompt and change the focus to the root of the C: drive. Enter the following command and press **Enter** (notice that if the rule name has a space in it you must enclose the name in quotes):

   ```
   C:\Httpfilterconfig.vbs import "Publish OWA Site" c:\webpol.xml
   ```

3. You will see a dialog box confirming that the information was successfully imported into the rule (see Figure 7.16).

Figure 7.16 Successful Import Dialog Box

Importing an HTTP Policy into a Web Publishing Rule

HTTP policies can be imported into Access Rules that include the HTTP protocol and Web Publishing Rules. We use the same script we used when exporting an HTTP policy, the **HttpFilterConfig.vbs** file. To import an HTTP policy saved to an .xml file into a Web Publishing Rule named **Publish OWA Site**:

1. Copy both the .xml file and the **HttpFilterConfig.vbs** file from the ISA 2006 CD-ROM to the root of the C: drive. In this example, the .xml file is named **webpol.xml**.

2. Open a command prompt and change the focus to the root of the C: drive. Enter the following command and press **Enter** (notice that if the rule name has spaces in it, you must enclose the name in quotes):

   ```
   C:\Httpfilterconfig.vbs import "Publish OWA Site" c:\webpol.xml
   ```

3. You will see a dialog box confirming that the information was successfully imported into the rule (see Figure 7.17).

Figure 7.17 Successful Import Dialog Box

Investigating HTTP Headers for Potentially Dangerous Applications

One of your primary tasks as an ISA firewall administrator is to investigate characteristics of network traffic with the goal of blocking new and ever more dangerous network applications. These dangerous applications might be peer-to-peer applications, instant messaging applications, or other applications that hide by wrapping themselves in an HTTP header. Many vendors now wrap their applications in an HTTP header in an attempt to subvert your Firewall policy. Your goal as an ISA firewall administrator is to subvert the vendors' attempt to subvert your Network Usage policy.

As you can imagine, the vendors of these applications aren't very cooperative when it comes to getting information on how to prevent their applications from violating your firewall security. You'll often have to figure out this information for yourself, especially for new and obscure applications.

Your main tool in fighting the war against network scumware is a protocol analyzer. Two of the most popular protocol analyzers are Microsoft Network Monitor and the freeware tool Ethereal. Both are excellent, the only major downside of Ethereal being that you need to install a network driver to make it work correctly. Since the WinPcaP driver required by Ethereal hasn't been regression tested against the ISA firewall software, it's hard to know whether it may cause problems with firewall stability or performance. For this reason, we'll use the built-in version of Network Monitor included with Windows Server 2003 in the following examples.

Let's look at a couple of examples of how you can determine how to block some dangerous applications. One such application is eDonkey, a peer-to-peer file-sharing application. The first step is to start Network Monitor and run a network monitor trace while running the eDonkey application on a client that accesses the Internet through the ISA firewall. The best way to start is by configuring Network Monitor to listen on the Internal interface of the ISA firewall, or whatever interface eDonkey or other offending applications use to access the Internet through the ISA firewall.

Stop the trace after running the offending application for a while. Since we're only interested in Web connections moving through TCP port 80, we can filter out all other communications in the trace. We can do this with Display filters.

Click the **Display** menu and then click the **Filter** command. In the **Display Filter** dialog box, double-click the **Protocol == Any** entry. (See Figure 7.18.)

Figure 7.18 The Display Filter Dialog Box

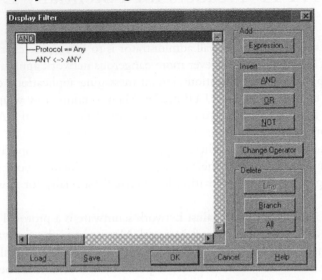

In the **Expression** dialog box, click the **Protocol** tab and then click the **Disable All** button. In the list of **Disabled Protocols**, click the **HTTP** protocol, click the **Enable** button, and then click **OK**. (See Figure 7.19.)

Figure 7.19 The Expression Dialog Box

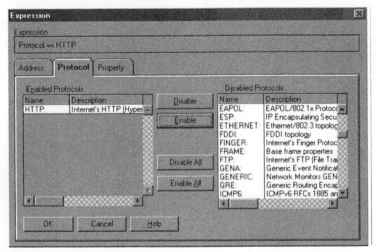

Click **OK** in the **Display Filter** dialog box. The top pane of the Network Monitor console now only displays HTTP connections. A good place to start is by looking at the **GET** requests, which appear as **GET Request from Client** in the **Description** column. Double-click on the GET requests and expand the **HTTP: Get Request from Client** entry in the middle form. This displays a list of request headers.

In Figure 7.20, you can see that one of the request headers appears to be unusual (only if you have experience looking at Network Monitor traces; don't worry, it won't take long before you get good at this). The **HTTP: User–Agent =ed2k** seems like it might be specific for eDonkey2000. We can use this information to create an HTTP Security Filter entry to block the **User–Agent** Request Header value **ed2k**.

Figure 7.20 The Network Monitor Display Window

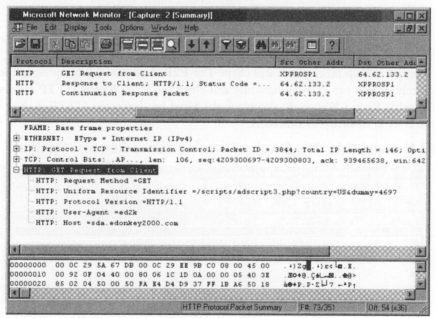

You can do this by creating an HTTP Security Filter signature using these values. Figure 7.21 shows what the HTTP Security Filter signature would look like to block the eDonkey application.

Figure 7.21 The Signature Dialog Box

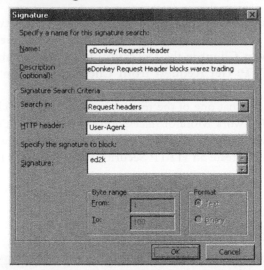

Another example of a dangerous application is Kazaa. Figure 7.22 shows a frame displaying the GET request the Kazaa client sends through the ISA firewall. In the list of HTTP headers, you can see one that can be used to help block the Kazaa client. The **P2P-Agent** HTTP request header can be blocked completely, or you can create a signature and block the **P2P-Agent** HTTP request header when it has the value **Kazaa**. You could also block the **Host** header in the HTTP request header when the value is set as **desktop.kazaa.com**.

Figure 7.22 Network Monitor Display Showing Kazaa Request Headers

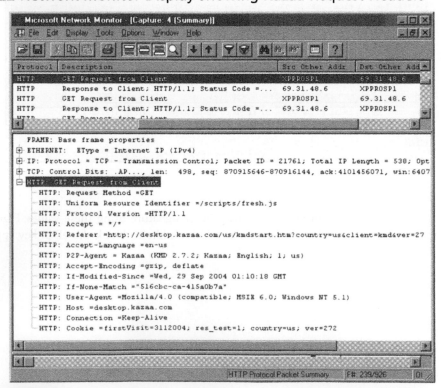

Example HTTP Security Filter Policies

Creating HTTP Security Filter policies can take some time. You need to run the required applications and then determine the required methods, extensions, headers, and other signatures that are specific for your application. While the effort is well spent, sometimes you need to get critical applications up and running quickly.

For this reason, we include a couple of example HTTP Security Filter policies you can use right away to protect IIS Web sites and Outlook Web Access sites.

Table 7.1 provides the defaults of a good default Web site HTTP Security Filter policy you can use. This policy allows the most common methods required for simple Web sites and restricts extensions that might allow an attacker to compromise your site. There are also several HTTP signatures included that block common strings that Internet criminals might use to compromise your Web site or server.

Table 7.1 Example HTTP Security Filter for Generic Web Sites

Tab	Parameter
General	Maximum header length is 32768.
	Allow any payload length is selected.
	Maximum URL length is 260.
	Maximum query length is 4096.
	Verify normalization is selected.
	Block high bit characters is not selected.
Methods	Allow only specified methods:
	GET
	HEAD
	POST
Extensions	Block specified extensions (allow all others):
	.exe
	.bat
	.cmd
	.com
	.htw
	.ida
	.idq
	.htr
	.idc
	.shtm
	.shtml

Continued

Table 7.1 Continued

Tab	Parameter
	.stm
	.printer
	.ini
	.log
	.pol
	.dat
Headers	No changes from the default.
Signatures (Request URL)	Block content containing these signatures
	..
	./
	:
	%
	&
Tab	Parameter

Table 7.2 provides settings you can use to configure an HTTP Security Filter policy for OWA publishing. Notice the methods required by OWA. You can see these in action by using the ISA firewall's built-in log filter and watching the HTTP Methods column.

ISA FIREWALL TIP

You may not want to include the **&** character and **.exe** extension. You need to allow **.exe** for downloading of the S/MIME control. However, because HTTP Security Filter policy is applied on a per-rule basis, we suggest you create a separate rule allowing access for specific Outlook Web Access needs, and order it before the rule that blocks access based on Table 7.3. The allow rule would allow access only to the OWA directory containing those controls. If you do not allow the **&** character in requests, certain functions, like Calendaring, will not work correctly.

Table 7.2 HTTP Security Filter Settings for OWA Web Publishing Rules

Tab	Parameter
General	Maximum header length is 32768.
	Allow any payload length is selected.
	Maximum URL length is 260.
	Maximum query length is 4096.
	Verify normalization is selected.
	Block high bit characters is not selected.
Methods	Allow only specified methods:
	GET
	POST
	PROPFIND
	PROPPATCH
	BPROPPATCH
	MKCOL
	DELETE
	BDELETE
	BCOPY
	MOVE
	SUBSCRIBE
	BMOVE
	POLL
	SEARCH
Extensions	Block specified extensions (allow all others):
	.exe
	.bat
	.cmd
	.com
	.htw
	.ida
	.idq
	.htr
	.idc
	.shtm
	.shtml

Continued

Table 7.2 Continued

Tab	Parameter
	.stm
	.printer
	.ini
	.log
	.pol
	.dat
Headers	No changes from the default.
Signatures (Request URL)	Block content containing these signatures
	./
	\
	:
	%
	&

Table 7.3 shows entries for an HTTP Security Filter policy you can use for an RPC-over-HTTP Web Publishing Rule. Notice the unusual HTTP methods used by the Outlook 2003 RPC-over-HTTP protocol.

Table 7.3 HTTP Security Filter Policy Settings for RPC-over-HTTP Web Publishing Rule

Tab	Parameter
General	Maximum headers length is 32768.
	Maximum Payload Length: 2000000000.
	Maximum URL length is 16384.
	Maximum query length is 4096.
	Verify normalization is selected.
	Block high bit characters is not selected.
Methods	Allow only specified methods:
	RPC_IN_DATA
	RPC_OUT_DATA
Extensions	No changes from the default.
Headers	No changes from the default.
Signatures (Request URL)	No changes from the default.

Commonly Blocked Headers and Application Signatures

While we consider it an entertaining pastime spending long evenings with Network Monitor and discovering how to block dangerous applications, not all ISA firewall administrators share this predilection. For those of you who need to configure your ISA firewall to protect your network from dangerous applications as soon as possible, we provide the information in Tables 7.4 and 7.5.

Table 7.4 lists the information you need to include in signatures to block commonly encountered dangerous applications. You use the information in this table to create a signature entry in the HTTP Security filter.

Table 7.4 Sample Signatures for Blocking Commonly Encountered Dangerous Applications

Application	Location	HTTP Header	Signature
MSN Messenger	Request headers	User-Agent:	MSN Messenger
Windows Messenger	Request headers	User-Agent:	MSMSGS
Netscape 7	Request headers	User-Agent:	Netscape/7
Netscape 6	Request headers	User-Agent:	Netscape/6
AOL Messenger (and all Gecko browsers)	Request headers	User-Agent:	Gecko/
Yahoo Messenger	Request headers	Host	msg.yahoo.com
Kazaa	Request headers	P2P-Agent	Kazaa Kazaaclient:
Kazaa	Request headers	User-Agent:	KazaaClient
Kazaa	Request headers	X-Kazaa-Network:	KaZaA
Gnutella	Request headers	User-Agent:	Gnutella Gnucleus
eDonkey	Request headers	User-Agent:	e2dk
Internet Explorer 6.0	Request headers	User-Agent:	MSIE 6.0
Morpheus	Response header	Server	Morpheus
Bearshare	Response header	Server	Bearshare
BitTorrent	Request headers	User-Agent:	BitTorrent
SOAP over HTTP	Request headers Response headers	User-Agent:	SOAPAction

Table 7.5 contains some HTTP header values you can use to block dangerous applications. In contrast to signatures that require the HTTP header name and value, the entries in Table 7.5 can be configured in the **Headers** tab of the HTTP Security filter. These headers are specific for the listed dangerous applications and are not used for legitimate HTTP communications, so you do not need to specify a specific value for the HTTP headers blocked here.

Table 7.5 HTTP Headers Used to Bock Dangerous Applications

Application	Location	Type	Value
Kazaa	Headers	Request Header	X-Kazaa-Username: X-Kazaa-IP: X-Kazaa-SupernodeIP:
BitTorrent	Extensions	None	.torrent
Many peer-to-peer clients	Headers	Request Header	P2P-Agent

The ISA Server Link Translator

Link Translation solves a number of issues that may arise for external users connecting through the ISA firewall to an internal Web site.

The ISA firewall Link Translator is implemented as an ISA firewall Web filter. Because of the Link Translator's built-in functionality, and because it comes with a built-in default dictionary, you can use it right out of the box to solve many common problems encountered with proxy-based Web publishing scenarios.

For example, when pages on the internal Web site contain absolute URLs pointing to itself, the Link Translator will return the appropriate links to the external user, even when those URLs contain http:// prefixes and the external user connects to the Web site using https://.

The default Link Translator dictionary can also appropriately translate requests made to nonstandard ports. For example, if users connect to a Web site that is published on a nonstandard port, such as http://www.msfirewall.org:8181, link translation will include the port number in the URLs sent back to the external client.

When you enable link translation for a Web Publishing Rule, a Link Translation dictionary is automatically created. In most cases, you won't have to add to the default dictionary.

The default dictionary includes the following entries:

- Any occurrence on the Web site of the computer name specified on the **To** tab of the Web Publishing Rule Properties is replaced with the Web site name (or IP address). For example, if a rule redirects all requests for http://www.microsoft.com to an internal computer called SERVER1 (or 192.168.1.1), all occurrences of http://SERVER1 in the response page returned to the client are replaced with http://www.microsoft.com.

- If a nondefault port is specified on the Web listener, that port is used when replacing links on the response page. If a default port is specified, the port is removed when replacing links on the response page. For example, if the Web listener is listening on TCP port 88, the responses returned to the Web client will include links to TCP port 88.

■ If the client specifies HTTPS in the request to the ISA firewall, the firewall will replace all occurrences of HTTP with HTTPS.

For example, suppose the ISA firewall publishes a site located on a machine with the internal name SERVER1. The ISA firewall publishes the site using the public name www.msfirewall.orgdocs. An external Web client then makes the following request:

```
GET /docs HTTP/1.1
Host: www.msfirewall.org
```

Note that the directory name in the request is not terminated by a slash (/). When the server running Internet Information Services (IIS) receives this request, it automatically returns a 302 response with the location header set to http://SERVER1/docs/, which is the internal name of the server followed by the directory name and terminated by a slash.

The ISA firewall's Link Translator then translates the response header value to http://www.msfirewall.org/docs/.

In this example, the following entries are automatically added to the Link Translation dictionary:

■ http://SERVER1 is mapped to http://www.msfirewall.org

■ http://SERVER1:80 is mapped to http://www.msfirewall.org

■ https://SERVER1 is mapped to https://www.msfirewall.org

■ https://SERVER1:443 is mapped to https://www.msfirewall.org

For security reasons, if an initial client request was sent via SSL, all links to the same Web server are translated to SSL. The following entries are automatically included in the Link Translation dictionary:

■ http://SERVER1 is mapped to https://www.msfirewall.org

■ http://SERVER1:80 is mapped to https://www.msfirewall.org

■ https://SERVER1 is mapped to https://www.msfirewall.org

■ https://SERVER1:443 is mapped to https://www.msfirewall.org

If the published Web site uses ports other than the default HTTP and SSL ports (for example, 88 for HTTP and 488 for SSL), links containing that port number will also be translated. For example:

■ http://SERVER1:88 is mapped to http://www.msfirewall.org

■ https://SERVER1:488 is mapped to https://www.msfirewall.org

In the same way, if the ISA firewall publishes the site using a Web listener on nondefault ports (for example, 85 for HTTP and 885 for SSL), links will be translated to the published ports:

■ http://SERVER1 is mapped to http://www.msfirewall.org:85

■ http://SERVER1:80 is mapped to http://www.msfirewall.org:85

- https://SERVER1 is mapped to https://www.msfirewall.org:885

- https://SERVER1:443 is mapped to https://www.msfirewall.org:885

ISA FIREWALL TIPS

- Don't end the search string in the Link Translator dictionary with a terminating character. For example, use http://SERVER1, not http://SERVER1/.

- When adding an entry for a site name, also add an entry with the site name and port. For example, if you add the search string http://SERVER1 in the Link Translator dictionary, also add the search string http://SERVER1:80.

- Use both http:// and https://.

- Use caution when changing directory structures, as this will affect the settings in your Link Translation dictionary.

- Dictionaries with a large number of entries when applied to Web sites that have many links requiring translation could detrimentally impact ISA Server performance.

While the default dictionary is effective for most simple Web publishing scenario, things get a bit stickier when you publish more complex Web sites. For more complex Web publishing scenarios, or when complex ASP code is involved (for example, with SharePoint services), it's necessary to configure dictionary entries that map to names returned by the internal Web site.

The Link Translator checks the Content-type header of the response to determine whether link translation should be applied to the body of the message. The default settings allow for link translation only MIME types belonging to the HTML document's content group. The ISA firewall's Link Translator works by first looking for a Content-type header to determine if it needs to perform translation. If no Content-type header is present, the filter will look for a Content-location header to perform translation. If neither header is present, the filter will look at the file extension.

The Link Translator maps text strings according to the following rules:

- The Link Translator searches for the longest strings, then shorter strings, and finally the default strings.

- If the Link Translator finds a matching text string, it will then look at the next character to the right to see if it is a *terminating* character. The following are considered terminating characters:

\t	\r	\n	;	~	<	!	"	&	'	)	$	)	*
+	,	–	/	>	=	?	[	\	]	^	{	|	}

- If the Link Translator finds a terminating character immediately to the right of the string, it will perform translation on that string.

For example, consider a scenario where the Link Translation dictionary is configured to replace "sps" with "extranet.external.net" and a response page returned by the Web server includes a hard-coded link to http://Sps/SpsDocs/. The Link Translator translates the string to http://extranet.external.net/SpsDocs/. However, if the response page includes a link to http://sps/sps-isa/, *both* instances of "sps" would be translated because they are both followed by a terminating character, resulting in http://extranet.external.net/extranet.external.net-isa/ being sent to the external client.

Because of these potential translation issues, it's critical that you understand the behavior of link translation mapping to prevent problems with your custom Link Translator dictionaries.

Determining Custom Dictionary Entries

You must test the behavior of the Link Translator to see if any custom dictionary entries are required. SharePoint Portal Services provides a fertile test bed for testing the Link Translator. Begin your test by connecting to a published SharePoint site using an external client and testing the functionality of the published site. You should look for links pointing to internal server names and links that use the wrong prefix (for example, http instead of https).

Be aware that some links will be included in client-side scripts returned to the browser for processing. You should therefore also view the HTML source code that is returned, not just the rendered HTML in the browser.

In the case of a published SharePoint site, it may be necessary to add custom dictionary entries. For example, even though the Link Translator is enabled, the search function on the SharePoint site may return results with both the wrong prefix (http instead of https) and internal server names.

In addition, after adding custom dictionary entries to fix these problems, the source code of the search results page contains JavaScript that includes references to the wrong prefix, causing errors to be returned to the browser when trying to perform an additional search from the search results page.

For example, after adding two dictionary entries to replace "http://" with "https://" and to replace "sps" with "extranet.external.net," the returned source code included the following strings in the client-side JavaScript code:

```
f.action='http:\/\/extranet.external.net\/Search.aspx', and
http:\\\/\\\/extranet.external.net\\\/Search.aspx
```

To fix this problem, it is necessary to explicitly map the shorter string "http:" to "https:". Importantly, it is necessary to include the colon (:) in the dictionary entry. Simply mapping "http" to "https" (without the colon) causes the entire site to be inaccessible.

It should be clear to you at this point that finding the correct custom dictionary entries can involve extensive and repetitive testing. Incorrect link translation mappings can break the Web site for external clients, so we highly recommend that you test configurations in your test lab before deploying link translation in a production environment.

Configuring Custom Link Translation Dictionary Entries

Custom Link Translation dictionaries are configured on a per-rule basis. Remember, link translation is only performed on links returned by Web servers published by Web Publishing Rules; you do not configure Link Translation for outgoing requests to Internet Web servers.

To configure Link Translation:

1. Right-click the Web Publishing Rule and click **Properties**.

2. In the Web Publishing Rule's **Properties** dialog box, click the **Link Translation** tab.

3. On the **Link Translation** tab, put a checkmark in the **Replace absolute links in Web pages** checkbox. Click the **Add** button.

4. In the **Add/Edit Dictionary Item** dialog box, enter the name of the string you want replaced in returned links in the **Replace this text** text box. Enter the value you want to replace the string in the **With this text** text box. Click **OK**. (See Figure 7.23.)

Figure 7.23 Add/Edit Dictionary Text Box

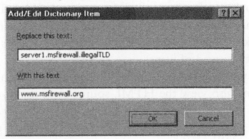

5. The dictionary entry appears in the list of dictionary entries. Click the **Content Types** button. (See Figure 7.24.)

Figure 7.24 Link Translation Tab in Web Publishing Rule Properties

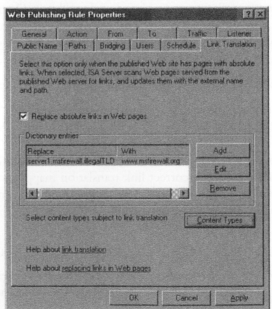

6. In the **Link Translation** dialog box, select the content types to which you want to apply Link Translation. By default, only the **HTML Documents** content type is selected. Your selection here is global and applies to all Web Publishing Rules. Even though you can create custom dictionaries for each Web Publishing Rule, the content types are the same for all dictionaries.

ISA FIREWALL WARNING

The Web Publishing Rule must list an explicit fully qualified domain name (FQDN) or IP address in order to perform link translation. If you configure the Web Publishing Rule to redirect for all incoming connections to the listener, you will see an error dialog box informing you that you must use an explicit FQDN or IP address on the **Public** tab of the Web Publishing Rule's **Properties** dialog box.

The Web Proxy Filter

The Web Proxy filter allows connections from hosts not configured as Web Proxy clients to be forwarded to the ISA firewall's Cache and Web Proxy components. If you want only hosts that are explicitly configured as Web Proxy clients to use the ISA firewall's Web Proxy feature set, you can unbind the Web Proxy filter by removing the checkmark from the **Web Proxy Filter** checkbox.

ISA FIREWALL WARNING

Be aware that disabling the HTTP filter for the HTTP protocol is a global setting and affects all rules that use the HTTP filter. While the filter is still active for Web Proxy clients, the configuration interface for the HTTP filter is removed, and you will not be able to configure the HTTP policy for the Web Proxy clients. This problem may be solved in the future, and we will post this information at www.isaserver.org when we find a solution to this problem. (See Figure 7.25.)

Figure 7.25 The HTTP Properties Dialog Box

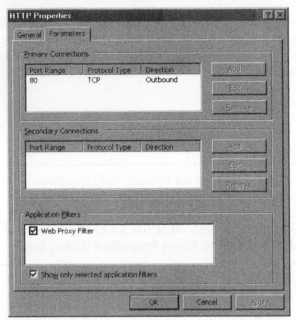

The OWA Forms-Based Authentication Filter

The OWA Forms–Based Authentication filter is used to mediate Forms-based authentication to OWA Web sites that are made accessible via ISA firewall Web Publishing Rules. Figure 7.26 shows the configuration interface for the OWA Forms-Based Authentication filter, which is accessible from the Authentication dialog box for the Web listener.

Figure 7.26 The OWA Forms-Based Authentication Dialog Box

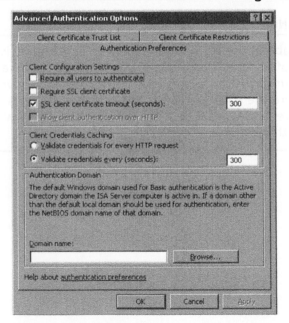

The RADIUS Authentication Filter

The RADIUS Authentication filter is used to mediate RADIUS authentication for Web Proxy clients and external hosts connecting to published Web sites via Web Publishing Rules.

The RADIUS filter is used by Web listeners when the listeners are configured to use RADIUS authentication. While the RADIUS filter provides you the ability to authenticate against any RADIUS-compliant directory (including the Active Directory), it does limit you to use only RADIUS authentication on the listener configured to use RADIUS. In contrast, when using other authentication methods, such as basic or integrated authentication, you can support multiple authentication protocols on a single Web listener.

IP Filtering and Intrusion Detection/Intrusion Prevention

The ISA firewall performs intrusion detection and intrusion prevention. In this section, we discuss the following intrusion detection and intrusion prevention features:

- Common Attacks Detection and Prevention
- DNS Attacks Detection and Prevention
- IP Options and IP Fragment Filtering

Common Attacks Detection and Prevention

You can access the **Intrusion Detection** dialog box by opening the **Microsoft Internet Security and Acceleration Server 2006** management console, expanding the server name, and then expanding the **Configuration** node. Click the **General** node.

In the **General** node, click the **Enable Intrusion Detection and DNS Attack Detection** link. This brings up the **Common Attacks** tab.

On the **Common Attacks** tab, put a checkmark in the **Enable intrusion detection** checkbox. Put a checkmark to the left of each of the attacks you want to prevent. If you enable the **Port scan** attack, enter values for the **Detect after attacks … well-known ports** and **Detect after attacks on … ports**. (See Figure 7.27.)

You can disable logging for packets dropped by the Intrusion Detection filter by removing the checkmark from the **Log dropped packets** checkbox.

Figure 7.27 The Common Attacks Tab

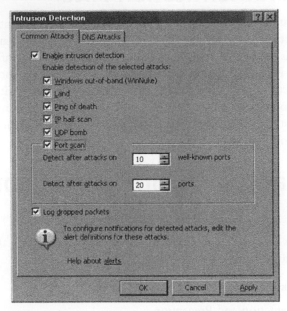

DNS Attacks Detection and Prevention

The ISA firewall's DNS filter protects DNS servers published by the ISA firewall using Server Publishing Rules. You can access the configuration interface for the DNS filter's attack prevention configuration page in the **Intrusion Detection** dialog box. Expand the server name and then expand the **Configuration** node. Click the **General** node.

In the Details Pane, click the **Enable Intrusion Detection and DNS Attack Detection** link. In the **Intrusion Detection** dialog box, click the **DNS Attacks** tab. On the **DNS Attacks** tab, put a checkmark in the **Enable detection and filtering of DNS attacks** checkbox. (See Figure 7.28.)

Once detection is enabled, you can enable prevention, and protect yourself from three attacks:

- DNS host name overflow
- DNS length overflow
- DNS zone transfer

Figure 7.28 The DNS Attacks Tab

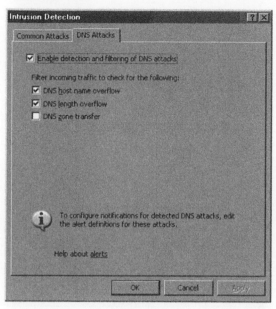

The *DNS host name overflow* and *DNS length overflow* attacks are DNS DoS type attacks. The DNS DoS attack exploits the difference in size between a DNS query and a DNS response, in which all of the network's bandwidth is tied up by bogus DNS queries. The attacker uses the DNS servers as "amplifiers" to multiply the DNS traffic.

The attacker begins by sending small DNS queries to each DNS server that contain the spoofed IP address of the intended victim. The responses returned to the small queries are much larger, so that if there are a large number of responses returned at the same time, the link will become congested and denial of service will take place.

One solution to this problem is for administrators to configure DNS servers to respond with a "refused" response, which is much smaller than a name resolution response, when they receive DNS queries from suspicious or unexpected sources.

Detailed information for configuring DNS servers to prevent this problem is contained in the U.S. Department of Energy's Computer Incident Advisory Capability information bulletin J-063, available at http://www.ciac.org/ciac/bulletins/j-063.shtml.

IP Options and IP Fragment Filtering

You can configure what IP Options are allowed through the ISA firewall and whether IP Fragments are allowed through. Figures 7.29 and 7.30 show the configuration interfaces for IP Options filtering and IP Fragment filtering. Figure 7.31 shows a dialog box warning that enabling Fragment filtering may interfere with L2TP/IPSec and streaming media services.

Figure 7.29 The IP Options Tab

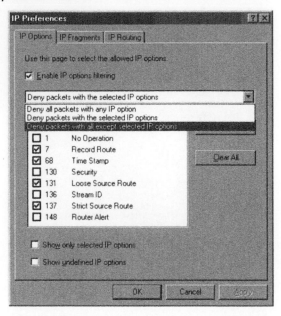

Figure 7.30 The IP Fragments Tab

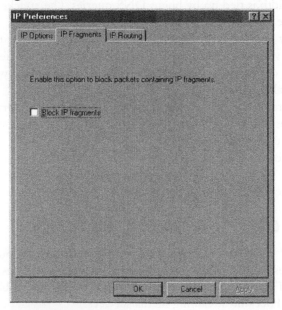

Figure 7.31 The IP Fragment Filter Warning Dialog Box

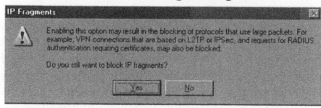

Source Routing Attack

TCP/IP supports *source routing,* which is a means to permit the sender of network data to route the packets through a specific point on the network. There are two types of source routing:

- **Strict source routing**   The sender of the data can specify the exact route (rarely used).

- **Loose source record route (LSRR)**   The sender can specify certain routers (hops) through which the packet must pass.

The source route is an option in the IP header that allows the sender to override routing decisions that are normally made by the routers between the source and destination machines. Source routing is used by network administrators to map the network, or for troubleshooting routing and communications problems. It can also be used to force traffic through a route that will provide the best performance. Unfortunately, source routing can be exploited by hackers.

If the system allows source routing, an intruder can use it to reach private internal addresses on the LAN that normally would not be reachable from the Internet, by routing the traffic through another machine that is reachable from both the Internet and the internal machine.

Source routing can be disabled on most routers to prevent this type of attack. The ISA firewall also blocks source routing by default.

Summary

In this chapter, we discussed the ISA firewall's application layer filtering feature set. We discussed the two main types of application filters employed by the ISA firewall: access filters and security filters. While we broke down the ISA firewall's filters into these two main categories, this is not to say that access filters are unsecure. Both the access filters and the security filters impose requirements that the connections meet specifications of legitimate communications using those protocols.

We finished the chapter with a discussion of the ISA firewall's intrusion detection and prevention mechanisms. You learned about common network layer attacks that can be launched against the ISA firewall and how the ISA firewall protects you against them.

Chapter 8

Accelerating Web Performance with ISA 2006 Caching Capabilities

Solutions in this chapter:

- **Understanding Caching Concepts**

- **Understanding ISA 2006's Web Caching Capabilities**

- **Configuring ISA 2006 as a Caching Server**

- **Comparing ISA 2006 to Third-Party Caching Solutions**

☑ **Summary**

With the growing emphasis on security and firewall capabilities, it's easy to forget that ISA 2006 provides a second important function: performance acceleration for your network's internal and external Web users. This is done via the caching feature, and it's a feature that most of ISA's top competitors in the firewall market don't include with their products.

The Web is a vital part of many of today's businesses. Members of your organization may access Web sites on the Internet every day, to gather information about particular subjects, conduct research on people and things, stay on top of the news affecting your industry, and so forth. At the same time, your own Web site(s) may be one of your best vehicles for advertising and promoting your business and providing information to partners and clients.

Within most Internet-connected organizations, the amount of Web traffic has been growing consistently. Users often visit the same Web sites on a regular basis, or multiple users within the organization visit the same sites and view the same pages. In addition, overall network and Internet traffic is steadily increasing, often to the point of near saturation of available Internet bandwidth. Caching can be the solution.

Understanding Caching Concepts

It can be costly to add additional Internet bandwidth. Some ISPs charge T-1 and T-3 users on a usage basis, so reducing bandwidth usage can result in real savings to the bottom line. Even if your organization buys bandwidth on an unlimited plan, reducing usage can increase performance for the network's users. There are two different types of caching – forward and reverse – that can benefit your organization, and we will discuss them in this section. Caching servers can also be deployed in groups, and these groups can be arranged in two different architectures, depending on your network's needs.

NOTE

Just in case you were anticipating that the two types of caching would be *active* and *passive*, please note that, as discussed in Chapter 2, ISA 2006 no longer supports active caching, although there is a setting for it in the interface.

In the following sections, we will look at the differences between the two types of Web caching, the architectures used to deploy multiple caching servers, and the protocols that are used by caching servers to communicate with one another.

Web Caching Types

As stated above, there are two basic types of Web caching:

- Forward caching
- Reverse caching

ISA 2006 performs both of these, so let's look at each a little more closely.

Forward Caching

One way to reduce Internet bandwidth consumption is to store frequently-accessed Web objects on the local network, where they can be retrieved by internal users without going out to a server on the Internet. This is called forward Web caching, and it has the added advantage of making access for internal users faster because they are retrieving the Web objects (such as pages, graphics, and sound files) over a fast LAN connection, typically 100Mbps or more, instead of a slower Internet connection at perhaps 1.5Mbps.

Forward caching is supported by all Web caching servers. Forward caching accelerates the response to outbound requests when users on the internal network request a Web object from a server on the Internet. Those objects that are requested frequently are stored on the caching server. This means they can be retrieved via the fast local network connection instead of over a slower Internet connection.

Forward caching takes place when a user on a network protected by the ISA 2006 firewall makes a request for Web content. The requested content is placed in the Web cache after the first user makes a request. The next (and subsequent) user who requests the same content from the Internet has the content delivered from the Web cache on the ISA 2006 machine instead of from the Internet Web server. This reduces the amount of traffic on the Internet connection and reduces overall network costs. In addition, the content is delivered to the user much more quickly from cache than it is from the actual Web server. This increases user satisfaction and productivity.

The primary "bottom line" benefit of ISA 2006's forward caching is cost savings realized by reduced bandwidth usage on the Internet connection.

Reverse Caching

Reverse caching, in contrast, reduces traffic on the internal network and speeds access for external users when the company hosts its own Web sites. Frequently-requested objects on the internal Web servers are cached at the network edge, on a proxy server, so that the load on the Web servers is reduced.

NOTE

In generic caching documentation, reverse caches are sometimes referred to as "gateway caches" or "surrogate caches."

Reverse caching is appropriate when your organization hosts its own internal Web sites that are made available to external Internet or intranet users. The caching server stores those objects that are frequently requested from the internal Web servers and serves them to Internet users. This speeds access for the external users and it also lightens the load on the internal Web servers and reduces traffic on the internal network.

Reverse caching takes place when a user on the Internet makes a request for Web content that is located on a Web server published by an ISA 2006 Web Publishing Rule. The ISA 2006 firewall retrieves the content from the Web server on an internal network or another network protected by the firewall and returns that information to the Internet user who requested the content. The ISA 2006 machine caches the content it retrieves from the Web server on the internal network. When subsequent users request the same information, the content is served from the ISA 2006 cache instead of being retrieved from the originating Web site.

There are two principle benefits to the reverse caching scenario:

■ Reverse caching reduces bandwidth usage on the internal network.

■ Reverse caching allows Web content to be available when the Web server is offline.

How Reverse Caching Reduces Bandwidth Usage

Reverse caching reduces bandwidth usage on the internal network when cached content is served directly from the ISA 2006 machine. No bandwidth usage is required on the internal network; thus, this bandwidth becomes available to internal network users. Corporate networks that are already having issues with insufficient bandwidth will benefit from this configuration.

How Reverse Caching Increases Availability of Web Content

There is an even more compelling advantage to reverse caching: its ability to make Web site content available when the Web server is offline. This can be part of a high-availability plan for your Web services.

Web servers can go offline for several reasons. For example, the Web server will be down for a time when routine maintenance needs to be performed or after the server experiences a hardware or software crash. No matter why the server is offline, downtime can create a negative experience, ranging from a minor inconvenience to a serious problem, for Internet users when they try to access content on the site. The big advantage of the ISA 2006 reverse caching feature is that it makes it possible for you to take the Web server offline and still have Web site content available to Internet users because the content is served from the ISA 2006 cache.

Web Caching Architectures

Multiple Web-caching servers can be used together to provide for more efficient caching. There are two basic caching architectures that use multiple caching servers working together:

■ Distributed Caching

■ Hierarchical Caching

As the name implies, distributed caching distributes, or spreads, the cached Web objects across two or more caching servers. These servers are all on the same level on the network. Figure 8.1 illustrates how distributed caching works.

Figure 8.1 How Distributed Caching Works

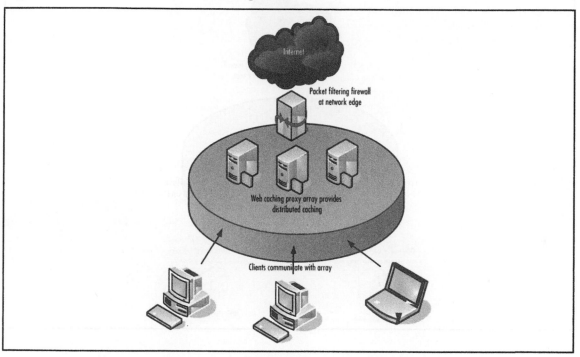

Hierarchical caching works a little differently. In this setup, caching servers are placed at different levels on the network. Upstream caching servers communicate with downstream proxies. For example, a caching server is placed at each branch office. These servers communicate with the caching array at the main office. Requests are serviced first from the local cache, then from a centralized cache before going out to the Internet server for the request.

Hierarchical caching is illustrated in Figure 8.2.

NOTE

Hierarchical caching is more efficient in terms of bandwidth usage, but distributed caching is more efficient in terms of disk space usage.

Finally, you can combine the two methods to create a hybrid caching architecture. The combination gives you the "best of both worlds," improving performance and efficiency. A hybrid caching architecture is shown in Figure 8.3.

Figure 8.2 How Hierarchical Caching Works

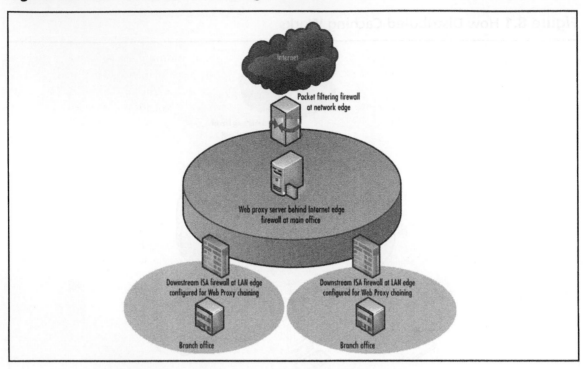

Figure 8.3 A Hybrid Caching Architecture

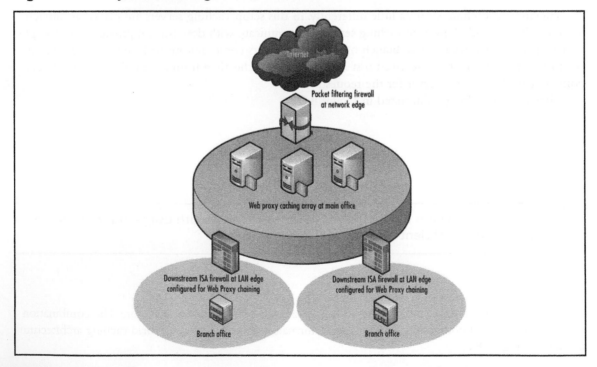

Web Caching Protocols

When multiple Web caching servers work together, they need a way to communicate with each other, so that if the Web object requested by the client isn't found in a server's cache, it can query other caching servers before the "last resort" of going out and retrieving the document from the Internet.

There are a number of different protocols that can be used for communications between Web caching servers. The most popular of these are the following:

- **Cache Array Routing Protocol (CARP),** a hash-based protocol that allows multiple caching proxies to be arrayed as a single logical cache and uses a hash function to ascertain to which cache a request should be sent. The hash function can also be used by the Web Proxy client to determine where the content is located in a distributed cache.

- **Internet Cache Protocol (ICP),** a message-based protocol defined in RFC 2186 that is based on UDP/IP and was originally used for hierarchical caching by the Harvest project, from which the Squid open-source caching software was derived.

- **HyperText Caching Protocol (HTCP),** which permits full request and response headers to be used in cache management.

- **Web Cache Coordination Protocol (WCCP),** a router-based protocol that removes distribution of requests from the caches and uses service groups to which caches belong. The router calculates hash functions.

- **Cache digests,** a hash-based protocol that is implemented in Squid, which uses an array of bits called a *Bloom filter* to code a summary of documents stored by each proxy.

ISA 2006 Enterprise Edition uses CARP for communications between Web caching servers.

Understanding ISA 2006's Web Caching Capabilities

ISA 2006 can act as a firewall, as a combined firewall and Web caching server (the best "bang for the buck"), or as a dedicated Web caching server. You can deploy ISA 2006 as a forward caching server or a reverse caching server. The Web proxy filter is the mechanism that ISA 2006 uses to implement caching functionality.

WARNING

If you configure ISA 2006 as a caching-only server, it will lose most of its firewall features and you will need to deploy another firewall to protect the network.

ISA 2006 supports both forward caching (for outgoing requests) and reverse caching (for incoming requests). The same ISA can perform both forward and reverse caching at the same time.

With forward caching the ISA firewall sits between the internal clients and the Web servers on the Internet. When an internal client sends a request for a Web object (a Web page, graphics or other Web file), it must go through the ISA firewall. Rather than forwarding the request out to the Internet Web server, the ISA firewall checks its cache to determine whether a copy of the requested object already resides there (because someone on the internal network has previously requested it from the Internet Web server).

If the object is in cache, the ISA firewall sends the object from cache, and there is no need to send traffic over the Internet. Retrieving the object from the ISA's cache on the local network is faster than downloading it from the Internet Web server, so internal users see an increase in performance.

If the object isn't in the ISA firewall's cache, the ISA firewall sends a request for it from the Internet Web server. When it is returned, the ISA firewall stores the object in cache so that the next time it is requested, that request can be fulfilled from the cache.

With reverse caching, the ISA firewall acts as an intermediary between external users and the company's Web servers. When a request for an object on the company Web server comes in from a user over the Internet, the ISA firewall checks its cache for the object. If it's there, the ISA firewall impersonates the internal Web server and fulfills the external user's request without ever "bothering" the Web server. This reduces traffic on the internal network.

In either case, the cache is an area on the ISA firewall's hard disk that is used to store the requested Web objects. You can control the amount of disk space to be allocated to the cache (and thus, the maximum size of the cache). You can also control the maximum size of objects that can be cached, to ensure that a few very large objects can't "hog" the cache space.

Caching also uses system memory. Objects are cached to RAM as well as to disk. Objects can be retrieved from RAM more quickly than from the disk. ISA 2006 allows you to determine what percentage of random access memory can be used for caching (by default, ISA 2006 uses 10 percent of the RAM, and then caches the rest of the objects to disk only). You can set the percentage at anything from 1 percent to 100 percent. The RAM allocation is set when the Firewall service starts. If you want to change the amount of RAM to be used, you have to stop and restart the Firewall service.

The ability to control the amount of RAM allocated for caching ensures that caching will not take over all of the ISA firewall's resources.

NOTE

In keeping with the emphasis on security and firewall functionality, caching is *not* enabled by default when you install ISA 2006. You must enable it before you can use the caching capabilities.

Using the Caching Feature

Configuring a *cache drive* enables both forward and reverse caching on your ISA 2006 computer. We'll show you how to enable caching in the section titled *Configuring ISA 2006 as a Caching Server* later in this chapter.

There are a few requirements and recommendations for the drive that you use as the cache drive:

- The cache drive must be a local drive. You can't configure a network drive to hold the cache.

- The cache drive must be on an NTFS partition. You can't use FAT or FAT32 partitions for the cache drive.

- It is best (but not required) that you not use the same drive on which the operating system and/or ISA firewall application are installed. Performance will be improved if the cache is on a separate drive. In fact, for best performance, not only should it be on a separate drive, but the drive should be on a separate I/O channel (that is, the cache drive should not be on a drive slaved with the drive that contains the page file, OS, or ISA program files). Furthermore, if performance of the ISA firewall is a consideration, MSDE logging consumes more disk resources than text logging. Therefore, if MSDE logging is used, the cache drive should also be on a separate spindle from the MSDE databases.

TIP

You can use the convert.exe utility to convert a FAT or FAT32 partition to NTFS, if necessary, without losing your data.

The file in which the cache objects are stored is named dir1.cdat. It is located in the urlcache folder on the drive that you have configured for caching. This file is referred to as the *cache content file*. If the file reaches its maximum size, older objects will be removed from the cache to make room for new objects.

A cache content file cannot be larger than 64GB (you can set a smaller maximum size, of course). If you want to use more than 64GB for cache, you must configure multiple drives for caching and spread the cache over more than one file.

WARNING

You should never try to edit or delete the cache content file.

Understanding Cache Rules

ISA 2006 uses cache rules to allow you to customize what types of content will be stored in the cache and exactly how that content will be handled when a request is made for objects stored in cache.

You can create rules to control the length of time that a cache object is considered to be valid (ensuring that objects in the cache don't get hopelessly out of date), and you can specify how cached objects are to be handled after they expire.

ISA 2006 gives you the flexibility to apply cache rules to all sites or just to specific sites. A rule can further be configured to apply to all types of content or just to specified types.

Using Cache Rules to Specify Content Types That Can Be Cached

A cache rule lets you specify which of the following types of content are to be cached:

- **Dynamic content** This is content that changes frequently, and thus, is marked as not cacheable. If you select to cache dynamic content, retrieved objects will be cached even though they are marked as not cacheable.

- **Content for offline browsing** In order for users to be able to browse while offline (disconnected from the Internet, all content needs to be stored in the cache. Thus, when you select this option, ISA 2006 will store all content, including "non-cacheable" content, in the cache.

- **Content requiring user authentication for retrieval** Some sites require that users be authenticated before they can access the content. If you select this option, ISA 2006 will cache content that requires user authentication.

You can also specify a **Maximum object size**. By using this option, you can set limits on the size of Web objects that will be cached under a particular cache rule.

Using Cache Rules to Specify How Objects are Retrieved and Served from Cache

In addition to controlling content type and object size, a cache rule can control how ISA will handle the retrieval and service of objects from the cache. This refers to the validity of the object. An object's validity is determined by whether its Time to Live (TTL) has expired. Expiration times are determined by the HTTP or FTP caching properties or the object's properties. Your options include:

- **Setting ISA Server to retrieve only valid objects from cache (those that have not expired).**   If the object has expired, the ISA will send the request on to the Web server where the object is stored and retrieve it from there.

- **Setting ISA Server to retrieve requested objects from the cache even if they aren't valid.**   In other words, if the object exists in the cache, ISA will retrieve and serve it from there even if it has expired. If there is no version of the object in the cache, the ISA will send the request to the Web server and retrieve it from there.

- **Setting ISA Server to never route the request.**   In this case, the ISA relies only upon the cache to retrieve the object. Objects will be returned from cache whether or not they are valid. If there is no version of the object in the cache, the ISA will return an error. It will *not* send the request to the Web server.

- **Setting ISA Server to never save the object to cache.**   If you configure the rule this way, the requested object will never be saved to the cache.

NOTE

The default TTL for FTP objects is one day. TTL boundaries for cached HTTP objects (which are defined in the cache rule) consist of a percentage of the age of the content, based on when it was created or last changed.

You can also control whether HTTP and FTP content are to be cached for specific destinations, and you can set expiration policies for the HTTP and FTP objects. You can also control whether to enable caching of SSL content.

TIP

Because SSL content often consists of sensitive information (which is the reason it's being protected by SSL), you might consider *not* enabling caching of this type of content for better security.

If you have multiple cache rules, they will be processed in order from first to last, with the default rule processed after all the custom rules. The default rule is automatically created when you install ISA 2006. It is configured to retrieve only valid objects from cache, and to retrieve the object from the Internet if there is no valid object in the cache.

We show you how to configure cache rules in the section titled *Configuring ISA 2006 as a Caching Server.*

Understanding the Content Download Feature

The content download feature is used to schedule ISA 2006 to download new content from the Internet at pre-defined times so that when Web Proxy clients request those objects, updated versions will be in the cache. This enhances performance and ensures that clients will receive up-to-date content more quickly.

You can monitor Internet access and usage (see Chapter 13, *Using ISA 2006's Monitoring, Logging, and Reporting Tools*) to determine which sites users access most frequently and predict which content will be requested in the future. Then you can schedule content download jobs accordingly. A content download job can be configured to periodically download one page (URL), multiple pages, or the entire site. You can also specify how many links should be followed in downloading the site. You can configure ISA 2006 to cache even those objects that are indicated as not cacheable in the cache control headers. However, a scheduled content download job won't complete if the Web server on which the object is stored requires client authentication.

To take advantage of this feature, you must enable the system policy configuration group for Scheduled Content Download Jobs, and then configure a content download job. We'll show you how to do that in the section titled *Configuring ISA2006 as a Caching Server*.

TIP

When you enable the **Schedule Content Download Jobs** system policy configuration group, this causes ISA 2006 to block unauthenticated HTTP traffic from the local host (the ISA firewall) – even if you have another policy rule configured that would allow such traffic. There is a workaround that will make it possible to allow this traffic and still use content download jobs. This involves creating a rule to allow HTTP access to All Networks and being sure that another rule higher in the order is configured to allow HTTP access from the local host.

Tools and Traps

How Webmasters Control Caching via HTTP Headers

There are two different factors that affect how HTTP (Web) content is cached. The configuration of the caching server is one, but Webmasters can also place information within the content and headers to indicate how their sites and objects should be cached.

Meta tags are commands within the HTML code of a document that specify HTTP expiration or non-cacheable status, but they are only processed by browser caches, not by proxy caches. However, HTTP headers are processed by both proxy caches and browser caches. They aren't inserted into the HTML code; they are configured on the Web server and sent by the Web server before the HTML content is sent.

HTTP 1.1 supports a category of headers called cache control response headers. Using these headers, the Webmaster can control such things as:

- maximum age (the maximum amount of time the object is considered valid, based on the time of the request).
- cacheability
- revalidation requirements

ETags and Last-Modified headers are generated by the Web server and used to validate whether an object is fresh.

In Microsoft Internet Information Services, cache control response headers are configured in the HTTP Headers tab of the property pages of the Web site or Web page.

ISA 2006 does not cache responses to requests that contain certain HTTP headers. These include:

- cache-control: no-cache response header
- cache-control: private response header
- pragma: no-cache response header
- www-authenticate response header
- set-cookie response header
- cache-control: no-store request header
- authorization request header (except if the Web server also sends a cache-control: public response header)

For more information about how the Webmaster can control caching with HTTP headers, see www.mnot.net/cache_docs/#IMP-SERVER.

Configuring ISA 2006 as a Caching Firewall

Although caching is not enabled by default, it is easy to configure ISA 2006 to perform forward and/or reverse caching. In this section, we will show you the step–by–step procedures for the following:

- Enabling caching
- Configuring the cache size and memory allocation for caching
- Creating cache rules
- Configuring content download jobs

Enabling and Configuring Caching

In this section, we'll look at how to enable, disable, and configure general properties of caching. The first step in using ISA 2006 as a caching server is to enable caching.

How to Enable Caching in Enterprise Edition

From the **Configuration | Cache** node of the ISA management console:

1. In the left pane of the ISA 2006 MMC, expand the server name (first expand the Arrays node if you are using Enterprise Edition) and then expand the Configuration node.
2. Click the **Cache Drives** tab in the middle pane.
3. On the **Tasks** tab in the right pane, if caching has not been enabled, you will see a selection labeled **Define Cache Drives**, as shown in Figure 8.4.

Figure 8.4 Defining the Cache Drives

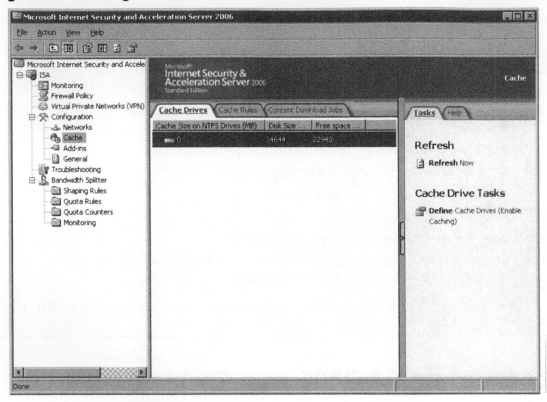

4. On the **Cache Drives** tab of the server's properties sheet (shown in Figure 8.5), select an NTFS drive and type the desired number into the **Maximum cache size** field, then click the **Set** button.

Figure 8.5 Setting Maximum Cache Size

5. Click **Apply** and then **OK.**

How to Enable Caching in Standard Edition

From the **Configuration | Cache** node of the ISA management console:

1. In the left pane of the ISA 2006 MMC, expand the server name (first expand the **Arrays** node if you are using Enterprise Edition), and then expand the **Configuration** node.

2. Right-click the **Cache** node in the left pane and select **Define Cache Drives,** or click the **Cache Rules** tab in the middle pane, and select **Define Cache Drives (enable caching)** from the right **Tasks** pane.

3. In the **Define Cache Drives** dialog box, select an NTFS drive and type the desired number into the **Maximum cache size** field, then click the **Set** button.

4. Click **Apply** and then **OK.**

How to Disable Caching in Enterprise Edition

After you have enabled caching, a new selection, **Disable Caching,** will appear in the **Cache Drive Tasks** section on the **Tasks** tab in the right pane, as shown in Figure 8.6.

Figure 8.6 Disabling Caching

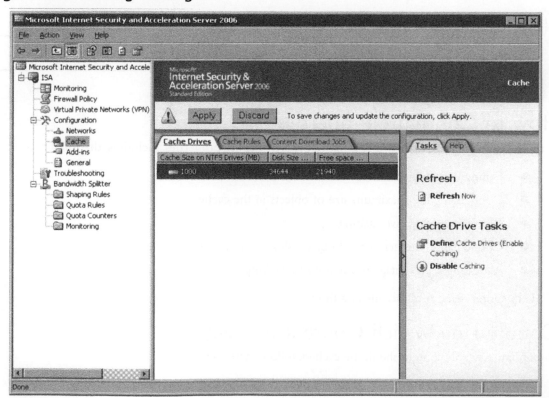

If you click **Disable Caching**, you will receive a dialog box advising that when you set the cache size on all drives to zero, caching is disabled. To enable caching, you'll have to reconfigure the cache drives. You are asked if you're sure you want to disable caching. Click **Yes**, and the cache size will automatically be set up to zero on all drives.

How to Disable Caching in Standard Edition

In ISA 2006 Standard Edition, you can disable caching by performing the following steps:

1. In the left pane of the ISA 2006 MMC, expand the server name (first expand the **Arrays** node if you are using Enterprise Edition), and then expand the **Configuration** node.

2. Right click the Cache node in the left pane and select **Disable Caching,** or click the **Cache Rules** tab in the middle pane and select **Disable Caching** in the right **Tasks** pane.

NOTE

Another way to set the drives to zero is by using the **Reset** button on the **Cache Drives** tab of the server's properties dialog box (in Enterprise Edition) or the **Define Cache Drives** dialog box (in Standard Edition).

NOTE

As long as at least one cache drive has a size greater than zero, caching is enabled.

How to Configure Properties

In this section, we look at how to configure general caching properties, including the following:

- Configuring which content to cache
- Configuring the maximum size of objects in the cache
- Configuring negative caching
- Configuring whether expired objects should be returned from cache
- Allocating a percentage of memory to caching

Let's address each of these, one at a time.

Configuring Which Content to Cache

To configure which content should be cached, follow these steps:

1. In the left pane of the ISA 2006 MMC, expand the server name (first expand the **Arrays** node if you're using Enterprise Edition).

2. Click the **Cache Rules** tab in the middle pane.

3. Click the **Tasks** tab in the right pane.

4. Click **Configure Cache Settings** in the **Related Tasks** section.

5. Click the **Advanced** tab in the **Cache Settings** dialog box.

6. Here you can select whether to cache objects that have an unspecified last modification time and objects that do not have an HTTP status code of 200 by checking or unchecking the appropriate checkbox, as shown in Figure 8.7. Both boxes are checked (thus, caching of these objects is enabled) by default.

Figure 8.7 Configuring Which Content to Cache

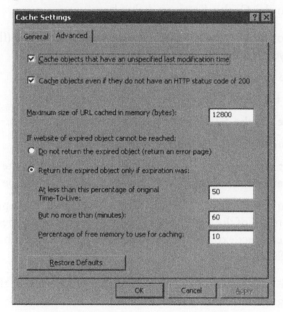

NOTE

HTTP status code 200 means "OK," or that the request sent by the client was successfully fulfilled. Caching objects that do not have a status code of 200 is referred to as "negative caching."

Configuring the Maximum Size of Objects in the Cache

This setting is made in the same **Cache Settings** dialog box as the previous setting.

1. In the left pane of the ISA 2006 MMC, expand the server name (first expand the **Arrays** node if you're using Enterprise Edition).

2. Click the **Cache Rules** tab in the middle pane.

3. Click the **Tasks** tab in the right pane.

4. Click **Configure Cache Settings** in the **Related Tasks** section.

5. Click the **Advanced** tab in the **Cache Settings** dialog box.

6. In the field labeled **Maximum size of URL cached in memory (bytes),** enter the desired number of bytes. This will limit the size of objects that can be cached and save space on your cache drive.

Configuring Whether Expired Objects Should be Returned from Cache

This setting, too, is made in the **Cache Settings** dialog box.

1. In the left pane of the ISA 2006 MMC, expand the server name (first expand the **Arrays** node if you're using Enterprise Edition).

2. Click the **Cache Rules** tab in the middle pane.

3. Click the **Tasks** tab in the right pane.

4. Click **Configure Cache Settings** in the **Related Tasks** section.

5. Click the **Advanced** tab in the **Cache Settings** dialog box.

6. If you prefer that an expired object not be returned if the Web site cannot be reached, select **Do not return the expired object.** An error page will be returned.

7. Alternatively, you can select to return the expired object if the expiration was less than a specified percentage of the original TTL, but no more than a specified number of minutes since the object expired. If you select this option, enter the desired numbers in the appropriate fields.

By default, ISA 2006 is configured to return the expired object only if the expiration was less than 50 percent of the original TTL and no more than 60 minutes.

Allocating a Percentage of Memory to Caching

This setting is also configured in the **Cache Settings** dialog box.

1. In the left pane of the ISA 2006 MMC, expand the server name (first expand the **Arrays** node if you're using Enterprise Edition).

2. Click the **Cache Rules** tab in the middle pane.

3. Click the **Tasks** tab in the right pane.

4. Click **Configure Cache Settings** in the **Related Tasks** section.

5. Click the **Advanced** tab in the **Cache Settings** dialog box.

6. In the field labeled **Percentage of free memory to use for caching,** enter the desired percentage.

The default amount of memory allocated for caching is 10 percent. When the percentage set here is exceeded, additional objects are cached only to disk (not to RAM).

Creating Cache Rules

In this section, we look at how to create and configure cache rules for various situations, how to modify an existing cache rule, and how to disable or delete a cache rule you have created, as well as how to change the order of rules. We also discuss how to copy, export, and import cache rules.

How to Create a Cache Rule

Creating a cache rule is made easy by the wizard that is built into ISA 2006. Just follow these steps:

1. In the left pane of the ISA 2006 MMC, expand the server name (first expand the **Arrays** node if you're using Enterprise Edition).

2. Click the **Cache Rules** tab in the middle pane.

3. Click the **Tasks** tab in the right pane.

4. In the **Cache Rule Tasks** section, click **Create a Cache Rule.** This will invoke the **New Cache Rule Wizard**, as shown in Figure 8.8.

Figure 8.8 Creating a New Cache Rule with the Wizard

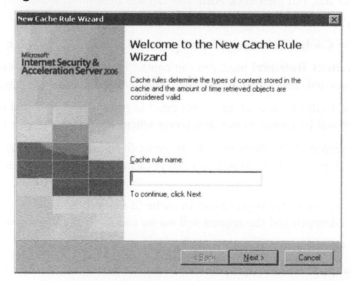

5. Type in a name for your new cache rule, and then click **Next**.

6. On the next page, you'll be asked to select destination network entities. The rule will be applied to requests that are sent to these destinations. Click the **Add** button and select from the entities listed in the Add Network Entities dialog box, as shown in Figure 8.9.

Figure 8.9 Selecting Destinations to which the Cache Rule will Apply

7. Expand the top-level entities to see the specific entities beneath them. Highlight the entity you want to add, and then click **Add**. You can add multiple entities.

8. When you're finished adding entities, click **Close**.

9. Back on the **Cache Rule Destination** page of the wizard, click **Next**.

10. On the **Content Retrieval** page, you can control how cached objects will be retrieved when they are requested. Select from one of three choices for retrieving the object from cache:

    ■   Only if a valid version of the object exists in the cache (if no valid object exists, the request will be routed to the Web server where the original object is stored);

    ■   If any version of the object exists in the cache (if an invalid version exists in cache, it will be returned from cache. If no version exists in cache, the request will be routed to the Web server);

    ■   If any version of the object exists in cache (if no version exists in cache, the request will be dropped and the request will *not* be routed to the Web server).

    ■   Make your selection and click **Next**.

11. On the **Cache Content** page, you can control whether particular types of content that are retrieved are to be cached. By default, an object is not stored in cache unless the source and destination headers instruct that it be cached. However, you can change that behavior here by making one of two selections: Never, (no objects will ever be cached); If source and request headers indicate to cache (the default setting). If you select to cache objects, you can also control which of the following should be cached: dynamic content, content for offline browsing, and/or content requiring user authentication for retrieval. By default, none of these is cached. You can select any number of these choices, as shown in Figure 8.10.

Figure 8.10 Configuring When to Store Content in Cache

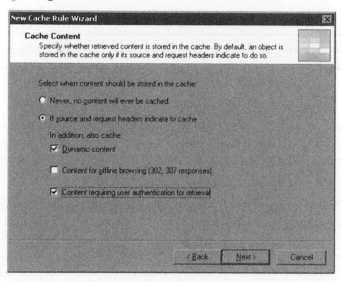

12. After you have made your selections, click **Next**.

13. On the **Cache Advanced Configuration** page, you can set a limit on the size of objects to be cached by checking the **Do not cache objects larger than:** checkbox and setting a size in kilobytes, megabytes or gigabytes, as shown in Figure 8.11.

Figure 8.11 Limiting the Size of Objects to be Cached and Caching SSL Responses

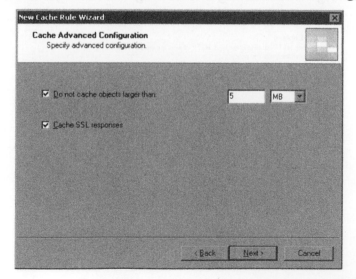

NOTE

By default, there is no limit set on the size of objects to be cached.

14. On this page, you can also select whether to cache SSL responses. By default, SSL responses are cached, but you might want to disable this for security purposes since SSL content may be sensitive, and you might not want copies of it sitting on the cache server.

15. After making your selections, click **Next**.

16. On the **HTTP Caching** page, you can enable or disable HTTP caching (it is enabled by default) and set the TTL of objects as a percentage of the content's age, based on when it was created or last modified. You can also set the TTL time boundaries, and select to apply the TTL boundaries to sources that specify expiration, as shown in Figure 8.12. By default, the TTL of objects is set at 20 percent of content age, and TTL time boundaries are set to no less than 15 minutes and no more than one day.

NOTE

The "created" and "last modified" dates are contained in the HTTP headers that are returned by the Web server.

Figure 8.12 Enabling HTTP Caching and Setting TTL Configuration

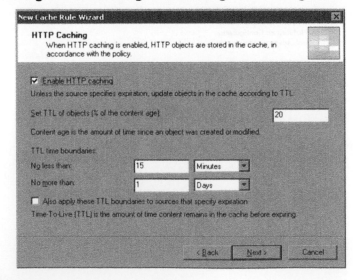

17. When you have made your selections, click **Next**.

18. On the **FTP Caching** page, you can enable or disable FTP caching (it is enabled by default). You can also set a TTL for FTP objects, as shown in Figure 8.13. The default TTL is one day.

Figure 8.13 Enabling FTP Caching and Setting the TTL Configuration

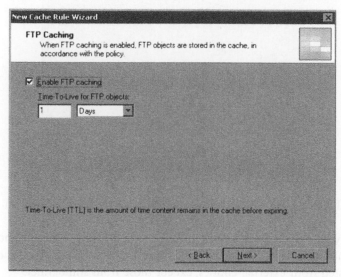

19. After making your selections, click **Next**.

20. The last page of the wizard summarizes all the choices you have made. If you need to make changes, you can click the **Back** button to return to the appropriate page and modify your selections. Otherwise, click **Finish** to create the rule.

How to Modify an Existing Cache Rule

If you want to make changes to a cache rule that you've already created, highlight it in the **Cache Rules** tab in the middle pane of the ISA 2006 firewall console, and click **Edit Selected Rule** in the right **Task** pane, or right-click the rule you want to modify and select **Properties**. Either method will open the **<Rule name> Properties** box, as shown in Figure 8.14.

Figure 8.14 Modifying an Existing Cache Rule

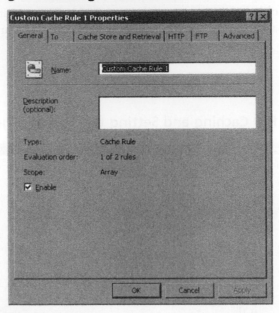

On the **General** tab, you can change the name of the cache rule or insert an optional description to describe the rule.

On the **To** tab, you can change, add, edit, or remove destination network entities. On this page, you can also configure exceptions, as shown in Figure 8.15. In our example, the cache rule will apply to all content requested from external entities, except those from shinder.net.

Figure 8.15 Configuring Exceptions to the Destination Network Entities

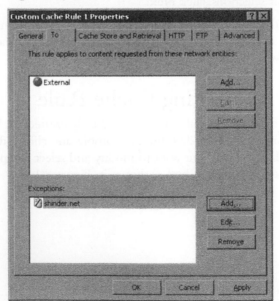

On the **Cache Store and Retrieval** tab, you can change the selections you made in the wizard regarding when to retrieve content from cache and when to store content in cache.

On the **HTTP** tab, you can enable or disable HTTP caching and modify your TTL configurations. You can also restore the defaults with the click of a button.

On the **FTP** tab, you can enable or disable FTP caching, change the TTL settings, or restore the defaults.

On the **Advanced** tab, you can set or change the size limit for objects to be cached and change your settings for caching SSL responses.

How to Disable or Delete a Cache Rule

If you want to disable a cache rule that you've created (but want to keep it because you might want to enable it again sometime in the future), you can do so by following these steps:

1. Highlight the rule you want to disable in the middle pane of the ISA 2006 firewall console and click **Edit Selected Rule** in the right task pane, or right-click the rule and select **Properties.**

2. On the **General** tab, uncheck the checkbox labeled **Enable**.

3. Click the **Apply** button, and then click **OK**.

The rule will still show up in the **Cache Rules** list, but with a red down arrow icon to indicate that it is disabled. You can re-enable it by simply checking the box.

If you want to do away with a rule completely (you will not want to use it again), you can delete it. Simply highlight the rule you want to delete in the middle pane, and click **Delete Selected Rules** in the right **Tasks** pane. You can highlight multiple rules and delete them all at once. Alternatively, you can right-click the rule(s) you want to delete and select **Delete** from the context menu. You will be asked if you are sure you want to delete the rule(s). Click **Yes** to do so.

How to Change the Order of Cache Rules

Remember that the cache rules are processed in order from first to last (top to bottom in the list on the **Cache Rules** tab in the middle pane), with the Default rule always processed last.

You can change the order of the rules by highlighting a higher rule in the middle pane and selecting **Move Selected Rules Down** in the right **Tasks** pane, or by right-clicking the rule you want to move and selecting **Move Down** from the context menu.

How to Copy a Cache Rule

You can also copy and paste the cache rules you've created. Why would you want to do that? Well, if you've created a rule and now you want to create another rule with only one or two properties that are different, rather than go through the whole wizard process, you can take the easy way out and just right-click the first rule, and select **Copy** from the context menu.

Next, right-click on the rule again (*not* in an empty area of the Cache Rules list as you might intuitively expect), and select **Paste** from the context menu. Now you can open the copy's **Properties** box, change its name and make whatever other changes you want to make to it.

TIP

Note that copying and pasting are tasks that don't appear in the right Tasks pane. Unlike with most tasks, you will have to do these from the right context menu.

How to Export and Import Cache Rules

You can export your cache rules to an XML file, which can then be used to import the data to another ISA 2006 firewall or back to the current machine. Here's how to export your cache rules:

1. In the left pane of the ISA 2006 firewall console, expand the server name (first expand the **Arrays** node if you're using Enterprise Edition).

2. Click the **Cache Rules** tab in the middle pane.

3. Click the **Tasks** tab in the right pane.

4. In the **Related Tasks** section, click **Export Cache Rules.** This invokes the **Export** wizard. Click **Next** on the first page of the wizard.

5. On the **Export Preferences** page, you can choose to include optional confidential information (which includes user passwords, RADIUS shared secrets, and other confidential information), along with the rules themselves. By default, confidential data is not exported. If you choose to export it by checking the checkbox, you will be asked to enter and confirm a password. This password will be used to encrypt the confidential data. Click **Next.**

6. On the **Export File Location** page, type in or browse to the path of the file to which you want to save the exported data. The file must be an XML file. If you have not already created a file, you can do so by typing in the desired path and filename (for example, **c:\files\cacherules.xml**).

TIP

Although you can create a new file by typing in the path and file name on the Export File Location page, you must specify an existing path (that is, you cannot create a new folder in this way; if you try to do so, you will get an error message stating that the path does not exist).

7. The last page of the wizard summarizes the selections you have made. If you want to change anything, use the **Back** button to return to the appropriate page and make your changes. If not, click **Finish** to export the data to the specified file. A dialog box will inform you when the configuration has been successfully exported, as shown in Figure 8.16.

Figure 8.16 Successfully exporting cache rules to an XML file

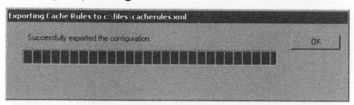

Now, to import cache rules that have been saved to XML files, simply follow these steps:

1. In the left pane of the ISA 2006 firewall console, expand the server name (first expand the **Arrays** node if you're using Enterprise Edition).

2. Click the **Cache Rules** tab in the middle pane.

3. Click the **Tasks** tab in the right pane.

4. In the **Related Tasks** section, click **Import Cache Rules.** This invokes the **Import** wizard. Click **Next** on the first page of the wizard.

TIP

If you have made changes to the configuration that have not yet been applied, you will see a warning message advising you that if an error occurs during the import process, these changes might be discarded. You are asked if you want to import anyway. You can click **Yes** to proceed, or **No** to stop the import process so that you can go back and apply your changes. To apply your changes, click the **Apply** button at the top of the middle pane.

5. On the **Select Imported File** page, you will be asked to type in the path or browse for the XML file from which you want to import cache rules, as shown in Figure 8.17. Enter this information and click **Next**.

Figure 8.17 Selecting an Import File

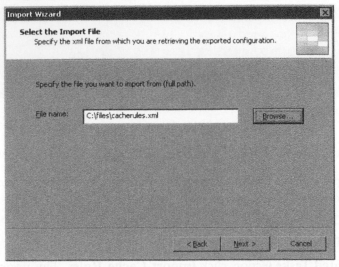

6. On the **Import Preferences** page, you can select to import server-specific information (such as cache drives and SSL certificates) by checking a checkbox. By default, server specific information is not imported. You should import server-specific information if you are importing information back to the same machine from which it was exported. If you import server-specific information to a different machine, you may find that the firewall service will not start because the machine does not have the same certificates.

7. The last page of the wizard summarizes the information you have entered. If you want to change anything, use the **Back** button and return to the appropriate page to make the changes. If not, click **Finish** to complete the import process. A dialog box will inform you when the cache rules have been successfully imported.

The process just described exports or imports all of your cache rules. You can also export or import just selected rules. To do so, highlight the rule you want to export or import and right-click it, and then select **Export Selected** or **Import to Selected** from the right context menu.

Configuring Content Downloads

Content download jobs are handy tools for administrators as they allow you to automate the process of updating cached content. In this section, we'll show you how to do the following:

- Ensure a content download job can run

- Create and configure a scheduled content download job

- Make changes to an existing content download job

- Disable or delete a content download job

- Export or import content download job configurations
- Run a content download job immediately

Let's look at each of these in the following subsections.

How to Ensure a Content Download Job Can Run

Several requirements must be met before a content download job will run. Specifically:

- You must configure the Local Host network to listen for Web Proxy client requests.
- You must enable the system policy rules to allow content download.
- You must ensure that the Job Scheduler service is running.

There are two ways to meet these requirements. The first automates the process and is easiest. If you try to create a content download job before making the configuration changes, you will receive a message advising you that these changes must be made and asking if you want the settings configured, as shown in Figure 8.18.

Figure 8.18 Making Configuration Changes Automatically

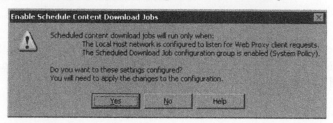

Click **Yes** to make the changes automatically (You will still need to click **Apply** at the top of the middle pane for the changes to take effect).

The second way is to make the configuration changes manually. In the following subsections, we show you how to make each of the changes.

Configuring the Local Host Network

To configure the Local Host Network to listen for Web Proxy client requests, perform the following steps:

1. In the left pane of the ISA 2006 firewall console, expand the server name (if you are using Enterprise Edition, first expand the **Arrays** node), then expand the **Configuration** node.
2. Click the **Networks** node.
3. In the middle pane, click the **Networks** tab.
4. Double click **Local Host** in the list of **Networks**, or right-click it and select **Properties.** This will open the **Local Host** properties dialog box.
5. Click the **Web Proxy** tab.
6. Check the box labeled **Enable Web Proxy clients** (it is unchecked by default), as shown in Figure 8.19.

Figure 8.19 Enabling Web Proxy Clients

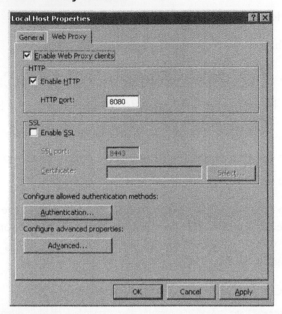

By default, when you enable Web Proxy clients, HTTP will be enabled, and SSL will not. You can enable SSL, if desired, by checking its box, and you can set different HTTP and SSL ports from the defaults (8080 and 8443), if needed.

NOTE

The CARP tab shown in Figure 8.19 appears only on ISA 2006 Enterprise Edition; Standard Edition does not support CARP, so you'll see only the General and Web Proxy tabs on SE computers.

If you enable SSL, you will need to select a server certificate by clicking the **Server Certificates** button, highlighting the server name and clicking **Select** to select from among the certificates installed on the server.

You can also configure authentication methods from among the following:

- Digest
- Integrated (the default)

- Basic

- SSL certificate

- RADIUS

To do so, click the **Authentication** button and check the box(es) of the authentication method(s) you want to use. You can also check a box here to require all users to authenticate.

You can select a default domain for authentication, select RADIUS servers, and configure OWA forms-based authentication.

NOTE

For more detailed information about configuring ISA to listen for Web Proxy clients and to configure authentication for Web Proxy clients, see Chapter 4, *Preparing the Network Infrastructure for ISA 2006*.

Enabling the System Policy Rules

To enable the system policy rule to allow content download, perform the following steps *after* you have configured the Local Host Network to listen for Web Proxy clients:

1. In the left pane of the ISA 2006 firewall console, expand the server name (if you are using Enterprise Edition, first expand the **Arrays** node).

2. Click the **Firewall Policy** node.

3. In the right Tasks pane, click **Show System Policy Rules.**

4. In the middle pane, scroll down to the rule **Allow HTTP from ISA Server computers for Content Download Jobs.** You will see a red down arrow on the icon that indicates that the rule is disabled.

5. To enable the rule, do the following: in the right **Tasks** pane, in the **System Policy Tasks** section, click **Edit System Policy,** or right-click the rule and select **Edit System Policy** from the context menu.

6. Under **Configuration Groups**, scroll down to the folder labeled **Various** and select **Scheduled Download.**

7. On the **General** tab, check the box labeled **Enable**, as shown in Figure 8.20.

Figure 8.20 Enabling the System Policy Configuration Group

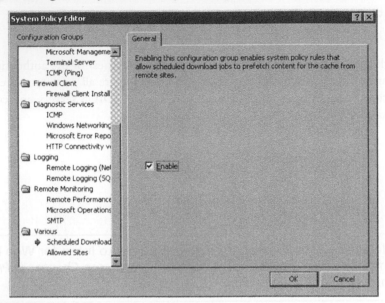

8. Click **OK**.

9. Click **Apply** at the top of the middle pane.

Running the Job Scheduler Service

To stop or start the Microsoft ISA ServerJob Scheduler service from within the ISA 2006 MMC, perform the following steps:

1. In the left pane of the ISA 2006 firewall console, expand the server name (if you're using Enterprise Edition, first expand the **Arrays** node).

2. Click the **Monitoring** node.

3. In the middle pane, under the **Services** tab, if the **Job Scheduler** status is shown as **Stopped**, right-click it and select **Start** from the context menu, or highlight it and click **Start Selected Service** in the right **Tasks** pane under **Services Tasks**, as shown in Figure 8.21.

Figure 8.21 Starting or Stopping the Job Scheduler Service from the ISA Console

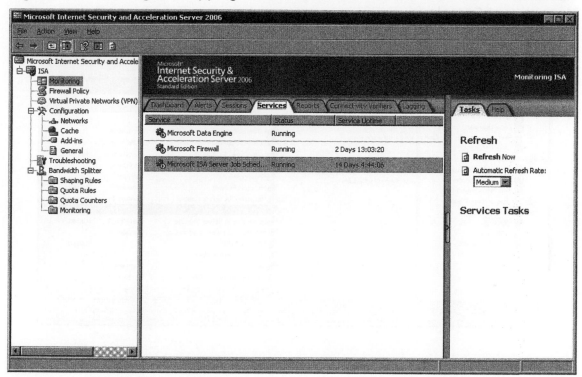

You can also start and stop the service from the **Services** node in the Windows Server 2003 Computer Management Console as you do with other Windows services. Click the **Start** menu and right-click **My Computer** (or right-click **My Computer** on the desktop) and click **Manage**, then expand the **Services and Applications** node in the left pane and click **Services**, as shown in Figure 8.22.

Figure 8.22 Starting or Stopping the Job Scheduler Service from the Computer Management Console

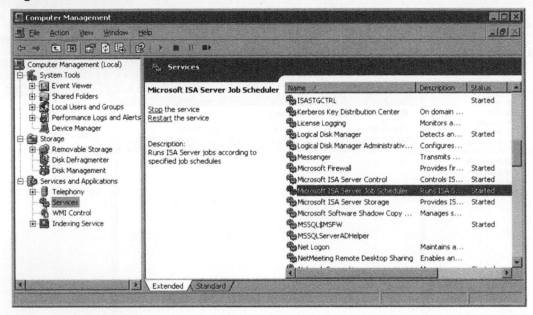

How to Create and Configure Scheduled Content Download Jobs

To create a scheduled content download job, perform the following steps:

1. In the left pane of the ISA 2006 firewall console, expand the server name (if you're using Enterprise Edition, first expand the **Arrays** node), then expand the **Configuration** node.

2. Click the **Cache** node.

3. In the middle pane, click the **Content Download Jobs** tab.

4 In the right **Tasks** pane, in the **Content Download Tasks** section, click **Schedule a Content Download Job.** This invokes the **New Content Download Job Wizard**.

5. On the first page of the wizard, give the content download job a name, and then click **Next**.

6. On the **Download Frequency** page, select how often to run the job. You can select from among the following choices: One time only, on completion of the wizard; one time only, scheduled; daily; weekly. Make your selection and click **Next**.

7. On the **Content Download** page, enter the URL of the page on the Internet server from which you want to download content. You can also set job limits, as shown in Figure 8.23. You can select not to follow links outside the URL's domain name, set a maximum depth of links per page, set a maximum number of objects to be retrieved, and set a maximum number of concurrent TCP connections to create for the job. By default, **Do not follow link outside the specified URL domain name** is disabled, so outside links will be followed. There is no maximum link depth set by default. The default limit on number of objects to be retrieved is 60,000, and the default maximum number of concurrent TCP connections is 4. After making your selections, click **Next**.

Figure 8.23 Specifying Content Download Details

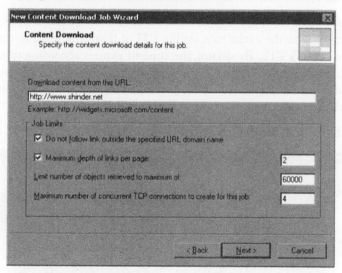

8. On the **Content Caching** page, you can control which content is to be cached and how long objects will stay in the cache before they expire (the TTL). First, select whether to cache all content, cache content if source and request headers indicate to cache *or* if content is dynamic, or cache if source and request headers indicate to cache (this is the default).

Figure 8.24 Configuring Content Caching

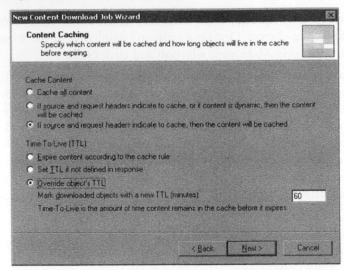

9. As shown in Figure 8.24, you can set the TTL according to one of three options: expire content according to the cache rule, set the TTL if it's not defined in the response, or override the object's TTL. By default, the content expires according to the cache rule. If you select to override the object's TTL, you can set a new TTL (in minutes) with which downloaded objects will be marked. The default is 60 minutes. After you have made your selections, click **Next**.

Figure 8.25 The New Job Appears in the Content Download Jobs List

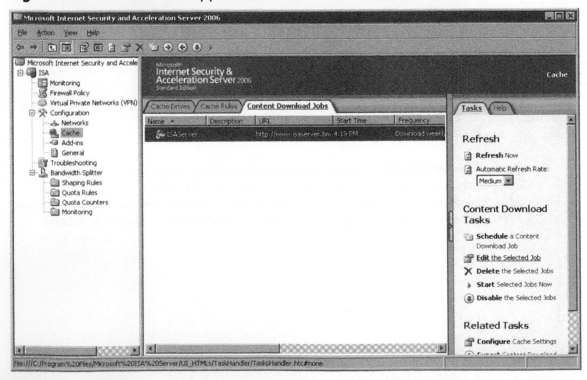

10. On the last page of the wizard, you'll see a summary of the selections you have made. If you want to make any changes, use the **Back** button to return to the appropriate page. Otherwise, click **Finish** to create the new content download job.

The new job you have created will now be listed in the middle pane on the **Content Download Jobs** tab of the **Cache** node, as shown in Figure 8.25.

Figure 8.26 Modifying the Job Schedule

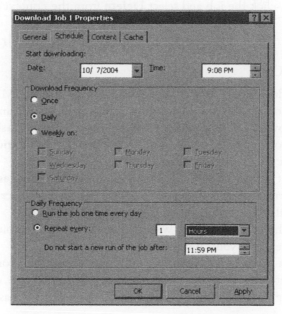

How to Make Changes to an Existing Content Download Job

If you want to modify a content download job that you previously created, highlight it in the middle pane, and click **Edit the selected job** in the right **Tasks** pane, or right-click the job, and select **Properties** from the context menu.

On the **General** tab, you can change the job's name and add an optional description.

On the **Schedule** tab, you can specify a date and time to start the download, and you can change the download frequency (once, daily, or weekly on a specified day of the week). You can also configure the daily frequency if you selected to run the job daily. As shown in Figure 8.26, you can have the job run once per day, or you can configure it to be repeated at specified intervals (either hours or minutes). You can also set a time after which a new run of the job should not be started.

On the **Content** tab, you can change the URL from which the content is to be downloaded, and you can modify the job limits that you set when you created the job with the wizard.

On the **Cache** tab, you can change the options for which content to cache and the TTL options that you set when you created the job with the wizard.

How to Disable or Delete Content Download Jobs

If you do not want a job to run as scheduled but you will want to start running it on the same schedule again in the future, you can disable the job. To do so, highlight the job in the middle pane and click **Disable the Selected Jobs** in the right **Tasks** pane. You can highlight multiple jobs and disable them all at once. Alternatively, you can right-click the job and select **Disable** from the context menu.

If you want to do away with a job, altogether, because you will not be using it again in the future, you can delete it by highlighting it in the middle pane and clicking **Delete the Selected Jobs** in the right **Tasks** pane. You can highlight multiple jobs and delete them all at once. Alternatively, you can right-click the job and select **Delete** from the context menu.

How to Export and Import Content Download Job Configurations

You can export a content download job configuration by saving it to an XML file, just as you have exported other ISA 2006 configuration settings. To do so, highlight the job in the middle pane and click **Export Content Download Job Configuration** in the **Related Tasks** section of the right **Tasks** pane. Alternatively, you can right click the selected job and select **Export Selected** from the context menu. This invokes the **Export Wizard**.

Click **Next** on the first page of the wizard. On the **Export Preferences** page, specify whether to export confidential information. If you choose to do so, you need to enter and confirm a password with which the confidential information will be encrypted. Click **Next**.

Type in or browse to the path where you want to save the XML file. You can create a file by typing its path and name here, but you cannot create a folder.

On the last page of the wizard, your selections will be summarized. If you want to change anything, use the **Back** button to return to the appropriate page. Otherwise, click **Finish** to complete the Export process. A dialog box will inform you when the configuration has been successfully exported.

You can import a content download job that you saved from this or another ISA 2006 computer in much the same way. Click **Import Content Download Job Configuration** in the **Related Tasks** section of the right **Tasks** pane. This invokes the **Import Wizard**. Click **Next** on the first page.

Type in or browse to the path where the XML file you want to import is located, and click **Next**. Select whether to import server-specific information (such as cache drives and certificates). By default, server-specific information is not imported. You should import server-specific information if you are importing the configuration back to the same computer from which you exported it. If you are importing it to a different computer and select to import server-specific information, the firewall service might not start if the new computer does not have the same certificates installed. After you make your selection, click **Next**.

On the last page of the wizard, your selections will be summarized. If you want to change anything, use the **Back** button to return to the appropriate page. Otherwise, click **Finish** to complete the Import process. A dialog box will inform you when the configuration has been successfully imported.

How to Run a Content Download Job Immediately

In addition to running the content download jobs on the schedule you have configured, you can run any existing content download job manually at any time. To do so, highlight the job in the middle pane, and click **Start Selected Jobs Now** in the **Content Download Tasks** section of the right **Tasks** pane. You can highlight multiple jobs and run them all with a single click.

Alternatively, you can right-click the job you want to run, and select **Start** from the context menu.

Summary

Although Microsoft's marketing emphasis with ISA 2006 is on its firewall and VPN gateway functionality, it also provides companies with a viable Web caching solution that can save hundreds or thousands of dollars that would have to be spent for a separate caching product if you implemented competing firewall products that don't include caching functionality (and that's most of them).

ISA 2006's caching capabilities enhance your network's productivity by providing acceleration of access to external Web sites by your internal users, via the forward caching feature. It can also accelerate the access of external users who connect to your internal Web sites, via the reverse caching feature.

In larger, more complex network environments, multiple ISA 2006 computers can be used in distributed or hierarchical caching arrangements to provide for the best possible performance. Distributed caching distributes, or spreads, the cached Web objects across two or more caching servers. These servers are all on the same level on the network. In a hierarchical caching setup, caching servers are placed at different levels on the network. Upstream caching servers communicate with downstream proxies. For example, a caching server is placed at each branch office. These servers communicate with the caching array at the main office. Requests are serviced first from the local cache, then from a centralized cache before going out to the Internet server for the request.

ISA 2006 uses the Cache Array Routing Protocol (CARP), for communications between Web caching servers. CARP is a hash-based protocol that allows multiple caching proxies to be arrayed as a single logical cache and uses a hash function to ascertain to which cache a request should be sent. ISA 2006 uses cache rules to allow you to customize what types of content will be stored in the cache and exactly how that content will be handled when a request is made for objects stored in cache.

ISA 2006 can act as a combined firewall and Web-caching server, or as a dedicated Web-caching server, in addition to its default configuration (firewall only). In this chapter, you learned about the concepts of Web caching and how to configure an ISA 2006 computer to perform caching for your organization.

Chapter 9

Using ISA Firewall 2006's Monitoring, Logging, and Reporting Tools

Solutions in this chapter:

- Exploring the ISA 2006 Dashboard

- Creating and Configuring ISA 2006 Alerts

- Monitoring ISA 2006 Connectivity, Sessions, and Services

- Working with ISA Firewall Logs and Reports

- Using the ISA Firewall's Performance Monitor

- ISA Firewall 2004 Upgrade Considerations

Introduction

One of the biggest complaints we hear about firewall products from almost all vendors concerns the monitoring and reporting capabilities. It's not enough for a firewall to provide protection from Internet attacks and control what comes into and goes out of the local network; the name of the game in today's business world is documentation. Network administrators need to be able to track attempted intrusions and attacks from outside, as well as their own users' Internet use.

Logs and reports serve several important purposes:

- Awareness of failed or successful intrusions and attacks so you can take additional preventative measures

- Evidentiary documentation for forensics purposes when pursuing civil or criminal actions against intruders, attackers or insiders who misuse the network

- Tracking of bandwidth usage for planning expansion of the network

- Establishment of performance benchmarks for planning future capacity requirements

- Justification to management for budgetary considerations

- Paper trail for management and outside regulatory agencies to show compliance with policies and regulations

ISA 2006 includes an array of tools that can be used to monitor ISA Firewall activities, create and configure alerts to keep you apprised of changes, generate reports to summarize information in an easy-to-read form and provide a document trail, and monitor the ISA Firewall's performance. All of these tools are located in the Monitoring node, accessed via the console tree in the left pane of the ISA 2006 management console.

TIP

To access the Monitoring node in ISA Firewall 2006 Standard Edition, expand the ISA Firewall name in the left console tree and select Monitoring. In Enterprise Edition, expand the Arrays node in the left console tree, followed by the required array name and then select Monitoring.

In essence, there has been little change in monitoring, logging and reporting aspects in the 2006 ISA Firewall when compared to ISA 2004. Subsequently, a majority of information contained within this chapter is equally applicable to ISA 2004. However, an interesting aspect to consider is that of the potential issues that may arise during an upgrade or migration from ISA 2004. Hence this subject is discussed in the section titled *ISA 2004 Upgrade Considerations* later in this chapter.

In this chapter, we will examine each of these tools built into ISA 2006 and provide step-by-step instructions on how to use them. Specifically, we'll address the following:

- How to use the ISA 2006 Dashboard (section by section)

- How to create and configure notification alerts

- How to monitor sessions and services on the ISA Firewall

- How to configure logs and generate reports

- How to use the ISA Firewall performance monitor (a specially-configured instance of the Windows Server System Monitor that is installed with ISA Firewall)

- How to preserve log information prior to an ISA 2004 upgrade

Configuring & Implementing...

ISA Firewall Supportability Update

At the time of writing, Microsoft has released an important ISA Firewall update which adds several enhancements specifically related to monitoring and logging. These enhancements include:

- Improvements to the ISA Firewall Management console with the addition of a new Troubleshooting node

- Enhanced log viewing functionality

- Additional log filter functionality

- Diagnostic logging, including over 200 new diagnostic logging events

Additional information can be found here: http://support.microsoft.com/kb/939455 whilst the actual update can be downloaded from this location: http://www.microsoft.com/downloads/details.aspx?FamilyID=6f629eac-d8c6-4437-9d20-b47b02db413a&DisplayLang=en

Exploring the ISA 2006 Dashboard

The Dashboard is an important feature in ISA 2006, and it's a handy way for the ISA Firewall administrator to tell, at a glance, what's going on in all the various monitoring subnodes. For more detailed information, you can click on the individual tabs for Alerts, Sessions, Services, Reports, Connectivity, and Logging, but if you want a "big picture" view, the Dashboard provides it in a single interface. The default Dashboard configuration on an ISA 2006 Enterprise Edition machine is shown in Figure 9.1.

Figure 9.1 The Dashboard on an ISA 2006 Enterprise Edition Computer

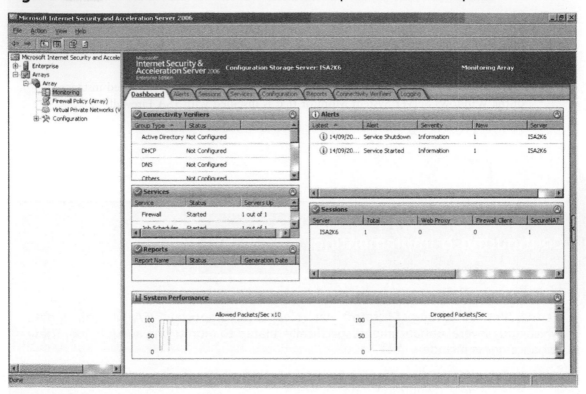

NOTE

You'll see an additional tab, called "Configuration Status," in the Monitoring interface for ISA 2006 Enterprise Edition; this tab is not present on a Standard Edition computer as it is not relevant in this version.

The Dashboard also provides you with system performance information. For example, you are able to see, in graph format, the number of packets allowed per second (times 10) and the number of packets dropped per second.

Each of the Dashboard sections contains an icon that indicates the status of that area:

- **Checkmark inside a green circle:**   indicates that all is okay.

- **Exclamation point inside a yellow triangle:**   indicates a warning.

- **X inside a red circle:**   indicates a problem or potential problem.

You can think of the Dashboard as the starting point for identifying any problems or issues that the ISA Firewall might be having. You can also perform some tasks, such as resetting alert instances, directly from the Dashboard interface.

You can "roll up" various sections of the Dashboard if you don't want to view them. Just click the icon in the top right corner of the section you want to "roll up" (a circle with two small up-pointing arrows) and the section will "roll up," making more room for other sections. In Figure 9.2, the Connectivity, Reports and Alerts sections are "rolled up".

Figure 9.2 Rolling up Dashboard sections

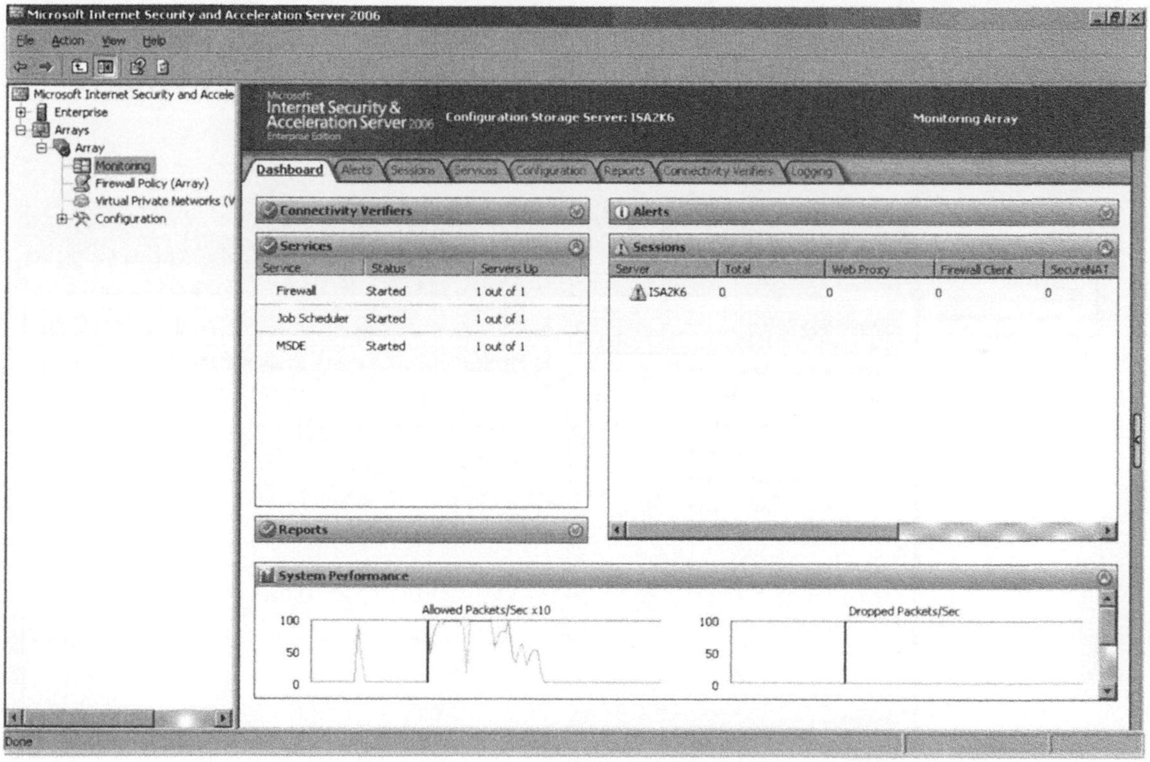

Dashboard Sections

The default Dashboard is divided into six sections:

- Connectivity
- Services
- Reports
- Alerts
- Sessions
- System Performance

Let's take a closer look at each of the Dashboard sections.

Dashboard Connectivity Section

The Connectivity section of the Dashboard allows you to monitor connections between the ISA Firewall machine and other computers. You can monitor specific computers on the network, or even a connection to a particular Web server, by URL.

However, before you can monitor connections to specific computers, you will need to create a connectivity verifier and assign it to a group. Until you do this, the Dashboard Connectivity section will show all group types as "Not configured," as shown in Figure 9.3.

Figure 9.3 Default Connectivity Status Prior to Creating Connectivity Verifiers

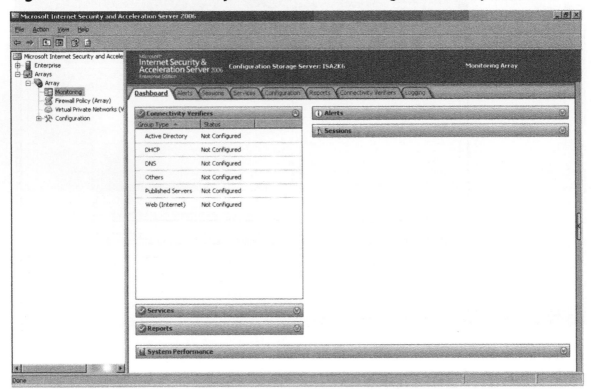

The groups to which computers can be assigned include the following:

- Active Directory
- DHCP
- DNS
- Others
- Published Servers
- Web (Internet)

After you've created one or more connectivity verifiers and assigned them to groups, the status will be shown for the configured group type, as shown in Figure 9.4.

Figure 9.4 Connectivity Status Shown After Creation of Connectivity Verifier

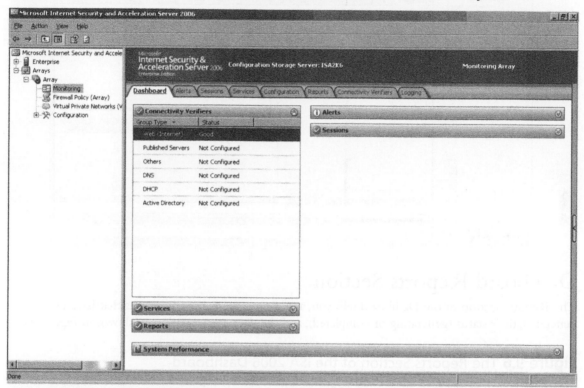

We discuss how to create connectivity verifiers in the section titled *Monitoring ISA 2006 Connectivity, Sessions and Services* later in this chapter.

Dashboard Services Section

The Services section of the Dashboard makes it easy for you to quickly check the status of the services that are running on the ISA Firewall computer. The following core services are installed during the installation of the ISA 2006 software:

- The Firewall Service
- The ISA Firewall Job Scheduler service
- The Microsoft SQL Server Desktop Engine (MSDE)

We discuss each of these services in more detail in the section titled *Monitoring ISA Firewall Connectivity, Sessions and Services* later in this chapter.

From the Services section of the Dashboard, you can view the status of each service (whether it is currently started or stopped). On ISA 2006 Enterprise Edition firewalls, a third column is displayed that tells you how many servers are up, out of the total number in the array, as shown in Figure 9.5.

Figure 9.5 The Services Section of the ISA 2006 Dashboard

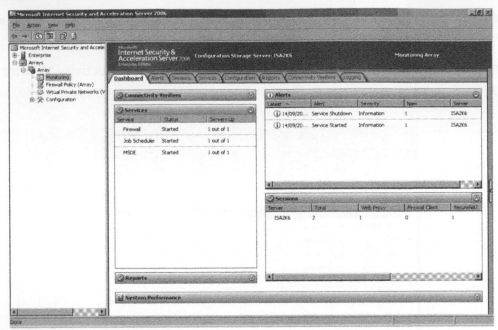

Dashboard Reports Section

The Reports section of the Dashboard tells you, at a glance, the names of reports that have been generated, their status (generating or completed), and the date of generation, as shown in Figure 9.6.

Figure 9.6 The Reports Section of the ISA 2006 Dashboard

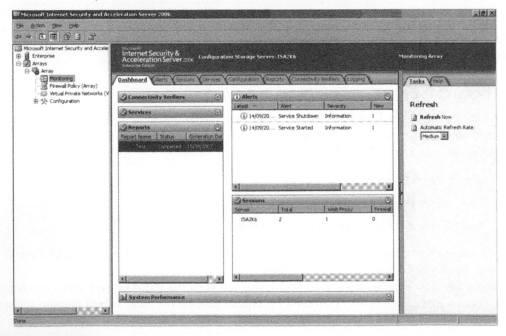

This section is handy for determining whether scheduled or manually generated reports have finished generating. You can open a listed report (if it has been completed) from the Dashboard interface by double-clicking its name in the Report Name column.

We discuss how to schedule automated report jobs, how to manually generate reports, and how to customize the content of reports in the section titled *Working with ISA 2006 Logs and Reports* later in this chapter.

Dashboard Alerts Section

The Alerts section of the Dashboard interface allows you to quickly determine the events that have been logged on the ISA Firewall computer, when each event occurred, the severity of the event (Information, Warning or Error), and the number of new instances when this event has occurred.

On ISA 2006 Enterprise Edition computers, this Dashboard section has an additional column that tells you on which server in the array the event occurred, as shown in Figure 9.7.

Figure 9.7 The Alerts Section of the ISA 2006 Dashboard

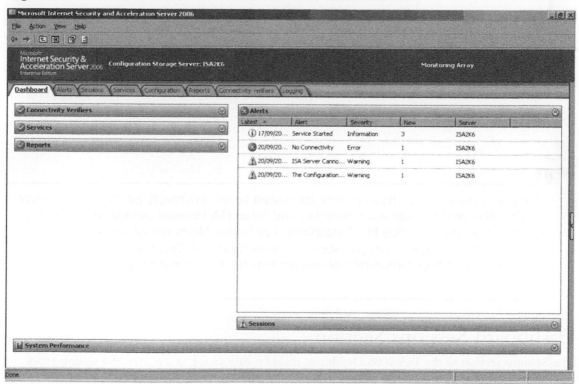

If you look in the Application log of the Windows Event Viewer (**Start | Administrative Tools | Event Viewer**), you'll see that the events displayed in the ISA 2006 Dashboard Alerts section are also shown there. In the Event Viewer, they will be shown with Microsoft Firewall as the source of the event, as shown in Figure 9.8.

Figure 9.8 Event Viewer Logs Show the Firewall Service Events Displayed on the Dashboard

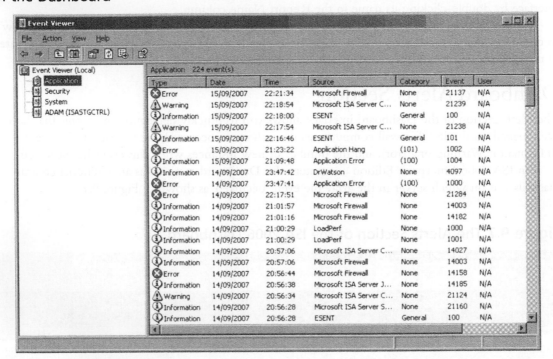

> **NOTE**
>
> The Event Viewer also shows events attributed to the Microsoft ISA Firewall Control service, Microsoft Server Job Scheduler, and other ISA Firewall services that are not displayed on the ISA 2006 MMC Dashboard or in the Alerts tab of the ISA Firewall management console. Thus, you should always check the Event Viewer for the most complete list of application-related events that have occurred on your ISA 2006 computer.

Dashboard Sessions Section

The Sessions section of the ISA 2006 Dashboard makes it easy to see, at a glance, the session types and number of sessions that are currently active through the ISA 2006 firewall that is being monitored. This includes the following session types:

- Firewall clients
- SecureNAT clients
- Web Proxy clients

- VPN Remote clients
- VPN site-to-site connections
- VPN quarantined clients

The total number of sessions is also shown, as you can see in Figure 9.9.

Figure 9.9 The Sessions section of the ISA 2006 Dashboard (Enterprise Edition)

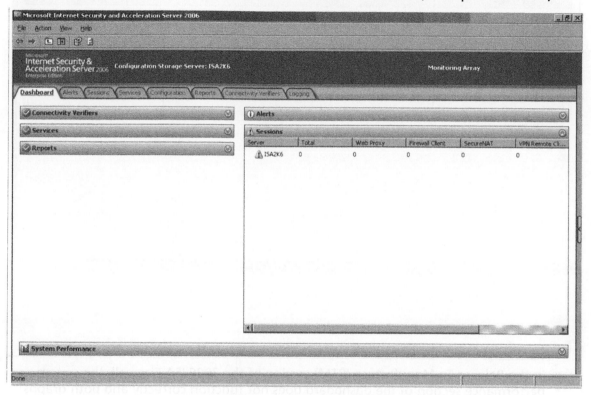

You can open the Sessions tab from the Dashboard interface to view details about each individual session by double-clicking the title bar of the Sessions section. We will discuss how to use the information on the Sessions tab in the section titled *Monitoring ISA 2006 Connectivity, Sessions and Services* later in this chapter.

Dashboard System Performance Section

The System Performance section of the ISA 2006 Dashboard interface provides a "quickie" view of the two most important performance counters for ISA Firewall:

- Allowed packets per second (times 10)
- Dropped packets per second

As shown in Figure 9.10, these counters are displayed in graph form on the Dashboard.

Figure 9.10 The System Performance Section of the ISA 2006 Dashboard

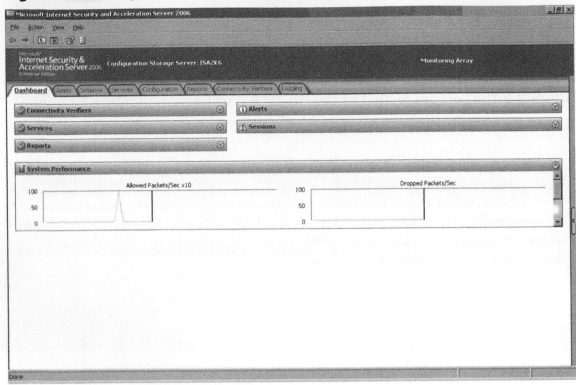

> **TIP**
>
> In the Release To Manufacture (RTM) version of the 2006 ISA Firewall, the system performance section of the dashboard does not function correctly and both graphs contain no data. This was a bug which was identified and fixed during the ISA Firewall's beta program, but was never fixed in the final RTM code.

These same counters, along with a number of other counters specific to ISA 2006, are displayed by default in the ISA firewall's Performance Monitor console that is installed during the installation of the ISA 2006 software, as shown in Figure 9.11.

Figure 9.11 ISA Firewall Performance Monitor with Default Counters

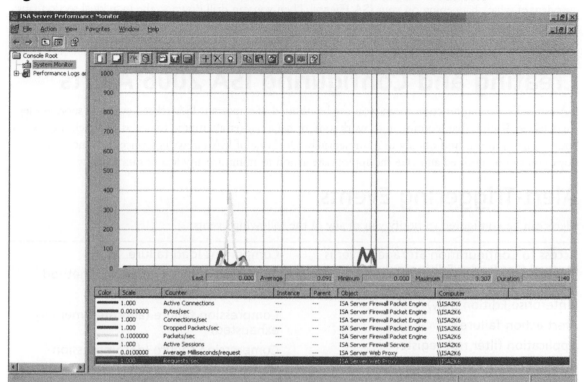

> **NOTE**
>
> The screenshots of the ISA firewall Dashboard and the ISA firewall Performance Monitor both show activity that occurred when Web sites were accessed through the ISA Firewall.

We will discuss how to use the ISA 2006 Performance Monitor in the section titled *Using ISA 2006's Performance Monitor* later in this chapter.

Configuring and Customizing the Dashboard

You can change the look of the Dashboard to suit your own preferences. As mentioned earlier, you can "roll up" or "unroll" any of the sections by clicking on the up- or down-pointing arrows in the upper right of the section.

You can also customize which columns are shown in each section by right-clicking one of the column headers (for example, Status) and selecting or deselecting column names.

To make more room for the Dashboard, you can close the console tree on the left by clicking its icon in the toolbar, and/or you can close the task pane on the right by clicking the right-pointing arrow between the Dashboard and task pane.

Once you have the Dashboard configured the way you want, you can use it as your "front page" overview of what's happening on your ISA Firewall. Then you can drill down to the individual section tabs to get more detailed information. In the following sections, we show you how to use the tools you'll find on those tabs to create and configure all of ISA 2006's monitoring, logging, reporting and alerting functions.

Creating and Configuring ISA 2006 Alerts

ISA Firewall's alerting function means you can be notified of important ISA-related events as soon as they are detected. Rather than coming in to work to find that a hacker attempted to access or attack the system hours earlier, you can find out about it immediately. Or if one of ISA Firewall's services unexpectedly stops, you can be notified and take the appropriate action to minimize any loss of functionality.

Alert-Triggering Events

Alerts can be configured to notify you of any of the following events:

Access to Configuration Storage server is blocked (Enterprise Edition only)

Account name resolution failed (Enterprise Edition only)

Alert action failure

Application filter not registered

Array member status verification failed (Enterprise Edition only)

Array member status verification succeeded (Enterprise Edition only)

Array-level policy rule was deleted (Enterprise Edition only)

Broken reference in cross-array configuration (Enterprise Edition only)

Cache container initialization error

Cache container recovery complete

Cache file resize failure

Cache initialization failure

Cache permissions insufficient

Cache restoration completed

Cache write error

Cached object discarded

Certificate on ISA Firewall about to expire

Certificate on ISA Firewall invalid

Code page invalid

Component load failure

Compression by unsupported method

Compression failure

Compression failure (allocated memory exhausted)

Compression failure (decompression failed)

Compression failure (filter misconfiguration)

Concurrent TCP connection from one IP address limit exceeded

Configuration Agent removed overlapping ranges (Enterprise Edition only)

Configuration changes cannot be loaded by ISA Firewall services (Enterprise Edition only)

Configuration changes overload (Enterprise Edition only)

Configuration error

Connection limit exceeded

Connection limit for a rule was exceeded

Credentials delegation failure

Credentials delegation using Kerberos constrained delegation failure

Cross-array link translation configuration inconsistency (Enterprise Edition only)

Denied connections per minute from one IP address limit exceeded

DHCP anti-poisoning intrusion detection disabled

Dial-on-demand failure

DNS intrusion

DNS zone transfer intrusion

Event log failure

Firewall communication failure

Free disk space limit exceeded

FTP filter initialization warning

Global denied packets rate limit

Host ID assigned to this server is not valid (Enterprise Edition only)

HTTP requests from one IP address limit exceeded

Intra-array configuration error (Enterprise Edition only)

Intrusion detected

Invalid configuration settings

Invalid CRL found

Invalid DHCP offer

Invalid dial-on-demand credentials

Invalid network adapter configuration

IP spoofing

ISA Firewall cannot connect to the Configuration Storage server (Enterprise Edition only)

ISA Firewall computer restart is required

ISA Firewall computer switched Configuration Storage servers (Enterprise Edition only)

ISA Firewall VPN tunnel redistribution is recommended (Enterprise Edition only)

LDAP server recovered

LDAP server unavailable

Link translation configuration insecure

Link translation configuration invalid

Link translation redirection unpublished site contains invalid character

Link translation redirection unpublished site length invalid

Local NLB configuration change

Log deletion failure

Log failure

Log storage limits

Logging resumed

Low non-paged pool

Low non-paged pool recovered

Misconfigured alert

Network configuration changed

NLB configuration failure

NLB inconsistent configuration detected (Enterprise Edition only)

NLB is draining and stopping (Enterprise Edition only)

NLB possible reduced load balancing performance (Enterprise Edition only)

NLB shutdown - Firewall service not responding (Enterprise Edition only)

NLB shutdown - Firewall service stopped (Enterprise Edition only)

NLB started (Enterprise Edition only)

NLB stopped - configuration failure (Enterprise Edition only)

NLB stopped - network adapter problem (Enterprise Edition only)

NLB stopped - NLB integration is unavailable (Enterprise Edition only)

NLB stopped - RRAS service not responding (Enterprise Edition only)

NLB stopped - VPN static address pool is empty (Enterprise Edition only)

NLB stopped manually (Enterprise Edition only)

No available ports

Continued

No connectivity

Non-TCP sessions from one IP address limit exceeded

OS component conflict

Oversized UDP packet

Pending DNS requests resource usage limit exceeded

Pending DNS requests resource usage limit within limits

POP intrusion

Propagate configuration change failed (Enterprise Edition only)

Published server certificate expiration warning

Published Web server name not resolvable

Quarantined VPN Clients network changes

RADIUS server recovered

RADIUS server unavailable

Report summary generation failure

Resource allocation failure

Revert to last known configuration failed (Enterprise Edition only)

Revert to last known configuration succeeded (Enterprise Edition only)

Routing (chaining) failure

Routing (chaining) recovery

RPC filter - bind failure

RPC filter - connectivity changed

Server publishing failure

Server publishing is not applicable

Server publishing recovery

Service initialization failure

Service not responding

Service shutdown

Service started

Slow connectivity

SMTP filter encountered an invalid bare CR or LF

SMTP filter encountered an invalid DATA terminator

SMTP filter event

SOCKS configuration failure

SSL connection failure with published server (name mismatch)

SSL connection failure with published server (no trust)

SSL connection failure with published server (server certificate not valid)

SSL connection failure with published server (unknown reason)

SYN attack

TCP connections per minute from one IP address limit exceeded

The Configuration Agent has restored its connection with the Configuration Storage server (Enterprise Edition only)

The configuration was reloaded (Enterprise Edition only)

The response was rejected because a compressed response was not requested

Total log size limit exceeded

Undefined account for intra-array authentication (Enterprise Edition only)

Unregistered event

Unresolvable remote gateway address on a VPN network

Unresolvable server name

Upload new configuration to services failed (Enterprise Edition only)

Upstream chaining credentials

VPN connection failure

Web farm servers unavailable

Web filter not registered

Windows NLB is not installed (Enterprise Edition only)

Windows user-based policy in workgroup (Enterprise Edition only)

WMI service connection was lost (Enterprise Edition only)

The alert service determines when an event occurs and whether an alert is configured to provide notification or perform some other action. It then initiates the specified notification or other action.

Viewing the Predefined Alerts

You can see the predefined alert definitions by clicking the Alerts tab and opening the task pane if it is not already open. Click **Configure Alert Definitions** under **Alerts Tasks** on the task pane **Tasks** tab. This will open the Alerts Properties dialog box, as shown in Figure 9.12.

Figure 9.12 The Alerts Properties Dialog Box (Enterprise Edition)

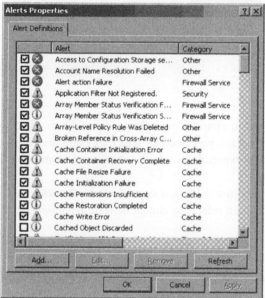

The Alerts Properties dialog box gives you a graphical representation of the severity of the alert, that is, whether it is an Error, Warning, or Information. You can modify the severity and other properties of the alert from this dialog box. You can also assign a level of severity to any new alert you create.

Creating a New Alert

To define a new alert, click the **Add** button. This will invoke the New Alert Configuration Wizard, as shown in Figure 9.13.

Figure 9.13 The New Alert Configuration Wizard

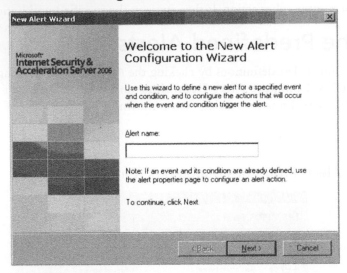

As you can see, you'll need to give the new alert a name. Then click **Next.**

On the next page of the wizard, you need to select an event and any additional conditions that will trigger the alert. The list of events from which you can select matches the list of events we described earlier in this section.

For example, as shown in Figure 9.14, you can select the **Access to Configuration Storage Server is blocked** event and then select for the alert to be triggered by an **Any connection failure** condition.

Figure 9.14 Selecting Events and Conditions to Trigger an Alert

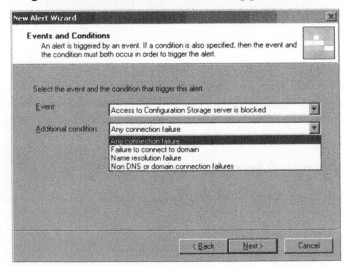

Next, you can assign a category for the alert from the following choices:

- Security
- Cache
- Routing
- Firewall Service
- Other

On the same page, as shown in Figure 9.15, you need to select a severity level (Error, Warning or Information).

Figure 9.15 Assigning a Category and Selecting a Severity Level for your New Alert

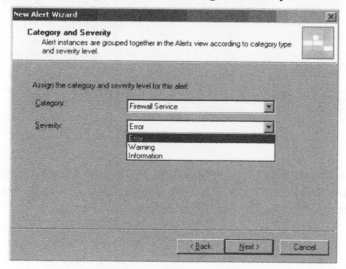

The next page allows you to define what action (if any) will be taken when the specified event and conditions occur. The ISA Firewall can be configured to do any or all of the following when the conditions specified for an alert have been met:

- Send an e-mail notification to yourself or another administrator(s)
- Run a program
- Log the event to the Windows event log (this option is enabled by default)
- Stop selected services on the ISA Firewall computer
- Start selected services on the ISA Firewall computer

You can select multiple actions. For example, you can select to send an e-mail message *and* report the event to the Windows event log, as we've done in Figure 9.16.

Figure 9.16 Defining Actions to be Performed when the Alert is Triggered

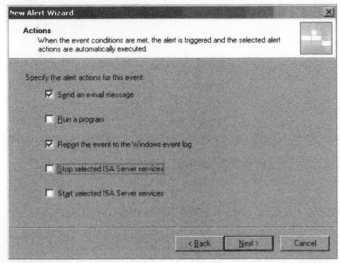

If you have selected to send an e-mail message, you will be asked to provide the name of the SMTP server to be used and enter "From" and "To" addresses for the message. You can send the message to multiple recipients using the CC: field, as shown in Figure 9.17.

TIP

You might be asked to enter the name and password of an account with permissions to access the SMTP server. In addition, you might need to create an access rule to allow the local host to access the External network using the SMTP protocol, if you configure the e-mail notification to use an external SMTP server. Furthermore, if SMTP messages to a server on the Internal network fail, a possible cause is that the "Allow SMTP from ISA to Trusted Servers system policy" rule is not enabled. (Note that the Help file suggests you must enable a system policy rule to allow the Local Network to communicate with the Internal Network via SMTP. However, by default this rule is already enabled, so you won't need to worry about this unless you have disabled it).

Figure 9.17 Sending E-Mail Notification Messages

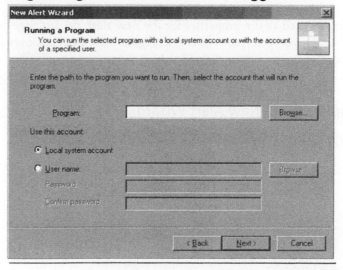

Similarly, if you select to run a program, you'll be asked to provide a path to the program's executable file and an account to use in running the program, as shown in Figure 9.18.

Figure 9.18 Running a Program when an Alert is Triggered

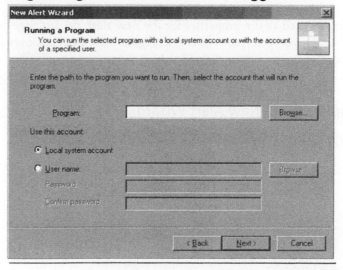

TIP

One of the more common uses of Running a Program is to invoke an executable that will send a pager message to an administrator. However, if the administrator's cell phone supports text messaging, it may be possible to use SMTP to deliver a message to the administrator's cell phone, eliminating the need to support paging mechanisms.

If you select to stop or start a service, you will be asked to choose the service(s) to stop or start, as shown in Figure 9.19.

Figure 9.19 Stopping or Starting a Service when an Alert is Triggered

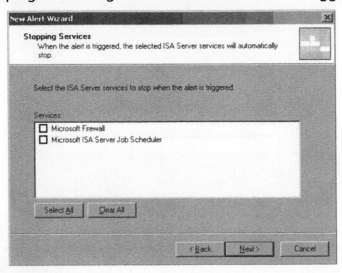

When you have configured all the properties for the new alert, the last page of the wizard summarizes the information you entered, as shown in Figure 9.20. Check it over and use the **Back** button to make any corrections, and then click **Finish.**

Figure 9.20 Completing the New Alert Wizard

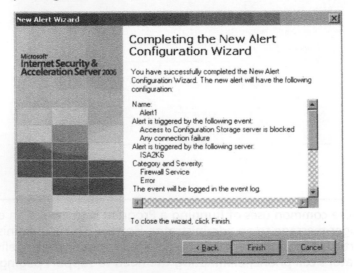

The new alert will now show up in the Alerts Properties dialog box, in the Alerts Definitions window, as shown in Figure 9.21.

Figure 9.21 New Alerts Show Up in the Alerts Definitions Window (Enterprise Edition)

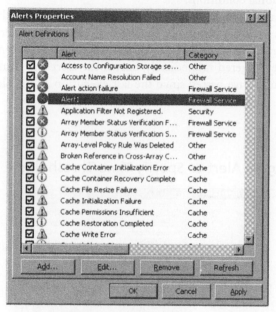

You can disable an alert here by unchecking its checkbox. You will notice that some alerts are predefined but disabled by default. These include:

- Cached object discarded

- Event log failure

- Network configuration changed

- Quarantined VPN Clients network changed

- Server publishing is not applicable

- SMTP filter event

The rest of the predefined alerts are enabled by default.

You can remove an alert completely by highlighting it and clicking the **Remove** button. You can refresh the view of the configured alerts after making a change by clicking the **Refresh** button.

You can rearrange the order of the alerts in the window by clicking the title of the column. For example, clicking the top of the Alerts column will rearrange the alerts in ascending or descending alphabetical order. Clicking the top of the Categories column will rearrange the alerts by category, in ascending or descending alphabetical order.

Modifying Alerts

You can modify the properties of your new alert, or those of any of the predefined alerts, by highlighting the alert you want to modify and clicking the **Edit** button. This will allow you to change the category and/or severity and disable or enable the alert from the General tab. On the Events tab, you can change the event and additional conditions.

When you modify an alert, you can specify the number of times that the event should occur before an alert is triggered, and/or you can specify the number of times per second that the event should occur before triggering the alert. You can also specify whether, when these time thresholds are met, the alert should be triggered immediately, only if the alert was manually reset, or only if a specified number of minutes have passed since the last execution of the alert. This is shown in Figure 9.22.

Figure 9.22 Modifying an Alert to Specify Time Thresholds

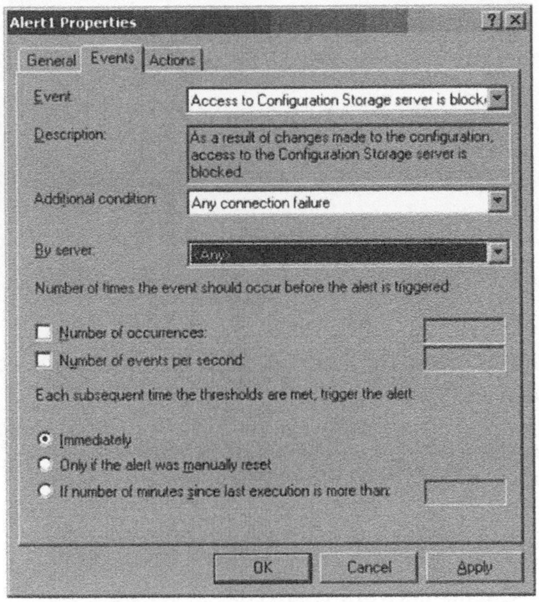

On the Actions tab, you can change, remove or add actions to be performed when the alert is triggered, just as you did when you originally created the alert.

Viewing Alerts that have been Triggered

When you click the Alerts tab in the Monitoring node, the alerts that have been triggered are displayed in the middle pane, as shown in Figure 9.23.

Figure 9.23 Viewing Alerts that have been Triggered

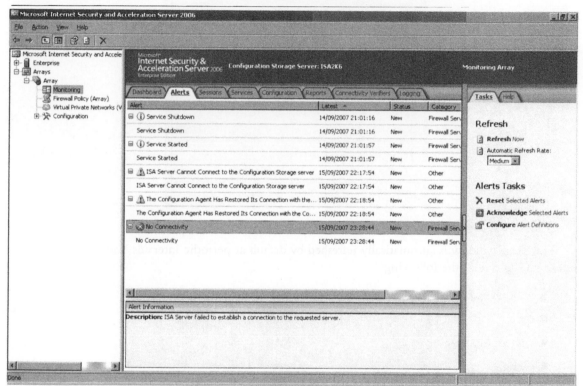

The display shows the alert name, the date and time it occurred, the status, and the category to which the alert has been assigned. Alerts are grouped together by alert type (such as "Service started"). Click the small square with a + sign to expand a group.

If you click on an individual alert, a detailed description will be displayed in the Alert Information window below the list of recent alerts. Again, this same information appears in the Event Viewer's application log, as shown in Figure 9.24.

Figure 9.24 Event Viewer Application Log Entry Showing Information Displayed in Alerts Windows

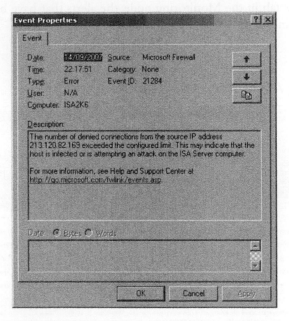

The alerts window is automatically refreshed by default at periodic intervals. You can set the refresh rate to one of the following:

- None
- Low
- Medium
- High

This is done in the right task pane. You can also force a manual refresh at any time by clicking the **Refresh Now** icon (refer back to Figure 9.23).

In addition to configuring alert definitions, you can perform the following Alerts Tasks:

- **Reset selected alerts:** You can reset alerts to remove them from the Alerts display. In the middle pane, highlight the alert that you want to reset, and click **Reset selected alerts** in the right task pane. You will be asked if you're sure you want to reset the alert. Click **Yes** to do so. The alert will then disappear from the middle pane. You can also reset a whole group of alerts by highlighting the group heading.

- **Acknowledge selected alerts:** You can acknowledge an alert to remove it from the Dashboard view. It will remain in the Alerts window on the Alerts tab, but its status will be shown as "Acknowledged." You can use this to indicate that you have seen the alert and are handling it. In the middle pane, highlight the alert(s) you want to acknowledge, and click **Acknowledge selected alerts** in the right task pane.

NOTE

When you reboot the ISA Firewall computer, all alerts will be reset.

Monitoring ISA 2006 Connectivity, Sessions, and Services

You can monitor connectivity between the ISA firewall and other computers from the **Connectivity** tab. You can monitor current sessions for Firewall, Web Proxy, and SecureNAT clients from the **Sessions** tab. You can monitor the status of ISA firewall services from the **Services** tab. In the following sections, we will look at each of these individually.

Configuring and Monitoring Connectivity

You can monitor the connections between the ISA Firewall and specific servers on any network (by server name or IP address) or between the ISA Firewall and a specific Web server (by URL). You can use one of three methods to verify the connectivity:

- **Ping:** The ISA Firewall will send a ping (ICMP ECHO_REQUEST message) to the server. When the server sends back an ECHO_REPLY message, this confirms that it is reachable by the ISA Firewall.

- **TCP Connect:** The ISA Firewall will attempt to make a TCP connection to a specified port on the server. This can be used to ensure that a particular service is running on the server.

- **HTTP Request:** The ISA Firewall will send an HTTP GET command to the specified Web server. A response indicates that the Web server is up and running and reachable by the ISA Firewall.

To monitor connectivity to a server by any of these methods, you need to create a connectivity verifier and place it into one of the predefined groups. The groups include:

- Active Directory
- DHCP
- DNS
- Published Servers
- Web (Internet)
- Others

The status of each group is shown in the Dashboard view. This will allow you to quickly determine if one of the servers in the group has a problem. Then you can click the **Connectivity** tab for details about which server(s) in the group has the connectivity problem.

In the following sections, we'll show you how to create connectivity verifiers, how to assign them to groups, and how to monitor connectivity with the verifiers you have created.

Creating Connectivity Verifiers

The first step in monitoring connections between the ISA firewall and other computers is to create a connectivity verifier. To do so, click the **Connectivity** tab in the Monitoring node, and then click **Create New Connectivity Verifier** in the right task pane. This invokes the New Connectivity Verifier Wizard. On the first page of the wizard, you need to give the verifier a name (for example, if you are going to monitor the connection to a Web site, you might give it the name of the site's URL).

Next, you'll be asked to provide connectivity verification details. First, enter a server name, IP address, or URL in the Connection details field (you can also browse to a location to monitor by clicking the **Browse** button).

Select the group type in the drop-down box, as shown in Figure 9.25.

Figure 9.25 Entering Connectivity Verification Details

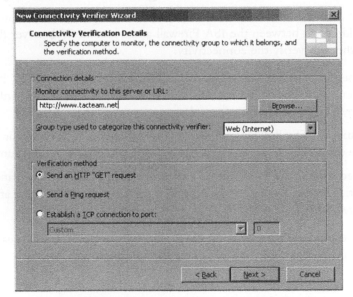

You can also select the verification method. If you are monitoring connectivity to a Web server (URL), you should select **Web (Internet)** as the group type and **Send HTTP "GET" request** as the verification method. If you want to verify that a specific program or service is running on the server connection you will be monitoring, select **Establish a TCP connection to port:** and select from the available applications in the drop-down box. The port number will be entered for you, or you can choose **Custom** and enter the port number.

Applications from which you can choose in the drop–down box include:

AOL Instant Messenger	IMAP5	PNM (Progressive Networks Media)
Charge (TCP)	IRC	POP2
Custom	Kerberos-Adm (TCP)	POP3
Daytime (TCP)	Kerberos-Sec (TCP)	POP3S
Discard (TCP)	LDAP	PPTP
DNS	LDAP GC (Global Catalog)	Quote (TCP)
Echo (TCP)	LDAPS	RDP (Terminal Services)
Finger	LDAPS GC (Global Catalog)	Rlogin
FTP	Microsoft CIFS (TCP)	RPC (all interfaces)
Gopher	Microsoft Operations Manager Agent	RTSP (Real Time Streaming Protocol)
H.323 Protocol	Microsoft SQL (TCP)	
HTTP	MMS (Microsoft Media Server)	SMTP
HTTP Proxy		SMTPS
HTTPS	MS Firewall Control	SOCKS
ICA	MSN	SSH
ICA session w/ Session Reliability enabled	MSN Messenger	Telnet
	Net2Phone Registration	Time (TCP)
ICQ 2000	NetBios Session	VPN Quarantine Protocol (RQS)
Ident	NNTP	
IMAP4	NNTPS	WhoIs

The last page of the wizard summarizes your choices. Use the **Back** button if you want to change anything. Otherwise, click **Finish.**

If you have selected to verify an HTTP connection, you will see a dialog box informing you that a rule allowing HTTP or HTTPS to the specified destination must be configured in order to do this, and asking if you want to enable the system policy rule to "allow HTTP/HTTPS requests from the ISA Firewall to the selected servers for connectivity verifiers." This is shown in Figure 9.26. Click **Yes** to enable the rule.

Figure 9.26 Enabling a Rule to allow HTTP/HTTPS Requests

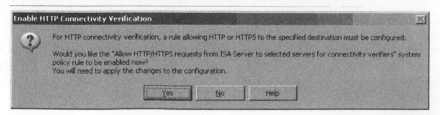

NOTE

If you delete or disable all of the verifiers that use the HTTP method, the system policy rule to allow HTTP/HTTPS requests for connectivity verifiers will be automatically disabled as a security measure. You'll have to enable it again if you later create or enable a verifier that is configured to use HTTP.

The new connectivity verifier will be shown in the middle pane when the **Connectivity** tab is selected, as shown in Figure 9.27.

Figure 9.27 The New Connectivity Verifier

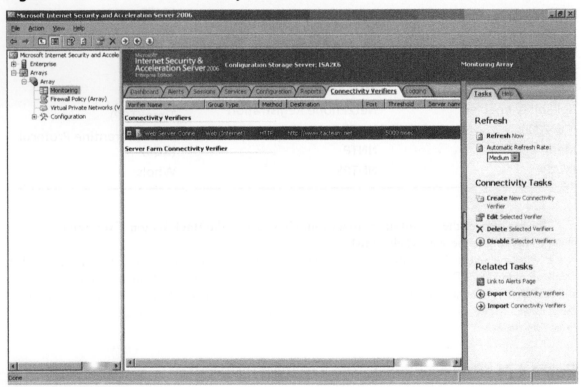

After you select to enable the rule, you must click **Apply** at the top of the console. This saves your changes and updates the configuration. You'll see a progress bar as the changes are applied, then the dialog box will advise that the changes to the configuration were successfully applied. Click **OK** to close the dialog box.

Now "Verifying" will disappear from the **Result** column and a result time (in milliseconds) will replace it.

You can delete or disable a verifier by right-clicking it and selecting **Delete** or **Disable** from the context menu. You can also export or import verifiers from this menu. Another way to perform these tasks is to highlight the selected verifier and click the appropriate task in the right task pane (**Delete Selected Verifiers, Disable Selected Verifiers, Export Connectivity Verifiers** or **Import Connectivity Verifiers).**

If you want to change any of the properties of your connectivity verifier, right-click it and select **Properties** from the context menu, or highlight it and click **Edit Selected Verifier** in the right task pane.

On the **General** tab of the properties box, you can change the name, enable or disable the verifier, and type an optional description. On the **Properties** tab, you can change the URL, server name or IP address of the connection being monitored, change the group type, or change the verification method. You can also specify a timeout response threshold (by default, 5000 msec). Finally, you can select whether to trigger an alert if the server response is not within the specified timeout period (by default, an alert is triggered), as shown in Figure 9.28.

Figure 9.28 Modifying Properties of a Connectivity Verifier

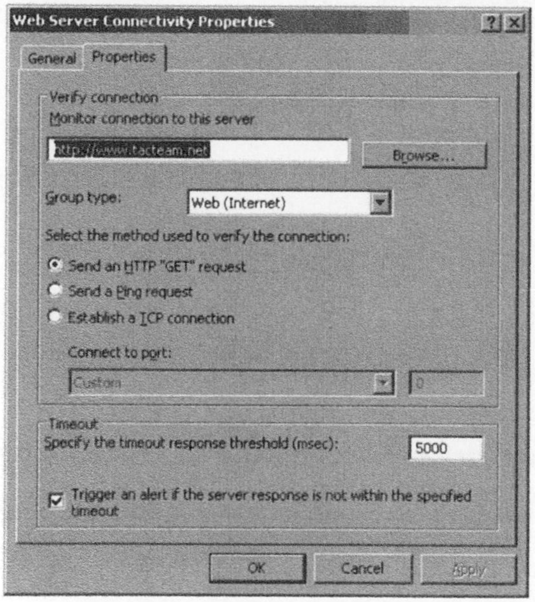

Monitoring Connectivity

Once you've configured your verifiers, you can tell at a glance whether there are any problems with the servers in a particular group by viewing the Connectivity section of the Dashboard. As you can see in Figure 9.29, the group types that have verifiers configured show a status of "Good" as long as the connections in that group type are verified.

NOTE

By default, connectivity is verified every 30 seconds. If required, this value can be changed by using a Microsoft script titled 'Refresh Rate Script' available at the following location: http://go.microsoft.com/fwlink/?LinkID=36764

Figure 9.29 Monitoring Connectivity from the Dashboard

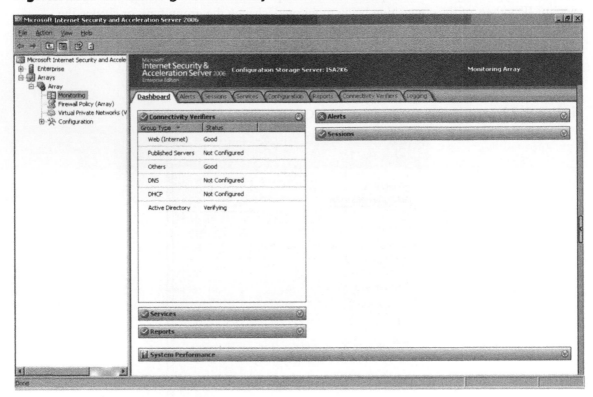

If there is a problem with one of the servers in a group, the group status will show the problem (even though other servers in the group may be connected without any problem). For example, if one of the servers in the 'Others' group is experiencing a slow connection, this will be indicated in the **Status** column on the Dashboard, as shown in Figure 9.30.

Figure 9.30 Connectivity Problems Displayed on Dashboard

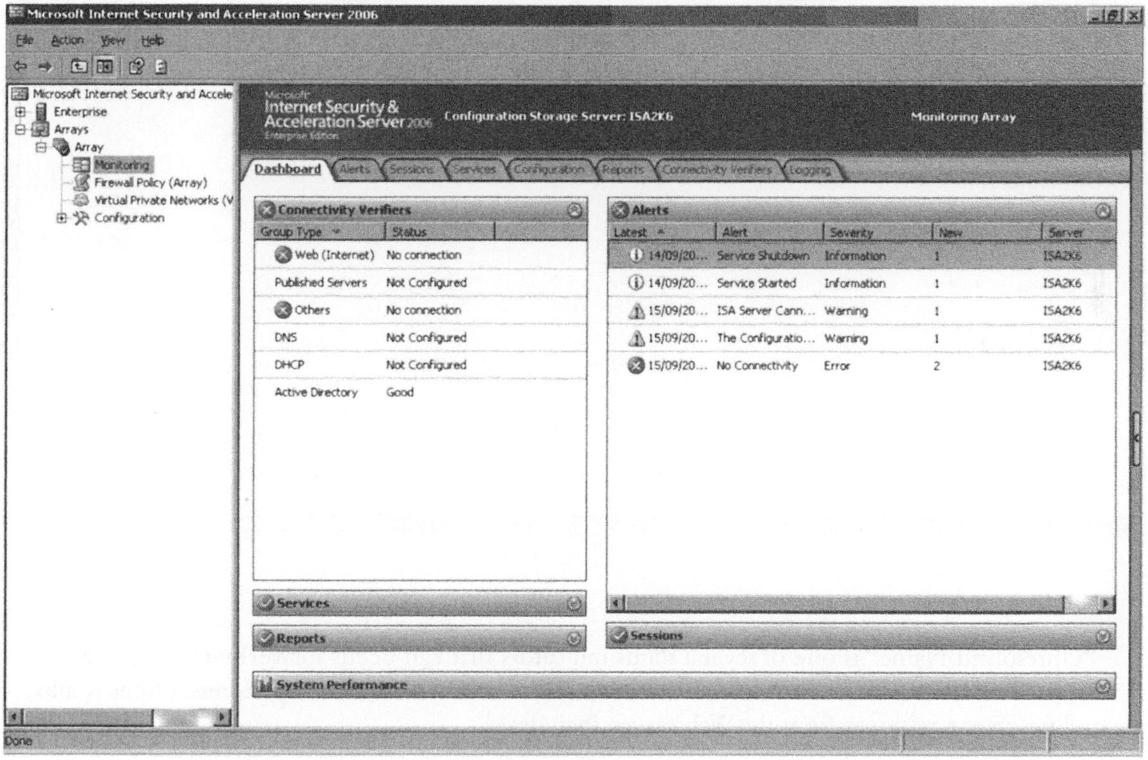

To determine which server has the problem, you'll need to go to the **Connectivity** tab. Then you'll be able to see exactly which verifier reports a problem, as shown in Figure 9.31.

Figure 9.31 The Connectivity Tab Shows Which Server Has a Problem

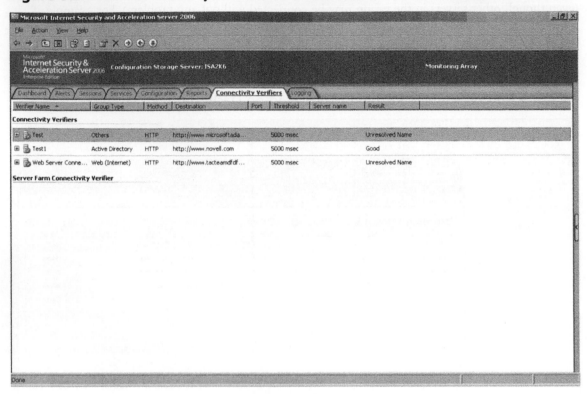

"Unresolved Name" is one of several status indicators that can occur for verifiers using the HTTP method. It occurs when the server's name cannot be resolved to an IP address. Other results, depending on the response from the Web server, include:

- **OK:**   This result is reported when a 401 message (Web server authentication required) is returned from the server.

- **Error**   (Windows Server 2003): This result is reported when a 407 message (proxy authentication required) is returned, because the ISA Firewall could not verify connectivity to the actual Web server.

- **Authentication required**   (Windows 2000 Server): This result is reported when a 407 message is returned if the server is running Windows 2000.

- **Error:**   This result is reported if any 4xx message is returned (except 401 or 407) or if any 5xx message is returned.

- **Time-out:**   This result is reported if the request times out before the server responds.

- **Unable to verify:**   This result is reported if the ISA Firewall is down or the Firewall service is otherwise unavailable.

Tools and Traps…

Why Monitor Connectivity?

When should you create connectivity verifiers, and to which servers should you monitor connectivity? If you have mission critical servers on the network (for example, your Exchange e-mail server) that have been published to make them available to external clients, you might want to create a connectivity verifier so you can easily keep tabs on whether it's working properly.

You might also want to create connectivity verifiers to some popular external Web sites that are considered reliable in terms of up-time, so you can tell at a glance if the ISA Firewall has connectivity to those external sites.

Monitoring Sessions

A handy feature in the 2006 ISA Firewall is the ability to monitor real-time *sessions,* that is, the activity of a particular client computer (IP address) by a particular user (account name). You can monitor sessions from all three types of clients: Firewall, Web Proxy, and SecureNAT.

NOTE

Because the ISA Firewall sees a session as a unique combination of a user plus an IP address, you might show more current users in the Firewall service performance counters than the number of sessions shown in the Sessions window. That's because if a new connection is made from the same IP address and the same user, it is considered part of the same session. The System Monitor denotes every connection as a current user.

Viewing, Stopping and Pausing Monitoring of Sessions

To view current sessions being conducted through the ISA Firewall, click the **Sessions** tab and you will see a list of sessions as shown in Figure 9.32.

Figure 9.32 Viewing Current Sessions

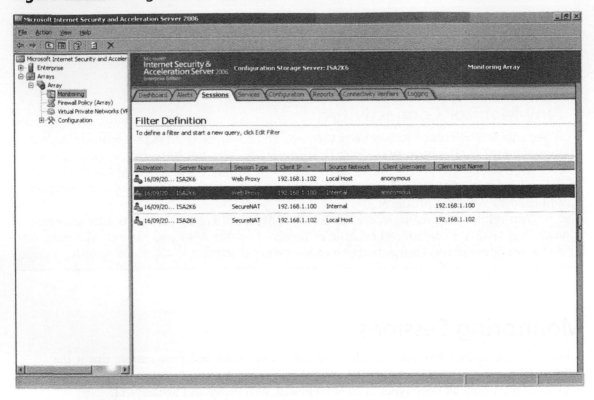

As you can see, the display shows you the following information about each session:

- Date and time the session was activated

- Session type (Firewall, Web Proxy, SecureNAT client, VPN client, or Remote VPN site)

- Client IP address

- Source network

- Client user name (if authentication is required)

- Client host name (for Firewall Client sessions)

- Application name (for Firewall Client sessions)

- Server name (name of the ISA Firewall)

NOTE

If the firewall client is installed on a client computer, but ISA firewall policies do not specifically require authentication, the username will be appended with a question mark symbol in the log entries to indicate that the username has been retrieved, but not validated.

The Server name and Application name columns are not displayed by default in Standard Edition. To display them, right-click on one of the column headers, and check **Server name** or **Application name** in the context menu.

NOTE

Even if you have blocked anonymous connections, you may see anonymous sessions because, for performance reasons, the Web Proxy client sends the first message anonymously; the server then returns a 407 message requiring authentication, and subsequent communications include client credentials.

If you want to stop monitoring sessions, just select **Stop Monitoring Sessions** in the right task pane. All the sessions information will then disappear from the Sessions tab. To start monitoring again, click **Start Monitoring Sessions** (which only appears when you have stopped monitoring).

WARNING

If you stop monitoring sessions, all the information that the ISA Firewall had collected about sessions up to that time will be lost.

You can also stop the ISA Firewall from adding new sessions to the display by selecting **Pause Monitoring Sessions.** When you do so, that selection will be replaced by **Resume Monitoring Sessions.** When you are paused, the sessions that were already in the display will stay there.

Monitoring Specific Sessions Using Filter Definitions

If you have many sessions going through the ISA Firewall, it can be difficult to find the ones in which you're interested. You can use ISA Firewall's filtering mechanism to sort the sessions data and display only sessions that meet specified criteria. If you specify multiple criteria, only the sessions that meet *all* of your specifications will be displayed.

To define a filter, do the following:

1. In the right task pane, click **Edit Filter,** or right-click in the middle pane and select **Edit Filter** from the context menu.

2. In the **Edit Filter** dialog box, select filter criteria for the **Filter by** field from the drop-down box, as shown in Figure 9.33.

Figure 9.33 Setting Filter Criteria

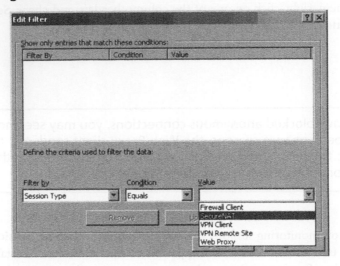

You can select to filter by any of the following:

- Activation
- Application name
- Client host name
- Client IP address
- Client user name
- Server name
- Session type
- Source network

3. Next, you'll need to select a condition ("equals" or "not equal").

4. In the Value field, your choices depend on which criteria you are filtering by. In our example, we chose to filter by session type, so our value choices are Firewall Client, SecureNAT, VPN Client, VPN Remote Site, or Web Proxy. We want to view all Web Proxy sessions.

5. Click **Add to list** to add your filter criteria to the list.

If you want to further narrow the scope of sessions listed, you can add more criteria by going through the same process again. In our example, as shown in Figure 9.34, we want to view only the Web Proxy sessions for client IP address 192.168.1.1 (the local host).

Figure 9.34 Specifying Multiple Filtering Criteria

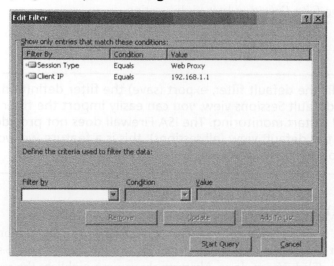

6. When you have added all the criteria that you want, click **Start Query** and the filtering process will begin. The session(s) that meet all of the specified criteria will be displayed as shown in Figure 9.35.

Figure 9.35 Result of Filtering

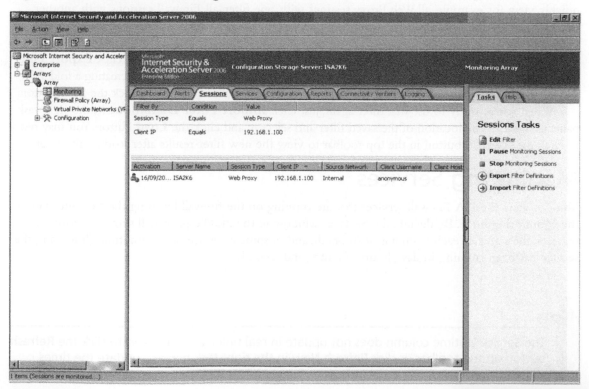

You can save a filter definition so you can use it again by exporting it to an .xml file. See *Exporting and Importing Filter Definitions* later in this section.

TIP

Before you edit the default filter, export (save) the filter definition. If you want to return to the default Sessions view, you can easily import the filter definition, and then stop and restart monitoring. The ISA Firewall does not provide a reset button to return you to the default view (all sessions); this is a feature we would like to see in a future version of the ISA Firewall.

Disconnecting Sessions

You can disconnect a session quickly and easily by right-clicking it in the Sessions window and selecting **Disconnect Session** in the context menu. You will be asked if you're sure you want to disconnect the session. Click **Yes** to do so. Alternatively, you can highlight the session, and then click **Disconnect Session** in the right task pane.

Exporting and Importing Filter Definitions

You can save filters by exporting them to .xml files, and then load them by importing them. If you do a lot of filtering, you will probably want to make a number of predefined filters so you can quickly view, for example, all Web Proxy sessions with one filter, all Firewall sessions with another filter, all sessions for a particular application with another, all sessions for a particular client user name with another, and so forth.

Once you have defined a filter you want to save and conducted a query with it, click **Export Filter Definitions** in the right task pane. Select a location in which to save it (we suggest creating a folder for all your filters) and give it a descriptive name (for example, FirewallSessionFilter). Click the **Save** button.

When you're ready to use that filter again, just click **Import Filter Definitions** in the right task pane, navigate to the location of the saved filter and select it, and click the **Load** button. You may need to click the **Refresh** button in the top toolbar to view the new filter results after loading the filter.

Monitoring Services

You can view the ISA Firewall services that are running on the firewall by using the **Services** tab in the Monitoring node. By default, the Services window in the middle pane will show the names of services, the status of each (running or stopped), and in some cases, the service uptime (how long the service has been running in days, hours, minutes, and seconds).

NOTE

The Service Uptime column does not update in real time. You will need to click the **Refresh** button on the toolbar or click **Refresh Now** in the right task pane to update the times.

You can stop and start services from this interface. Just right-click a running service and select **Stop,** or highlight a service and click **Stop Selected Service** in the right task pane. The service's status will change to "Stopped" as shown in Figure 9.36. You can then restart the service by right-clicking and selecting **Start,** or highlighting and selecting **Start Selected Service** in the task pane.

Figure 9.36 Stopping and Starting Services

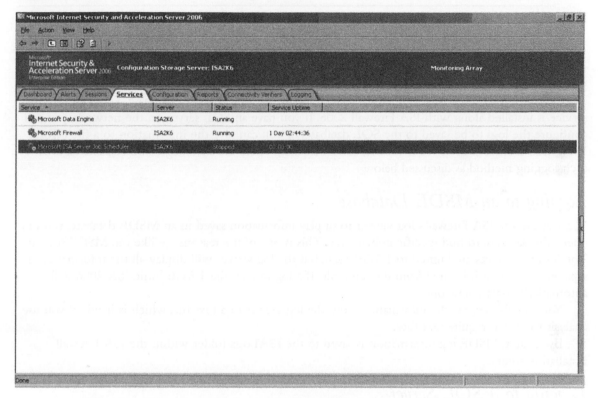

Working with ISA Firewall Logs and Reports

ISA Firewall 2006's logging and reporting features take monitoring a step further and provide you with permanent documentation of the activities related to your ISA Firewall. In the following sections, we take a look at how ISA Firewall logs data, how to configure the logs, and how to generate reports based on the logged information.

Understanding ISA Firewall Logs

ISA Firewall 2006 logs all components by default. These logs include the following:

- Web Proxy
- Firewall Service

NOTE

In ISA 2004 an additional log for the SMTP Message Screener was also included. However, this log has been removed from ISA Firewall as the Message Screener is no longer supported in this version.

Log Types

The default log type is a Microsoft SQL Server Desktop Engine (MSDE) database. The MSDE service is installed along with ISA Firewall 2006. If you have an SQL server on the network, you can configure the logs to be saved to the SQL database, or you can save the information to a file (World Wide Web Consortium or W3C format, or ISA format). There are advantages and disadvantages to each logging method as discussed below.

Logging to an MSDE Database

You can use the ISA Firewall's log viewer to display information saved in an MSDE database. You can query the database to find specific information. This is one of the reasons we like the MSDE format. The logs themselves are limited to 1.5 GB each, but the log viewer will display all the information in separate log files as if it came from the same file. If a log reaches the 1.5 GB limit, ISA 2006 will automatically start a new one.

You can also export the information from the log viewer to a text file, which is handy if you use analysis tools that require text files.

By default, MSDE log information is saved to the **ISALogs** folder within the ISA Firewall installation folder.

Logging to a SQL Server

Logging to a SQL server allows you to use standard SQL tools to query the database. There is also some fault tolerance in having the logs located on a remote SQL server. However, if connectivity with the SQL server is lost, the Firewall service shuts down.

There are also a number of security issues involved in logging to a remote SQL server. If you choose to do so, Microsoft recommends using Windows authentication rather than SQL authentication, and you should also consider encrypting the log information and implementing IPSec for the data transmitted from the ISA Firewall to the SQL server.

TIP

In order to log to a SQL database, you will need to ensure that the system policy rule to allow remote logging using NetBios transport to trusted servers is enabled on the ISA Firewall.

Logging to a File

If you select to use the W3C file format, the data is stored along with information about the version, log date, and logged fields. The W3C format creates a tab-delimited file.

If you select to use the ISA Firewall file format, only the data itself is saved, and all fields are logged, whether selected or not, but unselected fields are shown as empty (marked by a dash). This format creates a comma-delimited file.

Another difference between the two formats is that W3C files denote the date and time in Coordinated Universal Time (UTC), whereas the ISA Firewall format uses local time as configured on the computer.

The files are stored by default in the **ISALogs** folder. You can change this location if you want. If the partition on which the logs are stored is formatted in NTFS (which we recommend), you can compress the log files to save space, although this may cause a reduction in performance (access time).

W3C and ISA log files, unlike MSDE files, are limited to 2GB, but a new file is started automatically when the limit is reached. ISA Firewall monitors log file size at ten minute intervals.

NOTE

Regardless of the logging method you choose, logs should always be stored in a secure location. Access to logs should be tightly controlled to prevent accidental or deliberate modification. Ideally, logs should also be stored on a dedicated NTFS partition.

How to Configure Logging

You can configure logging separately for each of the two services (Firewall and Web Proxy). Click the **Logging** tab in the **Monitoring** node, and select **Configure Firewall Logging,** or **Configure Web Proxy Logging** in the right task pane, as shown in Figure 9.37.

Figure 9.37 Configuring Logging Separately

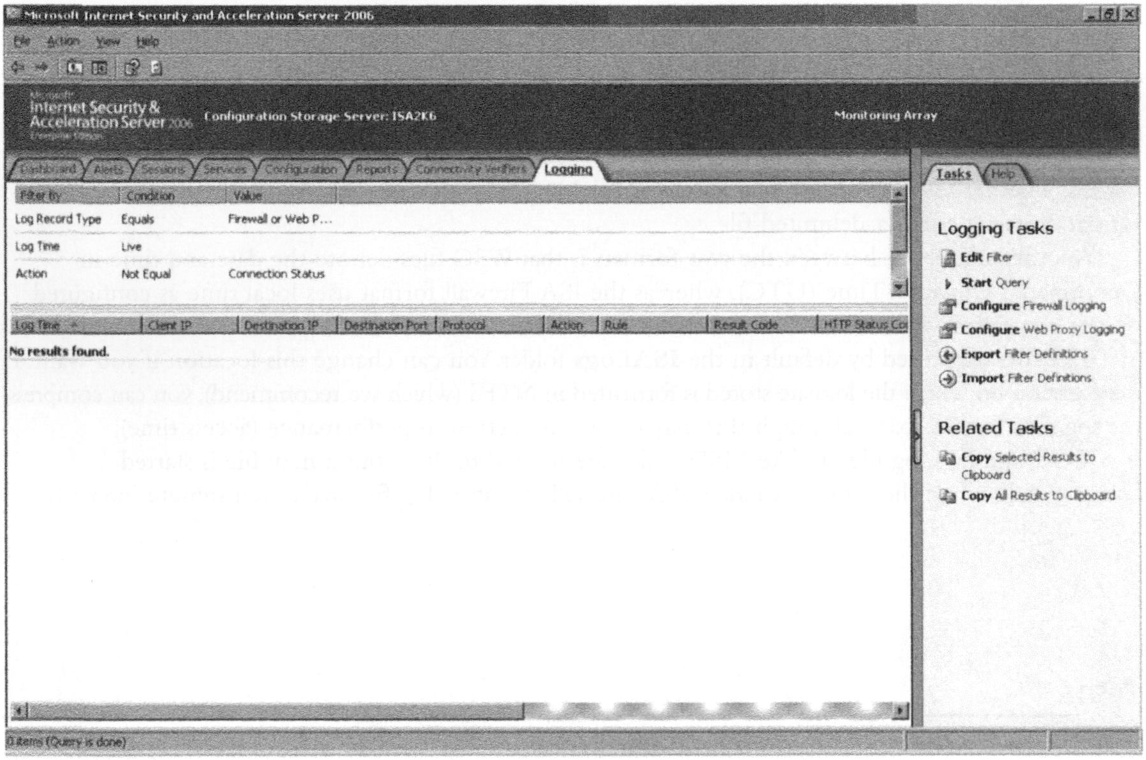

Configuration is basically the same for each service, with a few differences. In our example, we will configure logging for the Firewall service. The first step is to ensure that the **Enable logging for this service** box at the bottom of the **Log** tab is checked (it is enabled by default). Next, you need to configure the log storage format, as shown in Figure 9.38.

Figure 9.38 Configuring Log Storage Format

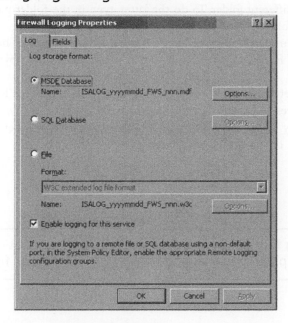

Configuring MSDE Database Logging

By default, the MSDE database format is selected. To configure it, click **Options**, which will display the **Options** dialog box shown in Figure 9.39.

Figure 9.39 Configuring MSDE Database Logging

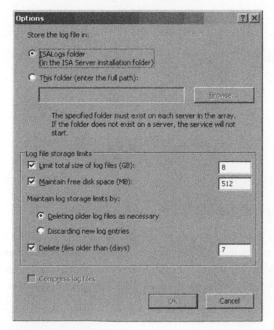

Here you can select whether to store the MSDE database files in the default location in the **ISALogs** folder, or in a different folder. To do the latter, type in the folder path or click the **Browse** button to browse to the folder where you want to store the logs.

Next, you can set a limit on the total size of all log files, in gigabytes. The default is 8 GB. You can also set an amount of free disk space that is to be maintained, in megabytes. The default is 512 megabytes.

You can select also determine what the ISA Firewall will do when the log limits are reached: either delete the oldest files to make room for new ones, or discard the new log entries. Finally, you can select to automatically delete files that are older than a specified number of days (by default, this option is selected and the default time period is 7 days).

> **NOTE**
>
> The **Compress log files** option is grayed out because you can't compress MSDE files. You can only compress when logging to a W3C or ISA format file.

On the **Fields** tab, you can check the fields that you want logged or uncheck those you don't want logged. If you want to log all fields, you can click the **Select All** button or you can clear all fields with the **Clear All** button. By default, all fields are logged except the following:

- Bidirectional
- Source proxy
- Destination proxy
- Client host name
- Destination host name
- Network Interface
- Raw IP Header
- Raw Payload
- GMT log time

You can log only the default fields by clicking the **Restore Defaults** button.

Configuring Logging to a File

If you choose to log to a file, you will need to select the file format from the drop-down box: either ISA Firewall file format or W3C extended log file format. When you click **Options**, you will see the same options you were given for MSDE logging (location to store the log file, storage limits, actions for maintaining storage limits), but you will also see that the **Compress log files** checkbox is now available.

Configuring Logging to a SQL Database

If you choose to log to a SQL database, you will first need to set up a SQL server for ISA Firewall logging. This involves configuring the SQL server to accept the connection from the ISA Firewall. You'll need to create a SQL server account if the SQL Server and the ISA Firewall aren't in the same Windows domain. If the two are in the same domain, you can use Windows authentication; if they are in different domains that do not have an appropriate trust relationship, you have to use SQL authentication.

NOTE

In previous versions of the ISA Firewall, SQL logging used ODBC; ISA 2006 now uses direct access and does not require the use ODBC. In addition, the ISA Firewall now supports the use of SQL Server 2005 as the logging database server along with SQL Server 2000.

Tools and Traps…

Setting Up the SQL Server for ISA Logging

To set up logging to a SQL server, you will first have to prepare the SQL database and tables. Fortunately, the ISA Firewall installation CD contains two SQL scripts, fwsrv.sql and w3proxy.sql, that will create the tables used to record the Web Proxy and Firewall service data. You will have to modify these scripts by adding SQL statements to use an existing database or create a new one to store the tables. You can use the SQL Query Analyzer tool that comes with SQL Server to run these scripts to create the tables. After setting up the SQL tables, you will have to configure appropriate permission for the Windows or SQL account used by the ISA Firewall to be able to query and insert data.

Once you have the SQL server set up, on the **Log** tab of the **Firewall Logging Properties** dialog box, you'll need to click the **Options** button and enter the name of the SQL Server in question along with port number, database name and a table name. Then you may need to set a user account. To do so, click **Set Account**, and enter the user name and password (twice) in the **Set Account** dialog box. You can browse for a user by clicking the **Browse** button.

You'll need to enable the necessary Remote Logging configuration groups in the System Policy Editor.

NOTE

There are many complex issues related to configuring SQL server authentication and creating SQL databases that are beyond the scope of this chapter. Please consult the SQL Server 2000/2005 documentation for detailed information.Additionalinformation is available at the following location: http://support.microsoft.com/kb/838710

To configure Web Proxy logging, the procedure is the same as for Firewall logging. The primary difference is in the available fields to be logged.

How to Use the Log Viewer

The log viewer will show you entries being logged in real time as they happen. The event is displayed in the log viewer as soon as it is logged. Click the **Logging** tab to use the log viewer. The default filter displays all log records for the Firewall or Web Proxy logs. To display these records, click **Start Query** in the task pane. Entries will continue to be added to the display in real time until you click **Stop Query.**

Because the log viewer contains many columns, you might want to close the console tree pane and/or the task pane to provide more room. Even if you do, you will probably still have to scroll to see all the default columns. The log viewer is shown in Figure 9.40.

Figure 9.40 The Log Viewer with Default Filter

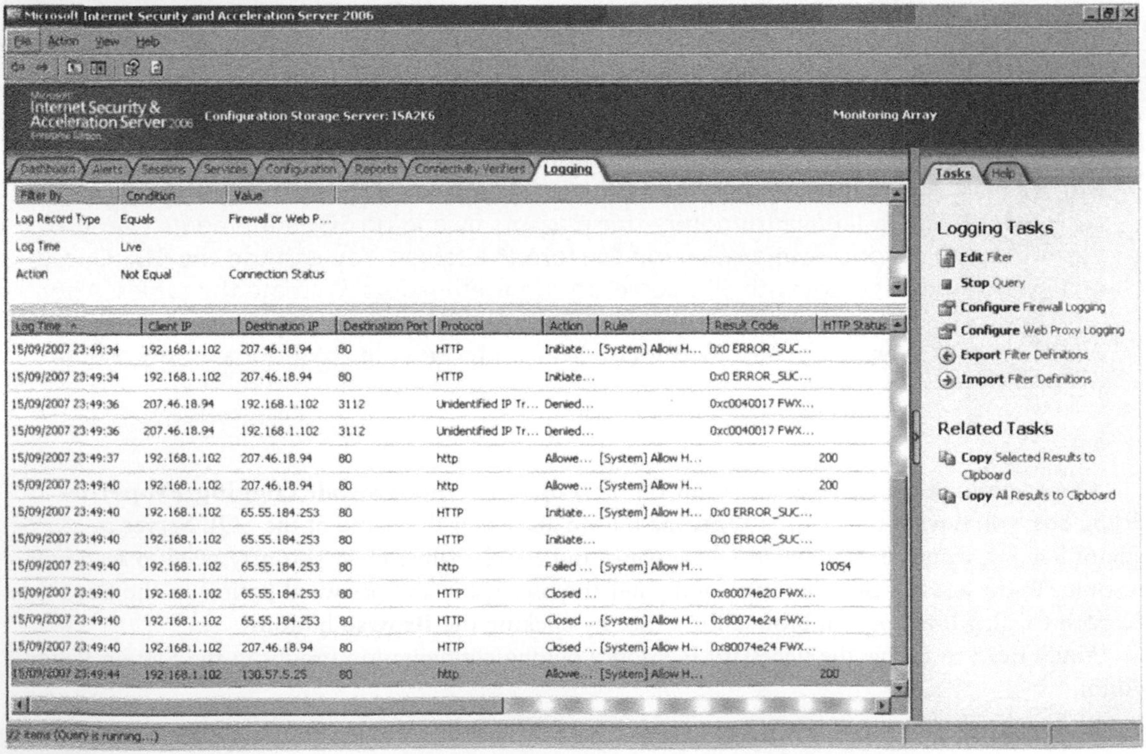

![The Log Viewer screenshot showing the ISA Server 2006 Logging tab with log records]

By default, the following columns are shown:

- Log time
- Client IP
- Destination IP
- Destination port
- Protocol
- Action
- Rule
- Result code
- HTTP status code
- Client username
- Source network
- Destination network
- URL
- Server Name (Enterprise Edition only)
- Log record type

You can add additional columns, such as MIME type, source or destination proxy, referring server, and many others. To do so, or just to view a list of available column headers, right-click any column header and select **Add/Remove Columns.**

How to Filter the Log Information

You can filter the information in log viewer similar to the way you filtered the sessions information. As with the sessions filters, only those entries that meet all of your specified criteria will be displayed.

If you have logged to an MSDE database, you can also filter by log time. This allows you to display log data entered during a specific time period (rather than live data). You can only set the log time to something other than live for MSDE databases. This is referred to as offline viewing.

To configure a filter, click **Edit Filter** in the task pane. The **Edit Filter** dialog box is shown in Figure 9.41.

Figure 9.41 Editing a Log Filter

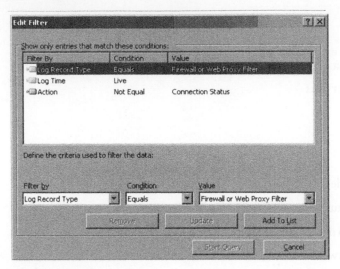

In the **Filter by** field, select the desired criteria.

ISA Firewall Mysteries...

Can't Remove The Default Criteria

Note that you cannot remove the default entries. When you click either the Log Record Type or Log Time entry, the **Remove** button is grayed out. If you try to create a new entry for Log Record Type or Log time, when you click **Add to List**, you will get a message that only one Log Record Type (or Log Time) expression is allowed in a query.

So how do you change these parameters? Here's the secret: Click the one you want to change to highlight it, make the change in the **Value** field, and then click **Update**.

You can choose from the following criteria by which to filter:

■ Action	■ HTTP status code
■ Authenticated client	■ Log Record type
■ Authentication Server	■ Log time
■ Bidirectional	■ MIME type
■ Bytes received	■ Network interface
■ Bytes sent	■ Object source
■ Cache information	■ Original client IP
■ Client agent	■ Processing time
■ Client host name	■ Protocol
■ Client IP	■ Raw IP header
■ Client user name	■ Raw payload
■ Destination host name	■ Referring server
■ Destination IP	■ Result code
■ Destination network	■ Rule
■ Destination port	■ Server name
■ Destination proxy	■ Service
■ Error information	■ Source network
■ Filter information	■ Source port
■ GMT Log Time	■ Source proxy
■ HTTP method	■ Transport
	■ URL

Some of these criteria apply only to one or the other log type (Firewall or Web Proxy).

When you configure the log record type, you can select to display entries from the Firewall or Web Proxy filter, from the Firewall filter only, or from the Web Proxy filter only.

When you configure the log time, in the **Condition** field the default is **Live** (and that is the only option if you are not logging to an MSDE database). If you're logging to MSDE, you can select any of the following:

- ■ Last 24 hours
- ■ Last 30 days
- ■ Last 7 days
- ■ Last hour
- ■ Live
- ■ On or after
- ■ On or before

If you choose one of the last two, you'll need to select a date and time in the **Value** field.

After you have specified all the desired criteria for filtering, click **Start Query** to display the entries filtered by your criteria.

NOTE

If the Firewall service is stopped, either manually or automatically, the log viewer will stop updating information, and the ISA Firewall will go into lockdown mode. The firewall service might shut down automatically because of an event trigger that is configured to stop the service if a particular event, such as an intrusion attempt, occurs. In lockdown mode, no incoming traffic other than DHCP traffic is allowed except for traffic specifically allowed by a system policy rule. To bring the ISA Firewall out of lockdown mode, restart the firewall service.

Saving Log Viewer Data to a File

You can save the data displayed in the log viewer to a file by copying all results, or only selected results, to the Windows clipboard. To copy selected results, highlight the entries you want to copy (you can select multiple entries by holding down the CTRL or SHIFT keys). Click **Copy Selected Results to the Clipboard.** To copy all results, click **Copy All Results to the Clipboard.**

Then you can paste the copied results into a text editor, such as Notepad, as shown in Figure 9.42.

Figure 9.42 Saving Log Viewer Data by Copying to the Clipboard

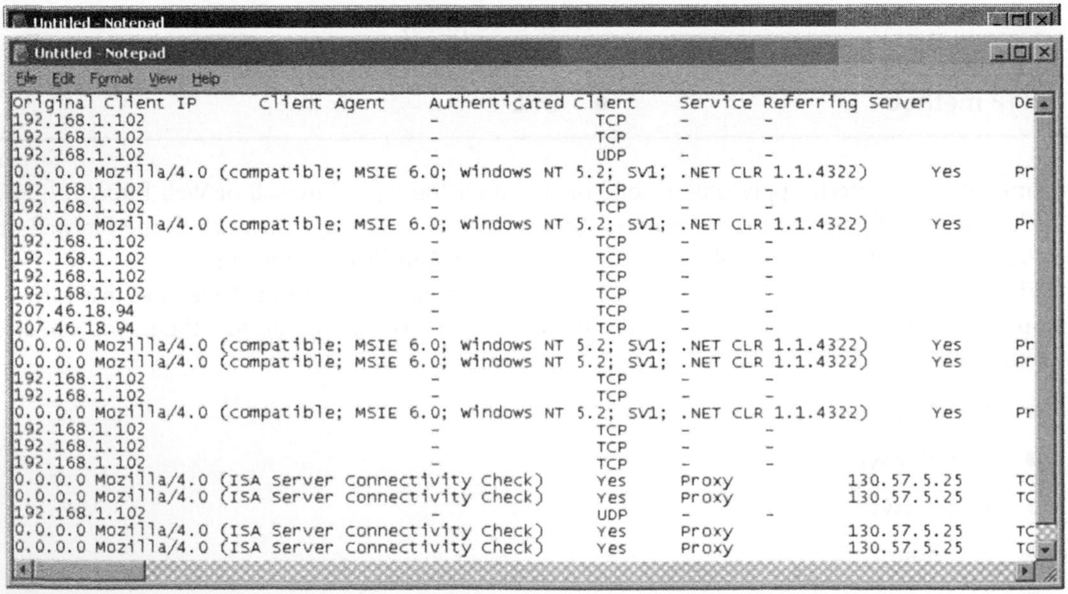

Once you have the data in a text editor, you can save it as a text file. However, note that you can only display up to ten thousand results in the log viewer, so even if you copy all results, you may not get all entries in the log.

Exporting and Importing Filter Definitions

You can save your filter definitions in the same way you did with sessions filters, by selecting **Export Filter Definitions** in the task pane and selecting a location and file name. The filters are saved as .xml files. You can then load them by selecting the **Import Filter Definitions** in the task pane.

Because there are so many different filtering criteria available for filtering log information, it is handy to be able to save a number of different filters and import them when they are needed.

Generating, Viewing, and Publishing Reports with ISA 2006

The reporting function is where it all comes together; this is where you create reports that summarize or detail the information in the log files in such a way that allows you to easily analyze the data and spot patterns, trends, and anomalies.

You can track usage for bandwidth allocation purposes, or you can track access for security purposes. With the reporting feature, you can generate reports manually or schedule report jobs to be run on a regular basis. The reporting component creates a database in the **ISASummaries** folder (by default) on the ISA Firewall computer. Reports are based on summaries of the Firewall and Web Proxy logs.

How to Generate a One-Time Report

To create a report, click the **Reports** tab in the Monitoring node. This will show you a listing of all reports that have been generated, or are in the process of generating, as shown in Figure 9.43.

Figure 9.43 The Reports Display

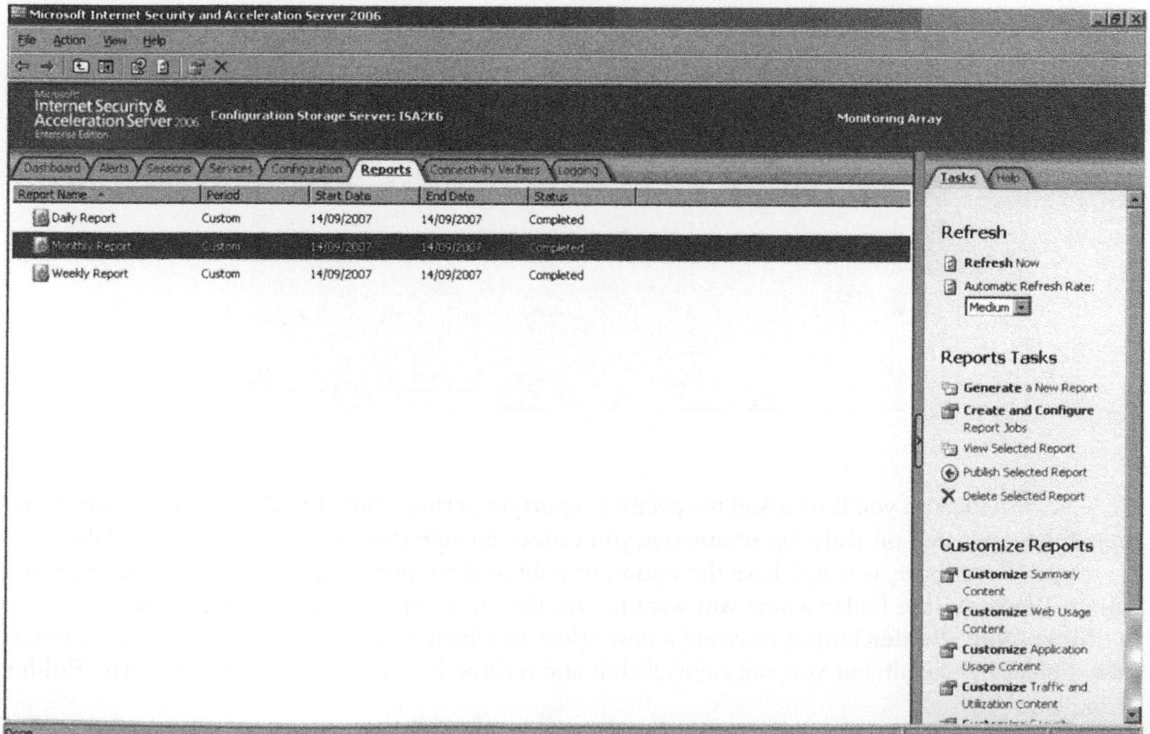

To create a new report, click **Generate a New Report** in the task pane. This will invoke the **New Report Wizard**. This wizard manually creates a single, one-time report as soon as you finish configuring the wizard. On the first page, you'll be asked to give your report a name.

On the next page of the wizard, you can select the type of content to include in this report. You can choose any of all of the following:

- Summary
- Web Usage
- Application Usage
- Traffic and Utilization
- Security

In our example, shown in Figure 9.44, we've selected to include all content.

Figure 9.44 Configuring Report Content

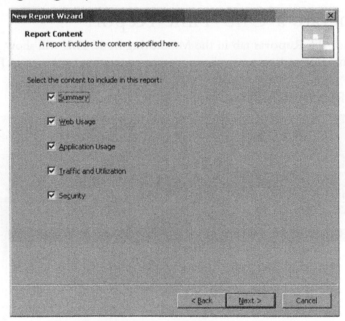

Click **Next,** and you'll be asked to specify a reporting period (start date and end date). Because the reports are based on daily log summaries, you cannot include the present date as the end date.

On the next page, you will have the option to publish the report to a directory. You can type in a path or browse to the folder where you want to save the report. If you click **Browse,** you can use the **Make New Folder** button to create a new folder in which to save the reports. It will be named New Folder by default, but you can right-click it and rename it from within the **Browse for Folder** dialog box.

You may need to enter an account name and password of an account that has permission to write to the specified directory. If so, check the **Publish using this account** checkbox, as shown in Figure 9.45, and click **Set Account** to enter the account name and credentials.

Figure 9.45 Configuring Report Publishing

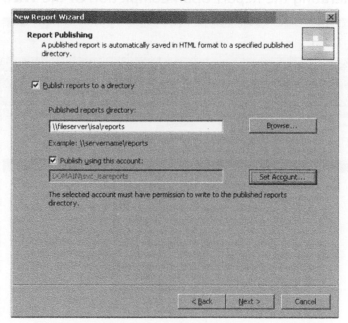

The report is automatically saved in HTML format.

On the next page, you can choose to have an e-mail notification sent when the report is completed. You'll need to enter the following information:

- SMTP server name or IP address
- Address from which the notification is to be sent
- Address to which the notification is to be sent
- CC: addresses of additional recipients, if any
- Message for the body of the e-mail.

You can also check a checkbox to include a link to the completed published report within the e-mail message.

The last page of the wizard summarizes your choices. Use the **Back** button to make any changes, then click **Finish** to begin generating the report. The report will immediately appear in the Reports list, with the status shown as "Generating," as shown in Figure 9.46.

Figure 9.46 Generating the Report Upon Completion of the Wizard

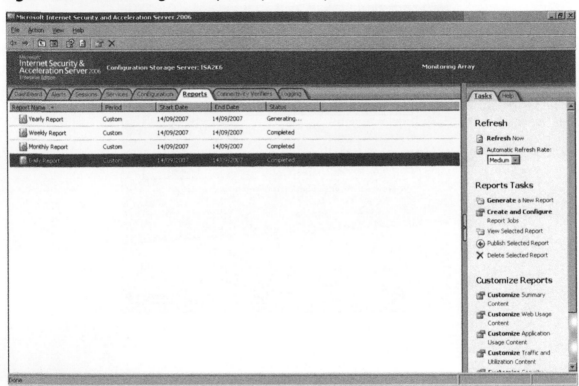

Because it is a one-time report, the **Period** column will indicate "Custom."

How to Configure an Automated Report Job

You can configure a report job to generate reports on a daily, weekly, monthly, or yearly basis. This is handy for comparative purposes. For example, you might want to create a daily summary report, or a weekly Web usage report.

NOTE

The ISA Firewall Job Scheduler Service must be running in order to generate reports from report jobs.

To create a report job, click **Create and Configure Report Jobs** in the right task pane. This will bring up the **Report Jobs Properties** dialog box, shown in Figure 9.47.

Figure 9.47 Creating Report Jobs

Here you will see a list of all scheduled report jobs. To add a new report job, click the **Add** button. This invokes the **New Report Job Wizard**. On the first page of the wizard, you'll be asked to give your report job a name (for example, Weekly Web Usage Report).

On the next page, you can configure the report content in the same way you did for a one-time report.

On the third page, as shown in Figure 9.48, you can select the time interval to run the report job: daily, weekly, or monthly.

Figure 9.48 Scheduling the Report Job

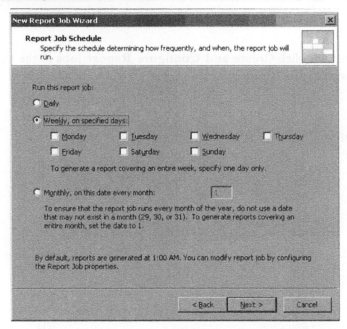

If you choose to run the job weekly, you can select on which day of the week to run the job. If you choose to run the job monthly, you will be asked to specify a day of the month on which to run the job. You should not use days that some months don't have (29, 30 or 31) if you want the job to run every month. If you want a report that covers the entire preceding month, you should set this value to 1.

On the next page, you can configure the job to publish the reports to a directory in the same way you did with the one-time report. The following page allows you to configure an e-mail message to be sent when the report completes, also in the same way as was done for the one-time report.

Finally, the last page of the wizard summarizes your choices. When you click **Finish,** the job will be scheduled to run on the day(s) you specified. By default, the report will start generating at 1:00 A.M. on the specified day. You can change this by selecting the report job in the **Report Job Properties** dialog box and clicking **Edit.** Click the **Schedule** tab, and you can change the generation hour, as shown in Figure 9.49.

Figure 9.49 Editing the Report Job Properties

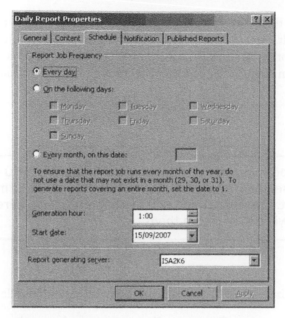

Other Report Tasks

There are a number of other report-related tasks you can perform from the task pane. You can configure the log summary by clicking **Configure Log Summary.** This brings up the **Log Summary Properties** dialog box, from which you can enable or disable daily and monthly summaries by checking a checkbox, as shown in Figure 9.50.

Figure 9.50 Configuring the Log Summary

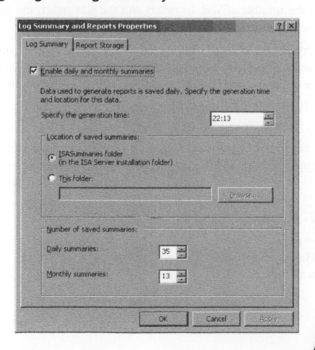

You can also change the default report generation time here, and specify where the summaries are to be saved (by default, they are saved in the ISASummaries folder). You can also configure the number of daily and monthly summaries to save (from a minimum of 35 to a maximum of 999 for daily summaries, and from a minimum of 13 to a maximum of 999 for monthly summaries).

> **NOTE**
>
> Remember: the log summaries are the basis for reports. If you disable the log summary database, the ISA Firewall will create the missing summaries if you generate a report. However, if you delete summaries that were previously created, the ISA Firewall will not re-create them.

You can also customize each of the report content types, using the following task pane selections:

- **Customize Summary Content:** You can specify the number of protocols to include, specify the number of top users to report on, specify the sort order for determining top usage, specify the number of top Web sites and the sort order for determining top sites, and specify the sort order for the cache hit ratio, either by requests or by bytes.

- **Customize Web Usage Content:** You can specify the number of top protocols to include and specify the sort order for determining top protocols (requests, users, bytes in, bytes out, or total bytes), specify the number of top Web sites and the sort order, specify the number of top users and the sort order, specify the number of object types and the sort order, specify the number of Web browsers and the sort order, and specify the number of operating systems and the sort order.

- **Customize Application Usage Content:** You can specify the number of top protocols and the sort order, number of top users and sort order, number of client applications and sort order, number of destinations and sort order, and number of operating systems and sort order.

- **Customize Traffic and Utilization Content:** You can specify the number of top protocols and the sort order for cache hit ratio.

- **Customize Security Content:** You can specify the number of clients who generate the most dropped packets and the number of users who cause the most authorization failures.

How to View Reports

Once a report has been generated, you can view it from the **Reports** tab in the **Monitoring** node of the **ISA Firewall Management** console. Double-click the report name, and it will open in your Web browser, as shown in Figure 9.51.

Figure 9.51 Viewing Reports

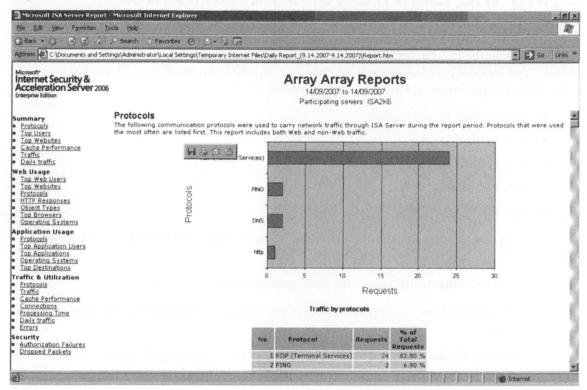

As you can see, the reports use graphs and tables to make the information easy to access and analyze. You can quickly move to different sections of the report by clicking the hyperlinks on the left side of the page.

Publishing Reports

If you didn't select to automatically publish the report to a directory when you configured the report job, you can publish it after it has been generated. Just highlight the report you want to publish and click **Publish Selected Report** in the task pane.

You will be asked to select a destination location for the report files folder. Click **OK**, and the report will be published to the folder. A new subfolder will be created within the selected folder (the folder name will be the report name plus the date). All the HTML and graphics files for the report will be stored there. To open the report itself from the folder, double-click the file named Report.htm.

Reports need to be published if you want to view them on computers other than the ISA Firewall computer.

Using the ISA Firewall's Performance Monitor

ISA 2006 installs the ISA Firewall Performance Monitor (a customized view of the Windows System Monitor that includes only ISA Firewall-related counters) when you install the ISA 2006 software. A list of the key performance objects is provided below:

- ISA Firewall Packet Engine
- ISA Firewall Service
- ISA H.323 Filter
- ISA Web Proxy
- ISA Cache

The following counters are added to the Performance monitor for the ISA Firewall Packet Engine object:

- **Active Connections**   shows the total number of active connections
- **Allowed Packets**   shows the number of packets that are permitted by the inspection engine
- **Allowed Packets/sec**   shows the number of packets per second that are permitted by the inspection engine
- **Backlogged Packets**   shows the total number of backlogged packets
- **Bytes**   shows the total number of bytes that have traversed the ISA Firewall
- **Bytes/sec**   shows the total number of bytes per seconds that have traversed the ISA Firewall
- **Connections/sec**   shows the total number of new connections created per second
- **Dropped packets**   shows the total number of packets dropped.
- **Dropped packet/sec**   shows the total number of packets dropped each second.
- **Packets**   show the total number of packets that the firewall packet engine driver has inspected.
- **Packets/sec**   shows the total number of packets that the firewall packet engine driver inspects each second.
- **TCP established connections/sec**   shows the number of TCP connections established each second (that is, a 3-way SYN handshake has been completed successfully).

The following counters are added to the Performance monitor for the ISA Firewall Service object:

- **Accepting TCP connections**   shows the number of connections that are awaiting a TCP connection from the Firewall client.

- **Active sessions**   shows active Firewall sessions.

- **Active TCP connections**   shows the total number of TCP connections currently passing data.

- **Active UDP connections**   shows the total number of UDP connections currently passing data.

- **Available UDP mappings**   shows the number of mappings that are available for UDP connections.

- **Available worker threads**   shows the number of Firewall Service worker threads that are waiting in completion port queue.

- **Bytes read/sec**   shows the number of bytes that are read by the data pump in one second.

- **Bytes written/sec**   shows the number of bytes that are written by the data pump in one second.

- **DNS cache entries**   shows the number of DNS name entries cached by the Firewall service.

- **DNS cache flushes**   shows the number of times the DNS domain name cache has been cleared.

- **DNS cache hits**   shows the number of times a DNS domain name was found in the DNS cache.

- **DNS cache hits**   % shows the percentage of DNS domain names retrieved by the Firewall service that are retrieved from cache.

- **DNS retrievals**   shows the number of DNS domain names retrieved by the Firewall service.

- **Failed DNS resolutions**   shows calls to resolve host DNS domain names and IP addresses for Firewall service connections that failed.

- **Kernel mode data pumps**   shows the number of kernel mode data pumps created by the Firewall service.

- **Listening TCP connections**   shows the connection objects awaiting TCP connections from remote computers following a successful listen.

- **Pending DNS resolutions**   shows calls to resolve DNS domain names and IP addresses for Firewall service connections that are pending.

- **Pending TCP connections**   shows the number of TCP connections waiting for a connect call to finish.

- **SecureNAT mappings**   shows the number of mappings that were created by SecureNAT.

- **Successful DNS resolutions**   shows calls to resolve host DNS domain names and IP addresses for Firewall service connections that were returned successfully.

- **TCP bytes transferred/sec**   shows the number of TCP bytes transferred by the kernel mode data pump in one second.

- **TCP Connections Awaiting Inbound Connect Call** shows connections from Firewall service to Firewall client after a connection from the Internet was accepted by the Firewall service on a listening socket.

- **UDP bytes transferred/sec** shows the number of UDP bytes transferred by the kernel mode data pump in one second.

- **Worker threads** shows Firewall service worker threads currently alive.

The following counters are added to the Performance monitor for the ISA H.323 Filter object:

- **Active H.323 Calls** shows the number of H.323 calls that are currently active.

- **Total H.323 Calls** shows the total number of H.323 calls handled by the H.323 filter since the Firewall Service was started.

The following counters are added to the Performance Monitor for the ISA Firewall Web Proxy object:

Active Web Sessions	Current Cache Fetches Average (Milliseconds/request)
Array Bytes Received/sec (Enterprise)	
Array Bytes Sent/sec (Enterprise)	Current Direct Fetches Average (Milliseconds/request)
Array Bytes Total/sec (Enterprise)	
Average Milliseconds/request	Failing Requests/sec
Average request speed	Failing Requests/Total Requests (%)
Bytes actually requested from server for range requests/Bytes in range requests (%)	FTP Requests
	HTTP Requests
Bytes Requested from Server in Ranges	HTTPS Sessions
Bytes Served from Cache in Ranges	Incoming Connections/sec
Bytes Served (Last Hour) From Cache in Ranges	IO Errors to Client
	IO Errors to Client/Total Errors
Bytes Served (Last Hour) in Ranges	IO Errors to Server
Bytes Served in Ranges	IO Errors to Server/Total Errors (%)
Cache Hit Ratio (%)	IO Errors to Array Member
Cache Hit Percentage for Range Requests	IO Errors to Array Member/Total Errors (%)
Cache Hit Ratio for the Last 10k Requests (%)	Maximum Users
	Memory Pool for HTTP Requests (%)
Client Bytes Received/sec	Memory Pool for SSL Requests (%)
Client Bytes Sent/sec	Outgoing Connections/sec
Client Bytes Total/sec	Requests/sec
Connect Errors	Requests from Array Member (Enterprise)
Connect Errors/Total Errors (%)	
Current Array Fetches Average (Milliseconds/request)	Requests from Array Member/Total Errors (%) (Enterprise)

Requests to Array Member
(Enterprise)

Requests to Array Member/
Total Errors (%) (Enterprise)

Requests with Keep Alive
to Client

Requests with Keep Alive to Client/
Total Errors (%)

Requests with Keep Alive to Server

Requests with Keep Alive to Server/
Total Errors (%)

Requests with Keep Alive to Array
Member

Requests with Keep Alive to Array
Member/Total Errors (%)

Requests with Multiple Ranges

Reverse Bytes Received/sec

Reverse Bytes Sent/sec

Reverse Bytes Total/sec

Sites Allowed

Sites Denied

SNEWS Sessions

SSL Client Bytes Received/sec

SSL Client Bytes Sent/sec

SSL Client Bytes Total/sec

Thread Pool Active Sessions

Thread Pool Failures

Thread Pool Size

Total Array Fetches (Enterprise)

Total Cache Fetches

Total Failing Requests

Total Pending Connects

Total Requests

Total Reverse Fetches

Total SSL Sessions

Total Successful Requests

Total Upstream Fetches

Total Users

Unknown SSL Sessions

Upstream Bytes Received/sec

Upstream Bytes Sent/sec

Upstream Bytes Total/sec

The following counters are added to the Performance monitor for the ISA Firewall Cache object:

Bytes actually requested from server
for range requests/Bytes in range
requests

Cache Hit Percentage for Range
Requests

Disk Bytes Retrieve Rate (KB/sec)

Disk Cache Allocated Space (KB)

Disk Content Write Rate (Writes/sec)

Disk Failure Rate (Failures/sec)

Disk URL Retrieve Rate (URL/sec)

Max URLs Cached

Memory Bytes Retrieved Rate (KB/sec)

Memory Cache Allocated Space (KB)

Memory URL Retrieve Rate (URL/sec)

Memory Usage Ratio Percent (%)

Total Disk Bytes Retrieved (KB)

Total Disk Failures

Total Disk URLs Retrieved

Total Memory Bytes Retrieved (KB)

Total Memory URLs Retrieved

Total URLs Cached

URL Commit Rate (URL/sec)

URLs in Cache

You can add or remove counters by right-clicking any column header in the bottom pane of the **System Monitor** view, and selecting **Properties.** On the **Data** tab, select the counters you want to remove, and click **Remove.** To add a counter, click **Add** and select the computer (local or a computer in the drop-down list), performance object and counter(s) to add. You can add counters for any performance object, not just those related to the ISA Firewall.

The ISA Firewall Performance Monitor is configured in the same way as the Windows Performance Monitor, and you can create counter logs, trace logs and alerts just as you do when monitoring other aspects of Windows computers.

Recommended Performance Counters

Of all the ISA Firewall performance counters available, you can use several key counters to provide general guidance on ISA Firewall system performance and important security threats.

In order to monitor general ISA Firewall performance, the following counters can be used:

- **ISA Firewall Firewall Engine:** Active Connections
- **ISA Firewall Firewall Engine:** Bytes/sec
- **ISA Firewall Firewall Service:** Active Sessions
- **ISA Firewall Web Proxy:** Requests/sec

In order to monitor general security threats faced by ISA Firewall, the following counters can be used:

- **ISA Firewall Firewall Engine:** Dropped packets/Sec
- **ISA Firewall Firewall Engine:** Packets/sec
- **ISA Firewall Firewall Engine:** Connections/sec
- **ISA Firewall Web Proxy:** Average Milliseconds/request

ISA Firewall 2004 Upgrade Considerations

With reference to monitoring, logging and reporting, two key considerations exist when performing an upgrade from ISA 2004 to ISA 2006. Firstly, ISA 2004 log files are not compatible with ISA 2006 and subsequently during the upgrade process all log files will be deleted, which is often not desirable. Secondly, settings defined for SQL logging are not migrated to ISA 2006, so these will need to be manually re-entered after the upgrade process is complete. Both of these manual procedures are discussed below.

> **NOTE**
>
> Remember: there is no direct upgrade path from ISA 2000 to ISA 2006. Subsequently, this upgrade scenario is not discussed within this section.

Preserving Log Files Prior to Upgrade

To allow you to preserve the existing log files prior to upgrade it is necessary to follow a manual backup procedure. This procedure is different depending on which log format you have chosen to use. An overview appropriate to each log method is provided below.

File Logging

Backup of file logs is the simplest procedure and merely involves copying log files from their default location of **%Program Files%\Microsoft ISA Server\ISALogs** to an alternate location. Figure 9.52 shows an example of the files contained within the ISALogs folder when using file logging.

Figure 9.52 ISALogs Folder

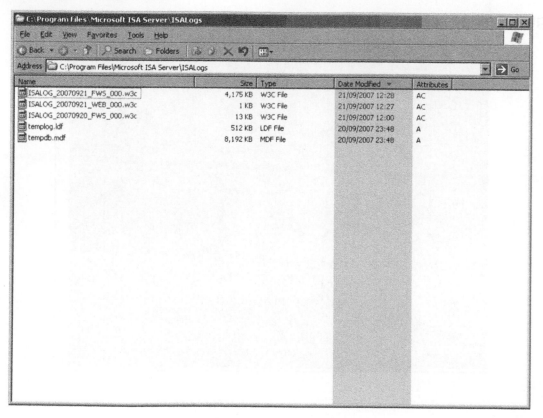

MSDE Logging

Historic MSDE logs files can be copied from their default location of **%Program Files%\Microsoft ISA Server\ISALogs** to an alternate location, however the current active logs files are held open by active MSDE processes and it is not possible to simply copy the files in the same way as for file logs. To enable us to copy the log files, we must first detach the database from the MSDE process. This can be achieved using the following procedure.

First we need to use the in-built **OSQL** command to select the correct Microsoft ISA MSDE instance using **OSQL –S** *ISA_Computer***\MSFW –E** where *ISA_Computer* is the name of the ISA Firewall in question. Once we have selected the correct MSDE instance, we then need to detach each of the Firewall and Web Proxy logging databases to allow them to be copied. This is achieved using the **sp_detach_db** *Database_Name* where *Database_Name* is the name of the required log files in the ISALogs folder, without the .mdf or .ldf file extensions. Figure 9.53 shows an example of the correct command syntax.

Figure 9.53 Detaching Databases from the MSDE Instance

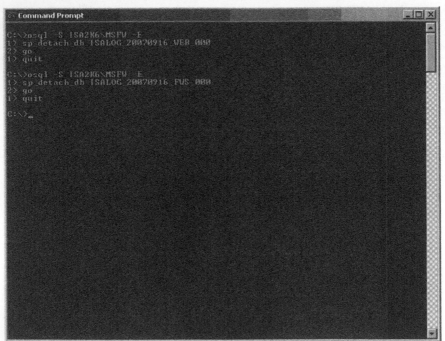

Once you have copied the log files to an alternate location, the original databases can be reattached to the MSDE instance again using **OSQL –S** *ISA_Computer***MSFW –E** followed by **sp_detach_db @dbname='***Database_Name***'**, **@filename1='***Path_To_MDF_File***'**, **@filename2='***Path_To_LDF_File***'** where ***Database_Name*** is the name of the required log files in the ISALogs folder, without the .mdf or .ldf file extensions, and ***Path_To_MDF_File*** and ***Path_To_LDF_File*** are the full path filenames of the required log files including their .mdf and .ldf references. Figure 9.53 shows an example of the correct command syntax.

Figure 9.54 Reattaching Databases to the MSDE Instance

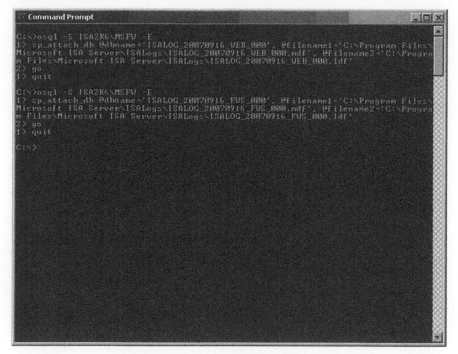

SQL Logging

When using SQL logging, log information is stored within the ISA Firewall databases held on the SQL Server. Subsequently, log files can be preserved by backing up the databases on the SQL Server, prior to the upgrade process. The exact details of this process are out of the scope of this book.

Preserving SQL Logging Options Prior to Upgrade

As part of the upgrade process, all options related to SQL logging will be lost and the ISA Firewall will revert to using MSDE logging for both Firewall and Web Proxy logs. Therefore, it will be necessary for you to make of note of these parameters *prior to the upgrade process* to ensure that you are able to reconfigure both firewall and web proxy logs for SQL logging once the upgrade has completed. Figure 9.55 provide details of the options parameters that need to be noted.

Figure 9.55 SQL Logging Options

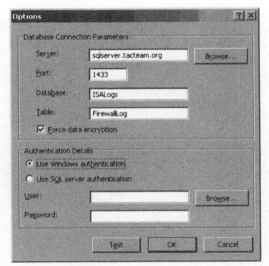

Index

A

access rules
  and block hosts on source network, 206
  built-in schedules for, 216
  context menu options for, 229–230
  destinations page creation of, 221
  general tab, for changing name of, 222
  MSN Messenger blocking by, 246
  ordering and organizing of, 232
  procedure for configuring outbound
    access through ISA firewall, 217
  properties of, 222
  source page creation of, 220
  sources, 453
acknowledgement (ACK) message, 25
Active Directory domain, 63
Address Resolution Protocol (ARP), 10
Advanced Encryption Standard (AES), 367
alert feature, of ISA firewall
  disable alert, 579
  event notification, 570–572
  modifiying alerts, 580
  new alerts wizard, 573–579
  predefined alerts, 573
  refreshing alert window, 582
  triggered alerts, 581
application-layer
  filtering, 266
  inspection, 391
Application Settings tab, configuring
    options pertaining to forms-based
    authentication, 343
ARP (Address Resolution Protocol), 10
authentication delegation
  features of, 341–343
  methods of, 296
  page, 295–297
  tab, 339
authentication port, 295
authentication preferences tab, 319
authentication settings page, 286–287

B

Authentication Settings Web Listener Wizard, 314
Automatic Web proxy connections for
    SecureNAT Clients, disabling of,
    234–235

biometric access control devices, 9
BITS caching, 367
bloom filter, 523
branch office
  access rules at, 424
  connectivity wizard, 378
  firewall, enable system policy rule on,
    434–435
  firewall request and installation of certificate
    for, 435–437
  network rule at, 423
  remote site network creation at, 421–423
  VPN connectivity wizard, 409
  VPN gateway dial-in account creation of, 424
Bridging tab, for configuring port or protocol
    redirection for Web Publishing Rule, 337

C

Cache Array Routing Protocol (CARP),
  523, 546
cache content file, 525
cache digests, 523
cache rules, in ISA 2006 server, 525–526
caching concept, in ISA 2006 server
  architectures in
    distributed caching, 521
    hierarchical caching, 522
  cache drive configuration, 525
  cache rules, 525–526
  content downloading, 527–529
  forward caching, 519–520, 523
  ISA firewall, role of, 524
  protocols for, 523
  reverse caching, 519–520, 523
  system memory usage, 524

CARP (Cache Array Routing Protocol), 523, 546

certificates
authorities, enterprise and standalone, 301–302
installation, details of, 313
MMC snap-in, 302
Tab features of, 318

Certificate Services Web enrollment pages, 401

CGI (Common Gateway Interface), 33

CIFS (Common Internet File System), 69

client authentication method, 319

client certificate
restrictions, features of, 322
restrictions tabs, 319
trust list, 319

Client Connection Security page, 284, 312

client credentials caching and authentication domain, 320

CMAK (Connection Manager Administration Kit), 370, 375

common attacks, detection and prevention, 511–512

common file extensions, default IIS MIME types for, 212

Common Gateway Interface (CGI), 33

Common Internet File System (CIFS), 69

commonly blocked headers and application signatures, 503

Communicator Web Access (CWA), 290

computer
virus, 34–35
worm, 35

computer security
designing of security plan, 35–36
detecting and preventing unauthorized external intrusions, 3
evaluation of security requirements, 36
objectives for, 7
overview of, 2

Connection Manager Administration Kit (CMAK), 370, 375

connections-advanced dialog, 318

connectivity monitoring
connectivity verifiers
creation, 584–586
properties modification, 587
Unresolved Name status indicators, 590
verification methods, 583

content type control, synchronization with HTTP and tunneled FTP traffic, 210

cookie-based affinity, load balancing of target web servers and, 329

corporate espionage, 21

corporate security policy, designing of, 40–41

Create Answer File Wizard, 378

custom dictionary entries determination, 507

custom link translation dictionary entries, procedure for configuring, 507–509

CWA (Communicator Web Access), 290

D

Dashboard feature, of ISA 2006
sections in
Alerts section, 565–566
Connectivity section, 562–563
customizing, 569–570
Reports section, 564–565
rolling up of, 561
Services section, 563–564
Sessions section, 566–567
System performance section, 567–569
use of, 559

Denial of Service (DOS)
attacks, 24
distributed, 18

dial-up
credentials, setting procedure for, 413
modem connections, 37
and Network Connections, 460

distributed caching, 521

DNS zone transfer, 474

domain functional level, changing procedure for, 448–449

Domain Name System (DNS), 33
attacks detection and prevention, 512–513
autodiscovery, making connection using, 115–116

DOS attack, 25
filter, 474–475
host name overflow, 475
length overflow, 475
server
  configuring to support Web proxy and
    firewall client autodiscovery, 108
  installing and configuring on ISA server
    firewall, 164
  placement of, 132
domain users, Windows authentication of, 371
Dynamic Host Configuration Protocol (DHCP),
    171, 421
  for autodiscovery, configuration of client
    browser to use, 105
  clients, procedure for configuring internal
    clients as, 184–186
  and DHCP Relay Agent, installing and
    configuring, 466–468
  installation and configuration on ISA server
    firewall, 170
  installation of, 98
  offer packet, network monitor
    capture of, 201
  reply from server rule, 180
  request to server rule, 178
  spoof attack prevention, 200

E

end-to-end encrypted connection, 316
enhanced key usage, 322
established corporate network name-resolution
    infrastructure, 134
EXCHANGE2003BE certificate, 402
exchange server, logon type
    provided to, 343
Extensible authentication protocol (EAP),
    389, 457
  configuration of ISA firewall software
    to support, 457–458
  users, enabling of user mapping
    for, 459
external intruders with internal access, 18
external network listener IP
    selection, 316

F

FBA (Forms-based authentication), 267–268,
    287, 322
fiber optic cable, 12
Firewall and Web Proxy Clients, autodiscovery
    information for, 146
firewall client
  communications, 75
  configuration files, 78–80
  installation, 117
  machines, 64
  software
    advantages of, 66–67
    authentication for all Winsock applications
      using TCP and UDP protocols, 63
    benefit of using, 64
    configuration of, 71
    enhanced support for network
      applications, 64
    installation of, 70–71
    proxy DNS support for firewall client
      machines, 64–65
    working of, 67–68
Firewall System Policy Rule, 69
fixed wireless services, 12
form customization, 323
forms-based authentication (FBA), 267–268,
    287, 322
forward caching, 519, 523
FQDN (Fully-qualified domain name), 73, 75,
    281, 303, 311
FTP access application filter, 477
FTP access filter, 477
FTP Policy, procedure for configuring, 231
FTP PORT-mode client, 477
FTP server, 338
FTP standard (Port) mode
    connections, 53
Fully-Qualified Domain Name (FQDN),
    73, 75, 281, 303, 311

G

Gateway caches. See Reverse caching
Generic routing encapsulation (GRE)
    protocol, 478

Generic Web sites, example HTTP security
    filter for, 499
Globally unique identifier (GUID), 253
GRE (Generic routing encapsulation)
    protocol, 478
group-based access controls, 373
group policy software installation, 121–124
GUID (Globally unique identifier), 253

H
hackers
    hybrid, 22
    profit-motivated, 20–21
    recreational, 20
    vengeful, 21–22
H.323 Filter, 477
Hide System Policy Rules, 155
hierarchical caching, 521–522
HTCP (HyperText Caching Protocol), 523
HTML
    form authentication, 287
    source code, 507
HttpFilterConfig.vbs script, 493
HTTP headers, 529
    investigating for potentially dangerous
        applications, 495–498
    used for bocking dangerous applications, 504
HTTPS traffic, 128-bit encryption for, 331
hybrid caching, 522
HyperText Caching Protocol (HTCP), 523
Hypertext Transfer Protocol (HTTP), 33
    authentication methods, 267
    communications, 479, 504
    compression, 367
    Host Headers, 267
    Listener (.160), 284
    policy
        export from Web publishing rule, 493–494
        procedure for configuring, 232
        for security filter, 499–500
    security filter
        logging of, 492
        overview of, 480
        settings, exporting and importing of, 493
        signature, creation of, 497

    signature of, 247
    use of, 246
    status code 200, 533

I
intentional internal security breaches
    detection of, 17–18
    motivation for, 17
    prevention of, 16–17
internal DNS server, 59
internal network adapter, 269
internal network computers, procedure for
    configuring, 184
internal publishing details, 309
Internet Authentication Server (IAS),
    88, 144, 440
Internet authentication services, RADIUS
    server configuration, 441
Internet Cache Protocol (ICP), 523
Internet-connected organizations challenges, 58
Internet Connection Firewall (ICF), 143
Internet Control Message Protocol (ICMP)
    router, 10
Internet Information Services (IIS), 211, 505
Internet Protocol (IP), 10
Internet Protocol (IP) addresses, 209
Internet Protocol (TCP/IP) properties, 417
intradomain communications, protocols
    required for, 252–253
intrusion detection, 474
IP address and DNS server assignment, 161–163
IP half scan attack, 32
IP Network Address Translation (RRAS NAT
    service) services, 143, 175
IP options and IP fragment filtering, 513–515
IPSec encryption protocol, 397
IPSec site-to-site connections, 378
IPSec tunnel mode, 367, 374, 378
IPSec Tunnel Mode Site-to-Site VPN, 440
IPSec VPN connections, pre-shared key support
    for, 375–376
IP Spoofing, 32. *See also* Internet Protocol (IP)
    addresses
ISA firewall
    access rule elements for, 208

alert feature
  disable alert, 579
  event notification, 570–572
  modifiying alerts, 580
  new alerts wizard, 573–579
  predefined alerts, 573
  refreshing alert window, 582
  triggered alerts, view, 581
applications in intrusion detection and
    intrusion prevention, 511
configuration of, 290
connectivity monitoring, 587–591
disk space for caching, 524
forward and reverse caching, 524
intradomain communications through, 251
logging feature, 597–608
performance monitor, 618–622
policy affecting new connections, 250
procedure for avoiding looping back through,
    244–245
procedure for configuring access rules for
    outbound access through, 217
protected networks, 267, 270–271
proxied access to Web sites protected by, 265
reporting feature, 609–617
service monitoring, 596–597
sessions monitoring, 591–596
types of
  application filters in, 472–473
  built-in protocols in, 208–209
  policy elements included in, 208
  pre-built Content types, 211
update, 559
upgrading, 622–626
VPN
  configuration, 380
  networking overview, 366–367
and VPN Clients, issue of certificates to, 397
Web proxy logs for, 246
Web publishing rules, 270
ISA firewall-protected network, 133
ISA firewall server publishing rules, 475
ISA firewall software
  access policy of, 206
  administrative roles and permissions, 187

assigning of static IP addresses to internal
    and external interfaces of, 161
basic processor, memory, disk space and
    network adapter requirements, 129–130
client roles for, 193
configuration of IP addressing information
    on external interface of, 163
configuration of network interfaces, 134, 161
configuration of routing table, 130
configuration of specific system policy rule
    for, 146
for controlling traffic between source and
    destination networks, 206
default post-installation configuration for,
    145–146
DNS server placement, 132
hardening and local security issues, 187
installation and configuration of DHCP
    server on, 170
installation via a terminal services
    administration mode session, 138
networks interface configuration
    scenarios for, 134
physical relationships with internal and
    external networks, 161
post-installation settings for, 145
post-installation system policy for, 146
pre-installation tasks and considerations, 128
procedure for configuring DNS service on, 165
procedure for single NIC installation of, 157
quick start configuration for, 159–161
requirements for installing, 128
service requirements for common tasks
    performed on, 187, 190
services on which ISA firewall software
    depends, 188
step for installing on dual-homed Windows
    Server 2003 machine, 138–144
system policy editor for, 155
system policy rules for, 155
ISA firewall Web filters
  features of, 504
  use of, 479
ISA management console, 117
ISA protected network, 278

ISA 2004's bridging mode page and ISA 2006, 315
ISA Server 2000
   caching-only mode simulation, 157
   firewall client software, 175
   service dependencies of, 187–189
   system hardening templates for, 187
ISA Server 2006
   centralized configuration options at, 72
   choice of appropriate client type, 95
   client type categories of, 48
   installation and management of, 48
   internal interface of, 51
   level of functionality and level of
     security in, 95
   methods available for automating Web Proxy
     and Firewall client configurations, 96–97
   multiple client type configuration, 93
   procedure for installing and configuring
     softwares for, 173–176
   publishing of autodiscovery information, 105
   role in protecting organization's security plan, 3
   SecureNAT client overview, 50
   security alert for, 68
   understanding firewall client, 62
   Web Proxy client, 84
ISA server firewall
   administrative roles and permissions, 195–197
   installation and configuration of DNS server
     on, 164
   lockdown mode functionality of, 197
ISA server link translator, 504–507
ISA Server *SecureNAT* clients, 184
ISA's Link Translation, URL rewriting with,
   266–267
ISA 2000 VPN server, 377
ISA 2006 VPN server, 395
ISA 2006 Web caching feature
   cache rules, configuration of
     copying, 541
     destination selection, 536
     disabling of, 541
     enabling HTTP caching, 538–539
     export and import, 542–544
     modification in existing, 540
     size of objects, 537

catch content, 533
content download
   changing existing, 553
   configure local host network, 545–546
   create and configure, 550–553
   disable, 554
   enable system policy rule, 547–548
   export and import, 554–555
   job scheduler service, 548–550
   requirements for, 545–548
disable caching, 532
enable caching
   in enterprise edition, 529–530
   in standard edition, 531
expired objects, 534
memory allocation, 534
size of cache objects, 533–534

L
Layer Two Tunneling Protocol over IPSec
   (L2TP/IPSec), 408
LDAP
   authentication, 290
   Settings Page, 291–293
Legacy firewall client/Winsock proxy clients,
   support for, 75–76
link translation
   applications of, 267
   features of, 340–341
listener SSL Certificates, features, 312, 314
list linking, 30
Local Address Table (LAT), 67, 140, 174, 206
local and remote sites, demand dial interface
   configuration on, 420
local host network traffic, 398
local site-to-site settings, summary of, 416
log analysis software, 269
logging and reporting, in ISA firewall
   configure logging
     log format, 602
     logging to a SQL Database, 603–604
     log storage format, 601
     log viewer, 604–609
     MSDE database, 601–602
   log types, 598–599

reporting
  generate, 609
  report content, 609–612
  report job, 612–616
  view report, 617
loose source record route (LSRR), 32, 515
L2TP connection, IPSec policy for, 389
L2TP/IPSec site-to-site VPN, creation
    of, 426
L2TP/IPSec VPN connection testing, 403

M

MAC. *See* Media Access Control
mail bomb attack, 29–30
mail server publishing rules, creation of,
    357–358
main office
  access rules at, 418–419
  creation of VPN gateway dial-in account at,
    419–421
  firewall, request and installation of certificate
    for, 428–430
  network rule at, 418
  system policy rule on, 427
malicious code trojans, 34
management by objective (MBO), 38
Media Access Control, 10
Microsoft encrypted authentication version 2
    (MS-CHAPv2), 389
Microsoft Exchange Server, 368
Microsoft Internet Security and Acceleration
    Server 2006, 71, 274
Microsoft point-to-point encryption (MPPE)
    protocol, 397
Microsoft SQL Server Desktop Engine (MSDE)
    database, 598
MMS filter, 478
monitoring node, 558
MSN Messenger Web Proxy Access rule,
    settings for, 250
multiple client configuration, machines
    application behavior on, 94
multiple Web-caching servers, 520
Multipurpose Internet Mail
    Extensions (MIME), 210

N

network adapters, default IP addresses for, 285
network address translation (NAT), 156, 206
network interface order, 163
network intrusion
  classification of types of attacks
    social engineering attacks, 22–23
  factors for, 4
  removal of opportunities for, 5
Network Listener IP addresses, 349
Network Listener IP selection page, 285
Network Load Balancing (NLB), 270
network monitor driver, 134
network operating systems, 17
network routing infrastructure, 65
network security
  education of network users on, 43–44
  legal considerations associated with, 39
  physical access control, 8–9
  responsibility for developing security plan
    and policies, 39–40
  responsibility for implementing and enforcing
    security plan and policies, 40–41
  specifications for rating of, 38
  tactical planning for enhancing, 19
  types of threat for, 19–20
  understanding intruder motivations for, 20
networks tab application, 316
network usage policy, for potentially dangerous
    applications, 495
New Access Rule Wizard, 222
non-encrypted firewall client connections, 175
non-native mode active directory
    domains, 392

O

Outlook 2003 RPC-over-HTTP protocol,
    HTTP methods used by, 502
Outlook Web Access (OWA), 368, 453
out-of-band data transmission, 29
out-of-band (OOB) attack, 29
OWA forms-based authentication filter, 510
OWA Web Publishing Rules, HTTP security
    filter settings for, 501–502
OWA 2003 Web site, 303

P

packet filter-based stateful hardware firewalls, 472
packet filter engine, 197
password management, 323
password policy, developing of effective, 41
path mapping, 335
paths tab, handling of request by
    Web Publishing Rule, 333
performance monitororing, in ISA firewall
  counters added for
    Cache object, 621
    Filter object, 620
    Packet Engine object, 618
    Service object, 619
    Web Proxy object, 620–621
    performance counters
      Cache object, 622
physical security plan
  keeping workstations secure, 9
  protecting network devices, 10
  protecting the servers, 9
  removable storage risks, 14
  securing the cable, 11–12
Ping, 583
Ping Flood (ICMP flood), 27–28
Ping of Death attack, 27
PNM filter, 478
Point-to-Point Tunneling Protocol (PPTP),
    408, 411, 421
POP intrusion detection filter, 475
Port Address Translation (PAT), 274
port and protocol redirection, 270–271
port scanning, 30–31
P2P-Agent HTTP request header, procedure
    for blocking, 498
PPTP filter, 478
PPTP site-to-site VPN, creating of, 408–410
PPTP VPN connection testing, 395
Progressive Networks Media Protocol, 478
Progressive Networks Media servers, 478
Protected Network Web servers, 265
Protocols page, features of, 218–220
Protocols Tab, for providing options available in
    New Access Rule Wizard, 223
Proxy autoconfiguration file (PAC), 118

Proxy autoconfiguration file (PAC) address, 73
Proxy Server 2.0 configuration simulation, 157
Public Key Infrastructure (PKI), 301, 375, 389
Public Name Details page, 281–282, 311
Public Name Details Wizard, 282
Published server logoff URL, 343
published Web sites
  deep application-layer inspection of
    connections made to, 265
  load-balancing of, 270
  method of securing connection between
    ISA firewall and, 315
  reverse caching of, 269
  single sign-on (SSO) for, 264, 268
publishing exchange Web client access, 360
publishing PPTP VPN servers, 374
publishing type page, 275–276
publish mail servers, 360
publish non-Web server protocols, 347

Q

quarantined VPN clients network, 156

R

radius/radius OTP server settings, 290
RDP protocol definition, 348
real-time log viewer, 377
refresh rate script, 588
Release To Manufacture (RTM) version,
    of ISA 2006 firewall, 568
remote access dial-in user service (RADIUS), 440
  authentication, 290
  authentication filter, use of, 511
  authentication, support for, 268–269
  compliant directory, 269
  features of, 88
  (OTP) authentication, 293
  server, remote access policies on, 386
  settings page, 293
remote access permission via remote access
    policy, controlling procedure for, 449–450
remote access policy, 445
remote access VPN client machine, issuing user
    certificate to, 460–462
Remote Procedure Call (RPC), 189, 478

remote site network at main office, creation of, 411
remote site network, configuring procedure for IP address range for, 414
Request for Comments (RFC), 35
reverse caching
  basic concept, 519–520
  benefits of, 520
reverse proxying, 264
root certification authorities, 321
routable local IP addresses, 416
routing and Remote Access Services, 376
routing table, configuration of, 130–131
RPC endpoint mapper, 258, 260
RPC Filter, 478
RPC-over-HTTP Web publishing rule, HTTP security filter policy settings for, 502
RPC Policy, procedure for configuring, 230
RPC Protocol, creation of, 220
RPC Server Publishing, 368
RTSP filter, 478
rule action page, features of, 217

S
scanning and Spoofing, 30
schedule tab, for configuring when user can configure to published Web site, 340
Secure Exchange RPC publishing, 358
SecureNAT client
  access procedure for, 478
  advantages of, 56–57
  applications of, 50
  approach fo disabling automatic Web proxy connections for, 234
  disadvantages of, 55
  DNS considerations for, 60–62
  improved performance for firewall client and, 85
  limitations of, 52–54
  name resolution for, 58
  support for VPN connections, 372
Security Account Manager (SAM), 63, 87
Security Administrator's Tool for Analyzing Networks (SATAN), 30
security terminology, 5–7

selected protocols, ways to block logging for, 233
Server Connection Security dialog, 315
Server Connection Security page, 276–277, 309, 311
Server-published server, 273
Server publishing HTTP sites, 355–356
server publishing protocol definitions, 344–347
server publishing rules
  for access to servers and services, 271
  application-layer filtering, 272
  creation of, 344
  fine-tuning of, 349
  inbound connections made through, 378
  list of protocol definitions used for, 355
  properties dialog box, 349
  publishing of IP level and TCP/UDP protocols, 272
  reverse NAT or port mapping, 271
  support for port redirection or PAT, 274
Server Publishing Wizard, 309
server-to-server communication, 358
sessions monitoring, in ISA firewall
  disconnect sessions, 596
  filter definitions, 593–596
  stoppping, 593
  viewing, 592
Sharepoint Portal Server, 290
silent installation script, 124
single sign on settings dialog, 290
single sign-on (SSO), for published Web sites, 268
site-to-site links, activation of, 425
site-to-site L2TP/IPSec VPN links, configuring pre-shared keys for, 439
site-to-site VPN and tunnel mode IPSec, 373–374
site-to-site wizard, 377
SMTP
  filter component, 473
  filter configuration interface, 473
  Message Screener, 598
  server, 576
Smurf attack, 28
Social engineering attacks, ways for protecting against, 23
SOCKS v4 filter, 475

source routing attack
  features of, 32
  types of, 515
Split-DNS infrastructure, 133
split tunneling, 372
SSL
  Bridging, 299
  certificate, 289
  certificate authentication, 87
  client certificate authentication,
      290, 331
  content, 527
  tunneling, 309
  Web sites, 242
SSL/TLS encryption, implementation of, 453
SSL-to-FTP bridging, 338
SSL-to-HTTP bridging, 299, 315
SSL-to-SSL bridging
  features of, 299
  and Web Site certificate configuration,
      302–304
SSL "Tunneling" versus SSL "Bridging," 300
SSL Tunnel Port range for Web, access,
      extension of, 242
SSL Web Publishing Rule
  creating and configuring, 299
  creation of, 308–309
SSO Domains, 324
streaming media services, 513
strict source routing, 515
switch jamming, 11
synchronization request (SYN) attacks, 25
system policy rules, 306
systems management server (SMS), 70, 125

T
TCP and UDP communications, 93
teardrop attack, 27
time streaming protocol, 479
time to live (TTL), 526, 527, 534, 538, 552
Total Quality Management (TQM), 38
traffic tab, 330
Transmission Control Protocol (TCP), 25
Trihomed DMZ, basic network configuration
      for, 252

Trusted Root Certification Authorities
      certificate, 306, 400
tunnel mode IPSec, site-to-site VPN using,
      373–374
twisted pair and coaxial cable, vulnerability to
      data capture, 11

U
UDP bomb/UDP flood, 29
UDP packet storm, 29
UDP Snork attack, 29
unauthorized external intrusions,
      prevention of, 18–19
universally unique identifier (UUID), 253
user account dial-in permissions, changing
      procedure for, 447
User Datagram Protocol (UDP), 25
user-defined access policy, 207
user sets page
  applications of, 298
  creation of, 221
users tab, for configuring published Web site via
      Web Publishing Rule, 338

V
Virtual Disk Service (VDS), 189
virtual intruders, 15
virtual private networking (VPN),
      37, 366, 450, 457
VPN authentication and remote access policy,
      440–441
VPN client
  connections
    firewall policy applied to, 368–369
    monitoring of, 404
  connections monitoring of, 377
  network, 369
  network access to resources, access rules
      allowing members of, 391–392
  remote access connections pre-shared
      key for, 406
  remote access policy, creation of, 442–445
  user mapping of, 371–372
VPN Quarantine (VPN-Q), 370
VPN remote-access client, 368